"Freedom is Indivisible"

Historical Materialism
Book Series

Editorial Board

Loren Balhorn (*Berlin*)
David Broder (*Rome*)
Sebastian Budgen (*Paris*)
Steve Edwards (*London*)
Juan Grigera (*London*)
Marcel van der Linden (*Amsterdam*)
Peter Thomas (*London*)

VOLUME 270

The titles published in this series are listed at *brill.com/hm*

"Freedom is Indivisible"

*Rudolf Hilferding's Correspondence with Karl Kautsky,
Leon Trotsky, and Paul Hertz, 1902–1938*

Edited and translated by

William T. Smaldone

BRILL

LEIDEN | BOSTON

Library of Congress Cataloging-in-Publication Data

Names: Smaldone, William, editor, translator.
Title: "Freedom is indivisible" : Rudolf Hilferding's correspondence with Karl
   Kautsky, Leon Trotsky, and Paul Hertz, 1902-1938 / edited and translated by
   William T. Smaldone.
Description: Leiden ; Boston : Brill, [2023] | Series: Historical materialism book
   series, 1570-1522 ; volume 270 | Includes bibliographical references and index.
Identifiers: LCCN 2022048685 (print) | LCCN 2022048686 (ebook) | ISBN
   9789004527379 (hardback) | ISBN 9789004527386 (ebook)
Subjects: LCSH: Hilferding, Rudolf, 1877-1941–Correspondence. |
   Socialists–Europe–Correspondence.
Classification: LCC HX254.7.H55 S63 2023 (print) | LCC HX254.7.H55 (ebook) | DDC
   335.0092 [B]–dc23/eng/20221024
LC record available at https://lccn.loc.gov/2022048685
LC ebook record available at https://lccn.loc.gov/2022048686

Typeface for the Latin, Greek, and Cyrillic scripts: "Brill". See and download: brill.com/brill-typeface.

ISSN 1570-1522
ISBN 978-90-04-52737-9 (hardback)
ISBN 978-90-04-52738-6 (e-book)

Copyright 2023 by Koninklijke Brill NV, Leiden, The Netherlands.
Koninklijke Brill NV incorporates the imprints Brill, Brill Nijhoff, Brill Hotei, Brill Schöningh, Brill Fink,
Brill mentis, Vandenhoeck & Ruprecht, Böhlau, V&R unipress and Wageningen Academic.
All rights reserved. No part of this publication may be reproduced, translated, stored in a retrieval system,
or transmitted in any form or by any means, electronic, mechanical, photocopying, recording or otherwise,
without prior written permission from the publisher. Requests for re-use and/or translations must be
addressed to Koninklijke Brill NV via brill.com or copyright.com.

This book is printed on acid-free paper and produced in a sustainable manner.

Contents

Preface VII
List of Figures IX
Abbreviations X

Part 1

1 Introduction to Part 1: Passing the Torch 3

2 Rudolf Hilferding's Letters to Karl Kautsky, 1902–07 29

3 Rudolf Hilferding's Letters to Karl Kautsky, 1915–18 87

4 Rudolf Hilferding's Letters to Karl Kautsky, 1924–33 128

5 Rudolf Hilferding's Letters to Karl Kautsky, 1933–37 164

Part 2

6 Introduction to Part 2: A Political Friendship? 181

7 Leon Trotsky's Letters to Rudolf Hilferding, 1907–12 191

Part 3

8 Introduction to Part 3: "Freedom or Slavery" 217

9 Rudolf Hilferding's Correspondence with Paul Hertz, 1933–38 231

Bibliography 499
Index 506

FIGURE 1   The new Finance Minister: Rudolf Hilferding in front of the Reichstag (1923)
AUTHOR: UNKNOWN, BUNDESARCHIVBILD 102–00144, CREATIVE COMMONS

Preface

Many years ago, while working on my doctoral dissertation on Rudolf Hilferding, I visited the Institute for Social History to read his correspondence. I remember my excitement as I sat in the reading room taking in the letters and thinking about the lives of the people whose world they revealed. In the years since then, as I have pursued other projects related to European socialism, I have found it useful to return to these materials for the rich insights they provide about the evolution of the European labor movement and some of the people who led it. The main purpose of this volume is to make these materials available to an English-speaking audience.[1]

Rudolf Hilferding was a major figure in the European socialist movement for the first four decades of the twentieth century. His work as editor of German Social Democracy's leading journals and newspapers, and his political activity, especially in Weimar Germany, placed him at the center of a far flung correspondence with thinkers and activists across Europe and, like many of his contemporaries, such as Paul Hertz, evidence indicates that he very likely made copies of many of his letters. Yet much of his correspondence has been lost. Forced to suddenly flee Germany in 1933 and then hunted down, imprisoned, and driven to suicide by the Gestapo eight years later, only a small fraction of his letters and private papers were salvaged. The three collections translated here, Hilferding's letters to Karl Kautsky, 1902–37; Leon Trotsky's letters to Hilferding, 1907–12, and Hilferding's extensive correspondence with Paul Hertz from 1933–38, contain almost all of this remnant with the exception of scattered letters in the papers of a few of his contemporaries.

Each one of these collections forms a separate part of this work. I have equipped each part with an extensive introduction designed to contextualize the letters and documents and to provide an overview and analysis of some of the major themes that arise. They are in no way intended to be comprehensive, however, and the reader will certainly find that many issues of interest are not touched upon in them. I have organized each collection of materials chronologically. In the sections dealing with Kautsky and Trotsky the reader should be aware that, while the archival numbering of the letters largely

---

1 Hilferding's correspondence has not been published in German or any other language. There is also no German version of his collected works, though Cora Stephan has published a useful selection. See Stephan (ed.), 1982. With Mark E. Blum I have translated and published a selection of Hilferding's most important essays in a broader work on Austro-Marxist thought. See Blum & Smaldone (eds.) 2016/2017.

follows their chronology, there are occasional exceptions. In the case of the very extensive Hertz collection, the individual letters and documents were not archivally numbered, so the problem does not arise. When I have occasionally encountered a word that was unreadable or the abbreviation or pseudonym of an individual whom I could not identify, I have alerted the reader in the notes.

Rudolf Hilferding regarded himself as an intellectual exponent of the socialist idea, a conception that, for him, combined society's ability to meet human material needs with the emergence of conditions in which, as Marx and Engels famously put it, "the free development of each is a condition for the free development of all".[2] To achieve that end, Hilferding believed that Marxism was an indispensable analytical tool for which "the sole aim of any inquiry – even into matters of policy – is the discovery of causal relationships". Therefore, "to know the laws of commodity-producing society is to be able, at the same time, to disclose the causal factors which determine the willed decisions of the various classes of this society".[3] The letters that follow shed light on the evolution of Hilferding's thinking on this project over the course of almost four decades. During that time, his understanding of the relationship between economic transformation and political and social consciousness would change considerably as did his view of the utility of Marxism for understanding that relationship. But, in the context of rising fascism and Stalinism, his conviction that freedom stands at the center of the socialist project grew ever stronger. Almost a century later, as authoritarianism again threatens democratic societies around the globe, his thoughts on the matter remain as pertinent as ever.

By way of thanks, I am indebted to Sebastian Budgen and the editorial board of Brill's Historical Materialism book series for supporting this project. I am also very grateful to Willamette University, whose financial support during my sabbatical year made the work possible, to the Institute for Social History for providing easy access to the original documents, to my colleagues at Willamette University's Mark O. Hatfield Library for their assistance with my research, to Darren Howard for the index, and to my colleague, Ortwin Knorr, for his generous assistance in translating Hilferding's Greek. Finally, I owe an enormous debt of thanks to Jennifer Jopp, whose indefatigable editorial skills and enormous patience made completion of the work possible.

2 Marx and Engels 1985, p. 31.
3 Hilferding 1985, p. 23.

Figures

1 The new Finance Minister: Rudolf Hilferding in front of the Reichstag (1923). Author: Unknown, Bundesarchivbild 102–00144, Creative Commons   VI
2 Rudolf and Margarethe Hilferding at the time of their wedding (1904). Author: Karl Hilferding, Creative Commons   XI
3 Karl Kautsky (circa 1904). Author: Unknown, Courtesy of the Archiv der sozialen Demokratie, Bonn   XII
4 Leon Trotsky in Vienna (sometime before 1915). Author: unknown   180
5 Rudolf and Rose Hilferding (June 1928). Author: Unknown, Bundesarchivbild 102–06069, Creative Commons   216
6 Paul Hertz in the 1920s. Author: Unknown, Getty Images   219

Abbreviations

ADGB	Allgemeiner Deutscher Gewerkschaftsbund (General Federation of German Trade Unions)
AfA	Allgemeiner freier Angestellten Bund (General Federation of Salaried Employees)
A–Z	Arbeiterzeitung
BVP	Bayerische Volkspartei (Bavarian People's Party)
DDP	Deutsche Demokratische Partei (German Democratic Party)
DSAP	Deutsche sozialdemokratische Arbeiterpartei in der Tschoslovakei (German Social Democratic Workers' Party of Czechoslovakia)
DNVP	Deutschnationale Volkspartei (German National People's Party)
DVP	Deutsche Volkspartei (German People's Party)
KPD	Kommunistische Partei Deutschlands (Communist Party of Germany)
LSI	Labor and Socialist International
LVZ	Leipziger Volkszeitung
NB	Neu Beginnen (New Beginning)
NSDAP	Nationalsozialistische Deutsche Arbeiterpartei (National Socialist German Workers' Party)
NZ	Neue Zeit
NV	Neuer Vorwärts
NZZ	Neuer Züricher Zeitung
PPS	Polish Socialist Party
RSD	Revolutionäre Sozialisten Deutschlands (Revolutionary Socialists of Germany)
SA	Sturmabteilung (Nazi paramilitary force)
SA	Sozialistische Aktion
SAP	Sozialistische Arbeiter Partei (Socialist Workers Party of Germany)
SdKPL	Social Democracy of the Kingdom of Poland and Lithuania
SDAP	Soziademokratische Arbeiterpartei (Social Democratic Workers' Party of Austria)
SFIO	French Socialist Party
SPD	Sozialdemokratische Partei Deutschlands (Social Democratic Party of Germany)
SS	Schutzstaffel (Nazi paramilitary force)
USPD	Unabhängige Sozialdemokratische Partei Deutschlands (Independent Social Democratic Party of Germany)
ZfS	Zeitschrift für Sozialismus

FIGURE 2   Rudolf and Margarethe Hilferding at the time of their wedding (1904)
AUTHOR: KARL HILFERDING, CREATIVE COMMONS

FIGURE 3 Karl Kautsky (circa 1904)
AUTHOR: UNKNOWN, COURTESY OF THE ARCHIV DER SOZIALEN DEMOKRATIE, BONN

Part 1

CHAPTER 1

Introduction to Part 1: Passing the Torch

Rudolf Hilferding's letters to Karl Kautsky spanned three of the most tumultuous decades in modern European history. Written between 1902–7, 1915–18, and 1924–37, the letters provide a window into the changing fortunes of Central European socialism from its halcyon days in the two decades prior to 1914, during which the growing labor movement in Germany and Austria seemed poised to challenge the ruling classes for power, to its fragmentation in the wake of war and revolution, and, after a period of recovery in the post-war era, to its collapse in the face of fascism during the 1930s. In 1902 Hilferding was a young Marxist thinker hungry for intellectual guidance. Kautsky, socialism's leading Marxist theoretician at the time, proved ready to provide that mentorship. He saw Hilferding as a kindred spirit, whose approach to theoretical problems and work ethic were similar to his own. The letters show how, over the course of many years, the two men reciprocally influenced one another intellectually and politically, and grew closer personally.

By the turn of the nineteenth century, Karl Kautsky had long been a central figure in the European socialist movement.[1] Born in Prague on 16 October 1854, his father, Johann, was a theatre painter and his mother, Minna, was an actress and novelist. After moving to Vienna in 1863, Kautsky's parents provided Karl with an excellent education, and he graduated from the University of Vienna in 1874 having studied history, economics, and natural science. He joined the fledgling Austrian socialist party in 1875 and soon began writing articles for its press. In the late 1870s he became acquainted with August Bebel and Karl Liebknecht, two of the most important co-founders of the German Social Democratic Party (SPD), who were also leading exponents of the ideas of Karl Marx and Friedrich Engels. In 1879 Kautsky began writing for *Der Sozialdemokrat*, the SPD's flagship newspaper, which, as the result of the German government's effort to suppress the party, was published from Zürich, Switzerland. In 1880 Kautsky moved to Zürich, where Karl Höchberg, a wealthy socialist scholar and publisher, provided a stipend for him to pursue research. While in Zürich he studied the works of Marx and Engels, whom he also met during a trip to London in 1881, and befriended Edward Bernstein, editor of *Der Sozialdemokrat*.

---

1 The literature on Kautsky is enormous. For this introduction I have drawn primarily from Steenson 1978; Salvadori 1979; Gilcher-Holtey 1986; and John H. Kautsky 1994.

A key moment in Kautsky's life occurred in 1883, when he founded *Die Neue Zeit* (*The New Age*) which, under his editorial guidance, soon became German social democracy's leading theoretical journal. This outlet, his close personal and intellectual relationship to Engels, as well as his role as co-executor, along with Bernstein, of Marx and Engels' literary *Nachlaß* (their unpublished papers) made Kautsky a central figure in the education of a generation of Marxist intellectuals in Central Europe and beyond. Kautsky's diverse works in the fields of history, economics, politics, and ethics brought Marxist and social democratic ideas to a broad, working class audience[2] and his co-authorship, again with Bernstein, of the German Social Democratic Party's *Erfurt Program of 1891* put his stamp on social democratic politics for decades to come. As a friend and ideological guide to Bebel, and as an often-decisive voice in the intellectual and political debates of the growing movement, many viewed Kautsky as the "pope" of socialism. Kautsky had prodigious energy, but his workload was burdensome. Having turned 50 in 1904, he considered giving up the NZ, but was concerned about finding a successor. Whoever it was had to pursue the journal's original mission – which Kautsky saw as his primary intellectual task – of promoting scientific socialism or Marxism.[3]

By the fall he thought he had found just the man in Rudolf Hilferding, a young Viennese physician who was also making a reputation as a Marxist theorist.[4] Born in Vienna on 11 August 1877, Hilferding was the son of Emil and Anna Hilferding, who were Polish-Jewish immigrants from Galicia. The head cashier of an insurance firm, Emil made a modest living but earned enough so that he and Anna could raise Rudolf and his younger sister, Maria, in the atmosphere of the "enlightened Jewish middle class", whose sons and daughters often displayed lively interest in the arts and sciences as well as in the socialist movement.[5] In a society in which few children could even dream of an academic education, Hilferding attended a Gymnasium from which he graduated in 1894. He then enrolled at the University of Vienna to study medicine. This was a common career path at that time for students of Jewish heritage, who were inclined to move into intellectual professions such as journalism, medicine, and law.[6]

---

2 For example, during the late 1880s he published *The Economic Doctrines of Karl Marx* (1887), *Thomas More and his Utopia* (1888) and *Class Struggles in the age of the French Revolution* (1889). His *Ethics and the Materialist Conception of History* appeared in 1906.
3 Steenson 1978, p. 52.
4 On Hilferding see Smaldone 1998; idem., 2008, pp. 71–100; Wagner 1996; and Gottschalch 1962.
5 Stein 1946, p. 5.
6 Kurata 1978, pp. 27–28.

During his student years, Hilferding developed the basic ideological and political perspectives that later guided his public career. While still in high school, he became interested in the growing socialist movement, and, in 1893, at the age of sixteen, joined the Socialist Student League, which consisted of a small group of Viennese students who met once a week in the café Zum Heiliger Leopold. There they discussed such classic Marxist works as *Capital*, but also new books by Kautsky and articles from the NZ. Although the group had no official connections with the Austrian Social Democratic Workers' Party (SDAP), it participated in SDAP-led street demonstrations, such as the May Day rally of 1893, during which Hilferding and student comrades such as Max Adler and Karl Renner joined in calls for a "red republic" that precipitated a melee with police. Soon these young radicals become close friends and intellectual collaborators. Along with Otto Bauer, who joined later on, all later rose to prominence in either Austrian or German Social Democracy.[7]

While earning his medical degree, Hilferding also studied political economy and, along with Bauer, Max Adler, and other social democratic students, attended classes taught by Carl Grünberg, one of Europe's few Marxist professors, Ernst Mach, a leading neo-positivist philosopher, and Eugen Böhm-Bawerk, the foremost anti-Marxist economist of the marginal utility school.[8] All three men strongly influenced Hilferding. Whereas Mach's materialist perspective reinforced his Marxist inclinations and Böhm-Bawerk challenged them, it was Grünberg's conception of Marxism as a social science that most decisively shaped his thinking. As Tom Bottomore has noted, Grünberg held that Marxism "should be developed in a rigorous and systematic way through historical and sociological investigations", and he argued that socialist intellectuals should not limit themselves to purely academic pursuits but should strive to develop the class consciousness of the workers.[9] Such notions – combining science and politics – fired the imagination of the young Hilferding. Although he received his medical degree in 1902, his real interest became political economy. After setting up a practice as a pediatrician, economics became his true passion.[10]

Hilferding first came to Kautsky's attention in April of 1902, just a month after earning his degree, when the twenty-four-year old sent him an essay regarded by many as the best defense of Marx's value theory against the

---

7   Kurata 1978, pp. 22–23, 28–29; Renner 1946, 245, 25, 278–79.
8   On Grünberg see Nenning 1973, pp. 126–28, and Bottomore and Goode (eds.) 1978, pp. 9–10. On Mach see Blum 1985, p. 20. For Böhm-Bawerk's influence on Hilferding see Rosner 1988, pp. 309–19.
9   Bottomore and Goode (eds.) 1978, p. 18; Nenning 1973, 65.
10 Stein 1946, p. 5.

criticisms of Böhm-Bawerk. Kautsky found the article unsuitable for the NZ due to its length and style, but he was impressed enough to invite Hilferding to become a regular contributor to the journal.[11] Hilferding then published several essays on important issues, such as the role of protective tariffs under modern capitalism and the use of the general strike as a tactic in political struggle, which confirmed Kautsky's assessment of the young man's talents. In an October letter to SDAP leader Victor Adler, Kautsky raised the issue of a successor, noting that Hilferding "had made a very good impression on him", and asked his friend what he thought of him.[12]

Ultimately, Kautsky decided not to relinquish control of the NZ, but, over the course of the next few years, he did persuade Hilferding to give up medicine and to devote himself to political economy full time. To facilitate that change, he arranged for Hilferding's appointment to teach political economy at the Berlin Party School in 1906. His recognition of Hilferding's talent proved prescient. After establishing a reputation as a leading economic theorist of what later became known as the Austro-Marxist School, in the wake of the World War and the advent of the Weimar Republic Hilferding would emerge as the SPD's most important thinker. In 1924, when the party created a new theoretical journal, *Die Gesellschaft (Society)*, to replace the defunct NZ, it named Hilferding as chief editor. Thus, twenty years after Kautsky had originally envisioned it, Hilferding truly stepped into his mentor's shoes.

Kautsky and Hilferding were among the leading Marxists of the second and third generations, respectively, of the Austrian and German labor movements. As Christina Morina has noted in her prosopography of nine of the most important Marxists of the second generation, including Kautsky, virtually all came from comfortable middle-class circumstances, were well educated, widely read, curious, and cosmopolitan. Self-assured and confident of their roles as intellectuals and political activists, they were convinced of their ability and right to intervene in the events of the day and to shape the course of history.[13] Hilferding was younger, but his background and outlook were similar to those of this group. He and Kautsky certainly had much in common. Both had attended Gymnasia in Vienna and studied at the university there, but their families had come from the provinces. Kautsky was born in Prague and spent part

---

11 Hilferding to Kautsky, April 23, 1902. The essay was published two years later as "Böhm-Bawerks Marx Kritik", in *Marx-Studien*, 1 (Vienna, 1904).
12 Karl Kautsky to Victor Adler, 18 October 1904, in Friedrich Adler (ed.) 1954, p. 434.
13 Wagner 1996, p. 10; Morina 2016, pp. 476–78. In addition to Kautsky, Morina included Edward Bernstein, Rosa Luxemburg, Victor Adler, Jaures, Jules Guesde, Georgi W. Plekhanov, Vladimir I. Lenin, and Peter B. Struve in her study.

of his childhood there, while Hilferding, born in Vienna, was of Polish Jewish background. Both men entered Austrian socialism as students at a time when national identity had become a burning issue in the Austro-Hungarian Empire, and life in Vienna could be difficult for anyone perceived to be non-German. Their response to this way of thinking was not to seek their political identity in nationality, but rather in the international labor movement.

The most important affinities, however, that drew Kautsky and Hilferding together were their fundamental agreement on matters of Marxist theory and their commitment to the achievement of socialism via democratic means. Although best known as the chief defender of Marxist orthodoxy against efforts by "revisionist" thinkers, such as his former friend Bernstein, to rethink key Marxian concepts such as historical materialism, the labor theory of value, and class struggle, Kautsky was also flexible enough to recognize that the world had changed a great deal since Marx's day, and that the latter's method had to be applied to recent developments even if that meant rethinking previous conclusions. Such an approach was fully in keeping with that of Hilferding, working in the field of political economy, and his Austrian collaborators such as Max Adler (philosophy), Renner (law), and Bauer (the nationalities question), who aimed to "further develop the social theory of Marx and Engels, to subject it to criticism, and to place their teachings in the context of modern intellectual life".[14] Like Kautsky, these young Austro-Marxists viewed themselves not as defenders of dogma, but as social scientists eager to apply Marx's method of analysis to new questions.[15]

Equally as important as their methodological approach was their attitude toward democracy. As Ben Lewis has recently observed, Kautsky used the term "democratic republic" to designate the conditions under which the working class, organized within the social-democratic movement, could come to power and create a socialist society. For Kautsky, the social revolution could "only be attained through political revolution, by means of the fighting proletariat conquering political power. And the sole state form in which socialism can be realized is the republic, the democratic republic".[16] Hilferding echoed these sentiments in no uncertain terms. In a letter to Kautsky written in August 1903 he asserted that "parliament, and its ultimate conquest, is the most suitable means of bringing about the victory of the proletariat". It was, therefore, "not an inappropriate instrument for the dictatorship of the proletariat".[17]

---

14   Hilferding and Max Adler (eds.) 1904, pp. ii–viii.
15   On Kautsky as a social scientist see John H. Kautsky 1994, p. x.
16   Lewis 2020, p. 16.
17   Hilferding to Kautsky, August 31, 1903 KDXII 582 (International Institute for Social History, herafter cited as ISH).

Thus, drawn together by similar attitudes towards scholarly work (*Wissenschaft*) and politics, Hilferding and Kautsky developed a firm political and personal bond. Over the course of their thirty-five-year friendship they would reciprocally influence one another on myriad issues such as the general strike, imperialism, and the nature of the Bolshevik revolution. As one might expect, the content of their letters largely reflected the issues of the moment, and some of their views on important matters, such as the socialization of industry in the context of the German revolution, are not discussed because both men were working together on that project in Berlin and their correspondence had ceased during that time. But the letters show quite clearly how their ideas and relationship evolved within social democracy's ever-changing context.

Just as the older man matured as a theoretician under Friedrich Engels's close mentorship, Hilferding did so under that of Kautsky. Between 1902 and 1907 he wrote over two dozen letters to Kautsky in which the student-teacher relationship is clear, but in which Hilferding's personal and political self-confidence and goals as a theorist also emerge. Focusing on the Böhm-Bawerk essay, the initial letters clearly reflect the insecurity of a novice writing to his master. Hilferding asks his "honored comrade" not only to consider whether the piece is suitable for the *NZ*, but also to judge "whether his efforts to write about economics are 'objectively' justified or not".[18] When Kautsky answered in the affirmative, Hilferding was jubilant and replied that, "It would be an inappropriate claim on your time if I were to fully describe how happy your letter has made me ... Because I was uncertain about how to judge my own work, it was essential to hear the opinion of someone who is, by far, the most competent judge of these matters since Engels' death".[19] Much encouraged, Hilferding then outlined his research agenda, which focused on developments in the capitalist economy that had arisen since Marx's death in 1883. It was this work that eventually formed the core of *Finance Capital*, his magnum opus.

Over the course of the next four years, Hilferding followed up on his economic agenda by writing several articles for the *NZ* on value theory and protective tariffs and by reading and reviewing a large number of books on recent capitalist development. At a time when Kautsky was heavily engaged in the struggle against revisionism, Hilferding also wasted no time in his letters in making clear where he stood in the debate. For example, he asserted that his critique of Böhm-Bawerk also aimed to criticize Bernstein, who had "misunderstood the problem of complex labor and its value".[20] Such views would have

---

18   Hilferding to Kautsky, April 23, 1902, KDXII 580 (ISH).
19   Hilferding to Kautsky, May 21, 1902, KDXII 581 (ISH).
20   Hilferding to Kautsky, April 23, 1902, KDXII 580 (ISH).

been welcomed by Kautsky, who needed allies in his effort to build an ideologically unified, class-based movement. Likewise, Hilferding's position on using the general strike as a weapon in social democratic politics. In the wake of Belgian workers' failed attempt in 1902 to use the strike to broaden the franchise and, three years later, of the Russian workers' efforts to use it against the Tsarist autocracy, Hilferding argued that, in Germany, where social democracy had made enormous gains using parliamentary methods, it should only use the general strike when its enemies, fearful of a socialist majority, moved to suppress the labor movement and thus unleashed what could only be the final struggle between the proletariat and the bourgeoisie.[21] Hilferding believed that the threat of the general strike in an advanced economy like Germany's, where the proletarian party and trade unions were well organized and prepared for battle, could keep reactionary forces at bay and thus preserve the party's parliamentary tactic. For him, "parliament was the terrain where economic power is transformed into political power. The proletariat, like the bourgeoisie currently, could use it in its own interest".[22]

Hilferding was very interested in comparing how the Austrian and German Social Democratic parties, operating in very different contexts, handled challenging problems. For example, according to Hilferding, when it came to big strikes, the SDAP's leadership generally played a much more direct role in their settlement than the SPD leaders did. In his view, it was imperative that the social democratic trade unions, cooperatives, and the party build institutional connections in order to facilitate communication and effective action, and he thought the Austrians had accomplished more in that regard than the Germans.[23] He and Kautsky agreed that the trade unions, which rejected the general strike as a dangerous threat to their organizations, should be subordinated to the party's political leadership, and both were critical of the revisionist inclinations of the SPD's flagship newspaper *Vorwärts*. Indeed, HIlferding believed that that paper had "failed in all important things" and that this failure was a result of careerists and opportunists permeating the editorial boards of the party press and the institutions of the party in general.[24]

Most fundamentally, as Hilferding's comments on parliamentary politics made clear, he agreed with Kautsky that, "Our task is not to organize the revolu-

---

21   Rudolf Hilferding, "Zur Frage des Generalstreiks", NZ 22, 1 (1903/04): 134–42; "Parlamentarismus und Massenstreik", NZ 23, 2(1904/05): 804–816.
22   Hilferding to Kautsky, August 31, 1903, KDXII 582 (ISH).
23   Hilferding to Kautsky March 14 and April 3, 1905, KDXII 588 and KDXII 589, resp. (ISH).
24   See, for example, Hilferding's letters to Kautsky of May 27 and October 30, 1905, KDXII 590 and KDXII 594, resp. (ISH).

tion, but to organize ourselves for the revolution; it is not to make the revolution, but to take advantage of it".[25] In fact, as the events of the Russian Revolution of 1905 began to unfold, he believed the revolution in the West was close at hand. In a letter to Kautsky in November of 1905 he wrote, "I can imagine how much the most recent events have moved you. The collapse of Tsarism is the beginning of our revolution, of our victory, that is now drawing near [...]".[26] But in 1905 he did not call for a change in Social Democracy's parliamentary tactics either in Germany or Austria-Hungary.

Hilferding's early letters illuminate how the two men grew increasingly close but, as was common in the Central European culture of the time, not too close. Hilferding wrote in detail about social democratic politics, about the qualities of various individual political acquaintances, and sometimes found himself a middleman conveying information between Kautsky and Austrian comrades such as Victor Adler. By 1905 Hilferding's "honored comrade" had become his "highly honored friend", and he and his new wife, Margarethe Hönigsberg, had visited the Kautsky home in Berlin Friedenau for several months. There they were welcomed into the Kautskys' social circle, and Hilferding became personally acquainted with leading socialist intellectuals such as Franz Mehring, Emanuel Wurm, and Rosa Luxemburg, who joined Kautsky in urging him to move to Berlin. Upon his return to Vienna, Hilferding expressed great longing for the Kautsky household and made clear his desire to leave Vienna for Berlin, but professional and familial obligations (his mother was ill) held him back. Meanwhile the two men continued writing letters, and Hilferding and Margarethe sometimes exchanged friendly notes with Kautsky's wife, Luise.[27] The letters seem open and frank, but Hilferding continued to use the formal "Sie" when addressing his mentor. A certain threshold had not yet been crossed.

Meanwhile, Hilferding faced some difficult personal decisions. By early 1906 Kautsky was pressing him to take the job teaching political economy at the new party school in Berlin. Hilferding had been one of the co-founders of the SDAP's own school in Vienna, called *Die Zukunft* (The Future), and placed great stock on the education of future worker leaders. For various reasons, however, he hesitated, and in a series of letters written in 1906, asserted that he was not suited to take the post because he had not yet really accomplished anything major and would be a foreigner, an outsider. While he wracked his brains about ways in which to become a German citizen, at one point even considering being adop-

---

25 Kautsky, "Verschwörung oder Revolution?" *Der Sozialdemokrat*, Nr. 8, February 20, 1881.
26 Hilferding to Kautsky, November 14, 1905, KDXII 597 (ISH).
27 See, for example, Hilferding's letters to Kautsky of March 14 and April 3, 1905, KDXII 588 & 589, respectively (ISH).

ted (by whom is unclear), he also thought that he might be more useful serving the Austrian movement, possibly as the editor of a soon to be founded new journal, *Der Kampf* (*Struggle*), which would be designed not to compete with the theory oriented NZ, but rather to focus on practical problems. He was also unhappy about the decision taken in Berlin to establish a trade union school that would be separate from the party's and feared that, because the trade union school was staffed by high quality revisionist teachers, a sharp divide would emerge between these two key branches of the labor movement. He did not think his presence would alter the balance significantly.[28]

In addition to these qualms, there was the matter of his family. Margarethe was a physician and a socialist intellectual in her own right.[29] They had met in the Socialist Student League, and Margarethe was the first woman to graduate from the medical school at the University of Vienna, receiving her degree in December 1903. In March 1904 Rudolf and Margarethe officially withdrew from the Vienna Jewish community and a month later married in a civil ceremony in which they gave their religious affiliation as "none". As a physician, Margarethe focused on women's concerns and was keen to establish her own practice, but this process was delayed by her first pregnancy in 1905 which ended in September with the birth of their first child, Karl Emil, named after Karl Marx and Rudolf's recently deceased father. During the following year, in addition to dealing with the new arrival, Rudolf pursued his own medical practice and was active in party affairs, while Margarethe restarted her practice and finished her training in gynecology at a local clinic. They were clearly very busy.

Yet very little is known about how well the pair actually got along. As Margarethe's biographer, Eveline List, points out, the two were clearly drawn together by similar intellectual and political interests, but the record is too thin to make any judgements about the level of passion in the relationship. No letters between them have survived and only one photo of them has been preserved. As was often the case in that period among middle-class intellectuals, even well-acquainted correspondents rarely discussed private affairs in any detail, and Rudolf's comments to Kautsky about his family life are usually brief and rather superficial. Still, there can be little doubt that Margarethe's professional future had to have played a role in their discussions. For two Austrian socialist intellectuals to move to Imperial Germany – not known for its tolerance toward its own dissidents – was risky enough, but issues related to their professional credentials and ability to work also had to be concerning.

---

28   Hilferding to Kautsky March 10 and August 20, 1906, KDXII 599 and 601, resp., (ISH).
29   On Margarethe Hönigsberg's relationship to Rudolf see List 2006, pp. 101–17.

In any event, they somehow reached a decision and in September 1906 Hilferding told Kautsky he was prepared to accept his suggestion that he take the job at the party school and co-edit the *NZ*. He told his friend that "The prospect of being able to work by your side and the hope of perhaps being able [...] to provide [you] with some relief are too tempting to resist".[30] Rudolf moved to Berlin in November. Margarethe stayed behind in Vienna to complete her training and arrived with Karl Emil the following spring.

Things did not go as planned. After one term Hilferding had to resign from the party school when Prussian authorities enforced a law prohibiting the hiring of non-Germans as teachers. To keep him in Berlin, the SPD leadership then offered Rudolf a position as foreign editor of *Vörwarts*, which he accepted. Since this was a full-time job, he also gave up his post editing the *NZ*. Matters worked out less well with Margarethe, who learned upon her arrival that she could not lawfully practice medicine in Germany. In January 1908 she gave birth to a second boy, Peter Friedrich, named after Friedrich Engels, but soon decided to return to Vienna with the children. By the fall she was practicing medicine there.

Rudolf did not follow. For him there could be no going back. Having made the decision to devote his life to the socialist cause, he was determined to stay in Berlin – the headquarters of the world's most important Social Democratic party – where his editorial post at *Vorwärts* and access to the pages of the *NZ* gave him real influence. He and Margarethe would remain in contact, but relations were sometimes rocky, and he was, to say the least, a distant father.[31] Meanwhile, by 1907 he and Kautsky had forged a close working relationship, though he was still the junior partner. Of course, he also had his own ambitions, especially in the realm of theory. In that sphere he made his career with the publication of *Finance Capital* in 1910. Drawing widely on the work of non-Marxist and Marxist thinkers, including Kautsky, who had also written

---

30 Hilferding to Kautsky, September 6, 1906, KDXII, 602 (ISH).
31 Margarethe essentially raised the couple's two boys alone. She continued to practice medicine and in 1910 was the first female member of the Vienna Psychoanalytical Association founded by Sigmund Freud. She also published extensively about birth control and worked as a school physician. Following Germany's annexation of Austria in 1938, the Nazis arrested her and son, Peter, an economist, and seized their property. After their release, Peter migrated to New Zealand, but Margarethe remained in Vienna under difficult circumstances. In 1942 the Nazis deported her to Theresienstadt and then to Treblinka, where she was murdered in September. Karl Hilferding, who was training to become a Catholic priest in Holland, was murdered in Niederkirch, a subcamp of Auschwitz, in December 1942.

about credit, protective tariffs, joint stock companies, and imperialism, Hilferding expanded and reformulated many of their ideas to produce a work widely hailed as the fourth volume of Marx's *Capital*.[32]

Three main points form the book's core: first, that the most characteristic features of "modern" capitalism are "those processes of concentration which, on the one hand, 'eliminate free competition' through the formation of cartels and trusts, and on the other, bring bank and industrial capital into an ever more intimate relationship. Through this relationship ... capital assumes the form of finance capital, its supreme and most abstract expression"; second, that there are, in principle, no limits to this process of centralization so that "the ultimate outcome of the process would be the formation of a general cartel"; and third, that this effort to introduce the "conscious regulation" of the whole of capitalist production would "inevitably come to grief on the conflict of interests [in society] which intensify to an extreme point". Such conflicts were exemplified by social polarization at home between the capitalist oligarchy and the mass of the people and abroad as imperialist rivalry among the capitalist powers made war likely and, in turn, opened the way to proletarian revolution.[33]

Hilferding believed that the development of finance capital and the introduction of large-scale planning laid the foundation for socialism but would not resolve the social conflicts engendered by capitalist property relations. Only the introduction of socialism, most likely via a violent revolution precipitated by capital, could resolve the property question and sweep away the basis of class conflict. Hilferding and Kautsky shared this basic outlook over the next two decades, although they would also adapt it in the face of rapidly changing conditions after 1914.

Theoretically, *Finance Capital* aimed to refute Bernstein's attacks on key elements of Marx's economic theory; politically, it suggested no changes in the movement's tactics. Between 1906 and the coming of the World War, Hilferding and Kautsky defended this position as leaders of the so-called Marxist center, which rejected the open reformism of the revisionist right while also opposing an emerging radical left, led by Rosa Luxemburg, which aimed to pursue a more aggressive extra-parliamentary strategy to prepare the masses for revolution and build the movement. Hilferding was able to put forward his views from his post at *Vorwärts*, where he soon became the paper's leading editor, and he published dozens of articles and book reviews in NZ and *Der Kampf* on a wide

---

32 Bauer 1909–1910, p. 397; Kautsky 1910–1911, p. 883; Gronow 2017, p. 3; Greitens, 2013, pp. 18–35. The most thorough recent study of *Finance Capital* is Greitens, *Finanzkapital und Finanzsysteme* (2012).
33 Rudolf Hilferding 1981, pp. 21, 234, 296–297, 370.

range of economic and political issues. At the same time, during these years Hilferding also began to make a career in the Social Democratic party hierarchy. In 1912 he was appointed to the Party Council, a body which advised the SPD's Executive Committee on a variety of issues. Unlike Kautsky, who never had official positions within the party, he now increasingly had to deal with day-to-day practical politics.

In August 1914 Hilferding and Kautsky opposed the majority of the SPD leadership's decision to support the government war effort. Together with party co-Chair Hugo Haase, Kautsky initially wrote a draft statement opposing the war, but it was rejected by the pro-war majority in the SPD's Reichstag delegation. His effort to add language attacking the ruling classes and demanding that any approval of war credits require the government to renounce any annexations of territory or violations of neutrality to the majority's official declaration also went nowhere. Hilferding supported these efforts and co-signed a declaration of a majority of *Vorwärts*' editors opposing the war.[34] Although they hoped to avoid a party split, both joined the opposition and were expelled, along with the rest of the anti-war dissidents, early in 1917. They then helped found the new anti-war Independent Social Democratic Party (USPD), which included representatives from all of the SPD's pre-war factions including Bernstein and Luxemburg. Drafted into the Austro-Hungarian Army's medical corps in 1915, Hilferding eventually was posted to various clinics, first in Vienna and later on the Italian front. He was not without spare time and continued to write essays on politics and economics. He also renewed his correspondence with Kautsky.

Hilferding's wartime letters show that their friendship had grown more intimate. Although he still addressed Kautsky using the formal "Sie", he also now greeted him as his "dear friend" and, in addition to the usual political and economic themes, also wrote occasionally of family problems. For Hilferding, Kautsky now served as a window to the outside world, especially when he was stationed nearer to the front. He depended on his friend not only for books and "conversation", but also for inside information about political affairs in Germany and elsewhere. In June of 1915 he expressed great joy after reading *The Demand of the Hour*, a manifesto written by Bernstein, Kautsky, and Hugo Haase, which condemned the government's war of conquest and called for a peace of understanding. A month later he urged the systematic organization of the opposition.[35] Over the course of 1915 and 1916 Hilferding published a series of sharp polemics against Social Democrats, including his old friend Karl

---

34   Steenson 1978, pp. 179–80; Smaldone 1998, p. 61.
35   "Das Gebot der Stunde" is reprinted in Eugen Prager 1970, pp. 72–74; Hliferding to Kautsky, June 22, 1915 & July 29, 1915, KDXII 608 & 609, resp., (ISH).

INTRODUCTION TO PART 1: PASSING THE TORCH

Renner, who urged cooperation with the autocratic state or who called for the creation of a post-war Mitteleuropa (Central Europe) dominated by Germany and Austria-Hungary.[36] Kautsky published many of these in the *Neue Zeit* until the party leadership took it away from him in 1917.

Hilferding and Kautsky had similar views of events in Russia. During the tumultuous summer of 1917, Hilferding initially dismissed the Bolsheviks' chances of taking or holding power, and, in the wake of the "July Days" fiasco in Petrograd, he expected Kerensky's government to "finish them off".[37] After the resilient Bolsheviks seized power in October, Hilferding noted to his friend on 3 December that they were still in agreement. "There is something tragic", he wrote, "in the fate of the Russian Revolution in general and the Bolsheviks in particular. One's heart is on their side [...] but reason does not follow. I fear they will not be able to keep their promises and their intentions are not clear". Did they want a separate peace? If so, on what terms? Did they think they could actually remain neutral with respect to the Entente? What about Trotsky's claim in 1905 that the dictatorship of the proletariat could only survive if the revolution spread throughout Europe? Hilferding asserted that "the situation is truly incomparable because the combination of revolutionary proletariat and revolutionary peasantry, armed and organized in one army in which the officer corps is in total disarray, has never existed. It has much power on its side, but on the other side stands not only the whole bourgeoisie, but also the power of all the other states. And that Germany should really make it easy for the Bolsheviks by repudiating its plans in the east, thereby helping to stabilize this great revolution in a neighboring country, I'll believe that when I see it". And what if the Germans don't cooperate and it comes to war, he asked? Only help from the western European proletariat could save the Bolsheviks, but he did not think such assistance seemed likely.[38]

These comments make clear Hilferding's early skepticism about the Bolshevik seizure of power. Like Kautsky and virtually all other Marxists at the time, he was dubious about the prospects for socialism in an economically backward, peasant society. But the decisive issue for Hilferding and Kautsky was

---

[36] See, for example, Hilferding 1915b, pp. 489–99. On his polemic against Renner, see Hilferding 1916, pp. 54–63.

[37] Between July 16 and July 20, 1917 (new style calendar) mass protests in Petrograd demanded that the soviets seize power from the Provisional Government. Although the Bolsheviks did not publicly support the protesters, they were blamed for the "July Days" unrest and subsequently proscribed (temporarily) by Kerensky's government. It is unlikely Hilferding had much detailed information about these events. See Hilferding to Kautsky, July 21, 1917 KDXII 579 (ISH).

[38] Hilferding to Kautsky, December 3, 1917, KDXII 631 (ISH).

the Bolshevik attitude toward democracy. For them, there could be "no socialism without democracy" and as the revolution became more authoritarian, their support for it waned.[39] With the abrogation of the Russian Constituent Assembly in January 1918, the suppression of all dissent within the soviets, the imposition of a single party dictatorship through the use of mass terror, and the effort to split the international labor movement, both men became vigorous opponents of the Communist regime and the targets of the Bolsheviks' unremitting hatred.[40]

In addition to the myriad political issues raised by the war, Kautsky and Hilferding were also thinking about theoretical matters. Drawing on Hilferding's concept of the general cartel, in September 1914 Kautsky published an article proposing that the imperialist war "represents only one among various modes of capitalist expansion". This had been true historically – witness the move from free-trade to protectionism in the late-nineteenth century – and also would be true in the future, as the ruling capitalists considered how the costs of militarism hindered capital accumulation. Kautsky foresaw the possibility of a shift, a new phase of imperialist development, in which capital translates cartelization into foreign policy. This "ultra-imperialism" would bring the great powers into a postwar "federation of the strongest" that would "renounce the arms race" and cooperate in the accumulation process. Workers must, of course, combat such a "Holy Alliance", which does not change their subordinate condition, but war as a result of economic imperatives would no longer threaten world peace.[41]

Hilferding was also rethinking the general cartel. Whereas earlier he had argued that cartelization under finance capital exacerbated economic crises, he now held that it actually shortened them, reduced chronic unemployment, and tended to transform the anarchy of capitalist production into an "organized capitalist" economic order in which state power – magnified by the war – would play an increasingly important role. Instead of socialism being victorious, it was now possible for an organized but undemocratic economy to emerge, controlled by monopoly capital and the state. Thus, the choice for the future was between organized state capitalism and democratic socialism. In a context of intensified class struggle, it was the task of the Marxists in the party to

---

39 Most clearly spelled out in Kautsky 1971, p. 6.
40 Kautsky fired the first round in what became a vicious and long-running polemic with the Bolsheviks with the publication of *The Dictatorship of the Proletariat* in Vienna in 1918. Lenin responded in that same year with *The Proletarian Revolution and the Renegade Kautsky*, which thereafter remained the touchstone of all Communist criticisms of Kautsky. In 1919 Kautsky followed up with *Terrorism and Communism*, which Trotsky answered with *Terrorism and Communism: A Reply to Karl Kautsky* in 1920.
41 Karl Kautsky, "Der Imperialismus", *NZ* 32, 2 (September 14, 1914): 920–922.

instruct the masses concerning their long-term interests. First put forward in 1915, within a decade the concept of organized capitalism would become the central theoretical principle guiding social democratic politics.[42]

During the last two years of the war it was sometimes difficult for Hilferding to keep fully appraised of what was going on at home and abroad from his differing postings. Nevertheless, he was able to receive enough information to comment frequently on developments in Germany, Russia, and elsewhere. He also found himself forced to cheer up the usually optimistic Kautsky, who was feeling low in the wake of the SPD's split and his loss of control over the NZ. Hilferding claimed that, although there were "practically no socialist groups" with whom they could identify, he remained relatively optimistic about developments in general because he did not expect too much from the USPD until matters had been settled on the battlefield. For him, the events occurring at home and in Russia were a mere prologue to the decisive developments that would follow the war and be centered in the West.[43]

In his last letters from the front in the fall of 1918 Hilferding indicated that he sensed the war's impending end. He was not sure when it would occur or where he would go when it was over. On 15 October he wrote to Kautsky that he was making inquiries in Berlin and Vienna but was sure that he would only be able to achieve something in the former. Without going into detail, he said he was "counting on" Hugo Haase to assist him, which most likely referred to his securing an editorial post at *Die Freiheit* [*Freedom*], the USPD's flagship newspaper.[44] Two weeks later, he noted that rising Pan-German nationalism was a major factor in Austria's deepening crisis, but he did not think the disintegration on the home front would advance so rapidly in Germany.[45] The sudden overthrow of both the Austrian and German governments in early November soon upended that assumption. By mid-November he was back in Berlin where he threw himself into revolutionary activity.

During the German Revolution, Hilferding played a key role in national politics as chief editor of *Freiheit* and as a member of the USPD's Executive Committee. Kautsky occupied no official party positions but participated in USPD policy debates and, along with Hilferding, was appointed to a government commission to study the socialization of the economy, which he also chaired. Both Hilferding and Kautsky held that the need for postwar reconstruction pre-

---

42 Rudolf Hilferding, "Arbeitsgemeinschaft der Klassen?" *Der Kampf* 8 (1915): 321–329.
43 Hilferding to Kautsky, October 13, 1917, December 3, 1917 and September 8, 1918, KDXII 630, 631, and 632, resp. (ISH).
44 Hilferding to Kautsky, October 15, 1928, KDXII 633 (ISH).
45 Hilferding to Kautsky, October 28, 1918, KDXII 634 (ISH).

cluded rapid and sweeping economic transformations. They argued, instead, for constructing a new socialist order based on the gradual socialization of large-scale industry, natural resources, and the big Junker estates, leaving small and medium-sized producers largely untouched. They also opposed creating a system run by a state bureaucracy or solely by workers' councils. In keeping with their pre-1914 commitment to parliamentary democracy, they believed that socialist majorities in parliament could oversee the establishment of an economy managed by new institutions in which the state, workers, and consumers were equally represented.[46] To their great disappointment, their commission's proposals met the effective resistance not only of the non-socialist majority dominating the Reichstag, but also of the SPD, which feared further economic disruption and civil war and was mainly concerned with consolidating the new republican polity.

Hilferding and Kautsky also fought tenaciously against the newly founded German Communist Party (KPD) on the left as well as against the resurgent nationalist right. By 1920 the USPD had become a major political force as many workers, disappointed with the SPD's hesitancy to push the revolution forward, swelled the ranks of the party which grew from 300,000 to 750,000 between January and October of 1919. Many USPD members, inspired by the Russian Revolution, favored the party's entrance into the newly founded, Bolshevik-dominated Communist International (The Comintern). The latter, in turn, aimed to detach the USPD's "revolutionary" left wing from the party's "reformist" elements by excluding "notorious opportunists", such as Hilferding and Kautsky, and merging the left with the miniscule KPD, which would then be transformed into a mass party effectively under Moscow's control. At the USPD's extraordinary Halle Congress of October 1920, it was Hilferding who was the chief spokesman for those who opposed this move. In a dramatic confrontation with the Comintern's special envoy, Grigori Zinoviev, he echoed many of Kautsky's views as he criticized the Bolsheviks' usurpation of soviet power, their elimination of dissent, their use of terror, and their effort to undermine the USPD's autonomy, but to no avail.[47] The resulting schism cost the party two thirds of its members, a blow from which it never recovered. Two years later, faced with the growing threat of counterrevolution from the nationalist right, Hilferding and Kautsky supported the reunification of the rump USPD with the SPD.[48]

---

46   See, for example, Hilferding 1919; Kautsky 1919.
47   Hilferding 1982, 133–65.
48   Morgan 1975, pp. 419–38.

Following reunification, Hilferding's star continued to rise. In addition to editing the *Gesellschaft*, he was elected to the SPD's Executive Committee and to parliament. At the height of the hyperinflation of 1923 and, again, in 1928–29, he served the republic as Finance Minister. Meanwhile in 1924, after drafting the party's new *Heidelberg Program*, which Hilferding presented at the party congress,[49] the now 70-year-old Kautsky decided to return to Vienna. This move led to the resumption of their correspondence.

By 1924 their friendship clearly had become very close. Hilferding now addressed Kautsky with the familiar "Du", and wrote to him in familial terms. Lamenting his decision to leave Berlin, he noted that Kautsky "had taken him in like a son", that their friendship had "made him feel secure and protected" and that his departure left him with "virtually no one with whom I can speak candidly and usefully about serious problems". Writing to Kautsky's son, Benedikt (Bendel), he referred to Karl and Luise as "father and mother". It is clear that Kautsky's leaving affected him deeply.[50]

Meanwhile, Hilferding continued to rely on his friend as a contributor to *Die Gesellschaft* and over the next nine years published 22 of his essays and reviews. He also depended on him as a sounding board on political matters. The two men certainly agreed that the SPD had to adapt its strategy to the new republican order. No longer could the party go it alone as it had done under the pseudo-autocratic imperial regime. Now, in a republic that was its own creation, it had to "conquer a majority or form alliances in order to carry out the demands it made in the opposition" and the use of extra-parliamentary means would be limited.[51] Hilferding knew that achieving this aim would not be easy. Concerned about the future of socialism, he missed having Kautsky nearby to discuss the challenges socialists faced in drawing workers into the task of economic management as well as addressing the moral and cultural aspects of their lives.[52]

Hilferding's influence on Kautsky's theoretical outlook also remained strong. In drafting the *Heidelberg Program*, Kautsky grounded this openly reformist road to socialism largely on Hilferding's theory of finance capitalism. Within the framework of finance capitalism, the labor movement had to use the new

---

49 For Hilferding's speech at the Heidelberg Congress and the subsequent discussion see Kampfmeyer (ed.) 1947.
50 See, for example, letters from Hilferding to Kautsky from July 19 and October 19, 1924, KDXII 636 & 638, resp. (ISH).
51 Rudolf Hilferding, "Wandel in der Politik", *Die Frankfurter Zeitung*, December 31, 1922 (second morning edition).
52 Hilferding to Kautsky, July 19, 1924, KDXII 636.

parliamentary order to achieve reforms in all spheres and gradually move society toward socialism.[53]

Meanwhile, Kautsky's theory of "ultra-imperialism" clearly shaped Hilferding's thinking, as he now argued that as finance capitalism developed into an increasingly stable system of organized capitalism on the domestic plane, it would have a similar impact on international relations. The victory of the West in 1918 had altered the relationship of the imperialist powers, which were now primarily concerned with holding onto their empires against rising colonial nationalism and were unwilling to unleash another destructive war to secure their economic interests. Instead, Hilferding thought they would pursue a policy of "realistic pacifism" in which they jointly exploited the world market. He suggested that, just as within each advanced capitalist state social democracy should use its enhanced postwar power to pursue socialist reforms, it also should create new transnational institutions to limit national sovereignty, promote disarmament, and pursue progressive economic and social policies.[54]

The period from 1924–1929, Weimar's "Golden Age", was one of relative economic and political stability and the calm was reflected in Hilferding's letters. While Kautsky, ever the scholar, focused on writing *Die materialistische Geschichtsauffassung* (*The Materialist Conception of History*), his two-volume magnum opus, among other works, Hilferding led the life of a busy politician. Having divorced Margarethe in 1923, he then married Rose Lanyi (1884–1959), a Czech-born physician and translator, and settled into a comfortable life in the middle class Steglitz neighborhood in Berlin. Hilferding's practical concerns as a leading SPD parliamentarian, as editor of the party's most important theoretical journal, as member of the Executive, to say nothing of his time as Finance Minister, were all consuming and, much to his chagrin, prevented him from executing large scale research projects. While he regularly produced essays on a wide range of subjects, these dealt largely with practical political problems facing the movement.

Hilferding's letters between 1924 and 1928 mainly concern publishing matters of various kinds with occasional extended observations about the political situation. One issue concerned Hilferding's desire to publish a review of the

---

53 "Programm der Sozialdemokratischen Partei Deutschlands beschloßen auf dem Parteitag in Heidelberg 1925", in Dieter Dowe and Kurt Klotzbach, eds., *Programmatische Dokumente der Deutschen Sozialdemokratie* (Bonn: Dietz, 2004), 194–203.

54 Rudolf Hilferding, "Realistischer Pazifismus", *Die Gesellschaft* 1, 2 (1924): 97–114; William Smaldone, "Can Capitalism Lead to Peace?" *Radical Philosophy Review, Special Issue, Violence: Systemic, Symbolic, and Foundational* 15, 1 (2012): 203–218.

first volume of the *Marx-Engels Collected Works*, edited by the Bolshevik scholar David Riazanov. Hilferding thought very highly of Riazanov's work and hoped that Kautsky, or his son Benedikt, would review it. Kautsky apparently thought that Hilferding's favorable view of Riazanov indicated that he was getting soft on the Bolsheviks, and Hilferding had to make a considerable effort to calm his mentor's fears. While he had no objections to polemicizing against Bolshevism in the pages of the magazine, he drew a distinction between Riazanov's considerable achievements as a scholar, and the politics of his party. In the end, Hilferding made sure to emphasize that he and Kautsky were united in their effort to "overcome communism".[55] Benedikt wrote the review.

Hilferding's letters make clear that he opposed any SPD participation in a coalition government if it meant sharing power with the business oriented German People's Party (DVP), which had fallen under the control of its right wing. Having been bloodied by its participation in the coalition government during the height of the inflation in 1923, the SPD needed time in the opposition to lick its wounds and rebuild its support. By the time of the Kiel Party Congress of 1927, however, Hilferding was convinced that the DVP had moved to the left and could be a cooperative partner. In his keynote speech at Kiel he argued that the SPD should go into the next round of parliamentary elections prepared to assume power, because the working class needed to use the state to carry out much needed social and political reforms, broaden its base of support, and prevent the radical right from undermining the republic. Hilferding's outlook won the day, and in May 1928 the SPD won an impressive victory at the polls (just short of 30 per cent of the vote) and took the helm of a new "Great Coalition" that included representatives from the Catholic Center Party, the Democratic Party, the Bavarian People's Party, and the DVP. Hilferding was appointed Finance Minister in a cabinet headed by his friend Hermann Müller.

Kiel marked the high tide of Hilferding's theoretical and political influence. As the liberal *Vossiche Zeitung* put it on the occasion of his fiftieth birthday in 1927, even though at that moment he was neither a member of the cabinet nor the SPD's official chief, he was "without question the intellectual leader of Germany's largest party".[56] Once the new cabinet was formed, however, it soon became clear that Hilferding's hopes at Kiel had been far too optimistic and sharp differences over military, economic, and other policies would make governing extraordinarily difficult. The onset of the Great Depression in late 1929 resulted in the coalition's collapse in March 1930.

---

55   Hiferding to Kautsky, January 13, 1928, KDXII 649 (ISH).
56   *Vossische Zeitung*, August 27, 1927.

Between June 1928 and April 1931 Hilferding's correspondence with Kautsky appears to have come to a temporary halt. It is possible that some letters have been lost, since we know Kautsky continued to publish in *Die Gesellschaft* during that time, but he may have dealt with one of Hilferding's editorial assistants. In any case, Hilferding was certainly extremely busy during these years and was, no doubt, rather depressed given political developments. Indeed, things went from bad to worse following the fall of Müller's government. In the Reichstag elections of September 1930, the National Socialist German Workers Party (NSDAP or the Nazis) increased its vote from 2 percent in 1928 to 18 percent, while the Communists, contrary to Hilferding's hopes, also did well with 14 percent. Over the next two and a half years, the growth of these extremist anti-republican parties paralyzed the Reichstag and, since none of the other increasingly conservative bourgeois parties were willing to cooperate any longer with the SPD, the formation of a stable, majority-backed government became virtually impossible. As a result, Germany was governed by a series of minority governments headed by increasingly anti-republican Chancellors, such as the conservative Catholic Center leader Heinrich Brüning, who secured the agreement of the reactionary President Paul von Hindenburg to use emergency powers granted by Article 48 of the Constitution to rule by decree. Thus, as the economic misery of the depression intensified and politics became more polarized, the republic began dying a slow death.[57]

Isolated in the Reichstag, the SPD's dilemma was profound. Brüning's cabinet had little support, and his policy of economic austerity further impoverished workers and only deepened the depression. A parliamentary vote of no confidence would have brought Brüning down and thus triggered new elections, but fear of further Nazi and Communist gains made that an unacceptable option for the Socialists. As an alternative, Hilferding urged the SPD leadership to "tolerate" Brüning's government in the hope that, by supporting the lesser evil, the party would buy time during which the economic crisis would bottom out and a subsequent upswing would take the wind out of the extremists' sails. Unfortunately for the SPD, when its leaders adopted this approach, they then associated themselves with Brüning's policies and alienated many workers from the party.

Understandably, Hilferding found this situation very depressing and told Kautsky on 15 April 1931 that he found it very hard to write. Still, over the next two years, he wrote frequently and sometimes at length about the party's

---

[57] The literature on Social Democracy's dilemma is immense. For a summary discussion see Smaldone 2008, pp. 1–21.

dilemma and his fears about the future. Two issues were particularly important. The first was Hilferding's dismay at "the terrible [political] immaturity of broad sectors of the people and the infuriatingly primitive way in which they react to material conditions". It was this immaturity, he thought, that led many to abandon their faith in the democratic republic and to turn to the Nazis and Communists. In a situation in which "the fight for the maintenance of democracy no longer satisfies the psychological needs of the broad masses", he despaired at having nothing to offer beyond the policy of toleration.[58]

Secondly, while Hilferding was able to effectively apply Marxist methods to gain an understanding of capitalist development, these were of no use to him in responding to the crisis. Indeed, in October 1931 he asserted that "the basic evil is that we cannot say anything to the people about how and by what means we can end the crisis". While capitalism had been shaken "far beyond our expectations", no socialist solution was at hand, deepening the political crisis and allowing the Communists and Nazis to grow.[59] Chastened by the experience of post-war hyperinflation, Hilferding feared any options that would have involved Keynesian-style deficit spending to stimulate demand. The few policy recommendations he did offer remained largely within the framework of capitalist orthodoxy.[60]

Brüning fell from power in May 1932, but his successor, right-wing Catholic leader Franz von Papen, had even less parliamentary backing. In subsequent elections to the Reichstag in July and November of 1932 the SPD's fortunes declined as its support fell to 20 percent of the electorate. Although the Nazis more than doubled their support to 37 percent in July, in November they sustained a setback and slipped to 33 percent. Meanwhile, the Communists with 17 percent seemed poised to overtake the SPD for the first time. Still unwilling to appoint Adolf Hitler to the Chancellorship, Hindenburg appointed a general, Kurt von Schleicher, to the post on 3 December. Hilferding remarked to Kautsky that he thought this move might bring "a certain easing of tension", but he was also fearful that, threatened by the forces of extremism, some in the SPD might make "adventurist mistakes".[61]

Hilferding had always asserted that supporters of the republic had the right to resort to any means necessary, including violence, to defend it against myriad enemies.[62] His letters to Kautsky and his published writings in the early 1930s

---

58 Hilferding to Kautsky, April 15, 1931, KDXII 652 (ISH).
59 Hilferding to Kautsky, October 2, 1931, KDXII 653 (ISH).
60 Smaldone 1998, pp. 120–23, 166–67.
61 Hilferding to Kautsky, December 1, 1932, KDXII 658, (ISH).
62 See, for example, Hilferding in Kampfmeyer (ed.) 1925, pp. 22.

show that he clearly understood that the Nazis' aim was to use parliamentary means to destroy the parliamentary order. Fearing that, if invited to share power in a right-wing coalition, they would take control of the state's administrative apparatus, the military, and the police, he asserted that "Once such a government is formed it would be very difficult to remove", and the Nazis and their reactionary partners would be able to destroy the republic.[63] Yet, when Hindenburg made the decision to appoint Hitler Chancellor on 30 January 1933, Hilferding joined with the majority of his colleagues in the SPD leadership and advocated a wait and see policy instead of calling for mass action. As in July 1932, when Reich Chancellor von Papen had illegally removed the SPD-caretaker government from power in Prussia, in January and February of 1933 the SPD leaders were unprepared to mobilize the party and trade unions for a general strike. Fearful of launching a civil war that they felt they could not win against the Reichswehr and Nazi paramilitary formations, they never seriously entertained overthrowing Hitler's government to save the republic. While the Social Democrats waited to act until Hitler violated the Constitution, the Nazis used a combination of their control over the state and police apparatus, a pseudo-parliamentary strategy, and a campaign of terror to destroy their enemies one by one and consolidate power. By June 1933, they were able to outlaw or absorb all other political parties, crush the trade unions, and drive those opponents not yet imprisoned either underground, into exile, or into silence.

Warned of his impending arrest following the Reichstag's passage of the Enabling Law giving Hitler full power on 23 March, Hilferding fled to Denmark a few days later. After stopping in Saarbrücken – still under French administration – and Paris, where other German exiles were gathering, he moved to Zürich in June and remained there until 1938. From Zürich he resumed his correspondence with Kautsky, who was now almost eighty, but remained intellectually vibrant and productive.

There can be no doubt that, in the spring of 1933, Hilferding was in shock. Just a few months before he had been among the top leaders of Europe's most important Social Democratic party. As a former government minister, leading parliamentarian, and well known intellectual, he could count himself a member of the republic's political elite, living a comfortable, interesting, if sometimes exhausting life. He had accomplished a great deal, even if there had also been disappointments. Now he had lost virtually everything. The party to which he had devoted his life was banned, and he was an outlaw, soon to be stripped

---

63   Hilferding 1930, pp. 290–97; Hilferding to Kautsky, April 15, 1931, KDXII 652 (ISH).

of his citizenship, who had left everything behind. He (and Rose) would have to find a way to make a living, and he would have to come to grips intellectually with what had happened.

The problem of making a living was resolved fairly quickly. During the spring of 1933 the SPD remained a legal political party in Germany, despite the harassment, arrest and brutal treatment of hundreds of its leaders and a ban on its press. Anxious to rejuvenate the party's disintegrating organization, on 26 April the SPD leadership organized a conference in Berlin to elect a new Executive Committee. The new twenty-member body still consisted of a majority of the core Weimar leadership, headed by Co-chairs Otto Wels and Hans Vogel, but it also included representatives from all the party's factions and a number of new and younger comrades.[64] Following the Nazi seizure of the Free Trade Unions' headquarters and the arrest of their leaders on 2 May, the Executive decided to send six members abroad, along with the treasury, to set up a party center in exile. These included Wels, Vogel, Treasurer Siegmund Crummenerl, Friedrich Stampfer, Paul Hertz, and Erich Ollenhauer, who soon established an office and an exile press in Prague. When the Nazis finally banned the party in June, this group – the Social Democratic Party Executive in exile (Sopade) – claimed to be the SPD's sole legitimate leadership body. Hilferding was no longer officially a member of the Executive, but he worked for the Sopade as editor of its new theoretical journal, *Die Zeitschrift für Sozialismus* (*The Journal of Socialism, ZfS*), and as a regular contributor to the new party weekly, *Neuer Vorwärts* (*New Forward, NV*), edited by Stampfer. From Zürich he was also able to serve as Prague's liaison with German exiles in the West and with the Labor and Socialist International, based in London. With a modest income from the Sopade, supplemented by Rose's work as a translator, Hilferding lived in the Touring Hotel Garni in Zürich, which was a decent accommodation in which each room had running water, and residents had access to a telephone.[65]

Hilferding spent the rest of his life grappling with the intellectual and political fallout from the collapse. As editor of the *ZfS*, he attempted to facilitate a discussion of the party's recent failure and of the theoretical and practical con-

---

64 The nine "new" personalities included Paul Hertz, Erich Rinner, and Otto Ollenhauer representing the "youth"; Karl Böchel, George Dietrich, Franz Künstler, and Seigfried Aufäuser representing the "left"; and Paul Löbe and Wilhelm Sollmann representing the "right." See Edinger 1956, pp. 23–24.

65 Hilferding initially received a salary of 400 Swiss francs per month. Barring other possible income, if he paid the daily room rate of 7.50 francs, he would have only had 175 francs remaining to cover all other expenses. It is possible, of course, that he paid a cheaper weekly or monthly rate. The salary was reduced to 300 francs in 1936 as the Sopade's resources dwindled. See Buchhoz and Rother (eds.) 1995, pp. 94–95.

sequences for the movement going forward. This was a difficult task given the sharp criticisms, especially from the left, of the Weimar SPD leaders, including Hilferding, who were still at the helm of the Sopade. Along with his assistant editor, Paul Hertz, Hilferding was constantly on the hunt for high quality contributors, while also writing regularly himself. At the behest of the Sopade, in January 1934 he completed and published what came to be called the *Prague Manifesto*, certainly the most radical programmatic document ever put forward by the SPD. In it Hilferding asserted that "in the fight against National Socialism there was no place for reformism or legality". The struggle was for "the conquest of state power, its consolidation, and the realization of socialism" and, in this new political situation, the old party apparatus had to be discarded. Thus, the SPD had to be transformed from a reformist into a revolutionary organization.[66]

The SPD did little, however, to actually carry out this transformation. Subject to brutal repression in Germany, divided about how to move forward, facing competition from new socialist groups, such as Neu Beginnen (New Beginning), for leadership of the movement, and increasingly short of resources, the Sopade made little headway in unifying the resistance in exile or challenging the Nazis at home. I will discuss these problems in more detail in the introduction to Part 3 below. For the present, suffice it to say that this situation left Hilferding feeling increasingly frustrated and isolated.

We have a dozen letters from Hilferding to Kautsky from the spring of 1933 until the latter's death in 1938. Of course, in some ways the letters remain routine since, as he had done at *Die Gesellschaft*, Hilferding opened the pages of the *ZfS* to his old mentor, and the latter's contributions had to be discussed. At the same time, they show how Hilferding's thinking was changing and sometimes differed from Kautsky's. In particular, they highlight Hilferding's deepening pessimism regarding the future of the labor movement.

On 13 April 1933, in his first letter to his friend since fleeing Germany, Hilferding commented right away on a recent debate between Kautsky and Friedrich Adler on the Soviet Union in which Kautsky reiterated his conviction that dictatorship is incompatible with the creation of socialism and that the collapse of the USSR was imminent.[67] Hilferding told Kautsky that he still agreed with his basic viewpoint but had his doubts about his optimism in regard to the future of democracy. Mulling over the SPD's recent defeat, he did not see the need for a sweeping rethinking of Marxist theory, but rather of the movement's political conduct. And in that regard, he did not think that any other tactical approach

---

66 For the text see Dowe and Klotzbach (eds.) 2004, pp. 204–15.
67 F. Adler 1933, pp. 58–69.

would have been more successful in the later years of the republic. Instead, he was more concerned with how socialists had "underestimated the will of the working class to preserve democracy at all costs and to place the political [sphere], freedom, over the material one". He was stunned at the ease of the fascists' victory and predicted that they would have little difficulty seizing control over Germany's public and private institutions and sweeping away the unions and other any remnants of opposition. He noted that the worst of his depression had passed, especially since Rose's recent arrival, but he was pretty pessimistic about the future and about the possibility of dislodging the Nazis. He thought "it [the dictatorship] could last a long time".[68]

Hilferding returns to these themes repeatedly in later letters, and he was no less pessimistic as he considered the western powers' ability to resist the rise of fascism. In the fall of 1935, he told Kautsky that his deep-seated pessimism stretched back to 1917–18, though there had been some interruptions. Now, as the Radical, Socialist, and Communist Parties of the French left coalesced into the Popular Front, he was most concerned with preventing the outbreak of war, but he did not think the western powers, and especially their socialist parties, were up to the task. Ideologically confused by a mix of "Tolstoian pacifism, an antiquated anti-militarism, the subordination to an idealized Soviet foreign policy, and the hope of a war of liberation", he saw no concrete policy in the making that could hinder the coming conflict. He preferred Churchill's attitude to the Nazis to that of the Labor Party, and he regarded the Popular Front as an exercise in demagoguery that would intensify the fascist danger at home while failing to develop a coherent foreign policy.[69]

Hilferding may have been depressed about the state of the labor movement and the prospects for peace, but his letters to Kautsky also reveal his openness to rethinking aspects of Marxist theory and to ideas for new projects. In the fall of 1936, for example, he engaged Kautsky in a discussion on the concept of class in which he asserted that the Marxist perspective on class, both from an objective and a subjective standpoint, had to be considered anew. Indeed, such an investigation would require a large-scale project examining capitalist development from at least 1914 and would be "a difficult work which also involves a new investigation of the 'foundation.'"[70] Thus, Hilferding was clearly considering problems that he would attempt to address years later when, while under house arrest in Arles, he undertook his final work "The Historical Problem".[71]

---

68   Hilferding to Kautsky, April 13, 1933, KDXII 660 (ISH).
69   Hilferding to Kautsky, September 30, 1935, KDXII 665 (ISH).
70   Hilferding to Kautsky, September 2, 1937, KDXII 668 (ISH).
71   Hilferding, 1954, 293–324.

Hilferding never forgot what he owed to Kautsky intellectually and personally. In the public sphere he never tired of reminding comrades what his mentor had contributed to the social democratic movement, and in private he often reminded his friend that the respect he had had as a young man for the editor of the *Neue Zeit* had, over the years, grown into friendship and love. For Hilferding, "the most beautiful time" of his life was "when he was learning and working" with Kautsky in Berlin and "felt like a son and friend" in his home.[72] It was, no doubt, difficult for Hilferding when Kautsky left Berlin for Vienna, but it was certainly much worse when his friend had to flee Vienna to escape the clutches of the Nazis when they marched into Austria in March 1938. Karl and Luise managed to reach Amsterdam, but the strain must have been great on the 83–year-old, and he died in October.

Hilferding's letters to Kautsky over three decades provide us with a view into a world transformed. When Kautsky first considered Hilferding as his replacement as editor of the *Neue Zeit* in 1904, he was certainly aware that he would have been handing him European socialism's most important editorial perch. Indeed, perhaps that is why he never voluntarily relinquished it. Nevertheless, having recognized Hilferding's deep commitments to Marxism as a science of society and to democracy in the process of revolutionary transformation, he did everything he could to integrate him into Social Democracy's leading intellectual circles and to secure him employment. Hilferding, for his part, more than lived up to Kautsky's expectations as a thinker, political ally, and friend. By the time Kautsky finally stepped back from active political work, he was able to pass the torch of intellectual leadership to a comrade from the next generation who had clearly shown his continued commitment to the ideas that had brought them together in the first place. That less than a decade later they would see the mass movement that they had helped build crushed under the boot of fascism would have seemed farfetched. And when the unthinkable did occur, neither was able to fully explain it or effectively conceive of how it could be reversed. It was not revolution driven by reason, as they would have hoped, but Allied military power that would overthrow Nazi tyranny.

---

72 Hilferding to Kautsky, October 15, 1934, KDXII 662 (ISH).

CHAPTER 2

Rudolf Hilferding's Letters to Karl Kautsky, 1902–37

(KDXII 580)

Vienna, April 23, 1902
II. Kraftgasse 6

Honored comrade,

Permit me, honored comrade, to send you a challenge to Böhm-Bawerk's criticism of Marx with the request that you publish it in the *Neue Zeit*.[1] I hope that the work, the content and tone of which is geared exclusively for the *Neue Zeit*, isn't too long. It is organized in such a way that it can easily be put in series form, and it only appears to be longer than it really is.

Unfortunately, due to his influence on the vulgar Marxists, an anti-critique of Böhm's misconceptions and sophistries has become necessary. It is only a question, then, of whether the anti-critique is up to the demands of such an undertaking. In that regard, honored comrade, I request your judgement. And it was no less my desire to receive your judgement, a judgement upon which I place the greatest weight, and from which I hope to learn whether my engagement with political economy is "objectively" justified or not, that moved me to send you this work, which initially was intended more for self-clarification than for publication.

In part one, I take the opportunity to show the significance of the most important point of Marx's teaching, fetishism, and to show the relationship of value theory to the materialist conception of history, as well as to treat the problem, frequently misunderstood, by Bernstein for example, of complex labor and its value. In part two, it was necessary to penetrate the jumble of Böhm's misunderstanding of Marx's price theory. It wasn't hard, then, in part three to show the source of this confusion in Böhm's subjective outlook and to characterize [it] as the self-abrogation (*Selbstaufhebung*) of economics. The latter [point], however, is only by way of suggestion, for that task would require a separate

---

[1] Hilferding is referring here to Eugen Böhm-Bawerk's, *Zum Abschluß des Marxschen Systems* [*Karl Marx and the Close of his System*] published in 1896.

confrontation with marginal use theory. Finally, if my work is accepted and does not encounter major difficulties, please allow me to ask that you send the printer's proofs to me.

In the hope that I have not delivered a completely worthless contribution to the discussion of Marx,

Yours truly,
 Rudolf Hilferding

(KDXII 581)

Vienna, May 21, 1902

Honored Comrade,

First of all, please forgive me for taking so long to reply. I was not sure, however, how I should answer a letter that surprised me as much as yours did in every respect.

What I mean to say is that it would be an inappropriate claim on your time if I were to fully describe how happy your letter has made me. Just allow me to say that it has helped me make an important decision. Because I was uncertain about how to judge my own work, it was essential to hear the opinion of someone who is, by far, the most competent judge of these matters since Engels's death. My wish to convince myself, whether I am at least to some degree fit for economic work or whether, in the end, it was a waste of time, has been splendidly fulfilled, and your letter has encouraged me to continue along the path upon which I had started. There is so much to do in this field of which bourgeois economics, like revisionism, can scarcely dream. When assessing the sterility of its critique, [consider] that it is completely in the dark about the direction in which Marxism should be further developed. It is not in the back and forth about value theory, but rather in the study of developments not observed by Marx, above all a theory of capitalist competition, which one can best study in New York, that new knowledge can be sought. To be sure, having little time at my disposal for economics makes this a task that I myself will scarcely be able to fulfill. Apart from everything else, I have no possibility of devoting all my time to these matters.

I especially want to thank you for your invitation to become a contributor to the *Neue Zeit*.

By and large I liked Sombart's book, despite his being unable to fulfill the great expectations evoked in his preface.[2] As opposed to the prattle of the "ethicists", the description of the triumphant advance of capitalism is much needed. The systematic sections, which, of course, were already known from Braun's *Archiv*, are very good.[3] I believe, however, that behind Sombart's book stands Schalk, who appears in the volume on economic policy.[4] What Sombart has in mind is, fundamentally, a type of capitalist reception of Marxism for which revisionism has paved the way by dividing Marxism up into individual pieces. Indeed! One only needs to place the proof of the necessity of capitalism in the foreground, to introduce the final goal arriving later on, necessarily and automatically out of the steady development of capitalism, to present the conscious class struggle as an annoying moment, and one has a theory from which one has certainly driven out the proletarian spirit, but which, in its superiority over bourgeois eclecticism, very much eases the transubstantiation of the "extraordinary" into the "ordinary". That is, to be sure, more a prediction about the content of future volumes rather than of those that have appeared, but some signs indicate that the prediction won't be wrong.

Liebknecht's book has eluded me.[5] Here in Vienna one scarcely hears anything about a new publication in this field, to say nothing of a library having it. Would you be so kind as to send me a review copy? In any case, I intend to go through some of the new works in this field (Nordenholz, Worms, etc).[6] Liebknecht's book interests me for that reason and not only because of the author's personality.

And now to the child of sorrow.[7] Aside from the difficulty of finding a publisher, to publish the article as a separate work above all comes with the disad-

---

2 Werner Sombart (1863–1941), *Der moderne Kapitalismus* (*Historisiche-systematische Darstellung des gesamteuropäischen Wirtschaftslebens von seinen Anfängen bus zur Gegenwart*), the first two volumes of which were published in 1902.
3 The reference is to the *Archiv für soziale Gesetzgebung und Verwaltung* edited by Heinrich Braun, a Viennese friend of Kautsky's and former co-editor of the *Neue Zeit*.
4 Hilferding is referring to Henriette Roland Holst-van der Schalk (1869–1952), a Dutch socialist and author of *Kapitaal en arbeid in Nederland* [*Labor and Capitial in the Netherlands*] (1902).
5 It is likely that Hilferding is referring to Wilhelm Liebknecht (1826–1900), a friend of Marx and Engels, co-founder of the SPD, long-time parliamentarian and, after 1891, chief editor of *Vorwärts*. It is not clear to which of Liebknecht's books he was referring.
6 Anastasius Nordenholz (1862–1953) and René Worms (1869–1926). It is not clear what specific works Hilferding is referring to. The former wrote a book called *The General Theory of Production in* Society in 1904. The latter was a French sociologist publishing widely at the time. The *Neue Zeit* did not review works by either author.
7 Hilferding's critique of Böhm-Bawerk (see the letter of April 23, 1902), which Kautsky decided not to publish for the reasons discussed here. It eventually appeared as "Böhm-Bawerks Marx-Kritik" in Rudolf Hilferding and Max Adler (eds.) 1904, *Marx-Studien*.

vantage that it will have much less impact. Its distribution would be less and in other circles than those upon whom the *Neue Zeit* exerts influence. The book of an unknown would not get the attention that a theoretical article [would receive] if it appeared in a review edited by you. Economic theory can also be taught to resistant readers much more easily in article form. In book form it would have less of an effect on just those circles – workers and socialist intellectuals – for whom it is meant. And naturally what concerns me is its impact upon party comrades. What professors have to say about it, is really of no concern.

I think that dividing it into three parts would also have a negative effect. The article is directed against a complete and, in terms of its form, one of the few respectable efforts to annihilate Marx. It is conceived as an integrated whole and its division is purely superficial. Only when I had finished it did I remember that any decent tapeworm would have its sections and so I inserted the three headings. But the parts don't stand completely on their own and it would require a complete rewrite to deal with this dismemberment. I had hoped that, despite the fatal length, it could be published in the summer, when Mehring is on vacation and the letters from Berlin do not appear.[8] Only when something decent has appeared in the *Neue Zeit* and one is no longer a complete unknown, can one perhaps attempt to publish something independently later on. I can, therefore, perhaps promise that I won't do anything so long again. Also, it could only come out in independent form in the late fall, when the dead season has passed. I fear that someone else easily could preempt me. Thus, C[onrad] Schmidt has announced something about "recent value theories".[9]

Regarding the form, I am well aware of its shortcomings. To be sure, the people who are interested in the Marx-Böhm dispute may well have some previous knowledge. I would of course happily be prepared to accede to your wishes in this regard as best I can. Still, you put it as if the skill with which you and Engels apparently know how to present the most difficult problems in generally understandable form is only a matter of good will. I am not so presumptuous as to suppose that I could manage to present difficult theoretical problems anywhere nearly as splendidly as you. I would be very thankful for your friendly advice in that regard. I ask that you not get annoyed when I have made counter suggestions in all too specific a form. They are only recommend-

---

8 Franz Mehring (1846–1919) was one of German Social Democracy's leading journalists and a pioneering Marxist literary critic and historian. Between 1891 and 1912 he wrote lead articles for the *Neue Zeit* and oversaw its Feuilleton.
9 Conrad Schmidt (d. 1932) was a Marxist economist who published extensively on wages, profits, and value theory in the 1880s and 1890s. He served as an editor at *Vorwärts* and for decades was a regular contributor to the revisionist *Sozialistische Monatshefte*.

ations; the decision lies with you. I only wanted to put forward the reasons that would speak in favor of publishing the work of an unknown author under your auspices in the *Neue Zeit*.

Perhaps I am also effected by an emotional moment. For the longest time my ideal was to announce my presence in the world of political economy with an economic study worthy of publication in the pages of the scientific journal of German social democracy.

Since your letter has calmed me down about whether the content of my article has effectively demonstrated, against one of their most outstanding representatives, the powerlessness of the bourgeois critique of Marxism, it is important to me to ensure its impact through the form of its publication.

Pardon me, honored comrade, for the impertinence with which I have taken up so much of your time. One cannot cure one's self so quickly from a tapeworm. Once again, please accept my most heartfelt thanks for the kindness of your letter and for the all-too-positive critique that you provided to the work of one of your pupils.

Respectfully, yours truly,
Rudolf Hilferding

(KDXII 582)

Vienna, August 31, 1903

Honored comrade,

Enclosed is the promised article on the general strike. I had already gotten the idea of writing it after the Belgian defeat[10] and wrote it up after the blocking of the protective tariff, when it seemed for a moment that universal suffrage was under immediate threat.[11] However, I intentionally refrained from any ref-

---

10 Universal male suffrage in Belgium was established in 1893, but the class-based electoral system strongly favored the rich. In April of 1902 striking coal miners pressed the issue of democratic reform and the Belgian Workers' Party called a general strike on April 10. Although 300,000 workers answered the call, the strike failed in the face of repression and government intransigence. Another general strike in 1913 brought promises of reform that were delayed by the First World War until 1919. Braunthal 1978, 298–99; Cole 1956, 633–34.

11 Hilferding is referring here to the new German tariffs on grain introduced by Chancellor Bernhard von Bülow in 1901 but not passed until December of 1902.

erence to the concrete events in order to lay out my basic ideas in as generally applicable a way as possible and to avoid any detailed tactical arguments. Of course, the article loses the advantage of dealing with an issue of the moment. But perhaps that can be achieved if one realizes that we are dealing with a problem that is not just related to Germany, even if it might soon become a burning issue there. For us, I think it is a question of how we protect universal suffrage, and thereby [our] parliamentary tactic when, through the use of this electoral right, the ruling classes really begin to feel threatened. It is about the possibility of maintaining our previous tactic at the moment when our successes put it in question. And I believe that the sole effective protection of the right to vote consists of the power of the proletariat as producer, which becomes visible when applied in the form of the general strike. To me it is a question of the proletariat, especially the German proletariat, familiarizing itself with the idea of making use of this weapon under extreme circumstances to protect the right to vote. In my opinion, the general strike is only valid in the limited sphere of either establishing or maintaining the parliamentary tactic.

Naturally, that also means that parliament, and its ultimate conquest, is the most suitable means of bringing about the victory of the proletariat. Anyway, that is my view and I seek to ground it by showing that it is a characteristic of bourgeois society for economic and political power within it to diverge (*auseinanderfallen*). Parliament is the terrain where economic power is transformed into political power. This transformation, which today can occur only to the advantage of the bourgeoisie, can, however, ultimately unfold to the advantage of the proletariat. Parliament itself is not an inappropriate instrument for the dictatorship of the proletariat. To be sure, this is difficult to explain in just a few words, but I hope that, in general, you will concur with the explanations in the article. I am at least not aware of having diverged from any of the main ideas that have been prevalent in the party up to now.

I am very keen to find out whether you ascribe any importance to these remarks, which, on some points, I would have happily elaborated. I thought of them as a contribution to the discussion of the international congress.[12] Please forgive the outward form. It was not possible to insert subtitles in the original text. I believe that the working class faces new and difficult struggles. One can expect a coming together of all of its opponents, who will provide difficult

---

12   The Amsterdam Congress of the Second International, August 14–20, 1904. At the congress, the SPD supported a resolution by Henriette Roland Holst, who argued in a similar, largely defensive, vein as Hilferding. She held that a total general strike was impracticable, but that extensive strikes in key industries could bring about important social reforms or defend already won workers' rights. See Cole 1956, pp. 55–57.

tasks for it to solve. It will be necessary to generalize this conviction through a delineation of capitalist development [and] through a thorough analysis of the change in the capitalist economic structure. Finally, I have yet another request for your opinion on my article on trade policy in the *Neue Zeit* and on my Sombart critique in the *Zeitschrift für Verwaltung*, etc.[13] It was, by the way, only due to a personal acquaintance that an essay by me accidentally appeared in a bourgeois review.[14] In that regard, I take an intransigent position. With social democratic greetings,

Yours truly,
   Rudolf Hilferding

P.S. Perhaps it would be better to call the article "The Power of the Proletariat?"[15]

(KDXII 583)

Vienna, September 7, 1903

Honored Comrade,

Thanks very much for accepting my article and for your interesting letter. However, I had no intention of inserting into it the demand you mention. Like you, I also think it is out of the question that workers today could respond immediately to the abolition of the franchise with a general strike. But in order to retain the general strike in the proletariat's arsenal, I seek to focus attention on this ultima ratio. To decide whether and when a general strike can be carried out requires, apart from everything else, such intimate knowledge of the party that a foreigner like me could not conceive of even suggesting it. It would not dawn on me to be so presumptuous. Therefore, I am happy to insert this correction into the text. Since I don't have the manuscript, I ask that, if possible,

---

13   Hilferding, 1903, "Werner Sombart", 446–553.
14   Hilferding thinks it necessary here to explain the appearance of his article in a bourgeois publication because, in the context of the heated debate between the orthodox Marxists and the revisionists, the idea of socialist writers publishing in non-socialist venues had led to considerable acrimony – and was condemned – at the SPD's Dresden Congress in September of 1903. See Pierson, 1993, 161–171.
15   It appeared as "Zur Frage des Generalstreiks", ("On the Question of the General Strike"). See Hilferding 1903/04: 134–142.

you send me the galley proofs. I am very keen to explore the investigation of the conditions under which a general strike is possible. I have given it a lot of thought. The most important thing, in any case, has been accomplished. With you also speaking about the issue, the problem will be discussed, something that my article alone could scarcely have precipitated.

I am very happy to know that, as in so many questions, we agree on this one, too. It makes me confident of being right. With social democratic greetings:

Yours truly,
   Rudolf Hilferding

(KDXII 584)

Vienna, November 15, 1903

Honored Comrade,

Do you still have the book by Oppenheimer available? I would be willing to review the book, some of the content of which I am familiar with from a lecture Oppenheimer gave here.[16] In regard to the Thompson book, I don't think that, on its own, it is very suitable for a review. I had been expecting more, but it disappointed me. It is not interesting. I would like to return to it, however, in a different context, if the work that you sent us some time ago about Ricardo and Marx has appeared in the Verlag des Volksbuchhandlung. That would provide the opportunity to sharply point out the difference between Marx on the one side and Ricardo, Hodgskin, Thompson and also Rodbertus [on the other].[17] In my view it seems that the work of the Russian – his name escapes me at the moment – did not do that at all.

I am very curious about the continuation of the general strike discussion. A few days ago, our party congress said some things about it that were not at all negative. I think the matter would have the greatest practical significance. To those people, such as Elm, who tremble continuously before the bourgeoisie's

---

16   The reference is likely to Franz Oppenheimer (1864–1943), a physician who, after 1890, published widely in economics and sociology. His *Großgrundeigentum und soziale Frage* appeared in 1898.

17   See Hilferding 1904/05a, p. 329 for his review of William Thompson's *Untersuchung über die Gründsätze der für das menschliche Glück dienlichen Verteilung des Reichtums* (*The Distribution of Wealth as the Basis of Human Happiness: A Study*).

power without seeing the counterweight on the side of the proletariat, it would be a cue not to eternally fret about the progress of the proletariat. The proletariat itself would gain enormous confidence in the struggle through the mere idea of the general strike. I hope that Bebel will change his mind about the general strike being undiscussable for the German party.

I would be curious about what Parvus has written on the issue.[18] Unfortunately, I cannot obtain it here.

Hopefully, the attack on Mehring will end soon and we'll soon have the pleasure of reading his articles in the *NZ*.[19]

Best regards,
R.H.

(KDXII 585)

Vienna, December 20, 1903

Honored Comrade,

Forgive me for answering so late, but my free time is currently so limited that I can scarcely get to the work.

Aside from Thompson, at the moment I have no review commitments. Of the authors you recommended, I would be interested in Inama Sternegg and eventually also Cossa. I would take up Worm's confusion later on, if it were

---

18   Alexander Lvovich Parvus (1867–1924) was born Israel Lazarevich Gelfand (often referred to as Helphand). A Russian revolutionary Marxist, Parvus was trained as an economist in Basel. He moved to Germany in 1891, joined the SPD, and wrote for the *Neue Zeit*, the *Gleichheit*, and the *Leipziger Volkszeitung*. In 1896 he became chief editor of the *Sächsische Volkszeitung*. In the debates on revisionism and the general strike he stood with the party left wing. In 1905 he moved to St. Petersburg and played a major role in the revolutionary events there. After his arrest and escape, he returned to Germany but eventually moved to Turkey where he made a fortune in business. During the First World War he promoted Russia's defeat by aiding revolutionary groups there to overthrow Tsarism. He was a key figure in facilitating Lenin's return to Russia from Switzerland via Germany in 1917.
19   The reference is to attacks on Mehring at the Dresden Party Congress of 1903 (see footnote 14 for a description of the issue). Accused of being a political "chameleon", a "salon socialist", and of inciting comrades against one another, Mehring survived the assault, but his reputation was damaged. He resigned his editorship of the *Leipziger Volkszeitung* and withdrew from the *Neue Zeit* but soon returned to both publications.

necessary to demonstrate the psychological school's failure to produce any results. At the moment there is no need.

On the other hand, Max Adler told me he would be prepared to report on the works of Aschaffenburg,[20] Löning, und Goldscheid.[21]

If you want to take on Oppenheimer yourself, I'd be very happy. Have you already heard from Zetterbaum?[22]

Regarding myself, above all I am interested in the economic-theoretical, sociopolitical, and economic-historical phenomena associated with the most recent development of capitalism about which I would like to write something if I only had the time. By comparison, I am not really suited to the discussion of juridical issues, excluding perhaps political and constitutional problems.

The shortage of space in the *Neue Zeit* is a cancerous sore not only for the editors and staff – that would be, ultimately, the least important aspect of the problem – but [also] for the dissemination and further development of theory, for which it is the sole organ. In that regard, there is not very much that *Marx-Studien*, which is finally due to appear at the end of the month, can change.[23] It is dependent on the publisher and must cover its costs, which depend upon how often it appears and especially upon whether it pays honoraria to its contributors. Additionally, it is set up primarily for longer works. We need space, however, for works of medium length and this is only possible through the enlargement of the *NZ*, even if that entails a price increase. Forgive this remark, which I am making primarily as a reader of the *NZ*. Hopefully, another strike article will arrive soon. It is disturbing that Vliegen has had the last word for so long.[24]

---

20 Gustav Aschaffenburg (1866–1944) was a German psychiatrist whose pioneering work, *Das Verbrechen und seine Bekämpfung* (1903), examined individual-hereditary and social-environmental causes of crime. Reviewed in the *Neue Zeit*, 23, 2 (1904/05): 679–80.

21 Rudolf Goldscheid (1870–1931), Austrian sociologist and pacifist. Co-founder, with Max Adler, Karl Renner, Rudolf Eisler, Josef Redlich and Wilhelm Jerusalem of the Vienna Sociological Society.

22 Max Zetterbaum (1871–1927) was a Jewish Social Democrat from Galicia. A co-founder of the Polish Social Democratic Party in 1892, he was acquainted with Kautsky and contributed articles to the *NZ*. See Nora Rodman's biographical entry on Zetterbaum posted on January 26, 2017 at https://libcom.org/library/zur-revision-des-parteiprogramms-max-zetterbaum.

23 *Marx-Studien: Blätter zur Theorie und Politik des wissenschaftlichen Sozialismus* was the theoretical journal of Austro-Marxism, whose main representatives were Hilferding, Max Adler, Karl Renner, and Otto Bauer. Edited by Hilferding and Max Adler, five volumes appeared at irregular intervals between 1904 and 1923.

24 Willem Hubert Vliegen 1903–4, pp. 193–99. Vliegen (1862–1947) was editor of *Het Volk* (*The People*) and a leader of the reformist wing of the Dutch Social Democratic Workers' Party.

Victor Adler told me he would like to write about the matter. Perhaps it would be good if the request came from you. With best regards.

Yours truly,
Rudolf Hilferding

(KDXII 586)

Vienna, April 27, 1904

Honored Comrade,

Forgive me for the late reply. I am so busy, that I have practically no free time at the moment. That is also the reason why I have not yet sent the reviews. To be sure, the content of the books is so insignificant that it does not matter much. As I certainly hope, I'll have more free time for a while beginning in June, and then I will catch up quickly. This lack of time also keeps me from returning to the discussion of the general strike. I am looking forward to that not because I have anything against your article, which brilliantly refutes Vliegen's error treating the economic impact of the general strike as the most important thing, but rather because I want to argue against the views of David and Heine, whose rejection of the general strike results in political agnosticism and skepticism, which can only with difficulty be camouflaged through liberal phraseology.[25] But I cannot get to it now. Perhaps the course of the Amsterdam Congress will allow me to return to it.

I'm very sorry that you will not be reviewing *Marx-Studien* yourself. This is not only because all three of us personally place the greatest value on your judgement.[26] It will also be much harder for anyone else to review the three works together. Of course, we also desire a review very soon after the recent publication of Bernstein's criticism.[27] Would it be too much to ask you

---

25 Eduard David (1863–1930) and Wolfgang Heine (1861–1944) were leading representatives of the revisionist wing of the SPD in the decade prior to the First World War. Both supported the SPD's leadership's decision in 1914 to back the government's war effort.
26 Hilferding is referring to the three Austro-Marxist authors of the first volume (1904) of *Marx-Studien*. Hilferding published his *Böhm-Bawerks Marx Kritik*; Karl Renner wrote on *Die soziale Funktion der Rechtsinstitute*; and Adler addressed *Kausalität und Teleologie im Streit um die Wissenschaft*.
27 Bernstein 1969, pp. 153–158.

initially to give notice to the volume and to reserve for yourself a critique of the individual works? Moreover, a review of the first two works will be easier, and only Adler's is more demanding because of the length and the material. Perhaps it would also be possible for you to do us the greatest favor and say something about us? Perhaps Rosa Luxemburg could make a presentation in *Vorwärts*. You see, Bernstein actually was right for once when he infers a certain lack of modesty in my work.

At the moment I don't know anything about Zetterbaum. I have written to him and await his reply. He is taking his law boards and, therefore, probably will scarcely have time to write.

As soon as I have time, I will do a new article on the theoretical problem of economics (*Nationalökonomie*) that I would like to briefly elaborate either following a critical review of Rosenberg's "Ricardo und Marx" or in some other form. At the same time that would give me a chance to return to Bernstein's critique.

Best regards.
 Yours truly,
 Rudolf Hilferding

(KDXII 587)

August 13, 1904

Honored comrade,

I'm sending you two reviews on Inama and Cossa.[28] Finally, I now have some more free time. I'll soon send you a critique of Rosenberg's "Marx and Ricardo".[29] Some time ago, you sent me Thompson's first volume. When was the second published? I would like to review both volumes simultaneously. To that end, please send me the second volume. Also, would it be possible for me eventually to again take on some reviews? You will probably want to review the new book by Dr. Levy on the "Establishment of Large Enterprises in England" yourself.

---

28 For the reviews of Karl Theodor von Inama-Sternegg and L. Cossa, see Hilferding 1903/04 a & b, pp. 497–50, and 700, resp.
29 Hilferding 1904/05b, pp. 101–112.

Do you happen to have a copy of Warschauer's "Physiologische Banken?" Perhaps one could say something about banking in the *Neue Zeit* in the form of a review.

Hopefully, a review of *Marx-Studien* will soon appear in the *Neue Zeit*. I still hope it will be by you.

Best regards.
 Yours truly,
 Rudolf Hilferding

P.S. Is Strieder's "The Rise of Capitalism" still available for a review?

(KDXII 588)

Vienna, March 14, 1905

My highly honored friend!

I am homesick for Berlin and long to see you. I feel so strongly about it that I would prefer to chuck everything here and come to Friedenau, permanently if possible. To me, being here seems so unnecessary; it is not at all the right place, and I often think what a mistake it was not to have listened to you and Rosa and to have stayed in Berlin. Still, for the moment, it is a good thing that I am back. My mother is sick, much more than before, and requires constant attention, which, given our situation, only I can provide. And I also think that, in Germany, I would immediately have gotten engaged in politics and would not have gotten my feet on the ground for theoretical work. To be sure, thus far I have not yet been able to get much done here. My office gave me a lot to do last month and I could not concentrate. Therefore, day after day, I put off writing to you despite my intentions. It is incredible to me how long I could put it off. However, I've been thinking all the more often about you and yours, and I hope that my silence has not greatly offended you. I come out the worse for it, since I otherwise would have long had an answer in hand.

Recently, I've had a little more time and can work a few hours in the afternoon in the library. At the moment I'm working through the literature on money and banking and I hope to have found some interesting material. Unfortunately, the older English literature is not available here. Then I want to read the rest of the literature on cartels and the stock market and hope to be done with the description of "modern capitalism", but to do it a bit differently than Sombart. Meanwhile I will finish up the few things that I owe the *Neue Zeit*. This week I finally hope to be able to send you the critique of Thompson. Have you spoken already with Hans Deutsch and looked through his book?[30] It would be very interesting to hear your opinion. I will be doing that soon as well.

The coal miners' strike interests me very much. I believe it has made the problem of the relationship of the trade unions to the party acute. The separation, as it now stands, damages not only the party but also the unions. I think the strike was called off too quickly, because one treated it as a math problem rather than as a class struggle. This ignoring of the party, as just occurred among the trade union leaders, is impossible here. In such cases here, Victor Adler himself would be a member and spiritus rector of the strike committee. In a conversation with me about it, he told me that at the time of our coal miners' strike he was on the phone every day for hours negotiating with all the shop stewards in the various centers, and the trade unions had to cover a telephone bill of a couple of thousand kronen. But that was how we won our strike. Such a strike can only be won on a political and centralized [basis] and not on a trade union and local one. At the same time, we had much, much more unfavorable conditions than in Germany. In my view, it is, therefore, above all an organizational challenge to build the necessary connections in such cases. It seems that organs and authorities have to be created which connect the trade union, political, and also the cooperative leaders, if we want to avoid the risk of them gradually losing touch. I think it would be very important to stress this with new organizations of the party. That this is possible is shown not only by Austria, but also by Belgium in regard to cooperatives. I hear very little about Russia outside of what is in the newspapers, but I do have contacts with Russian comrades. Yesterday, I heard that, unfortunately, Plekhanov is very sick.[31] Tuberculosis or cancer of the throat were mentioned.

---

30   Hans Deutsch (1878–1953) was a civil engineer. It is unclear to what book Hilferding is referring. After 1909 Deutsch became technical director of the "Hammer" bread factory, a social democratic institution, in Vienna. He married Leopoldine Renner, the daughter of Hilferding's friend, Karl Renner, in 1913.
31   Georgi Plekhanov (1856–1918) was widely regarded as the "father of Russian Marxism." Initially an adherent of Russian populism, to avoid arrest he went into exile in Western Europe in 1880 and remained there until 1917. He turned to Marxism and co-founded the first Russian Marxist organization, Liberation of Labor, in Geneva in 1883. His application of Marxism to Russian conditions influenced a whole generation of young activists, including Lenin.

In Poland the PPS [the Polish Socialist Party] appears to dominate, and people here in the party and the Polish comrades in particular are enraptured by its energetic and successful approach. They are annoyed that people in Germany don't give the impact of the PPS more attention.

For all that, it seems to me that their demand for Polish independence is not very opportune. I've been told, however, that without it, it would not have been possible to unleash a movement in Poland. In any case, the local Polish comrades very energetically claim that the party is of a pure social democratic character. Be that as it may, it seems to be one of the most important factors among the revolutionary parties, for whom finding a modus vivendi would be important, certainly for the Russian Social Democrats. "One step forward is more important than a dozen programs".[32]

In any case, now even the worst doubters must grasp what proletarian power means and the Russian example must open the period of socialism's realization in Europe. You are right again: one can't be optimistic enough.

Were you satisfied with my Marx critique? Victor Adler initially thought it was too long and delayed its publication in the AZ [*Arbeiter-Zeitung*]. How do you like the economic policy review? Nobody reads it here and I get no comments. In case you read it, I'd be very grateful for a couple of critical remarks. Unfortunately, my information is still unsatisfactory.

Oh, how I would love to pick you up tomorrow afternoon to go for a walk and chat, instead of writing. I am constantly reminded of how it feels to have to do without your company after having thoroughly enjoyed misusing it for so long. And how are your wife and boys doing? If only I had the chance to visit everyone this summer! At the moment the chances don't look very good, but perhaps I will be able to change that.

You should really come some time to inspect our workers' school. You'd be pleased when you heard how these workers already know how to argue about the difference between surplus value and profit and between value and the price of production, like no bourgeois professor. We have one who, after two years of instruction, already gives lectures and really good ones, too. It goes well when one takes it on correctly. Bauer, who does it beautifully, lectured on economics.

---

32 Hilferding is attempting to quote a comment by Karl Marx in a letter to Wilhelm Bracke on May 5, 1875. The actual sentence reads: "Every step of real movement is more important than a dozen programs." The letter, along with Marx's "Marginal Notes to the Program of the German Workers' Party", was first published by Friedrich Engels in the *NZ* in 1891.

Very best regards to your wife. Your dear ones were a pleasure for us, best regards to Felix, Karl, and Bendel. I'd be glad to get a few lines from Rosa. Also, please give my best to the Thursday round, above all to the Mehrings, Cunow, and Wurm. Don't be mad about my long silence. Again, very best regards.

Your
 Rudolf Hilferding

(KDXII 589)

Vienna, April 3, 1905

My highly honored friend,

Thanks so much for your letter, which once again made me very happy. I always have a bit of a guilty conscience when I "provoke" you to write a letter, because I think it's another interruption of your precious time, but the desire to receive another always wins in the end. And especially now, as I still suffer from a kind of hangover in the wake of those days in Friedenau. Hopefully, it will gradually clear up the more I return again to sensible work. Yet, the task I have decided to take up is so big, that I often doubt whether I have the necessary talent and time to carry it out to the end. But the efforts to achieve something in the sphere of theory are already panning out, at least for anyone interested. So, the second volume will come by Pentecost?[33] I am extraordinarily curious; I hope that from it one will be able to learn about the methods and problems of economics. Perhaps it will make clear to the bourgeois how different Ricardo and Marx are, and how the same value theory has a completely different meaning for each. It is good that just now two thick volumes by Karl Diehl have appeared, which I believe will also enlarge upon this relationship. I'd be very grateful if I could get this work to review, if you haven't decided otherwise. To be sure, I know that it is presumptuous to ask for new review assignments when I still have older ones to deliver. But I am just now getting back into the work, and this time you must have a little patience with me. I recently became acquainted with Sombart, who is now in Vienna and is

---

33 Hilferding is referring is referring to the second volume of *Marx's Theories of Surplus Value*, which Kautsky was preparing for publication. It appeared in three volumes between 1905 and 1910.

giving two lectures. One, on economics and art, was painful and showed all of Sombart's disagreeable attributes. The second, which should be better, will be given today and is on "American socialism". Unfortunately, I won't be able to hear all of it, because I have to give a lecture, too. He told me, however, that he believes firmly in the future of American socialism. He will write about it in his archive.[34] Sombart has two souls that he can't combine at all. On the one side he is shabby, decadent, and poses as a refined man of taste. On the other he is a talented scholar who is serious and hard working. His misfortune is that he lives and feels like a corrupt bourgeois, while to a certain degree he has to think like a proletarian. He illustrates that to be a social scientist today requires character, but he only has that of a Prussian Extraordinary Professor. It is interesting that, as he told me, his "modern capitalism" is already sold out and a second edition will soon appear. What you write about the changing carriers of development [*Entwicklungsträger*] is very interesting. The complete overview of technical and economic institutions, indeed, in their fully developed form, is very important for [understanding] economic and political development and its variations in different countries. This explains the late onset of capitalist development in Germany and the various differences in the development and organization of its banking system in comparison to England. Moreover, the degree to which the rebellion of the petty bourgeoisie against capitalism is successful is largely dependent on the stage or the level of capitalist development as it initially emerged in this country. And, finally, it explains, as you say, the changeover of leadership from one country to another.

What you say about Austria is, to be sure, unfortunately mostly correct. Only here, in my view, we have realized the correct principle of the complete unity of the party, the trade unions, and the cooperatives. I believe that this gives rise to such strength and such direction-giving power that it protects us, above all, from wrong turns and all too serious mistakes, and reduces the danger rooted in the lack of satisfactory basic education. By the way, that [condition] will also change. Moreover, such articles as the one about France's militaristic democracy only make a strange impression. Of course, it had to have been by Leuthner, who now has the privilege of making the greatest blunders. He has been pushing an even stupider policy in the Morocco matter.[35] However,

---

34   Sombart was coeditor of the *Archiv für Sozialwissenschaft und Sozialpolitik*.
35   Karl Leuthner (1869–1944) was a member of the pro-imperialist, pan-German far right of the revisionist wing of the SDAP, editor of the *Arbeiter-Zeitung*, contributor to the *Sozialistische Monatshefte*, and member of the Austrian Reichsrat. Hilferding is referring here to the Moroccan crisis of 1905, when Emperor Wilhelm II attempted to drive a wedge

this will pass without a trace because, in contrast to Germany, our party is too weak and without influence for it to have any more than a platonic interest in these discussions. That explains the lack of opposition, the lightness with which such things are laid aside. To be sure, this is a condition of immaturity, but it is in no way a particular danger in Austria, whereas in Germany it has to be combatted with the greatest energy. Similarly, something else also played into the discussion of "away from Rome": the effort to smash the Reichenberg [party] organization, to take it in hand, to make an end of this North Bohemian, unfruitful Fronde against the party leadership. The bottom line was that the Reichenberg electoral district now belongs to Adler and no longer to Hannich.[36]

On the issue of the unity of all the branches of the labor movement, Austria is important to Germany. And I don't think that there will be a satisfactory solution in Germany. In your really excellent examination of the miners' strike you yourself have pointed out how trade union and political action have to be combined. And the Americans are promoting the same development, cartelization, in liberalism. In Germany, the critical phase of trade union neutrality will be all the more quickly overcome when the party does what is necessary. And, in my opinion, here we don't just have a problem of recognition – I remember Bebel going off the rails – but rather also a problem of organization. The centralization, which the party must undertake, has to be supplemented through a centralization of the workers' movement as a whole.

---

between England and France as they negotiated Morocco's fate in the context of their overall colonial interests in North Africa. By personally landing in Tangiers on March 31, 1905 and guaranteeing Morocco's independence, Wilhelm precipitated a major crisis that resulted in Germany's humiliation. Ultimately, France took control over Morocco and the Kaiser's action brought France and England into a closer alliance.

36 "Away from Rome" was a movement calling upon Austrians to abandon Rome, i.e., Catholicism, for Protestantism. It was an attack on the Habsburg monarchy promoted by Pan-German nationalists such as Georg Ritter von Schönerer. Hilferding uses the term here to sarcastically describe the Reichenberg's electoral district's refusal to heed the wishes of the Vienna-based party leadership. Due to Austria's unequal franchise, there were few electoral districts where the SDAP could win seats in the Reichsrat. Reichenberg was an exception and the SDAP leadership wanted the local party organization to nominate Victor Adler, the party founder and leader, as its candidate there in 1896. The locals thought otherwise, however, and despite enormous pressure, including an appeal from German Party leader August Bebel, nominated their long-time leader, Josef Hannich (1843–1934), who then represented the district for eight years. In 1905, with the push for equal manhood suffrage in full swing, the party leadership finally prevailed over the locals. Hannich stepped down and Adler won the seat. See Braunthal 1965, pp. 146–48.

I haven't heard much new about Russia. There is more about Poland, but mainly hymns of praise for the PPS, and I know of little by way of contrast.

Just now I've come across the prospectus of the *Neue Gesellschaft* [*The New Society*] – a beautiful society. It is nice how the enterprise presents itself in lily-like innocence as social democratic. Hopefully, the disavowal won't take long. What's funny is that it could become serious competition for the *Sozialistische Monatshefte*. But who is financing it?

I very much enjoyed Clara Zetkin's speech in Berlin; it appears that the idea of the political strike is beginning to catch on. What a shame that Frau Roland [Holst] missed it.[37] Will it come out soon as a pamphlet?

You wrote that you'd like to talk to me about something. You can imagine how incredibly curious I am about that. Now, excuse me for bothering you for so long with this lengthy letter. My very best regards.

Yours truly,
R.H.

Dear madam [Luise Kautsky],

I should also have written to you much earlier to tell you how grateful I am to you for making me feel so at home during my stay in Berlin. I felt as well at your home as I would at my mother's. But I am terribly awkward at saying thank you, even in those unusual cases when it is such a pleasure, as with you. The boys are certainly annoyed that they haven't heard from me. Hopefully, I can reconcile with them once again. Do you [still] have Thursday evenings? How is Frau Rosa? Actually, she owes me a letter. She had so firmly promised to write to me as we parted that I expected to have it long ago. But now it means woe to you if you are not a Russian!

Nevertheless, please give her my best regards. Now I have to leave some space for my wife (a superior force as Rosa would say) and can, therefore, only send my best regards to you, Karl, Felix, and Bendel. Please also give my regards to Grandie.

Yours truly,
R.H.

---

37 Clara Zetkin (1857–1933) was a leader of the SPD's women's movement, editor of its newspaper, *Die Gleichheit*, and later a co-founder of the German Communist Party. On Roland Holst see footnote 4 above.

(KDXII 590)

Vienna, May 27, 1905

Honored friend,

Maybe this time I can quietly complain about having heard no news from Berlin for so long. But I know that you have better things to do and are probably deep into the work on volume two of the "Theories".[38] Will it be possible for you to publish them before Pentecost? How is *Volume One* selling?

I myself have had lots to do lately because we moved to Lichtenstein Straße 30 and had to get ourselves set up, with a carpenters' strike making things that much more difficult. Now the most aggravating part is over, and since I have less medical work in the summer, I can start again on the [economic] work. I would now like to finally attack my "Finance Capital", which still amounts to no more than a title. But June still belongs to Deutsch, which is already driving me crazy anyway. I have seldom had so little inclination to review a book, and I have already regretted taking it on a thousand times. I don't think there is much to it, but I'll still get on with the work.

Did you perhaps by chance read my comments on the recent issue of currency in the *Sächsische* [*Volkszeitung*]? I think the position taken by the fraction on the government's proposed law is totally wrong, although the matter is itself very minor. Bernstein's reasoning was childish and would be more embarrassing if the others understood more about it. However, in these matters, although they are very simple and clear, a level of ignorance predominates, long sanctified by tradition and general respect, that is astounding. One could perhaps discuss that in the *Neue Zeit* sometime, if it wouldn't be received so apathetically. I'm very curious about the decision of the trade union congress on May Day and the general strike. However it comes out, I hope it will result in the party press – which usually plays down these matters – finally being forced to take a clear position, and I believe the outcome of the discussion will be very positive. Anyway, it is the party leadership and above all the press and, especially, the infuriating, miserable *Vorwärts*, which have completely failed in all important things, and are responsible for allowing matters to reach the point where the great influence that the party could exert, if it only knew how, is so completely wasted that such resolutions were at all possible. They are really a mockery of the international congresses that cannot be more maliciously con-

---

38 See footnote 33.

ceived. Nevertheless, I view this attitude as a moment, which will soon pass and more quickly than revisionism. The increasingly rapid sharpening of conditions in Germany will ensure that.

I really enjoy the *Leipziger Volkszeitung*, which I now read regularly, but I regret that it is not the flagship paper. I am very curious about Frau Roland's brochure. I will see if I can advertise it in the *Arbeiter-Zeitung*. Maybe Adler himself can write about it.

The Russian Revolution has not completely lived up to its promise. From here, too, it seems the internal struggles were damaging. On the other hand, the Poles – and that means the PPS according to the dominant views around here – are performing heroic feats. Zetterbaum, who is an expert, claims that the PPS is a good social democratic party. Zetterbaum was recently here on the occasion of the foolish founding of a Jewish party in Galicia.[39] He will soon edit a strictly Marxist, Polish, scientific organ [and] we have promised to collaborate. The second editor should be Kelles-Kraus, but he is hopelessly sick.[40] He has a severe case of tuberculosis and I fear – I have seen a lot of him – that it won't be long. It is an incredible shame – such an active person, totally dedicated to the cause, and only just thirty-five.

Otherwise, in Austria not much is new. We are waiting for the solution to the Hungarian crisis; otherwise, we make small steps forward and are more interested in Germany than in the states represented in the Reichsrat. And I still long for Berlin. Very best regards from me and my wife to you, your wife, the boys, and friends.

Your,
R.H.

P.S. Thanks very much for sending Schüllers' *Handelspolitik*. Will you be reviewing Tugan-[Baranovsky] yourself or is Rosa interested in it?

---

39   The Jewish Social Democratic Party of Galicia was founded in 1905 after a split with the Polish Social Democratic Party of Galicia.
40   Kazimierz Kelles-Kraus (1872–1905) was a Polish Marxist philosopher and sociologist particularly well known for his writings on nationalism.

(KDXII 591)

Vienna, July 4, 1905

My honored friend,

Your last letter embarrassed me somewhat. Recently, I've done so little that I had absolutely no idea what to send you. In addition, I have to send a review of Roland Holst's pamphlet to the *Dresdner Arbeiter-Zeitung* that should have been delivered already. The paralyzing heat, which we've had here for some time and which makes even the nights unbearable, makes work difficult, and this year I am less able to deal with the heat than normally. Add to that that I am very busy with my medical work, then you'll be forgiving when I make no promises. Right now, my only wish is to get away, and I want to see you very much. Hopefully, you won't be prevented [from traveling], and I'd like to ask, therefore, that you write to me about whether you are sure you will be going to St. Gilgen on the ninth. Once I know, I can find someone to substitute for me. I'll come, then, around noon or perhaps a little earlier or a little later. I am so looking forward to it. If you don't come, then despite everything I'll probably stay in hot Vienna. Thanks again for all the information about your summer holiday. Victor Adler, who is traveling to Konstanz, might visit you. I'll probably talk to him about it in the next few days and I'll let you know. So, don't be annoyed that I have to leave you in the lurch for now and let me know soon about your travel plans.

Thanks very much for your wife's kind words and give her my best regards.

Best wishes,
R.H.

(KDXII 592)

Vienna, August 9, 1905

Honored friend,

I've had a lot to do and just today have I been able to get around to thanking you and your wife for the wonderful get together in St. Gilgen. I am fully restored and can get a decent amount of work done again. I was rather ashamed of my laziness. Roland Holst is already reviewed; unfortunately, not well enough.

[That is because,] in part, the content is very difficult to recapitulate and, in part, the essential material on the mass strike has already been discussed. In addition, the contradiction and the counter argumentation are on such a low level that it doesn't offer anything very stimulating. I believe that the next stage of the discussion will be the argument between the *supporters* of the mass strike, [one resulting in] the rejection of those who view the mass strike as an especially forceful means of demonstrating, but think that after such an event the bourgeois order would calmly carry on as if nothing had occurred, except maybe a change in the franchise in the commune of Stir-Neusiedl. It would be better if this [debate] was put off until the principle opponents of the mass strike are defeated. Hopefully, that will occur at Jena.

I recently talked briefly with Victor Adler. He has little desire to write about the organizational question. His chief reason is that he is a foreigner, and as such, he does not want to peer into the internal affairs of the German party. He believes that that would be resented by onlookers. In addition, it is more a question of morale and concrete execution than one of formal rules. I think, though, if you press him again, he'll write the article, despite [these objections]. If he doesn't, then how about you?

In this silly season [*saure Gurkenzeit*] of prosperity in the realm of theory, it is the theoretician who can least escape punishment upon entering the editorial office. Thus, on Tuesday, I found out that Saturday is the one hundredth anniversary of Rodbertus's birth.[41] Therefore, I would have to write an article – in four days! Maybe I can do it. But it is such a shame that I have not read Rodbertus for years, and the book is just now at the bookbinder. In the wake of the Marx critique, it would be especially interesting to write about Rodbertus, who was an honest, gifted man and became a victim of his time and of his country. I always believed that Engels did not entirely do him justice, and I suspect that he would have made out better with Marx. I would be very curious to hear your opinion on that sometime. I read Schüller and will be able to send you a review soon.[42] I am very excited about Marx's Nachlaß and would be extraordinarily grateful if I could receive it soon, because I am supposed to review it for Zetterbaum's new journal.[43] He is [by the way] now in Vienna. I just received

---

41 Johann Karl Rodbertus (1805–1875) was a Prussian landowner, lawyer, philosopher, and economist who advocated a gradual path to socialism within the framework of the monarchy.
42 The reference is most likely to Richard Schüller, *Schützzoll und Freihandel* (*Die Voraussetzung und Grenzen ihre Berechtigung*), Vienna-Leipzig: F. Tempsky, 1905.
43 Marx's *Nachlaß* consisted of his literary estate, which, following Engels's death, Eleanor Marx entrusted to Kautsky. The reference here is to that part of the Nachlaß that Kautsky edited and published as *Theories of Surplus Value*.

the card from Schafberg. Please tell Frau Luise that her mocking grin doesn't do her justice at all. I have to gather up the last remnants of my gallantry and the beginnings of what Bauer claims is my upbringing by Margaret in order to maintain the "good breeding" that I once despised. By the way, I just received a second card from a friend, and it, too, was of the Schafberg peak. Did you at least have a view? One more thing in closing. Wegmann is a good and reliable party comrade, an Austrian citizen, but a Russian, whom I know well and who is thoroughly trustworthy. [He] translates and writes a lot and understands his business. The translation is almost done. He [would be] very grateful for your permission as well as a short preface from you.[44] What happened to your article in *Vorwärts*? Best regards from Margret and me to you all.

Your,
    Rudolf Hilferding

(KDXII 593)

Vienna, August 28, 1905

Most honored friend,

You should probably have received my letter while still in St. Gilgen. Bauer just told me that you had not received a post card from Sesäuse that my wife and I had sent. I mention that in order to prevent my laziness as a correspondent from appearing to be even greater than it is.

Now, about the Russian translation, comrade Wegmann urgently asks again that you provide, first of all, your authorization, second a preface or introduction, and third, in case *you* think it necessary, any changes in passages relating to Russia. At the moment the thing is in the hands of the censor in Odessa. Once it is approved, changes are very difficult. Therefore, it would be best if you, in case you are so inclined, as I hope, send the preface soon.

It is beginning to get more interesting here. It seems that in Hungary the Habsburgs, helpless and cursed by nature and clericalism as they are, will attempt to implement an absolutist policy to the extent that they are able. Of course, for us that means raising the franchise question. The *Arbeiter-[Zeitung]*

---

44   Wegmann was translating W. Cohnstaedt, *Die Agrarfrage in der deutschen Sozialdemokratie von Karl Marx bis zum Breslauer Parteitag* (Munich: E. Reinhard, 1903). Pravda published a Russian edition, equipped with Kautsky's forward, in Kiev in 1906.

has modified its position and is now taking the matter more seriously than before. The situation is now difficult for our Hungarian comrades, who, not entirely blameless, have come under suspicion of cooperating with the government. If universal suffrage comes to Hungary, then the national question will become a burning issue just like in Russia after the victory of the revolution. It will become the most important issue for Austria, Hungary, the Balkans, and Russia. It can only be resolved on the democratic path and will be a means that can be championed by the proletariat to accelerate the victory of democracy. On the other hand, Europe will remain in an uproar as the nationalist struggles in the East are a constant temptation for Western Europe to meddle there, which in turn multiplies the seeds of violent conflict. In any case, the relative calm in Europe is basically over.

On Saturday, Adler traveled to Wurmsdorf. At the district conference there he was nominated as the candidate for Reichenburg. He will probably appear in Parliament in the fall, perhaps at just the right moment. He was in very good humor and sends his best wishes. He will *not* write the article on organization. Instead he intends to send you an article on internationalism (against Pernerstorfer).[45] Hugo Schertz will send you an article about our view on war. What he told me about it seemed interesting. Though not important, it is the stuff of an interesting discussion. I will soon send you a review of Schüller. I'll hurry up with it in order to study the Marx volumes in peace. Yesterday, I received the first part and I should get the second in a few days. Once again, you've made me very happy and I am very grateful to you. Thereafter I'll finish off Diehl[46] and then, aside from medicine, I hope there will be no more disturbances and I can concentrate fully on my finance capital.

I'm very curious about what you think of the Duma. From the beginning I agreed with Martov that it would deliver a powerful new shock to the revolution.[47] Surely you will now have many difficulties in Germany. Eisner under-

---

45 Engelbert Pernerstorfer (1850–1918) was a leading Austrian Social Democrat who, after joining the SDAP in 1896, served for many years in the lower house of the Reichsrat and eventually as its Vice President.

46 Karl Diehl (1864–1943) was a well-known German economist and academic. It is not clear which of his early works Hilferding is referring to here, but most likely it was either *Ueber das Verhältnis von Wert und Preis im ökonomischen System von Karl Marx* (Jena: G. Fischer, 1898) or *Kornzoll und Sozialreform* (Jena: G. Fischer, 1901). Neither was reviewed in the *Neue Zeit*.

47 Julius Martov (1873–1923) was one of the early leaders of the Russian Labor movement. He joined the Russian Social Democratic Labor Party in 1900 and was a co-founder and editor, with V.I. Lenin of its newspaper, *Iskra*. At the RSDLP's second congress in 1903 he split with Lenin over organizational questions and became a leading figure of the Menshevik faction of the RSDLP.

stands that this time we are dealing with his senior [editorial] position, and he is frantically trying to steer the struggle into the personal sphere and [into] the *Leipziger Volkszeitung* instead of *Vorwärts*.[48] Hopefully the *LV* will make that impossible: but that will require tremendous skill given the apparently uncertain morale. Will you publish your article? Also funny is how *Vorwärts* suddenly wants to publish theoretical articles again. I cannot judge whether the separation of *Vorwärts* from the Party leadership is a good idea. In itself it seems senseless. Under German conditions, where the party executive is not in a position to influence the editors themselves, it may even be useful. It is also shabby how the executive plays off Friedeberg against radicalism.[49] Sorry for the long letter, which surely has bored you. Please give my best to Frau Luise and the boys and Margret also sends her best to you and your wife. Best regards to comrade Wurm. Best wishes,

Your,
R.H.

---

[48] Kurt Eisner (1867–1919) joined the ten-member editorial board of *Vorwärts* in 1898 and soon became chief editor. In this letter and especially the one that follows, Hilferding comments extensively on the political and personal conflicts that emerged within the editorial board and between it and the SPD executive committee. Eisner was not a revisionist, but he was not an orthodox Marxist either, and he and a majority on the board attempted to maintain an independent policy that kept the newspaper open to a broad spectrum of views. If they thought it appropriate, they were even willing to reject articles from leaders like August Bebel. In the context of the debate between revisionism and orthodoxy, this policy raised the ire of many in the executive committee, especially Bebel, and also drew fire from Kautsky and his orthodox supporters. Personal conflicts complicated the ideological issues, as did the Berlin party organization's desire to take over the paper. The struggle came to a head in September of 1905 when the Party Executive and Press Commission decided to replace two of the editorial board members with new ones closer to its views. In response Eisner and five editors announced they would resign in April of the following year which then precipitated their summary firing. See Pierson 1993, 176–182.

[49] Like Hilferding, Raphael Friedeberg (1863–1940) trained in medicine and developed an interest in political economy. At first a contributor to the reform oriented *Sozialistische Monatshefte*, after 1900 he moved steadily leftward and sharpy criticized the SPD's focus on parliamentary tactics and the trade unions' conservatism and advocated increasingly anarcho-syndicalist ideas. Forced out of the party in 1907, he remained the personal physician of both Kautsky and August Bebel. See Karl Kautsky Jr. (ed.) 1971, xiii, 380–81.

(KDXII 595)

Vienna, September 29, 1905

Honored friend,

I'm writing today because yesterday I met with some acquaintances to whom I explained the matter. Deutsch is not in Vienna; we've had no news. Your letter may not have reached him. Bauer can't do it now, which is also the case with another comrade who would otherwise be suitable. In contrast, Fraulein Dr. Herzmark told me that she would be pleased to take the job. She speaks Russian and German perfectly, she is well educated in the socio-political, philosophical, and natural sciences, discrete, and absolutely reliable. Her parents live in Berlin, and she would be happy to spend some time there. Of course, it is totally up to you whether to you want to try things out with her. I regret very much that I cannot place myself at your disposal; it would have been a great pleasure for me to again spend some time in Berlin. But it just won't work. Wurm wrote to me yesterday about whether I'd like to write an article on Brentano for the *Berliner Tageblatt*.[50] However, I don't read that paper here and have not been able to get it. Otherwise I'd be inclined to write something for him about welfare institutions and the congress of the Association for Social Policy.[51] It seems to be a unique kind of scandal, in particular I would like to hammer home the idiocy of Schmollers' proposal on cartels. If there is enough time, I'd like to ask you to please have the articles sent to me. I will then also wait for the congress reports to appear in the *Frankfurter Zeitung*, to which I've subscribed, and write about it. What does Wurm really need? Please give him my best regards and express my deepest regret. Hopefully, it isn't all that bad.

---

50   Emanuel Wurm (1857–1920) was a leading socialist editor, long-time member of the Reichstag and of the Berlin City Council. From 1902–1917 he was a co-editor of the *Neue Zeit*. Lujo Brentano (1844–1931) was an economist who promoted social reforms via state intervention in the economy. Part of a group of academics known as *Kathedersozialisten* (socialists of the chair), he believed such a policy would hinder the radicalization of the working class and thereby undercut the growth of social democracy.

51   The reference is to the Verein für Sozialpolitik, founded in 1872 by economists such as Bentano and Gustav Schmoller (1838–1917) to address social issues that arose from German industrial development. Max Weber, Werner Sombart, and Friedrich Naumann joined later on. They sought a middle path between socialist and laissez-faire economics.

I am very curious about what happened in Jena.[52] Aside from the newspaper reports, the only thing I've heard is as follows: Ströbel and Mehring attacked one of Eisner's articles especially sharply as ethical-aesthetic, idiotic, etc. Eventually, Eisner very calmly conceded that he had forgotten to use quotation marks. The incriminating passages are taken word-for-word from your (and Schönlank's) "Erfurt Program".[53] On the basis of these developments, the chairman of the [party press] commission will make a decision.

Is there any truth to that? Around here that is largely what people are saying and believing, including Victor Adler, who told me the same story yesterday. It would be good to hear something [from you] in order to be able to counter the story if necessary.

On the issue of the [general] strike, V[ictor] Adler sides with Bebel. My article is suspended in mid-air; your conception postpones the strike indefinitely [and] robs it of its effectiveness as we plan for the dominant classes to steal the right to vote. Moreover, in the *Vorwärts* discussion he thinks that in many respects you have been unjust, and that Eisner had done much too much. I told him that you were very annoyed by his article and had viewed it as a betrayal of Marxism. That hit him hard, and he asked me if I thought the article was so bad. I said it was Eisner's most effective support, the only one that really carried weight, leaving you exposed. He did not want to concede that, [and said] Eisner wasn't even mentioned and so on. He will write to you. I am telling you all this in such detail, just as I also have explained your outlook to V. Adler, because I believe that it can help more easily overcome the conflicts that have recently arisen between you. I would be really pleased if you would write to V. Adler and fully explain things. Recently he has seen matters too much from the Austrian perspective and in too partisan a fashion.[54] I hope that you will pardon any indiscretions I might have committed in regard to either of you.

---

52 The struggle for control of *Vorwärts* came to a head at the Jena Conference of September 17–23, 1905. Heinrich Ströbel (1869–1944) and Franz Mehring, two of Kautsky's allies in the fight against revisionism, led the charge there against what Kautsky called Kurt Eisner's "ethical-aesthetic" viewpoint. See also footnote 48 above.

53 Bruno Schönlank (1850–1901) was a leading social democratic editor and parliamentarian. From 1894 until his death he edited the *Leipziger Volkszeitung*, one of the SPD's most radical and successful dailies. A colleague of Kautsky's at the *Neue Zeit*, in 1892 they co-edited *Grundsätze und Forderungen der Sozialdemokratie. Erläuterungen zum Erfurter Programm*, which appeared in many editions.

54 Instead of patching things up by mail, Adler and Kautsky met personally to hash it out. On October 11, Adler wrote to Kautsky that he would come to Berlin "essentially to have it out with you", because your letter to Hilferding "gives me no rest." He signed his note with "yours despite everything and always your loyal Victor Adler." See Friedrich Adler (ed.) 1954, 469.

What has changed at *Vorwärts*? Will Stadthagen join the editorial board? This time, your recommendations to the party organization received too little attention. Perhaps they came too late. However, something like the make-up of the Party Executive is not possible without a change in the statutes and will be difficult to implement.

Margret and the littlest Karl are doing well.[55] Please give my best to your wife and the boys. Please let me know what you think of Dr. Herzmark. Very best regards,

Your,
R.H.

(KDXII 596)

Vienna, October 24, 1905

Honored friend,

Frau Luise poured hot coals on my guilty head. Once again, I haven't written for much too long. First, Dr. Adler was not in Vienna; then, I wanted to send an article along with [the letter], but it wasn't ready, and, annoyed at having run out of steam, I did not write, though every day I planned to do so. Concerning V. Adler, I have told him about your letter. You will hear from him what he thinks about it. Therefore, I can be very brief. He was, first of all, personally sickened that you would think him so impressionable and, on top of that, by Heinrich Braun with whom he does not even correspond, and, second, that you would think that he would allow himself to be influenced in his article on the general strike by anything other than purely factual considerations. He had not thought of Eisner at all, but rather only on the political failure [that would result] if your conception – the general strike as proletarian *revolution* and not as a struggle for any particular concrete demand – would be victorious at Jena. He thinks Bebel's resolution also opposes your view, which I myself do not believe. He was also personally upset, and that might have had an impact on your meeting. I greatly regret that I did not alert you to that earlier. Now, in other respects, there are indeed also contradictions or, better put, differences

---

55 On September 12 Rudolf and Margret's first child, Karl Emil, was born. Named after Karl Marx and Hilferding's father, Emil, he was the "littlest Karl" compared with Kautsky, senior, and his own Karl junior. See List 2006, 110.

of views. But these have nothing to do with greater or lesser honesty. V[ictor]. Adler is honest in every fiber of his politics, which is something that I, of course, need to tell you least of all. I have unlimited respect for his character. But he sees or strives to see only the matter at hand (*die Sache*) and forgets to take the people involved into consideration, sometimes to the point that by injuring the person he does harm to the issue that person has brought forth. Then he always sees things more exclusively in purely political [terms]; he asks less often: how should things unfold, but instead how can I influence them. That is an outlook, of course, of a Social Democratic politician in Austria, where the party has a disproportionately large influence. Today, not only do we have almost unlimited freedom of the press, association, and assembly as well as considerable freedom to organize unions, but under certain circumstances we can wield what are practically terroristic methods, and we will perhaps conquer the franchise without all too great a sacrifice. To be sure, that is in essence only the consequence of exceptional conditions. But on the other hand, we very shrewdly take advantage of these conditions. Despite the party's power, class antagonism is still limited, and the conditions remain rather comfortable. No wonder it is widely believed here that German Social Democracy pursues a poor tactic and has too little understanding of how to take advantage of its power. For that reason, V. Adler also opposes your conception of the mass strike. He fears the party would lose its ongoing ability to discourage those who wish to eliminate the franchise. Furthermore, there is his inclination toward mediation, a necessity under Austrian conditions. First of all, they arise from the difficulties that the national conditions create for the party. One judges the Czechs too favorably when one judges them according to their principled behavior at international congresses. At home, this attachment to principle is a hindrance just where it is most important, because its immediate practical impact comes to a head on the terrain of ethnic politics. The Czechs constantly put not only the unity of the party but also of the trade union movement in question out of fear of coming up short in the face of bourgeois nationalist agitation. The only thing possible in this situation is persistent, laborious negotiation, as disagreeable as that is, and as conscious as V. Alder is about the dangers of this tactic. In regard to other political matters, the [nationality] principle plays a less decisive role because militarism, foreign policy, and even economic policy (the whole tariff policy) are excluded. Moreover, one must consider the less than fully developed class antagonism, which makes all conceivable elements into temporary allies. In spite of this, our party essentially has maintained its proletarian character and by and large carries on without making many compromises. Still, for that reason, to a certain degree Adler maintains a certain antipathy toward "theoretical" discussions. And because he has great personal influence through his efforts to overcome a lot of stupid mistakes and to prevent errors, etc., he therefore prefers this manner of "leadership" more than the open airing of party affairs as is common in Germany. [While the latter] is in my view largely unavoidable, in Austria the nationality issue is very harmful and, as long as the party was small, could be avoided to a certain degree. That has changed here recently and, characteristically, Czech questions that Adler cannot control any longer have to be hashed out, even if cautiously, in public. And that will also be the case when universal suffrage, especially the elimination of the curial system, is imposed for all important political business in our sphere of influence. Your discussions of principles will be a necessary result, and I believe that Victor's "opportunism" will not amount to very much. Indeed, I hope that, in the interest of the German party, Bülow delays your deportation, but if that occurs later on, then you can return to Vienna comforted in the knowledge that you and Victor are not at odds. For him, on the other hand, it would be very good. For us Jungen, and particularly for me, it would be much too nice. What I'd most like to do right now is write a long report to Bülow about how damaging and dangerous you are for the German Reich.

There was a misunderstanding about the social-political article in so far as I thought that the business had been settled following Mehring's article about Mannheim. Politically, he had treated the matter in full, but scientifically it offered little. Furthermore, the reports are vague, and so I thought that one could return to the matter on another occasion after the appearance of the official report. However, on 12 November I have to give a lecture on the subject at the Social Science Association. If it goes well, then I'll send you something. I *never* received the book by Kropotkin. Therefore, although I searched carefully to be certain, it is not in my library. Also, I never asked for it, because I had no intention of reading it. So, there has been a mistake. I have spoken with Renner about an article on our electoral movement and you will have it probably by Tuesday. I will remind him about it this evening. It would be good, however, to write to Austerlitz. He said to me the other day that he wanted to send you two articles. But you have to request it, because otherwise, overworked as he is, he doesn't get to it.

Regarding the *Vorwärts* issue, which has now really become a struggle among the literati, I cannot judge whether the Executive Committee's firing of the editors was the right move. In terms of facts, the Executive was right, because otherwise we'd wind up with a dictatorship of the editors. Eisner is now fighting with everything he has. Hopefully, you will be able to prevent the Workers' Press Association from taking his side. It has been awhile since I was in the editorial office, but like you I fear that the action of the party Executive will be condemned here. But journalistic solidarity is apparently enticing to many of our people and also to the Dresdner editorial board. Hopefully, we will still succeed in disposing of the matter without too much racket. As matters get ever more critical, there are now much more important things to deal with than the "Eisner question". These include foreign policy. I would have been glad to write something. But now, in the winter, there is more to do with my medical practice and I also have the firm intention of finally moving ahead with the work on my finance capital. I think that Mehring and the editorial board in Leipzig judge the matter too optimistically or, at a minimum, purely historically. He is, of course, sure that Delcassé can't go to war.[56] But all the conditions for war are available with the single exception of the proletariat's willingness to go to war. Therefore, the proletariat's hostility to war must be strengthened, and internationalism must come to the fore better and more *concretely* than previously. In that connection, not only can the May Day demonstration be used, but it its content would be enriched, it would gain in political significance, and it would thereby lose its purely celebratory character. At the same time, the question about the purpose of May Day would get an answer that would have to satisfy Bömelburg and Bringmann.[57] It is also necessary to express our internationalism more clearly in parliament and to cultivate it at reciprocal conferences. If not to Paris, then it seems to me that Bebel should go in any case to the next French party congress. It should also be a point on the agenda in Stuttgart and I don't think it is asking too much for the French, Germans, and English to draft a concrete international program whose main points would be: the elimination of the standing army, an alliance among the western powers, and the protection of open doors. If that were supported simultaneously by the socialists in the three [respective] parliaments, it would certainly have a good effect. I don't believe that, in the end, that could prevent a war. But the war would immediately create a revolutionary situation, the successes of which would redound to us.

Otherwise, not much is new. The movement for the franchise is going very well. I don't think it will come to a mass strike. I could deceive myself, but if in Hungary there is no appeasement, then we must also get the franchise as well. Indeed, given the public mood right now, if we don't get it the mass strike

---

56   Théophile Delcassé (1852–1923) was French Foreign Minister from 1898–1905. He pursued a strongly anti-German policy and cultivated close relations with Russia and Britain.

57   Theodor Bömelburg (1862–1912) was a Social Democratic trade union leader, a member of the Hamburg Assembly, and a member of the Reichstag. Although a supporter of the unity of the party and trade union leadership, he also was a sharp opponent of the general strike. August Bringmann (1861–1921) was a German Social Democratic leader of the carpenters' union and a newspaper editor.

will be unavoidable. The masses are impatient, the party congress in any case will declare the mass strike as an appropriate means, and agitation will be fully unleashed. Then we get a state and relief from our peculiar and in the long run dangerous situation.

Margret and little Karl are doing very well. Victor Adler told me that you are doing well, too. I am very grateful to Frau Liuse for her lovely letter. In the next week or so, Gustav Eckstein should be coming here. I am already looking forward to seeing him; he should be doing pretty well now.[58] Bauer is taking exams and yesterday passed his law exam with distinction. But otherwise he is doing quite respectably. Best regards to all the Berlin friends and on you and the boys.

Your,
R.H.

(KDXII 594/7)

Vienna, October 30, 1905

Honored friend,

For days I have been furious. First of all, the *Vorwärts* story, which is significant because it is a *symptom*, a symptom of the kinds of people ensconced in the most important posts in our party. Every word in the *Leipziger Volkszeitung* is correct and hits the mark. It is a nameless obscenity. I also believe that here, where initially only the information about "the six" is known, the mood changes, although at first there was only one voice against the Party Executive, which in any case was inept, either beforehand or afterward. The declaration would, at a minimum, have had to appear along with the resignation. Until that difficult document was ready, one could have put off the decision about the latter. All this, however, is only of incidental importance. But that one is always so naïve not to recognize people and not to know with whom one is dealing, people for whom the party has become a source of income and who, after losing this income can only think of one thing: revenge. And I am afraid that, if one does not take energetic and decisive measures, then we are only at the begin-

---

58 Gustav Eckstein (1875–1916) was an Austro-Marxist intellectual and journalist. He became a regular contributor to the *Neue Zeit* in 1902 and joined the editorial board in 1910. Like Hilferding, he taught at the party school. Hilferding's comment here about his health probably refers to his chronic lung disease which eventually killed him.

ning of the scandal. There are many people in the party who want to rise to the top using all means, including the *bourgeois* press, and who want to be liberated from Bebel, Mehring, Kautsky, etc., at any cost. One speaks openly of a boycott of the Party Executive by the six. That's a joke. But one also talks about publishing [something] about why Stadthagen has to give up providing legal counsel to *Vorwärts*.[59] Perhaps those are only empty threats from the Café des Westens.[60] However, I don't think Eisner, Gradnauer[61] or the others are capable of that. I do believe, however, and it is really simply a feeling – upon which I can mostly rely – that there are people in the party who are capable of anything. That being the case, the business has to be dealt with rapidly and energetically, above all it has to be made clear that the issue is not about revisionism, but rather about whether one is comradely [*parteigenößish*] or not.

In the end you have to carry out another policy or simply any policy. It's impossible for us to remain passive in all important world historical questions and to be satisfied when the government decides to summon the Reichstag and, after the fact, to make a few speeches that, coming so late, can exercise no influence – almost like the idle prattle of the [parliamentary] factions. Since the Reichstag's failure is ever more pronounced, its meeting depends increasingly on the whims of the government. Because the "tough summer work" and the winter work is increasingly carried out by Wilhelm and Bülow,[62] the party must ultimately do its work in the press and in the people's assembly, which are always at its disposal. What, then, did our press say about the Delcassé affair,[63] and while one might disagree on that matter, what does it say about the Kaiser's audacious, provocative speech announcing immediate increases for naval armaments. Almost nothing, worse than nothing. Instead of facing off against the Kaiser with the dignity and energy that the moment demands; instead of setting the proletariat's conviction against the Kaiser's talk in order to undercut the chauvinists' ability at home and abroad to make use of the

---

59 Arthur Stadthagen (1857–1917) was a legal expert and long-time SPD delegate in the Berlin City Council and the Reichstag. After his expulsion from the bar for political reasons in 1893, he became a journalist at *Vorwärts* and served on its editorial board from 1905 until 1916 when he was removed due to his opposition to the war.
60 The Café des Westens was known as a gathering place for revisionists in the SPD.
61 Georg Gradnauer (1866–1946) co-edited *Vorwärts* from 1896–1905 and sided with Eisner in the board's conflict with the SPD executive committee. See footnote 48 above.
62 Bernhard von Bülow (1849–1929) served as Kaiser Wilhelm II's Chancellor from 1900–1909.
63 Théophile Delcassé (1852–1923) was French Foreign Minister between 1898 and 1905. After signing the Entente Cordiale with Great Britain in 1905, his effort to assert French control over Morocco and to exclude German interests there precipitated a crisis that led to his fall in 1906.

Kaiser's speech; instead of answering the Kaiser immediately in the people's assemblies with peace demonstrations; [it made] a few foolish remarks. The only good thing was the publication of the article by Jaurés, who, it seems, has now undertaken to make foreign policy for Germany. And the Russian Revolution! Except for the *Leipziger*, no paper is worthy of this great moment. No stirring up of public opinion, no response, [and] no idea that above all in Germany, as in no other country in the World, it is necessary to treat the revolution as a separate thing. It seems that in Germany one thinks that international obligations increasingly can be paid off in marks and pennies. No wonder that the German Kaiser calmly sends his warships to Peterhof, as reported in the *Neue Freie Presse*. That can mean the beginning of an intervention which, perhaps, was long been agreed upon by Wilhelm and Nicholas in their well-known meeting. What did our press do in order to make the event, which was in any case possible, indeed, very probable, impossible? Nothing, absolutely nothing. Whenever possible, anything that was disconcerting was denied. Our press is surprised by all political events; it sees nothing in advance; it doesn't know what to prevent; it doesn't seek to influence anything. In a word, it promotes not policy but rather purely perfunctory agitation. Of course, it is easy to criticize, but how should it improve if the party does not criticize it where necessary? That applies to our whole press, whether revisionist or not. In addition, how can you make a policy which is essentially dependent upon whether the government chooses to hear our speeches on the budget? How can you make policy without politicians sitting on the editorial board? I certainly don't agree with Austerlitz about everything. But what had this man learned since joining the editorial board? There is no political law, no political event, with which he is not familiar and that he does not understand. His political opponents cannot escape his criticism, because he fully grasps the material. Today he is recognized as one of the best political and constitutional jurists, and that makes the politician. He places the whole of his knowledge in the service of the political situation, which he always sees in advance and which he, therefore, also always masters. And, despite all the legalese, he never loses the connection with the masses, whose power he knows how to bring to bear at the decisive moment. I know all that is much harder in Germany, but I still think that is no reason for nothing to happen. When will we really accomplish something politically? When will be actually take a position aside from those dealing with indirect taxes and trade policy? (Even there we let Schippel plague us.[64] I would like

---

64   Max Schippel (1859–1928) was a leading revisionist journalist and intellectual who published frequently for the *Sozialistische Monatshefte*.

to know what would happen to the Austrian who now says something against universal suffrage.) Even our position on militarism and navalism suffers due to passivity of our foreign policy.

I am also worried, because the reputation of German Social Democracy is undeniably harmed by its view of foreign parties. It is not surprising when Russian or Polish comrades, whose sense of self naturally grows as a result of the enormous heroism that they have demonstrated, look upon the German party with less admiration than before, because they are unfamiliar with the real difficulties faced by German Social Democracy. At the same time there is the outlook of the German party, which has not satisfactorily supported the Russian Revolution, does not seem to be in a position to prevent its government from perhaps soon actively intervening on the side of Tsarism, and will make no attempt to do so, as [anti-Tsarist] circles feared. And furthermore, one acknowledges and supports Plekhanov alone, or practically alone, while he, as those in these circles bitterly comment, sleeps away the revolution in northern Italy. [The German] attitude toward the PPS has exactly the same effect. I have to say that, after informing myself as much as possible, I am becoming increasingly convinced that these complaints are not unjustified. To be sure, the PPS does not have one Marxist of Rosa's prominence. But the PPS certainly is a proletarian party that has achieved a great deal and is no less social democratic than any other party. Regarding its leaders, the most important of whom I am acquainted with personally, their attitude toward Marxism is not hostile. That they are much more hostile toward the bourgeoisie than the Russians arises directly out of Polish conditions which lead necessarily to real class struggle. The issue of Poland's independence is a tactical question, which has now lost much of its importance and also within the PPS has been increasingly supplanted by the demand for autonomy. It [the PPS] cooperates fully with the Russian Revolution in all practical matters and is a powerful driving force of the whole movement. Perhaps it has sometimes underestimated the Russian proletariat, but it has also sometimes overestimated the power of the intelligentsia. That is now scarcely the case and, in any event, has lost its significance. There are no grounds for the hostile attitude of the German party and there is no reason for the party to withhold financial support. I can't resist [saying]: here in Austria not a single person approves of this [policy]. I have spoken with Zetterbaum, who is a very good Marxist, with Häcker, who is also a Marxist, and with many others. In connection with the PPS, a purely Marxist scientific journal should appear in Cracow. That proves that no hostility toward Marxism exists from the side of the PPS. They have all solemnly assured me that they regard the party as a good social democratic one and I, for one, share this conviction. I believe that today, with the party engaged in a magnificent struggle, the German party has no right to boycott it any longer. It has not been pleasant to write all this to you. I know that Rosa, whom I highly respect, has the opposite view, but, after my long and careful investigation, carried out as far as possible for a non-Slav, I really felt duty bound to explain my view to you. Dixi et salvavi animam meam. [I have spoken and saved my soul.] *Austerlitz* will write the article about Austria for you himself, indeed right after the party congress.[65] He plans to write one about Hungary, one about Austria, and eventually a third about the international obligations of the proletariat. Best regards, and please send news of you and Frau Luise. Otherwise, everything is good here.

Your,
 Rudolf Hilferding

(KDXII 597)

Vienna, November 14, 1905

Honored friend!

I've been meaning to write to you for some time but have not been able to get to it. I can imagine how much the most recent events have moved you. The collapse of Tsarism is the beginning of our revolution, of our victory, that is now drawing near. The expectation, which Marx had mistakenly expressed about the movement of history in 1848, will now, we hope, be fulfilled. In Austria we are at least in the happy situation that the tremendous excitement that every Social Democrat must feel can be channeled into a struggle for the franchise that is being conducted with élan and real revolutionary energy. Perhaps victory is made too easy for us, perhaps our need to exert the energy, which internal tension has created within us, in the struggle against our opponents, won't quite be enough to meet the slight resistance we encounter. Yet, we can console ourselves in the knowledge that our struggle is just the beginning of a whole series of shocks and crises that Austria will go through until it is restructured or goes under. And today the latter possibility seems more likely than the former. The Russian Revolution raises anew all the unsolved and unsolvable national questions. At the same time, it complicates them with the question of

---

65 Friedrich Austerlitz (1862–1931) was chief editor of the Social Semocratic *Arbeiter-Zeitung*.

the liberation of the proletariat. It opens the road for the struggle of nations and simultaneously for the struggle of classes within the nations. Austria has lived, however, from the irresolvable [nature] of the national question. The disintegration of Austria would have meant the disintegration of that empire in which they most easily found the conditions for their national development. The Russian Revolution signifies a total change in this situation. How Europe will be reconfigured in the future depends completely upon its progress. And here the Polish question is most important. I am not speaking here from special sympathy for the Poles or even in light of information from the PPS, but rather – considering matters as a Marxist – I mean that a free Poland is now in the strongest interest not only of the Russian Revolution but also of the European proletariat. I think it is a reliable instinct that leads the reaction from Witte[66] to Wilhelm II to immediately ally themselves against Poland. A free Poland means a constant threat to Prussia, which would have to radically change its policy toward Poland and could not change it without becoming democratic. In other words, it would have to radically change itself, which is impossible. But the Prussian reaction would also simultaneously mean an immediate threat of war and could not hold out against the assault of the proletariat. A free Poland would also mean the liberation of Austria's Slavs [and] the democratization of Austria. That would be the result of peaceful development, which is, however, unlikely. Much more likely is that Prussia intervenes, which would mean war, a war that probably would not be limited to Prussia and Russia but would sweep across Europe. In this war, Prussia would have everything going against it at home as well as abroad. It would mean catastrophe for the rulers and revolution in Germany. Free Poland, therefore, is the most effective catalyst, the strongest driver of permanent revolution. As much as I agreed with the view that, as long as the revolution was still in preparation, as long as it remained firmly in its early stage, the policy of Polish Social Democracy had to be closely tied to that of Russian Social Democracy and had to place all national demands on the back burner, I now believe just as strongly that the time has come when – without damaging the Russian Revolution – it must go much further and take advantage, for its own benefit, of the demand for as much autonomy as possible or perhaps even for independence. It can scarcely do anything else in the face of Witte's provocative manifesto, against which even the Russian liberals

---

66 Count Sergei Yulyevich Witte (1849–1915) served in a number of high positions in the Russian government under Alexander III and Nicholas II. As Finance Minister he promoted Russian industrialization. After the outbreak of the Revolution of 1905, he supported reforms that ended Tsarist absolutism and created a pseudo-parliamentary regime. He served as the government's first Prime Minister from November 1905 until May 1906.

are protesting, and after the declaration of martial law. Now it can't possibly retreat, without harming the Russian Revolution, without giving the counter-revolution the chance – through its cheap triumph – to appear as the savior of the fatherland. If it continues to move forward, it will rescue not only the Russian Revolution, but it will create the conditions under which revolution must spread across Europe. I think that, politically, the proletarian revolution is now in a situation similar to that of the bourgeois [revolution] in 1848. The Polish Revolution will be decisive above all for the victory of the revolution in Europe.

I would be eager to know whether you share this view and what Rosa says about it. To be sure, I know that you are extraordinarily busy and would be happy to wait [for a reply]. Unfortunately, you are busy not only with the revolutionary events, but also with the shameful developments connected with the struggle of the six. It has gradually dawned upon me that there must be elements involved about which we here (and also the editors of the *A–Z*) don't know anything. What happened then to the position of the general commission? Firstly, it did not participate and, secondly, what kind of interests did it have in Eisner and his associates. It really seems to me that some people believed that the moment for a palace revolution – there is no other word for it – had come. To believe in any kind of sincere intention is almost impossible. But if that is the way it is, then only the greatest energy, paired with the greatest caution, and the greatest openness, which appeals to the healthy instinct of the masses, will be able to purify the party of the corruption that is consuming it there. As repulsive as the matter is, it is also infuriating that German Social Democracy concerns itself with *that* at just this moment, as unavoidable as it might be. But, hopefully, my view is too dark. If not, then the struggle has to be taken to the enemy camp and all the trade union leaders, journalists, and parliamentarians put before the people and held to account. I would very much like to see matters more clearly, because I'd like to get Adler and Austerlitz to take a position. For that, however, I have to know more. Adler asked me recently if I'd heard any news from you. I very much hope that you are feeling well and that these nuisances don't rob you of your happiness and joy about the advent of the new age, our age, our victory. It is the epoch of fulfillment. The preparations are complete, the detail work is done, and we can hope for the harvest now that the fields have long been plowed and the seeds spread. It is a time in which one can feel proud and happy to be a Social Democrat.

We are all doing very well. Best regards to you and yours.
 Your,
 Rudolf Hilferding

[P.S.] Hans Deutsch has been in Vienna since Saturday. Unfortunately, his sister is quite sick and therefore he did not come via Friedenau. How is your work on ethics going?

Dear Frau Luise,

I won't, of course, be writing to you about the Russian Revolution and about Poland. Don't think, though, that I've lost interest due to the demands of the nursery. At the moment there is just no chance of participating. In accordance with my husband's admonitions I've even stayed away from the demonstrations.

Now I have to report to you, the mother of the family – not the party. The baby is growing and developing about as much as one could expect. Today, at nine weeks, he weighs almost 11 pounds. Everyone who sees him assures me that he is a beautiful child, even those who have no reason to provide such compliments. He also cries very little. The nights are quiet and I only nurse him once in the early morning. With a lot of effort, I've even managed to get the household in order, so that I've been able to work again since early November. Forgive me for writing so much about myself, but I thought you might find it interesting. Among my friends it is now raining children. Leonie Hock-Gombrich started things off a few days before me. Today I heard about the tenth and now an eleventh is in sight. There is one on the way at the Heller's too.[67]

Gustav Eckstein was in Vienna for a few days. We tracked him down and he looked extraordinarily well. He seemed a bit resigned, which is understanding given his isolation, but he is hopeful about the future.

Best regards to you and your boys. Next time I'll more rationally.
  Your,
  Margret

---

67   Leonie Hock-Gombrich was a pianist who had studied with Margarethe's sister. Margarethe had met Hugo Heller, an Austrian Social Democrat, in the Socialist Student League. His bookstore was a well-known meeting place for intellectuals. See List 2006, p 111.

(KDXII 598)

Vienna, December 18, 1905

Honored friend!

You are right a thousand times over, but it is now so hard to write about theoretical matters as practice moves forward so splendidly. In addition, I have my finance capital, which expands slowly enough, far more slowly than it should, and this awful medicine, which is also a miserable way to make a living. Despite everything, I agree that I've inexcusably left you in the lurch. But I have communicated with the others as I have been able to and, indeed, with Austerlitz. Saturday, I spoke with him again and he promised me to send you two articles before Christmas. Hans Deutsch also promised to write something by Christmas and you've already received something from Bauer. I'm very curious about what you say about that. Maybe I'll respond to it in the *Neue Zeit*. Furthermore, today I'm sending you the programmatic article of the first number of *Natschalo*, which is probably by Parvus and is not only interesting historically. It is up to you to publish it either in the *Neue Zeit* or *Vorwärts*.[68] I received it with the request that I pass it on to you from comrade Klatschko, a Russian who lives here, is a consul in the party office of the Russian revolutionaries, and who you may know. If it seems unsuitable to you, please send the manuscript back to me. I have not done all of that in consequence of your threats. The Pope who threatens with apostasy, *non liquet* [not proven], contradicts my economic-historical thinking. In regard to me, however, I don't exactly know what to do. I would very much like to review the Marx *Nachlaß*, but I don't know if it would go quickly enough. I have to then read both volumes again and what I'd most like to do is take note of those points that have become halfway clear to me in my finance capital. Still, I'll probably write to you next week that I'll review it. When will the final volume appear? One could then take care of it all at once. I would have been happy to read your "Ethics" also in manuscript form.[69] Will you allow it to be published soon? Cuno and Rosa will probably be lost to theoretical work for some time. Rosa will probably now be writing in slavish. You yourself are probably overworked. Hopefully you will be able to take a proper rest

---

68   For background on Parvus, see footnote 94 above. Kautsky published the manuscript in the *Neue Zeit* 1(1905/06): 451–58.

69   The reference is to Kautsky's *Ethik und materialistische Geschichtsauffassung. Ein Versuch* (Stuttgart: J.H.W. Dietz, 1906).

at Christmas. Will you be traveling? I feel wistful and strangely emotional when I think about those days in Berlin and the joy I felt at that time in your home. I increasingly regret having left, my wife almost more than me. Recently I looked at the rules for adoption in the German states, but for that, too, one needs the approval of a minister and without citizenship I can't do much in Germany.

I believe that now the most important thing in Germany is purposefully to promote the movement that has spontaneously started in Saxony and, in regard to its goals, to raise the ante. I think the slogan most suitable for this critical situation would be down with Junker rule. It goes without saying that I am keenly aware of how improbable a purely political revolution in Germany is, and how much Junker domination today corresponds with that of the big bourgeoisie. Nevertheless, initially the movement will have to consider this aim, and it does not depend on us how far it will take it. Therefore, [first] the fight for the franchise in Saxony and Prussia, but then, shortly after getting the struggle started in Prussia, the fight for the franchise in the Reich, the demand to redraw the electoral districts [and], finally, when possible, the raising of constitutional issues such as the reduction of the competencies of the state assemblies, a concomitant increase [in the power] of local (Kreis) government, a reduction or elimination of the authority of the Bundestag (a demand which Engels, I believe, had asserted was necessary), in short an action program that is geared to set the masses in motion. I don't think it's a mistake for the program to appear to be purely political and only democratic. It would be our fight and our victory. The achievement of democracy in Germany would rapidly result in the transformation of a bourgeois into a proletarian democracy. That our opponents know this speaks only for the difficulty of the struggle. But it simply has to be fought out in order to set the classes in motion again [and] to revolutionize them. That is necessary right now, when we cannot know how soon the situation will demand a revolutionary show of force by the German proletariat. I know that the foregoing appears to be rather sketchy and is therefore very much open to attack, but on the one hand I have to send the article off today, and on the other I could only write hastily, because I have to leave. I will write more extensively very soon and ask for your indulgence for today's hastiness. Victor Adler sends his best regards. He was welcomed in parliament with great respect, and every conceivable person hurried over to introduce themselves to him, for example, old Randa, the Czech minister.[70] He replies with sharp retorts

---

70 Antonin Ritter von Randa (1834–1914) was a minister representing the Czechs (Landsmannminister) in the Austrian government from 1904–06.

and the fellows are still thankful. The Minister of the Interior, Count Bylandt-Reidt, was recently honored in this way when V[ictor] A[dler] said to him: You know, your reputation with us isn't too bad. From Linz one assures us that you are not the usual councilor of the forests and fields.[71] The man had no idea how to respond to this recognition. Bebel and Eisner should be able to say that. Best regards to your dear family and don't be too mad at your lazy correspondent,

Rudolf Hilferding

(KDXII 599)

Vienna, February 7, 1906

Honored friend,

I did not want to answer your letter immediately, because I intended to do it at the same time as an article on the question of electoral rights in state assemblies. Now I have neither the article nor the letter and I am aggravated about both. One can only say in a letter a fraction of what one wants to say.

Concerning my "transfer" to Berlin, I think that it is better if I stay here for seasoning or, if you would prefer, to mature. Today, I would come to Berlin "young", [or] "half-baked", and I don't know with what other epithets one might use to describe a man who would have to listen to the advice of every conceivable – experienced, etc. – comrade. If I come a bit later, when I have something to show that is worth seeing, then I'd have the prospect of being able to do something, if I'm good for anything at all. Now I very much fear being seen by Ströbel and some others as a disagreeable intruder. In addition, there is also the biggest difficulty of being a foreigner. Not because of the danger of deportation – if it were only that I'd just as soon risk it today as tomorrow without any commitment from the party. But it is extraordinarily difficult to really pursue social democratic politics without the support of the masses. What I find problematic in the German policy is that it understands so little about how to allow the masses themselves to act, which does not always have to mean

---

71 Artur M. Graf Bylandt-Rheidt (1854–1915) held a number of important posts in the Austrian government between 1897 and 1906. These included Minister of Agriculture, Minister of Education, as well as Interior Minister. He supported universal manhood suffrage.

street demonstrations, and carries out its entire policy in an exclusively parliamentary [fashion] and through its press. In Austria, in contrast, we have the necessary resonance for our parliamentary approach. The people's assemblies are a broad and independent tribune for us from which we can raise our voices at any time on any issue, even when parliament is not available. In Germany, the people's assembly is merely a means of agitation, here it is also an instrument of politics. Now, I know that that is much more difficult in Germany than here, but it would still meet with some success, certainly with the masses, perhaps also with the ruling classes. In addition, one has a whole other authority within the party itself when one has the support of the masses and is in contact with them. Otherwise, one is, with just a few exceptions, as you yourself are, just a party employee, whose opinion requires little consideration. That is why I place so much importance on citizenship. Do you think it might actually be possible that I could receive it in southern Germany through adoption?

In regard to the issue of universal suffrage, in my view the right to vote in Prussia and Saxony has the greatest significance, and I don't agree at all with the opinion of those who see it only as a means of agitation and hold that, when it brings us a million votes in the next election, the job is done, an opinion that I fear Mehring also shares. The reason that drives me to ascribe so much importance to the right to vote in state assemblies is not so much its authority in the spheres of railroads, mining, and so on, which concern administrative and welfare policies, but much more its important authority in matters of state that flow from the nature of the Reich constitution. The state assemblies make decisions about the federal governments, including the Bundestag. A majority in Saxony and later on in Prussia would mean our arrival in the Bundestag and, thus, our participation in the Reich government. Now, I don't think that is immediately possible at all. Our representation in the Bundesrat would be in effect the end of that institution. But exactly for that reason does the raising of the suffrage question in Prussia and more immediately in Saxony mean the immediate raising of the issue of the conquest of political power, if not in its entirety then a major and significant portion of it. The dominant classes themselves can only avoid this problem by changing the constitution and shifting the decisive power into the Reichstag, where we are a minority, and taking it from the state assemblies, where we are decisively in the majority or soon will be. By conquering the right to vote in the state assemblies, we would place the ruling elites before a terrible dilemma. Either leave the constitution as it stands, thereby paralyzing the Bundesrat and with it their whole policy, or change the constitution by fleeing into a Reichstag elected by universal suffrage. Of course, that leads to the extraordinary resistance of the dominant classes against any change in the right to vote for the state assemblies, but on the other hand, for us, it shows the extraordinary importance of success. And the struggle has some good prospects for success because of universal suffrage in south Germany and in the Reichstag. In any case, the latter can be best protected by an offensive in Prussia and Saxony if it is energetically led, and it must be, because a defeat here would be the signal for the firebrands to go on the attack against the franchise in the Reichstag.

Therefore, putting on the brakes here accomplishes nothing at all and can only hurt us, as would moving too quickly or, again, too cautiously, as Bloch, who is thinking of a demonstration strike, would like. The demonstration strike, however, is only the lips and here one has to whistle. Of course, not immediately, but only after long preparation. The masses first have to know and have a sense of what it is all about. The issue must be moved to the foreground of our policy and has to be dealt with unremittingly in the Reichstag and in the people's assemblies. These don't always have to be announced so dangerously. But, likewise, the question has to be treated as one for the whole German party, not just as an issue for Prussia and Saxony, and the south German comrades have to co-operate. (A real mass strike could in no way remain limited to Prussia and Saxony; its chances would then diminish from the outset). In short, all forces have to be concentrated on it. There is no need to say how important a real success would be for Social Democracy in Germany both at home and abroad. It finally would bring an end to the dumb talk about our powerlessness. It would also mean taking the fight against Junkerdom onto its own ground in the Prussian Landtag. The struggle against the grain tariff would have to be linked with a struggle for suffrage rights in the assembly. I think that such an energetic, consequent, and untiringly pursued fight, which must also be appropriately supported in the party press, could give the power of Social Democracy such a momentum that it could break the ranks of our opponents and silence the intolerable grousing [within the movement]. [The letter breaks off here and resumes a month later.]

Vienna, March 10, 1906

Honored friend,

The last time I wrote, I'd gotten so far, but annoyed that I had to write instead of being able to talk to you, I broke it off and let it lie there. Despite my intentions, it was only today's letter from you that roused me again. I have to openly concede that I am rather dissatisfied with myself and, therefore, I understand that you also would have had every reason not to write. Recently, I have worked much less than I should have. It is unpleasant when you are in the middle of a major effort and then get bogged down somewhere and don't have the patience or desire to do anything else, like the small things. Yet, I hope that now this period will soon be over, and I will be able to move ahead. Chapter I on money is basically done, and I'll now begin with chapter II on the role of money in the circulation process of capital. From there I will work on the emergence and necessity of credit. The boring part of it is that a large part of the description has to be dedicated to the reproduction of volumes II and III of *Capital*, and such repetitive work is difficult and uninteresting.

For a long time, I've wanted to ask you if Marx's manuscripts of volumes II and III are accessible. Not that I would now have the time to study the manuscripts thoroughly. But I'd really like to do it sometime, perhaps later on. To wit, I suspect that Engels did not always grasp the issue at hand. I think that some of his polemical remarks against Marx are incorrect. It would also be interesting to examine whether the passages that are important for the investigation of competition are left out. Copies of the manuscripts must exist. Further, I wanted to ask whether you might know of a manuscript by *Engels* on the *stock market*. It is rumored that he worked on it late in life. Finally, I expected that the final volume of *Theories of Surplus Value* would have appeared. Therefore, I put off the review for the *Dresdner [Zeitung]* and our *Arbeiter-Zeitung*. Will it be out soon?

Now on to a reply to your last letter. You write that you fear I will become a doctor and give up the party. You don't have to fear that at all. I don't know *when* I'll be able to give up medicine, but I know that, first and foremost, I will remain a socialist and I will allow no external circumstances to change that. There is only the other "danger" that I become an "Austrian" and then eventually more of a practical politician. However, the latter is, in any case, in the pretty distant future, and, at all events, I would do it only when I'm done with my theoretical work. It is also wholly untrue that I have applied for a job on the editorial board of the *Dresdner*; I've not taken a single step in that direction and have no intention of doing so. Recently I was very surprised when Victor Adler asked me if it was true that I aimed to compete with Gradnauer in Dresden. But he did not want to name his source. Perhaps you'll be so good as to tell me where this rumor comes from? I have never considered Dresden but only *Vorwärts*. I've also never applied there, as you know. On the contrary, I've always believed that I still needed years of training. Indeed, now comes the change in Austria on top of it all. For the next few years I am pretty secure. But it is possible that the party will need me more than previously and then I can scarcely say no. The start might come very soon, and I've wanted to write to you about it for quite a while. The plan has emerged to establish a journal, indeed a monthly. This is certainly a necessity. Victor Adler has long been in favor [of the idea] and I think that this plan may be realized by the end of the year. We've already had a few discussions about it and a committee was set up including Winarsky,[72] Renner, and me. We have a program in mind that should provide this review essentially with practical content. It should deal with all ongoing problems from a socialist standpoint, and for problems specific to Austria material has to be provided and a socialist viewpoint found. Purely theoretical, very specific scientific discussions should be avoided as much as possible (much to the chagrin of my friend Max Adler). Thus, the journal should develop its own character and not come into competition with others. It is particularly the national question, which will continue to exist here, and the issues of the constitution and administration that have become significant for us in ways rather different than before. In addition, all questions of Austria's economic policy and, finally, the issues of the political and trade union movement, of tactics, and so on [should be covered]. The magazine should not be an official party journal, but it should be close to the party. If the thing should get done – and I am very curious to hear your opinion about it – then I'll probably be editor, a prospect that does not make me unabashedly happy. It is not only a great responsibility, but it would also be a difficult and thankless task that would take up a frightful amount of time that I would otherwise devote to my studies. But it would be very difficult for me to be able to avoid taking the job, because there is no one else available. But maybe it will take a while before the founding occurs.

Of course, at the moment one thinks only about the right to vote. In that regard the *Arbeiter-Zeitung* can really be proud. It has led the campaign masterfully (one could be critical, perhaps about this or that detail), even if the foreign comrades cannot always know how necessary it was not only to present our tactics in the paper, but also to show the bourgeoisie, especially the [Austrian] Germans, how it has to do politics. In fact, Gautsch's speech (written by Sieghardt, who you might know) consisted of nothing other than extracts from articles in the *Arbeiter-Zeitung*.[73] The swing in public opinion is also thanks to an outstanding journalistic performance, in which above all Austerlitz and

---

72 Leopold Winarsky (1873–1915) was a member of the SDAP secretariat and a delegate to the Reichsrat.
73 Paul Gautsch (1851–1918), leading educator and three-time Austrian Minister President. His government tried, but failed, to pass legislation granting universal male suffrage. He resigned in May 1906. Rudolf Sieghart (1866–1934) was a key figure in the Austrian President's Office from 1902–10 and laid the groundwork for the suffrage reform.

Renner were involved, that was unrelenting, devastating, and on target against all opposing views. From abroad one cannot really imagine the effectiveness of the direct and indirect influence we exercise on the policy of the government, which [the latter] had initiated. By the way, our current Minister of Justice[74] is now on familiar terms with V[ictor] A[dler], an accident that is characteristic [of the situation]. In addition, Adler's most recent speech is a brilliant example of genuine socialist argumentation. Certainly, one hopes for the realization [of our policy] and the fact is that our chances get better every day. Everyone is already counting the number of seats; I bet on forty-five. Personally, I am interested in Renner getting a seat. That will probably happen, to the great benefit of our party.

Regarding the reviews, I ask that you send me Knapp. Only I am worried that the book is totally silly. I ask that you give me a little more time with Diehl, so that I can finish reading it. Then I will get into contact with Eckstein, but I myself won't write about it. I think it is fine that he wrote about Marz.

Now, concerning the "Economic Review", I'd be happy to take it on for material reasons.[75] In any case I have to keep track of economic conditions abroad. The difficulty is only in acquiring the material. I managed [to get the *Sächsische* [*Zeitung*] with a sub-subscription to the *Frankfurter* [*Zeitung*], but that does not suffice for *Vorwärts*. Now the issue is whether *Vorwärts* will make the material available to me or not. Above all, I would need the reports of the Chamber of Commerce and similar stuff. Regarding the dailies, the *Berliner Tageblatt*, the *Rheinisch-Westfälische* [*Zeitung*], the *Kölnische* [*Zeitung*] and the *Frankfurter Z*[*eitung*], would be necessary. I'll check at the *Arbeiter-Zeitung* to inquire whether I can use the economic sections of these papers and that will probably work out. I'll let you know what happens.

In other respects, I can only promise an improvement. Once I'm through the toughest part of my finance capital, then a flood of economic criticism will be unleashed to flow over the fields, but until then I ask for your patience and hope you haven't given me up for lost.

By the way – an understandable thought – why has Rosa disappeared?

I'd like to write about a lot of other things, such as the prospects in Russia, but I've truly misused your time – and your eyes – already. We are doing very

---

74 Franz Klein (1854–1926), Austrian Minister of Justice from 1906–1908. Serving in the cabinet of Gautsch's successor, Minister President von Beck, he oversaw the introduction of universal male suffrage.

75 Hilferding seems to be responding here to a suggestion that he become a regular reviewer of works on economics for *Vorwärts*. It is unclear who made the suggestion and why it did not pan out.

well. Hopefully, Frau Luise will soon be feeling better. If I take on the "Vorwärts Rundschau", I will accumulate and invest the money productively for a trip to Berlin. With best regards to you, Frau Luise, and the boys,

Your,
  Rudolf Hilferding

[P.S.] My wife promises to send the reviews within eight days.

(KDXII 600)

Vienna, June 30, 1906

Honored friend,

My reply to the charming letter from your wife, which is long overdue, has been delayed for such a long time because I still cannot say with any certainty whether I can be in Thumersbach on the fifteenth of July. The decision will be made in the next few days, and then I'll let you know immediately. I also have so much on my mind that I couldn't resolve to write a letter. But today I'm driven to it by immense anger over the most recent event in the party. Silberschmidt's indiscretion is an unbelievable matter in itself, but apparently it gets worse. The trade union commission seems to think the moment is favorable to move against the party, to reveal the conflict over this vital question in public, and thereby lay bare the party's complete powerlessness. Because in Germany the party is nothing the moment union support is lacking. In other words, without the trade unions, without the most active, enthusiastic trade union participation – one prepared to make any sacrifice – then to even think about a mass strike is mad. Without the mass strike as a last resort, the German party is completely defenseless. Here is where the form of organization comes into play, one that has allowed a split, which appears to be getting worse, to emerge between the unions and the party along with the lack of any unified leadership. Where this lack of discipline, this constant putting on an act, by cliques that are perhaps small in number but hold influential and responsible posts will lead is not at all clear. In addition, there is the press, which in general has no opinion [and] the rest of which only enlarges the conflict instead of seeking the means to end it. I'm very sorry only now to be able to write about the preparations for the mass strike. I'll do it until the issue is decided, whether or not it occurs. It is still up in the air. The committee is working, indeed terribly slowly, but still [it is working], and it is possible that it will be avoided. Certainly, one could almost wish for it to occur in the interest of German Social Democracy. However, what unity, what enthusiasm, what discipline is prevalent in our preparations is not a matter solely for the trade union commission or the party leadership, but rather is known to hundreds of shop stewards from around the whole empire without a word having been said in public, to say nothing of it having been used for low intrigue. The trade unions are not passive, but on the contrary, they are out in front, carry out all organizational preparations, they are identical to the party, and a conflict between them is unthinkable. It is crazy that the unions have drawn greatest advantage from the rising political movement and were able to sharply increase their membership. Nevertheless, our press participates in trade union struggles very differently than its German counterpart. In Germany the incredible decision was made that only the party can lead and finance the mass strike. Besides the silliness of a resolution to finance the revolution and, indeed, to divide the finances of the German working class along political and trade union lines, so that when the political money runs out, the revolution is interrupted leaving the trade union money intact and before which, in the face of the celebratory declaration that this money is for reformist rather than revolutionary purposes, the enemy will respectfully call a halt – apart from this insanity, that means that one has no grasp of the possibilities and requirements of the mass strike if one thinks that such an enterprise can be carried out without the total and united power of the whole working class. Does one think that one is dealing with a trivial matter like calling for a series of assemblies in which the most important question for the organizers is raising the money to pay the rent? A life and death struggle and both bodies ask who has to pay the costs! A revolution considered from a fiscal point of view! Only, what a shame that there is no fiscal revolution. One can only say that the German working class may well be spared from a revolution under this leadership. And it will be, because this leadership will carry out neither a revolution nor anything else. A[nd] then the idea of [using] the mass strike for the practical right to vote! I won't deny that the revolution could be sparked by the [struggle] for the right to vote in Prussia. But to debate the mass strike before a serious movement is present, before public rallies, demonstrations, and conflict have occurred, means putting the cart before the horse. It means gabbing about distant goals and doing nothing at the moment. And, on top of that, now there is the awkwardness of discussing the matter in declarations, where the only declaration could have been the rejection of any declaration on the expulsion of Silberschmidt. And if there were only hope that the party would like to learn something from such sad incidents! That it would finally get rid of an organization from which conflict *must* arise, and that it would get down to the business of reconstructing the unity of the movement, without which any effective action is impossible. It must take the matter firmly in hand and get control over those who have been unconscionably playing games with the party.

Just to make sure that satire is not lacking, today's *Vorwärts* contained a reproach for Austria. I am talking about the article "Only Because" about Ellenbogen's speech. If you only knew how intolerable such – I can't find the right word, let's say nonsensical – things are at such a moment, when we might be facing a revolution! Reprimands from this newspaper, which fulfills its mission so miserably and has no conception of how to do it, are unbearable.

Forgive this outburst of anger, my dear friend. I had to speak my mind. I can only imagine how aggravated you must be. To be sure, in your optimism you console yourself with Russia and you are right. We had a great time with your wife, and I long to be able to see you and yours in Thumersbach (please send your address there). Best wishes,

Your,
Rudolf Hilferding

(KDXII 601)

Vienna, August 20, 1906
Thermal-Curanstalt
Herztliches Institute für partielle heissluft-Behandlung
Vienna, I., Dorotheergasse Nr. 6 (Graben)

Honored friend,

If by writing again today I am out of sync with my usual habit, it is because the latest developments in Germany have once again touched a nerve. The trade union protocol is uniquely illuminated by the plan for the trade union school, which *Vorwärts* published – for the moment without comment – and which goes beyond the worst of our expectations. Upon reading the protocol, I was surprised by the insignificance, naivety, and shortsightedness of the union leaders. They seem to be people who, when dealing with a vital question, such as that of the relationship of the unions to the party, obviously give it cursory consideration and can never express themselves clearly about it. From this lack of clarity arises this confused language, which, stemming from all kinds of personal frictions, wounded vanities, and certain difficulties in agitational work, in so far as they encounter opponents who take advantage of their individual assertions, never arrives at concrete conclusions and thus misses the heart of the issue entirely. Evidently, they remained chagrined at the party and itch to show: we are important to you, indeed more important than the others. And the program of the school illustrates how this sole purpose of annoying the others emerged. One cannot accept that people who are conscious of their responsibility, who understand what is at stake, two men like Calwer and Schippel,[76] could both attach themselves to bourgeois policies of the most reactionary stamp, and, as representatives of the proletariat, go over to the protective tariff supporters, to the expansionists, and [promote] the training of their successors. Calwer and Schippel, who are isolated on all the issues and stand in sharpest antagonism to the party, an antagonism that is related to the most important practical questions now confronting the party's entire policy – as teachers of future trade union leaders! It is an absurdity that would be impossible in any other country. What would English trade unionists say if one presumed to make agrarians and protectionists into their leaders?

Generally speaking, it is a misfortune that it could come to the establishment of this competing school, a misfortune that is the fault of the party executive. It would have been a thousand times more prudent to create a school as a school of the Berlin [party] organization, indeed of the political and trade union [organizations], if possible with a certain amount of independence from both, as is true here, where the unions provide the money and the party dispenses blessings. But I also think that the school can only be established with the agreement of the unions. Its main value should be that it produces people schooled in trade union and party politics, who come into personal contact in the school and would be guided by ideas that would secure unity in the future. To be sure, if one had thought it important, then besides books used jointly, two or three special books with only trade union content could have been introduced. But now one has created a school only for trade unionists and citizen lecturers where participants are educated against the party and absorb bourgeois confusion instead of the proletarian world view. At the same time, the division between the party and unions is sharpened, because in the future the unions will draw their personnel from this school. This story is probably the worst to come out of Germany thus far.

When one wonders what to do, the answer is extraordinarily difficult. In the discussion of the protocol in the press, an extraordinarily cooperative path is

---

76   Richard Calwer (1868–1927), leading revisionist journalist and economist. For Max Schippel, see footnote 140 above.

clearly discernable. I think it is correct politically, if I don't share the optimism that is frequently expressed. It is very hard, therefore, to openly come out against the trade union school, especially since the unions, as a consequence of the party's independent actions, are formally within their rights, though it is also politically outrageous to appoint the most outspoken opponents of the party's policy [as teachers]. But maybe it might be possible successfully to create a unified school, as I said, perhaps by adding courses dealing purely with trade union matters, by pursuing it with skill and energy, and if the union members arouse themselves against the contradiction. It is unthinkable that the trade unionists really want to support the protective tariff, the agrarian policy, the colonial policy, Marxism, and so on in this splendid manner! On the other hand, they can only return [to the fold] if one uses the recommendation of a common school to build a bridge to them. Of course, one has to provide instruction for the trade union leaders, too, in order to combat mistrust from the start. If one brings forward this recommendation to support the unity of the party and the trade unions, given the current morale and the proper timing in catching the attention of the masses, it would be hard to reject. For the school itself, it would only be an advantage. It would be set up on a much broader material basis, the school material itself would, perhaps, be much more diverse, there would be positive reciprocal influence, and the school itself would have much greater significance and be much more useful. On the other hand, a pure party school would conflict with a trade union [school] from the outset.

And there is yet another related matter. The trade union school disposes over the best known of our opponents and its program is rich and comprehensive. In contrast, the party school cuts a very poor figure both in terms of personnel and content. Its teachers are too little known and too few for its purpose and, due to the separation and the trade union students' refusal to enroll, it will only be able to partially achieve its aim. You understand that, as a result, my concerns about coming to Berlin have grown markedly. Nevertheless, now I feel myself far too committed to be able to back out without your approval, especially since you have already communicated with Bebel about my last letter. To speak plainly, however, I think that my coming is pretty useless. The balance has to rest on a different basis; it has to be for the coming generation of both party and trade union leaders and must have the very best instructors. That means you and Mehring and, perhaps for a political course, Bebel, too – he won't have more to do than Legien[77] – will have to participate as teachers, at least at the beginning.

---

77 Carl Legien (1861–1920), a turner by trade, was the leader of the General Commission of German Trade Unions from 1891–1919.

Given the choice between you or Calwer and Schippel, people will have to yield out of fear of the masses and that seems to me to be extraordinarily important.

Not much is new here. Margret is with the boys in Gleichenberg. [She] became ill and has to remain there. The boys are doing well. This week I myself am filling in as "director" of a hot air clinic, which takes up my time into the evenings. Along with the book-keeping, it is about enough. Next week I'm free again, [but] unfortunately, time is not money. The article by Roland Holst is very nice, but perhaps it is too optimistic in light of the conclusion. Regarding Parvus, I hope that he escapes soon, when possible via Vienna. I am curious about news from Rosa [...]. Is Wurm already back? Please give him my best regards.

With my very best wishes for you, Frau Luise, and the boys [...].
Your,
Rudolf Hilferding

(KDXII 602)

September 6, 1906
Juridisch-politischer Leseverein
Vienna, I., Rotenturmstraße 13

Honored friend,

Of course, I must accept your suggestion. The prospect of being able to work by your side and the hope of perhaps being able in some respects to provide [you] relief are too tempting to resist. When I know that my work will enable you to have more free time, then I know that it will be useful. The timing of my vacation has still not yet been formally arranged, but I think I can count on it with certainty. The people involved will return from their vacation next week and I will then push for a definitive decision. Nevertheless, as I said, there is no doubt about the vacation.

Of course, with my joining the NZ, I would definitively go to Berlin. But I would like to keep the possibility of my return open for the first half year. Initially, because of my possible deportation, but also in order to see whether I am really up to the demands of the job. I hope that it will go well. As I said, I look forward to the activity at the NZ perhaps more than [that] at the school. Hopefully, the party executive has nothing against that [feeling].

Please write and let me know when the school will open. As far as I am concerned, the later the better. Mauerenbrecher wrote me a letter about his plans for his class.[78] There is not much to object to in these plans [since] everything depends on the execution. Now, he was very awkward and politically childish, but whether he can lecture well in history I don't know. It is just that I would not want to recommend that as a major field. Shortly after my first letter, I wrote you a second in which I wrote about the trade union school and, in connection with that, I asked again, whether you, or if that would be absolutely impossible, then Mehring, could take on the history of the party. As before, I still believe that is very important. At that time, I was very pessimistic and wrote that I would not really want to go to Berlin. Your current suggestion makes the whole thing much more palatable to me. But it seems that you have not received that letter? I am very sorry that Wurm is not doing better. You must be plagued by lots to do just before the party congress. Frau Luise must remain patient, I am not giving up my hope to dance a waltz with her. Margret is back and is doing well. The son will first report for duty in a few days.

Your article about the trade unions was very good. But I hope that in Mannheim no definitive result is achieved. The whole thing is essentially a question of organization, and it has not matured to the point where a decision is warranted. I would not view reciprocal delegations of the P[arty] E[xecutive] und the T[rade] U[nion] C[ommission] as very fruitful.

Mehring's article about flags and commodities is, once again, brilliant. Margret sends her best regards to all. Please also give my best to Wurm.

Your,
Rudolf Hilferding

(KDXII 603)

August 2, 1907
Die Neue Zeit
Berlin-Friedenau, Saar Straße 19

Honored friend,

Frau Luise writes that none of you know how my handwriting looks anymore. But I think that must at least be aesthetically pleasing. My conscience does

---

78   Max Mauerenbrecher (1874–1929), evangelical pastor and writer, began his political activity in the Christian Social Party before becoming first a liberal and then, in 1903, a Social

bite, however, and not only because I have not written to you. Nothing important has happened, and I did not want to disturb your peace and quiet. But I'm writing today because something has come up. I spoke with Mehring yesterday about the Congress of the International.[79] Naturally, he wanted nothing other than to write his lead article and asserted that *you* must write. When I told him that you did not want to and that I should do it, that did not seem right to him. Because it was not difficult to guess what he was talking about, I accommodated him and said that I also think it would be somewhat immodest [for me] to greet the international congress and to write something about its agenda. Mehring enthusiastically agreed and said he will write to you today and emphasize that it is all the more necessary for you to write, because the congress is meeting for the first time on German soil and it would be odd if you don't provide the welcome. That is also my opinion. You are the representative of German and of international socialism and I am an unknown comrade. Now, it is distressing to me that your relaxing vacation has to be interrupted, and I ask that you drop the belief that I *don't want* to write the article. I could write it, but I really do think that the only correct thing, the only possible thing, is that you write it yourself. I hope it won't be too much work. (I thought of the following: one could point to the Amsterdam Congress and its consequences, such as French unity, and tie it to the hope or the demand for the *Russian* comrades to unify (which supposedly is not so terribly important). That would only be successful if you did it, because you are not only the Pope, but also the Tsar of all those who wish to overthrow the Tsar). The *Sozialistische Monatsheften* published an entire issue on the congress without much substance, though with some cheek from Bloch[80] against the French comrades, who are to blame for the right-winger Clemenceau,[81] but with the consistent tendency, especially stressed by MacDonald,[82] Fourniere,[83] and Bloch himself, to "warn" the congress against allowing itself to be misled by passing resolutions "a la Amsterdam", which had harmful (!) effects on the international development of individual parties (as in France). However (and that's the funny thing), it had

---

Democrat. Initially considered to teach political history at the Party School, his unorthodox views met with suspicion in the party leadership and he was dropped. He left the SPD in 1913.

79   Held in Stuttgart from August 18–24, 1907.
80   Josef Bloch (1871–1936) edited the *Sozialistische Monatshefte* from 1897–1933.
81   Georges Clemenceau (1841–1929) was a leader of the French Independent Radical Party and Prime Minister from 1906–1909 and 1917–1920.
82   Ramsey MacDonald (1866–1937) was co-founder of the British Labor Party in 1906, and later party leader, parliamentarian, and two-time Prime Minister.
83   Eugene Fourniere (1857–1914) was a French socialist and member of parliament.

to energetically cast off Hervé[84] and to declare his principles to be incompatible with ours, so that it would be possible for the French comrades to finally find the courage [also] to dispense with Hervé. Bloch demanded that directly. I did not want to take action against the most disgusting of all these toads in order not to bring attention to their croaking, but I wanted to tell you in order to be conversant with the hopes and fears of revisionism. Bernstein wrote a passably rational article about the position of the trade unions; Schippel [wrote] one on the emigration question, which he does not think has been adequately explained. Therefore, he recommends a further postponement of the question, which I think is untimely, an embarrassment for the congress, and unnecessary. In Vienna, Bauer has become the secretary of the [party's Reichsrat] delegation. He starts on 1 October. His article has received a lot of attention, as has the *Neue Zeit*'s emigration issue. Otherwise, there was not much in the party press worth mentioning. Some trade unionists and revisionists have turned against the importation of potash. Bertrand writes about the participation [of socialists] in political power, and I believe Bloch stresses that we can stop rejecting colonialism where party comrades (!) like Augagneur and Sydney Olivier have become governors.[85] But in my view the whole thing is too insignificant, ridiculous, and unimportant for you to take on. I would like to ask that you answer me directly and I ask, as well, for your pardon. I would not have written to you at all and I would not have even brought up the issue if Mehring had not initially declared that he wanted to write to you. By the way, he doesn't know that I am writing to you. I am doing well. I have a lot of work. Margret and Karl Emil are doing well. I got a letter yesterday from Parvus from Wartenberg [...] in Bohemia. He writes that he is buried in work up to the roof top and does not know if he can come to Stuttgart. The letters are anxious. A Russian bill that arrived today also belongs to [Kostia] Zetkin. Frau Luise did not write anything about that. I'll send it to him in any case. Please thank Frau Luise and ...

[The letter breaks off and is unsigned]

84　Gustave Hervé (1871–1944), at the time of Hilferding's letter was one of French Socialism's most radical anti-militarists. With the unification of French socialism in 1905 in the form of the SFIO, Hervé stood on the far left. In 1912, however, after years in prison, he reversed course and became an ultra-nationalist. As a co-founder of the French National Socialist Party in 1919, he was a pioneer of French fascism.

85　Victor Augagneur (1855–1931), a parliamentary deputy of the French Independent Socialist Party and Mayor of Lyon, served as Governor of Madagascar from 1905–1910. Sydney Olivier (1859–1943) was a Fabian Socialist and later member of the Labor Party. He had a long career in the British Colonial Office and served as Governor of Jamaica between 1900 and 1903.

(KDXII 604)

Berlin, October 9, 1907

Honored friend!

I am rather disturbed about your health. [I] have no information at all, although actually that, as I hope, might be a positive sign. Yesterday I wrote an article about Stuttgart and saw to it that the proofs were sent to you. If you have the desire and it doesn't interfere with your need for rest, I'd be very pleased if you could review it. It would also be very agreeable to me if you were of the opinion that it could appear unsigned as an editorial commentary, because it does not seem right to have Karl Emil insert himself in place of K[arl] K[autsky].[86] I am not very satisfied, but this time, since the emigration problem was dealt with, there is not much more to be said, or rather I don't know what more to say. In any case, it seems to me that Wurm was satisfied. Hopefully, you are having better weather there and are not taking the episode too hard. The cold-water cure wasn't too strenuous? When are you traveling to Stuttgart and where will you stay? Best regards to you, Frau Luise, and the boys.

Your,

Rudolf Hilferding

---

[86] The article, "Der Internationale Kongress in Stuttgart", appeared under the pseudonym Karl Emil 1906–07, pp. 660–67. To avoid attracting the attention of the German police and the risk of deportation, Hilferding used this penname for many of his early lead articles in the *Neue Zeit*.

CHAPTER 3

Rudolf Hilferding's Letters to Karl Kautsky, 1915–1918

(KDXII 607)

April 29, 1915
Rudolfsspital III, Rudolfsgasse 1

Respected Frau Luise,

Your letter made me very happy. I would have answered sooner, for I have become – for the moment at least – a real letter writer here out of sheer desperation, and [because] I'm so pleased to hear something from Germany, which, unfortunately is only possible when one also writes, but I was prevented from doing so due to the double duty that I have undertaken at [Der] Kampf.[1] Karl's first article was excellent, both in tone as well as in content; the second, against the Mecklenburger,[2] suffers from a degree of consideration that I would rather apply to myself; while I have not yet seen the third, concluding, article, because it often takes forever for the mail to get here and sometimes it never does.

The Mecklenburger is a real puzzle; his position is at the same level as the region he hails from and his enthusiasm for the circus. If the office worker's character is indelible, then that of a Hamburg "businessman" [Koofmich][3] is obviously an even more indestructible character flaw. But that does not explain the depth to which he has sunk. Compared to him, the worthy Lensch is a skilled lawyer. And as damaging as the business is with the misguided Heinrich [...], who is now galloping toward a reversal of his politics, this effect remains inexplicable. I can only imagine how disturbing this polemic must be for Karl and also for Gustav [Eckstein]; I myself am less impacted, because I knew him as a politician. But it remains a disturbing story.

---

[1] It seems that, after being posted to a hospital in Vienna, Hilferding also helped out at *Der Kampf* after Otto Bauer had been drafted and sent to the front. Hence his "double duty" (*Parallelschichtung*).

[2] The Mecklenburger was Heinrich Cunow (1862–1936) a long-time collaborator at the *Neue Zeit*. After having initially opposed the war, he switched his position in October of 1914 and, along with Konrad Haenisch and Paul Lensch, gave enthusiastic support to the war effort.

[3] The term *Koofmich* was a derogatory expression for a businessman or a salesman (*Kaufmann*).

One can console oneself that events ultimately will prove us right, though this bleak period also will last a long time. In Austria, matters will move even more quickly, because here the material prerequisites for a politics a la Wolfgang[4] are less available than abroad. I'm curious about Otto's perspective, which can become important. Recently, after months of waiting, there was finally a telegram from him. He is doing well and is busy with literary work.

You can imagine how wretched things are for me. Perhaps I could have acted more prudently, and calmly let matters take their course in Berlin; [here that] will be all the more [necessary] because it is not at all certain I can remain in Vienna. Doctors are being continually sent away. Otherwise, medicine (in a hospital and in an internal department, of course) would be a bearable change. I have settled in sooner and better than I expected, and even the twenty-four-hour duty every third day is bearable. I see a lot of what one otherwise does not see, for example, smallpox, and even two cases of the feared spotted fever; typhus is our daily bread. Margret should be writing to you soon. She is not doing particularly well and for no apparent reason has gotten very thin. In contrast, the children have gotten very big, Bendel would be embarrassed, [and] they look good. Since they don't have much school, they are very cheerful.

Things are so-so with my friends. Fritz [Adler] is doing the best (in that regard, Victor is of the opposite opinion; his view is little changed). He wanted to go to Zürich, and it took a lot of effort to keep him here. He will, however, probably soon take a vacation, perhaps in Nauheim, because he has been under great strain and become very agitated. On the other hand, in this time of instability Karl [Renner] is now thinking unstably (in total contrast to Max [Adler]. Engelbert [Pernerstorfer] says it's a religious conflict) and sometimes that makes everything worse. So, you see, I also have not been granted pure joy among my closest friends. Sometimes, I think I'm going crazy; I have the feeling I can't stand it anymore and have to abscond to Berlin.

Hopefully, it won't be all that long before we celebrate our reunion under your chairmanship with caviar [...].

Best regards to Charles the Great [Karl Kautsky] and the medical men. Please write soon.
  Very best regards from your exiled
  Rudolf Hilferding

---

4   It is unclear to what "a la Wolfgang" refers.

(KDXII 608)

June 22, 1915

Dear friend!

It has been a long time since I've been as happy as I was when reading the opus that you wrote with Hugo and Ede.[5] It was terribly important, just as it is correct, that you and not the party secretaries step forward as spokesmen. By the way, I assume that the thing was only released after the others had rejected it, which would increase its value even more.

I am now in a new hospital, a "war hospital", set up to deal with epidemics. It is a big camp with barracks for 2,500 beds. Unfortunately, you have to live in such barracks in a very primitive room on the ground floor. At the moment, however, there are no major epidemics, so the hospital will be temporarily open only for internal illnesses. For now, there is not much to do.

You must have received the pamphlet from Max [Adler] by now.[6] He would be pleased to have you review it in the *NZ*. I just finished the essay by Emil Lederer, "Zur Soziologie des Weltkrieges", in *Archiv*.[7] The history is really interesting and perhaps I'll follow up and finally write an article for you. Just in case you or Gustav might think otherwise, I'd be very grateful to you for such initiatives (including book reviews).

Nothing is new here. The doctor [Friedrich Adler] and Fritz [Adler] are back from Edlach and are rested. It is uncertain if they are going to Nauheim. Hopefully Frau Luise won't need an operation. Does she still have feverish episodes? The fact is that, even if bacilli are present, that in itself is not so important. I am not comfortable with the idea of an operation. To be sure, if there are frequent bouts [of fever] and [her] general condition does not improve, one would have to resign oneself to it.

Otherwise, things at home are good. My boy [Karl Emil] is taking his entrance exam for the Gymnasium. Just when it seems as if you, yourself, have just [finished] ...

---

5 The opus to which he is referring was "Das Gebot der Stunde", ("The Demand of the Hour"), authored by Kautsky, Hugo Haase and Edward Bernstein. Appearing in the *Leipziger Volkszeitung* on June 19, 1915, the article criticized the SPD leadership's pro-war policy, condemned the war of conquest, and called on the party to fight for peace.
6 Hilferding is referring to Max Adler's, *Prinzip oder Romantik! Sozialistische Betrachtungen zum Weltkrieg* (1915). He eventually wrote the review. See Hilferding 1914/1915, pp. 840–44.
7 Lederer (1915), pp. 347–84.

Give Hugo my best. He is acting astutely, prudently, and courageously. One cannot do more. How it will turn out ultimately will depend on the others. Provisionally, it looks like the thing is going to last a long time. I think one can't exclude the possibility of complications. As for the rest, I so look forward to seeing and talking with you all again. But I don't know whether that will be possible in the foreseeable future. And one can dispense with me without changing the outcome very much. But, quantilla prudentia ...![8]

My very best regards to you, Frau Luise, and the boys. Felix is probably done, and you can congratulate him [for me].[9]

Your
R.H.

Please write to Favoritenstraße 67.
Please give my best to Gustav [Eckstein]. I'm very pleased that he is back in Berlin. Ask him to write to me occasionally.

(KDXII 609)

July 29, 1915
Vienna, Favoritenstraße 67

Dear friend and honored Frau Luise,

Thank you so much for your letter and for that of Frau Luise. I am very glad that you are treating yourselves to a vacation and wish and hope that you have a really good rest [...]. My people are in Perchtoldsdorf, and I am traveling there on Sunday. The hospital will be fully operational next week and after that there will be no getting away. I will temporarily lose the whole morning, which is really too bad because of the impossibility of using the library. I still have the afternoons free, but a lot of time is lost with commuting and reading the paper in the editorial offices. Margret was very nervous, but she is now already doing better after an eight-day vacation. For the moment she is no longer on service

---

8 From the question, "Do you not know, my son, with how little wisdom the world is governed?" posed by the Swedish statesman, Axel Oxenstierna (1583–1654) to his son, Johan, in 1648, as the latter set out to participate in the negotiations that led to the Peace of Westphalia.
9 The reference is to Felix Kautsky (1891–1953), Karl and Luise's eldest son. It is likely that he had just completed his studies.

in the hospital and is staying, instead, in Perchtoldsdorf. To be sure, she has to spend the whole afternoon in the surgery in town. The boys are very big and are cheerful, though they could put on a few pounds. Karl is quite proud of his Gymnasium, and I think about how Frau Luise observed that, just when you, yourself, are done with high school, then it's someone else's turn. My efforts to convey to the boys that I am their elder brother have failed in the face of Margret's resistance. She insists on no further compromise and in Vienna I am defenseless against that.

Regarding the operation, Frau Luise, I stand by my opinion and am pleased that the problem is no longer pressing. Typhus bacilli are really by nature obliged to decrease in virulence and ultimately become harmless. In addition, one does not know for certain if one has caught them all gathered together in the gall bladder or whether they haven't thrown themselves into the now so popular policy of colonial expansion. Of course, the final decision depends upon whether your condition steadily improves or not. If you are feeling better, then in this case I would be for conservative treatment. After all, these days the conservatives are the most respectable. Naturally, this is a judgement with reservations, because Karli obviously has become illiterate and only eats with a knife and tongs, which he occasionally changes out for a fork, but never for a pen. And since parental authority fails with him even more than with the party (temporarily), do you think intervening with your spouse would be useful? I would love to talk shop.

Now, concerning other matters, things are not especially good. What you, my dear friend, say about Victor Adler doesn't surprise me at all. Viktor is, by the way, in Nauheim. He is now an old, tired, sick man. He has never taken a position of his own regarding these problems, and his desire to mediate has become a mania which has transformed his skill in that sphere into its opposite. I have the feeling that a part of the irritation against us is rooted in our representing his own, better conviction. In addition, he was angry that Hugo had taken the step without consulting the party executive. As dictator (at least formerly), he cannot grasp that. Moreover, he has no conception of the danger that David[10] and, above all, Legien represent. Whether Nauheim can help a bit in that respect is rather questionable. He was pretty passive here in Vienna and didn't say anything against our Karl [Renner], who is ever more hopelessly wrongheaded. In that regard, a complete switch has taken place. Now the two of them, the son and the bellowing boss, practically are united, while Karl stands

---

10   Eduard David (1863–1930) was a leading Social Democratic revisionist intellectual, newspaper editor, and, after 1903, a member of the Reichstag. He strongly supported the pro-war majority in 1914.

completely on the other side. By the way, Victor himself, as he told me, was quite satisfied with his stay in Berlin. Unity appeared to be assured in spite of everything, and he only regretted that his "clear, moderate line" was not really discernable. I, myself, am less sanguine about it. To me, the others, especially the trade union action center, are working busily and successfully. They will have read the declaration of *the I[nternationale] K[orrespondenz]*. In relation to that it will be necessary to do more. Unfortunately, *V[orwärts]* is now obviously forced to be even more cautious after Müller's departure. I would like to try and say something political in the *NZ*, but unfortunately the connection is pretty poor. I sent the *NZ* a review of Max Adler's pamphlet on June 18, but never received notice of its arrival. For that reason, I've written to Gustav. I've written an article on Rakowski for *Der Kampf*. You will like his pamphlet. I hope that it circulates here, more than abroad. I haven't yet received your last article.

Hopefully, Hugo is recovering well; he will have lots of work to do and he must do it. It would be good if he organized support systematically and pushed his colleagues, who share his views, to become more active. The shortage of people is really shameful.

And now, once again, get a good rest. Egotistically, I wish you would be a better writer and I'd be very happy to one again get some news soon. All the best to you, Frau Luise, Felix, and Karl.

Your,
R.H.

[P.S.] What is Bendel up to?

(KDXII 610)

Postcard, December 27, 1915
Flützersteig, Kriegsspital, Nr. 1

Dear Friend,

I am pleased that you [have] written about Naumann.[11] The publication is coming along quickly. I advise letting it appear separately both in the *NZ* and,

---

11   Kautsky published a series of essays in the *NZ* criticizing Friedrich Naumann's liberal imperialist work *Mitteleuropa* (1915). For Hilferding's critique of Naumann, see 1915a, pp. 357–365.

eventually, if possible, in the V[*orwärts*] publishing house. The matter is very important, because our people are disoriented and our Karl [Renner] wants history to intercede, though not completely openly. He'll be arriving soon in Berlin at the beginning of the second week of January. It would be good if a copy could be provided to the members of the [Reichstag] delegation. Of course, this should all be done privately.

I'm very happy about old Fritz. Hopefully, a continuation will soon follow. Now that means not only holding out but being victorious. I have a lot on my plate, but I hope to get to work soon. You'll soon receive Prueß and Jansson. Give my very best to Hugo and Gustav.

Your,
R.H.

(KDXII 626)

Postcard, June 14, 1916
Landsturmarzt Dr. Rudolf Hilferding
Notreserve-Spital
Steinach am Brenner, Tirol

Dear friend,

You have probably received the cards I sent earlier. There is nothing new here. The weather is bad and therefore it isn't too much fun, but it is bearable. I am writing primarily to point out to you that this year it would be very advisable for you to take your vacation in Austria, indeed in northern Tirol, or to spend some time where one lives better and cheaper than over there or in northern Austria. The same goes for Hugo. I'm telling you this without any egotistical notions, because I don't know where I'll be at the time.

Otherwise, I'd really like to hear some news from you and yours as well as Gustav. [Do you have his] address? Letters are my only nice change of pace except for Innsbruck, which I will be visiting today. You'll get a long letter from me at the end of the month. Meanwhile, I wish you, Frau Luise, the boys and Hugo all the best.

Your,
R.H.

(KDXII 611)

July 1, 1916

Dear friend,

The manuscript is enclosed. Please don't be alarmed, it can easily be divided into seven more or less independent parts. I thought the trade policy sections are important enough to warrant more extensive treatment. Because I want it to be read, I urgently ask you to publish it as soon as possible in the *NZ*. Any stylistic or censor related changes I leave up to you, indeed, I was in such a rush to complete the work that I ask you to please give some attention to improving the style. I also ask that you have as much of the thing as possible typeset as soon as possible, and that you send the offprints, without further comment, or just with the comment that here are the desired corrections, to the address of the *Innsbrucker Volkszeitung*. For all that, I don't actually have to read the proofs myself; above all I would like to prevent any delays from occurring.[12]

I am, as always, curious about your judgement. At some point one could publish a modified and somewhat extended history drawing on the economic and political section of *Finance Capital* as a pamphlet. To be sure, I don't know if one can procure all the necessary material here, in particular for a chapter on colonialism that must be added. But, in any case, one can consider it. I'd also like to ask your opinion about that. One would have to then ask Dietz whether he'd publish it. The thesis of the article could then be retained. I ask that you send me your answer in a somewhat shortened form for my summer holiday.

I hope that you are seeing events somewhat too pessimistically. I believe that the events in the Berlin General Assembly, about which I have only read short reports (today I hope to get V[*orwärts*]), are not all that unwelcome. The act of placing the Berlin representatives of both groups of opportunists in the committee [showed] perfectly well that the factional differences are not of an essential nature. At the same time, the rejection of the ban on publishing articles demonstrates healthy good sense and serves as a useful box on the ear for Rosa. However, it is characteristic of the "center's" impoverishment that it did not know of anyone other than Arthur to make the presentation. But, in my view, the important thing is that the bureaucracy's restraints on the masses and their energy be thoroughly loosened, and that is happening, whereby, and here

---

12 Hilferding is referring here to a long essay on trade policy (Handelspolitische Fragen), which, as he had recommended, was published in seven installments. See Karl Emil (Hilferding) 1916/17, pp. 5–11, 40–47, 91–99, 118–26, 141–46, 205–16, 241–46.

I cannot help myself, it [the center] is doing extremely good pioneering work. In general, I see no differences in principle and we can talk about tactics only when a fight is really possible. Provisionally, however, I see no necessity in taking a "centrist position", since we are actually on the extreme left and must be there, within the limits of pure and practical reason, the overstepping of which little Rosa, as in the article ban, cannot always resist.

And likewise, I hope, though in this matter I cannot make a judgement from out here, that it still doesn't come to a split.

In this world historical situation, by the way, that issue is of secondary importance. What is really at stake is solely whether after the war, which, in spite of everything, could still last a long time – it seems to me the winter campaign is still probable if France somehow holds out – a revolutionary situation emerges that forces the masses to fight and unites them in the struggle. As long as this prospect exists, we only have one thing to fear and that is to throw away our chances of taking advantage of this situation and of leading by too strongly adhering to a centrist position.

Please reply soon. Very best regards on everyone and on Wurm, too!
Your,
R.H.

July 5: Unfortunately, though not due to anything on my part, the matter [of the article] has been delayed a bit. Through another revision I hope that the story has some effect. Hopefully, it will appear *soon*. Please send the honorarium to the Deutsche Bank, Depositenkasse, G.H. Steglitz, Schloßstraße 88. I am hoping for eight marks per page. I don't understand why one should give money to the accounting office of the social patriots, since that is where they cheat one out of one's salary anyway. Fritz will inform you of the transcription costs. Here, of course, I am only a doctor, so please pay attention to the address: *Innsbrucker Volkszeitung*. I'd love some books, only nothing by Lensch, because I don't want to polemicize with that blackguard. One more thing: In my work, conflicts, such as those with Schumacher, have been discussed in the NZ. That is not a problem, because it occurred in a completely different and especially necessary context. I ask, therefore, not to cut it, but to relegate it to the notes. How is Hugo? Once again, my very best wishes.

Vienna, July 12: P.S. The manuscript will follow as soon as it has been transcribed. Best wishes [signature unclear, possibly Margarethe Hilferding]

(KDXII 625)

Postcard, July 3, 1916
Landsturmarzt Dr. Rudolf Hiferding
Notreservespital
Steinach am Brenner, Tirol

Dear friend,

Thanks very much to you and Frau Luise for your letter. I wanted to answer sooner, but at the same time I also wanted to let you know that the business has been taken care of. I am doing that here. It is rather large, but as I hope, also very useful. To me you are a bit too pessimistic. I see things now, despite some difficulties, on the whole optimistically. The earlier relationship has to some extent reversed itself. We are, of course, very sad that you aren't coming to Tirol, but naturally Karli comes first (and Lotta?).

There is not much new here and at the moment I also don't wish for anything new; indeed, long term it would be bitter. If you have any literature that is halfway interesting and appropriate for me, please send it. I will suffer most from the shortage of literature. Otherwise, one can be satisfied with Berlin; the temperature is neither too hot nor too cold? For Karl [Liebknecht] it has gone better than I'd feared.[13] Please, have Frau Luise give my best to Sonja.[14] Frau Luise, you have always had a soft spot for Diefenbach[15] hopefully, you are right, we have terribly few useful people. "Terribly few useful" is a phrase appropriate for Bendel, who should write about what he is up to and how his dissertation is

---

13   Karl Liebknecht (1871–1919), the son of SPD co-founder Wilhelm Liebknecht and a leader of the party's emerging left wing in the decade preceding the outbreak of the First World War. An outspoken opponent of the war, he was the first member of the SPD Reichstag delegation to break ranks and vote against war credits in December of 1914. With Rosa Luxemburg and others, he organized the anti-war Spartacus League. Arrested and sent to the front in 1915, he returned home due to illness, was arrested again for anti-war agitation in May of 1916 and sentenced to two and a half years in jail. Released in the wake of the liberalization of the regime in October 1918, he was a key figure in the November Revolution in which he co-founded the Communist Party. He was murdered by the military as it crushed a radical rising in Berlin in January of 1919.

14   Sophie "Sonja" Liebknecht (1884–1964) was Karl Liebknecht's second wife and a close confidant of Rosa Luxemburg. Like them, she began her political activity in the SPD and later joined the Communist Party.

15   Hans Diefenbach (1884–1917), wartime correspondent and intimate friend of Rosa Luxemburg, was well known in the Kautsky household. He was killed on the Western Front in October 1917.

going. What is new with Gustav? Adolf [Braun][16] seems to have become childish or only concerned with finding an alibi. But who should make history from that?

Regards,
Rudolf

(KDXII 612)

Postcard, August 1, 1916
Landessturmarzt Dr. Rudolf Hilferding
Steinach am Brenner
Notreservespital

Dear friend,

The news of Gustav [Eckstein's] death has stunned me all the more, because just a few days previously Frau Luise had written that the operation (which would have been better had it not occurred) was successful. All of us have lost much with [the death of] this talented, hard-working, steadfast person, who is irreplaceable, especially now. You have lost more than anyone. To you he was a loyal assistant and he gained much from you.

I would have been so happy to have spoken with Frau Luise. She made me hopeful that we might meet during your vacation. In any case, while it is easy, get yourself a passport. It is really important to me to talk with you, because our community does not seem very active. (Indeed, I can hear you say – unwillingly – what it is that people want.) How is Hugo and what is he up to? Why doesn't that damned Bendel write at least once? If we don't see each other this summer, I fear it will be a long time before we see each other.

With my very best regards,
Rudolf

---

16 Adolf Braun (1862–1929) was an editor of *Vorwärts*. After being expelled from Prussia he took over the *Fränkische Tagespost*, in Nuremberg. His sister, Emma, was Victor Adler's wife and his older brother, Heinrich, was, with Kautsky, co-founder of the *Neue Zeit*.

(KDXII 613)

Steinach, August 30, 1916

Dear friend!

I haven't written for so long first of all because I did not want to disturb your vacation, but also because I thought that the tiresome gift affair would have wrapped itself up. That certainly is not the case. Happily, a duplicate exists, which you will receive in the not too distant future. Fritz will tell you about it. You can imagine how uncomfortable the delay is for me. I hope you have had a good rest. I often miss you a great deal and I'd give so much just to be able to talk things over with you. Unfortunately, there is no chance of that.

There is not much new here. I often have the desire to write to you at greater length. But the distance is such a huge obstacle. One never knows to what extent one can effectively gauge what people are thinking [or] whether one's views seem farcical from so far away, as, for example, the most recent petition of our fathers,[17] which has to be judged differently on the spot. Meanwhile, events continue on their relentless path and individuals can do almost nothing about it – a comfort for one far away. History works with astounding precision, and we are still a long way from the end. I think we will experience an intensification of the war as a result of its expansion, and the historical perspectives are becoming increasingly colossal. One can only hope that the epoch finds the right men and that they can find the correct line of action.

How is Hugo doing? I hope he finds his old energy and that which is needed above all: generosity and consistent clarity toward all sides.

I think that you, too, don't cherish much hope after the lack of results at the last conference of neutrals in the Hague.[18] I don't believe much good could come of it. But just because little that was practical could be achieved there, it would be dangerous to allow theoretical confusion to arise.

I've been happy to have seen so much by you recently. You handled that blackguard Paul [Lensch] wonderfully.

---

17   It is not clear what petition is referred to here. By "fathers" Hilferding is probably referring to either the party leadership or the leadership of one of the SPD's dissident factions. The matter may concern the struggle of the dissident majority on the *Vorwärts* editorial board (of which Hilferding has been a part) with the party leadership or with the government over the paper's content. The matter was "resolved" in October 1916 when the SPD leadership purged the board of those who opposed its wartime policy.

18   The Hague Conference of July 31, 1916 was convened by the International Socialist Bureau of the Socialist International. It was attended by representatives of socialist parties from

I don't hear much good news from Vienna. Fritz [Adler] cannot be convinced not to leave. I almost hope that the call will upset his plans.[19]

Best regards to Frau Luise and the boys as well as to Hugo. All the best to you,
Your,
Rudolf

(KDXII 615)

Postcard, September 10, 1916
Landessturmartzt Dr. Rudolf Hilferding
Notreservespital
Steinach am Brenner, Tirol

Dear friend,

I very much hope that you have the gift in hand, and I am on the edge of my seat waiting for you to confirm it. There is nothing new here. My Karl [Emil] has been here for a few days which is a really nice change. Hopefully, all of you are doing well. What is going on with the call up of the boys? I've written to Hugo; he'll probably tell you about it. It is just a shame that we cannot see one another. You should have received my letter of two weeks ago. Fritz [Adler] will resign his post, which I think is a really big mistake. Perhaps I'll write to him about it.

Best wishes to all,
Your,
R.H.

---

nine neutral states. The conference passed a number of resolutions asserting that capitalism was the cause of the war, condemning economic warfare, and calling for, among other things, peace negotiations, free trade, and the self-determination of nations.

19   Friedrich Adler had studied chemistry, math, and physics. After earning a doctorate in physics, he taught for a time. In 1911 he returned to Vienna to become a secretary in the SDAP. In protest over the SDAP leadership's decision to support the war, he quit that post in September of 1914. In 1915 he considered leaving Vienna and answering a "call" from Zurich, where he was offered the editorship of the *Volksrecht* or Berlin, where Kautsky hoped to hire him at the *Neue Zeit*. Instead of accepting either offer, he decided to assassinate the Austrian Prime Minister, Count Stürgkh on October 21, 1916. He was arrested, tried, and condemned to death but his sentence was commuted to 18 years before he was released and hailed as a hero in the revolution of November 1918.

[P.S.] Please send Nestriepke's address.[20] I was pleased about Franziscus.[21] Will there be more frequently something from him to read?

(KDXII 616)

Steinach, September 15, 1916

Dear friend,

Thanks very much for your letter of September 11. I am very glad that you are refreshed. Hopefully, that will last awhile. I am also very happy that the story has been straightened out, the present has finally arrived, and it has pleased you to some degree.

Regarding Karl Emil's work, I can't deny the length. But I fear that, following your recommendation, the connection will be lost to those of lesser intelligence. As I see it, the point here is to demonstrate the falsity of the "theory of collapse" in various individual cases.[22] I'm happy, by the way, that you obviously agree with the author. Perhaps you can add a note somewhere that fat Heinrich [Cunow's] newest effort to derive the viability [of capitalism] from increasing concentration (as if the fatter he got, the healthier he would become) is the theory of collapse in pure form. In contrast, K[arl] E[mil] is correct when he silently passes over Rosa's effort to save the theory of collapse; she is not mentioned. It might be in the interest of the article and of the youthful, and therefore really impatient, author, for the thing not to be delayed all too long. Now, I don't fully understand you: do you want to return the article to the author, or do you wish to undertake what is required *yourself*. I think the latter is the *only* practicable practical path. I would favor keeping a general title. The space question has no relation to the shortage of co-workers, and the subject will attract enough readers. Therefore, I definitely would recommend getting the *typesetting started*.

---

20   Siegfried Nestriepke (1885–1963) was a Social Democratic journalist who joined the *Vorwärts* editorial staff in 1914. Opposed to the war, he joined the USPD and, in the fall of 1918, became chief editor of the USPD's flagship paper, *Die Freiheit*. Hilferding replaced him in that post in early November.
21   Hilferding may be referring here to Franz Mehring.
22   Hilferding is discussing the revisions to his essay "Handelspolitische Fragen", written under the pseudoym Karl Emil. See Chapter 3, footnote 12.

By the way, what do you think about a pamphlet with similar content? I would like to eventually recommend that to the author.

You have misunderstood the business with Fritz [Adler]. I am firmly of the opinion that he should stay where he is and not seek a new position. I think that alone is appropriate. I was thinking that you would eventually write to him along those lines. You could invite him to write to you again. Like the rest of us, he needs a poke in the ribs. By the way, do you have anything interesting for me?

What do you think of the problematic Karl [Renner]? That was Gustav's territory. He was an extraordinary loss for us. By the way, it's funny that Karl flatters himself that the excerpt of Hammers in *Finance Capital* is originally from Renner's own work! Psychology is very funny sometimes.

It is sad that we cannot see one another. There remains only one thing to be done: in the winter, you will have to take up winter sports. It would be really nice.

My very best greetings to Frau Luise and to the boys, with lots of luck! I hope to hear from you soon. My very best wishes,
    Your,
    Rudolf

Dear Bendel!

The reasons [you give] for the interruption are obviously a means of excusing laziness! Enough of that, please. Where did you find the Ramsey? I would also like to read that sometime. Unfortunately, I am unfamiliar with Storch, but if you find something questionable, sit down and write to me. I have enough time for such inquiries here.

That you are pursuing the natural sciences makes a lot of sense. What have you done [so far]? You should also study a little advanced mathematics, one needs that. I would like to take that up during the winter. And you also have Felix there. Then, after the mathematics, work through the basics of physics and chemistry. Then Mach. In the meantime, I would advise you to read Lang's *Geschichte des Materialismus* and the *Geschichte der Philosophie* by Schwegler or Vorländer. Then the philosophers themselves starting with Schopenhauer's "Satz von der vierfachen Wurzel", [*sic!*][23] and "Ethik", etc. More later. Go to lectures. You and Bortkiewicz? Say hello to him.

---

23   The actual title of Arthur Schopenhauer's essay is "Über die vierfache Wurzel des Satzes vom zureichender Grunde."

That you want to work on statistics over the winter is also sensible. Are you planning to attend any seminars? It would be important to do a statistical and an historical one, the latter because of the information about sources. Write to me separately and at length, as is proper for a young man!

(KDXII 617)

Postcard, September 21, 1916
Landessturmarzt Dr. Rudolf Hilferding
Notreservespital
Steinach am Brenner, Tirol

Dear friend,

I hope that you have received my letter from two weeks ago, in which I requested finishing quickly. The matter has become more pressing, because I will only be staying here until 20 October. Then I'll be moving out, but I don't know where. In any case, I'm not happy about it, because I have no idea how communications will be. I would like to ask, then, that we wrap things up ahead of time.

I am very curious about what you and Hugo think the result of today's demands will be and I hope for news from you soon. Also, about what is happening with the boys.

It has been snowing here since yesterday and is terribly cold, which is even more uncomfortable for me because I am housed in an unheated room. Possibly, Margret will be coming to visit in the next few days.

My very best greetings to you, Frau Luise, and the boys.
  Your,
  R.H.

(KDXII 618)

> Postcard, October 4, 1916
> Landessturmarzt Dr. Rudolf Hilferding
> Notreservespital
> Steinach am Brenner, Tirol

Dear friend,

Your card from the twenty-ninth arrived today. Thanks very much. I'm glad the article is under way. If you want to go above and beyond, send the copies of the photography to the office in Innsbruck. That is not absolutely necessary, because I can rely on your taste and, in any case, I don't want a delay.

I am pleased that you are satisfied. I also believe that once the most difficult thing has been overcome, one must make an even greater effort. I am already curious about Hugo and send him my best regards.

The business with Bendel is stupid. Hopefully, he won't be sent too far away. Give him my best regards, I wish him all the best. Tell him to send me his address right away.

I'm here until October 20 and then I'll keep you posted. Best wishes to all.
Your,
R.H.

The tough critic was probably Emmo?

(KDXII 619)

> Postcard, October 6, 1916
> Landsturmartz Dr. Rudolf Hilferding
> Notreservespital
> Steinach am Brenner, Tirol

Dear friend,

I hope that this card arrives on time for your birthday. From the bottom of my heart I wish you all the best and I hope you will long retain your vigor, clarity, and confident optimism. I think back to the day that I could congratulate you for the first time in person – it was your fiftieth and only August [Bebel] was still there. How much has happened since then! You have remained the same and during this historic time the years have left no mark on you. The war thwarted the planned celebration of your sixtieth. Some who wanted to celebrate were not there, but, nevertheless, life is still beautiful for them only because you live for a great goal and you have the good fortune to see its future realization so clearly. My heartfelt wish for you is that you may still experience and accomplish a great deal. Farewell and my very best regards to you, Frau Luise, and the boys.

Your,
  R.H.

(KDXII 620)

> Postcard, October 25, 1916
> Landsturmarzt Dr. Rudolf Hilferding
> Mobiles Epidemie-spital Nr. 2
> Feldpost 613

Dear friend,

I am now in a new location. It is, once again, very beautiful. Working conditions are promising, and in spite of the distance, initially it has gone tolerably well, if not for the external matters that could spoil everything.

I can't wait to hear from you, especially about what's happened to Bendel. Is Karl [Jr.] still in Frankfurt? I'd be very grateful if you could send me books. The thicker and weightier the better and especially theoretical and philosophical [works] that don't need to be reviewed right away.

What do you think of the assassination in Vienna?[24] It is the purest and most incomprehensible idiocy, which generally seems to be spreading.

I wish the winter would soon end. Then I could hope for a vacation and perhaps also to see you again. I ask that you and Frau Luise write soon. Best regards to Hugo and to you all.

Your,
  R

---

24 The reference is to Friedrich Adler's killing of Austrian Prime Minister Count Stürgkh. See Chapter 3, footnote 19 above.

(KDXII 621)

> Postcard, November 21, 1916
> Landsturmartz Dr. Rudolf Hilferding
> Reservespital "Jagerndorf"
> Feldpost 613

Dear friend!

Hopefully, I'll soon get some news from you or from Frau Luise. There is nothing new here. It is still the case that I might possibly come to Berlin at the beginning of January. I would like to know if the date works for you and for Hugo. Have you heard again from Breit[scheid][25] and Nestriepke? And what is going on with Bendel? I hope Ede is doing well and send him my best regards. In addition to my desire to receive some books, I would also like to ask for the edition of *NZ* with the review of the book from Kestner on the compulsion to organize. Please also send Karl Emil's honorarium to the Deutsche Bank in Steglitz. I am quite busy and have lots of medical work. You probably hear more than I do from Vienna. By the way, the worst might not actually occur, and the patient may escape with his life.[26] Regarding the outlook for peace, I remain skeptical. What do you think about it? I long to see you again and I hope that nothing can interfere with that. My very best regard to you all.

Your,
  Rudolf H.

---

25 Rudolf Breitscheid (1874–1944) was a liberal journalist who turned to socialism in 1912 and soon became friends with Hilferding, wrote for the *Neue Zeit*, and became a vehement opponent of the war. In 1916 he was sent to the Western front but remained politically engaged. Along with Hilferding and Kautsky, he joined the USPD in 1917.
26 The "patient" was Friedrich Adler.

(KDXII 622)

Postcard, December 7, 1916
Landsturmartz Dr. Rudolf Hilferding
Reservespital Jägarndorf
Feldpost 613

Dear friend,

I'm writing to tell you that I've been transferred back to my earlier hospital: Landsturmarzt Dr. R.H. Mobiles Epidemie-Spital Nr. 2, Feldpost 613. Hopefully I'll get some news soon. Also, I'd like to know if I'll be able to meet with you and Hugo at the beginning of January in Berlin. Will Hugo be absent at Christmastime? Best regards to all,

Your,
   Rudolf

(KDXII 623)

Postcard, November 12, 1916
Landsturmartz Dr. Rudolf Hilferding
Mobiles Epidemie-Spital Nr. 2
Feldpost 613/II

Dear Frau Luise,

Your letter arrived yesterday a bit late due to my transfer. It was really nice to hear from you again. I am glad that you are all doing well, especially in Berlin. As far as I know, you can write to me in a sealed envelope. The censorship is piecemeal. I am doing passably well. I'd rather be in this hospital than in the former one. It is true that I have a quite enough to do, but I'd like to have the new volume. I can review it in any case. It would be best if you sent it to my wife at Favoritenstraße 67. I hope to finish one small matter for you before my vacation. I am thinking of coming to Berlin around the tenth of January. I don't want to delay my leave any longer, yearn to see everyone, and am especially looking forward to seeing Karl and Hugo. I hope that Hugo is generally feeling better and is not suffering from his old illness. Hopefully, his wife is feeding him well, that is important. It's too bad I can't have him stay awhile in my department. Please say hello to him for me. Otto [Bauer's] address is: Prisoner of War Lieutenant Dr. O.B., Troitzkosansk, Transbaikal. I use the Red Cross cards for prisoners of war. He can now, once again, receive Russian newspapers, which for a time had been denied to him. I get the same news from Vienna. Recently, however, for certain reasons I've hardly written at all. Please write again soon. My very best greetings to you all.

Your,
   R.H.

(KDXII 624)

Postcard, December 5, 1916
Landsturmarzt Dr. Rudolf Hilferding
Reservespital Jägerndorf
Feldpost 613

Dear Frau Luise!

I am impatiently waiting for some sign of life [from you]. I know that Karl cannot write, but that you can't find the time to set aside an hour I find hard to understand. Since I am solely dependent on the B.T.,[27] I am cut off from all contact and therefore would love to hear your opinions and impressions. And I have no idea about what is going on with Bendel, although I really should not even worry about the guy, who never picks up a pen. So please, let me hear from you. There is nothing new here. And the business with the leave is still up in the air. Hopefully, though, it will happen. My very best regards to you all.

Your,
   Rudolf Hilferding

---

27   It is probable that Hilferding is referring here to the *Berliner Tageblatt und Handelszeitung*, an important left-liberal daily that had a national audience.

(KDXII 627)

December 20, 1916

Dear friend,

I received your letter of 5 December, your card from 11 December, and subsequently your letter from 17 October, as well. Meanwhile, I'd answered the letter from Frau Luise [but since then] I've been so overburdened that I could not write and I'm sorry about that.

Your letter to Vienna made me very happy, though I also know that you overestimate me to some degree. But if I, personally, can replace a few of the heavy losses, then I am proud. Certainly, I still place my trust in Otto Bauer. The dangers to which he will be exposed after his return are, of course, very large and it is to be seen whether he is strong enough, and whether the situation will be favorable enough, to overcome them. Indeed, otherwise the milieu will ruin him in the end, like all the others, especially Viktor (aside from his illness). At the moment it looks bad enough, more hopeless than just about anywhere else. Certainly, there are many more possibilities, and it is to be expected that people will be forced to behave more decently much against their will. At the moment there appears to be great disappointment once again, people were excited about Körber and Klein.[28] Upon the death of the Kaiser our people behaved themselves very correctly. Ellenbog[en], Renner, and Seitz[29] were in St. Peter's Cathedral. Diamand, [an SDAP Reichsrat member], and two of his friends laid wreaths. Thus, after some misunderstandings, [our] tactical approach is becoming more unified, which is very welcome.

Regarding the fate of our patient [Friedrich Adler], I am somewhat disturbed. Of course, from here I can't make a firm judgement, I am less optimistic than the Vienna doctors.

I am quite burdened here, more than I was earlier, and I have less time for myself, but I think matters will improve after my leave.

---

28   Ernest von Koerber (1850–1919), a leading Austrian liberal politician, replaced the assassinated Count Stürgkh as Minister President in late October 1916. He resigned on December 13 after myriad disputes with the new Kaiser, Karl I. The liberal Franz Klein served as Minister of Justice in November and December 1916. See also Chapter 2, footnote 74.
29   Karl Seitz (1859–1950) was an SDAP expert on educational policy. Elected to the Imperial Council in 1900, with the collapse of the Empire in 1918 he played a leading role in the National Assembly and served as President of Austria until 1920. He became SDAP Chairman in 1919 and Mayor of Vienna in 1923.

I am very glad that your family is there, and I hope that it stays that way. I hope, too, that, despite everything, you have the nicest possible holiday and I wish you all the best for the coming year. Will it be the last Christmas of the war? I strongly doubt it. In any case, one won't be able to judge before the fighting that is expected this spring. The peace offering was a smart move, especially in relation to the domestic situation.[30] Now a general intensification of the war is likely along with renewed enthusiasm in the parliaments. Hugo's statement was good. Otherwise, I can hardly wait to see you again. I long for Berlin much more than Vienna, although [having the] the boys [here] is very nice.

I must, of course, get Dictaeus's new publication.[31] I can also write about it – there are various possibilities. I'd also like to have the second edition of Sombart's *Capitalism*, because I've recently been reading about this topic. Have you received that book? Personally, I'm doing quite well and would almost rather be here than in Vienna. The medical work is also very interesting. In addition to the Typhus Department, where I am in charge, I'm in a department for special cases of diphtheria and scurvy, where one gets a pretty good sense of life on the front. The personal and working conditions are comfortable; living conditions and food are excellent. Finally, being stuck in such a compulsory, but personally most comfortable, mechanism, can also prevent you from doing much else.

All the best to you and Frau Luise and the boys. Please give my best to Hugo and, again, I wish you a pleasant holiday and a toast to the New Year! Send letters here until January 2, thereafter to Vienna, Favoritenstraße 67. I hope to leave here on the January 2 or 3. Hopefully, nothing will intervene to prevent that. Thanks so much for your letters.

Again, best regards,
Your
Rudolf

---

30   On December 12 Germany and its allies made a "peace offer" to their opponents, though no concrete terms were proposed. Like Hilferding, most members of the opposition regarded this action merely as a means of satisfying public opinion and mobilizing support for continuing the war.
31   The identity of Dictaeus is unclear.

(KDXII 628)

January 31, 1917

Dear friend,

I've been back in the old shit for the last couple of days. At least being stuck in the gears of the automatic machine has the positive attribute of calming one's nerves a bit. I know damned little about what is happening anywhere else. As you might imagine, I spend much of the time thinking about you and Hugo. Above all, what is happening with the *NZ*? What are the practical consequences? And what comes next? I'd be very grateful if Bendel or Frau Luise would write to me about it. You will have noticed Austerlitz's attitude. Privately, he expresses himself in an even-tempered manner. In contrast, Viktor is just depressed and lets things drift as they will. Wilson's willingness was very interesting, as was its reception.[32] It is really telling that the leading German and Austrian Social Democrats dismiss this proclamation of democratic principles as utopian, and they only wonder whether it is targeted at one or the other centers of power instead of grasping that it is directed at the earlier power politics and thus provides that principled alternative solution, which should have been the task of the Bureau [of the International].[33] It is also international. It is also significant that, in contrast to *V[orwärts]*, the unified declare themselves to be in solidarity with Wilson. Nevertheless, now the psychological moment might be more favorable for the Bureau. I fear, however, that Troelstra, will do some damage in his eagerness. Viktor [Adler] is skeptical, and his hopes for the meeting are outweighed by his fears.[34] I suspect this is because of the rather unfavorable position of the German majority, but also because he does not have any hope for practical success. Certainly, the latter would be very doubtful. And besides, the whole business would be technically very hard to carry out.

Otherwise, everything in Vienna is in order. I saw Fritz [Adler] and could speak to him for 45 minutes. I found him to be pretty much the same, perhaps a bit pale. Otherwise, he seemed to be in high spirits and was cheerful, more

---

32 In January 1917 U.S. President Woodrow Wilson (1856–1924) gave a speech calling for a "peace without victory" and the establishment of an international organization to maintain peace.

33 The International Socialist Bureau was the primary administrative organ of the Socialist International. It failed to respond effectively to the outbreak of the war in 1914.

34 This discussion centers on a call by Pieter Jelles Troelstra (1860–1930), a co-founder of the Social Democratic Workers' Party of the Netherlands, for a peace conference of Social Democratic Parties. The meeting was planned for Stockholm but was never held.

talkative than usual, and made a few too many jokes. To me, he appeared a little unsteady. The meeting had the character of a coffee house conversation. [It was] uncanny and sad.

Otto [Bauer] is in steady communication and he is healthy and working.

It is really freezing here, and I only hope that you are not nearly as cold. Personally, things with me are quite good. I'm now reading the Dietz volumes and the new Sombart [book], which would make for good reading if it wasn't for the foppish and pompous layout: the style is the man.

I hope to hear from you soon. My very best to you all.
Your,
Rudolf H.

(KDXII 577)

April 13, [1917]

Dear friend,

Thanks very much for your letter of March 30. I have felt rather guilty taking a lot of time away from you, but in other ways I don't feel that way at all about what interests me most. Nevertheless, I did not answer you right away, because, firstly, there was a break in communication here, and secondly, I did not want to write during the Easter hullabaloo, because then the letter might not get there.

Regarding me, I just have very little time. The day is completely broken up, it is hard enough to read and even worse for writing. Now I have to express my opinion at length about the two volumes to Victor. Something could be said about it now, but not about what is decisive. Hopefully, I'll get to that and then I'll write to you, although I'm not sure yet about what.

That you can keep your job, despite everything, is very good. I hope it stays that way. It is so important especially now. I read the last issue (numbers 13 and 14, I think). I liked the second article more than the "Ice Palace", which contained too much pacifistic speculation.[35] In the end, it is just that one knows so little about what is going on. Even the émigrés. Intervening might not be very advantageous. I am very anxious to see what happens internationally. What

---

35   The reference is to Kautsky's article on the Russian Revolution of February 1917 titled, "Der Eispalast" (*The Ice Palace*). See Kautsky, 1916/17, pp. 609–13.

Ebert wrote was silly, and Stampfer's view was wretched. I am waiting in great suspense for a report about the Easter meeting.[36] Perhaps Frau Luise will write to Bloch that he should send it to me. Also, I'd be very [happy] if Hugo could send me the protocol of his speech. What you write about him is not very good. If one could only do something. He must get a certificate of service that will grant him extra [ration] cards. He must get that. Otherwise, the only other option would be a stay in a sanitarium in Bavaria or, perhaps better, in Austria.

Otherwise, there is certainly reason for optimism, though the focal point of development might change. In any case the Russian and also the American events mark an enormous acceleration. The American intervention might also be of world historical significance as it brings the whole Anglo-Saxon world together – a sweeping perspective.

How is Bendel? Max Adler's address is VIII Josefstädterstraße 43. He will already have a theme in mind. In Bavaria, Adolf [Braun]'s compromise tactic has already been successful. Under those who are currently in charge, that is welcome. Have you heard anything at all from Nestriepke? What are Ströbel, etc., doing. Be well and please give my best to all the friends, Frau Luise, and the boys. I hope to hear from your soon.

Your,
    Rudolf

(KDXII 579)

July 21, [1917]

Dear friend,

Thanks very much for your card. I was very indecisive about my leave but am now inclined to put it off until September. A visit to the big city is not very attractive and I also fear that some of the people I want to see won't be around. The *only* reason to travel there would be to speak with you. But I think it will be more important in September. The only problem is that [the delay] would put off my next leave from January to March. In case you or Hugo think it important

---

36   On 6 April 1917 the recently expelled anti-war elements of the SPD met in Gotha to create the Unabhängige Sozialdemokratische Partei Deutschlands (Independent Social Democratic Party of Germany, USPD, often referred to as the Independents). Hilferding and Kautsky joined this party.

to see me *before* you travel, please send a telegram to Margret at Favoritenstraße 67. In that case, I would take my leave and come at the beginning of August. In any case, I ask that you please confirm receipt of this letter by return post.

The German "crisis" is succumbing to neglect, as I thought it would from the beginning. In the domestic sphere, too, it was a function of foreign events.[37] The latter are not yet decisive enough to have powerful internal effects. The behavior of all the parties confirms the judgement we made at the beginning. At best, the Scheideleute are more childish than we had supposed.[38] Such striking images have been created by the words of gentlemen like Erzberger[39] and David, of whom the former is, to be sure, the much more impressive. The only good thing is that the history is just starting to unfold, and future development will probably be very different than the above-named gentlemen, whose desire for ministerial posts I can only imagine, suppose. The war has other functions than making Renner and David into ministers.

For the moment, the most decisive thing remains the path of Russian development, which has become critical. I think Tsereteli[40] and Kerensky[41] will succeed in finishing off Lenin, but they don't have a lot of time. Lenin in power for any length of time, even a few months, is impossible, but it would be enough to create such anarchy that it would be fateful for the peace and for the revolution. To me, Kerensky's policy seems to be the only realistic one. Trotsky and Lenin are making the totally wrong assumption, which they, and especially Trotsky,

---

37 The key event here was the Peace Resolution put forward in the Reichstag on July 19 by the Social Democrats, the Catholic Center Party, and the Progressive People's Party. Calling for a peace without annexations or indemnities, with freedom of the seas and international arbitration of disputes between states, it was ignored by all the warring parties.

38 The reference is to SPD co-Chair Philip Scheidemann (1865–1939) and his allies.

39 Matthias Erzberger (1875–1921) was a leader of the Catholic Center Party. Initially an enthusiastic supporter of the war, by 1917 he had turned against it and he put forward the peace resolution in the Reichstag.

40 Irakli Tsereteli (1881–1959) was a Georgian politician and member of the Menshevik faction of Russian Social Democracy. After the February Revolution, he returned from Siberian exile and rose to become Interior Minister in the Provisional Government of Prince Georgy Lvov. His efforts to affect a compromise among the Socialist factions and to also gain middle class support failed and he lasted only three weeks in office.

41 Alexander Kerensky (1881–1970) was a Russian lawyer well known for defending jailed revolutionaries against the Tsarist regime. A prominent member of the Socialist Revolutionary Party and a key parliamentary leader of the socialist opposition, after the February Revolution he was active in the Petrograd Soviet and in the Provisional Government, eventually becoming Minister of War and then Prime Minister on 21 July 1917. The Bolsheviks overthrew his government in October.

made in 1905, that the situation in Western and Central Europe is a revolutionary one. That is not yet [the case] and could only occur as a result of military and other external political events. Kerensky seems to sense that; hence the offensive.

I suppose that, after the most recent events, you, too, don't expect all that much from Sc[andinavia]. Nevertheless, it would be very good to be able to get a sense of what is real. The method preferred by the Scandinavians to reconcile the irreconcilable is not only without prospects, but it is also damaging and would just be grist for the mill of Thomas,[42] [Victor] Adler, David, and the rest.

Right now, one cannot be realistic enough and one has to fend off seductive illusions. And, for the moment, war remains the only reality, and its length and results determine the internal developments of the countries involved. It is clear that the speeches and resolutions of parliaments must remain without direct impact on the run of events and that is not their purpose. They buttress – hence their utility – the policy of holding out, at the moment the only possible choice available in the current framework of power. When we last saw each other in January, you did not want to believe that the war would last longer than this year. But, to me, that still seems most probable. Could you please send me Hugo's speech, when possible from the protocol? I look forward to hearing from you soon. Best regards to all.

Your,
R.H.

(KDXII 629/1)

Postcard, August 1, 1917
Landsturmarzt Dr. Rudolf Hilferding
Mobiles Epidemie-Spital Nr. 2
Feldpost 136

Dear friend!

This card might arrive just in time before you leave for your trip on the fifth. Therefore, I'll put off writing at greater length. Your letter made me very happy

---

42 Albert Thomas (1878–1932) was a leading French Socialist who, as party of the wartime coalition government, became Minister of Armaments in 1916.

and was very interesting. I also got the impression that all manner of doubtful influences is in the mix.[43] I know Hanecki[44] [sic] slightly and don't think much of him, Helphand [Parvus] is certainly corrupt, Sobelsohn [Radek][45] is at least corruptible. Meanwhile, it appears that the matter probably will take care of itself. The Bol[sheviks] might be less excluded, but I think a reorganization is probable. I now expect clarification from St.[46] That is very necessary [...].

The new historical supplement is very good as is the explanatory material that goes along with it. I only hope that your trip is not postponed or that it does not take too long. I would like to be in Berlin at the beginning of September and I don't want any delay. In any case, I ask that you keep me informed about where you and Hugo will be.

I am displeased with Frau Luise. In Vienna it seems that she had little to say and spent her time mainly pursuing ... psychology. As punishment she should send me an eight-page letter and commentary with all manner of gossip and news. Bendel doesn't write either. What is going on with Felix and Karl? I hope that things aren't going badly for you personally. With me nothing special is happening. I very much long to see you again. Best regards,

Your,
Rudolf

---

43   Hilferding is referring here to acquaintances involved in the Russian events of the spring and summer.

44   Yakov Hanecki (1879–1937), real name Jakob Fürstenberg, known in Russia as Yakov Stanislavovich Genetsky, was a Polish revolutionary initially active in the Social Democracy of the Kingdom of Poland and Lithuania. He cooperated closely with the Bolsheviks, was active in the post-1905 community of revolutionary exiles, engaged in business dealings with Parvus, and helped facilitate Lenin's transit to Sweden in 1917. After the October Revolution he held important posts in the Soviet government. He was executed during the purges of 1937.

45   Karl Radek (1885–1939) was born in Austria-Hungary as Karol Sobelsohn. A member of Social Democracy of the Kingdom of Poland and Lithuania and of the SPD, prior to the war he criticized Kautsky from the left. Charges of corruption and personal antagonisms made him unwanted in both parties, but Lenin, Trotsky, and others defended him. During the war he moved to Switzerland and was on the sealed train that transported Lenin and his entourage to Sweden. After the October Revolution he became an important figure in the Bolsheviks' effort to promote revolution in Central and Eastern Europe. Initially an ally of Trotsky, the Communist Party expelled him in 1927 and sent him to Siberia. After capitulating to Stalin, he was readmitted to the party in 1930 but was later purged and sent to a penal colony where he died.

46   The identify of St. is unclear.

(KDXII 629/2)

Postcard, August 2, 2017
Landsturmarzt Dr. Rudolf Hilferding
Mobiles Epidemie-Spital Nr.2
Feldpost 136

Dear friend,

I just read that you will probably be absent from Berlin from September 9–15 and I assume that will change your earlier travel plans. I am writing to ask that you keep me informed about what you have in mind. I am not concerned about just a couple of days. However, I don't want to postpone my leave too long, because the next will first be scheduled six months after this one. To be sure, it would be very desirable to see you after your return rather than beforehand. Don't you agree?

Best regards,
  Your,
  Rudolf

(KDXII 630)

October 13, 1917

Dear friend,

I had certainly hoped to be in Berlin on 16 October in order to finally be able to tell you, personally, how I wish you the very best and how close I feel to you, closer than ever. [But] it won't happen, and I don't know when this letter will actually reach you. I hope, however, that your strong optimism, from which others have so often drawn renewed confidence, will not have deserted you at the moment in which you have borne such a personal blow.[47] Ultimately, you stand

---

47   After Kautsky joined the USPD in the spring of 1917, it was a matter of time before his editorship of the *Neue Zeit* was challenged. At the end of September, the SPD leadership unceremoniously transferred control of the journal to Heinrich Cunow, Kautsky's former associate editor now turned ideological and political opponent. After 35 years at the helm, Kautsky was not permitted to write a farewell article.

far above the vileness [...] of the ungrateful jerks' ability to reach you or to seriously affect you. What the riffraff, which owes what it knows to you, has done, and the way in which they did it, is so grotesque that the outrage that must result from this action is actually reduced by its ridiculousness and by certainty of the chastisement that will soon follow. "Ἔσσεται ἦμαρ! [The day will come!][48] You, however, are [living] in an epoch in which there are more pressing things to do. Freed from the petty details of daily work, you are already taking on greater, more important matters. The world is renewing itself, though very differently than the new representatives of all the [political] currents believe, and your clarity of vision is necessary to recognize what is essential and to teach us what is new. I have no doubt that you will succeed. Above all, for your birthday I wish that you get to see the great and thoroughgoing impact of your efforts.

I had believed that I would be able to travel together with Bendel to Berlin. Even yesterday I thought I'd be able to go. Now I am stuck sitting here and have no idea for how long. Frau Luise is also somewhat responsible for that, because it took too long making arrangements. As a result, I submitted [my application] one day too late. Otherwise, I would have left on 15 September. For the moment, I don't know a thing. I only hope that I can at least get out of here this month. I fear, though, that I will miss Fritz [Adler], whom I would have liked to see, and presumably Otto [Bauer], who is supposed to report for duty on 20 October.[49] At the moment, I cannot communicate with anyone in writing. Otto had only written to me earlier very briefly. As I've always said, essentially, he seems to agree with our view. It would have been hard to be any different, because he is one of the few real Marxists. I only fear that, in this dreadful milieu, his full strength in many respects will be wasted.

I am not well-informed right now, but it seems that one can be halfway satisfied with things. My skepticism regarding the Russian Revolution has, indeed, proved justified. However, in spite of everything, what is occurring there is not decisive. Or, rather, what has begun there can only be secured and completed in the West. That will probably occur, however, after the war. The war will last at least through next summer. Military events will probably become even more important.

---

[48] This is an abbreviated quote, stemming from a famous line in Homer's *Iliad*, book 4, line 164 (Hom. *Il.* 4.164). I am grateful to Professor Ortwin Knorr for the translation and source.

[49] In May 1917 Friedrich Adler's death sentence was commuted to 18 years at hard labor. He was transferred to a new prison on October 12. Otto Bauer was released from Russian captivity after the February Revolution and returned to Austria in September. Still subject to military discipline, he received a four week leave and returned to duty in Vienna.

Once again, my very best regards to you, to Frau Luise, to the boys and to [our] friends.

And, hopefully, we will see each other soon!

Your,

Rudolf

(KDXII 578)

November 10, [1917]

Dear friend,

I received your letter of 2 November on 8 November, but not yet the one [you sent] to Vienna. I've asked Margret to forward it to me. I was recently caught up in a lot of hubbub, because I changed to another hospital about an hour's wagon ride away. At the moment, I am living very comfortably, I am pretty busy with medical matters and, of course, I have less freedom of movement than before. In particular, I have lost access to Innsbruck. I'll soon have the right to take a leave, because I will have belonged to the "field army" for six months. I am thinking about coming to Berlin for a few days to see you and Hugo. I think that December would be less appropriate than mid-January, since the Reichstag would be meeting, but in any case, I'd like to hear what you and Hugo think about it. Hopefully, Hugo is doing better, and I very much hope it is only exhaustion and nothing else. I'd be very happy if he could drop me a few lines. I cannot write to him now. Please give him and his family my best regards. Is Ernst still with the radio?

The story with Bendel is very disconcerting, but I don't think it will be too bad. I have the feeling that he won't be able to stand all too much marching and will have to allow himself to be reevaluated and reassigned to some lighter duty. In any case, he could write to me and let me know what is happening with his leg.

I have not been able to get any work done here but hope to find some time for that soon. Of the things [that you mention], nothing strikes me as particularly interesting, except please send me Heimann's "Methodologisches" and Wiese. Only send me Schneider's "Mitteleuropa" if it is halfway decent.

Of course, I am out of touch here and I'm all the more interested in hearing from you. For a while I had the impression that Hugo always hung a nose length behind, and not a small one but one more like Rosa's. Under pressure, he was forced to do tomorrow what he refused to do yesterday, when our friend

[Rosa] demanded it. Often no other way was possible, but, on the other hand, it too strongly gave the appearance of his being pushed. But, of course, from the outside it is hard to make judgements about the legitimacy of such actions. I've heard as good as nothing from Vienna, so there is not much to be said about it. I agree with you and to me the affair seems inexplicable.

The [appointment] of new ministers will really awaken all possible illusions in our people. It is completely in keeping with their wishes. Even better: the experiment will be carried out. We'll see how it turns out. The Polish story is interesting, once again it shows the heterogeneity of goals, and opens up a Pandora's box of all possible difficulties. The whole thing is, of course, more than problematic. In Germany, the whole matter will probably meet with stiff opposition.

I received numbers two and three of the *NZ* and expect the others today. Ede [Bernstein]'s [article] in number two was really good. He is becoming pluckier all the time. Please give him my best regards.

It has been very beautiful here and was warm and sunny until a few days ago. It's been raining nonstop since yesterday. The hospital is very nice, and one learns new and interesting things. I was in a muddy trench, heard and saw planes, and sometimes was fired upon. The work itself is quite agreeable, sometimes there are movies, and, on All Saints' Day, there was a theater performance of Der Müller und sein Kind [The Miller and his Child] put on exclusively by soldiers who also played the women's roles.[50] You should have seen it. I am curious about whether I'll be staying here for a while.

I am looking forward to my leave especially if it results in my seeing all of you again. Please thank Frau Luise very much for her letter. I hope she lives up to her promise and toasts with me in her letters as she would verbally in better times. Have you heard from Breitscheid again and could you provide me with Nestriepke's address? Sometimes I'm glad to be forced to be elsewhere. I don't envy the situation of my former colleagues. Frightful ... And now so much else is horrible. We have lost so many. And, in spite of everything, I still believe things are moving forward and will go well in the end. Be well. Again, many thanks for the letter. Such things now count twice as much. My very best regards to you, Frau Luise, and the boys.

Your,
R.H.

---

50   *Der Müller und sein Kind* was a 1911 Austrian silent film based on a late romantic drama by Ernst Raupach, first staged in 1830 in Vienna.

(KDXII 631)

December 3, 1917

Dear friend,

Your letter arrived yesterday evening. It gave me great pleasure and was interesting. It was, by the way, the first news I've had since my departure. I only note this, because something might have gone missing. Bendel is most probably in Bruck? Everything should be fine for Karli in Prague. It is too bad that he isn't being housed here; I could have steered him my way because our hospital is being greatly enlarged. As a result, I am *very* busy. I spend practically the whole day in my department, and I have to waste my historical interest by keeping records on the sick – it is a bit too much like rather ephemeral contemporary history. I did not even have time to read Renner all the way through. Furthermore, the mail connection here is miserable, the papers (from Munich and Vienna) are two or three days old and the *Berliner Tageblatt* is five to seven days old. How nice and just now. Moreover, [there is] the terrible laziness of my Viennese [correspondents] ...

Now to more important things. I am very pleased that your work, which I'm very excited about, is ready. It is important, because Renner's work, through its form, stakes out the ground and, above all, satisfies the needs of the majority leadership.[51] Now [about] publishing it: Max Adler is working on publishing a fourth volume of *Marx-Studien*, which, I believe, should appear in March on the occasion of Marx's one hundredth birthday. Now, it is not necessary for the whole thing to appear in a single volume; the edition could also – as in volume one – appear in the form of individual installments. Your work could, therefore, be published as the first installment. Indeed, it could be printed *immediately*. A second installment could be Gustav [Eckstein]'s, for which Otto [Bauer] or Karl Emil would write a foreword. I think Max would write the third. This form of publication would not only fulfil an old desire of the editors to bring out your work, it also makes sense in terms of substance. Renner is, after all, of great local importance. The framework of *Marx-Studien* would be more appropriate than a Leipzig publishing house. The issue of the honorarium would be more delicate due to the difference in the rate of exchange. But, because you will

---

51   Kautsky was working on *Kriegsmarxismus. Eine theoretische Grundlegung für die Politik des 4. August* (*War Marxism. A Theoretical Basis for the Politics of August 4*), published in 1918 in reply to Renner's *Marxismus, Krieg und Internationale* (*Marxism, War, and the International*) which appeared in 1917.

eventually be taking a summer vacation in Austria and would need Austrian currency, the difference in value would not be very great. And, by the way, the publisher would also certainly pay a half-decent honorarium. I would be very happy if you were to accept my suggestion, and, in any case, I will write to Max today along these lines. Your agreement, which ensures the volume's publication, would also relieve the editors of their important concern that Gustav's work see that light of day. Karl Emil cannot write this time. Right now, the poor devil can hardly find the time to read. I don't think it is a good idea to publish an overly large work in a journal. In my view, the new must be at least more up to date than the old and that is hindered by a work that is too massive. I hope that it finally comes together; at this moment it is very important.[52]

Your view of the Bolsheviks was also extremely interesting, likewise the article. Here, too, I see new evidence of the large measure of agreement in our points of view and conceptions. There is something tragic in the fate of the Russian Revolution in general and of the Bolsheviks in particular. The heart stands with them (as heartless as they themselves are in every sense), but reason does not really want to follow. I also fear that they will not be able to keep their promises. At the same time, their intentions are not very clear. Unlike before, do they now want a separate peace, and do they really believe they could maintain their neutrality against the Entente in the long run? And wouldn't a separate peace, if it were possible (and under what conditions?), mean a lengthening of the war on the other fronts? In 1905, Trotsky argued that the dictatorship of the Russian proletariat would be possible if the rest of Europe followed Russia into revolution. He must expect something similar now. But this expectation does not seem very justified. And, therefore, I also fear that the current regime will not be able to hold out. The situation is truly incomparable, because this combination of revolutionary proletariat and revolutionary peasantry, armed and organized in one army in which the officer corps is in total disarray, has never existed. It has much power on its side. But on the other side stands not only the whole bourgeoisie, but also the power of all the other states. And that Germany should really make it easy for the Bolsheviks by repudiating its plans in the east, thereby helping to stabilize this great revolution in a neighboring country – I'll believe that when I see it. And if it doesn't happen, what then? Should Trotsky and Lenin declare war? As they must know, the continuation of the war would

---

52   Hilferding's general plan did work out, though not exactly as envisioned. Kautsky did publish his reply to Renner in volume four of *Marx-Studien* (1918) under the title, "Kriegsmarxismus. Eine theoretische Begründung der Politik vom 4. August. Beleuchtet von Karl Kautsky." The work first appeared, however, as a separate pamphlet published by the Verlag der Wiener Volksbuchhandlung.

have to mean the reorganization of the army and, with that, their fall, as would the signing of an unfavorable peace. Help out of their dilemma could only come from the outside, from the Western European proletariat. But the outlook there is poor. Still, if the French and the English succeed in getting to Stockholm, perhaps now would be the moment to do something. I very much fear, however, that they will be less inclined than earlier to push for the granting of passports. Nevertheless, it would be worth a try.

In Austria it appears that there is a bit more liveliness in the party. As I expected, Otto's influence is pretty noticeable. Everyone can derive something from the Russian articles in the *AZ*. They are very optimistic, but they make it rather difficult publicly to adopt a different viewpoint when, as I fear, the eventual disappointment comes. Unfortunately, he has not written to me in a long time. He is also overworked. In any case, the situation is extraordinarily interesting and taking shape in extraordinarily dramatic ways. The Russian action, should it continue, must bring forth one good thing: greater clarity in respect to the real war aims of all the powers. That could have very positive consequences. Hopefully, the Russians will really make sure that the negotiations take place in the open.

In any case, I'd like to ask you not to leave me in the lurch and to write to me soon, regardless of your own lack of time. Written discussion is the only thing I've got here. I hope for good news from you regarding *Marx-Studien*. Please thank Frau Luise very much for her letter and the newspaper cuttings she sent. I've asked her to subscribe to the *Berliner Tageblatt* for December and to let me know how much I owe her. The address is K u K Etappenpost 197. I hope that you are doing well and that you have not felt the shortage of fats too noticeably.

I'm very sorry about Westmeyer, his life was full of suffering and now this terrible end.[53] I only knew Diefenbach fleetingly, it is also too bad about him. Do you know anything about Nestriepka and Breitscheid? I've written to both from here but have not received any replies. Perhaps Frau Luise [could] tell that to Frau Breitscheid, so that he replies to me or, if my letter was lost, writes to me himself. Please give Hugo my best. He promised me that he'd send the newsletter. Perhaps you could remind him about it?

Again, thanks so much for your letter. Very best regards to all from your,
Rudolf

---

53   Friedrich Westmeyer (1873–1917), chimney sweep, socialist trade unionist, journalist, and member of the state assembly in Württemberg, after 1914 he joined the anti-war Spartacus League. Drafted into the army and sent to the Western Front, he died in a military hospital in France.

(KDXII 632)

September 8, 1918

Dear friend,

I hear that you have decided to hold back the anti-Franz [article], and I am very happy about that. Because I am hoping to come to Berlin in early October, we could talk over the matter then.[54] Meanwhile, I've read his Marx biography.[55] There is nothing new there at all. The best is the chapter about the young Marx, in which he summarizes his introductions to the edition of Marx's works. The remaining material is simply unsatisfactory. For example, the whole section on Marx's view of the oriental question [and] on Marx's position on war and development is superficial and, more or less, generally known. Of course, Schweitzer and Bakunin come off well – since Mehring doesn't like you and August [Bebel]. In short, this depiction is undeniably very useful as an introduction for beginners – that which is unsatisfactory or incorrect, such as the treatment of the International, does not weigh so heavily. In my view, this account makes a scientific biography more necessary than ever. Hopefully, Goldendach will get to it *soon*.[56]

By the way, do you know what the situation is with the publication of the volumes on the International? And what is going on with your [work] and the economics of transition?[57] I am also curious about your new manuscript.[58] Otto [Bauer] and Robert Dann[eberg][59] write that they are in complete agree-

---

54   Kautsky did not wait very long to publish his critique of Mehring. See his *Franz Mehring und die deutsche Sozialdemokratie. Ein Beitrag zur Parteigeschichte* (1918).
55   Franz Mehring, *Karl Marx. Geschichte seines Lebens* (Leipzig: Verlag der Leipziger Buchdruckerei, 1918).
56   David Borisovich Goldendach (1870–1938), better known as David Riazanov, was a lifelong Russian revolutionary, a Marxist, and a self-trained historian. In 1917 he joined the Bolsheviks and, despite holding unorthodox views, served in a number of important positions. After co-founding the Socialist Academy of Social Sciences, in 1921 he established the Marx-Engels Institute, which he led for ten years until his arrest, internal exile, and execution in 1938. He completed a biography of Marx ten years later than Hilferding had hoped. See Riazanov 1927.
57   Published as *Sozialdemokratische Bemerkungen zur Übergangswirtschaft* (*Social Democratic Remarks on the Transitional Economy*) in 1918.
58   The reference is most likely to *The Dictatorship of the Proletariat* (1918), which led to Lenin's furious rejoinder *The Proletarian Revolution and the Renegade Kautsky* published in the same year.
59   Robert Danneberg (1882–1942), a member of the SDAP and Austro-Marxist thinker, played

ment but have concerns about opportunity. Now, ... the matter must be discussed; naturally, we would never have avoided that. Provisionally, the criticism of weapons is still more decisive than the weapon of criticism, and I suspect that the former will be more decisive than the later against the Bolsh[eviks]. How much damage Asiatic Marxism, which the good Franz much prefers to Austro-Marxism, has caused will then also be clear to the blind.

By the way, I don't fully understand your bad mood, which Frau Luise wrote to me about. That you are unhappy about the I[ndependent] people I can understand.[60] You were expecting too much from these illustrious gentlemen, and you projected too much of your own love for the party onto them. Because early on I had estimated the political capacity of the working class differently, I am somewhat less affected by this development. Therefore, I believe one has to clarify matters to one's self. Today there is scarcely a socialist faction with which we could identify. There is also hardly any place where we can represent our own viewpoint. It is a very painful thing, but the latter is eased somewhat because the decisive events must occur on the battlefield. (The other, domestic possibility can only be exploited when it is a reality und for the time being cannot be influenced). Only when there is possibility of free activity will we again be in the position to attempt to exert influence on the party. What is occurring now is just a prologue. And I admit, it is all the same to me whether the Independents make one mistake or another, because their entire effectiveness, for the moment, is at an historic low, not through any fault of their own or that of their leaders, but rather due to the historical state of the German working class, which, to be sure, will change. But before that change, one cannot expect or do much.

And I think that you should, least of all, get upset by the idea that you bear a responsibility for the views and actions of others, such as Georg [Ledebour].[61] That would not occur to any sensible person and things will be determined later, but also in a timely way. And, in the same way, I would not view the enthusiasm of the Berliners or the Leipzigers for the Bolsheviks as such a tragedy. I feel rather sorry for the poor devils. In the end, what will they do when they are inspired by a foreign revolution, but subsequently have to kiss the local Canute (after issuing a resolution of protest, of course) at home? And paving stones are

---

a leading role in the party's pre-war educational work. After 1914 he joined the anti-war opposition.
60   Hilferding is referring to the leaders of the Independent Social Democratic Party.
61   Georg Ledebour (1850–1947) was a journalist and parliamentarian on the SPD's left wing. He was a significant figure in the anti-war opposition and in the USPD's efforts to push the German revolution to the left in 1918–19.

paving stones, revolution is revolution, and anyway the joy is gone tomorrow, and your criticism will soon be your only consolation; the same criticism which weighs upon you today as treason. And such a platonic enthusiasm will never cause practical difficulties. In Germany the danger stems only from the right, not from the left.

But history is once again the best Marxist and completely in the old Hegelian mode to boot, because the war is the most powerful negation of consciousness, and from this negation history develops the most beautiful negation of the negation, a new political consciousness in which the old phrases are wiped out and the old content is realized. Today I see fewer reasons than ever for despair and you, the old steadfast, convinced optimist, who thereby has always been right, you allow yourself to get depressed? I hope it is only a temporary attitude and in October I'll see you as confident as ever.

Why is Luise coming? And what is with Bendel? Might I plan not only to see you all and Hugo, but also most of the other friends in October?

My very best regards, your
Rudolf

(KDXII 633)

Postcard, October 15, 1918
Landsturmarzt Dr. Rudolf Hilferding
Mobiles Epidemie-Spital Nr. 2
Feldpost 483

Dear friend,

You can imagine how impatient I am sitting here. Moreover, I hear very little and very much hope that you will write to me more often or that you will urge Stein[62] or Breitscheid to write. I am very curious about whether Hugo has been able to get anything going. I fear that for me it will only be possible to achieve

---

62   Alexander Stein (1881–1948), born in Latvia in the Russian Empire, joined the revolutionary socialist movement in 1901. Following the revolution of 1905, he fled to Zürich and then to Berlin, where he wrote for various publications including *Vorwärts* and the NZ. As an opponent of the war he joined Rudolf Breitscheid, Kautsky, and Bernstein as an editor of *Sozialistishe Außenpolitik*. A member of the USPD, he later worked with Hilferding editing *Die Freiheit*.

anything from Berlin. To be sure, I've also written to Vienna, but I don't know whether it will be of any use. In any case, I am counting on Hugo.

Naturally, first I'd like to know what is going on. Did the thing appear in the *LV*? At the moment I don't receive any Berlin papers, although I've subscribed to *V[orwärts]*, which is also not very pleasant. Oh well, that will also eventually come to an end. Again, please send me news. My very best regards to you, Frau Luise, Felix, and friends.

Your,
   R.H.

(KDXII 634)

October 28, 1918

Dear friend!

I hope that you have received my letter. It is disconcerting to hear nothing at all from Berlin, and I repeat my request to tell Stein that he should write to me (I don't know his address). Is Breitsch[eid] already in Berlin? Does Hugo know anything new? Nothing is happening here, and you can imagine my impatience. I read your article about Austria's problems and am anxious for the next installment. The feeling for the Pan-German idea appears to be gaining strength and I also believe that this development ultimately will be realized. Regarding peace, as before I believe in it, and with a somewhat bolder tactic on the part of Scheidemann and his supporters it would surely have already arrived.[63] But in any case, it [the war] cannot last much longer. For Austria, by the way, it [peace] is even closer at hand for the most urgent reasons, and it is the most exalted insanity that even now so many victims are killed. The next phase of Germany's domestic development is unclear to me. I think that matters will move most slowly there. However, I have never been as poorly informed as I am now. Today, for a change, no newspapers arrived except for

---

63   Aware that the war was lost, the German Supreme Command prevailed upon Kaiser Wilhelm II to appoint the liberal Prince Max von Baden Chancellor in early October 1918. He was charged with simultaneously seeking an armistice with the Entente while introducing parliamentary reforms that would make his government responsible to a majority. As part of the latter transformation, he invited representatives of the SPD, such as party co-Chair Philip Scheidemann (1865–1939) to enter his cabinet.

a few old issues of *Vorwärts*. They are talking about greatly restricting the delivery of newspapers to the front. All kinds of rumors are circulating. Hopefully, you've found time to write me a few lines. I hope you are all doing well. Best regards to you, Frau Luise, and friends.

Your,
   Rudolf

CHAPTER 4

Hilferding's Letters to Karl Kautsky, 1924–33

(KDXII 635)

May 30, 1924
Die Gesellschaft: Internationale Revue für Sozialismus und Politik
Berlin NW 6
Schiffbauerdamm 26

Dear Karl,

As you will see, unfortunately it wasn't possible in the June edition to find space for Most, whose article had gotten too long. Therefore, I published the one by Korsch. The episode in Thüringen [sic] passed unnoticed and is too insignificant to give special consideration. It would have taken up too much space if we'd published the critique.[1]

Thanks very much for the article on Countess Hatzfeldt. Now we've seen everything: Karl as sex researcher or father as peeping Tom!

Although I would like to, I can't come to Vienna. Crispien,[2] Wels,[3] and Müller[4] are members of the Executive and Müller has nominated Adolf [Braun][5] as his deputy, which is completely in order. If the political situation permits, Müller will possibly go as well. There is no room for me. I'm sorry that you are

---

1 The discussion concerns an article Kautsky had submitted about late nineteenth century anarchist intellectual and political leader Johan Most (1846–1906). It appeared in *Die Gesellschaft* later in the year.
2 Arthur Crispien (1875–1946) was co-Chair of the SPD from 1923–33, a member of the Reichstag from 1920–33, and a member of the LSI executive committee from 1923–36. In 1933 he went into exile in Zürich where he worked in the LSI office and represented the Sopade in Switzerland.
3 Otto Wels (1873–1939), co-chair of the SPD from 1919–1939, member of parliament, later leader of the party executive in exile (Sopade).
4 Hermann Müller-Franken (1876–1931) joined the Party Executive in 1906, was one of the SPD's most important politicians under Weimar and a good friend of Hilferding. He served as Foreign Minister from 1919–1920 and Chancellor in 1920 and again from 1928–1930.
5 Adolf Braun (1862–1929) initially joined the Austrian Socialist movement before moving to Germany in the 1890s. Well known as a scholar specializing on economics and trade union matters, he also edited *Vorwärts* and the *Fränkischer Tagespost*. After serving in the National Assembly, he became the secretary to the Party Executive and was also elected to that body.

not coming to the party congress, but I am hoping you will come to Berlin in the foreseeable future. As before, I would rather have you here all the time. Despite everything, it is more agreeable here now than in recent years. I'll write about politics next time, as soon as I can get a sense of the overall situation. The Lassalle article is already at the printer and you will soon receive the proofs. Since you already have a copy of the Most manuscript, I've only enclosed the last page, on which you had made some additions by hand. Best wishes from Rose and me to you, Luise, and the boys.

Your,
   Rudolf

[P.S.] Please tell that loathsome Bendel that he should finally send me the promised review.

(KDXII 636)

July 19, 1924
*Die Gesellschaft. Internationale
Revue für Sozialismus und Politik*
Berlin NW 6
Schiffbauerdamm 26

Dear Karl,

Thank you so much for your letter, which also shows how much I am losing with you gone from Berlin. I had also very much hoped that, in the end, you would be here in the fall, and I was very saddened when I received a call from Dr. Deri that you suddenly had an apartment. I have a dark memory of this apartment, because I have visited Fritz Herz there a few times.[6] Deri, who has become Herz's brother-in-law, wanted to know something about your finances in the

---

6   Friedrich Otto Herz (1878–1964), an Austrian Social Democrat, studied law and economics at the University of Vienna and the University of Munich. After serving in the Austrian Ministry of War during the First World War, he became a Ministerial Councilor in the Office of the Federal Chancellor in Vienna and worked to improve Austrian relations with Great Britain and the newly independent states of the former Austro-Hungarian Empire. After teaching world economy and sociology at the University of Halle-Witttenberg in Germany from 1930–33, he fled the Nazis first by returning to Vienna and then, after the Anschluß of 1938, by moving to Britain.

wake of the settlement.[7] And so, in this grotesque way, I learned about your luck in finding an apartment. Of course, I understand your reasons, though – despite your intention of concentrating on theory – I still think that you will miss Berlin's politics, which are much livelier [than Vienna's]. It makes no sense, however, to discuss what is already decided. I only hope that, once again, you find it agreeable and tranquil there. Through your decision, though, I lose an awful lot. To me, right now, in this critical period – I mean critical for socialism – contact with you is all the more urgent, since I scarcely have anyone here with whom I can talk about difficult problems with total frankness and with real practical benefit. I'm not worried about the future of the workers' party as such. But I am not sure how things stand in regard to socialism itself. It is not just a question of tempo. We need to identify more concretely than before the organizational forms that must be brought into the economy. And there it seems to me, without having come yet to a definitive result, that it would be necessary for workers to move up into the leadership of their enterprises before one could carry out a more sweeping centralization and more comprehensive social regulation. Because otherwise it is to be feared that, given its current condition and its moral and intellectual abilities, the advantages of socialization would be lost through falling productivity, through the indolence of the leadership, and because the cartels and trusts have [already] realized a large portion of these advantages by reducing the costs of free competition, at least in the decisive branches of production. Promotion within enterprises would be possible, of course, only for the able, and presumes, firstly, non-partisan selection, and secondly, appropriate educational opportunity, in other words, a real, thoroughgoing democratization of our educational system. Of course, that would also mean that, next to the earlier focus on primarily economic matters, our agitation must now more strongly emphasize moral and intellectual elements.

Aside from that, of course, there are a huge number of things to talk about and, more than anything, I had hoped for your advice with the *Gesellschaft*. I think the thing has gotten off to a fairly good start. The print run is 6,000. It would be nice, at least for now, to expand distribution abroad. We have also successfully attracted a number of young people. It wasn't easy, and how little fire, lust for battle, and, above all, how little real knowledge and especially knowledge of Marxism there is!

At the moment, it does not look too bad in the party. On the other hand, our overall situation is really uncomfortable. In reality, since we left the government,[8] the [internal party] opposition has no more opportunity for heavy

---

7 The nature of this "settlement" is unclear.
8 At the height of the great inflation of 1923 and following the French occupation of the Ruhr

attacks. That was very noticeable at the party congress.⁹ I also don't think that there are grounds to speak of the rape of the opposition. One must, finally, combat this misuse of co-presentations: the matter was set up through the long hand of Dissmann at the party assemblies.¹⁰ Everywhere that a member of the party executive or someone else rose to speak, the opposition demanded a co-speaker of its own. I don't believe that when Otto Bauer agrees to give a speech, he would tolerate it if a Pölzer [sic] or a Dr. Leichter (whose article in the AZ was so idiotic!) were allowed to stand against him.¹¹ In the same way, we don't want to allow an incapable rascal like Dissmann to put on airs as the leader of a so-called opposition. Since the discussion began with about eight opposition representatives speaking one after another, one cannot really talk about any kind of reduction in the freedom of speech. The party congress behaved calmly in every case. But the government's proposed tariff legislation and its stupid position on the eight-hour day has put us in a tight spot. The masses must now have the feeling that you can do what you want with the Social Democrats. The government will now get back the Dawes recommendations¹² and then come the demands from the bourgeois bloc for the lengthening of the working day, grain tariffs, and so on. The opposition here, which is inspired by [Paul] Levi,¹³ will seize upon that and demand that, in return for accepting the

---

industrial region, the SPD had participated in a broad coalition government headed by Gustav Stresemann of the German People's Party. Hilferding served as Finance Minister from August until October. After his monetary policy and support for the eight-hour day encountered resistance from the right-wing forces in the coalition, he was replaced. The SPD left the cabinet altogether in November.

9   The reference is to the SPD's Berlin Party Congress of June 1924.
10 Robert Dissmann (1878–1926), leader of the German Metal Workers' Union and a co-founder of the USPD. After the reunification of the latter with the SPD in 1922, he was a key figure on the party's left wing.
11 Johann Pölzer (1872–1934) was a leader of the SDAP in Lower Austria and a member of the National Assembly from 1920–1934. Social Democratic thinker Otto Leichter (1897–1973) was a legal expert, co-founder the Association of Social Democratic Students and Academics, and served on the staff of *Der Kampf* and the *Arbeiter-Zeitung*.
12 Following Germany's decision to cease making reparations payments to the Entente powers and Frances subsequent decision to occupy Germany's Ruhr industrial basin, a committee of representatives from France, Britain, Belgium, Italy, and the United States, chaired by Charles G. Dawes, an American banker and Republican politician, was formed to resolve the crisis. The resulting Dawes Plan rescheduled Germany's reparations payments and ended the Ruhr occupation. It was also essential to ending Germany's hyperinflation.
13 Paul Levi (1883–30), Social Democratic lawyer, defense attorney (and lover) of Rosa Luxemburg, and co-founder and, briefly, leader of the German Communist Party. As a result of internal conflicts with the KPD's left-wing, Levi was expelled from the party in 1920 and

recommendations, we make certain demands, which, if rejected, should result in our voting no. That would put us in a totally confused and impossible situation for the coming elections. And, as unfavorable as our position in new elections would be if they occurred as a result of their rejection by the German nationalists, it would be just as unfavorable if we, who have fought for their acceptance, rejected them for internal political reasons that have little directly to do with the decision. On the other hand, we cannot allow the impression to arise that we would not do as much as possible for the eight-hour day and for tariff exemptions. You understand that it is not easy to find a way out of this dilemma, because our situation in parliament is not particularly strong, and also the fighting power of the masses on the outside, if not as low as it was in the fall of last year, is also not yet strong enough.

I am, of course, extraordinarily interested in what you write about your book. I thought about whether I could recommend a biologist to you, but I did not come up with a satisfactory result. Perhaps I'll think of someone. It is interesting, how you have returned to your first love. You have always had a bit of the natural philosopher in you.[14] By the way, yesterday Riazanov told me that manuscript on the critique of ideology begins something like: There is only one science, history, which is divided into the history of nature and that of society. Perhaps there you could also refer to Marx.[15] Riazanov is now very upbeat and it seems he is publishing or editing an extraordinary amount. Most important, however, is the complete works of Marx and Engels. In my view, despite everything, he must have our help, and, above all, I'll try to talk to Bernstein. One cannot really say that Bernstein has administered the Marx-Engels papers as they should have been.

I myself can hardly do any scientific work, although there are two things continually swirling around in my head. First, an expansion of my theory of money, and, at the same time, a critique of the most recent English and American crises, banking, and money matters, which, if perhaps not theoretically significant, are interesting in a practical sense, particularly the problem of influencing the conjuncture via the credit policy of the central bank. Then a "political the-

---

eventually returned to the SPD in which he became a leading figure on the left. He served the SPD in parliament until his suicide in 1930.

14 The reference here is to Kautsky's magnum opus, *Die Materialistische Geschichtsauffassung*, (*The Materialist Conception of History*) which appeared in two massive volumes in 1927.
15 Hilferding is referring here to Marx and Engels's, *The German Ideology*, of which only a small portion had ever been published. A section on Feuerbach was published in 1926 and the entire work finally appeared in 1932, after Riazanov's arrest (See Chapter 3, footnote 56 above).

ory of the state", which could also have practical significance. But where to find the time? German parliamentarianism demands much more time than its Austrian [counterpart]. Your words of consolation came at the right time.

Now to editorial matters. I will simultaneously send you the Müller [article]. I would be grateful to you, however, if in one swoop you'd also take on Williams's "Die soziale Geschichtsauffassung". If circumstances allow, it would be enough to just write two pages on each, just in case you don't find them too stimulating.

Furthermore, I have another request. If it is not important to you whether your preamble appears in the *Gesellschaft*, then I'd like to pass it on to *Der Kampf*, in which its form would be more appropriate. On the other hand, I'd be very grateful if, since you've already read it, you'd write a few lines on [Emile] Vandervelde's little book, which would be good for Vandervelde and the *Gesellschaft* and would come at no cost to us.[16] Essentially, you only need to repeat what you've already said in the preface. Finally, I'd ask your pardon, because I could not publish Rocker in the August edition. It is, I'm afraid, twenty pages. It will certainly come out in September.

In regard to the international situation I am pretty optimistic in the wake of the French elections, which to me felt like liberation. When it comes to our International, though, the behavior of the English is very shabby. After Amsterdam[17] they sent Mieße Bell, while the others were represented by [Emile] Vandervelde, [Leon] Blum,[18] H[ermann] Müller, and so on. The English trade unionist (Purcel?) supported the rejection of the [Dawes] recommendations because the English workers would be damaged by the required German exports. You can just imagine how the standing of the International, which can only be secured through much struggle, gained nothing from this action.

By the way, have you read Paul Levi's "Das Gutachten und nachher" ["The Judgement and its Aftermath"]? If it interests you, I'll send it right away. Along with Müller, I am enclosing the corrected galleys of Rocker. If it is too much bother, you don't need to read through them any further, but if you find any typos, I'd appreciate it if you would send them back.

---

16 Emile Vandervelde (1866–1938) was a leader of the Belgian Labor Party. He had ministerial posts in wartime and post-war Belgian governments and was a co-founder and then longtime President of the Labor and Socialist International in 1923.
17 The reference is to an international meeting of mainly European free trade unions that took place in Amsterdam in February of 1919 and created the International Federation of Trade Unions.
18 Leon Blum (1872–1950) led the SFIO during the interwar period. He served three times as Prime Minister, including the crucial period of the Popular Front during which he introduced a wide array of radical economic and social reforms.

At the moment, Rose is at her mother's in Czechoslovakia.[19] Hopefully, the Reichstag will soon be done. I could use a vacation right now.

Be well and give my best to all the friends and the evil boys, who have lured you away from Berlin. My very best to you.
From your,
Rudolf

P.S. At some point do you want to review Bogdanov's "Entwicklungsformen der Gesellschaft und die Wissenschaft" ["Science and the Forms of Social Development"]?[20] I just noticed that I already sent the Müller piece to Dr. Marck in Breslau. If that is important to you, I could ask for the pamphlet back. But you don't miss much there, as I gather from a critique in the *Rote Revue*. It seems to consist of a completely insignificant ethnic objection to the materialist conception of history.

(KDXII 637)

Postcard, August 14, 1924
Reichstag
Berlin NW 7

Dear Karl,

I'm sending you Bogdanov. The [article] from Below, unfortunately, went to Otto Landsberg some time ago. He had asked me for it, and I cannot very easily get it back. I don't think it would be of essential interest to you. I'll be more careful in the future and ask you in a timely way about books that might interest you. Karli should tell me whether he can write the essay for *Die Gesellschaft* and when.

Best wishes,
R. Hilferding

---

19   Rose Hilferding (d. 1959), a Czech-born physician and translator, married Rudolf in 1923 just after his divorce from Margarete.
20   Alexander Bogdanov (1873–1928), a physician, scientist, and revolutionary Russian intellectual whose works ranged widely from Marxist philosophy to science fiction. An early member of the Bolshevik faction, he was a rival of Lenin until his expulsion from the group in 1909. After 1917, he was active in Soviet politics, criticized the Bolsheviks from the left, and was subject to their frequent harassment.

(KDXII 638)

October 19, 1924
Schiffbauerdamm 26

My dear Karl,

As Rose says, you, who know yourself never to be a "believer in the calendar", will forgive me for not writing to you hastily in the midst of the political crisis and for waiting, instead, for a calm moment.

What I had to say to you as a party comrade, I have tried to say in *Vorwärts*. Only, [it was] incomplete and one aspect of your activity came up very short: your part in the development of political tactics. You, yourself, have said little about that [and] the correspondence with Engels, Bernstein, and [Victor] Adler is unpublished. In addition, after Engels's death and your move to Berlin, your influence on Bebel was very strong, but to write about that in a newspaper article was not possible.

Let me thank you today for that for which I am personally grateful. That is not just thanks to the teacher and advisor. You decisively and formatively intervened in my life, because you brought me to Berlin. Then you and Luise took me in like a son and your house was more and more like home to me. To me, you were the benevolent friend, and I felt increasingly secure and protected in this friendship. You've only ever disappointed me once, when you left Berlin. I knew right away what I was losing. The longer you are gone, the more strongly I feel the loss. I have a peculiar feeling; I will never really feel at home here, today even less so than when you and Bebel represented the party. I have no real friend here, scarcely anyone with whom I can talk about serious problems and – strange, but true – I can't get over 1914 as easily as you. I couldn't keep you [here], however, and believed I had no right to do so, because I think that Vienna, where the boys are and where the atmosphere is warmer and more human, must be more comfortable for you than Berlin. Only for me, sometimes, it is even more difficult.

That had to be said, so that you know how strongly my feelings, and my gratitude, toward you have always been, and how happy I was to be able to work together with you intellectually. Perhaps in 1914 and 1918 I had tactical differences with you on some isolated issues, but on all the important and essential matters we were united.

Hopefully, London and the holiday have left you refreshed and upbeat, the work goes steadily forward, and will enrich us all anew.

The crisis is continuing. Today, some sought to dissolve [the Reichstag] again. The whole thing is basically a boring episode. If the right-wing bloc can be successfully stopped this time, then the fight will occur later. We first have to get caught up on the political-democratic debate, before we can have the social one. Of course, that won't occur as a purely separate matter, and it means [going forward] in two stages, which also will shape our different tactics. Now we have to make the German working class aware of the singular character of the republic and of democracy, which it still does not fully grasp. Therefore, I'm glad that the Democrats, as insignificant as they themselves might be, remained firm; it eases the working out of the *political* problems rather than those concerning immediate, material, class interests. It could also lead to the easier decomposition of the [Catholic] Center [Party], which is a prerequisite for the recovery of Germany's party system and is also a precondition, if necessary, for coalition politics.

Hopefully, you'll find something for the *Gesellschaft* again, which would please me very much. The November edition contained Baade's guidelines for an agrarian program, the start of a discussion. Perhaps that will get you going. Would you like to review [Antonio] Graziadei's "Wert u[nd] Mehrwert bei Marx", ["Value and Surplus Value in Marx"], an effort to refute [Marx's] teachings on value and price! Graziadei has urgently requested that his pamphlet be reviewed. When I think about your book, I wish – in a totally self-interested way – for its rapid completion so that the *Gesellschaft* will receive more from you.

Be well. Rose also sends her love and wishes you her very best. She would have written herself but is visiting friends in the country until Sunday. Best regards to Luise and the boys!
Your,
Rudolf

(KDXII 639)

November 6, 1924
Berlin W6
Schiffbauerdamm 26

Dear Karl,

On January 6, 1925 Eduard Bernstein turns seventy-five. It is necessary to do something. I ask that you please write an article about Ede for the *Gesell-*

schaft.²¹ I wouldn't know of anyone else who could do it. Nothing was done for the old fellow's seventieth birthday because of the circumstances at that time. Now one must make up for that. I'd be very grateful if you could send the article during the first week of December. You have probably already received my letter. Will you review the Graziadei [pamphlet]? I've received Karli's manuscript.

Rose also sends her best regards to you and Luise.
Your,
Rudolf

(KDXII 640)

December 29, 1924
Die Gesellschaft
Berlin NW 6
Schiffbauerdamm 26

Dear Karl,

First of all, thanks very much for your letter and your article about the [Paris] Commune. I'm happy to publish it and cannot conceive of any objections. The fight against nationalism, also, indeed, especially within the party, is of overwhelming importance. Actually, I could be a bit offended because of your belief in my "diplomatic" mission, but you won't believe how thick skinned I am. I am thinking of publishing your article in the March edition. Perhaps when making corrections you can observe that the article is at the same time in remembrance of the Commune. Otherwise, at most I'd like you to insert a sentence after the remark about the confiscation of the fleet, which safeguards us against [any] possible malevolent interpretation.

Politically, I am in complete agreement with what you've written in your letter, including your remarks about Ebert. I also liked the article about that in the *Arbeiter-Zeitung*. We will scarcely have to worry about stronger effects of the trial within the party, but the Communists, of course, are exploiting it commensurately.²² Regarding the outcome of the [December Reichstag] election,

---

21   Kautsky agreed and wrote the article. See Kautsky 1925, pp. 1–22.
22   In 1924 Reich President Ebert took one of the editors of the *Mitteldeutsche Presse* to court for slander after his paper had accused Ebert of contributing to the defeat of 1918. Despite

perhaps I will have to say something in the February edition. Naturally, for the party itself it is a turning point. Things are moving in a positive direction. One should not forget that, as Social Democrats we are not as strong as in 1912 (26 percent vs. 35 percent). Only when one adds the Communists' 9 percent back in, do we reach the level of 1912. The slowness of the Communists' decline is disappointing, and worst of all is the indecisiveness of the outcome of the election and the difficulty of forming a government.

In any case, I hope that we can stay out of the government. At the moment, one speaks of [forming] a cabinet of officials (*Beamtenkabinett*), which would be the worst solution, because then all the parties could avoid political responsibility. The conflict over the withdrawal from the zone around Cologne, which could have been avoided with some skill and good will, is having a very bad effect. The victory of the English Conservatives is fateful for world politics and increasingly destabilizes Herriot's position as well as the situation in Germany. I doubt whether Macdonald's tactic, which might have been understandable from the standpoint of English domestic politics, grasps the future clearly and was correct from the European point of view. A better relationship with the Liberals would have made the continuation of a Labor government possible. It seems to me that the weakening of the Liberals came at great cost.

I have a guilty conscience about the Bogdanov article. If I had known how much work it would have meant for you, I would never have tempted you. The man seems to be too insignificant for you to have found it necessary to deal with him in such detail. Maybe you can do some cutting when you get the proofs, but I fear the article will be too long. How is your book going? I hope it is moving forward briskly. Just in case you see Otto [Bauer] before his trip to Brussels, tell him that I would value it greatly if he returned via Berlin.

Best regards to you and yours from Rose and me.
    Your,
    Rudolf

"winning" the case, the trial did not go well for Ebert and was an embarrassment for him and for the SPD.

(KDXII 641)

> July 5, 1925
> *Die Gesellschaft*
> Berlin NW 6
> Schiffbauerdamm 26

Dear Luise,

I've wanted to write to you and Karl for a long time, but currently I am terribly overworked. I'm in the Reichstag ten to twelve hours [each day]. On top of that, there is the preparation for the committee meetings, so I have scarcely any time to take care of the most important work at the *Gesellschaft*. I ask that Karl please send the article about Axelrod. But I have an even more important request for him. Recently, he wrote to Adolf [Braun] that he intends to edit Engels's letters. I would be very grateful to him if he would perhaps place a couple of the letters, along with a short commentary, at the disposal of the *Gesellschaft*. I had forgotten that it is the thirtieth anniversary of Engels's death and, otherwise, would not have anything to include in the *Gesellschaft*. It does not have to be anything very thorough and, therefore, would still be manageable.

I sent the books to Bendel. [Vladimir] Woytinsky,[23] had already asked Adolf Braun to do the review and he has already delivered it. (Note to Bendel) As soon as I can look through the review copies, and as soon as I receive the two [reviews] from him, he'll get new ones.

Your complaints about the party's operations in the bookstore are certainly justified. I'll try to talk to Adolf about it and see what can be done.

We were so glad to receive your card from Belgrade. You are a world traveler, and I almost suspect that you would rather linger around Belgrade for fourteen days than bore yourself for fourteen hours in Vienna. Rose wanted to answer right away. But recently she has been working overtime and two days ago went to visit her mother in Czechoslovakia. She will surely write to you from there. She wants to leave from there for Switzerland, where we will meet. We are not sure about exactly when. It depends upon the end of the parliamentary [session],

---

23   Vladimir Woytinsky (1885–1960) was a Russian trained economist who became a Bolshevik in 1905, was imprisoned and exiled to Siberia. He joined the Mensheviks during the First World War, was a leading figure in the Soviets and edited *Isvestiia*. Released from Bolshevik imprisonment, he moved to Germany where he worked at the *Die Gesellschaft* as an editorial assistant and eventually became Director of Research for the German Federation of Trade Unions. He migrated to the United States in 1935 and played a key role in the establishment of the Social Security system.

and we are in a critical situation in foreign as well as in tariff policy. Whether we'll be successful in preventing the passage of the tariff legislation is unclear. The agenda is set up in such a way that obstruction is almost impossible. It is also hard to say how long the others will tolerate our exhaustive discussions.

From Switzerland I'll naturally go to Marseilles, unfortunately with a lecture. I'm not sure yet, if Rose will also be coming.

Thanks to Otto [Bauer]'s good offices, for which I am very grateful and through which I finally learned what it was really all about, the differences with Margret are on their way to being reconciled. Regards to Peter. Bendel should write to me.

Best regards to Otto and the generations of Kautskys and the very best to you and Karl.
Your,
Rudolf

(KDXII 642)

January 8, 1926
Die Gesellschaft
Berlin NW 6
Schaffbauerdamm 26

Dear Karl,

It has been quite a while since I've heard anything from you, and I am a bit concerned. Woytinsky recently said you were not well. Now, you are among those people who generally don't bear up very well in the winter. But, naturally, I would like to know how you are doing. There is not a lot that is new here. Politically, we are still grappling with [the issue] of the Great Coalition.[24] Like Hermann Müller, Breitscheid, and many others, I am absolutely opposed [to it], because I don't believe that we can achieve anything positive with the German People's Party even if [the coalition] were limited to a short period. After such a short time, a second collapse of a government in which we are particip-

---

24 The term "Great Coalition" was used to describe a government consisting of the pro-republican SPD, the Democratic Party, the Catholic Center Party, and the business-oriented German People's Party, which harbored powerful anti-republican elements as well as some, like Gustav Stresemann, willing to make their peace with the republic.

ating would do extraordinary damage to the party. I hope that this nonsense can be avoided. The situation is not very good. The crisis is very serious, especially in the Rhineland and in Westphalia, where the workers have had to deal uninterruptedly with terrible conditions since 1914. Our organization there has suffered the most due to the split, Communism, and unemployment. At the moment it is the weakest point in our movement. The crisis and unemployment will deepen, however, especially in heavy industry, and we don't know how long they will last. One cannot count on a strengthening of the party until a new period of prosperity sets in.

On the other hand, I don't think there will be a Communist revival, although we have to consider that the crisis could lead to a temporary flareup. Otto [Bauer]'s optimistic evaluation of the Russian economic situation is noteworthy. I don't share it at all, and I think that not only the Mensheviks, but also Bolshevik observers, share my view. I expect a serious crisis as soon as it becomes necessary to replace worn out constant and particularly fixed capital. Then the Russians will be forced to make a decision. They must then try to get credits from the Anglo-Saxon powers, which would be possible only if they liquidated their own foreign policy, or they could once again attempt to return to pure communism and terrorism, especially in respect to the peasant masses, and that would be a truly catastrophic development. I expect the first alternative to be the most likely [choice], and that would mean a further internal development of Bolshevism itself, which would be characterized by newly forming class antagonisms and would mark the beginning of its political transformation.

[Paul] Cassirer's suicide was frightful. He was at our place on 1 January for the whole day. The idea that Tilla wanted to leave him for good was unbearable for him. The attempt to set things right again failed due to Tilla's total inflexibility. Although I was together with him less frequently in recent years than earlier, his death hit me really hard. He was one of Berlin's most interesting and unique people.[25]

My very best greetings to Luise and the boys. I would be grateful to Karli, if he did not make me wait too long for the review of Oda Ohlberg's book. Please write me a few lines. Rose also sends her best to all.

Sincerely yours,
Rudolf

---

25   Paul Cassirer (1871–1926), gallery owner, publisher of *Pan* and *Die weissen Blätter* (*White Pages*) was a leading promoter of Expressionist art.

(KDXII 643)

July 13, 1926
Die Gesellschaft
Berlin NW 6
Schiffbauerdamm 26

Dear Karli,

Along with this letter I'm sending you three books which might interest you, and which I am asking you to review for the *Gesellschaft*. Parts seven and eight, which were produced behind schedule at Dietz-Verlag, are missing from Hirschfeld's book and I'll request that they be sent to you. I'd appreciate it if you'd keep the reviews short. I've got a big backlog, and the longer the reviews, the harder it is to reduce the pile. Above all I ask that you write the shortest possible review of Frau Dr. Lazarsfeld's collection, because when one considers the tiny scale of these works, the review easily could be longer than any of the individual books themselves.

On Friday I am traveling to Sils Maria with my wife and, from there, before I return to Berlin, I am thinking of surprising your parents on the Ossischersee.

My very best regards to you all.
   Your,
   Rudolf

(KDXII 645)

July 21, 1926
Hotel Margna
Sils-Baselgia

My dear Karl,

It weighs heavily on me that I've not written for so long. But one cannot allow even the interesting stuff to get old for a short time, and in recent months I have been so overwhelmed with parliamentary and editorial work that, in spite of all good intentions, I could not get to it. But writing, after all, isn't actually very satisfying and I so wish to see [you] and to talk. I now intend, when it works out, to come to Vienna on 23 September for a conference of the Verein für Sozialpolitik. I never know, though, whether something will intervene. Therefore, if it is okay with you, [I'd like to] come for a few days to visit at the end of my vacation if that is at all possible. That would be between 8 August 8 and 15 August. I assume that you are still be in Ossischer See (Who is still there?), and I'd be very thankful if you would tell me where you are and how one can get there from Engadin. I'd then write to you in advance about when I'd come, assuming that I would not upset your peace and quiet too much. If that is the case, then I'll stay in Vienna. Rose and I have been here since the seventeenth. This is my first time in Engadin. It is extraordinarily beautiful, and the weather has been glorious. There is nothing ostentatious about the hotel in contrast to those big hulks filled with the Berliner bourgeois, who circulate here as *faux frais*[26] not only of the capitalist process of production, but of nature in general.

Hopefully, you've enjoyed Gastein and in the fall you'll finish your book. I am already very curious; in Germany and elsewhere the ignorance and, at the same time, the disdain for Marxism is grotesque. At the moment, [Hendrik] De Man is in vogue![27] But, hopefully, we soon be able to talk in person about all that and more.

Meanwhile, Rose and I send our very best to you and Luise.
Your,
Rudolf

(KDXII 644)

Postcard, November 11, 1926
Reichstag
Berlin, NW 7

Dear Karl,

Thanks very much for your letter. I think the article is already on its way here and that I will be able to publish it, even though, unfortunately, there is too

---

26 Faux Frais is a term used by Karl Marx and other classical political economists to refer to "incidental operating expenses" which do not add new value to capital in the process of production. See Marx, 1967, pp. 134–135.
27 Hendrik de Man (1885–1953) was a Belgian socialist leader and theoretician. During the interwar period he asserted that without middle class collaboration the proletariat could not achieve socialism and advocated state-led economic planning that directed most of

much publicity for [De] M[an].[28] In any case, I'll write to you right after I've received it. I am too busy to write during the meetings of the [Reichstag] delegation. The situation is very unstable, and I don't think there is much chance of the government surviving. The [SDAP] congress in Linz appears to have gone reasonably well. I'm in a hurry. Best regards.

Your,
  Rudolf

(KDXII 646)

December 10, 1926
Reichstag
Berlin, NW 7

Dear Karl,

The galley proofs are enclosed. I'm sending you two, just in case you undertake more thorough changes. I've taken the liberty of shortening the text in a few places, because the article is rather long and the book has already required four essays, which is really more than it is worth. I hope you agree. Perhaps you still can shorten it here and there, for example, the comparison with modern painting, which is not really imperative, because one cannot really argue about matters of taste. In addition, this type of expressionism is already old hat.

I've also toned down a few passages. First of all because the polemic becomes more effective and, furthermore, because the younger people are very sensitive. Then, if possible, I would also like to avoid another reply from De Man, and that would be much easier if there are fewer personal attacks. I hope you agree on that as well.

I am so glad that you are almost done with your work. I am very excited about it. We are once again at a critical moment. What will happen in the end remains unclear. In the Reichstag it is very difficult to find a rational solution, because the [German] People's Party holds the balance [of power]. The result of a dissolution [of parliament], even if [President] Hindenburg could be convinced, is uncertain, because the Democrats and the People's Party would probably lose

---

the means of production in private hands. During the Second World War he collaborated with the Nazi occupation regime and was discredited.

28   The reference is to Kautsky 1927, pp. 62–77.

seats to the Economic Party. Under certain circumstances, the Economic Party could become a decisive factor. You see, it is not easy to do politics in Germany. Besides that, I have quite a lot to do, especially concerning the budget. Personally, I have the usual fall cold. Otherwise it's going okay and Rose is already going out again. The operation seems to have been a complete success.

My very best regards to you, Luis and the boys.
Your,
Rudolf

ISH (KDXII 647)

October 10, 1927
Die Gesellschaft
Berlin NW 6
Schiffbauerdamm 26

Dear Karl,

I returned from Brazil at the beginning of the month. It was very interesting but exhausting. The tropical heat is not very refreshing, and the long ocean voyage is rather monotonous. You can't beat the mountains! And the most beautiful thing at sea is the land, which is confirmed every time an island or the coast comes into view. The immense possibilities for development in South America made a very strong impression on me, even the tropical areas. First of all, the fertility of the soil is extraordinary, and industrial development is also moving ahead very quickly. For example, using a high protective tariff, Brazil's textile and shoe industries have developed to the point where they can satisfy practically the whole domestic market. If in Europe we had to wait for socialism until capitalism abroad had done its work, it could take a really long time. Fortunately, that is not necessary. Of course, the stay was much too brief to be able to make more than a superficial judgement. But I don't really want to become a researcher on Brazil.

Now to something else. During my absence, Bendel had asked for and received the first volume of the *Marx-Engels Collected Works* [edited] by Riazanov. Originally, I'd intended to review it myself, but then I thought I'd ask you, whether you, as the most qualified, would like to take it on yourself, for which, of course, I'd be most grateful. Despite the delay, I think the edition is a terrific thing and, as far as I can tell, Riazanov's remarks are very objective. I would like to stress that point in order to be able to finally overcome the narrow-minded opposition to him from, unfortunately, Adolf Braun. Naturally, it would be very good if you wrote about it yourself. Bendel will understand and not be annoyed and I am once again overwhelmed with day-to-day work.

Of course, I'd also like to know how you are doing, whether you have the corrections done already and what you are planning. Hopefully, all is well. Rose is delighted with the trip and, like me, sends her best regards to you and Luise.

Your,
   Rudolf

(KDXII 648)

> January 4, 1928
> *Die Gesellschaft*
> Berlin NW 6
> Schiffbauerdamm 26

Dear Bendel,

Thanks very much for the review but, hopefully, you won't be mad when I tell you that I don't find it completely satisfying. Although a long way from finished, in view of the colossal achievement which Riazanov has begun and, above all, organized, it is too sober and dry. And there is another reason. Adolf Braun and, along with him, the party Executive, have made what are in my opinion unjustified and petty difficulties for him, which, unfortunately, I cannot overcome. It is all the more important to me, [then], to emphasize the great achievement to the public, and to thereby indirectly exert some pressure. I also do not think the polemic against Bolshevism is appropriate here, as much as I am otherwise so inclined to give space to any polemic against Bolshevism.

Now, I've attempted to help my [cause] by revising the thing myself, and I'd like to ask you to accept the altered form because it is important for the review to appear right away. I hope that you agree and ask that you send it back as soon as possible.

How are things otherwise? It seems to me that the tensions in the Austrian party have grown stronger again. At least, that is the conclusion I drew from Otto [Bauer]'s remarks in the December issue of *Der Kampf*. What is going on?

It is a bit calmer here now and I am using the time to read at least part of father's work. Of course, I am interested above all in the political, and [I've read] some of what he says about democracy and the modern state with great satisfaction. Hopefully, I'll have the chance at some point to read it systematically. It will be very difficult to find an appropriate reviewer; I cannot take it on myself in the foreseeable future. I have considered Alfred Braunthal, who, among the few Marxists, is probably the best. Please give my best to father and mother as well as to your brothers and their wives. Write to me at length.

Best regards,
   Your,
   Rudolf

(KDXII 649)

January 13, 1928
Die Gesellschaft
Berlin NW 6
Schiffbauerdamm 26

Dear Karl,

That is a nice mess. I thought I was dealing with an equal and suddenly Wotan steps forth and points his spear at my fountain pen. A pleasant situation.

More seriously, I'm very sorry that you have made such an effort in regard to something that is really not all that important. Substantively, there are no differences of opinion. I completely share your views, particularly in regard to the Bolsheviks, and I have long intended to formulate my judgement very sharply and ruthlessly. As is generally the case with political commentaries, I have waited until the time is ripe. In my opinion, the psychological moment has arrived, and I hope to follow through on my intention soon. For me it is all about uniting against the false slogan of the "unity of the Internationals", which would presuppose the unification of the national parties. For us, that can only mean overcoming communism. Thus, you can see that I have nothing against a polemic. Nevertheless, it has to be effective and certain psychological attitudes have to be considered, not in order to make allowances for them, but to weaken them.

But with the *Collected Works* we are not dealing with Bolshevism, but rather with a scholarly feat and with Riazanov's individual achievement. I am also skeptical about whether he will personally complete the thing. In any case, it will take a long time, but no academic publication is completed quickly. Of course, a change of regime in Russia can change the matter completely. But in just such a case, it would be important from the beginning to take the position that the edition had nothing to do with Bolshevism, and that any other Russian government is committing an outrage against science if it prevents the continuation of the edition. By the way, Riazanov has done more than execute the printing of the first volume. As far as I can see, the material for the *Collected Works* has already been organized by his institute, so that his successor could continue the work without insurmountable difficulties. I regard Riazanov life's work extraordinarily highly, all the more so because none of the more productive Marxists wanted or were able to do it. I have never regarded the fate of Marx's papers as a happy one. Without R[iazanov] the manuscript of the "German Ideology" would still be lying in some basket at Bernstein's, [or], in the best case, unused in an archive, while it now is published and is of great importance for the history of the creation of Marxism. My appreciation of the value of such editions is, to be sure, different than yours. You are surely right from a political standpoint: perhaps not much will come of it in terms of the social impact of Marxist teachings. We will probably not derive any fundamentally new insights. From a scholarly perspective, however, one will not only gain much biographically and in terms of the history of ideas, but certainly also in respect to a much more detailed knowledge of the branching out of theory. Thus, it is an old desire of mine to finally look through Marx's economic manuscripts themselves. I am convinced that there are important scientific insights to be garnered, especially from the preliminary drafts of volumes two and three [of *Capital*]. What political and social impacts would result from these insights is, of course, unforeseeable. Under no circumstances, however, do I think that it is simply crap. It is also a totally different thing to have a scholar's complete work before you than the hunting down of personal details which are fairly irrelevant to the impact of a poetic work. Moreover, as I just wrote to Bendel, one had caused so many difficulties for Riasanov here that I want to strongly emphasize his achievement.

Regarding Mehring I see no differences. I myself have noted that Mehring's edition is indispensable as an introduction and for popular purposes. If that still needs further emphasis in one sentence, I have no objections. Riazanov is right, however, that the deletions are substantial and, therefore, the purely scholarly value is markedly reduced. These are two incomparable things.

I have already said that I agree with you substantively about everything you say about Bolshevism. But to me it goes against the grain to carry on this polemic *en passant* on this occasion. Furthermore, it doesn't seem effective in this context. Every Communist will say: Marx stood for press freedom in the class state. We demand that, as well. But then comes the unavoidable period of the dictatorship and there all the rights of the class enemy must be withdrawn until classes are abolished. Against this point, one must prove that the elimination of democracy damages the proletariat and the carrying out of its aims. We are dealing with a different kind of argumentation than Marx could use in 1844. But that is just by the by. It seems to me that what is decisive is in this polemic, which occurs often, should receive a great deal of space in a review of the Collected Works. I had the feeling that it was added artificially and therefore cannot be made with good effect.

In this issue I'll be publishing an article by Abramovitch about the Russian political situation.[29] According to what he has told me, he will criticize the regime with appropriate sharpness. I also have the prospect of another article by someone else. As I said, I also hope to contribute a fundamental settling of accounts. Therefore, you don't need to worry that Bolshevism will be spared somehow by [our] silence. That is a point where I find Bauer's tactic, and even more so that of Kunfi but also of some the Mensheviks, unsatisfactory.[30]

Matters are now moving fast. I must publish the review in this issue. I would suggest that Bendel send the proofs with your absolutely indispensable corrections back to me as quickly as possible. If I can accept them, at least in the main, then the article can appear under Bendel's name. If not, then a pseudonym has to be selected. In this case I find that rather disagreeable. I have considered whether I might ask Bendel to allow the article to come out under my name. I have no substantive concerns, because I agree with Bendel about that part. Personally, I find it naturally somewhat strange to drape myself in some of Bendel's plumage. What do you think about it? The best thing would be if Bendel would make a few changes that take into consideration the arguments I've made here and that I can accept.

Now that's enough. *Tant de bruit* [so much noise] over one article.

In your book, which I've only been able to read rather cursorily up to now, I really liked the discussions about democracy. I am considering whether or not I should publish the chapter in the *Gesellschaft*. It is too bad that you did not send it to me before it was published. In regard to the review, the great difficulty is that we no long have any such encyclopedists. But I think the solution

---

[29] Raphael Abramovitch (1880–1963), a Russian socialist intellectual, a member of the Jewish Bund and a leading figure in the Menshevik faction of Russian Social Democracy. He fled Russia in 1920 and settled in Berlin, where he edited the Menshevik exile journal *The Socialist Courier*.

[30] Zsigmond Kunfi (1879–1929), a leading Hungarian socialist intellectual and journalist. A member of the National Council in 1918, he also served as People's Commissar of Education in the Hungarian Soviet Republic. After the latter's collapse, he moved to Vienna and became chief editor of the *Arbeiter-Zeitung*.

will be to allow a number [of authors] to write and I'm grateful to you for your suggestion. By the way, I already have the impression that the whole [work] is an admirable achievement. I heard from [Julius] Braunthal[31] that you are writing a pamphlet again. That's really terrific. Did you see the *Klassenkampf* [*Class Struggle*]? Max Adler attacks me uninterruptedly. To preserve my peace of mind, I have not read any of it and know the story through hearsay. Perhaps you might want to write an article about the Adler pieces, which aim to pass themselves off here as a kind of new platform for the opposition (alias Saxony). In no way Marxist, it is the worst kind of eighteenth-century deductive reasoning, rather than historical-political analysis. I think you could do us all a great service if you took on the issue. From what I can gather in your book, you have read the stuff.

What else are you planning? In particular, what are your plans for a vacation? After holding out for so long, maybe it would be smart to stay home for a while and only to go south at the beginning of the spring, when one can be more certain about the weather. But your doctors will know more about that. In closing, once again many thanks for your letter and my very best wishes to you and yours …

Your,
   Rudolf

[P.S.] Rose also sends her best regards.

(KDXII 650)

Postcard, May 12, 1928
Bad Oeynhausen

Dear Karl,

Driven here by the electoral agitation, which counts as one of the pleasures amidst the unpleasantness, I want to send you and Luise my very best greet-

---

31   Julius Braunthal (1891–1972), Austrian socialist, a leading journalist, and historian of the labor movement. During the interwar years co-editor of the *Arbeiter-Zeitung* among other publications. In exile after 1934, after 1945 Braunthal played an important role in the revived Socialist International and published his monumental three volume *History of the International*.

ings. If only the twentieth had already passed and with useful political results. How are you and what are you up to? I hope that you have rested well. Greetings to all [and to] Otto.

Your,
    Rudolf

(KDXII 651)

> Postcard, June 25, 1928
> Reichstag
> Berlin NW 7

Dear Karl,

Thanks very much for your letter, which I enjoyed very much. I completely agree. Your contribution also came just in time and appears in this issue. The appetite, however, comes with the eating. I believe you could perform a very great service for us all if you would undertake a critique of the Russian Communists' new program. In case you don't have it, I'll try to provide one from here. But surely the editors of the *A–Z* have a copy.

Meanwhile, I hope that a political decision here will finally be made this week. Personally, I'm doing tolerably well. Best regards to you and yours.

Your,
    Rudolf

(KDXII 652)

> Berlin, April 15, 1931

Dear Karl,

I have a very bad conscience and hope you understand. It is terribly hard to write. Just the notion of writing a very long letter hinders the act of just writing a few lines. And in that I am the loser, because that is how I get to hear your views. Meanwhile, I very much hope that you have recovered from your illness, that your admirable ability to work has returned, and I would be very grateful if you and Luise or Karli would write a few lines. I would very much like to come to Vienna, mainly to be able to talk with you, but I don't know whether that will be possible before July.

And now we have to get to the long disquisition about Germany, Russia, and ..., but then there would be another disturbance and no conclusion. Therefore just a few words, [meant] primarily to prompt a reply.

The time that passed between the elections and [Hermann] Müller's death[32] was really terrible. The most depressing thing is the terrible immaturity of broad sectors of the people and the infuriatingly primitive way in which they react politically to material conditions. One cannot view the working class as an exception, and the intellectual and moral status of the Communists is not much different than that of the National Socialists. Therefore, one has to consider that they will continue to grow as long as the economic crisis persists. Naturally, this expectation results in growing pressure on the policy of the party and the tendency to become more "radical" again. In the face of this [sentiment], it was difficult for political reason to prevail. The funny thing is that the new "radicalness" is most often supported by groups that were more or less revisionist and for the most part they have remained so mentally. Trade unionists, sentimentalists in pants and petticoats (which for female comrades, I fear, are still made from wool), who demand success every minute and disregard long term class interests. The death of H[ermann] Müller was a great loss. I was consistently able to work really well with him, and through him I could carry out my policy. Now it will become very hard, and how shameful is the fact that we have no one to replace him. The party has grown poor and it is its own fault. It does not undertake anything substantial to develop new talent. The position of the intellectuals has become more difficult, especially in the wake of war and revolution and the growing self-confidence of the workers, and proportional representation has had increasingly destructive effects on the selection of delegates to the Reichstag. The situation there will remain difficult. The National Socialists will try to realize their aims as a parliamentary party; in other words, they will get rid of their wildest men, present themselves as the point of crystallization for the broad reactionary right, and thereby gain access to the government. Then, as before, they could become a great danger for democracy. I don't see any easing of the situation through the breaking away of the Stennes people.[33] Anyway,

---

32 The reference is to the Reichstag elections of September 1930, in which the growing Nazi and Communist parties gained 18 and 13 percent, respectively, while the SPD won 24 percent, and Müller's death in March 1931.

33 Hilferding is referring here to a faction within the Nazi Party led by Walter Stennes (1895–1983), a leader of the Nazi SA. He mobilized supporters to oppose Hitler's decision to

a violent *Putsch* would have no chance; access to the government makes fragmentation easier. The unfortunate thing, however, is that the party [the SPD] does not understand that and is very much inclined to making fateful errors.

Matters also don't look very good internationally. The German-Austrian tariff affair was an effort that made the situation abroad much worse and endangered the whole system of trade agreements.[34] But the black and yellow painted Germans are enthusiastic, inside the party too, though, fortunately, they are not very numerous.[35] On 25 April I'll be going to Zurich (along with Breitscheid, I'm being taken along by our dictator [Otto] Wels);[36] Dan also would like Russia to be discussed. That does not seem promising to me, because people are taught only by facts. What is noteworthy is Otto Bauer's optimism. It is inconceivable to me that the five-year plan has anything to do with socialism. And if it were so, if socialism could only be achieved if beastliness is a required means, then I would reject that goal. It is just the opposite, however, and one might have many factories but neither socialism nor democracy. But one cannot do anything there and one will have to wait for the results.

My health is very good, but otherwise I'm dissatisfied and listless. I write that although I'm also a little embarrassed in front of you, the tireless worker and indestructible optimist, and although you are right and I'm not. I am also missing the personal here. It is so different than when Bebel, Eckstein, and you were here. I feel much too alone, and I always have the feeling of never being able to discuss problems frankly without having to fear it could be used against me politically. So, it is rather unpleasant.

I'm very curious about your book.[37] Hopefully, part of it will appear before the fall, so that I can read it right away. Here the fine topic of the "capitalist crisis" or the "crisis of capitalism" is being discussed on a level that undercuts any desire to read the stuff, to say nothing of getting engaged [in the debate].

---

pursue power via parliamentary means and to relegate street fighting to a secondary role. Easily defeated in April of 1931, Stennes went into exile in 1933.

34 In March of 1931 the German and Austrian governments concluded an agreement to create a customs union between the two states. The French and Czechoslovakian governments and, eventually, the World Court quickly blocked the action as a violation of the Treaty of St. Germain (1919), as well as subsequent agreements signed by Austria.

35 Black and yellow were the colors of the Habsburg Monarchy and the Austrian Empire from 1700–1867.

36 Otto Wels (1873–1939) was trained as a paper hanger. After joining the SPD as a youth, he moved up through the ranks of the trade union and party organizations. Elected to the SPD Executive Committee in 1912, he became co-chair in 1919 and its most important political leader until his death in 1939.

37 The reference is most likely to Kautsky's *Krieg and Demokratie* (*War and Democracy*) published in 1932.

I am curious about the next installment of Bauer's book.[38] I think that the chapter about "Fehlrationalisierung" [flawed rationalization] is wrong – [due to] flawed rationalizing. Do you, as well? Apart from a few survivors, however, the "Marxists" and the "Austro-Marxists" soon will resemble one another in their total lack of familiarity with Marx's ideas and method. What a shame, that one can't get a timely patent for "Marxism". And Riazanov! I am frightfully angry that these thugs are destroying the man himself and, above all, his work. But if there are a few more electrical plants, then of course socialist democracy will follow ...

Now, be well and recover your health quickly! Please give Luise and the boys my very best and forgive my long silence. Rose also sends her very best.

Your,
  Rudolf

(KDXII 653)

October 2, 1931
Die Gesellschaft
Berlin NW 6
Schiffbauerdamm 26

Dear Karl,

I fear that you are somewhat annoyed with me, but I was not only extraordinarily busy, but Rose was away, and dictation was difficult. I did not send your first article for corrections, because it could not appear in this issue. Since your second article had already been sent in, the matter was taking too long which perhaps would have made you still more impatient. I read the galleys attentively myself, so I hope that I did not miss any typos. I think that one comment, dealing with Sinclair's nervous breakdown, was superfluous, because the tone is moderate and incontestable. The second article will be sent to the printer today and I'll send it to you punctually. I hope that I've acted in accordance with your wishes.

---

38 Hilferding was reading Bauer's *Kapitalismus und Sozialismus nach dem Weltkrieg: Rationalisierung, Fehlrationalisierung* (*Capitalism and Socialism after the World War: Rationalization and Flawed Rationalization*) published in 1931.

In regard to your book [*War and Democracy*], I had talked with [Paul] Hertz. The issue was not discussed in the party executive, because Hertz had talked about the matter with Wels personally. There is no difference of opinion that Dietz-Verlag must publish the work. The difficulty comes only from the scope of the work given the tight financial situation not only of the publishing house, but also of the party. Since Hertz has a reputation in the private sector, I let him do the negotiating. The recommendation that resulted from that is, indeed, not great, but perhaps you can consider it.

Otherwise, [the situation] is terribly unsatisfactory. My morale is so bad that even the expulsion of Rosenfeld gives me no pleasure!![39] It is a pity that the opposition is so miserable that one can hardly get worked up enough to argue with it. It would have been better had the matter been handled somewhat differently, but even Victor Adler said that the mantle of Christian charity was missing from our party cloak room. On the other hand, it was hard to deal with these people. I don't foresee any particularly dangerous consequences, although the strife with the totally disoriented youth will intensify.

But the basic evil in this situation is that we can't say anything concrete to the people about how and by what means we can end the crisis. The blow to the capitalist system extends beyond anything we expected, but the solution to the credit crisis can only be expected from France and the United States, where we have little or no influence. I fear that the intervention of their financial power, a drastic [action] that would be necessary to solve the English and German credit crisis through the sweeping consolidation of their floating debts, will fail due to the fear of large gold transfers. That is, naturally, a possible solution along purely capitalist lines. A socialist solution is not present, and that makes the situation extremely difficult and allows the Communists and National Socialists to continue to grow. The political situation grows increasingly critical, because, by itself, the fight for the maintenance of democracy no longer satisfies the psychological needs of the broad masses. The Brüning government will now be powerfully assailed from the right, and I see the great danger of our people losing their nerve and playing Hugenberg's game. [That is] because our bringing down the government would drive the Reich President

---

39   Kurt Rosenfeld (1877–1943) joined the SPD in 1899 and practiced law In Berlin. Attracted to the SPD's pre-war left wing, he opposed the war, joined the USPD, and returned to the SPD in 1922. After the Revolution of 1918, he served briefly as Prussian Minister of Justice and was elected to the Reichstag from 1920–1932. A vocal member of the SPD's left-wing opposition, he was expelled in September of 1931 for violating party discipline and voting against his own delegation on the defense budget. He co-founded the Socialist Workers' Party and was elected its chairman in October.

and the [Catholic] Center Party much further to the right and toward the formation of a right-wing government with far greater powers than would be the case if it were the other way around and the right brought Brüning down. It is increasingly doubtful if a right-wing government can be avoided at all, though I am still of the opinion that one must attempt this even at great cost. I find it very difficult, personally, because of the absence of [Hermann] Müller's calm deliberation. You see, it is pretty bleak.

I can't say much about the Russian matter. I have not dealt with the question more intensively. I basically share your view and am extraordinarily skeptical. What those people are now doing is essentially mercantilism with all the accompanying misery of the early period of capitalism. I also have no idea how, after creating so many factories making means of production, the adjustment of the consumer goods industries should occur without major shocks [to the system]. But people will only believe that when they feel it. And I think it is more than doubtful that anything democratic will come of it.

And now please accept my somewhat early but very heartfelt good wishes for your birthday. May the next year bring the completion of your work and continue to give you the astounding energy that you have maintained. Best greetings [to you] and Luise. Rose sends her best.

Your,
    Rudolf

[P.S.] Dear Karl,

The [plan] mentioned above was already realized when your card arrived. The article was already typeset (on September 20), and I thought you would prefer that the answer followed right away rather than a month later. Should you find it absolutely necessary, you could come back to the second article on the description of the war and add a note or concluding remark. By the way, I must concede that I did not know that G writes political articles and German papers hardly deal with him as a politician. So, don't be mad. I believed I was fulfilling your intentions.

Your,
    Rudolf

(KDXII 654)

> November 23, 1931
> Reichstag
> Berlin NW 7

Dear Karl,

I could not answer your letter until today, because I was in Dresden. I have received a request to contribute to the commemorative volume for [Julius] Wolff [sic],[40] but I said no due to lack of time. Therefore, I did not need to solve the problem for myself of whether a socialist could participate or not. It would have been the same for me as for you: recently, Wolff [sic] had not expressed himself in any way against us. At the moment, he does not play a large role in the public consciousness. On the other hand, his earlier positions were not very apt. I cannot really give you conclusive advice.

Best regards to you and yours.
Your,
Rudolf

(KDXII 655)

> December 21, 1931
> *Die Gesellschaft*
> Berlin NW 6
> Schiffbauerdamm 26

Dear Karl,

Herr Dr. Kröner assailed me on account of your contribution to the commemorative volume for Julius Wolff [sic]. I already wrote to you that I rejected participating due to lack of time. Recently, Wolf's attitude has been quite progressive in

---

[40] Julius Wolf (1862–1937) was a well-known economist who taught at the Universities of Zürich and Breslau among others. Although he supervised Rosa Luxemburg's dissertation, he sharply criticized Marxism and socialism. He co-founded the *Zeitschrift für Sozialwissenschaften* (*Journal of the Social Sciences*) in 1898 and the International Society for Sexual Research in 1913.

regard to both foreign and domestic policy, and he stood up not only for a German understanding with France but also – and that requires more courage – with Poland. I know of no statements about social policy and similar matters to which we could object. At most what remains is what is past. I don't know if that is a satisfactory reason to withdraw the contribution.

Whatever is new here you can learn from the newspapers, and you can see my own political view in the January edition of the *Gesellschaft*. I hope that you agree. Whether Hitler comes to power is, above all, a matter of Brüning's nerve and that of the Center [Party]. The evangelical bourgeoisie lost its nerve long ago. By the way, the type of rabble one now has to deal with in politics is really outrageously depressing. Economically, it is no less grotesque; if the paralysis in the credit mechanism and the shutdown of world trade lasts much longer, one has no idea what can happen. But something good and reasonable cannot emerge from this kind of revolution.

I'm sending you a lecture that I recently gave on the crisis. Of course, it only is only a sketch; perhaps I will be able to expand it into a small pamphlet. Give a copy to Karl and Bendel. I did not have any more available for Felix.

Now, I wish happy holidays and a happy New Year to you, Luise, the boys and all of their wives.

With best wishes, also from my wife,
　Your,
　Rudolf

(KDXII 656)

February 27, 1932
Reichstag
Berlin NW 7

Dear Karl,

At last I have a chance to write to you. You can't be annoyed – this time everything happened at once. In particular, Rose had [to do] a translation, so I was robbed of my secretary. Moreover, I have never not published an article of yours in the *Gesellschaft* at the earliest possible time. This time, too, I sent the article right to the printer, and I cannot help it that some time passed before the print shop had it ready, because, after all, the editorial deadline was on February 20. I also had it set to allow for the text's possible use in the pamphlet and

I kept Hertz apprised, because I knew that he has been corresponding with you. Therefore, again, don't be mad, and be sure that what you want to have published, will – to the extent it is possible, and it is always possible – be published.

Concerning your question about the position on reparations, there are of course no differences [between us]. The issue has now become a purely political one and, at the moment, because of the clear declaration that we will pay nothing, we are at a dead end. A national psychosis now holds sway on this issue, and it has taken hold of some of our [own] people, especially the trade unions. I could have envisioned a "final solution", which would have included no payments during the crisis and would have made possible a low-cost settlement with the French. In every respect, that would have been much cheaper than the continuation of German-French tension, which makes any solution of the currency and trade crises, and, therefore, of the world crisis itself, almost impossible. In principle, of course, it would be most sensible to end reparations entirely. This is also the position you've adopted. But, in practical terms, taking this position strengthens the nationalist currents even more. For that reason, I have certain reservations. At the moment, for us as a party, the question is also very sensitive. We are going along with Brüning's declaration that we cannot pay, but, of course, we have to avoid everything that goes beyond that and makes any agreement impossible. Indeed, how this will be at all possible is a mystery to me, and, therefore, also [explains] my rather pessimistic view of the next development.

We are now concerned with defeating Hitler. It won't be easy, and the outcome is not certain. If Hindenburg wins decently in the first round, it could be a decisive success. However, I have two fears: firstly, that the very timid government will not take advantage of the success, and, secondly, that the worsening of the economic situation will place the political success again in question. How an improvement can occur here, given the insanity of the international policy, cannot be seen at present.

I hope you are all doing well. Rose and I are doing passably well, but we need a rest. I have not had a vacation in two years. Best regards to you and yours.

Your,
    Rudolf

(KDXII 657)

March 16, 1932
Die Gesellschaft
Berlin NW 6
Schiffbauerdamm 26

Dear Karl,

The proofs are enclosed. I am not completely sure if I can publish the article in the next issue, but I hope to do so. There is one issue with which I am not fully comfortable. Today, Engels's judgement of Lassalle can only be upheld with certain reservations. In any case, in the current situation, such assertions only provide fodder for the National Socialists and also have a terrible effect on our own youth. I don't know if it would be possible – while maintaining the Marxist critique – for you to nevertheless say something about Lassalle's great historical achievement. After all, Marx had expressed himself very differently about Lassalle in public, especially in his obituary. So, perhaps you could insert a few lines somewhere.

The elections went well, and the party performed marvelously.[41] The thing would have been decisive if, as a consequence of continued disruption of trade policy, economic conditions had not continued to worsen.

Best regards to your all.
Your,
Rudolf

(KDXII 658)

December 1, 1932
Düsseldorf

Dear Karl,

Thanks very much for your article. It is, indeed, somewhat long and I want to ask if you'd be very annoyed if I recommended some cuts, which in my view

---

[41] Although the SPD's support fell slightly between the elections of July and November 1932, the Nazis' decline from 37 percent in July to 33 percent in November indicated to many that their support was beginning to ebb.

would be easy to make without weakening the argument.[42] It would then be easier for me to publish the article in the January edition. I would have the article typeset with the cuts and, where you did not agree [with them], you could restore the original text.

More difficult is the issue with Bienstock.[43] I had told him that I would not publish the article. In my view it is very confusing and adds nothing to the party's frame of mind other than the general sense of "democracy being shaken". However, his position in favor of the referendum and against parliamentarianism has no resonance at all, so I could not see much promise in that discussion. Bienstock then sent the article to *Der Kampf*. After I received your letter, however, I became somewhat doubtful [of my view], because an assertion from you on the basic issue would be very valuable. But I fear this would be sidelined by its association with Bienstock, who would also like to precipitate an argument about pre-war policy. Would it not be more fruitful if you would say something, perhaps in connection with Otto Bauer's remarks at the party congress or completely independently, about your thoughts on Bienstock's argument? Because [otherwise] I don't really see the use in publishing Bienstock's article.

At the time of this writing, I am in Düsseldorf and Essen at meetings, it is difficult to discern the political situation. If we get a Schleicher government and Papen is finally out of the way, then perhaps there will be a certain easing of tension. By the way, I share your view entirely and completely oppose making allowances for the undeniable nervousness in some party circles. The situation is, indeed, very disturbing, the fascist danger still threatens, and the growth of the Communists unsettles our people all the more, because further advances in this direction would bring the great danger that the Communists' attractiveness would grow as soon as they overtook us numerically. It is not pretty, but adventurist mistakes would make things even worse.

Best regards to all!
As ever
Your,
Rudolf

---

42   The article under discussion is Kautsky's "Heinrich Braun. Ein Beitrag zur Geschichte der deutschen Sozialdemokratie" ("Heinrich Braun's Contribution to the History of Social Democracy"). See Kautsky 1933, pp. 155–72.

43   Gregor Bienstock (1885–1954) was born in St. Petersburg and educated in Germany. A Bolshevik from 1904 until 1907, he later became a Menshevik, went into exile in Germany in 1922, and was active in Social Democratic politics.

(KDXII 659)

December 9, 1932
Reichstag
Berlin NW 7

Dear Karl,

The proofs are enclosed. You see that the thing has gotten very long and my cuts were not enough. I'd be very grateful to you if you could undertake some more cuts. The next editions of the *Gesellschaft* will be extraordinarily overloaded, the March edition must be mostly a Marx-edition, and in the January and February editions I will have to take up the party's tactical debates, because the party congress is scheduled for March, about which I am in any case fearful that it will be pretty confused. Therefore, I would be extraordinarily pleased to have more space.

Having once more read Bienstock's article, I cannot decide in favor of publishing it. [This is] not because of the ideas expressed in it, but rather because the ideas are of no relevance to the current situation. I need the *Gesellschaft* for the discussion of problems that are likely to play a role at the party congress and the problem of authoritarian democracy certainly has no place there. After all, we have some possibilities for referenda and plebiscites in the constitution and practice has ensured that there has been very little use of them. For a moment it may have seemed that, as parliament grew weaker, the referendum could have taken on a more important role, but that [moment] seems to be over. On the other hand, I would be very pleased if you wanted to express your ideas on this subject in the *Gesellschaft* without polemicizing further.

Now, concerning the articles sent to Stein, I consider the "Die Überlegenheit des Marxismus über seine Vorläufer" ("The Superiority of Marxism over its Predecessors"), as more appropriate and, consequently, I'm returning the others to you as well.[44] To be honest, I had wished that you'd written an article for this particular purpose with a length of six to eight printed pages and I'd like to inquire again whether it might not be possible, even if it took a few days longer. When not, then we'll print the article you sent, even if Stein thinks that some cuts have to be considered due to the lack of space. At the same time, I

---

44 This work eventually appeared in a collection of essays published on the occasion of the fiftieth anniversary of Marx's death. See Walther Biehahn, ed., *Gedenkschrift: Marx der Denker und Kämpfer* (Berlin: J.H.W. Dietz, 1933), 41–53.

would like to ask you if you possibly could write an article about Marx for the March edition of the *Gesellschaft* that was not too long. I think that would be terrific.⁴⁵

I am very curious about your article on Bauer, which I would have very much liked to have published in the *Gesellschaft*. But perhaps you will write about the problem for us sometime.

Now I have to go, because I'm summoned to vote.

Best regards to you all,
   Your,
   Rudolf

---

45   Kautsky's article, "Marx und Marxismus", appeared in *Die Gesellschaft* 10, 3 (1933), 181–200. It was the last issue of the magazine, which ceased publication after the Nazi seizure of power.

CHAPTER 5

Hilferding to Kautsky, 1933–38

(KDXII 660)

April 13, 1933
Hotel Terminus
Vitznau (Vierwaldstättersee)

Dear Karl,

I've been wanting to write to write to you for some time, since the day I received *Der Kampf* with your article [on the Soviet Union] and the reply by Fritz [Adler].[1] He came here a few days later and we also talked about it. I was unable, however, to write to tell you that I share your basic point of view and only have my doubts about your optimism in regard to the possibilities for the future development of democracy. Like you, from the beginning I have regarded Bolshevism and its effects [as] the greatest danger and the Bolshevik seizure of power as a counterrevolutionary fact for the rest of the world, and we were quite right. So much has happened since receiving the article that everything else retires into the background. Everything is so difficult and so meaningful that, despite having enough time to think about it, I can't form a concrete picture of our defeat's historical significance and of what conclusions are to be drawn from it. Only it seems to me that the conclusions will be sweeping, and this will affect some of our basic views. This does not relate to Marxist theory, of course, but rather to our political conduct. And, again, here [I] am [referring] not to our tactical approach in recent years, which, in spite of the final fiasco was unavoidable and correct. In any case, any other policy would not have had a different result, as both the wholly different approach in Italy and the ongoing difficulties in Austria show. In many ways they remind us of our situation under Papen, and I very much fear a similar result in spite of the incomparable weakness of the Austrian ruling classes. However, we have underestimated the will of the working class to preserve democracy at all costs and to place the political [sphere], freedom, over the material one. The most depressing thing is the ease with which fascism won and consolidated its victory. The first act

---

1 See Kautsky 1933, pp. 58–69.

of the seizure of power is now over and the second act has begun. During it, fascism will stabilize its dictatorship. It has not only taken over state power, but also the economic organizations. First, the bourgeois [ones]. Germany's entire, expansive organizational apparatus has been placed under the leadership of the party, from the National Association of Industry, the chambers of commerce and agriculture, [and] the rural organizations, to the organizations of government officials, employees, teachers, etc. It will soon be the turn of the trade unions, as soon as one has agreed upon the form of their domination, and all of the desperate attempts of the functionaries will be of no use. The party still has a little bit of apparent room for maneuver; it is not banned – not yet. Individuals can still move around without hindrance, perhaps hold conferences, etc. I believe that will also soon be over. But as long as that is the case, it makes psychological sense for it to do everything [it can] to preserve this remnant, hence the individual, humiliating steps that have been taken. This is, however, only a transition stage and what happens there is of little importance. Only when that is over and the situation has clarified itself definitively will the new tasks emerge, and I only hope to have the chance to become active again in response to that, because the inactivity is maddening.

In a purely physical sense, I am okay since the worst of the depression passed. Also, my wife arrived on Saturday, which was a great relief. I look at the future pretty pessimistically. The thing could last a long time. Economically, despite everything, they will be pretty cautious. So far, they have not done anything special financially [...]. With the power of the state and of the organizations in their hands, they don't have to do much. And in foreign affairs it seems that England will help them reach a compromise, which, as bad as it might be, they can call a major success. All experience shows that resistance is extraordinarily difficult against a state power that has seized control of all organizations. The issue we are concerned with here is now less about Germany's fate than that of the western democracies, and I fear that the ideology we have maintained thus far will greatly hinder a realistic understanding of the situation [domestically] and also in relation to foreign policy.

I hope you are all doing tolerably well and ask [that you write] a few lines. Perhaps you might tell Otto [Bauer] about the content of my letter. Give him my best regards. He can also probably tell you a few things. Please write to Fritz [Adler]'s address. My very best regards to you, Luise, and the boys from your old,

Rudolf

(KDXII 661)

Zürich, September 23, 1933

Dear Karl,

As I said to you in Vienna, I have very limited space in the journal. I feel guilty, though, because unfortunately in my own article I went over the limit that I myself had imposed. But I had to use the introductory article to make the objective situation clear, and I could not do that more succinctly.[2] In any case, I had to defer the discussion of controversial problems, because that would have been way beyond the available space. With a total of 32 pages available, I have to maintain essentially a six-page limit for the articles. In addition, I have concerns about giving so much space to an argument with such a little-known pamphlet.[3]

I am in almost complete agreement with your comments. I think that a change of emphasis is needed in only one point. Our policy in Germany after 1923 was certainly more or less unavoidable due to the situation and could not have been much different. At that time, another policy would scarcely have led to a different result. But in the period after 1914, and especially from 1918 until the Kapp Putsch, politics were plastic and the worst errors were made at that time. We said that then and we don't need to take anything back now. In my view, this is not about simply being right. Nor is it about condemning the right-wing socialist leadership. It was a failure of the working class itself, [the actions of which] certainly are explainable by the historical situation, but which cannot remain uncriticized if one wants to combat the German working masses' lack of a will to freedom and repeated capitulation to nationalism. Leipart[4]

---

2   Writing under the pseudonym of Richard Kern, Hilferding published, "Die Zeit und die Aufgabe", ["The Time and the Task"] to introduce the inaugural issue of the exile SPD leadership's new theoretical journal *Sozialistische Revolution*. The magazine was later renamed the *Zeitschrift für Sozialismus* (ZfS).

3   Kautsky was responding to a recently published pamphlet called *Neu Beginnen!* [New Beginning!] by Walter Löwenheim (1896–1977), who used the pseudonym Miles. Löwenheim had joined the KPD in 1919 but moved to the SPD in 1929. Frustrated with the KPD's sectarianism and the SPD's increasingly bourgeois makeup, in 1929 he founded a clandestine "Leninist Organization", which, attempted to recruit cadre from virtually all the existing socialist organizations with the goal of creating a new, revolutionary party. Renamed Neu Beginnen after Hitler's seizure of power, the group eventually grew to about 500 members but dissolved due to differences over strategy in 1935. Miles then called upon his supporters to adhere to the Sopade.

4   Theodor Leipart (1867–1947) became the leader of Germany's social democratic trade union association (ADGB) in 1921 and shortly thereafter the chief of the International Association

and Löbe[5] are totally representative, but that is exactly why one should not cover up the German Social Democratic past with the cloak of Christian charity. You will find some discussions of this subject, however incomplete, in the journal.

So, don't be annoyed if I send the article back to you. I will be very happy, when you intervene in the discussion and everything that appears in the magazine is up for debate.

Otherwise, there is nothing new with me. Austria is now starting to become sinister.

Best regards, also from Rose, to you all.
Your,
Rudolf

(KDXII 662)

Zürich, October 15, 1934

My dear Karl,

Elsewhere I've tried to tell the public some of what there is to say [about you].[6] I was not completely successful, because that would have meant having to present the entire scope of the history of the socialist idea, in the shaping of which you had a large part, after Marx and Engels by far the largest, to a generation which knows less and less and has increasingly less desire to know more. In the struggle against eclecticism and against opportunism from the left and the right, your work before the war created the solidity and uniformity of the socialist outlook which guaranteed its superiority. It maintained such strong authority, even after the war, which so abruptly interrupted and so com-

---

of Free Trade Unions. Following Hitler's appointment to the Chancellorship he attempted to salvage some form of union autonomy by accommodating the regime but was arrested along with the rest of the union leaders on May 2 and only released after being beaten severely and hospitalized.

5   Paul Löbe (1875–1967), chief editor of the *Breslauer Volkswacht* (1900–1920). Elected to the National Assembly in 1919 and to the Reichstag from 1920–1933, he served as its President from 1924–1932. His efforts to preserve the SPD's legality by making concessions to some of Hitler's policies resulted in conflict with the SPD exile leadership. He was arrested in June 1933 and released in December.

6   See Richard Kern (Hilferding) 1934, pp. 369–75.

pletely undermined the work already carried out, that it seemed to friend and foe alike merely a matter of course that Social Democracy would take power. The violence of the war and the chaos of the split deeply wounded the conception and authority of socialism, but all the greater is the admiration of your work, through which you untiringly strive toward the resurrection of a socialism, which is not based on the belief in violence as the bringer of miracles and the blessings of dictatorship, but rather on discernment and knowledge and on the will of humanity.

But today I am driven to think not only about general and historical matters, but also about personal ones and to tell you how much I owe you and how your friendship has enriched me. Intellectually, even as a young lad I felt more closely bound to you than anyone else through the *Neue Zeit*, and this bond has become ever closer since the first time I approached you in person with that respectful shyness that was still present in the younger generation at that time. The respect is still there but bound up with friendship and love that grow ever stronger. And I can certainly say that, though there may have been differences in detail on some matters of approach to individual things and individual moments, our views were also most closely bound together and today I feel I stand as close to you as ever. And since the most beautiful time of my life was when as I was learning and working in Berlin and felt like a son and friend in your home, I'm always pained to think of how much I've lost as a result of the geographic distance between us. How annoying it is that I can't shake hands with you tomorrow; how lamentable these times are in which this day cannot be celebrated as a proud holiday in the whole socialist world.

Be well, Karl, and I wish you the very best on your eightieth birthday. You know that the best of us today are with you in spirit and only desire that we may continue to receive your advice and knowledge for a long time to come. You can also think of them, when you spend the day with your and our Luise and with the "boys", and not for a moment should you forget, that you have accomplished great things and your life's work will bear fruit.

With my very best regards,
 Your,
 Rudolf

(KDXII 663)

Postcard to Karl and Luise Kautsky
July 30, 1935
Adelboden, Switzerland

Warmest greetings from our little convalescence tour. From here I'm going to my mother's and either on the way or on the way back I'll stop in Vienna for a day just to see you. Meanwhile, very best regards from your

Rose H[ilferding]

Dear Karl, [my] very best regards to you, Luise, and the boys. I'll be back in Zürich on 6 August.

Your,
    Rudolf

(KDXII 664)

Postcard, August 18, 1935
Brussels

Dear Karl,

Thanks very much for your warm letter, which made me very happy. I completely agree with your remarks about W. I was also very pleased about the publication of your correspondence with Engels. I hope you and Luise are doing well. Warmest regards to all!

Your,
    Rudolf

(KDXII 665)

September 30, 1935
Touring Hotel Garni
Zürich

Dear Karl,

I am extremely sorry that I've annoyed you, but I am really innocent, and it is clear that we are dealing here with misunderstandings, about which there is nothing I can do, but which are connected to the objective difficulties of achieving agreement under today's circumstances.[7]

When the thing arrived, I prepared it right away and sent it to Graphia. In doing so I decided to forego what I myself had planned [to publish], which was made good later on. Meanwhile, Paul [Hertz], to whom I'd also written on the matter, was in Vienna and perhaps had not yet received the letter. I had to assume that you would come to an understanding with Paul. In addition, after I had taken care of the issue in the sense *you* intended and thought I was finished with it, I heard from Paul that [Max] Klinger will take over the matter, about which I assumed you and Paul were in agreement and no further action was required. My own role in this affair was limited to dealing with it in the sense you intended. I had no part in making the change, the possibility of which I hadn't even considered. To redress the matter now would, nevertheless, hardly be possible because it would probably already be too late.

Dear Karl, I cannot ever remember having hindered you and today less than ever. This time, too, it did not enter my head for a moment, although I found your outlook disconcerting, especially at this point in time because it collides with facts on the ground. So, I hope that you can take back the "in spite of everything" and greet me again without reservation.

Concerning the matter itself, I agree with you on the basics as you stated them in your recent letter, which pleased me very much. But I am not as optimistic as you; I lack your sense of history, which allows you also to relativize defeats more easily. I am basically quite pessimistic. This pessimistic attitude actually goes back to 1917, grew stronger in 1917 (Moscow!), and really set in after 1918. Of course, there were interruptions, but they silenced my doubts only temporarily. I don't really believe in the capacity of uniform conceptions, also dur-

---

7 The discussion concerns an article by Kautsky on the issue of the united front. See Kautsky 1935, pp. 825–38.

ing the storm of war, and [I don't really believe] in the means of creating them. The main concern is to prevent war. Thus, at the decisive moment, the key parties, the French and the English (ideologically, however, almost all the others as well) failed completely. Today it is not much better. It is certainly progress when the L[abor] P[arty] allows Eden and Hoare to make foreign policy rather than Lansbury, but Blum, who was otherwise the International's best, was and remains confused and is practicing ever more emotional demagoguery in his foreign as well as in his domestic policy. There is no clear, *concrete* position. All possible oscillations are present between Tolstoian pacifism, an antiquated anti-militarism, the subordination to an idealized Soviet foreign policy, and the hope for a war of liberation. A concrete foreign policy of the French and English parties does not exist – the others don't matter at all and are merely followers of their respective governments. Nevertheless, only a real alliance between England and France could perhaps still save the peace, just as, if it had been concluded in time, it could have prevented the current chaos, for which the left parties and left governments are wholly responsible, while men like A[usten] Chamberlain[8] and [Winston] Churchill [...] have understood matters correctly and in a timely way. If I were an Englishman or a Frenchman today, I would in no way vote for the L[abor] P[Party] or the W[orkers'] P[arty]. Moreover, I would not vote for the French Socialists because of their "anti-capitalist" demagoguery, which will in the end make it possible for French fascism to become a real danger.

From this perspective, your article is too abstract and too mild, which of course would not have been a reason not to publish it.

Furthermore, internationalist sentiment has ebbed enormously. The working-class today is supporting a nationalist economic policy virtually everywhere; it is a representative, along with the peasants and the old middle class, of the most backward and economically restrictive demands. And in foreign policy I've had no illusions since 1914.

The situation is damned serious. Until a few months ago, I had resisted believing in a new general conflagration, but today it is getting damned close. I still have hope that the [political] turn in England might prevent war in Europe and that, in a competition between bankruptcy and war, bankruptcy reaches the finish line first. But that is not a sure thing, and it will be even less likely

---

8 Austen Chamberlain (1863–1937) was a long-time leader of the British Conservative Party, serving in Parliament and in many ministerial posts, including First Lord of the Admiralty (1931). Like Winston Churchill (1874–1965), who became Prime Minister in 1940, he was one of the few members of parliament to call for rearmament against the German threat in the mid-1930s.

if the Popular Front wins in France and throws the country into incalculable chaos.[9] This type of Socialist domestic policy kills any foreign policy. It has gotten to the point that today one must wish for stable conservative governments for England and especially for France.

I hope, Karl, that you don't get angry with me for my candor, but once in a while one really needs to vent, and you are, after all, my father confessor.

Be well. Warmest regards to you, Luise, and the boys. Don't be mad.
Your,
Rudolf

(KDXII 666)

Postcard, October 13, 1935
Brussels

Dear Karl,

Warmest best wishes for your health and your so admirable vigor. I am traveling from here to Paris, to the Hotel Langham at 19 Avenue de Friedland where I'll stay for about a week. I hope you received my lengthy letter. Best wishes to you, Luise, and the boys.

Your,
Rudolf

(KDXII 667)

Postcard, November 16, 1935
Zürich

Dear Karl,

Thanks very much. Your acquaintance has already left for Carlsbad. He left part of his luggage behind, however, but I still think it will work out.

---

9 The Popular Front was a coalition of the French Radical, Socialist, and Communist parties which came to power in 1936 and governed until 1938. Under Leon Blum's leadership, it intro-

I hope you are feeling well again. One needs to be careful with such eczema. I got quite a fright, when I read the first sentences from Luise, but in every respect you are amazingly indestructible. Nikolaevsky has told you some interesting stuff and I am glad that in this matter, too, we are in agreement. I should also think of Bendel.

Forgive the card, but I did not want you to have to wait any longer. Warmest regards to all of you.

Your,
Rudolf

(KDXII 668)

April 29, 1936
Touring Hotel Garni
Zürich

My dear Karl,

I was very glad to once again receive a few lines from you. After London (Executive), I was in Paris, but not because of the [Marx-Engels] archive. I did not participate in the negotiations, about which I was just as glad as you. I don't fully share your view; I think that neither side behaved very well. But that is now over, and the negotiations ended unsuccessfully. In spite of all the information, I don't really know why. I regret that very much, first of all for political reasons, since the continued ⌊production⌋ of the works becomes increasingly difficult, and also for personal ones, because my expectation of again being able to undertake scholarly work has come to naught. To me it is doubtful that it will come to new negotiations.

In regard to your issue, I haven't heard anything from Paul yet. I will be happy to take it up, even though it collides with my own intention. But that does not matter.

For the rest, I am very depressed about how things have developed and, therefore, I will gladly make use of your permission to not write a long letter. I would so much like to talk with you. Paul wrote to me about how fresh and

---

duced a series of radical economic and social reforms very favorable to workers but refused to intervene on the side of the republic in the Spanish Civil War.

busy you are, but I don't know when I will again have the opportunity for that. Hopefully, it won't be too long.

Letters always reach me via the Touring Hotel, because they are forwarded. In any case, I will be staying here for a while.

Best regards to Luise, you, and the boys.
   Your,
   Rudolf

(KDXII 668)

September 2, 1937
Touring Hotel Garni
Zürich

Dear Karl!

Thank you so much for your letter. I value your remarks not only for their valuable stimulation and significant support, but also for their encouragement. This is because it is very important to me to know that I'm in agreement with you on most things. I've never feared the truth, and I believe that "non-conformism", as one calls it now, the rebellion against received opinion, dogmas, and simplistic conception, forms a part of the essence of my way of thinking. Perhaps the only advantage that the exiles have is that of complete independence and the liberation from the considerations that every active politician has to weigh. But that does not exclude one's fear of being on the wrong path, when one has to face conclusions that deviate substantially from one's long held conceptions. It is very encouraging to me that you confirm that I have seen the problems themselves correctly, and that you, too, are working on them.

Today I don't intend to respond to your letter in detail. That also isn't really necessary because I essentially agree with your remarks. So, let's deal solely with what you say about class analysis. Here, however, we are talking about two things: firstly, the analysis of class strata objectively, as they emerge from economic tendencies but then [also] from the repercussions of politics (which we have perhaps underestimated) on the preservation of social strata; secondly, the examination of the extent to which what we understood as class consciousness – indeed as a psychologically imperative result of a certain objective situation – actually must arise. It seems to me that, in regard to both points, the Marxist perspective must be considered anew. If one wants to take on the whole thing scientifically, in other words to do it in a way that is unassailable, that requires a new analysis of capitalist development at least since 1914, and it would be a large-scale and difficult work which also involves a new investigation of the "foundation". I am still very far from "formulations", because I would take on the whole enterprise without presuppositions. To me, the results to which one would arrive are not yet at all discernable. It is precisely this doubt about what positive results are possible that is somewhat discouraging.

This is a preliminary confirmation of the receipt [of your letter]. I was so happy to get the letter and with the personal warmth that emanated from it, about which I had never doubted. I have no copy of my letter. I would be very grateful to Frau Luise if it would not be too much trouble to have one made and to send it to me. My very best greetings to you, Luise, and the boys. My desire to be with you is surely greater than yours, but one has become, after all, in cruel ways the slave of circumstances. Nevertheless, I hope to see you in the not too distant future.

Your,
    Rudolf

[P.S.] I'd be grateful for a brief confirmation of receipt.

(KDXII 669)

October 15, 1937
Touring Hotel Garni
Zürich

My dear Karl,

My very best wishes for your birthday! I am just starting to study your latest work, which has riveted me and given me much to think about.[10] More about that later, when I'm done. The awful newspaper reading, which is indispensable, takes up too much of my time and attention. For today, just the wish that your amazing ability to work and your energy remain unchanged and that your expectations are soon fulfilled.

---

10   The reference ist to Kautsky's *Sozialisten und Kriege* [*Socialism and War*], published in 1937.

Indeed, your book is all the more topical since the question of war dominates everything and suppresses everything else. What passionate engagement the socio-political progress and experiments in France would have encountered in other periods! Today, it is much more important whether and how France can resist Italian and German attack, and the fate of Minorca is much more important than the forty-hour week. In that regard it is tragic how the foreign policy of Labor and the French Socialists has totally failed. Then there is the objective situation: for England and France the issue of war and current foreign policy are not class or party issues, because all classes have the same interest in the victory of these *states*, with which the fate of democracy and culture are intertwined. The policy of the workers' movement has been reduced, therefore, to that of daily material concerns, while on the great and decisive issues it has become an appendage of the government, if not, as in Belgium for example, the leading element of a dangerous and reactionary policy of isolationism. What is necessary is to think about our great ideals and, hopefully, your book will contribute to that. That is turns out that way is my wish for your birthday.

My very, very warmest regards to you, Luise, and the boys!
Your,
Rudolf

(KDXII 670)

November 5, 1937
Hotel Touring Garni
Zürich

Dear Karl!

It has been a long time since I've heard from you and Luise. I hope that you received my last letter (for your birthday). I'm reading your book with great interest and feel, at least intellectually, as close to you as ever. I've stopped in the middle, however, because the journalistic work has slowed me down a bit. If nothing interferes, I hope to finish it in about ten days. I can already see, however, that you have succeeded not only in writing a comprehensive history of ideas concerning one of the most important aspects of socialist intellectual development – not only relation to war but, going further, also in relation to foreign policy – but, at the same time, despite all efforts to stay focused [on the ideas themselves], you also have made clear their objective causes. The book is extremely topical and is exciting to read. If one reads the book with discernment, one can learn a lot from it. The evidence supports your thesis that, with the expansion of war into people's or mass war, which is still developing steadily and rapidly, the next war will largely eliminate the last differences between combatants and civilians and will primarily have reactionary-nationalist effects, rather than revolutionary-progressive ones. The same can be said concerning the criticism that you direct against the illusions of civil war. It also does one good to read a book that is not filled with propaganda, but rather with scholarly seriousness and with such a relentless love of truth. The book gives you so much to think about, such as the limits of the use of the materialist conception of history, and I also found your occasional remark very interesting, where you talk about the great simplicity of the notion that all history is the history of class antagonisms, a formulation to which Marx himself only rarely succumbed. Indeed, the state apparatus and its interests are a factor which is gaining autonomy, especially in moments of dictatorship, when dominant interests strive to subjugate other social interests – often with decisive success in historically critical situations.

Violence, too, as Marx understood very well, is an often decisive but also unpredictable factor, but modern war in particular is gaining independent potency. With its heavy weight, it temporarily flattens all class differences, and it has economic, psychological, and, therefore, political effects that cannot be derived simply from the class relations of the pre-war period. The sociological determinism that undergirds the Marxist outlook remains correct, but it is much more complicated than the vulgar [Marxists] ever dreamed. In the next war, if it comes, these specific systems of laws, accidents of the total state's policy, and the results of total war will be of much greater influence on concrete historical development than the strivings of classes. Therefore, you are absolutely right to reject the ideologies of war and revolution. Whether it will come to war, who can say? But that one cannot say it – before 1914 it was easier to foresee, even if that war was not "necessary", just as today eliminating war, from a class standpoint, is a real necessity – shows how enormous the power of the total state has become and how weak the influence of classes. Because it is characteristic that everywhere where the classes have the possibility of political participation, a partially damaging, dumb, pacifist policy is pursued, while the dictatorial state's policy of war encounters no resistance worth mentioning.

But I won't write an essay for you here; perhaps I'll have occasion to do that after I finish reading. I just wanted to tell you how thankful I am for your talent and how highly I estimate its value.

Be well, Karl. All the best and warmest regards to you, Luise, and the boys, from your
    Rudolf

Part 2

FIGURE 4   Leon Trotsky in Vienna (sometime before 1915)
AUTHOR: UNKNOWN

CHAPTER 6

Introduction to Part 2: A Political Friendship?

Leon Trotsky is best known to the world as one of the architects of the Bolshevik Revolution of 1917.[1] An outstanding speaker, brilliant theorist, and masterful writer, Trotsky cut a dashing figure during the revolution, and his many works in Marxist theory and history, as well as those on politics and literature, continue to provide insights on both the past and the present. Working closely with V.I. Lenin, his erstwhile opponent in Russian Social Democracy's earlier factional squabbles, Trotsky played a decisive role in the overthrow of Kerensky's provisional government, as the revolutionary government's first Foreign Minister, and, most importantly, as the creator and leader of the Red Army during the Civil War. Later, after Lenin's death in 1924, he became Stalin's most important opponent in the struggle for power inside of the Communist Party. Trotsky and his allies were completely defeated in their efforts to reverse the concentration of authority in Stalin's hands. Driven out of the leadership, in 1927 he was expelled from the party and a year later sent into internal exile in Alma-Ata. In 1929 the Bolsheviks deported the unrepentant Trotsky to Turkey, and from there he wandered first to France, then to Norway, and finally to Mexico. Trotsky continued organizing against the regime until 1940 when an assassin sent by Stalin silenced him.

Trotsky, whose real name was Lyov Davidovich Bronstein, was born in 1879 in Yanovka (today Bereslavka), a rural settlement in Ukraine. His parents were prosperous Jewish farmers whose success enabled them to provide their son with a nanny. After attending a local Jewish elementary school, Lyov completed his secondary education at high schools in the cosmopolitan Black Sea ports of Odessa and Nikolaev. An outstanding student, he gravitated toward literature, but soon was swept up in the discussions of political and social revolution percolating among students in many of Russia's urban centers at the time. Initially, Trotsky was drawn toward the peasant-oriented populist movement, which viewed the use of terrorist methods as a viable means of overthrowing Tsarism. In 1897, however, under the influence of his soon-to-be first wife, Alexandra Sokolovskaya, he converted to Marxism. After beginning his studies in mathematics at the University in Odessa, he and Alexandra became involved

---

[1] There is a vast literature on Trotsky. For what follows I am relying primarily on Deutscher 2015; Trotsky 1984; Service 2009; and Volkogonov 1996.

in the local clandestine labor movement and were arrested. While in prison, first in Odessa and then in Moscow, he read widely, including Marxist literature, and married Alexandra. Sentenced in 1900 to four years in a colony near Siberia's Lake Baikal, the pair were soon parents to two daughters, but Trotsky chafed at their isolation. Determined to get involved in the activities of the newly founded Russian Social Democratic Labor Party (RSDLP), with Alexandra's agreement he escaped in the summer of 1902.

By early October Trotsky was knocking on Lenin's door in London. At that time, Lenin was a leading figure among a small group of Russian revolutionaries attempting to organize the fledgling RSDLP from exile in western Europe. Key to this project was the publication and underground distribution of their newspaper, *Iskra* (*The Spark*). Since during his years in exile Trotsky had already established a good reputation as a journalist – he was nicknamed "the pen" – Lenin initially welcomed his contributions and hoped to bring him onto the paper's editorial board. Like his colleague on the board, Julius Martov, Lenin recognized Trotsky's myriad talents as a writer and a speaker, but also that the new arrival still needed a bit of "schooling" especially on theoretical matters.[2] In contrast, Lenin's most important rival within the board, Georgi Plekhanov, disliked Trotsky, regarded him as a prima donna, and feared that his support would give Lenin a majority in *Iskra*'s factional squabbles. As a result, Trotsky's cooptation to the board was blocked.[3]

Trotsky's cooperation with Lenin did not last long. At the Second Party Congress, convened in Brussels at the behest of the *Iskra* board in July 1903, he came to oppose Lenin's rude, divisive and authoritarian behavior in the heated dispute over the party's definition of membership. Trotsky sided with Martov's "Menshevik" (minority) faction, which aimed to open the party to a broad membership of those who agreed with its principles, while Lenin's group, the "Bolsheviks" (majority), supported a narrower definition insisting that members also must actively work for one of its clandestine organizations.[4] The differences were not actually very great, but the debate degenerated into such

---

2 Service 2009, p. 72.
3 At the time, the six-member editorial board was divided between leaders of the older generation of Russian exiles, which included Georgi Plekhanov, Vera Zasulich, and Pavel Axelrod, and the younger generation that included Lenin, Julius Martov, and A.N. Potresov. On the makeup of the board and Plekhanov's antipathy to Trotsky see Deutscher 2015, pp. 69–73.
4 Which group actually had a majority depended on the moment and the issue. Martov's proposals on membership actually carried the day but, after the delegates of the Jewish Bund and other Menshevik allies, disgruntled by defeats on other issues, walked out of the meeting, Lenin's faction won a majority on the *Iskra* board. For an excellent summation of the Second Congress and its immediate aftermath see ibid., pp. 82–107.

hostility that the party never recovered. Going forward, the RSDLP's two factions effectively would function as separate and competing parties, despite several efforts to reunite them. Although Trotsky stood with the Mensheviks in Brussels, over the course of the next year he grew impatient with their openness to cooperation with liberals against the Tsar. Thus, he oscillated between the factions, a position he would maintain until 1917.

Meanwhile, early in 1903, on a visit to Paris, Trotsky met Natalya Sedova, a revolutionary who was then studying art at the Sorbonne and soon became his second wife. They had two sons and spent the rest of their lives together. Settling down, however, was not in the cards. Following the Brussels Congress, Trotsky left London for Geneva, where Plekhanov and other Mensheviks lived. When his personal and political differences with the Mensheviks made residing there untenable, he and Natalya moved to Munich, where they befriended the radical social democratic thinker, Alexander Helphand (Parvus), and lived for a time in his house. Parvus's ideas about revolution and the development of the world economy strongly influenced Trotsky, who later brought them to bear in his theory of "permanent revolution".[5] Developing that theoretical construct had to wait, however, as the outbreak of revolution drew him back to Russia in February 1905. Moving first to Kiev and then to St. Petersburg, Trotsky worked with Bolsheviks and Mensheviks during that tumultuous year of mass strikes, mass demonstrations, and street fighting in which, along with Parvus, he edited a major newspaper, the *Russian Gazette*, along with other publications. Most importantly, he became a major figure in the Petersburg Soviet of Workers' Deputies, in which, as a result of his energy and speaking ability, he rose to the Presidency. Trotsky believed that peasant Russia was experiencing a bourgeois-democratic revolution in which the land question stood at center stage. He thought that, under Social Democratic leadership, the working class, not the recalcitrant bourgeoisie, could lead the peasantry to complete the democratic revolution in Russia. In addition, depending on the balance of domestic class forces and the international situation, it could also begin with the implementation of socialist measures.[6]

But it was not to be. In early December the Tsarist military closed down the Soviet and arrested its members, including Trotsky. Tried for supporting armed rebellion, he defended himself energetically in court, but was again sentenced to exile in Siberia. In January 1907 he escaped in route, making his way to London in time for the Fifth Party Congress of the RSDLP in mid-May.

---

5 Ibid, 108–26; Scharlau and Zeman 1964, 72–77.
6 Trotsky 1984, p. 177.

According to Trotsky's memoirs, he and Hilferding first became acquainted when he visited Kautsky's house in the summer of 1907, but their correspondence shows that they had been in brief contact four years before.[7] There are 22 letters and postcards from Trotsky in Hilferding's papers. All but one were written after Trotsky's return to London. The outlier was a picture postcard of Maxim Gorky sent by Trotsky from Zürich on 11 November 1903, in which he thanks Hilferding for sending him copies of the *NZ* and compliments him for his recent article "The Functional Change of the Protective Tariff". The next contact for which we have evidence was written by Parvus on Trotsky's behalf in the early summer of 1907. It is a simple request for Hilferding to retrieve some items Trotsky had left behind at his landlord's after that first visit to Kautsky's. The most interesting thing about the letter was Trotsky's postscript, in which he apologizes for not writing himself due to his poor German. His lack of skill in the language, which did not last long, would be a sore point with Trotsky, who complained about it repeatedly in his early letters. In a note to Hilferding from 8 July 1907, he made clear that he intended to remedy this shortcoming over the course of the next month and vowed to return to Friedenau "fully armed".[8] Later that summer he wrote that, "you should always read my letters with the understanding that I am not nearly as dumb in the Russian language as in the German translation".[9]

Trotsky clearly disliked being at a disadvantage when dealing with Hilferding on complex matters, but the issue also had practical implications. While in Russia, Trotsky had published translated articles in the *NZ*, which, according to his memoirs, Hilferding had praised.[10] Once Trotsky was back in the West, Hilferding was in a position to help him earn his living by securing him continued access to the journal and to the large social democratic readership of German speaking Europe. Indeed, Trotsky was brimming with ideas about his theory of permanent revolution, as well as on Russian socio-economic and political development, but he was frustrated that the *NZ* did not accept articles in Russian. He was able to solve the problem by finding translators, which made it possible for the journal to publish eleven of his articles between 1908 and 1914.[11]

In his early letters Trotsky addressed Hilferding using formal salutations such as "Dear Doctor" and "Esteemed Comrade", along with the "Sie" form of you. Soon, however, he switched over to the informal, claiming later on that Hil-

---

7　Trotsky 1984, p. 212.
8　Trotsky to Hilferding, July 8, 1907, TH 2 (ISH).
9　Trotsky to Hilferding, August 31, 1907, TH 3 (ISH).
10　Trotsky 1906–07a; pp. 76–86 and 1906–07b, pp. 377–85.
11　Trotsky to Hilferding, August 31, 1907 and March 16, 1908, TH 3 & TH 8, resp. (ISH).

ferding, "quite unexpectantly [...] insisted from the very first" that they address each other as "Du". To modern day English speakers this might seem like a trivial matter, but, given the norms of Central European culture at the time, and the fact that it took Hilferding twenty years to address Kautsky informally, it may also say something about how Hilferding regarded his new Russian acquaintance. The two men seemed to have much in common. Roughly the same age, both were well-educated Marxist intellectuals who had abandoned their parents' Judaism, were living abroad, were newly married with young children, and regarded themselves as representatives of the revolutionary wings of their respective parties. Taking Trotsky at his word that the informality was at Hilferding's behest, it is possible that he saw this mode of address as a reflection of these commonalities and as a sign of mutual respect.

In any case, Hilferding was certainly very helpful to Trotsky. In addition to accepting his essays for publication in the NZ, he also helped him find temporary lodging in Vienna, where Trotsky and his family finally settled in the fall of 1907.[12] In 1907 and 1908 Trotsky sent Hilferding at least 14 letters and, its seems from his comments, most of these were answered. The two men visited one another in their respective cities, and Trotsky later noted that it was Hilferding who introduced him to the Austrian Marxists as they socialized in Vienna's cafes. In Berlin they even attended political demonstrations together, along with Kautsky, Rosa Luxemburg, and others.[13] Most of Trotsky's letters are cordial and concern his articles, his lack of money, and his efforts to adapt to Vienna, its press, and its politics. Early on Trotsky was at pains to catch the attention of Otto Bauer and Karl Renner, who seemed to be so busy with their own affairs that they paid him little mind. He expressed great admiration for Renner's publications in *Der Kampf* but thought that Bauer was too pedantic. Trotsky could be charming, but he was also arrogant and touchy. At one point he seems to chafe at Hilferding's condescension by remarking, "Sometimes I can also reach the heights upon which you stand in [our] correspondence. An eye for an eye."[14]

Trotsky could also be quite blunt in his judgements about his friend. After finding out that, in order to make ends meet, Hilferding had given up his post at the NZ, "a living part of the international", to take a job at *Vorwärts*, he expressed his shock and accused him of selling out "for a mess of pottage". This must have stung Hilferding, who not long before had been fulminating about the problem of careerism in the German party press. To soften the blow, Trotsky conceded

12   Trotsky to Hilferding, August 31, 1907, TH 3 (ISH).
13   Trotsky 1984, pp. 212–213, 220.
14   Trotsky to Hilferding, March 16, 1908, TH 8 (ISH).

that he, too, needed to make a living and had "lowered himself" to write on art and literature for a bourgeois paper in Odessa.[15] In any case, with Hilferding now at *Vorwärts*, Trotsky used the connection to write brief reports for the paper on events in Russia and the Balkans.

Of course, Trotsky was also keen to keep Hilferding appraised of relations between the factions of Russian Social Democracy. In July 1908 he made clear to his friend that, in the wake of the Tsarist counterrevolution in Russia, he was increasingly appalled at the RSDLP's continued division and especially at the behavior of the "rotting, toothless, Mensheviks", who were "sinking into the swamp of vulgar opportunistic prejudices".[16] Hoping to play the role of unifier, a few weeks later Trotsky wrote enthusiastically about his founding of a new bimonthly newspaper, *Pravda (Truth)*.[17] As he told his sponsors from the Ukrainian Social Democratic Union, "the newspaper must be a *workers' paper*, it must have a decidedly revolutionary outlook; it must stand above both factions; it must be *political* and not *polemical*, and its goal cannot be to establish a third fraction, but rather to maintain contact and political ties between the workers of both fractions".[18] In subsequent letters he described his efforts to promote the paper and complained that his "German comrade has no time to write for *Pravda*".[19] The latter remark, made in 1909, reveals a simmering resentment in Trotsky's attitude toward Hilferding that would eventually boil over.

Trotsky wrote few letters to Hilferding from 1910 until 1912, but the ones he did write focused on *Pravda*'s financial problems. Trotsky poured his heart and soul into *Pravda*, but it was a money loser from the beginning, and he kept it going only by plowing his own sparse income from writing into its operations, sometimes even selling his books or sending his wife to the pawn shop as a last resort. Loans from the SPD helped keep the paper afloat, and it actually achieved significant readership in Russia, but its finances were in perpetual crisis. In 1910, however, *Pravda*'s fortunes seemed to revive. In January of that year the Bolsheviks and Mensheviks met in Paris for another attempt at unity and, against the odds, cobbled together an agreement to disband their separate organizations, to merge into a single group, and to pool their financial resources, which would be placed temporarily under the trusteeship of a

---

15 Trotsky to Hilferding, March 24, 1908, TH 9 (ISH); idem. 1984, 212; Hilferding to Kautsky, October 30, 1905, KDXII 594 (ISH).
16 Trotsky to Hilferding, July 21, 1908, TH 13 (ISH).
17 Usually referred to as the Vienna Pravda to distinguish it from the one founded in St. Petersburg in 1912.
18 Trotsky to Hilferding, August 5, 1908, TH 14 (ISH).
19 Trotsky to Hilferding, undated letter, spring 1909, TH 15 (ISH).

INTRODUCTION TO PART 2: A POLITICAL FRIENDSHIP?

committee consisting of three German Socialists, Kautsky, Mehring, and Clara Zetkin. Best of all for Trotsky was that the arrangement recognized *Pravda* as the party's flagship and granted him a subsidy of 150 rubles per month. It seemed his troubles were over.[20]

Of course, it was too good to be true. Within weeks the agreement broke down and Trotsky found himself in the middle of heated recriminations from both sides. By the summer of 1910 the Central Committee had withdrawn its subsidy to *Pravda*. In reply, Trotsky assailed "the conspiracy of the [Bolshevik] émigré clique against the Russian Social Democratic Labor Party" and soon carried his attack into the German press, where he asserted that the émigré leaders no longer represented the real movement in Russia, a view that was not uncommon among underground workers at home. These accusations so infuriated the émigré leaders that, in October, the RSDLP's delegates to the Copenhagen Congress of the International attempted to take disciplinary against him, an effort that failed but left Trotsky wounded.[21]

This decision did not end the struggle, however, as both sides then sought to gain control over the funds administered by the German trustees. During the summer of 1911, Trotsky and the Menshevik, Pavel Axelrod, attended the SPD's Jena Congress where they attempted to make their case with the trustees. The discussions were secretive and complicated. Since Zetkin seemed friendly to the Bolsheviks, they concentrated their effort on winning Kautsky's support. He seemed sympathetic but, with Mehring sick, in the end no majority could be won to release the money, and nothing came of the venture. The split between the two factions was made permanent the following year when, at a conference in Prague, Lenin declared his faction to be the party and began publishing a new version of *Pravda* in Petersburg. Trotsky fulminated in the face of this theft of his paper's title but undertook no concrete steps to reverse the Bolshevik action.[22]

In a letter to Hilferding written in September 1911, Trotsky made clear that he felt abandoned by the Germans. He fumed at Zetkin's support for the Bolsheviks, claimed that the trustees had transferred significant funds to them, and blamed Rosa Luxemburg for influencing her as she precipitated Russian Social Democracy's "deepest humiliation".[23] About a month later he wrote again, this

---

20 On Trotsky's work on *Pravda* see, Deutscher 2015, pp. 201–09.
21 Ibid., p. 207.
22 Ibid, pp. 208–9; Trotsky to Hilferding, September 20, 1911, TH 19 (ISH).
23 Trotsky to Hilferding, September 20, 1911, TH 19 (ISH). Rosa Luxemburg's role in all this is difficult to discern. Her party in Poland, the SDKPL, received subsidies from the Bolsheviks and had a stake in their receiving access to the RSDLP's money held in trust. As J.P. Nettle

time expressing his frustration of having not heard from him and inquiring if he had been able to get information for him from the SPD Executive Committee. It is not clear exactly what information he was looking for, but apparently he expected Hilferding to be actively working on his behalf. This frustrated tone is repeated in the next letter, written almost a year later, in which he accused the SPD leadership of having "hidden behind the principle of non-intervention", while capitulating to Lenin's schismatic politics.[24]

Trotsky's frustration with his political situation and his personal anger and resentment toward Hilferding finally came to a head in a letter written either at the end of 1912 or in early January 1913. In it, Trotsky effectively declared an end to their "friendship", which, he asserted, was "of a very peculiar nature", and rested not upon a personal basis, but rather upon a political one. And even this "political friendship" was of little substance, because, although Hilferding had taken Trotsky's side with regard to Russian party politics, his support had been "platonic" rather than concrete. For Trotsky, "the decisive moment of their estrangement" came when Hilferding failed to openly defend him against Lenin's calumnies at the Copenhagen Congress, and Trotsky claimed that he would have acted very differently if the situation had been reversed and Hilferding had been subject to the judgement of the Russian party's Central Committee.

Finally, Trotsky accused Hilferding of using spurious pretexts in order to avoid writing for *Pravda*, because he feared "compromising" himself concerning debates in the Russian party. Worse yet, Hilferding's café jokes about Russian politics indicated that he did not take them seriously. Indeed, they "reveal[ed] your disinterest in the bitter struggle that is now being waged in the bitter time of emigration". Trotsky had had enough. It was no longer worth pursuing a political friendship that rested on such a "doubtful basis". It was his last letter to Hilferding.[25]

Looking back on these events many years later, Trotsky had little positive to say about his erstwhile friend or the other Austrian Marxists he had come to know. Noting that in 1907 Hilferding was at "the peak of his revolutionism", he asserted that this was largely of a "fireside character". "In practice, Hilferding remained a literary official in the service of the German party – and nothing

---

notes, she seemed at pains to take a non-partisan position in the dispute over the money, but she supported Lenin in his heated polemics against Martov at the time. See Nettl 1969, pp. 349–50.

24   Trotsky to Hilferding, early October 1912, TH 22 (ISH).
25   The letter breaks off suddenly and is unsigned. See Trotsky to Hilferding, Late December or early January 1912/13, TH 21 (ISH).

more". Indeed, for Trotsky, Hilferding, Bauer, Max Adler, and Renner were "well educated people whose knowledge of certain subjects was superior to mine. I listened with intense and, one might almost say respectful interest to their conversation in the 'Central' Café". Yet, "These people were not revolutionaries [...] they represented a type that was furthest from that of a revolutionary. This expressed itself in everything – from their approach to subjects, in their political remarks and psychological appreciations, in their self-satisfaction – not self-assurance but self-satisfaction. I even thought I sensed philistinism in the quality of their voices".[26]

Trotsky wrote these words fifteen years after leaving Vienna, having passed through the fires of 1917, the Civil War, and his catastrophic defeats of the 1920s. At the time, his revolutionary experience and his situation as a defeated exile stood in stark contrast to the fates of his former Austrian comrades, who had risen into the political elite of the German and Austrian Republics. While Trotsky wrote his memoirs isolated on Prinkipo, Hilferding was Finance Minister in Germany, Bauer was the effective head of the SDAP, Austria's second strongest party, and Renner was its leading parliamentarian. In 1929, Trotsky was prepared to draw a sharp distinction between his conception of revolution and theirs and, as Isaac Deutscher notes, his reminisces of the Viennese milieu are marked by "disdainful irony". Yet his writings from his years in Vienna suggest that he actually reveled in his experience there. Indeed, he participated enthusiastically and fully in local political and cultural life, joined the SDAP, and enjoyed the company and the friendship of its leaders. Perhaps he became disillusioned with their Marxism and political attitudes as time went on, but there was little sign of this prior to 1914. Indeed, the friendships he established in Vienna gave him entre to the socialist elite of Western Europe and helped establish his reputation as a representative of Russian socialism.[27]

As his letters show, Trotsky's broke with Hilferding when he perceived the latter as unwilling to "compromise" himself by intervening in the disputes of the Russian Social Democrats. But the long simmering tensions between the two men had deeper causes. When Trotsky arrived in Central Europe after the Revolution of 1905, he was a heroic figure in a revolution that had inspired deep admiration and much enthusiasm among socialists in the West. Well-known as he was, however, he was one among many Russian émigrés from one of Europe's smallest, most fractious, and least understood socialist parties in the Second

---

26 Trotsky 1984, pp. 212–13.
27 Deutscher 2015, pp. 194–97.

International. A hard-working journalist, Trotsky lived hand to mouth and his professional and political prospects seemed dim. As the years passed his star seemed to be in eclipse.

Meanwhile, Hilferding's star was rising. His posts as Kautsky's protégé at the *NZ*, as a teacher at the party school, and then his editorship at *Vorwärts* placed him in proximity to the leadership of the world's most important socialist party, and with the publication of *Finance Capital* in 1910 he became one of the movement's best-known intellectuals. As Trotsky teetered on the brink of relative obscurity, Hilferding moved from one success to the next. His future, politically, intellectually, and financially, seemed secure. Thus, the commonalities that seemed to draw the two men together in 1907 were, indeed, superficial. More deep-seated were the differences. Hilferding's Viennese background, education, and political experience were very different than Trotsky's, who, after leaving the family farm, was never at home anywhere for very long, and he had participated in a full-blown revolution that had resulted in his flight from his homeland. Trotsky's self-confidence and intellectual sovereignty often bordered on arrogance, and his dependence on Hilferding, himself no shrinking violet, no doubt got under his skin. Trotsky's letters make clear that, as the struggles among the Russian Social Democrats intensified, his hopes that his "political friendship" with Hilferding would be of use came to naught. Hilferding was not prepared to invest much energy into the affairs of the small and obscure Russian party. At that point that break became inevitable.

CHAPTER 7

Leon Trotsky's Letters to Rudolf Hilferding, 1907–12

(TH 1)

[No Date. Early summer, 1907]

Dear Hilferding,

We are now in the middle of enjoying our vacation and have become somewhat befogged, which does us good. Now [we have] a request for a big favor from you as a friend.[1] Trotsky left things at his landlord's, but the landlord would like to dispose of them. Could she perhaps leave them with you? It is just a *small* basket, a small suitcase, and a bag of laundry. If yes, then you will want to have them delivered. The landlord, Frau Haupt, knows you and the whole Kautsky family. When that occurs, you'll have to pay the fee, so you'll want to deduct that from the honorarium for Trotsky's last article in the *NZ*. Recently, we talked about the rapid development of the speed of monetary transactions in Germany. We want to be in the vanguard of that good model.

Kautsky will soon receive a package of […] from *Vorwärts*. The delivery is for Trotsky. It can be held by you or by Kautsky or forwarded to Agnetendorf general delivery. Best wishes to you and to your wife from all of us.

Parvus

[P.S.] Unfortunately my German is too unsatisfactory for even this short article and I had to turn to Parvus. My very best greetings to your wife. My wife and I hope to see you and your wife here in Agnetendorf.

Trotsky

Side note from Parvus: Could you perhaps also send us the most recent number of the *NZ*?

---

1 In his memoirs Trotsky says this vacation took place in late summer, but he seems to have erred. After his escape from his second imprisonment, he made it to London for the Fifth Congress of the Russian Social Democratic Labor Party. He then went to Berlin, where he met his

(TH 2)

Leipzig, July 8 [1907]

Esteemed comrade,

Once again, I have to turn to you regarding a practical matter. My honorarium is in danger. It arrived in Hirschberg after I'd already left. Now I'm traveling on to Mittwerde, Freiberg, and so on to give lectures, and I have no permanent address. The best thing would be if the editors of the *NZ* would request it [... letter damaged] [from] the post office ... Would you be kind enough to do that? I'll send you my new address.

What bothers me in my work for the *NZ* is not my time off, as you assume, but rather the simple fact that the *NZ* does not accept essays in the Russian language. And, unfortunately, Parvus is so driven by the need for independent literary activity that it is impossible for me to appoint him as my court translator. Doesn't the editorial board have its own translator? A Russian comrade with whom I have discussed this [matter] made draconian demands upon me. I would very much like to write an article on Russian liberalism – on its ideology and leading men with Peter [... letter damaged, W.S.] at the center.[2] Along with that, I'd like to say a few words about the political role of revisionism on Russian soil.

In the next month I'll turn my attention to learning the German language. From today going forward the German syntax will be my model. In August I'll come to Friedenau fully armed.[3]

This morning Parvus went hiking in Bohemia with his backpack. I'll be following him in four or five days.

Best regards to your wife and to the Kautsky family.
    Trotsky

[P.S] I ask for your constant pardon due to my German.

---

   wife and son and became acquainted with Kautsky, Hilferding and their circle of leading German socialists. He took this break before going to the Stuttgart Congress of the International and moving to Vienna in the fall. See Trotsky 1984, pp. 210–11.
2 It is likely that Trotsky was referring to Peter Struve (1870–1944), a former Russian Marxist who, by 1905, had become a liberal and a leader of the Constitutional Democratic Party.
3 Trotsky was clearly planning to meet Hilferding at Kautsky's home.

(TH 3)

August 31, 1907

My dear friend,

Once and for all: you should always read my letters with the understanding that I am not nearly as dumb in the Russian language as in the German translation …

It would be regrettable if the only thing you got out of our friendship was my poor umbrella. But it is actually not an umbrella, but a shadow, something transmitted from the past. I took the thing to Stuttgart with the joyful promise of losing it and thus creating the need to buy a new one.[4] And speaking of that: didn't I forget another, much better umbrella at Kautsky's?

For your recommendation to rent [Ankeso's][5] apartment I thank you much more heartily than for your concern about the fate of my umbrella. I would be most happy and grateful to take the apartment. That would be very nice. I should tell you, though, that I have a one and half year-old son, and in two or three months he'll be coming from Russia with the firm intention of living with me. I hope that won't prevent my renting the apartment. Then write to me, please, about how and when to pay.[6]

I would have gladly taken on a review of Maslow's *Agrarian Question* if only I'd had the book. Is this work pressing? I expect the arrival of my Russian library shortly. There I have written a complete article on Maslow's *Agrarian Question*, which I wrote in the margins (?) of his book while I was in prison. If you'd like to have a two to three paged review for the next issue, just send me a copy of his German book.

I want to write a series of articles for *Vorwärts* and the *Neue Zeit* on "Results and Prospects for the Russian Revolution".[7]

---

4 Trotsky was in Stuttgart for the congress of the Second International which took place from August 18–24, 1907.
5 The name of the landlord is difficult to read in the text.
6 Trotsky's preoccupation with word usage is illustrated well here. In German the last sentence of the paragraph reads, "Und dann schreibe mir bitte, wie und wann wird die Bezahlung effektuiert" and includes a footnote in which he says: "I fear that this expression (effektuieren) has the smell of Pavlovsky's Russian-German dictionary – no?"
7 Trotsky first published a Russian version of these essays in book form in 1906 under the title *Results and Prospects – the Moving Forces of the Revolution*. They were reprinted in 1919 with a new introduction in 1919 and appeared in English in 1921. Deutscher 2015, p. 160.

1. The social development of Russia and self-determination (already done in Russian)
2. The city and capital (also done)
3. The agrarian question in Russia
4. Russian liberalism
5. The proletariat
6. *The army and the revolution* (the mass strike, the uprising, and so on)
7. Russian Social Democracy (the differences in the party)

For the article about the mass strike, I'd like to have the pamphlet by Rosa. Perhaps you'll send it to me?[8]

I warmly shake your hand,
   Trotsky

[P.S.] My wife sends her best to you and your wife. Please give your wife my best regards as well.

ISH (TH 4)

Postcard, September 5, 1907

Dear Hilferding,

Enclosed is an article in Russian. It is a bit long (about 20,000 letters in German) and, what is still worse, somewhat boring. After the translation, please send my manuscript as soon as possible to the following address: Geneva, Bd du pont d'Arve – Editor's Office of *Radouga*.

I hope, dear Hilferding, that you will correct the translation. If the article is not suitable for the NZ, then I'll happily bear the costs of the translation. I'll then publish the whole work as a pamphlet. The longest article will be "The City and Capital". A part of this article is borrowed from my book *Our Revolution*. I await your reply.

Your,
   Trotsky

---

8 Trotsky is referring to Rosa Luxemburg's article "The Mass Strike, The Political Party, and the Trade Unions", published in 1906. Trotsky wrote "Für den Artikel über den Massenstreik

(TH 5)

September 19, 1907

My dear friend,

Today I must be brief, otherwise I'll miss the mail. Your letter made me very happy. It is always nice to hear positive opinions about one's articles and all the more so from the editor!

I am also very pleased that you will hold onto my article on revolution for the coming year, because that will give me time for a second article, which I will rewrite on the basis of new evidence that will improve my analysis.

However, have you sent the Russian manuscript to Geneva? I repeat the address: M. Khodjamiriantz 8 Bd du Pont d'Arve, Geneva. Do it, dear friend.

I'd very much like to come to Berlin – that is a given – and the Kubenstraße 19 speaks to my heart (as one says in Russian) – but it is a damned question of money. You suggest immediate payment of my honorarium. If you are comfortable with that, I'd be very pleased. Due to the lack of money, all three of us sit here in Wartenberg. After I get my honorarium from Petersburg, my wife will go to Russia. The honorarium from Friedenau will give me the opportunity to come to Friedenau. I've written two articles for Cunow on "Industry and Proletariat in the Revolution" and now I'm writing two new ones about the same theme – in other words about the connection between the industrial upswing in R[ussia] and the future destiny of the revolution. Have you heard nothing about the "future destiny" of this article? Cunow hasn't written a word to me. Perhaps he is at the party congress?

So, if possible, send me the honorarium immediately.

Best wishes, your loyal
Trotsky

---

wünschte ich [mir] die Broschur von Rosa haben. Vielleicht willst Du sie (die Broschüre selbstverständlich) mir senden". Here, he makes a joke by clarifying that the "it" (sie) he wants sent is the pamphlet, not Rosa.

(TH 6)

[December], 1907
Bronstein
Hüttelbergstr. 55
Vienna XIII

My dear Dr. Rudolf,

I am now finally in Vienna – fully settled in. I was in Zürich, Bern, Lausanne, Geneva, Karlsruhe, Mannheim, Darmstadt, Liege, Brussels, [and] Paris and gave 16 lectures. All of Europe is overwhelmed with Russians. Students, big landlords, expropriators, decadents, former dictators, mystical anarchists, delegates to the first and second Dumas, potential renegades – everything you want. Now I am free of this small people and thank my God for it.

I read your article on German imperialism closely.[9] Excellent! Only the connection with Prussian suffrage seem to me a little artificial and, if I might say – semiofficially – thin. But that concerns only a few lines.

Bauer told me that you have a lot to do at *Vorwärts*. I haven't read that [paper] for the last three months. Only after the first of the year will I get it.

I received my things. Thanks a lot! Write to me, dear Hilferding, if you need anything. I'd like to be useful to you for once. Maybe you or your wife need something here in Vienna?

A Russian publisher has now asked me for an article about Frank Wedekind.[10] Yes, yes, my dear doctor, in Russia one is no longer a writer if one does not concern one's self with erotic literature from this or that point of view. Could you perhaps recommend an interesting article about Wedekind to me? Aside from an essay by Pissin, I don't know of any.[11]

Two days ago, I heard [Victor] Alder speak on the budget in parliament. Splendid! Via the Russian delegation, at the protest in the wake of the Leuchthaus judgement, I got to hear Winarsky, Nemec,[12] and Daszynski[13] speak. I was very disappointed about Daszynsky.

---

9   The reference is to Karl Emil (Hilferding) 1907–08.
10 Frank Wedekind (1864–1918) was a leading German playwright and critic of bourgeois society known for his biting satire.
11 The reference is to Raimund Pissin's essay on Frank Wedekind published in 1905.
12 Anton Nemec (1858–1926) was a leading Czech trade unionist and Social Democrat.
13 Ignaz Daszynski (1866–1936) co-founded the Polish Social Democratic Party in 1892 and served as delegate to the Austrian parliament until 1918 when he briefly became Prime Minister of the newly founded Polish Republic.

I now hope to write the second and third articles for the *N[eue] Z[eit]*. Parvus in still in Dalmatia. I have not had a letter from him for a long time.

Best greetings from your friend,
   Leon Trotsky

[P.S.] Best regards to your wife!

(TH 7)

February 27, 1908

I've already said repeatedly that you, dear Hilferding, in your soul are a Russian in so far as you are terribly inaccurate.

I am waiting most impatiently for my article on the revolution. I need it for my German book. Now I cannot write about the Russian Revolution for the *NZ*, because in that regard I have to rob my own book. My dear Rudolf, send me the article (with the Russian text) immediately. Was my article on Wedekind unsuitable for the *NZ*?[14]

Best regards,
   Lev Trotsky

(TH 8)

March 16, 1908

My dear Dr. Rudolf,

Sometimes I can also reach the heights upon which you stand in [our] correspondence. An eye for an eye.

Comrade Klatschko received a letter from Wurm today, which inquired about my Parisian address. What is the meaning of this? Are you trying to hide the location of my stay from the editorial board? Wurm writes that I would receive an honorarium of 45 marks. I think the editor forgot that last fall I

---

14   Hilferding did publish he article. See Trotsky 1907–08b.

received 50 marks for *two* articles, of which only one appeared in the NZ (I withdrew the other for my book). I'd be very satisfied, if I could cover my debt to the publisher with the Wedekind article. In this case, however, it would be good if Fraulein Herzmann received her honorarium for the Wedekind translation. But if the honorarium has already been sent, write to me, please, about how much of it the translator receives.

I am living in absolute isolation from the entire world – except for my family. I see no one. I visit no one, and no one comes to me. Why is this the case? First, because I live in Hütteldorf; second, because I always have pressing work; third, because my parents are staying here for the whole winter; and fourth, fifth, and sixth, because when the circle of Austrian comrades comes out of the [the meetings of the] parliamentary delegation or the editorial office I feel absolutely superfluous. I could not read your letter about German politics or parliamentary affairs to Bauer or Renner, because I saw neither the former nor the latter even once the whole time. Regarding the NZ, woe is me, the sinner, I haven't read a single issue for three months. I will get it tomorrow. I read the *Arbeiter-Zeitung* and I'm satisfied with that. In the March edition of *Der Kampf* there is a splendid article by Renner on Marx and the workers. The guy has something athletic in his style. With him, the spirit of socialist abstraction assumes the form of living flesh on the bones. To be sure, sometimes the cherished I is too much in evidence; indeed, sometimes our athlete with the biceps plays only out of pure love of the game. Still, I always see the *person who moves freely and expressively* in the realm of ideas. Otto Bauer – in so far as I have a mental image of him – seems to me to be too pedantic. From definition via definition to conclusion. What you write about German party affairs seems to me to be too absolute. You stand in the middle of the work, in particular in the middle of the contradiction between parliamentary organization and tradition and the social-revolutionary tasks of the movement, and *as a politician* you also have *the duty*, metaphysically (and absolutely), to take up this contradiction. But from the historical (dialectical) standpoint, it is always only the contradiction between the machine and the steam. The machine is inert, and the large and dismembered party machine is much, much to sluggish. The steam, meaning the energy of the class, has the task of overcoming the machine's ability to resist change. But after that is overcome, the slothful party machine will fulfill an incomparable task.

It is very late, and I have to go to bed. Otherwise, I fear that you will find my philosophy too dull.

Best regards to your wife. Write to me, please, before the end of 1908.
   Your,
   Trotsky

(TH 9)

March 24, 1908

You grumble, my dear Hilferding, about the brevity of my letter. [But] you see, I am sympathetic, and I would rather not overly burden the Franz Mehring of the future, who will want to systematize our papers ...

You are no longer at the NZ? How is that possible?[15] To me you are a part of the NZ, and the NZ is a living part of the International. No doubt, *Vorwärts* is an upright paper, but for me it remains Berlin's local organ and Bebel's monitor. Thus, you sold yourself for a mess of pottage. I know, I know, the honorarium does the same thing. I have even lowered myself to take on the role of art and literature reporter and critic of a bourgeois-radical Odessa paper. You ask how things are with me when it comes to earning money? Ni shatko ni valko.[16] one says in Russian. So far it has not gone brilliantly, but I have hope – and that is the most important thing. At the moment, Marxism has very low standing on the Russian literary market. One can smuggle it in only in small doses when one talks about the fine technical details of historical conditions – or, like your obedient servant – about Franz Wedekind (which, by the way, amounts to the same thing). Now I have received another invitation to write a pair of articles for two collections of Marxist-pornographic works. One pays 250 Kronen for 40,000 letters, which, from the German standpoint, is a very high honorarium. But this work takes a lot of time and distracts from the more important issues. Still, in no way do I want to emerge as a critic of the modern ...!

Two Russian Social Democratic newspapers are now appearing in Geneva: *Golas sozialdemokrata* [*The Voice*] published by the Mensheviks and *Proletari* [*The Proletariat*] by the Bolsheviks. I have received invitations from both and have answered with *no*. The Mensheviks now sit like the Russians of Babylon (Lake Geneva) and cry the bitterest tears in the world – the tears of powerlessness. "We are not a party". "We are demoralized". "We won't become a party". And the Bolsheviks are free of any Marxist culture and work happily at the loom of counterrevolution to create a truly boorish literature.

What is the situation by and large? That is a difficult question to answer in a letter, especially if you don't want to create too much work for the Franz

---

15 By this time, Hilferding had given up his post at the Party School because German law forbade non-citizens from teaching. To earn a living, he took on the full-time job of editing the international pages of *Vorwärts*. As part of the switch, he also no-longer helped edit the *Neue Zeit*.
16 Literally "neither good nor bad."

Mehring mentioned above. I will comment on one thing. It would be absolutely wrong to draw an analogy between this moment in Russia and the year 1793 or 1848. At that time the fundamental problems of revolution were solved (in the second case accommodated but still solved). One had satisfied the peasants and that is the most important thing. Even the Bourbons after 1815 could only give the emigres a billion [francs], they did not touch the new landowners. And we have still not created new landowners. Everything is like it was. We have absolutely nothing to restore [sic]. That is most clearly demonstrated by the peasant delegation to the Third Duma, which demanded the expropriation of the land. We are not heading toward a long lasting feudal-bourgeois reaction [but, rather] toward the most radical outbreak of social revolution. The damned peasants, however, need a few dozen more blows from the vagaries of history in order to get behind the workers in the great cause. I am waiting patiently for that and have no intention of intervening in the petty business of the Geneva emigres.

I have written an article about the Third Duma for the Poles (Rosa's firm).[17] The article is now being translated in Berlin. I think it would also be appropriate for the *Neue Zeit*, but under one condition: it may not be translated by Fraulein Herzmann, because she is supposed to translate my book. In any case, it will appear three months later than planned. I hope the book will be interesting. [It includes] a substantial theoretical introduction, historical description, the evaluation of individuals, and even many illustrations. The book takes all of my time. And then the translation! Fraulein Herzmann translates pretty well, but everything is flattened out. One doesn't notice that too much in a theoretical article, but in a description, where the style makes the music, it is terrible to see how one applies formless, ponderous terms from the foreign language lexicon to your thoughts.

Best regards to your wife and I hope to see you here in the next few months.
    Your,
    Trotsky

---

17 "Rosa's firm" was the Social Democracy of the Kingdom of Poland and Lithuania, (SDKPL) in which she played a leading role. It opposed the nationalism of the Polish Socialist Party.

(TH 10)

April 30, 1908

My dear D[octor],

Here is an article about the Third Duma. You can do with it what you'd like: correct, shorten, lengthen, or throw it in the waste basket. The latter would perhaps be the most appropriate. However, if you decide to publish it, after the title you can write: "Sent to us from Petersburg" or "A Russian colleague writes to us". Or something like that. Or mark the top of the page with a "t". Then I'll use that notation for all my short pieces. Every week I'll send you a short notice for *Vorwärts*.

It never goes right with Dresden. I wanted to travel on the weekend, but Wallfisch told me that he will be away on Saturday and Sunday.[18]

Brobrinsky has been appointed Governor of Galicia and the party says nothing, as if it is none of its business. The *Arbeiter-Zeitung* has extensively discussed the need to make use of the agenda in parliament [but] can't find any space for Galicia. Why? One doesn't want conflict with the government. One doesn't want to have anything to do with "empty demonstrations". One dares no serious protest in which the Ruthenians are abandoned to a wild butcher, to a Polish Plehve.[19] It that an accident? A momentary mistake? It is treason! Not against the Ruthenians, but against the revolutionary faction. In time, revenge will be had. And then I'll laugh with malicious pleasure ...!

Be well. Best regards to you.
 Trotsky

---

18 Hermann Wallfisch (1862–?) was a Social Democratic organizer in Dresden and administrative coordinator of the *Sächsische Arbeiter-Zeitung*.

19 Vyacheslav Plehve (1846–1904) was chief of the Tsarist police, including the secret police (the Okhrana). In 1902 he became Interior Minister. Reviled for his repressive policies and for his ruthless Russification of Poland and other ethnically non-Russian territories, he was killed by a Socialist Revolutionary assassin in 1904.

(TH 11)

[Early July 1908]

Dear H,

Here you once again have a small monstrosity of the German language (unfortunately it is too big for *Vorwärts*). In it you will find a minor polemic with the *Arbeiter-Zeitung*. What Leutner has written about Russia and Russian politics is unbelievable. He understands these matters as much as a streetlight at today's Vienna's anniversary parade (The *Arbeiter-Zeitung* published an article about the parade in the style of moderate Byzantinism. Disgusting …!)

It could be that you, the gentlemen of *Vorwärts*, find it inappropriate to polemicize with the *Arbeiter-Zeitung* … then you will, of course, correct the relevant passage. But I will keep it in reserve.

Why don't you write to me about what you've done with my article about Tscherevanin?[20] I am still of the opinion that it would work out best if you gave it to the *Neue Zeit*. [And] how are you doing? What are you writing about? What is your family up to?

Be well.
Your,
Trotsky

[P.S.] *Reply to me soon*[!]

(TH 12)

[July 1908]

My dear Dr. Rudolf,

Here is another article on Russian Social Democracy. If you like it, print it. During the week, I'll also send you a brief notice summarizing the results of the Third Duma and (perhaps) the Tscherevanin review – Tscherevanin has written

---

20 V. Tscherevanin was a Menshevik writer who published *The Proletariat and the Russian Revolution* (1908).

a new book, "The Current Situation and the Possibilities for the Future". In this book, he concedes, first of all, that it was *not the errors* of the faction that caused the defeat and openly contradicts the argument of his first pamphlet. Then he raises the question, "Why the idiotic faction of Trotsky and Parvus dominated in 1905 and not the rational Menshevik faction?" And [then] the "rational" jackass replies: "Because the genuine Menshevik faction is impossible in the fog of revolution". Listen to that my friend. *The revolution is an obstacle for the rational Tscherevanin faction.* Marvellous! That is a world historical aphorism from the treasury of the former Royal Austrian War College.

Do you know why after such a long time my [earlier] Tscherevanin article has not appeared in the *NZ*?[21]

Pardon my mistakes and my handwriting. I am very tired and must go to bed. Best regards to your family. Salutations, brotherhood, and good night.
Lev Trotsky

(TH 13)

July 21, 1908
Sieveringerstraße 19
Vienna XIX

My dear and much, much too quiet friend,

Enclosed is an article on Russian foreign policy. Thanks very much for your effort in correcting my articles. But when, according to the law of the distribution of energy, you don't write me any letters that make it possible for me to improve my essays, then I will feel the need to turn to someone else with my articles. But, in any case, I do not wish to do without your letters my dear Hilferding. I ask you, then, to inquire again about the fate of the Tscherevanin article. I fear that Kautsky does not think that the brief remarks on the relationship of some European socialists to the Russian Revolution are very tactful. Perhaps he has other concerns. I'd be happy to rework the article if Kautsky thinks it necessary, not for the sake of the article or for my sake, but for that of the cause. The reaction gives the opportunists courage. In his second book (I'd like to write a post-script to my article about it), Tscherevanin says that Kautsky's views on

---

21   It appeared soon afterward. Trotsky 1907–08a.

the Russian Revolution have value only Reductio ad absurdum. The most recent issue of the Mensheviks' Geneva paper asserts that Kautsky has expressed some fantastic opinions. You know very well that I am not an intransigent nor am I a rescuer of principles: in regard to that I have too much trust in the objective logic of things. But precisely now, in this moment of political depression, it is our duty to fight for the maintenance of the party, and this fight must, first of all, be directed against the rotting, toothless Menshevik faction. The more the Mensheviks sink into the swamp of vulgar opportunistic prejudices, the stricter and more tenacious they become in questions concerning the purity of "teachings". In the issue I mentioned, Plekhanov writes a major article against Bogdanov in which he declares: he cannot and may not call Bogdanov "comrade", but only "sir", because Bogdanov is no philosophical materialist, but rather, a Machist. Doesn't this sound a bit insane to you? But that is the bitter truth.

I think it is important, that the NZ makes clear that it does not think it necessary to change its views of the Russian Revolution. *For these reasons* I wanted to see my article in the NZ. Please write and tell me what you know about it.

With best regards,
Lev Trotsky

(TH 14)

August 5, 1908

My dear friend,

On 8 [August] you are going to the Tirol and I fear that this letter will no longer find you in Berlin. Meanwhile, it is very important to me that you get this letter. [Once] again it concerns the honorarium that I've not yet received. There were three articles: on Russian Social Democracy, on the summary of the third session of the Duma, and on Russian imperialism. It is unclear to me what has happened to my article on Tscherevanin, because I haven't received *Vorwärts* since the first of the month.

Dear friend, I ask you to tell the administration: 1) to send me this month's *Vorwärts* (from August 1) and to cover the cost of my subscription from my honorarium and 2) to send me the rest of the honorarium *immediately. I need it very badly right now.*

It its very unpleasant for me to complain to you about my petty problems, and I would have dealt with the administration directly, but I don't know if the people in the administration have any idea that I am the author of the articles. And so, I turn to you again.

Do you know, dear friend, that in the next two or three weeks I will start publishing a new newspaper? A month ago, I would not have been able to believe it myself. But that's how it is. The thing developed as follows. A month and a half ago I received an inquiry from one of the "practical" ones, an old acquaintance, about whether I would support a newspaper of the Spilka Organization with my articles. (Spilka is an organization that encompasses five or six southwestern territories and it has influence mostly over rural workers.)[22] I replied with a programmatic letter: the newspaper must be a *workers' paper*; it must have a decidedly revolutionary outlook; it must stand above both fractions; it must be *political* and not *polemical*, and its goal cannot be to establish a third fraction, but rather to maintain contact and political ties between the workers of both fractions. I received no answer, and I forgot about the whole matter. Suddenly, the above-mentioned "practical one" came to me in Vienna along with another comrade. They told me that, after receiving my letter, they traveled to Russia, visited every significant point in the Spilka region, and, together with me, are now charged by the organization with founding a new newspaper, *Pravda (Truth)*. Although the paper will be published by a local organization, it is not meant for a local audience, but rather for the proletariat of the whole country. It will appear twice per month (published from abroad). – I have accepted the proposal. The two comrades confirm fully what I have published in *Vorwärts* about the evolution of the party: the intelligentsia falls apart like an old fur coat and the workers have outstanding morale, are not psychologically depressed, are ready to fight, courageous, and active. They demand a political newspaper and the first issue will already be of great significance for the whole party. The two other comrades will manage the trade union section and the correspondence. I will have the political section. Parvus is very satisfied with the enterprise and is getting to work. For a long time, I rejected [establishing] an independent literary enterprise in order to avoid inadvertently creating a third fraction. But now it is high time to begin. The conditions for the recovery of the party are very good. And in six months you will call me a scoundrel if the Mensheviks and the Bolsheviks are as divided then as they are now. Write to me, write to me! Otherwise, when you come to Russia, and I am your only connection to the outside world, I'll leave you pining away and without letters.

Your,
Trotsky

---

22   The Spilka (The Ukrainian Social Democratic Union) was established in 1904. It was an autonomous, regional adherent to the Russian Social Democratic Labor Party and sided

(TH 15)

[Between March 7 and June 20, 1909]

Dear friend,

Naturally you are mad at me. We are always dissatisfied with one another. Now, I am highly satisfied with your article about Leuthner. The article is well written with good Marxist irony – it was truly a pleasure to read it.[23] I doubt whether one can label Leuthner a revisionist. He is not even an opportunist. He is a Prussian National Liberal, and he isn't an opportunist, because he makes no compromises with socialism. But that you criticize the Italian party and treat Leuthner only as a contributor to the S[ozialistischer] M[onatshefte] is hypocrisy for which the Austrian half of your heart bears responsibility. Is it still an "accident" that the stylistic dandy of the second rank makes the Austrian party's foreign policy? And the position of the party in the history with Serbia is also an accident? On Berlin's soil you are more Marxist than on that of Vienna.

I could not come to the Café Central [because] my wife was very ill (even today she is still sick) and was totally absorbed in family matters.

I am now writing a big article for the NZ on the Russian Revolution. I have had too little time to write for *Vorwärts*, just as my German comrade has no time to write for *Pravda*.

Tomorrow I'm moving. My new address is XIX Friedlgasse, 40, F. 10. On the fifteenth I am traveling to Paris via Switzerland and I'll be back on June 1.

Don't be mad.

Your,
Trotsky

P.S. I just got your card. Thanks a lot. I had quite a guilty conscience when I noticed your handwriting on the cover. But, even if it is only by way of justifying myself, I wrote the letter before I'd received yours.

Two days ago, I sent two telegrams on *Pravda*'s behalf to Ströbel and to *Vorwärts* because of the decision of the commission investigating elections. Will the telegram appear in V[orwärts]? We want to promote P[ravda]. Yesterday I organized a closed meeting of party comrades here. It was about fifty people.

---

with the Mensheviks. Trotsky's hopes for the new newspaper and SPILKA eventually came to naught and by 1912 the group had largely collapsed.

23 Hilferding 1908–09.

Of these, thirty voted to support *Pravda*, 7 abstained for official reasons, 10–15 left in order not to vote against. Of course, a Viennese gathering has no great political significance, but it is highly characteristic of the attitude of the party comrades of all currents (there were Bolsheviks, Mensheviks, Bundists, and so on. More than half were workers).

Trotsky

[P.P.S.] What is actually the name of your street? Write it out clearly.

(TH 16)

[June 1910]

Dear theoretician of finance capital,

I'm sending you an article about Finland. Once again, I'm not receiving *Vorwärts*, and I don't know what you have recently carried about Finland. Make sure you place the article as soon as possible. If it doesn't work out, send it to the *Leipziger* [*Volkszeitung*]. In May, I had a very unpleasant episode with my right ear; an internal infection in the middle ear. The pain was unbearable – ten days and ten nights! Professor Alexander cut through the tympanic membrane. Now I can hear pretty well, only the subjective noises bother and immiserate me. Hopefully, they will also go away.

I've only just begun to read *Finance Capital*, I've not gotten very far, just the first twenty pages. I can already say one thing: the book is nicely written, and if the tone is the same all the way through, then it will be a fabulous achievement from a literary standpoint. When I've reached the end, I'll write an article for a Russian monthly about it.

In expectation of your reply.
Lev Trotsky

P.S. My article actually was written for *Pravda* and was translated by a Russian comrade. It will appear in *Vorwärts* earlier than in *Pravda*.

(TH 17)

Postcard [July 25, 1910]
[*After a major assembly of workers in Belgrade.*]

Dear friend,

You should come to the Balkans some time in order to see what kind of an impression the behavior of the V[ienna] *Arbeiter-Zeitung* during the annexation crisis has had on the Serbian comrades.[24]

Your,
   Trotsky

(TH 18)

Postcard [December 25, 1910]
Maxim's Restaurant "Baar"
Geneva

Dear Hilferding,

I received your letter and Cunow's confirmation. Thanks a lot! Please don't worry about the fate of the article. That is really not so important. I am not on a very interesting trip [sic]. At the moment, I'm in Geneva, but tomorrow I'm going to Bologna. Ten days later I'll return to Vienna. I'm very sorry that I won't be able to see you in Vienna. Best regards.

Your,
   Trotsky

---

24   In October 1908 the Austro-Hungarian Empire unilaterally annexed the territories of Bosnia-Herzegovina, which had formerly been under the control of the Ottoman Empire. This act caused a profound crisis that intensified tensions between the Empire and neighboring states such as Italy, Serbia, and Russia. It was one of the major steps on the path to the outbreak of the First World War.

(TH 19)

[September 20, 1911]

Dear friend,

Enclosed is a notice about Bulgaria. I wrote the notice in order to have the possibility of saying a few words about Rakowsky's journal. Here is Rakowsky's address: Herr Kr. Rakowsky, Editorial Offices of "Napred", Sofia. I think that in him *Vorwärts* would have a very useful collaborator on Balkan matters. In any case, he is the most skilled and the most European of the people on the outside.

My mission with Axelrod did not lead to any result. Kautsky agreed that the decision that has been taken is completely wrong. But to Rosa, [Clara] Zetkin's action is the right one. Mehring is sick. In any case I hope that the depositors don't give any money to the S.G. Technical Commission (the Lenin-Tyschna group). But we did not get any money either, even to cover expenditures already made. *Pravda* should receive a subsidy for nine months (9 × 400fr = 3,600fr). With this in mind, we have already run up big debts (2,000kr). In Jena, Kautsky was prepared to pay off 6,000fr of past debts to the foreign office and to *Pravda*. Zetkin had rejected the idea, however. And now *Pravda* is in an impossible situation. We are not in a position to pay the debts from our own resources, we can't get the paper from the printer, the organization of transport is in a state of dissolution, and I am expecting the printer, Verney, to send the court bailiff to my apartment. But the worst thing is that Zetkin has delivered 10,000fr to the Lenin-Tyschna group (it calls itself the Organizing Committee for the Calling of a Party Conference) without having any right to do so. The depositors have simply attempted to elevate a fractious group that came into existence though a vile Bonapartist coup d'tat by giving them the party's money. It is really the deepest humiliation for Russian Social Democracy, where Clara, informed by Rosa, destroys party institutions and gives life to new ones. It's disgusting!

That Stolypin was murdered by his "guard" is really very impressive.[25] The immediate result could, indeed, be the strengthening of the reaction; one will attempt to exterminate everything there is to exterminate. But that can only go on a few weeks. The sense of indecision and confusion in government circles

---

25   Pyotr Stolypin (1862–1911) was a conservative Prime Minister of Russia from 1906–1911. He was assassinated on 14 September 1911 by Dmitry Bogrov (1887–1911), a member of the Socialist Revolutionary Party and also an agent of the secret police. There has been considerable debate among historians if this action may have been carried out at the behest of reactionary forces opposed to Stolypin's agricultural reforms.

must unavoidably set in. Because it is now fully clear that the matter of "order" is not completely in order. In any case, one could already observe the onset of the hangover some time ago. The assassination has interfered with the process [and] even conjured up a (brief) reaction. But the more drastically and deeply the hangover expresses itself, perhaps even as this winter unfolds, then once again our time will come.

I am not yet writing to you on the matter of the petition, because I can't know when we'll have the possibility of once again having access to the printer ...

Best regards. Write a few lines to me.
Your,
Trotsky
Address: N. Trotsky
XIX/1 Rodlergasse 25

P.S. I was completely unprepared for this great embarrassment to Rosa. She could not have defended her cause more stupidly.

Unfortunately, the nastiest speeches leave me unsatisfied. I find some things incomprehensible.

In one and a half to two months I'm coming to Berlin.

(TH 20)

[October or November 1911]

Dear Hilferding,

Your silence is completely incomprehensible to me. Were you unable to get the necessary information from the [Party] Executive? Did you not want it? That is something I could accept. But you should at least write to me about it. Then I would have long ago turned directly to the Executive and *Vorwärts* and of course received the reply.

In expectation of your answer.
Your,
Trotsky

P.S. Enclosed is an article. When you find it suitable, you can write "from our Russian correspondent" or "from Petersburg".

(TH 22)

[Early October 1912]

Dear friend,

I hoped to see you in Chemnitz,[26] therefore I didn't answer your letter. I also had an awful lot to do.

The behavior of the German Party Executive is regrettable. It was much too apparent that the matter is in [Hermann] Müller's hands – this embodiment of socially necessary obtuseness. The Party Executive *had intervened* in the Russian matter by putting forward its very reasonable approach (by which it said: unity is possible!).

However, it hid behind the principle of "non-intervention" after Lenin had written his terroristic letter. The Party Executive always placed our communications under Lenin's control, [even] after he had rejected the Executive's recommendation for a joint discussion. That was disgraceful!

A few words about the Radek affair. I can understand very well that the German party wishes to cast out this man. [However,] that one wants to do it by taking advantage of the Polish matter is infamous. Dr. V[ictor] Adler and Otto Bauer had the same impression, only they did not express themselves so sharply. *Vorwärts*'s opinion on the issue is pitiful. *Vorwärts* trembles before Rosa.*[27] The polemic with Bremer makes the undeniable impression that *Vorwärts* wants to make peace with Rosa on the bones of Radek. Good luck! But allow me to say that your [the German leadership's] entire behavior in this matter was not noble. To take revenge in this way for the Göppinger Affair,[28] to defend Müller's tranquility in this way – no ...! (And whether Radek really had stolen [anything] or not doesn't matter. "He may be a scoundrel", I say, along with our friend Henne.)

---

26 The reference is to the SPD's Chemnitz Party Congress which took place in mid-September 1912.
27 In a footnote to his letter, Trotsky adds: "And in the Göppinger Affair (see footnote 28 below) Radek acted only as Rosa's disciple."
28 The Göppinger Affair refers to the successful effort of revisionist forces to remove the radical editor, August Thalheimer (1884–1948) and his widely unpopular deputy, Karl Radek (1885–1939), from the editorial board of Göppingen's *Freie Volkszeitung* in June 1912. The pretext for their ouster was the controversial publication of an article in December 1911 in which they asserted that, in the event of war, the press must light the fire of revolution in the streets.

We are now publishing a pamphlet on Russian Social Democracy in German. It would be very good if you would take a look at and comment on the proofs (from the standpoint of the German reader). Lenin put the matter before the public and we have to shed light on it. (not on the miserable money issue, of course, but rather on our entire effort to free the party from the shame of Leninism and strengthen its ability to act).

Tomorrow I'm traveling to the Balkans on behalf of two Russian newspapers. The moment is highly inappropriate for me, but I can't do anything else because I have to save myself financially ...

My address during this time will be S. Bronstein (not L but S!), general delivery, Belgrade, Serbia.

With best regards.
Your
Trotsky

(TH 21)

[Late December 1912 or Early January 1913]

Dear Hilferding,

Comrade Klatschko[29] told me that you've complained that I don't write. I must tell you openly that this is no accident. What people call our "friendship", and what Warski[30] in Copenhagen in front of the Party Executive had denounced using that name, was of a peculiar nature. We are hardly ever together, we scarcely know one another, and are perhaps too different of character to base our friendship solely upon psychological inclination. However, [until now] we have been mature enough to maintain our relationship as comrades in the Café.[31] I have always regarded our relationship as a *political friendship*, as a

---

29   Samuel Klatschko (1851–1914) was a Russian Narodnik who became a socialist and moved to Vienna in the 1880s. He joined the SDAP in 1905 and befriended Victor Adler as well as Trotsky.
30   Adolf Warski (1868–1937) joined the Polish socialist movement in 1889 and became a member of the executive committee of the Socialist Party of the Kingdom of Poland and Lithuania (SDKPiL). He later became a leader of the Polish Communist Party and was murdered in Soviet Union during the Great Purge of 1937.
31   In other words, the familiarity one might cultivate among acquaintances in a café that would not be regarded as appropriate under other social circumstances.

convergence that rested upon agreement in important political questions. I never underestimated or overestimated the analytical differences between us regarding the policies of the German and Austrian parties. I have even discerned that these differences have pretty much become less pronounced in the last two years. In regard to Russian party politics you have always taken my side – but – purely platonically. For me that was the decisive moment of estrangement. I have become most firmly convinced that, when it counts, you don't dare to step forward with your view of Russian party affairs in order to avoid compromising yourself. That is what happened in the matter with the Executive Committee. After Lenin did not withdraw his accusation against me in Copenhagen, he repeated the claim for months in his journal – and even just a month ago – that I was officially charged before the German Executive with having slandered the party in my "propaganda" article. In previous years, after months of silence, you have responded to my entreaties [by saying] that the Executive could not be moved to answer [because] the accusation had been withdrawn, even if this withdrawal had only occurred on purely formal grounds. How remarkable! I demand to be told whether I am subject to the judgement of a party court or not and I'm told: no reply can be given *because* (!) the accusation had been withdrawn for purely formal reasons. When you are in a similar situation before our party Central Committee, then I will behave very differently! In any case, in answer to your letter, I said that the matter no longer interested me, but as you well understood, only in order to not to give a totally different reply.

And then another moment. I asked you many times to write for *Pravda*. You always said no under various pretexts. You, yourself, don't want to make me believe that it was always due to the lack of time. Your time is not that precious, and *Pravda* is also not so insignificant for that to be a valid reason.*[32] The real reason seems to be your fear of "compromising" yourself. Who knows, yesterday Trotsky appeared to be right, but today, perhaps, it is Riazanov ... By the way, you don't take it at all seriously and – in a Café joke (!) you reveal your disinterest in the bitter struggle that is now being waged in the bitter time of emigration. I am not called to discern whether you have objective grounds to question my standpoint in the party. That this doubt is not expressed in open criticism or with a suggestion, but rather is hidden [behind] the mask of skeptical cautiousness, you will have to concede, results in a very doubtful basis for a political friendship.

---

32   * In contrast, Otto Bauer has sent us another splendid article, which he had openly written with Russian conditions in mind.

Now you will ask why I am writing all this? In order not to have on my conscience that I have alienated a political friend without attempting to have an open and honest exchange.

But enough of that –.

[The letter breaks off here.]

Part 3

FIGURE 5   Rudolf and Rose Hilferding (June 1928)
AUTHOR: UNKNOWN, BUNDESARCHIVBILD 102–06069, CREATIVE COMMONS

CHAPTER 8

Introduction to Part 3: "Freedom or Slavery"

Unlike Hilferding, Kautsky, and Trotsky, Paul Hertz never achieved international renown as a leading theoretician or charismatic political leader. He was, however, a political workhorse of the type whose skills are indispensable to any successful mass party. Smart, versatile, and energetic, he played a wide range of roles in the Social Democratic leadership over the course of his long career. From 1918 until 1938 he collaborated closely with Hilferding on the editorial board of *Die Freiheit*, in the Reichstag, and in the work of the SPD Executive Committee in exile, the Sopade. As a trained economist, skillful editor, and principled political leader, Hertz was a figure with whom Hilferding could correspond as an equal. After both were forced into exile in 1933, their letters reflected the emotional, intellectual, and political shock of the experience and the intensity of their struggle to salvage the movement to which they had dedicated their lives.

Hertz was born in Worms, Germany, in 1888 but grew up in Hamburg and Stettin. His parents, Carl and Hermine, were Jews engaged in the commercial clothing business. For financial reasons Paul left school at fifteen and became a commercial apprentice at a wholesale firm that exported men's and boys' clothing. According to Hertz's biographer, Ursula Langkau-Alex, young Paul had a pronounced sense of justice and fairness that drew him to the labor movement. It is not surprising, then, that in 1904 he joined the salesmen's union and a year later, at the age of 18, the SPD.[1]

Hertz's early engagement in the labor movement soon opened doors for him. In early 1906 he accepted an offer from his union in Hamburg to be trained as an organizer/administrator and, as a part of his preparation, he was sent to study theory at the General Commission of the German Trade Union's school in Berlin. By the end of the year Hertz was an official responsible for dealing with workers' problems on the job, disseminating propaganda, and doing various kinds of administrative work. He was good at his job, which took him to many regions of the country and allowed him to cultivate his skills as a public speaker and administrator.

---

[1] There is still no full-scale biography of Paul Hertz and works focusing on his personal life and political activities are scarce. I have drawn heavily here on Langkau-Alex (1988), pp. 145–169.

But Hertz was also hungry for knowledge. After four years of union work, he decided to undertake university study, a very difficult path in Germany for those who had not attended Gymnasium. He was determined, however, and with the assistance of knowledgeable superiors at his union, he gained entrance to the University of Munich and later transferred to Tübingen, where he studied political economy, sociology, and history. In February 1914 he completed his doctoral thesis on "The History of the Trade Union Press in Germany", a work which reflected his Marxist perspective about the function of the trade union press under capitalism and its future role in the creation of a socialist society.

Hertz's efforts to rise from an apprentice salesman to a Ph.D. in economics says much about his tenacity and independence. Initially, his family was displeased with his choice to undertake union work, but his success eventually brought them around. In 1910, when he decided to seek an advanced degree, his father at first suggested that he only would help with the finances if Paul agreed to remain a Jew and never to marry a non-Jew, but Paul rejected such pressure and Carl soon relented. Indeed, Paul made clear to his parents that for him science, not religion, undergirded his view of the world, and that intellectual and emotional affinity should stand at the heart of close personal relations rather than material considerations or religious affiliation. While working in Frankfurt in 1909 he met Hanna Loeb-Gernsheimer, a socialist, feminist intellectual who was an acquaintance of Rosa Luxemburg. They married in 1914, had two children, Wilfried (1915–?) and Hilde (1919–2012), and remained together until Paul's death in 1961.

In a growing labor movement in which well-educated writers and editors were in short supply, Hertz had no trouble finding a post after finishing his dissertation. In April 1914 he joined the editorial board of the well-known *Leipziger Volkszeitung* (LVZ), but the coming of the World War in August cut short his sojourn there. Like many other young Social Democrats eager to defend the fatherland, Hertz had immediately volunteered, although we do not know exactly what his motives were at the time. By the fall of 1917, however, he clearly had turned against the war. In October, as a result of Hannah's intercession with the authorities, the emaciated corporal was released from military service for work in the government department in Berlin responsible for the distribution of vegetables. He also joined the USPD and, when revolution came to Berlin the following November, participated in the armed seizure of the Reich Telegraph Office. Meanwhile, his party comrade, Kautsky, arranged a job for Hertz at the Reich Food Office, which was responsible for managing Germany's dwindling stocks. Hertz's boss, Emmanuel Wurm, had formerly been Kautsky's long-time associate editor at the *Neue Zeit*.

INTRODUCTION TO PART 3: "FREEDOM OR SLAVERY" 219

FIGURE 6   Paul Hertz in the 1920s
AUTHOR: UNKNOWN, GETTY IMAGES

It is unclear when Hertz and Hilferding first met. Hertz continued to work at the Reich Food Office until early 1919, when he joined the editorial board of *Die Freiheit*, which Hilferding had been running since his return from the front in November. It is very possible that Hilferding's longtime friends, Kautsky and Wurm, introduced them and recommended Hertz for the job. In any case, it seems they got on well and were in general agreement on most major issues. In 1919 and 1920 both hoped that the labor movement could somehow overcome its divisions to win parliamentary majorities that would pave the way for thoroughgoing socialist reforms, they opposed the creation of a soviet style republic, and they rejected subordinating the USPD to the authority of the Bolshevik controlled Communist International. Following the USPD's split in October 1920, Hertz, like Hilferding, came to believe that reunifying the remnant of the party with the SPD was the most sensible policy to secure the republic against the counterrevolutionary right and the Communist left.

Meanwhile, Hertz also embarked on a career in electoral politics. Between 1920 and 1925 he represented the Charlottenburg district in the Berlin City Council, but more importantly, he became a major figure in the Reichstag. Initially elected on the USPD list, after 1922 he represented the SPD in that body until 1933. Best known for his economic expertise, but also engaged with a wide range of other issues, Hertz was a disciplined, skilled parliamentary tactician and an excellent speaker upon whom the party often relied to put forward its position. Indeed, during his first four years alone, Hertz addressed the Reichstag 335 times and sat on numerous parliamentary commissions dealing with such matters as the economy, taxes, and the budget. In 1923 the SPD Reichstag delegation selected Hertz as its secretary, a crucially important post for managing its legislative agenda and mobilizing members to get party policies passed into law.

This work kept Hertz in regular contact with Hilferding, who was also one of the party's major parliamentary figures and who dealt with similar issues, especially those related to economics and finance. He and Hilferding occasionally had differences on policy matters. In 1928, for example, Hertz worked to block the funding for a pocket battleship that Hilferding was willing to countenance in order to hold the SPD-led coalition government together, but, in general, they were in basic agreement on political and economic questions. Most importantly, both men believed that for the SPD to achieve its policy goals it had to do more than fire broadsides from the comfort of the parliamentary opposition. While they may have disagreed at times concerning the efficacy of entering into particular coalitions, they agreed that to exercise power the party had to be prepared to take on governmental responsibility – if necessary, in cooperation with the pro-republican bourgeois parties – and to accept the inevitable compromises that such combinations entail.

Like Hilferding, Hertz recognized that the emergence of Nazism represented a serious threat to the republic. Unlike his comrade, however, he initially opposed the policy of tolerating Heinrich Brüning's conservative government and was prepared to bring it down and risk new Reichstag elections. In 1931, however, he changed his mind once Brüning threatened to withdraw the Catholic Center party from the SPD-led coalition government in Prussia. Like many other Social Democrats, Hertz feared the loss of long-time Socialist control over Germany's most important state. In the end, along with Hilferding, he remained wedded to parliamentary political tactics and economic orthodoxy; he had no alternative approach to stave off fascism. Indeed, even after the Reichstag granted Hitler full power at the end of March 1933, Hertz momentarily believed it might be possible for the SPD to carve out a legal space in Hitler's Germany. When the Nazis indicated they would end the ban on the socialist press if leaders like Hertz went abroad to counter reports about Nazi atrocities against their opponents, he accepted the offer and traveled to Denmark and Sweden for that purpose. Of course, Nazi behavior soon disabused Hertz of these illusions. The destruction of Germany's free trade unions on 2 May and the arrest of union leaders sent a clear signal to the SPD that it would soon suffer a similar fate. Instructed by the Executive to participate in the establishment of a party center abroad, by mid-May he was in Saarbrücken with his family. In early June they joined other members of the leadership in Prague.

It is unclear whether Hertz was able to flee Germany with any of his own financial resources. Like Hilferding, his family had lost its personal possessions, and he and Hannah had to reestablish their household. With two teenage children they certainly had much to worry about, but fortunately for them, the SPD had been able to move a part of its treasury abroad, which it then used to reconstitute its organization. As a member of the Executive, Hertz was entitled to a salary of 2,500 kronen per month.[2] This was enough to allow them an adequate, if modest, living, and Hertz soon had a regular work routine.

Between June 1933 and March 1938 Hilferding and Hertz exchanged hundreds of letters dealing with a wide range of subjects. The content of their correspondence naturally flowed largely from their respective functions within the SPD leadership in exile. As a member of the elected leadership, Hertz was involved in the Executive's day-to-day political decision-making and was an active participant in the many debates and crises experienced in the group.

---

2   Buchholz and Rother (eds.) 1995, p. 124.

Engaged in a variety of publishing projects, his most important job was as the editor of *Sozialistische Aktion* (*Socialist Action* or SA), a party weekly intended for underground dissemination in Germany. In addition, he co-edited the *Zeitschrift für Sozialismus* (*The Journal of Socialism* or *ZfS*), to which he also contributed, and wrote for *Neuer Vorwärts* (*The New Forward* or NV), the party weekly distributed in Europe's democratic countries.

Hilferding, for his part, was the chief editor of the *ZfS* and wrote weekly for NV. Already in exile in April 1933 when the SPD's Berlin conference had chosen the new leadership, Hilferding was not reelected to the Executive. Although most of its members remained interested in his views and called upon him frequently to participate in its activities, he did not need to be regularly present in Prague for its deliberations. The freedom from day-to-day practical political responsibilities allowed him to settle in Zürich, which had a long tradition of accommodating left-wing exiles, and the location of which gave Hilferding easy access to the Labor and Socialist International's office in Brussels and to émigré centers in Saarbrücken and Paris. Importantly, despite his complaints to the contrary, it also gave him time to consider the factors that had led to German Social Democracy's catastrophic defeat and to ponder the way forward.

Naturally, many of the letters concern issues relating to publishing matters, especially those related to the *ZfS*. Virtually everything connected with publishing was more difficult from exile; with Hilferding in Zürich and Hertz in Prague, reviewing and editing manuscripts, sending them on time to the printer in Karlsbad, and distributing the journal were onerous undertakings. Once the journal's mission was defined, the editors were also faced with the constant challenge of recruiting contributors, paying honoraria, marketing the magazine, and keeping the whole enterprise afloat financially. As the letters make clear, it was often difficult and frustrating work, and Hilferding repeatedly, but in vain, requested to be relieved of the responsibility, because it robbed him of time to devote to research and writing. He was disappointed in 1936 when the Executive cancelled the *ZfS* for financial and political reasons, but also clearly relieved to be free of the burden.

In addition to the daily business of publishing, the letters also reflect how the two men dealt with the stress of their situations. Hilferding was frequently depressed, and it was often difficult for him to respond to Hertz's letters, even when they were time sensitive. There were moments in which he basically became immobilized and unable to function, as is shown most clearly in a letter from Rose Hilferding to Hertz in July 1935, when she described him as so "downcast, hopeless, and disconsolate" that "he just dragged himself around, couldn't work, slept for hours, *ate practically nothing at all*, was irritable, and unapproachable".[3] Hertz was generally very understanding, though there were times when he scolded Hilferding for his silence. He was less patient when Hilferding hesitated to support him in the factional infighting in Prague, especially if that meant going there in person to fight it out. Hertz was an indefatigable factional infighter whose minority views generally were not welcome to the majority of the Sopade's members. That Hilferding tried to stay aloof from these squabbles, even if it meant the demise of the *ZfS*, caused much tension between them.

Of course, the political issues of the day stand at the heart of the correspondence. When the members of the Sopade arrived in Prague in early June, the party organization in Germany was collapsing in the face of Nazi repression and the leadership was split. A majority of the twenty-member Executive consisted of the old guard of the Weimar leadership, headed by Otto Wels and Hans Vogel, but nine of the members were "new" personalities. Hertz, Erich Ollenhauer, and Erich Rinner had been selected to represent the younger generation of party comrades; Karl Böchel, Siegfried Aufhäuser, George Dietrich, and Franz Küntsler represented the "left"; and Paul Löbe and Wilhelm Sollmann the "right". While some, such as Löbe, hoped that the SPD could continue to operate legally within Hitler's Germany, most quickly concluded that this was chimerical and recognized that resistance to the Nazis would have to be organized from outside the country. From their headquarters in Prague they set up a series of new publications to disseminate their message to their comrades in Germany, to the exile community scattered throughout Western Europe, and to foreign audiences whose support they needed in the fight against Hitler. They also built up a cadre of border secretaries whose task was to assist with moving people and propaganda across the border and began efforts to create an underground operation inside Germany.[4]

What the content of the party's message would be also generated considerable controversy as the factions debated the extent to which they should engage in self-criticism for their recent defeat and their specific immediate and future goals. While under Weimar the party had championed a reformist road to socialism, now their early manifestos of June 1933 called upon German workers to "break the chains" of Nazi oppression and carry out a "revolution against Hitler". Asserting that freedom and socialism were inseparable, the Sopade aimed to "mobilize the widest coalition of all strata of society", for an uprising "in the spirit of the liberal democratic revolutionaries of 1848", and it clearly

---

3 Rose Hilferding to Hertz, July 18, 1935.
4 Edinger 1956, pp. 23–24, 56–59.

rejected establishing a proletarian dictatorship along Bolshevik lines.[5] What these goals concretely meant, however, and how they would be achieved in practice remained the subject of heated discussion.

While the Sopade had to rethink its message, it also had to fend off rival groups challenging its claim to be Social Democracy's sole legitimate leadership. One of the most important of these groups, known as Neu Beginnen (New Beginning, NB), called for a break with the mechanistic "economic determinism" of the Social Democratic "old Left", demanded the party's complete reorganization along democratic centralist lines, and advocated the training of a new cadre of elite revolutionary fighters to organize and lead the struggle against the Nazi regime. NB rejected the dogmatism of the KPD and its subordination to the dictates of the Comintern, but its criticisms and demands left the Sopade's conservative majority cold. Ultimately, the Sopade spurned NB's claims to a share of its resources and avoided cooperating with it.[6]

Another dissident group, the Revolutionary Socialists, was led by Böchel and Aufhäuser, who had been leading Social Democratic trade unionists under Weimar and were now members of the Sopade itself. Its demands to reorganize the party and to jettison its reformist ideology were similar to those of NB, but they also emphasized the necessity of reuniting the labor movement by joining together with the Communists in the quest for a soviet Germany allied to the Soviet Union and opposed to western imperialism.[7] These positions were completely unacceptable to a majority within the Sopade, and it soon became apparent that Böchel and Aufhäuser's membership in that body was untenable.

Much of Hilferding and Hertz's correspondence grapples with their responses to these issues as they unfolded over the span of many years. As Langkau-Alex has observed, for Hertz the cause of Social Democracy's weakness was rooted in a lack of self-confidence and a lack of a will to power among the leaders of the SPD and the Labor and Socialist International (LSI). Once in exile, Hertz thought, the Sopade had reproduced the hierarchical and authoritarian structure and mode of thinking of the Weimar period and was, therefore, unable to fully grasp the movement's new situation and tasks. As a result, Social Democracy's fragmentation had intensified after 1933, and the weakened movement was in no position to become the motor of anti-fascist resistance and revolution. To remedy this situation, Hertz argued vehemently in favor of reorganizing or concentrating all socialist forces, including NB and the Revolu-

---

5 Ibid., pp. 42–47.
6 Grasmann 1976, pp. 115–23.
7 Edinger 1956, p. 148; Grasmann, 22–23.

tionary Socialists, in an alliance that would centralize resources and activities inside and outside of Germany and promote unity. He was also open to cooperation, if on a limited basis, with the Communists.[8]

For his part, Hilferding began the exile period with a sharp turn to the left.[9] Many of his early letters, his proposal for a new theoretical journal, and, most importantly, his publication of the "Prague Manifesto" in January 1934,[10] arguably the most radical program ever put forward by the SPD, reflected his view that "the turn away from reformism is not only a subjective one, but one brought about by the objective situation, one that became a fundamental necessity".[11] Expecting Nazi policy to wreck the economy and fuel discontent, he was also convinced that material want and political disillusionment alone would not be enough to bring down the Nazi "total state". Its downfall could only be the result of a "total revolution" backed by mass movements. This revolution required much mental, technical, and organizational preparation, but most of all it needed leadership. The SPD, he asserted, had two main tasks: first to organize illegal operations in Germany and build cadre to carry on the struggle; and second, to prepare itself intellectually to lead the fight and exercise power after the revolution.[12]

Much of this language was similar to that used by NB and other radical Social Democratic groups. Hilferding was now advocating the violent overthrow of Nazism by a class-conscious proletariat led by a Social Democratic movement that had reorganized itself along lines necessary to carry out underground mass work. Moreover, Hilferding also argued that a successful overthrow of fascism would have to involve a set of radical economic and political actions to secure the revolution and lay the groundwork for a new democratic and socialist era. These programmatic ideas pushed the limits of the acceptable for the Sopade's majority. It soon became clear that most SPD leaders were not willing or able to realize them in practice.

Indeed, although Hilferding never repudiated the ideas he laid out in the Manifesto, within a short time he became increasingly doubtful that the SPD or any of the other socialist groups could realize them. Early in 1935 he expressed his agreement with Hertz that Otto Wels and the rest of the Sopade were not really capable of leading the party forward, but unlike Hertz, he thought little of

---

8   Langkau Alex 1988, p. 164.
9   On Hilferding's years in exile see Smaldone 1998, pp. 173–207.
10 For the text see Dowe & Klotzbach (eds.) 2004, pp. 204–215.
11 Hilferding to [Max] Klinger (Curt Geyer), January 10, 1934, (NPH).
12 Richard Kern (Hilferding) 1933–1934, p. 10.

the splinter groups like NB and the Revolutionary Socialists, and he would have nothing to do with the Communists. When considering the various groups, he wrote, "*one thing was decisive*":

> the position on democracy and, therefore on communism. Ever since Bolshevism produced a socialism based on force and oppression, for me there has been only one correct question: freedom or slavery. In any case, socialism can mean both, and the real tragedy is that freedom and socialism are no longer identical, as they were before 1917. I cannot, therefore, compromise on the issue of dictatorship; there can be no equivocation. There can be no "furlough from freedom". Dictatorship is not transitional or educational, but makes the dictators increasingly despotic, and that is the case in Russia as well as in Italy or Germany. For this reason, I reject any cooperation with Communists, as long as they are for dictatorship and terror. I cannot understand how one can protest together with murderers and terrorists (and today, more than ever, that is what Stalin's worshippers are) against murderers and terrorists. And I will not change my mind. I don't care a rap if workers somewhere want to get together or not, because I am not the servant of the workers, but the representative of an idea [...].[13]

Here we have, in a nutshell, Hilferding's basic political attitude after 1933. Despite Hertz's energetic efforts to change his mind, he remained basically loyal to the Prague leadership primarily because they remained firmly anti-Communist and because, among the groups, they had more organizational capacity, however poor it might have been, than all the others.[14]

Throughout his intellectual career Hilferding had often been willing to rethink his earlier views in light of ongoing changes in the economic, political, and social realms. While he considered himself a Marxist until the end of his life, he remained true to the aims he had put forward with his Austro-Marxist friends many years before, namely not to treat Marxism as a dogma, but rather to subject it to criticism and to develop it further in light of new knowledge. The defeat of 1933 and the failure of the underground to make headway in Nazi Germany forced him to begin rethinking earlier assumptions about the relationship between the development of capitalism and the emergence of class

---

13 Hilferding to Hertz, January 29, 1935.
14 See, for example, Hertz's letter to Hilferding of February 11, 1936 and Hilferding's reply of March 5, 1936.

consciousness among the workers. It had not worked out as most Marxists had expected. The "most crucial and dangerous thing", Hilferding noted to Hertz in March 1936, "is that events in Italy, Germany, and, above all, in Russia itself have shown very clearly that workers' own longing for freedom is not as strong as we once imagined. The freedom of science, the development of individuality, the self-determination of one's personality, in short, all the things that led me to socialism, because I thought that the securing of material [existence] via the social control of the economy would mean the consummation of freedom, is hardly a vital factor which, under all conditions, actually drives the historical behavior of today's labor movement [...]. The consciousness of freedom must be obtained by or reawakened in the working class".[15] Problems like this one increasingly preoccupied Hilferding in his last years and are clearly reflected in his letters to his friend.

Hilferding's concern with individual and group subjectivity also was reflected in the growing emphasis he placed on the importance of the political realm as a driver of social and economic transformation, first under Weimar and later in exile.[16] Indeed, his becoming a "political thinker" led him to gradually discard traditional Marxist thinking in which capitalism must ultimately give way to socialism and instead to see that other developmental possibilities were possible, of which the "total state", in either its fascist or communist garb, is an example. For Hilferding, to insist that the great contradiction of the day was "socialism or capitalism" rather than "freedom or slavery" and to associate with the Communists, whose leaders were "detestable" and who saw "all ideals of freedom as a bourgeois swindle", would only obfuscate the importance of freedom in the minds of the workers and undermine their struggle against fascism.[17]

As his letters to Hertz and other documents in the Hertz collection make clear, over time Hilferding came to believe that there was little chance of a revolution from below destroying Nazism. Having argued that from the beginning of their regime the Nazis were bent on a war of conquest, he increasingly looked to the western democracies to stop them. Therefore, he consistently criticized the pacifist foreign policies of the interwar Socialist parties in the West as well as the outlook of the Labor and Socialist International and instead, as German power grew, urged them to support rearmament.[18] Indeed,

---

15   Hilferding to Hertz, March 5, 1936.
16   Behring 2019, pp. 115–48.
17   Hilferding to Hertz, March 5, 1936.
18   See, for example, Hilferding's report on "The French Situation and Foreign Policy", of March 1934 and his letter to Friedrich Stampfer, August 28, 1936.

eventually he began to look more to the British Conservatives rather than the Labor Party or the French Socialists, whose policies disappointed him again and again.

As time passed, life in exile took on a certain routine, but all Social Democrats were certainly aware that their initial breathing space – in both material and political terms – was constantly narrowing. By the summer of 1936, as the Sopade's financial resources dwindled, there were heated debates about how to distribute remaining resources and how to raise more funds, including the possibility of selling the SPD's archives, which included many of the papers of Marx and Engels, to the Soviets as a means of salvaging the party's finances. Hilferding and Hertz's discussions of the practical and ethical aspects of such a move reflected the seriousness of their dilemma. Should the Sopade accept an offer of millions in support from a group that it condemned both politically and morally? Did the goal of saving the organization justify the use of such means? Interestingly, in this matter Hilferding was more open to the sale if it supported Social Democratic purposes than Hertz, who felt it would only fuel corruption and undermine the moral standing of the organization.[19] In the end the Sopade elected to sell the archive for a modest sum to the Institute for Social History in Amsterdam, but the financial crisis continued.

Hilferding's relationship with Hertz was both political and personal. Although over their twenty years of working together they never spoke or wrote to one another in the familiar, their personal relationship was strong enough to survive often heated disputes. The two knew one another's family members, occasionally offered advice or to help with the affairs of the other's children, and, after some blunt speech, knew how to cut one another some slack. Each recognized that, despite substantial differences, the other was completely dedicated to the socialist cause, and both were in it for the long haul. Thus, the two men had enough in common politically and enough mutual respect, to continue their relationship.

It seems, however, that their friendship did not survive their move to Paris in 1938. Both men moved there for political reasons. Following the fall of Austria, Nazi pressure on Czechoslovakia made the Sopade's position in Prague untenable, forcing it, along with Hertz and Hannah, to relocate to Paris. At the same time, similar political pressures in Switzerland made it increasingly difficult for Hilferding to remain in Zürich, and he and Rose followed their comrades to

---

19   The issue recurs frequently in letters from late 1935 and throughout 1936. For a good summary of their views see Hertz to Hilferding, February 11, 1936. On the background see Buchholz and Rother (eds.) 1995, pp. xxix–xxx.

the French capital. Once there, matters did not go well for Hertz. His continued effort to promote his proposals to concentrate the forces of the left made no headway in the Sopade, and matters came to a head when his open association with NB led to accusations of disloyalty and to disputes over money. By June, he had been expelled. Meanwhile, Hilferding began to attend the meetings of the Executive, though he did not become a formal member. In regard to Hertz's actions, he felt that Hertz had clearly "compromised himself" and did not speak in his favor.[20] We have no record of further contact between them.

Hertz remained in Paris until 1939 when he was able to move to the United States where he became a citizen but remained involved with the left wing of the German exile community. Concerned about the post-war reconstruction of Germany, he participated in such organizations as the American Friends of German Freedom and the Council for a Democratic Germany and was also influenced by his work with the Congress of Industrial Unions and the American labor leaders Walter and Victor Reuther. He returned to Germany in 1949 where he played a major role in Berlin's reconstruction as financial advisor to Social Democratic Mayor Ernst Reuter, as the Chairman of the European Recovery Program Advisory Committee and as a Senator for economics and finance.

Unlike Hertz, there is no evidence that Hilferding entertained the idea of leaving Europe until it was too late. He remained in Paris where he continued working with the Sopade and writing for *NV* until June 1940, when the Nazi invasion caused him to flee the city. Separated by unknown circumstances from Rose, he fled with his friend Rudolf Breitscheid, Breitscheid's wife Toni, and a few others to Marseilles, where they arrived after an arduous journey in early July. Although they knew they were being hunted by Nazis, they hoped that they would be protected by the French government in Vichy, and attempted to make arrangements to board a ship that would eventually take them to the United States, from which, through the intercession of the Emergency Rescue Committee led by Varian Fry, they had received entrance visas.

These plans came to naught, however. In September the French police arrested Hilferding and Breitscheid and confined them to a hotel in Arles. For the next four months they tried in vain to procure exit visas to leave the country, while Hilferding used the local library to begin his last major project, a critique of Marxism posthumously published as "Das historische Problem" ["The His-

---

20   Buchholz and Rother (eds.) 1995, pp. XLI–XLII, 220–225, 332.

torical Problem"].[21] It was a work that would remain unfinished, however. On 10 February the French police drove Hilferding and Breitscheid to the demarcation line separating Vichy from German occupied France and handed them over to the Gestapo, who then took them to dungeon of Le Sante in Paris. At that point Hilferding decided that the fight was over for him. Having successfully concealed veronal on his person, he took his own life.[22]

21   See Hilferding 1954, pp. 293–324.
22   Breitscheid was taken to Germany and eventually housed in Buchenwald concentration camp where he was killed in a bombing in 1944. Rose Hilferding arrived in Arles soon after Hilferding's extradition to Germany. She was able to escape France by ship and make her way to New York. On Hilferding's final months see Smaldone 1998, pp. 200–7.

CHAPTER 9

Rudolf Hilferding's Correspondence with Paul Hertz, 1933–38

Zürich, June 14, 1933

Dear Paul,

Thanks very much for your letter. I'm doubly thankful for being kept up to date. Matters in Germany are certainly frightful. What is disconcerting is that this behavior will drive the workers away from Social Democracy and into the arms of the Communists. Nevertheless, I think we are dealing with an episode, if also a very bad one.[1] For the result will be one of two possibilities: either people will limit themselves to collecting dues and, through good behavior, purchasing Nazi toleration for a short time, which might appeal to the Nazis as a way to confuse and sabotage us, and then we lose any of the working-class following that we might have maintained. Or they attempt to carry on modest political activity and are then suppressed by the National Socialists, thus also bringing this illusion to an end. I don't believe that the National Socialists are clever enough to allow a semblance of opposition. For them that would probably be too dangerous.

It is, unfortunately, correct that our organizational work is very difficult at present. On the other hand, we can really rely on the people who now are following us. Hopefully, we will succeed in getting the best group of leaders on our side.

The business with [Hans] Vogel[2] is very unpleasant. Hopefully, he'll think it over. His return would not only be dangerous for him personally, but it would be completely useless. Legal political work cannot be carried out in Germany and the fake work only does harm. I am waiting impatiently for the final step

---

1 Hilferding is referring to the behavior of the remnant of SPD leaders in Berlin, primarily in the Reichstag delegation, who hoped to salvage a modicum of legal existence for the party by refraining from criticizing the Nazis and behaving cautiously. This placed them at odds with the émigré leadership, which recognized that the SPD had no future in Nazi-dominated Germany.
2 Hans Vogel (1881–1945) trained as a sculptor but made his career as a Social Democratic politician, first on the regional and then on the national stage. A supporter of the pro-war majority in the party, he served in the National Assembly in 1919 and then in the Reichstag until 1933.

to be irrevocably taken.[3] As before, I prefer that the manifesto be published as it stands.[4] I would also accept an appeal with the same content. It would be wrong to simply do an article. The form must also express that a new epoch, an epoch of radical and revolutionary resistance has begun. Otherwise, we will lose our influence and strengthen the Communists. In regard to the signature, I would not hesitate to include the names of all of those working abroad. Otherwise, Wels could sign on behalf of the Party Executive in exile. Have you read and corrected the article on economics? Once again, I ask that you send me the galley proofs as soon as possible. I'd be grateful for ideas and material.

For me, the political difficulties were not completely unexpected. Perhaps, in the long run, the work will only be possible in a big country, in France or, eventually, England. When the final decision is reached, the fate of Vienna will weigh heavily on the scales.

Breitscheid is inclined to go to Paris, not London. I would think the latter would really be much better, because it is much more important to influence British public opinion than French. At the moment, his concerns about going [to London] have been strengthened because of America, but he has probably written to you about that directly.

Hopefully the other things – journals and informational reports – are gradually moving ahead. For the rest, one must be aware of the difficulties, but the path we have chosen is the only possible one if the future of Social Democracy is to be saved. And, therefore, I think that any further delay is senseless. The supposed threats of expulsion are ridiculous. Please, write to me really soon. Best regards to you and the friends. I am especially pleased that Cr[ummenerl] is coming here.[5]

Your,
    Rudolf

The Executive Committee of the SPD
Sopade, Prag-Karlin

He joined the party Executive in 1927 and became SPD Co-chair, with Otto Wels, in 1931. He was reelected to that post in April 1933 and migrated, via Saarbrücken, to Prague with the Sopade in June.
3 Hilferding is referring to the outlawing of the SPD, which finally occurred on June 22.
4 Bearing the title "Zerbrecht die Ketten!" ["Break the Chains!"], the manifesto was published in the inaugural issue of *Neuer Vorwärts* on June 18, 1933.
5 Siegmund Crummenerl (1892–1940) became the SPD's treasurer in 1930. In May 1933 he joined the leadership in exile first in Saarbrücken and then in Prague.

Palackeho trida 179
Prague, June 24, 1933

Dear Rudolf,

Stampfer gave me your letter with the article, which, unfortunately, arrived so late that we could no longer include it in the second issue [of *Neuer Vorwärts*]. The laying out of the paper occurs on Thursday. The latest possible time for the receipt of a manuscript here in Prague is, therefore, early Wednesday. But even then, its inclusion is doubtful. You always have to remember that the printer is in Karlsbad, and forwarding it there, as well as the typesetting, takes much more time than we are used to.

I don't think we can publish the article in its current form in the next issue. We have already dealt with trade and the rising cost of fats ourselves. One can summarize the issue of Hugenberg and the London Conference in a notice.[6] Therefore, I recommend that you send us a new article right away. If you don't have any concrete material at your disposal, write something more general and, indeed, as accusatory as you'd like to see reflected in the journal's overall content.

I am in full agreement in respect to this critique, but it is very difficult to create the publication that we want when there are no co-workers and when all the other conditions are so primitive. Still, I hope that we will come closer to this goal.

Crummenerl has probably spoken to you personally about everything else. He told us that the proposal for the magazine will come soon. Hopefully, you will keep this promise, otherwise we won't get anywhere.[7]

Best regards,
[Paul]

6　The London Economic Conference of June 12 to July 27, 1933 brought together representatives of 66 nations to discuss measures to end the Great Depression. Minister of Economics, Alfred Hugenberg (1865–1951), leader of the German National People's Party – a partner in Hitler's coalition government – represented Germany and caused a scandal when he called for German colonial expansion, overseas and in Eastern Europe, as a means of reversing economic decline. Although Hitler also cherished such goals, he responded to the public scandal by firing him.
7　See below the document entitled "On the Need for a New Theoretical Journal."

Zürich, June 26, 1933

Dear Paul,

Thanks for your letter. I should have written before, but I thought it would be better to take care of things verbally with Cr[ummenerl]. Unfortunately, his return was delayed until tomorrow evening at the earliest. My collaboration at [*Neuer*] *V*[*orwärts*] has not gone well thus far. I did not know the day of the editorial deadline. That's why the earlier article came too late. Only I thought that, with changes, it could still be usable. I'm still of the opinion that the Hugenberg matter deserves attention and easily could be brought up to date. Because it is, on its own, characteristic – especially its rejection – but, then [again], it is not yet settled. Yesterday, Litvinov[8] officially protested in Berlin and Bülow[9] rudely sent him away. I don't think the Russians will want to put up with that. Today's *Temps* reports that emissaries are preparing a visit to London by Göring.[10] Göring wants to suggest a joint action against Russia (an old idea of Rosenberg's).[11] As fantastic as that sounds, perhaps it suits the Russians to act as if they are taking it seriously. It could, for example, provide a good pretext to delay payments to Germany. In any case, it appears that the Russians want to exploit Germany's situation. Therefore, I would not drop the matter, especially after Litvinov's impertinence.

Thus, I was not prepared today to write for [*Neuer*] *V*[*orwärts*] when your letter came, and [Friedrich] Adler told me what happened on the phone. I had written this morning about the most recent plan to provide employment by means of highway [construction], but I already sent the article to Saarbrücken, which I feel badly about. I then tried to put something together for [*Neuer*] *V*[*orwärts*], but I fear *it did not go particularly well*. Still, maybe you can use

---

8   Maxim Litvinov (1876–1951) was Soviet Foreign Minister from 1930–39.
9   Bernhard Wilhelm Otto von Bülow (1885–1936) was State Secretary in the Foreign Office from 1930–36. A nationalist opposed to the Versailles settlement, he accommodated himself to the Nazi regime and justified the Nazi purge of Jews and others from state service.
10   Hermann Göring (1893–1946) was a World War One fighter ace and early adherent to the Nazi Party. A member of Hitler's inner circle, after the seizure of power he took control of the Prussian police and Gestapo, became head of the Air Force, was put in charge of the war economy, and in 1941 was named Hitler's successor. Later tried for war crimes at Nuremberg, he was found guilty and committed suicide while awaiting execution.
11   Alfred Rosenberg (1893–1946) was a "Baltic German" born in Estonia. Educated in Russia, he emigrated to Germany in 1918 and became one of National Socialism's leading intellectuals. He edited the Nazis' flagship daily, *Die Völkischer Beobachter* and later became Minister of the Eastern Occupied Territories. He was found guilty of war of war crimes and hanged at Nuremberg in 1945.

it. Perhaps the contrasting of behavior to the entrepreneurs is effective. In the future, I'll see to it that you receive the articles by *Tuesday*. The only very difficult thing is [getting] *material*. Don't we have anyone left in Berlin who can provide us with some information?

Now, to the other thing. I am thinking of providing Cr[ummenerl] with an extensive plan for the *journal*.

Concerning [*Neuer*] *V*[*orwärts*], one can only say *Die Freiheit* is excellent.[12] (That was always so – but only for you!) Thus far it lacks impetus, *elan*. But I grasp the difficulties. A daily has it easier than a weekly, and I understand the inhibitions when considering Berlin. I'm very glad that B is free, please give him my best. Now, to more important matters.

The violent liquidation of the party, which was to be expected, now marks the actual endpoint. The party has every reason to say that clearly and to proclaim the closure of the old and the beginning of a new epoch. It needs that in order to strengthen trust. For that reason, I am coming back to the recommendation regarding the *manifesto*. Of course, the old must be changed in some respects, the end underlined, [and] the new emphasized. I will attempt to provide Cr[ummenerl] with *a revised manifesto*. It can't be too short, because some things must be said for it to be effective. St[ampfer] makes his judgements, however, based only on the space available in *N*[*euer*] *V*[*orwärts*]. But perhaps it does not actually have to appear there, but could come out as a flyer, on thin paper if necessary. But that is secondary.

Regarding the *signature*, here one must liberate one's self from old notions. The authority of Prague does not primarily, or, in any case solely, rest upon its being an elected leadership (Saarbrücken now is getting one, too),[13] but rather is derived from it *having done the right thing*. The authority of Plekhanov, Axelrod, Martov, Lenin, and Trotsky [also] rested upon it. The appeal opposing the [party's] wartime policy was signed by Haase, Bernstein, and Kautsky – not by any institutional authority – and it was effective. Therefore, I think the manifesto should be signed by you [in Prague], but also by the leaders in Saarbrücken, by Breitscheid and me and, just in case there is somebody else there with a good name, by him, too.

Also, very important is what Cr[ummenerl] will report on the trade unions. I have to catch a train, so I have to end the letter and can't say much about it. I

---

12   *Die Freiheit* [*Freedom*] was Social Democracy's newspaper in the Saarland region, which, as a result of the Versailles Treaty, remained under French administration until it was returned to Germany following a referendum in 1935.

13   The reference is to the regional SPD leadership based in Saarbrücken, the capital of the Saarland.

have spoken at great length with S about it and I have a splendid impression.[14] He is irreplaceable right now, but the trade union matter is just as important as the political, and it is a now or never moment to gain influence upon it. It is you who must keep an eye on this issue. I'll talk about it with Cr[ummenerl], when I'm next able to see him.

I have to close now, but I'll write soon, and I hope you'll write soon, as well. Please give my regards to all the colleagues, and please read the corrections and make any changes that you think would be good.

My very best regards,
    Rudolf

Der Parteivorstand der SPD
Sopade, Prag-Karlin
Palackeho trida 24
Prague, July 15, 1933

Dear comrade Hilferding,

On Sunday we had a discussion with comrade Arthur [Arnold][15] and I'm writing to you on the same subject. We urgently require the last five years of *Vorwärts*. Arthur believes that Dr. Emil Oprecht of Zürich[16] could order the back issues in Berlin from the *Vorwärts* publishing house. The letter would be given to him [Artur], and he would ensure that the papers would be delivered to Oprecht. Oprecht could probably send them via Leipzig directly to our address. Of course, we are prepared to pay all the necessary costs.

Now it depends upon you speaking with comrade Oprecht and making arrangements with him to order the *Vorwärts* editions in Berlin from *Vorwärts's* publishing house. It would be even better if we could get the paper going back ten years. Perhaps Oprecht can write expressing his interest in acquiring all back issues of *Vorwärts* since its founding.

---

14 The identity of S is unclear.
15 Arthur Müller (1891–1940?) supplied paper for *Vorwärts* under Weimar. He emigrated to Prague in 1933, served as secretary to the Sopade and temporarily directed the publishing house of *Neuer Vorwärts*. In exile he went by the name Arthur Arnold and eventually migrated to South America.
16 Emil Oprecht (1895–1952) was a leading Swiss publisher and bookseller with Social Democratic sympathies. He helped many German political and artistic emigres and was an important publisher of exiled authors.

Let me know, please, when you've spoken with Oprecht and whether he is prepared to meet our request.

Freedom!
[S. Crummenerl]

Zürich, July 17, 1933

Dear comrade Crummenerl,

Oprecht will write to you directly regarding the [*Vorwärts*] matter. If you need anything else done, I'm happy to help.

Oprecht is traveling today, but I spoke with his wife and the letter will be mailed to Berlin today. We asked initially for the last five volumes, but with the possibility of acquiring the last ten.

I've just called Bern, but the envoy himself was unavailable to speak; the secretary said a courier would come on Wednesday. I'll call again early tomorrow morning. At the same time, there seems to be a misunderstanding. The envoy, [Zdenek] Fierlinger, is in Vienna.[17] The person from Bern is named Künzl-Iserski.[18] I assume we are just dealing with a mix up of names and, in any case, I will let you know what is happening after the morning call.

In regard to use, I am *against* your recommendation. Not only because I think that the gold-backed currencies that still exist, especially that of France, are more secure, but, above all because, if France drops the gold standard, then no country can continue to have gold-backed currency. It is unclear to me how the price of gold will change. Historically, there is no analogous situation. It is possible we'll enter a period of confusion with strong swings in the exchange value of gold in the various currencies. I would recommend that we invest in French francs and, perhaps, once again in defense bonds. How long do you think we will be able to maintain the reserve? If for many months or one to two years, then it would be best to buy first class shares in French or possibly

---

[17] Zdenek Fierlinger (1891–1976) was a Czech businessman, diplomat, and Social Democrat. During the interwar period he served as a Czechoslovakian ambassador in the United States, Switzerland, and Austria. From 1937–45 in Moscow, he mediated between the USSR and the Czechoslovak government in exile. After 1945 he supported a merger of the Social Democratic and Communist Parties in Czechoslovakia. He was Prime Minister of Czechoslovakia from April 1945–June 1946.

[18] Künzl-Iserski had replaced Fierlinger as Ambassador to Switzerland in 1932.

Dutch firms, about which there would be more to say, if possible (without special purpose fees) [...]. In any case, please let Fritz [Adler] or me know what you think. Scheidemann[19] should work through Hilquit[20] to sue the *New York Times* for falsifying his article. The aim should be, above all, to rouse American public opinion about the hostages. It has to happen right away, however, because the statute of limitations is short.

Finally, Henderson's visit to Berlin is very unpleasant.[21] But he would not have been dissuaded by either us or Fritz. We thought about it. In Paris, however, one will have to discuss the International's view of disarmament, etc.

Best regards to you and to the friends,
 Rudolf Hilferding

[P.S] A couple of days don't matter. Fritz and I think that for the moment the money should be deposited in Swish Francs until we know your opinion.

Zürich, July 18, 1933

Dear comrade Crummenerl,

Following up from yesterday's letter, I'm writing to tell you that I'll be in Bern tomorrow (the courier won't get there until the evening). I have come to an understanding with the envoy there. Fritz is also coming to Zürich tomorrow in order to take care of the business we discussed yesterday in the manner I had proposed. We are awaiting further news from you. Also, after giving it further thought, I stand by my advice.

Concerning the Scheidemann matter, an American told me that using Hillquit as a [legal] representative would not be very practical. Samuel Untermeyer is the lawyer who usually deals with such political trials. Depending on the circumstances, he would probably take on the case, possibly at no cost, because

---

19 Philip Scheidemann (1865–1939) joined the SPD in 1883. Prior to 1914 he edited a number of important socialist newspapers and served in the Reichstag. A supporter of the SPD's right wing, he backed the war. After the monarchy's fall, he served in the revolutionary government and briefly as Chancellor in 1919. He fled Germany in 1933.
20 Morris Hilquit (1869–1933) was a co-founder and a leading figure in the Socialist Party of America.
21 The reference is to British Labor Party leader Arthur Henderson (1863–1935) who, as Chairman of the Geneva Disarmament Conference, was working to prevent Germany's departure from that body. He failed and Germany withdrew on October 14, 1933.

it would be sensational. I don't know his address, but one could easily make contact with him through a comrade in New York.

Finally, I'd be grateful if you could tell me something to pass along to George D. from Erfurt. I told you already, that we are dealing here initially with possibilities for activity, not a salary.

Hopefully, my article for [*Neuer*] *V*[*orwärts*] has arrived on time. I sent it airmail on Sunday.

Best regards to you and the colleagues,
Your,
[Rudolf Hilferding]

[On the Need for a New Theoretical Journal. Document written by Hilferding sometime in 1933]

The need for a journal results from the necessity to renew the discussion of the tactical problems facing the party and socialism in general, to validate our conception of democratic socialism, and to draw conclusions for socialism stemming from the stormy economic and political upheaval of the current epoch. However, before discussing this set of problems – if only by way of suggestion – I initially would like to say something concrete about the form and content of the first issue, as I imagine it right now, of course bearing in mind that the planned content would have to be modified depending on the timing of its appearance and the staff we recruit.

In regard to the journal's form, the articles will have to be clear and written for a popular audience. The *Gesellschaft* had the task of making new problems accessible to the elite of our [party] functionaries. The scholarly form could not be avoided. The content of the new journal must be fully understandable to the masses. It must leave broad space for discussion. I imagine a magazine something like the *Neue Zeit* at the time of the revisionism discussion, of course without the personal polemics. The articles' form would have to be something along the lines of the political articles written by the young Kautsky. The individual articles must be short. They must forego complicated theoretical problems of political economy, philosophy, or law.

The journal should appear every fourteen days; a monthly would undercut its topicality too much. It should be thirty-two pages long. For printing, besides Karlsbad perhaps Vienna could be considered. The printers there are more efficient, and the communications are just as good. Of course, the decision would also depend on the costs. The editorial board probably would be located in Prague.

As content for the first issue, I'm thinking along the following lines: 1) Tasks of the magazine – Hilferding; Social Democratic politics and organization in the struggle against dictatorship, a declaratory article that must be written by Otto Wels; problems of trade union struggle by Leuschner[22] or Aufhäuser;[23] an article about the tasks of the emigration, especially the historical role of national and social revolution, by Otto Bauer; an article about finance policy by Hertz or Rinner;[24] an article by Vandervelde, not just a greeting, but rather a substantive statement about the fight against fascism in the democratic countries; the young generation of Social Democracy by Ollenhauer;[25] [and] a political letter from Berlin by Geyer.[26] For the series, there should be a lead article of a political or tactical nature by me, Geyer, or Stampfer.[27] Foreign policy should be handled by Breitscheid and Schiffrin [sic].[28] The latter should also be con-

---

22   Wilhelm Leuschner (1890–1944) led the wood sculptors' union and was an SPD leader in Hesse. He served in the Landtag, became Interior Minister in 1928, and joined the Executive Committee of the ADGB in January 1933. Arrested in June, he spent a year in various camps. Later active in the underground, the Nazis arrested him August 1944 in connection with the failed July bomb plot against Hitler. He was executed on September 29, 1944.
23   Siegfried Aufhäuser (1884–1969) was leader of the German Association of White-Collar Workers (AfA-Bund) and a major Social Democratic political figure under Weimar. In exile, he was on the left-wing of the Sopade until 1935, when he was expelled due to his opposition to majority's reformist course. He eventually moved to the United States but returned to Germany in 1951 and continued his trade-union activities.
24   Erich Rinner (1902–1982) was a functionary in the SPD Reichstag delegation under Weimar. In April 1933 he was coopted onto the party executive as a representative of the younger generation and remained in Berlin until the SPD was banned in June. After operating underground, he joined the Sopade in Prague in October 1933. His major charge was to edit underground intelligence reports later published as *Deutschlandberichte der Sopade, 1934–1940*.
25   Erich Ollenauer (1901–1963) became the leader of the SPD youth organization in 1928 and joined the party executive committee in April 1933. Along with Wels, Vogel, and others, he emigrated to Prague in 1933. After later fleeing to France and England, he eventually returned to Germany and became SPD Chairman in 1952.
26   Curt Geyer (1891–1967) was a major figure on the SPD's left-wing. A co-founder of the USPD, he joined the KPD in 1920 but, disillusioned, returned to the SPD in 1924. There he became managing editor of *Vorwärts*, where Friedrich Stampfer was chief editor. After arriving in Prague in October 1933, he became Stampfer's deputy at *Neuer Vorwärts*.
27   Friedrich Stampfer (1874–1957) was a non-Marxist socialist who joined the SPD in the nineties. A skilled journalist, he directed the party's national news service before the war. A supporter of the pro-war majority in 1914, he became chief editor of *Vorwärts* in 1916, joined the party Executive, and became a leading SPD parliamentarian. In exile he remained in the Executive and was chief editor of *Neuer Vorwärts*.
28   Alexander Schifrin (1901–1951) was active in the Ukrainian Menshevik Party. After his arrest in 1922, he moved to Germany and joined the SPD. A collaborator with Hilferding

sidered for the altercation with Communist ideology. As a first article in that regard, I am thinking of a piece on the attitude of the Russian government and the Communist International, as well as the German Communist Party, toward the National Socialist seizure of power. Space must also be preserved for the concrete debate with the National Socialist program, thus, on the corporate state, on the problem of providing employment, [and] on economic policy, in order to constantly reveal the contradictions between ideology and reality. Two outstanding specialists, Friedrich Hertz[29] and [Hugo] Iltis,[30] can write against the racial teachings. In connection with the Paris discussion of the International, a series of statements of principle will be necessary, and for these we should draw on foreign Socialists, too.

Concrete discussions of illegal work, in so far as they are possible, can only be carried out by you and in a scope that you determine.

For the moment, I would like to limit myself to these suggestions; the main concern and the main difficulty will be the recruitment of coworkers from Germany itself. That alone makes it necessary for the editorial board to work in close collaboration with Prague. To these comments I'm adding yet another, more general, section, because from a broader view of the situation flow additional consequences for the creation of the journal.

The new phase of capitalist development raises new questions not only for Germany, but for the whole world. German development had only occurred in an especially extreme form, in part as a result of historical preconditions, [such as] the lack of democratic and, to some extent, political experience; and, in part, as a result of general psychological and sociological developments of a peculiar nature: the sudden collapse of national self-confidence as a result of the defeat, the stimulation of nationalism as a result of the Versailles Treaty, the expropriation of the middle class by the inflation, a series of crises including the Ruhr occupation, the stabilization crisis, the world crisis, the hatred of the rising working class, etc. However, the world crisis had created similar, if

---

at the *Gesellschaft*, after 1933 he became a prominent figure on the left wing of the exiled party and an expert on military affairs.

29   Friedrich Hertz (1878–1964) studied law and economics at the University of Vienna where he completed a PhD in 1902 and joined the SDAP. After a distinguished career in the Austrian government, he became a Professor of World Economy and Sociology at the University of Halle-Wittenberg in 1930 but the Nazis removed him in 1933. He then moved to Vienna and, ultimately, to London.

30   Hugo Iltis (1882–1952) was a Jewish Czech biologist who, in addition to his full-time teaching job as a high school teacher, also taught at the Germany Polytechnical Institute in Brünn from 1911–1938. A socialist and vocal opponent of Nazi racial teaching, he fled Czechoslovakia in 1938 and eventually emigrated to the United States.

not exactly the same, conditions in many other countries, some of which are of key importance. Sociologically, the change is characterized by the heavy blow to the big bourgeoisie's position. These strata, the big banks and big industries, formerly so decisive in determining economic policy, and which had at least exhibited certain progressive tendencies in the capitalist world economy – even if in ever weaker form as a result of monopolistic tendencies – have lost much influence to the petty bourgeoisie,[31] and to the peasants in particular. The expansion of democracy after the war strengthened the political and economic influence of these groups and especially of the peasants. Their rebellion grows as the crisis drags on, and it is remarkable how strongly developments in the United States parallel those in Germany. In the rural areas the rebellion of the farmers takes on very similar forms, as in Holstein. The influence of bank capital is in complete retreat, while the struggle against interest slavery, the expansion of credit, and, thereby, the creation of employment becomes the content of politics. Sociologically, despite certain strong qualifications, Roosevelt is not too far from Hitler. Similar developments have occurred in many other countries as exemplified by the rapid progress of the middle-class fascist movement in Switzerland.

In addition, there is the enormously increased power of the state over the economy, which in part involves the direct violation of bourgeois private [property] rights, for example, the confiscation of the property of creditors to the benefit of debtors in a variety of forms. These interventions are especially strong in the agricultural areas – [e.g.,] a complete or partial grain monopoly and the fixing of state guaranteed minimal prices, as in France; the spread of ideas about capitalist economic planning, etc. In short, the rebellion against the crisis leads to the progressive revolutionizing of intellectual, political, and economic [life], from which social democracy, too, must draws its conclusions. I am far from believing, as do many others, that fascism, whether in its Italian or German form, is a necessary phase of capitalist development.

It is precisely the dispute about this matter which can form the focal point of debate and provide us with grounds to constantly move the significance of democracy to the center of the discussion.

The dispute about that leads to another important task of carrying on a continual debate with Communist ideas. The problem of socialist tactics in the conquest and maintenance of political power will presumably be rekindled as

---

[31] I have translated Hilferding's term "die gewerbliche Mittelschicht", as the petty bourgeoisie rather than "commercial middle class", because the latter is too broad a term given the context. The craftsmen and small retailers of the petty bourgeoisie were the urban counterparts of the peasantry. All three groups formed major elements of the Nazi constituency.

a result of the discussions at the Paris conference of the International. In that regard, it will likely become plain how different the situation of the parties in the fascist countries is from the others. In the fascist countries the tactical situation is only too simple. It aims to overthrow the dictatorship with all means; it is, in the technical sense of the term, revolutionary work. It is natural, then, that this work leads to an extremely radical ideology. Certainly, there is then the danger that thereby the difference with pure Bolshevism becomes blurred, and democracy is pushed into the background. To be sure, there are countertendencies, [since] the loss of freedom results in the recognition of its value. [Thus], to maintain the importance of democracy in the consciousness of the proletariat remains a vital issue, because it is not only a prerequisite for a socialism that raises economic productivity and, in contrast to Bolshevism, brings about a noticeable and constant improvement in material life, but rather, it is also a prerequisite for the maintenance and augmentation of culture, which cannot exist without intellectual freedom. The clarification of the concept of dictatorship is also necessary, as is the clarification of the illusion that a dictatorship in Bolshevik form can be a temporary condition. This is because the dictatorship, despite having the opposite intentions at its founding, itself creates the prerequisites for its continuation. In spite of being aware that the form of the seizure of power and its consolidation certainly does not depend on theoretical argument alone, but rather on the dynamism of the political struggles and the actual situation under which the seizure of power occurs, the formation of democratic consciousness is one of the most important prerequisites of future development.

It is evident that we must add the continual analysis of political problems to the theoretical clarification of our own ranks and to the debate with Communist ideology on principles.

Questions of foreign policy require exhaustive discussion and, in part, clarification. The Communist catchword of imperialism stokes confusion. Today the issue of war is much more a question of the warlike outlook of broad masses of the people. The International's foreign policy versus the dictatorships must be discussed anew. Certain ways of thinking, strongly represented recently in our own ranks, require revision. This is particularly true regarding military policy and the demand for equality of rights. It must be shown how their content depends on whether they are put forward by nationalists or socialists. In that regard, all illusions about the possibility or even the use of preventative wars must be opposed.

The annihilation of all the organs of Social Democracy makes it necessary for the journal consistently to discuss the fundamental problems of trade union policy, social policy, actual German economic and financial policy, and also cultural policy. Whether this can occur in the form of a panorama, like the *Sozialistische Monatshefte* had, is above all an issue of whether we can find enough co-workers, which under today's circumstances is questionable. In addition, these considerations, in so far as they are of an economic nature, are to be raised within a framework that starts from the perspective that economic development itself, especially through the unfolding of the crisis, and through the collapse of the political attempts to resolve it, gives rise to the drive toward socialist production.

The Executive Committee of the SPD
Office: Sopade, Prague, Karlin
Palackeho trida 24
[no date]

Dear Rudolf,

The article arrived punctually. It will be published. I've not read it myself yet, because Stampfer immediately forwarded it to Karlsbad.

We have recently been discussing the journal in detail regarding a sale price. I was initially for a low sale price but became convinced that it cannot fall below five kronen if we don't want to go broke in the process. Printing in Karlsbad is, indeed, substantially cheaper than in Vienna. Nevertheless, one copy costs 3.50 kronen. That can be broken down into 1 krone for layout, printing, and paper, .15 krone for mailing, .25 krone for administration, .5 for taxes and miscellaneous expenses and 2.10 kronen for honorarium and editorial costs. This calculation is based upon a circulation of 2,000 copies. I think that it is very optimistic. That's because this number is to be sold in German-speaking territories outside of Germany. It won't be easy, and it can only succeed at all when the magazine has something outstanding to offer. Of course, we cannot consider domestic sales at all in this estimate, because I don't believe that Siegmund [Crummenerl's] assumption that we might earn some money there is correct. By the way, I don't believe that, at the moment, we will be able sell any appreciable number in Germany. Regarding payment for the editors and authors, [we have] initially set aside 3,000 kronen for the editors and 1,200 kronen for honoraria. That amounts to 40 kronen per page or about 5 marks. To be sure, that is not very much and is even less than the *Gesellschaft* [paid], but we now have to calculate differently. We cannot pay more than the local party press, whose rates we have used as a basis for [*Neuer*] *Vorwärts*. If we don't sell more than 2,000 copies, then the magazine will be a money loser from the beginning, because with a sale price of 5 kronen we will see only 3 kronen in cash, while we will have costs of at least 3.50 kronen. So, in leading the editorial board, you constantly will have to remember that increasing circulation is a vital issue for the magazine.

In my opinion the journal should be published on 1 October at the earliest. The content of the first edition should create a stir. Therefore, I think that it is correct to do it in the wake of the Paris Conference. You and the other comrades there will, first of all, view problems flexibly. Something that I think is absolutely essential is that the magazine not be viewed as a continuation of the *Gesellschaft* but will be welcomed as something new that will provide guidance going forward. I also don't really understand why you want a programmatic article from Otto [Wels]. You have to write that, and if you don't know yet what the content should be, then how should Otto know? Meanwhile, I don't know yet what I should write for the magazine. In any case, a factual appraisal of the economic situation or of Germany's financial condition scarcely belongs in the first issue. Maybe later, we'll soon see. I also don't believe we'll get an article from Stampfer. For the moment he has no intention of writing. But I think it would be best to discuss all this in Paris. The planned conference for our agents in the West should take place after Paris. You will surely get lots to think about there.

We will name the delegation for Paris on Friday. I assume that it will consist of Otto [Wels], Friedrich [Stampfer], you, Rudi [Breitscheid], and Erich O[llenauer] as International Youth Secretary. I also think that Siegmund should go. It seems to me that Böchel[32] will also assert his right to join the delegation. On Friday we will have to discuss what we will do with Sollmann,[33] Aufhäuser, and so on.

---

32   Karl Böchel (1884–1946) trained as a locksmith and became active in the German Metal Workers' Union. After joining the SPD in 1910, he made a career as a journalist and during Weimar served as chief editor of the *Chemnitzer Volksstimme* while also a leader in the Saxon state assembly. A left-wing critic of the SPD's Weimar policies, he was appointed to the party executive committee in April 1933 and joined the Sopade in March 1934. He was expelled a year later due to his sharp criticism of the latter and calls for SPD cooperation with the KPD.

33   Wilhelm Sollman (1881–1951) was long-time editor of the social democratic *Rheinische Zeitung*, a member of the National Assembly in 1919 and of the Reichstag from 1920–33. He served as Interior Minister in the coalition government led by Gustav Stresemann in 1923, he was an important representative of the SPD's right wing. Arrested and tortured by the Nazis in March 1933, he managed to flee to the Saarland where he edited the *Deutsche Freiheit*. Later he emigrated to England and the United States.

M-Helf was here today.[34] He went to Vienna and won't likely return to Germany. He views matters in Germany very soberly and thinks that all reports about S.]A unrest are exaggerated. Above all he disputes the idea that these isolated rebellions bear any kind of revolutionary character. Bad food and similar petty complaints are what's driving them. We hear little from Erich and Kurt.[35] It appears, however, that they still are doing well.

Best regards,
   [Paul]

Karlsbad, August 16, 1933

Esteemed comrade,

Unfortunately, I'm just now writing to you about the journal and I ask you to pardon the delay. Because I don't know if this letter will reach you in Switzerland, I'm sending a copy under your name to Paris in order to be certain [that you receive it] and to ensure the most rapid reply.

First of all, the technical and organizational matters pertaining to the journal: Dr. Hertz has already told you that the Party Executive has decided that the title will be "Sozialistische Revolution" ["Socialist Revolution"]. I am very happy about it and I think it has great promise. In my view, however, we also have to agree on a subtitle, which will make the essence of the magazine clear. Have you come up with any formulations thus far? Finding the title is a pressing matter for me, because otherwise I'll find it difficult to move ahead with the technical preparations and propaganda. It would be very good if you could make a decision right away and let me know. Is there anything in particular that you want on the title page? Do you prefer or find it more practical to put the magazine's table of contents on the title page (of course, I am referring only to large format here) or is it enough to put it on inside page of the cover?

For propaganda purposes it is of decisive importance for you to send me the most recent and detailed documents about the content of the journal and the first contributions to it.

---

34   The identity of M-Helf is unclear.
35   The reference may be to Erich Rinner and Curt Geyer. For background see above footnotes 383 and 385, resp. If Hertz is referring to Kurt Geyer, then he is misspelling his first name using a K rather than a C.

I assume that you have created a new conception for the organization of the magazine, and I ask that you make that available to me. If we are to market the journal, then we have to know the direction the advertising should take, and we don't want to come into conflict with the editorial board.

Now, to political matters and, as the case may be, editorial ones. Comrade G[36] has been recruited for domestic affairs. He asked me to tell you that thus far he has found 12 domestic collaborators for the journal. The contributions that you receive from him (in future I will only refer to him as the home editor) and his colleagues will of course be anonymous. The home editor places the greatest importance on this, and strongly requests that all other contributions also be anonymous or published under a pseudonym. According to our friends at home, it is not only a matter of security for those who need it in order to avoid a repetition of the taking of hostages, as in the Scheidemann case,[37] but rather it is also absolutely necessary stemming from psychological and political considerations. I should tell you in total frankness that the idea has also come up that none of the old names should be allowed to appear in the journal as the author of an article. Naturally, that goes also for all later articles of welcome.

An additional request of the home editor is to meet with you as soon as possible. He suggests Holland and asks that you let him know whether you agree, when, and what location you prefer. If Holland is not acceptable to you, then he'd agree to come to Czechoslovakia, but under no circumstances should the meeting occur in Prague.

I ask that you communicate your decision and send all other correspondence with the domestic affairs editor to me. I will then make every effort to forward it on the fastest and most secure routes. This task has been assigned to me from the local comrades as well as from those in Berlin.

Finally, the home editor urges some consideration for a satirical collaborator. He recommends Hermann Wendel[38] or, even better, trying to recruit Kurt Tucholski [sic].[39] Initially, the recommendation for a satirical contribution had

---

36 Curt Geyer (see above footnote 26).
37 After Philipp Scheidemann began writing articles from exile critical of the Hitler regime, the Nazis responded by arresting his parents, children, and a grandchild. Two of his daughters and the grandchild perished.
38 Hermann Wendel (1884–1936) was born and raised in Metz in the French-German border province of Lorraine. A social democratic politician, historian, and journalist, he was well known as an excellent stylist. In exile, he contributed to *Neuer Vorwärts*.
39 Kurt Tucholsky (1880–1935) was an outstanding journalist and satirist whose many works, especially as editor of *Die Weltbühne* (*The World Stage*) made him one of Weimar's most influential left-wing critics.

flabbergasted me a little, but if it occurred in the same way that Jaffle Schemend, a British comrade in the *New Leader*, does it, then I think it would be promising.

I request that you reply to all these questions as quickly and securely as possible.

With socialist greetings!
[Fritz] Heine[40]

The Executive Committee of the SPD
Office of the Sopade, Prague-Karlin
Palackeho tride 24
Prague, October 9, 1933

Dear Rudolf,

Today I received your letter of October 5. I assume that, meanwhile, you've received the galley proofs. According to the printer, the articles, the notice about the labor struggle, and the two book reviews total 48 pages. We have to be published eight sided. I assume that the article by Vexator takes up about six pages and that by shortening the articles by Klinger, Schifrin, and the Catholics we can easily save two pages. Today I hope to look through the complete set of galleys. If you agree with these arrangements, then on Thursday Heine can undertake the changes and the first issue will be published in mid-October.

Regarding the publication dates of coming issues, like you we would basically like to stick with the first of the month. That won't be possible for the November and December issues, but the January issue should appear punctually on the first.

Today I spoke with O[tto] W[els] about the article "On our Tasks". I favor his writing the article. I myself lack the time and also the inclination. I gave O.W. a copy of the letter I wrote to *The Times* that he can use as he likes. I'm enclosing a copy for you. Nevertheless, the letter should not appear in this form, because the local representative of *The Times* has already incorporated its content into an article he wrote at the request of his editors. I can't say if there are other pro-

---

40   Fritz Heine (1904–2002) trained to be a salesclerk. After joining the SPD in 1922 he worked on the staff of the Party Executive. He moved to Prague with most of the party treasury in May 1933 and served as secretary to the Sopade.

spects for the journal. This afternoon, Siegmund [Crummenerl] and I will be talking with Seydewitz.[41] For notices or book reviews I have collaborators here.

What's happening with your suggestion to list an address from which we can send free copies of S[ozialistische] R[evolution]? I'll mention your request to Aufhäuser.

Not much is new here. We have now come to a fundamental agreement that the large edition of N[euer] V[orwärts] will be fully separated from the small edition. I intend to mainly concern myself with the small edition. However, since I simultaneously want to be involved in the production of Sopade *Information* – I have pushed through [its] publication in three languages – it is not at all certain that I can cope with all these things. At the moment, the preparation of Klinger's book is quite a lot of work, because it became clear that a large section that was written in April has to be revised.

By the way, are you familiar with the book that Oprecht is publishing: *Deutschland wohin?* [*Whither Germany?*] I have the impression that it is a poor work and I cannot very well imagine that Werner Pahl[42] is the author, which Siegmund claims. Do you know anything more concrete about it?

We still haven't received a letter from Wilfried [Hertz],[43] but he should get here tomorrow or the next day. I hope to find out something about Otto N, who is now beginning a job at Princeton (new address: 10 Greenholm, Princeton NJ). By the way, [Fritz] Naphtali[44] has also written to me that he could work for SR and NV. (His new address: Tel Aviv, Elieser ben Jehuda Strasse, Buchholz House).

Best regards,
Your,
[Paul]

---

41   Max Seydewitz (1892–1987) joined the SPD in 1910. During Weimar he led a left-wing dissident faction that was expelled from the party in 1931. With Kurt Rosenfeld (1877–1943), Seydewitz then founded the Socialist Workers' Party of Germany. In exile, he favored cooperation between the Sopade and the KPD, and in 1935 he joined the Revolutionary Socialists, which advocated this policy. The group disintegrated by 1937.

42   Walter Pahl (1903–1969) was a trade union functionary in the ADGB and a writer. On the SPD's far right, he was among those in the union leadership who thought they could come to an accommodation with the Nazis in the spring of 1933. After 1933 he publicly praised Nazi imperialist foreign policy and discrimination against Jews.

43   Wilfried Hertz (1915–?) was the son of Paul and Hanna Hertz. He eventually moved to the United States where he changed his name to Fred W. Berg and became an official of the American Federation of Labor. He later returned to the Federal Republic of Germany where he taught courses for the Deutsche Gewerkschaftsbund.

44   Fritz Naphtali (1888–1961) was an economic expert and leader of the ADGB. In 1928 he and

The Executive Committee of the SPD
Office of the Sopade, Prague-Karlin
Palackeho tride 24
Prague, October 25, 1933

Dear Rudolf,

As far as I can tell, Stampfer has published your article without changes. I cannot concern myself now with the editing of the *Neuer Vorwärts*, because we have separated the small edition completely from the large one (it appears now under a different title and with a different script). In so far as your articles are of interest to German readers, we want to accept them, but then, as a rule, shortened, because one has to operate totally differently with four pages instead of eight.

At the moment, we don't intend to have [*Neuer*] *Vorwärts* bound, at least not quarterly. We will send you a copy of the issues that have appeared thus far. Meanwhile, have you received the journal? Wels started the article we discussed but did not finish it. Siegfried A[ufhäuser] has little desire to write. I told him about your request. You can now write to him directly. His address is: S.A. c/o Ing. W. Strauss, Prague XVIII, Vorechovka Lomena 3.

Best regards,
[Paul]

Touring Hotel
Zürich October 30, 1933

Dear Paul,

Thanks for [*Neuer*] *Vorwärts*. My article was mailed yesterday.

I urgently need you to intervene in a matter concerning the journal. On 18 [October] I sent the manuscript of three articles to Graphia with a request to send the galley proofs as soon as possible. A few days ago, I sent two additional manuscripts with the same request. I have received neither the galleys nor a confirmation of receipt. Since I would like to be able to send one or the

---

Hilferding were part of a commission that worked out a widely hailed social democratic approach to creating "economic democracy" within the republican framework. He fled to Palestine in July 1933.

other manuscript to the author for corrections, or because of the need to bring it up to date, this manner of doing business is impossible, completely apart from the fact that given the unreliable state of the mails, a brief confirmation of receipt is also necessary. Today is already the thirtieth and I have no idea when the next edition will be published. Since someone goes to Karlsbad every Thursday, it must be possible to speak with the printer. Is there anyone there in a responsible position to whom I could turn and correspond with personally?

I have not received the promised article that is in Prague's interest. The same goes for articles from Seydewitz [sic] and Aufhäuser. Could something more be sent by [Max] Klinger[45] or his friends? In addition, I still need reviews. Can [Alexander] Stein write one or the other, for example, on the pamphlet by Max Adler on left socialism that was just published in Prague? I'd be very grateful to you if you could urge Dr. Strauss and a couple of the young German-Bohemian comrades to become collaborators. When you are able to establish the necessary connections, I'd really appreciate it if you could let Klinger know that I'd like to publish a review of *Neu Beginnen* [*New Beginning*] preferably written by him or someone close to the circle around Miles.[46] Kautsky has written one for me that I have to publish, but the pamphlet requires another appraisal. I found the viewpoint in [*Neuer*] *Vorwärts* to be very awkward. I am not referring to the substance, but tactically the review threatens to undercut what we wanted to achieve by publishing it, namely, to demonstrate our tolerance.

There is a hitch in the administration. Here the brochure was sent to various bookstores, but, as I've been told, without a price, so that it initially could not be sold. I don't know if that has been rectified in the meantime. It seems that, except for ten copies that were sent directly at my request, the journal has not yet been mailed. In any case not a single one has been delivered to the secretariat. I've run out of my own copies and, because I need to send more, I request that you send me ten additional copies.

Furthermore, I request that you send the issue (with the enclosure that exchange copies be sent to me at the Touring Hotel), to the Vienna *Arbeiter-Zeitung*; to Julius Braunthal [at the] *Kampf*, to *Le Vie Socialiste*, Paris (9e), 32, Rue Rodier; to Th[eodor] Dan, Paris (6e), 9 Rue Mézieres, für *Le Révolte*; Mr. William Gillies, International Secretary [of the] Labor Party, Transport House, South Block, Smith Squire, London S.W. 1; in exchange for *Labour*; if possible

---

45 Curt Geyer's pseudonym after 1933.
46 Miles was the pseudonym for Walter Löwenheim. See Chapter 5, fn. 3.

[send to] to *Die rote Revue*, Ernst Nobs, Zürich, c/o *Volksrecht*, Postfach Hauptpost, Zürich; and to the German-Bohemian academic organ, always with the enclosure that all exchange copies must be sent to me. Also, I ask that the first edition be sent to Breitscheid; Dr. Arthur Rosenberg, 32 Goldhurst Terrace, London N.W. 6; Vandervelde; Grumbach, Ville d'Avray (S. et O.) Avenue Halphen 4; Dr. Alexandre Bracke; Huge Dalton, 5 Carlisle Mansions, Carlisle Place, London S.W. 1; H.N. Braislford, 24/27, High Holborn, London, W.C.; Dr. Egon Wertheimer, Genéve, 2, Rue de Cloîtrex, who would like a half-year subscription; to Dr. Nathan; Professor Lederer, and Dr. Arthur Feller, The New School for Social Research, 66 W 12th Street, New York; to Dr. Otto Bauer, Vienna VI, Kasernengasse 2; Dr. G. Denicke, Saarbrücken, Varziner Strasse 9, c/o Weyrauch; Dr. Mendelsohn, Amsterdam, Bieybosch Straat 20; and Dr. Alfred Braunthal, Bruxelles-Kule, 11, Rue Robert Scott; Dr. Fr. Brügel, Sozialwissenschaftliche Studienbibliothek, Vienna I, Ebendorferstr. 7; and Kautsky. If, later on, I think of anyone else, I'll write again.

I would be thankful if you now would send me the illegal *Neuer Vorwärts*. By the way, send me your private address again.

The slogan for the elections is correct. But, from the outset, more important than the illusory electoral agitation will be characterizing the brazen fraud in the foreign press. In that respect the *Temps* already published a very good article yesterday.

At the moment, the most important thing is the disarmament issue. The position of the Labor Party is becoming ever more impossible. I've written about this extensively in *Der Kampf* and had a copy sent to Wels, of which you and Crummenerl should avail yourselves.[47] I hope that there will soon be a meeting of the Executive, and this time I think it is very important that I also get to present this view, which, hopefully, you share. Because the Saar question is now a very hot topic in France, in accordance with the agreement with you and Max Braun,[48] and with Breitscheid's concordance, I'll be going to Paris for a few days. On the way I'll stop in Saarbrücken. From an administrative point of view, things with *Die [Deutsche] Freiheit* obviously are going very badly. The business is in disarray, there are delays paying the bills, and inquiries are either answered late, inadequately, or not at all. The editorial board is also not very good. Since, in any case, I have to talk with [Max] Braun about political matters,

---

47   Richard Kern (Hilferding) 1934, pp. 41–47.
48   Max Braun (1892–1945) was the chief editor of the Social Democratic *Volksstimme* in the Saarland. From 1933–35 he led the regional SPD. In French exile after 1935, he edited the SPD exile publication *Deutsche Freiheit*.

I'll combine the trip to Paris with one to Saarbrücken. As I learned today, the party congress will be on the twelfth in Saarbrücken. Will any of you be going?

Best regards to you and all the colleagues.
  Your,
  Rudolf

[P.S.] Please reply quickly!

The Executive Committee of the SPD
Prague-Karlin
Palackeho tribe 24
Prague, November 3, 1933

Dear Rudolf,

I wrote to you yesterday and received your letter of 30 October today.

As Heine told me, the manuscript and corrections have, meanwhile, been sent to you. By the way, I wrote to you yesterday that Kurt is here. He will write to you himself. In the future, I'm leaving everything regarding the journal to him. I cannot take care of everything and I have no inclination to relieve Kurt of the useless work that he finds here. I will leave to him the task of pressuring Seydewitz and Aufhäuser to write the promised articles. Stein will deliver some reviews, including the one about Max Adler. O[tto] W[els] has not yet finished the article. He wants to write it, so that you can count on him for the next issue. The current issue should be full anyway.

I have passed along your complaints about the agitation. I hope they are dealt with. I have seen to the sending of ten copies to you and to all the addresses you provided. I've enclosed the issue of the small [*Neuer*] *Vorwärts*.

I'll read your article in *Der Kampf* in the next few days. I'll let you know what I think and your also get news about Saarbrücken.

Best regards,
  [Paul]

Prague, November 14, 1933

Dear Hilferding,

I think we have to limit ourselves to 40 pages. You certainly will have to cut quite substantially. Please send the page proofs to Karlsbad as quickly as possible. You can alter or enhance the agrarian article as much as you want, a pre-publication arrangement with the author is not possible.

A decision must be made about the journal's new title. The title *Sozialistische Revolution* has been banned. "Sozialistische Aktion" ["Socialist Action"] is not usable, because another publication has it. We have to choose something like "Sozialistische Erneuerung" ["Socialist Renewal"] or "Sozialistischer Kampf" ['Socialist Struggle'], or just plain "Sozialismus" [Socialism]. I am for the latter.

Best regards,
 [The letter is unsigned][49]

Prague, November 30, 1933

Dear Hilferding,

With this letter you will also receive a draft of a platform written by Max Klinger [Curt Geyer] and Ernst Anders [Erich Rinner] with my assistance. We regard you and Denicke [George Decker][50] as part of our commission and would initially like to clarify the earlier question about how to carry on our work. It won't be possible for the five of us to sit down together for any length of time to carry out our task, but to save time and money it will be necessary to proceed using a mixture of written and verbal communication. Therefore, we request that, within a week of receiving the draft, you tell us what you think of it on the whole, whether you are satisfied with it, have recommendations for changes,

---

[49] Given the salutation, it is unlikely that this letter stemmed from Hertz, but rather from either Friedrich Stampfer or his assistant Curt Geyer.

[50] Georg Decker [Iurii Denicke] (1887–1964) began his political activity as a Bolshevik but in 1917 joined the Mensheviks. After teaching history and sociology at the University of Moscow, in 1926 he emigrated to Germany and worked as Hilferding's assistant at the *Gesellschaft*. After 1933 he was very active as a publicist in Menshevik and German emigre circles.

cuts, or additions, or whether you think it necessary to start all over and to create a wholly new draft. Whatever your response might be, we will let you know of our recommendations concerning how to proceed.

Clearly, we are not expecting that within eight days you will provide us with a detailed evaluation of the draft, but only in relation to the question of whether you think the draft is a useable foundation for further work.

Best regards,
[Friedrich] Stampfer

Zürich, January 10, 1934

Dear Klinger [Curt Geyer],

My draft is enclosed. I have the sneaking suspicion that you have strongly suspected me of sabotage. But that would be wrong. I fully understand the need for a new work plan and a new guideline. But I was somewhat taken aback by the idea of creating a program that, at the moment, notwithstanding everything, would of necessity be directly influenced by the German crisis, and also by the ongoing economic catastrophe, whose features one is all-too-inclined to absolutize, and from which it would be all-too-easy to derive political conclusions, which, viewed over the long term, could easily prove to be illusory. That would include, for example, the whole complex of "anti-capitalism", which requires, first of all, precise scientific analysis and a level of understanding that I myself have not yet achieved. Therefore, from the first I have advised not creating a fixed program, but rather simultaneously to show in the manifesto what is necessary right now and what the concrete goals are. My preference would be to see a program emerge like the *Erfurt Program* did, which means [following] the publication of a draft and a thorough discussion. And the moment and frame of mind for that have not yet arrived.

Now, concerning your draft, from the start I ask your indulgence for a frank critique. Stylistically it is a failure, which is all the more remarkable since two stylists like you and Stampfer worked on it. It is an agglomeration of declamations, programmatic phrases, [and] political declarations that don't hang together well. Now, I completely agree with you both that the appeal to the will, the commitment to an idea, and idealistic ardor must play a bigger role than previously. But the will is not awakened by a declaration that one wants to awaken the will. The National Socialists have done it by means of fueling the fantasy of their followers: cut off heads, drive out the Jews, destroy the department stores, etc. In my view, we must do the same by making socialism much more concrete, not least in its ideological content. But not by means of simple appeals. For me the thing is somewhat too rhetorical.

On the other hand, I think it is absolutely necessary that it finally be shown in what sense *work will really be done*. Only by [means of] demonstration and through high quality work will be able to rebuild trust and win the upper hand. Along with the program, topicality must be ensured. But, above all, on this occasion I think it necessary and more useful – because it is more effective – to show that the turn away from reformism is not only a subjective one, but one brought about by the objective situation, one that became a fundamental necessity. Therefore, I think it is of key importance to make clear the conditions of revolutionary work. And the slogans must be developed from those. So, I would place the *revolutionary organizational work* and the *tasks of the party leadership* at the beginning, and they would then appear again in the conclusion in a different context. Besides, I think that what is said there is already familiar and cannot be open to doubt (in this context I want to remind you again of my article on the tasks and functions of the party leadership in emigration that I've written for the journal).[51]

Of course, a lot can be said about the specific formulations. Some of it is much too detailed. Why should a future Reichstag have 400 members and why should that be programmatically established today? Decker's draft also contains far too many details [and] plans, which could provide the basis of a discussion, but must not be set today. On the other hand, there is a substantial lack of imagination and insight concerning what must be said about the exercise of power. I think that on this occasion it is superfluous to again analyze the nature of fascism at length, and it is damaging to express remorse [for past errors]. All that belongs in the commentary, which is absolutely necessary. I am certainly for sharp self-criticism, which should be carried out without limits in [our] publications. But a programmatic manifesto must be a *manifestation* of the new outlook. It must be clear that the turn has already occurred, and that [claim] is weakened, when one asserts that new self-criticism is needed to finally achieve it. Moreover, some things are badly expressed, so, for example, on page 2. At least, many of us have never imagined that socialism could ever be achieved without radical inroads into the economic order. It is even less so [the case] that not winning over the middle classes was due to a failure of the party. In that regard, I'm happy to wait and see which party, at least when placed in a similar situation, would have done better. However, I can't continue with a

---

51 Richard Kern [Hilferding] 1933–1934, pp. 1–3.

detailed critique, because I have to close due to the mail. I hope that my draft speaks for itself, even where it deviates politically. For example, in the case of a future war, I would not think it useful to speak in favor of Trotsky's tactic versus Lenin's at Brest Litovsk. All that depends so much on the actual conditions that taking a position today can only be damaging. I'll write to you soon at greater length or I'll call you after the manuscript arrives. You can reach me on the phone regularly in the morning from 10:00 to 10:30 at 35.755. Hopefully, the draft will be so convincing, that I won't have to go to Prague, which would strongly hinder my other work, as much as I'd like to talk to you all. Otherwise, of course I'd come.

I'm very unhappy about the delay of the *Zeitschrift*. It is really an impossible situation and all the more so since a change was not at all necessary.

Best regards.
Your,
RH

[P.S.] I assume that my draft will be brought to the attention of the other comrades (including Böchel and Aufhäuser), before a third is put forward.

Zürich, January 11, 1934

Dear Paul,

Thanks very much for the letter. I sent my draft yesterday. I would prefer that it not remain among the circle of three to be reworked by them into a new version, but rather that it be copied and distributed to the other members of the Party Executive including, above all, Aufhäuser, Crummenerl, and Böchel. I think it is very important that, apart from the details, the form, the mode of thinking, and the content remain essentially unchanged. The draft by the three is remarkably poor, except for the section on socialization, which, in its essentials had been prepared [earlier] by the research institute and the AfA-Bund.[52] I've adopted most of this here, despite having some inner reservations, which I will have to clarify for myself by carrying out a systematic study. I've also incorporated as much "anti-capitalism" as one can and still have a halfway

---

52   The AfA-Bund was the Allgemeiner freier Angestellten Bund (General Federation of Salaried Employees), basically a union for white collar workers.

good conscience. As I said to Klinger in the letter accompanying [the draft], I find the mix of declaiming about human rights, appeals to the will, and the call for the most reactionary groups to march in step, if you please, the least promising. Instead, it must be shown that the slogans and aims of the struggle flow from the conditions determined by the enemy, and it must be demonstrated that the struggle has already been unleashed and is being organized and supported by the leadership. Instead of eternal self-criticism, which people make in their own names or in the name of the right-wing socialists, but not in our name, the end of reformism, a clear commitment to revolution, and the revolutionary work already underway has to be placed in the foreground. That's because people don't think much of subjective assertions. I still hope that the draft speaks for itself and that, together with the others, you'll be able to win its acceptance essentially unchanged without me. If that proves to be impossible, I'm prepared to come to Prague, although I balk in the face of the high cost for the party, which perhaps already lives beyond its means, but, above all, because it interrupts my work again. Be that as it may, I have so much to do with the everyday stuff that I can hardly get to any scholarly work. In any case, write to me after you've read the draft or call me in the morning between 10:00 and 10:30 at the hotel at 35.755.

And there is something else. The tall Rudi [Breitscheid] writes that you had warned him again about Max Braun. From the start I've thought that such an action was completely wrong and totally unfounded. My view of this matter was strengthened by a detailed conversation with [Emil] Kirschmann,[53] with whom I've often been at odds, and Fritz [Adler] feels the same way. I regard Klopfer [sic] as very evil and would think it completely wrong to accept his assertions or to cooperate in any way with him or his clique, which Otto Wells is prone to do. In any case, Max is straightforward and consequent on the main issue with which we now are concerned. We have every reason to dismiss that evil gossip about him.[54]

---

53 Emil Kirschmann (1888–1949) joined the SPD in 1906 and was active in the trade union and cooperative movements. From 1919–26 he edited the *Rheinische Zeitung* before taking a position in the Prussian Interior Ministry. He also was a member of the Reichstag. In 1933 he fled to the Saarland and later to France where he worked for the Sopade and organized assistance for refugees. In 1940 he fled from France to the United States.

54 Ernst Klopfer was the business manager of the *Volkstimme* publishing house in Saarbrücken. He was fired in May 1934 in the wake of a scandal. See Buchholz and Rother (eds.) 1995, p. 57. Max Braun, as editor of the *Volkstimme* and regional party leader, played a key role in the SPD's effort to prevent the Saarland from voting for annexation to Germany in a referendum planned for 1935. Contrary to the Prague leaders wishes, he favored cooperation with the KPD in that effort.

I don't have your letter at hand and, consequently, I don't know if I've answered all your questions. But to me it is not only pleasant, but I also think it urgently necessary, that you often keep me appraised.

Best regards and also to Hannah.

[the letter was unsigned]

[P.S.] Will the pamphlet by Decker be published and when? I am very much in favor of that. Should I urge Schifrin to write a brochure in reply to "New Beginning" under my supervision and with my support? The business with the *Zeitschrift* is an unheard-of scandal. I could really describe it as sabotage. Why in the world did one have to change the width of the lines and thereby reduce the space without even asking me? And how could that take three weeks!! That the good Curt [Geyer] did not take care of matters on time is quite incomprehensible to me. Today (!) I received the first (!) galleys, which were probably just typeset. That is a complete waste of money.

Today, I received a manuscript of my last article back from Stampfer without comment; "The Financial Policy of the Dictatorships". What does that mean? Will it not be published, or will it just be mutilated?

You must also read my accompanying letter. I've enclosed it here, because I have doubts about whether I enclosed it with the draft.

Please send it back immediately!

For the P[arty] E[xecutive]. Not for publication.
The French Situation and Foreign Policy[55] (March 1934)

---

[55] The context in which Hilferding wrote this document was an existential crisis that rocked the French Third Republic in the winter of 1933–1934. At the time, the government was led by the Radical-Socialist Party, which in fact, was not "radical" at all but occupied a position in the center of the French political spectrum and itself contained diverse political currents. At the end of January, the left-of-center cabinet of Camille Chautemps (1885–1963) resigned in the wake of the collapse of the Crédit Municipal in Bayonne, as the result of a massive fraud carried out by financier Alexandre Stavisky (1886–1934), in which a number of Radical leaders were implicated. To win the parliamentary backing of the SFIO, the new Radical Prime Minister, Édouard Daladier (1884–1970), fired the reactionary Parisian police chief, an action that on 6 February triggered a massive and violent demonstration by a variety of French right-wing groups on the Place de la Concorde and a large counter-demonstration organized by the Communist Party. The police used force to restore order and the result was 15 dead and over 1,500 injured, mostly demonstrators. On 7 February the General Confederation of French trade unions carried out a general strike to pressure the government to take stronger action against armed right-wing groups. Despite having adequate parliamentary support, Daladier wanted a broader coalition and resigned. As a

I.

I was in Paris from March 6–10. For the French politicians with whom I spoke, the domestic situation is very opaque. The scandals have called forth terrific excitement, the cause of which is the state leadership's apparent involvement. As a result of this, one gets the impression, strengthened by the right-wing and part of the left-wing press, that small, personal parliamentary cliques exercise such influence on the administrative and justice systems that the objective administration of the state and the courts can no longer be guaranteed. The executive [branch] has become, in part, so dependent upon personal groups of parliamentarians, who themselves are tied to financial and industrial circles often of an evil type, that the call for reform has become general. It is clear that this attitude can become a danger for parliamentarianism as such and prepares the ground for fascist currents. This is all the more the case, since no comprehensible reform plan exists. Nevertheless, voices from various quarters claim that there is no large-scale danger to democracy. The self-confidence of the left, especially of the socialists and the unions is very high due to the success of the general strike, which was beyond their expectations. On the other hand, this has strengthened certain radical tendencies in the old Socialist Party.[56] The slogan of a united front with the Communists is in keeping with this trend. The slogan has arisen from sentiments among the mass of the workers, and the Socialist Party hopes, in spite of the opposition of the Communist Party leadership, to strengthen its influence on the masses through this tactic. The formation of a government of concentration, which allows the party to go into ruthless opposition, is also contributing to these radical tendencies. Like a part of the right, it has made the slogan of parliamentary dissolution its own. Blum[57] says he is reckoning on this occurring before the end of the year. The prospects for a new election under the current circumstances are doubtful. In Blum's opinion, the Socialists would not just win, but they'd get stronger. The real losers would be the Radical-Socialists. They are, first of all, terribly comprom-

---

result, he was replaced by Gaston Doumergue (1863–1937), a center-right Radical Socialist, who appointed a more conservative cabinet. This government survived, but without the support of the SFIO or the Communist Party.

56 The "old Socialist Party" was the French Section of the Workers' International (SFIO). Founded in 1905, it split in 1920 when a majority of its members left to form a new Communist Party of France. The SFIO revived but split again in 1933, when it expelled its right-wing minority which then formed a "neo-socialist" movement.

57 Leon Blum (1872–1950) was a long-time leader of the SFIO, three-time Prime Minister, and a friend of Hilferding.

ised by the scandal, although Herriot[58] and some others remain unscathed. They are discredited, because they bear the responsibility for the victorious left not being able to rule following the [last] election. (Indeed, at least on the left the responsibility for the political failure is ascribed more to the Radicals then to the Socialists. Also, the majority of the young Radicals seems to be of this opinion). Of course, the defeat of the Radicals would mean that the right comes to power again. It is thought, however, that this would result in a reactionary parliamentary regime but not in fascism. To be sure, there is the concern that the latter could be the case if there were a substantial sharpening of the economic crisis. At the moment, though, the situation is such that the formation of the Doumergue government and, especially the comprehensive work of the two parliamentary committees on the Stavisky Affaire and on the mutiny of 6 February, has brought about a certain calming effect. Nevertheless, the situation remains very tense, and a minor cause could easily lead to new and severe convulsions. In addition, there are undoubtedly currents among the young Radicals and the Neo-Socialists which vaguely support all possible constitutional and electoral reforms and thereby support the game being played by the right and the extreme right. In the near term, much will depend upon whether the Doumergue government survives. That depends upon the Radical-Socialists. The postponement of their party congress until May appears to indicate that up this point the government-friendly forces in the party have the upper hand. Because the Radicals have much to fear from the new elections, the majority will probably attempt to avoid a renewed governmental crisis. It remains questionable, however, whether the party can hold together. A substantial weakening of the party, whether via a split or an electoral defeat, would, of course, fundamentally weaken the resistance against fascist currents within the bourgeoisie.

II.

In regard to the situation of the two socialist parties, following the split the earlier balance of forces between right and left within the old party has shifted strongly in favor of the left. As before, the antagonism continues to exist, and tough fights are being waged about future tactics. Whether this will lead the right to break away in another split is doubtful, perhaps even improbable, because, as it stands, the tactic of the left (united front, sharp opposition not only against the government but also the Radical-Socialists) is in keeping with

---

58   Édouard Herriot (1872–1957) was the interwar leader of the Radical Socialist Party.

the sentiment of the masses. But then the attractiveness of the Neo-Socialists has strongly declined. Renaudel,[59] who, personally, should be very pessimistic, is still sick and is not in Paris. Déat[60] is pursuing a confusing anti-capitalist and, in part, demagogic anti-parliamentary policy and is encountering resistance in his own ranks. Marquet,[61] who should do good socio-political and general political service in the Labor Ministry, appears to be at odds with him as well. In any case, this movement is currently completely stagnant, though perhaps it hasn't lost ground. It seems to me that the International's attempts to reestablish unity have no chance given the unclear situation. At best, a chance might occur when Renaudel is once again in a position to exert influence.

III.

The [moment of] decision is approaching in foreign affairs. In a certain sense the situation has become simplified. France is becoming isolated, which means that, without England and Italy, it won't undertake anything decisive in spite of the much greater determination with which [Louis] Barthou is carrying out foreign policy. The English memorandum is regarded as finished. The issue is whether there will be an agreement, based largely on Mussolini's proposal, or none at all. Mussolini's proposal essentially means German rearmament within the framework of German demands, the maintenance of the armaments of the other signatories to the agreement, no further increase of armaments, and the establishment of controls that will ensure the implementation of the agreement. Within the French party there will be different answers to the question of concluding such an agreement or of repudiating any kind of agreement. One

---

59   Pierre Renaudel (1871–1935) was editor of the SFIO's flagship daily *L'Humanité* from 1914–1919, a long-time member of the Chamber of Deputies, and an important figure on the party's right wing. Expelled in 1933, he then co-founded the Socialist Party of France and edited the weekly *La Vie Socialiste*.

60   Marcel Déat (1894–1955) joined the SFIO in 1920 and became an important exponent of its revisionist right-wing which advocated for class collaboration rather than struggle, national solidarity rather than internationalism, a corporate form of social organization, and for "anti-capitalism" instead of socialism. He was expelled in 1933 and joined the Socialist Party of France. His rightward political trajectory resulted in his ultimately collaborating with the Vichy regime during the Second World War.

61   Adrien Marquet (1885–1955) was elected Mayor of Bourdeaux as a Socialist in 1925. Along with Déat, he borke with Marxism and socialism to advocate a "neo-socialist" authoritarianism and was expelled from the SFIO in 1933. Like Déat he also collaborated with the Vichy regime.

can say, however, that among the left parties the conclusion of some kind of agreement is preferable to total failure, while the militarists would prefer an open arms race. Essentially, the decision will be strongly influenced by whether the French can establish a stronger alliance with England, in case the agreement is violated, an action that one certainly expects from Germany. It is not out of the question that, to save the convention, the British will acquiesce. The Labor Party, which it appears wants to have this convention under any circumstances, would support such a concession. Objectively, the differences concerning armament are not very large. In every case they lead to an arms race. France seeks security by drawing closer politically to England and Italy and by foregoing any isolated action.

If Germany can expect complete success in regard to the disarmament question, it is different in respect to the Austrian issue. As before, Dollfuß[62] will get every support from English and French policy. But, at the moment, the Austrian question is dominated by the German-Italian antagonism. The French hope that, in line with their foreign policy goal, it will lead Italy to draw closer to them. On the other hand, out of consideration for the Little Entente, they are not in a position to allow a political alliance between Hungary, Austria, and Italy and they have made that very clear in Rome. Austria should remain a buffer state and an economic hub of Central Europe, including Italy, but excluding Germany. England does not have an independent policy in this matter and platonically supports independence for Austria, but it would accept Italy's absorption of Austria and acts indifferently even in respect to the German solution. In contrast, it appears that in official circles in Paris one thinks that Mussolini will not forcefully impose his solution, because, in fact, the rapid strengthening of Germany seems too dangerous. It is probable, therefore, that the Austrian question will get bogged down, that there are, perhaps, certain economic agreements with Italy and Hungary, and that Austria's political status will remain unchanged with Italy maintaining its strong influence on its foreign and domestic policy. In this case, French policy will again continue to attempt to shape relations with Italy and to improve relations between Italy and the Little Entente.[63]

---

62 Engelbert Dollfuss (1892–1934) was a leader of Austria's right-wing Catholic Christian-Social Party. Appointed to the Chancellorship in May 1932, a year later he shut down the parliament and assumed dictatorial powers. In February 1934 he crushed a Social Democratic uprising. He was killed by Nazi assassins in July 1935.

63 The Little Entente was a French-backed alliance of Czechoslovakia, Romania, and Yugoslavia formed in 1921. It was designed to protect against Hungarian revanchism and the return of the Habsburg monarchy.

At the moment, with respect to the issue of disarmament, Hitler's complete success is the most likely outcome. In regard to the Austrian question, in contrast, at least initially his policy will fail. Bearing in mind that nationalist circles, particularly in Prussia, have always considered the annexation of Austria very skeptically, one may still conclude that the Austrian debacle will hardly cause a break between the nationalists and Hitler, because the extraordinary success in the struggle to reestablish the army and to tear up the arms provisions of the Treaty of Versailles have raised enormously the prestige of the regime.

This outcome is not only a major defeat for the Socialist International, but the future of the foreign policy of the western Socialist Parties is now severely threatened. With their agreement, the rearmament of Germany and indeed, a general arms race will probably be sanctioned – a direct result of the behavior of the Labor Party. In addition: because international law has proven itself to be nothing more than a scrap of paper [and] established treaties no longer need to be observed, then any League of Nations' policy and any treaty in the international sphere becomes utopian. Blum, too, concedes that in this situation the foreign policy of the socialist parties has become an irresolvable problem.

IV.

Finally, I'd also like to mention Wirth's[64] impression from Rome that the Vatican's attitude against Germany is becoming ever sharper. The Pope has reserved for himself the decision in the German question. There is no intention of making further concessions in the implementation of the Concordat; one would rather resume the struggle. In Rome the view of the German Catholic Bishops is considered too subdued. There is a strong movement among Catholics in Germany itself; the workers and their leaders are also maintaining their opposition to the regime.

---

64 Karl Joseph Wirth (1879–1956) was a leader of the Catholic Center Party, held many important governmental posts under Weimar, and was Chancellor from 1921–1922. A sharp critic of the right, he emigrated to Switzerland in 1933. In exile he was in frequent contact with Vatican circles, as well as many émigré resistance groups.

Prague, March 23, 1934

Dear comrade Hilferding,

We have received a package from Czech[65] that was brought over via courier. I opened it and ascertained that it contains excerpts (e.g., *The Liberation of the Peasants* by Knapp, The *German Stock Exchange Inquiry of 1893*, *The Economic Crisis* by Eugen von Bergmann, etc.), manuscripts, letters, etc. Please decide if we should hold the package here or send it to you. Since it weighs at most 5 kilos, it would not cost much to send it.

After my conversation with Käte Rosenberg, you can publish the enclosed notice with a good conscience.

I just sent a report about Vienna to F[riedrich] A[dler]. It should be added that Karl and Luise are physically and psychologically in good shape. Karl is already writing another pamphlet! It will be a response to Franzel, against whom O[tto] B[auer] has also written in *Sozialdemokrat*.[66]

In regard to the publisher for Engels's letters, Karl is in touch with a Dutch publisher who had also taken on Gustav Mayer's Engels letters[67] from Ullstein. The second volume of *Krieg und Demokratie* [*War and Democracy*] might be published by Orbis. Karl is also thinking about him as a publisher of his Engels-letters if it doesn't work out with the Dutch publisher. Oprecht has rejected publishing the Engels letters.

I found O[tto] B[auer] in good spirits. I spoke with him for two hours. He thinks that Hitler has given up the fight for Austria and that Dollfuss and Fey[68] are consolidating their power. He does not believe that the internal contradictions of the government will create a wholly new situation. One the other hand,

---

65   Ludwig Czech (1870–1945) was the leader of the Sudeten German Social Democratic Workers' Party.
66   This letter was written just five weeks after the Dollfuss dictatorship crushed a Social Democratic uprising in Austria and created a one-party state. Many Social Democrats were killed, imprisoned, or driven either underground or into exile. Many SDAP leaders, such as Otto Bauer, escaped to Czechoslovakia, where they attempted to organize resistance from abroad.
67   The letter writer has confused Engels' letters with Gustav Mayer's biography of Engels titled *Friedrich Engels: Eine Biographie, Bd. I: Friedrich Engels in seiner* Frühzeit and *Bd. 2 Friedrich Engels und der Aufstieg der Arbeiterbewegung in Europa* (Den Haag: Martinus Nijhoff, 1934).
68   Emil Fey (1886–1938) was an important leader of the fascist militia, the Heimwehr, which supported the Dollfuss dictatorship. He became Dollfuss's Vice Chancellor in 1933 and played a major role in crushing the Social Democrats the following year.

he thinks that the workers' movement, which hitherto has proven itself very capable of resistance, will have to reckon with strong persecution.

I also talked to him about working together. He said no for the same reason as Fritz [Adler]. In Austria the party's tactical situation is completely different; one can't burden the movement there with the Germans' problems, and the different situation will last a long time. One thinks of common ground with the *Tribune*. O.B. stressed very strongly that there is no money and one is forced to be frugal.

Best regards,
 [Paul]

Zürich, April 12, 1934

Dear Paul,

The packet consists of scholarly excerpts which are very important to me and should not get lost, at least if they are the right ones, as I hope. I'd like to have the thing sent here as *speedily* as possible. If it is the case that you think the usual route is secure, that's good. Otherwise it will have to be sent via diplomatic [pouch] via Bern. In any case, I'd like to have it as soon as possible. Please make certain of it.

Hopefully the business with S[chönherr] is now over. Your traveling acquaintance essentially did not know anything new. He is now back home and in a really bad state. I only hope that nothing appears.

It is not a very comfortable situation for the *Zeitschrift* if the *Kampf* actually would appear in association with the *Tribune* and the *Rote Revue*. Only, I also fear that there is nothing to be done to oppose it. I was not very satisfied with the last issue; I found the discussion miserable and that it really undercut any desire to participate. Someone from among you ought to write something about practical activity, in particular pointing out the fact that transfer of the Executive, indeed as such, to Prague, was the beginning of a new politics, and the maintenance of the form of the Executive was necessary at the time, because of the threat of a new leadership forming in Berlin under Löbe.[69] The role played

---

69 Paul Löbe (1875–1967) trained as a printer, began his political career as a journalist and edited the Social Democratic *Breslauer Volkswacht* from 1903–1919. During Weimar he was a member of the Reichstag and served as its President. In April 1933 he was elected to the SPD executive committee in which he argued that the SPD could survive by acceding to

by Prague against Berlin at the time has not yet been described, but that is the best justification. In addition, one must raise the question of what the critics would have wanted aside from a different choice of individuals. In any case, it would be good if one of the practical people said something about that.

Please urge comrade Crummenerl to answer my last letter. I have to leave for Geneva before the 20th in order to discuss the matter with Horkheimer,[70] and I'd like to then go to Amsterdam but, in any case, to Paris. Crum[menerl] should write to me immediately. Further, remind Arthur [Arnold] of his promise to send me the earlier issues of [*Neuer*] *Vorwärts* in bound form.

From Germany, one now hears a lot of pessimism from the side of the bourgeoisie. The hard currency situation is difficult. Nevertheless, I don't think it is out of the question that credits for raw materials will be found and with that they would have gotten through the worst. For the rest, everything in the world is so unstable that one really can't say what will happen. Certain is only the increasingly poor situation of all the Socialist Parties, especially in France, and of the trade unions' growing tendency to distance themselves from the party and to ruin themselves by resorting to Tarnow's idiotic policy.[71]

You've probably received the material about your protégé Sch[önherr]. I was a bit amused that that would happen to such a schooled smeller of corruption.

Please ask Klinger whether he has anything for the *Zeitschrift*, whether he has reworked his old article, and what the editorial deadline should be.

What do you hear from Wilfried? I'd be happy to have an article from Nathan or at least his private views about Roosevelt's policy. Tell him when you write. Give my best to your wife, Else [Lehmann],[72] and Arthur, and answer right away.

Best regards,
Your,
Rudolf

---

some of the demands of the Nazi regime. His viewpoint put him at odds with the Sopade and soon proved to be illusory. He was arrested in June 1933 and released in December. He survived the war and resumed his political activity for the SPD in West Germany.

70   It is not clear what the discussion concerned. Max Horkheimer (1895–1973) was a German philosopher and sociologist, developer of "critical theory", and, after 1930, the Director of the Institute for Social Research at the University of Frankfurt. Due to its association with the ideas of Marx and Sigmund Freud, the institute was forced to close in 1933. Horkheimer moved to Geneva and then, in 1934, to New York City, where the institute was reopened.

71   Fritz Tarnow (1880–1951) was member of the ADGB leadership, of the Reich Economic Council, and of the Reichstag. In this passage, Hilferding is most likely criticizing his role in the trade unions' futile effort to reach an accommodation with the Nazis.

72   This reference is to Else Lehmann who had been a secretary to the SPD Reichstag delegation under Weimar and moved with the Sopade to Prague and then to Paris. I am indebted

Prague, April 12, 1934

Dear Rudolf,

As I understand it, Klinger has already written about the A.B.S. program.[73] I'll read it in the next few days. I've enclosed Stampfer's marginal comments, which I think are good. Of course, I'm very interested in your view, indeed not only about the substantive, but also the tactical material. In that regard, up to now, I've been inclined also to print nonsense. But when the nonsense contains a fundamental abandonment of Social Democratic principles or the abdication of Social Democratic organizations in favor of the Communists, then my view changes. Today, I am just as unwilling to make any kind of concessions to the Communist way of thinking as in 1920.

I spoke with Otto [Bauer] about the *Zeitschrift*. He told me essentially the same thing as Fritz [Adler] told both of us. Nevertheless, with the difference that it is only the association with the *Tribune* that is in question and not that with the *Rote Revue*. He thinks the association with the *Zeitschrift* is impossible, both for us and the Austrians. For us, because we cannot forgo discussion of matters particular to Germany; for the Austrians, because the discussion burdens them with controversies that would cause confusion rather than clarification. This is true at least at a time when the political situation in Austria and the conditions of struggle for the working class are fundamentally different than in Germany. I don't think there is much one can say against the substance of these arguments. If you have a different opinion, than I suggest you write directly to O[tto]. That is certainly much better than all the conversations that involve people in between. Otto is always in Brünn and never comes here, so that we have to connect in writing or through the detour of Fritz Brügel.[74]

---

to Dr. Ursula Langkau-Alex of the Institute for Social History in Amsterdam for this information.

73 The reference here is to a draft platform put forward by two members of the Sopade, Siegfried Aufhäuser and Karl Böchel, who, along with former SAP leader Max Seydewitz, were critical of the Weimar SPD leadership and aimed to promote a more "radical" approach to party tactics and strategy that would also include cooperation with the Communists. In addition to these three, several other authors collaborated on the platform. See Buchholz and Rother (eds.) 1995, pp. 46–49.

74 Fritz Brügel (1897–1955) was raised in Prague and but trained as an historian in Vienna. In 1933 he founded the Association of Socialist Writers and joined the Austrian Communist Party. After the failed workers uprising in February 1934, he moved to Czechoslovakia and later to France and Great Britain. He returned to Czechoslovakia after 1945

I've noted the information about Schönherr. I cannot make out the signature. Who is this man? I cannot remember having spoken with him; probably that has to do with a conversation with you? I don't think the factual material is correct. In any case, I don't know whether he was the treasurer of the DMV [The German Metal Workers' Union]. Schäfer[75] had once made such a statement to a third party about what Sch[önherr] had done. If it had been mentioned in the trial and had really concerned the theft of 200,000 marks, then it is hard to fathom how it is that that it did not result in an investigation and conviction by the state prosecutor.

This information also completely ignores my having never spoken in favor of Schönherr's material integrity. I don't know anything about that. I regard him as politically reliable. I've spoken neither in favor of trusting him with money nor of giving him a job. Therefore, I also am not obligated to investigate all the accusations that one levels against him.

On the matter of Breitscheid-Saarbrücken, there were, as usual, a whole lot of misunderstandings. Of course, Breitscheid was very aggravated about it. Sollman, too. Breitscheid wrote furious letters to us about it. Now, I've given Breitscheid a dressing down and explained our intentions to him, which were intended only to benefit him. His last letter was, once again, reasonable, and he understands everything. Hopefully, he will finally become a collaborator at *Deustche Freiheit*. In spite of all my reservations, I can still imagine that that will give him satisfaction and be useful for the *Freiheit*.

[Georg] Bernhard's behavior is incomprehensible to me.[76] In spite of all the denials of [Carl] Severing's son, as well as those of Severing himself,[77] he has not retracted his accusation that Severing had gone over to Hitler, and he has not informed the readers of the *P[ariser] T[ageblatt]* even once that this report admittedly is a falsification of the Communists. I can't bring myself to write to him directly. I've written a notice against the *Pariser Tageblatt* for the *Sozialdemokrat* and the *Freiheit*, but it has turned out milder than I thought it would.

---

but fled back to England following the consolidation of the Communist dictatorship there.

75 Valentin Schäfer (1882–1938) was a former editor of the *Volksstimme* and a party leader in Saarbrücken. He was expelled in 1934 in the wake of his involvement in an internal conflict in the local party.

76 Georg Bernhard (1875–1944) under Weimar was chief editor of the *Vossische Zeitung*, a member of the Reich Economic Council, of the executive Committee of the DDP, and of the Reichstag. After emigrating to France in 1933, he founded the *Pariser Tageblatt*.

77 Carl Severing (1875–1952) was one of the SPD's most important Weimar political leaders and served as Prussian Interior Minister from 1920–26, 1930–32, and Reich Interior Minister from 1928–30.

If I did not know that Bernhard was basically a decent guy, then the behavior of his paper would give one the impression that it is led by scoundrels.

Best regards,
[Paul]

Zürich, April 17, 1934

Dear Paul,

At first, I attempted to write a lengthy report, but that would practically require a book, and it doesn't make much sense to create a large work as long as it isn't clear whether and in what form the matter will be discussed. Therefore, I'll limit myself to a few remarks.

The economic introduction is a superficial and, in part, inaccurate reportage about the current state of the crisis. This [crisis] is generalized, declared to be a long-term condition, and established as a "permanent". This is a shamefaced, clean sweep of the theory of economic collapse – reminiscent of Rosa Luxemburg and Fritz Sternberg[78] – which was rejected by all serious Marxists. The real problems, in particular the position of the middle classes, are hardly mentioned, their dynamics are not examined, or are dealt with through the unsupportable assertion of their impoverishment. In that regard, the pauperization of the peasants, for example, is a fairy tale, which is faithfully repeated by the National Socialist demagogues. A tendency towards the pauperization of the peasants under capitalism does not exist. Over the long haul the tendency was toward an improvement in the peasant's situation, because the cost of production and consumption goods for the peasants tends to fall faster than the cost of food. This tendency was interrupted first by the American agrarian crisis from about 1873–1885. After it ended the peasants' situation improved markedly, in part due to the employment of relatively modest state funds. The ongoing agrarian crisis is an immediate and exclusive result of the war. The peasants' situation is highly differentiated. *In terms of time*: an advantageous situation during the war and postwar period until the second agrarian crisis

---

78   Fritz Sternberg (1895–1963) was a German Jewish socialist economist who wrote on a wide range of issues but especially on imperialism and fascism. Initially active in the SPD, in 1931 he later joined the breakaway Socialist Workers' Party and, after fleeing Germany in 1933, remained active in its exile organization.

became acute. Now, *in terms of space*, there are substantial differences. The peasants' situation in the agricultural exporting countries is poor, especially where state power is weak as in Southeast Europe. In the European countries that import agricultural goods, the consequences of the agrarian crisis have largely been deflected from the peasants onto other classes through measures taken by the state. In Germany, this process of deflection, on the whole, has been successful. Further development depends on the development of the agrarian crisis, which has its own peculiar laws. All of that is ignored. One needs "pauperization" for the illusion that the peasants will want to strive for a proletarian dictatorship. The whole economic discussion is fabricated around this wishful thinking. It is the exact opposite of Marxism. One doesn't study the laws of economics in order to draw political conclusions from the results. On the contrary, one arbitrarily constructs the economic laws in order to suit the already established political conclusions. As result, false representations, incorrect generalizations of special cases, and contradictory economic conceptions slip into [the analysis]. I think that the "permanent crisis" is, economically, a wholly untenable construct. By the way, this construct returns from either the bourgeois or the socialist side in every crisis. The arguments find believers every time – until the next upswing. The massively increased role of state power is not even mentioned. Fascism is viewed in a wholly oversimplified way as the affair of big capital, [and] the role of the middle classes is played down in order to be able to represent them as future supporters of the proletarian dictatorship. One would have to write pages concerning incorrect details. All questions are not solvable with "radicalism", but rather with scientific insight. The issue here is not [to be] "radical" or "reformist", but rather true or false.

The political critique is so superficial that there is nothing to be said about it. It is simply the old story: the "leaders" (Carlyle's great men) make history, so the "leaders" are guilty. And it would have been so easy. The successful "radical" tactic in Italy or the "militant democracy" in Austria prove it! If only Wels and [Ernst] Thälmann[79] had listened to Rosenfeld and Seydewitz!

In foreign policy it is all dabbling of the most superficial type. In the introduction it states that the formally dependent regions are so strengthened when they become independent that their creditors can no longer extract debt payments, capital exports dry up, and the world economy collapses. But "imperialism", which to us can be understood as the foreign policy of finance capital, remains in the program as the policy of capital export and the [securing of]

---

79   Ernst Thälmann (1886–1944) was the leader of the KPD from 1925–33. The Nazis arrested him on 3 March 1933 and eventually executed him on 18 August 1944 in the Buchenwald concentration camp.

spheres of investment. Meanwhile, the "defensive policy" of France and England (?), who certainly also have something to say, becomes ever stronger and *therefore* the imperialist danger grows enormously! Simply put, the anxiety in the face of actual Russian foreign policy is odd and the confusing twaddle about disarmament and proletarian militancy is childish.

The militant catchword, Jacobin war, is charming (Otto [Bauer] really put his foot in it here): apparently all democratic countries – *usque ad finem* (fight to the death), only, unfortunately, without any announcement of war aims! And that gives one claim to leadership!

Enough, because nothing needs to be said about the ghastly democratic dictatorship of the soviets. Stampfer has already done that with his fatherly indulgence. As a specialist, Klinger can complete it. To that end, the economic is again humanistic. The economic council is exquisite, it is so central. As a Central European, of course it absolutely must meet in Vienna, in the Café Central, at the same table where I sat together with Trotsky. Because the *genius loci* (the spirit of the place) alone will be able to help. And how elegant in solving the most difficult problems! And the relationship of the public to the private sector? Very simple: The private sector is forced to become a state syndicate that is merged with the nationalized enterprises. It does not exist, but the name is retained. With this reliance on scholastic nominalism, the trickiest problem is resolved. And that passes for Marxism.

It seems to me that the liquidation of Social Democracy as a means of changing the makeup of the Party Executive and giving vent to the resentment against Wels and Stampfer goes too far, just as the united front with the Communist vultures of Viennese heroism is not appetizing right now.

But now to the single *serious* question. What should happen! I can only think that you, as the Party Executive, can only make a decision about the tactical issue of *publication*. There is nothing to be gained from a substantive discussion and, above all, I warn you against recommending any improvements. If at all, the story should be published *unchanged*, and I suggest discretion regarding my objections, whose form is not suited for passing along to the author to whom no details should be communicated. But I am *for* publication. Firstly, because I think it cannot be prevented, and then its effectiveness against you would be stronger. We would have no other tools than a refutation. Publication can occur in the *Zeitschrift* if we allow for an additional half sheet. Then, to be sure, at least one article to counter it (by Klinger against the council system!). If [publication] occurs separately, that causes a certain difficulty for the *Zeitschrift*, which then would have to repeat its content. I am against the attempt the suppress the article, however. If it is published in a different way, then, in any case, not in the regular series of brochures. It is very important to demand that the authors make *their names* public. Eternal anonymity sometimes makes attacks too easy.

By the way, the section on the councils is by Dr. Otto Friedländer[80] and it sounds like it (A viper nursing at Stampfer's breast!). An article he sent me upon Aufhäuser's recommendation contains the discussion in the draft almost word for word. Still, I had to publish the thing. In any case, I need to be informed about *your decision.* Who else *collaborated on it?* (not Schifrin, obviously). Why A.B.S.? I don't really agree with Stampfer's comments, especially at the end. The danger of the whole discussion up to this point is that, practically, the call for a dictatorship strengthens Hitler. It is insane utopianism to believe that the "assembled forces of anti-capitalism", which failed when the possibility of activity was greatest, will now succeed under the dictatorship. How much smarter the Miles people are! (By the way, how are relations now?) I fear that the discussion in the *Zeitschrift*, as carried on up to now, will not have an attractive effect.

Please tell Klinger that I did not receive *any* galleys from the printer, although the manuscripts were sent by the ninth. I need them immediately, because I have to proceed [with publication]. The article from [Wenzel] Jaksch[81] is very good, unusually [so]. In any case, I want to put it up front. The man, to whom I'm very thankful, should certainly write again.

The assertions about Schönh[err] were from Lück, who was present at the trial. The socialist building firms were also affected.

Please write to me on Friday. I also receive mail on Sundays.

Best wishes,
R

[P.S.] If the occasion should arise, call me, if necessary, Thursday or Friday between 10:00 and 10:30 a.m. Please send me the addresses for Amsterdam. Please have the letter transcribed and send the carbon copy to me [...].

---

80 Otto Friedländer (1897–1954) studied politics, was leader of the Socialist Student Association from 1923–29, and published a book about his travels to the Soviet Union in 1927. After fleeing to Prague in 1933, he remained active among émigré socialists. He eventually fled to Norway and then to Sweden.

81 Wenzel Jaksch (1896–1966) was a Sudeten-German Social Democrat, editor of *Der Sozialdemokrat* (published in Prague) from 1924 to 1938, a long-time member of the Czechoslovak parliament, and became Chairman of the DSAP in 1938. He eventually fled to Britain and moved to Germany after the war where he was active in the SPD.

Prague, April 20, 1934

Dear Rudolf,

Your letter of the 17th arrived promptly. You'll find the copy you wanted enclosed. We were very pleased that, in regard to our conclusions, there were scarcely any differences of opinion between us. In terms of the form of the presentation, too, we are in general agreement. From the beginning, I'd pleaded not to reject publication out of hand. Nevertheless, I had certain reservations not to mess up our pamphlet series, which is selling well right now. Then came your recommendation to use publication in the *Zeitschrift* as the way out, especially since those who were against publishing it at all could be won over. Only Arthur has certain concerns due to the large size the issue would have in which this tapeworm will appear. But these concerns can be overcome.

You ask: Why ABS? A is Aufhäuser, B [is] Böchel, and S [is] Seydewitz. I'd assumed you knew that. We first heard of the thing when we received a letter from Reinbold,[82] who told us about the plan put forward by Seydewitz. It seems to have been circulating with this title. That Seydewitz is one of the key people involved was confirmed today in a meeting of the [Executive] by A[ufhäuser]. He did not say who else was involved in the group, although he was asked to do so many times.

I'll provide a short description of today's meeting. From the start, in pretty strong terms, Wels said that he views this work, the way it came to our attention, and the demand for its publication as a serious betrayal, which he did not think was possible among members of the Executive. Aufhäuser calmly rejected this accusation. It is not about a proclamation by the minority in the Executive, but rather it the basis for a discussion put forward by a group that strives for a new intellectual understanding. Böchel asserted that one should not discern any disloyalty in the way communication took place, because the exposé was sent as the basis for discussion and was not ready for publication. Finally, I made a recommendation that the resulting work not be published as a brochure in our series, but rather as an essay in the *Zeitschrift*. Aufhäuser rejected that suggestion.

A[ufhäuser] and B[öchel] earlier had told us that they still intended to write a foreword. Wels and Stampfer, who had already complained that we'd received

---

82   Georg Reinbold (1885–1946), SPD and trade union activist in Baden. He became regional party secretary in the 1923–33 and was also a member of the national executive committee as well a leading figure in the Landtag. He fled to the Saarland in 1933 and later to France and the United States.

an unfinished manuscript, demanded to delay the decision, because, of course, one first had to familiarize one's self with the foreword. As a result, there was only one vote over whether to make the decision today, or to wait until later. An immediate decision was rejected. A[ufhäuser] and B[öchel] remained in the minority.

I don't wish to claim that this result is satisfactory. I would have preferred that my recommendation had been voted upon positively, so that A[ufhäuser] and B[öchel] would have been forced to either accept or to reject this mode of publication. Whether A[ufhäuser's] declaration that, for reasons of self-respect, he would not come back to us a second time, is his final word, I don't know. If yes, then that is something we will have to put up with, especially since we can rightly point out that we offered him publication in the *Zeitschrift*, through which all of those who are at all interested in the discussion, both domestically and abroad, could be reached. No one among us thought about a substantive discussion within the Executive, to say nothing of making any suggestions for improving [the manuscript]. Should publication in the *Zeitschrift* be considered later on, then I favor swallowing the toad in one gulp. That means that I would like not only to publish this tapeworm in the issue, but also three or four pregnant pieces along with it. That is a way one can call a halt to further discussion. Whether the authors are prepared to use their own names or to publish the whole thing anonymously has not yet been clarified.

Today's discussion also touched a bit on substantive matters. Stampfer needed to make some observations about the abandonment of the Social Democratic Party. I decided not to express myself substantively but left no doubt that I agree neither to any abandonment of the social democratic idea nor to any approach to the Communists. I think as little of the council system today as in 1919, and I'm as unwilling to offer obeisance as in 1920. By the way, have you read the article "A New Party" by Otto [Bauer] in number 7 of the *Arbeiter-Zeitung*? We will reprint the decisive parts in *Sozialistische Aktion*.[83] I think Otto will cross himself, when he reads this elaboration. Just like you, I pointed out in our internal discussions that the dictatorship and the soviet system are a gift from God for Hitler.

We had a long discussion with Miles-Mann. He put three demands before us, with which you are familiar from the conversations in Zürich and supported them with a very skillful presentation of their activity at home and abroad.

---

83 *Sozialistische Aktion* was the underground counterpart of *Neuer Vorwärts* smuggled into Germany.

However, as unambiguous as his assertions were, his intentions were less so. I don't hold it against him that he and his friends strive for power. Since they apparently dispose over many qualified people, it is their right and, perhaps, it will also be the result of their work. But, without having expressed myself with finality about his demands – none of us did so, we only wanted to inform ourselves – I made clear to him that, for example, the demand for representation in the International cannot mark the beginning of cooperation, but rather can only be fulfilled, when what he rightly calls required trust-building cooperation has become a reality. The decision concerning the demands of the Miles group was postponed because Siegmund [Crummenerl], who is not in good health, is gone for a few weeks for a cure in Karlsbad. There was general agreement, especially since we are essentially united about the material.

I think it would be good if you let F[riedrich] A[dler] know. I've informed Klinger because of the *Zeitschrift*. For Amsterdam, I can give you the following addresses: Mendelsohn, Biesboschstraat, 24, III; Landsberg, Emmastraat 16 b. Beckers (mailbox only, not an apartment); Asch, Büro Heerengracht 48; Parteivorstand, Tesselschadestraat31; Het Volk, Hekelveld 15.

Best regards,
 [Paul]

Brünn, June 2, 1934
Auslandsbüro (Foreign Office)
österreichicher Sozialdemokraten (Austrian Social Democrats, ALÖS)

Dear Rudolf,

In Brussels I did not get the chance to see you to exchange views about some misunderstandings that arose during the course of the meeting of the Executive committee. In order to prevent them from lingering, I'd like to deal with them by mail.
1. You obviously took it badly that I accepted the invitation to listen to a young comrade from the Miles group. Indeed, to me it seemed not only to serve my purpose of gaining information, but also, due to the situation in Austria, it seemed useful to go. In Austria we also have a group with the same standpoint as that of the Miles group and they are in contact with it. The young German comrade wanted to put forward the demand, that one of the three seats that you have should be transferred to his group. I talked him out of it and recommended to him, instead, to write a letter

to the Executive requesting support for the calling of a conference, which should deal with German representation in the [LSI] Executive. He accepted the advice. I don't think that this action of mine was disloyalty against you.

2. In the meeting of the Executive, you gave a half hour speech against me. I spoke later and in a single, parenthetical sentence remarked that I very much doubt whether your view is in line with the outlook of the comrades active in Germany. In response you took the floor again and again gave an extended speech against me. I don't take offence at such things. But that you take it badly when I reply to your whole speech against me with half of a sentence, is overly sensitive.

3. A general problem underlies all of this. We should not deceive ourselves about the fact that the emigration is not an expression of the outlook of the comrades at home. And what is more, we should not deceive ourselves that the movement in the fascist countries cannot be reestablished under the old firm, under the old leadership, and with the old ideology. That is true for us just as it is for you, but for you certainly not to a lesser degree than for us. That is why at the meeting I justified a letter from the Vienna Committee, although it was sent without my advice being heard, and although I would have advised against its being sent if someone had asked me. Therefore, I am also of the opinion that it is in the interests of both parties and also in the interest of the International to allow representatives of the domestically active groups into the meetings as soon as that is feasible. This is important, because, morally, the émigrés in the Executive naturally are in a weaker position than the representatives of those who are active at home, and because the authority of the Executive itself would be strengthened by these groups. I think that this point of view should be subordinated to considerations of an organizational nature, which stem all too much from the organizational routine of the past.

I hope that these considerations to some degree will ease the touchiness and pique you've exhibited toward me this time.

From an old friend,
   [Otto Bauer]

Prague, July 3, 1934

Dear Rudolf,

Geyer gave me your letter from 29 June so that I could reply regarding his perspective on the publication of the draft program. Because he was and is an opponent of publishing it, he does not want to have anything to do with the modalities of its publication. I don't really understand this viewpoint well, but I also don't see any reason that would prevent me from not relieving him of unpleasant correspondence.

So far, the shortened version of the draft program has not yet arrived. I don't see any reason to speed up publication in such a way that it would appear in the August issue. Perhaps A.B.S. have had second thoughts and are themselves delaying publication. We can calmly wait. I would be in favor of your planning the next issue in the normal way and that you concern yourself with the publication only after the draft has been sent to you.

I don't want to make the final decision about whether it would be advisable to carry out publication in one issue (which would have to be enlarged) or in two. I would make it dependent upon the best possible way to publish two articles on fundamentals at the same time as the draft. One article could include the polemic against the utopia of the councils, and the other, which I consider more important, would have to be a polemic against the abandonment of Social Democracy to the advantage of a revolutionary centralist party. It is extraordinarily interesting that rumors of such intentions have led to substantial discord at home. Thus, a few days ago comrades from home appeared, and the first thing they asked our agent was whether it was true that we wanted to give up the name "Social Democrat". They were very happy when they heard that that is not the case and promised their collaboration just to maintain this position. I can imagine that such an article could be published at the same time as the draft program, perhaps even before it. Indeed, it would be best in the form of a letter from Germany, because as the case I mentioned shows, the problem is now already acute and not dependent upon the draft program. The draft program will only substantially deepen the issue.

I think it is absolutely necessary that the authors of the draft program bear personal responsibility for it. We need that not only in order to protect ourselves from the unwanted assertion that we support a dictatorship of the councils. It [also] seems necessary, because in the introduction the left opposition in the party Executive is mentioned and one can in fairness demand, that this formulation be complemented with the names of those concerned. To be sure, we have not discussed this issue very much in the party executive, but I think I can say that both Crummenerl and I have presumed the personal signature as a matter of course. If you take the position that they must attach their names to it, A[ufhäuser] and B[öchel] would demand that the Party Executive make a decision, so the result is not absolutely certain. Finally, I'm also of the opinion that the personal signature is necessary in order for the Sopade to avoid difficulty in carrying out its activities in Czechoslovakia. I could imagine that the local authorities, who are in a tough fight with the Communists, would take a position opposing any strengthening of Communist tendencies by German Social Democratic emigrants. Anyway, with this in mind, I intend to talk with [Siegfried] Taub[84] and [Ludwig] Czech before publishing. To me, it seems to be a mark of loyalty and politically astute to inform these comrades about what is going on.

It would be good if you'd let me know your opinion soon. I am not counting on publication in the August issue, but rather in the September issue at the earliest. A prompt reply from you is also necessary, because we have to speak with Arthur about increasing the length if we go forward with publication in a single issue.

Leeb will be bringing you a letter from O[tto] W[els]. We talked with Fritz Adler about writing him a letter in response to the attitude of the Labor Party on the transfer issue. He wants to forward this letter. This agreement will probably be invalid by the time of your next visit to London. There you could undertake this step personally. If that is not the case, then it would probably be best if you drafted such a letter yourself and to give directly to Fritz Adler. I don't think we need to do any further work on the wording.

Karl Kautsky's brochure will soon be published. (He urgently desires to use a pseudonym, to which you will have to give attention.) We don't yet have a title. I am also in touch with K[autsky] in order to prevail upon him to use his name. O[tto] B[auer] told me that he could take legal action against our publishing the brochure. Of course, he would be of a different opinion. Fritz [Adler] has a copy of the manuscript. Have him show it to you.[85]

Best regards,
    [Paul]

---

84 Siegfried Taub (1876–1946) was a leading member of the DSAP, Vice-President of Parliament, and a member of the International's Executive Committee.
85 The discussion concerns Kautsky's critical analysis of the February debacle in Austria in *Grenzen der Gewalt: Aussichten und Wirkungen bewaffneter Erhebungen des Proletariats* (Karlsbad: Graphia, 1934). Published anonymously.

Prague, August 9, 1934

Dear Hilferding,

Enclosed is the last issue of our Sopade-*Information* with the declaration about the publication in the *Manchester Guardian*.[86] Also enclosed is a copy of a letter to Breitscheid. If you find out something about this matter, we would also like to quickly be informed. I called Comrade Sturmthal today.[87] He was already familiar with the article in the MG, which I thought was remarkable. Is my assumption correct, that he was informed about this article from the other side?

Geyer gave me the proofs of the article by Seydewitz three days ago. I am quite astounded that you are going to print this entire article. You told me earlier that you wanted to cut it. I will not follow through on my intention to reply to the article. Two considerations have led me to that decision. The length of the article makes it impossible for me, as I originally intended, to merely make a couple of short comments in those places where we were expressly mentioned. Such a brief reply would appear pathetic and give the impression that one would want to skirt taking a position on the other problems brought up in the article. If one wants to respond to the Seydewitz article at all, it has to be a reply that includes taking a fundamental position on the methods of illegal work. I cannot provide that, because, first of all, I have a different view as the one otherwise represented here. My views deviate particularly from those represented in Part B of the July report. And since Seydewitz and others possess this report, then it would not be hard for them to construct conflicts in the organizational spheres, as they are able to construct antagonisms between the conceptions [sic] which are again described in the Appeal of 30 June and in Part B of the July report.

Best regards,
 [unsigned, probably Friedrich Stampfer]

---

86 The Sopade's *Informationsblätter* was published from 1934–1939. The article in the *Manchester Guardian* reported that Wels was negotiating with the German government to conclude an "conservative-military" similar to the "labor-military" alliance that Chancellor von Schleicher had attempted to cobble together in December of 1932. The Sopade vehemently denied the report, which may have been planted by their opponents. See Edinger 1956, p. 139.

87 Adolf Sturmthal (1903–1986) was an Austrian Social Democrat who became Friedrich Adler's assistant in the offices of the LSI, first in Zürich in 1926 and later in Brussels when, under pressure from the Swiss government, the International relocated there in 1935. From

Zürich, August 14, 1934

Dear Paul,

I am writing to you because I hear that Klinger is on vacation. If that is the case, then I must ask you to make an exception and to take care of the page proofs. Otherwise just pass the request along to Klinger.

Issue 11 has the following content:
Richard Kern: "The German Crisis"
Alex[ander] Schifrin: "The Split in the Dictatorship"
Max Seydewitz: "Hitler's Counterrevolution"
Commentary: "Hindenburg – Hitler"

I estimate that about 70 lines are missing and ask, in any case, that Stein send a short review to Graphia.

Since the commentary on Hindenburg is uncorrected, and, this time, I had to make major changes and additions to the proofs, I now ask for careful revisions, especially to my article. Also, please complete the work quickly.

Now to the next issue. The draft from A.B.S. has been removed. I wrote to Graphia to send you the prints; if necessary, demand them directly. As I feared, the size substantially exceeds one printed sheet. Unfortunately, the printer did not tell me the exact size, but I estimate it to be two printed sheets! If we stick with the plan to publish the thing in the *Zeitschrift*, then it will have to comprise at least three printed sheets. Above all, I now need the promised articles from Klinger and your article right away. The [latter] should, first of all, contain something about the *true* state of the real work, if only as a correction of Seydewitz, and it should be linked with a description of your work, for example, in terms of the scope, tasks, and goal of illegal work. But I need the article immediately.

Now to the *Zeitschrift* in general. Up to now, it is not working, in the first place it is a technical failure. For issues 9 and 10, I've tried to send in the manuscripts before the twelfth of the month, a deadline, which was arrived at in the hope that the magazine would be able to appear about the first of each month. Nevertheless, the issues come out only around the twentieth, at least I receive them around that date. Of course, that means that the articles are six weeks old, and the magazine cannot be up to date.

Because I was not finished with my own article earlier and I wanted to wait for a certain clarification, this time I sent the articles to G[eyer] on 23 July with

---

1933–34 Sturmthal organized assistance for Socialist refugees from Germany and Austria. He eventually moved to the United States in 1938 where he became an academic.

the urgent request to deal with them expediently. I got back the first part of the proofs on the evening of 9 August and the second on 11 August. In that case there was luck in the bad luck, because the deaths of Hindenburg[88] and Dollfuss could be taken into account when doing the corrections. In the long run, however, it is impossible if the articles need six weeks or longer to reach the reader. I'd like to ask you to discuss the situation with Arthur [Arnold]. There must be agreement on a set deadline for sending in manuscripts. If I sent some earlier, it would not matter, because the printer would send all the proofs together. In the same way, the deadline for sending the proofs has to be fixed, and to accomplish that it must be made certain that the manuscripts and the proofs are dealt with expediently. I don't need to describe to you the kind of editorial confusion that sets in when I accept articles that are current and then watch them get old.

And if order arrives in the technical realm, which presupposes that someone – Arthur, I hope – takes matters in hand, the content could also be different. I've already told you that I want to keep the "theoretical" discussion as narrow as possible. I think it would be a mistake to exclude it altogether. In the current situation, it is unavoidable. But it would be necessary for you [all] to comply in your articles and not just complain. That the workers in Germany have little time for it is understandable, and to a certain degree, gratifying. But that alone cannot be decisive in this matter. Without a certain unification of socialist ideology, we will not regain our force of attraction and, without better orientation, the influence we've won back will lead all the more to chaotic conditions. So, it can't work completely without theory, as Otto [Wels] likes to imagine (and toward which you, too, are sometimes inclined).

I am also enclosing Kleinberg's manuscript, which Stein sent me. It came too late, although I would have otherwise taken it, shortened, as a commentary. I don't think there is enough room for it in this issue. If I've made an error (as a result of additional cuts in the corrected proofs), you could publish it now as a commentary, in two columns, shortened by cutting the part about Karl Kraus,[89]

---

88 Paul von Hindenburg (1847–1934) commanded the German military for the last two years of the First World War and, with General Erich Ludendorff (1865–1937), was the de facto head of state. Elected President of the republic in 1925 and 1933, the arch-conservative appointed Hitler to the Chancellorship. When he died on 2 August 1934, Hitler consolidated his power by combining his office with that of the presidency.

89 Karl Kraus (1874–1936) was an Austrian writer and journalist whose magazine, *Die Fackel*, established him as a major literary and social critic. Sympathetic to Social Democracy, by the 1930s he also held it responsible for the rise of National Socialism and in 1934 he looked to the Dollfuss dictatorship as a last chance of defending Austria.

who has no significance for us. Kleinberg does not formulate things particularly well and the [*Neuer*] *V*[*orwärts*] articles also are too long. Otherwise, send the manuscript with my regrets directly back to him.

Hindenburg's death was very convenient for Hitler. According to pretty reliable information, the Reichswehr appears to have had the intention in the fall of undertaking the creation of something approximating a state grounded in the law (Rechtsstaat). That moment has now passed. It will have to be seen to what extent Hitler can succeed in taking control of the decisive posts with his own people. One will be able to ascertain that depending on whether Fritsch[90] remains or not. For the rest, what happens down the road will probably be determined above all by economic matters. In any case, as before, I find the uncritical optimism questionable, if also, on the other hand, the anxiety of the "patent radicals" (*Patentradikalen*) in the face of any energetic activity, and their expectation that the illegal "elite" will one day bring about the miracle, is childish.

I may be leaving in a few days, if only because I have to interrupt my stay. My address will remain the same, however.

Wrote to me soon. Best regards,
Your,
Rudolf

Prague, August 21, 1934

Dear Rudolf,

Yesterday I received the page proofs of issue number 11 of the *Zeitschrift*. Today it goes back. I've read your article carefully. There were just a few minor errors to consider. I've asked [Alexander] Stein for a review and he will deliver it today. I estimated that it would take up two pages, but we only have one and one-quarter available. So, I'll cut the reviews accordingly. I'm sending the article by Kleinberg back, which I'm very happy about, because I get aggravated whenever

---

90   Werner Freiherr von Fritsch (1880–1939) was a reactionary German general who enthusiastically supported Hitler's regime and became Chief of the German Army High Command in 1935. Fritsch initially balked at the suggestion that Hitler combine the offices of President and Chancellor, but eventually acquiesced. He was sacked in 1938 for his lack of enthusiasm for Hitler's plan to go to war earlier than Fritsch thought prudent.

I see anything by him in [*Neuer*] *Vorwärts*. I don't understand Stein's love for him or your recognition of him as well. I will make sure that a publisher's blurb is produced and that the *Zeitschrift* is advertised.

We have received the proofs of the ABS-Program. The length is 35 pages. Even if one wanted only to publish articles by Klinger and myself along with it, it would require at least three print pages. However, meanwhile, as you have seen from Otto Wels's letter concerning Karl B[öchel], the conflict has entered into an acute phase. Consequently, the question has arisen about whether the prerequisites still exist that underlay the decision to publish the ABS-Program. What do you think about it? Thus far, no decision has been reached. It would be important to hear your viewpoint, especially after the typesetting is already done. If, nevertheless, publication goes forward as planned, I am for coming out with a double issue that is four printed sheets long. I am of the opinion, however, that it is necessary to have an article on fundamental principles from you, along with one from C[urt] G[eyer] on the councils' system, and the one you want from me. You are not wrong, when you criticize me for thinking little of theoretical debates. If we publish the ABS-Program, then I'll learn from this mistake, but I think it absolutely imperative that you take a position on the fundamental issue and, thereby, in a way, deliver a new platform for our work and, above all, draw a clear line between us and the ABS group. Furthermore, I think that we should only go forward with publication either when the commentary about the left in the Party Executive becomes known or if the left goes public by name. The advantage of the double issue would be that no special costs would arise, and that it would be difficult to continue the discussion four weeks later. Let me know what you think about these things.

I have spoken with Sattler in regard to the technical preparation of the *Zeitschrift*. He wanted me to submit an exact date. So far that has not happened, but it can be made good in a short time. Since number 11 will appear at the end of August, number 12 can come out in mid-September at the earliest. By the way, I also need a few days to write the article. I'll write to you again in the next few days and tell you what's up in the Böchel matter. In any case, note my private address: Praha XIX, 1044, Na Nicance. For the moment, I cannot be reached by telephone.

Very best regards,
[Paul]

Zürich, August 28, 1934

Dear Paul,

I was away for eight days, which, along with the lack of material, helps to explain why I wrote so little for [Neuer] Vörwarts. Thanks very much for your letters and efforts. But even today I'm still not in possession of the *Zeitschrift*. I also don't have your article or Klinger's. That means, according to previous experience, that the September issue will appear just before 11 October, which is really impossible. Therefore, and also due to the cost savings, the idea of a double issue (September–October) is more appealing to me. But it also raises the technical difficulty that the September issue would be the twelfth and thereby close out the first year of publication. But we cannot begin the second year with the November edition. The difficulty can be overcome if we continue the first volume until December and begin the second on 1 January. Under the current circumstances I think that is the best solution. Talk to Arnold about it. I really wish that he would take over the *Zeitschrift*. Tell Arnold that I've forwarded the two letters from Arosa.

The problem of the double issue remains the same, whether the draft program is printed or not. I personally am inclined, especially after the typesetting and under the prerequisites you have mentioned, to go ahead despite everything. Assuming we would be dealing with people who are part of a completely independent group, I would have some misgivings about failing to publish. I don't need to tell you how unpleasant I find publishing the thing, but we cannot avoid the debate.

It is different when it comes to the relationship with Böchel as a member of the Party Executive. His letter confirmed the picture that I've had of the man. My feeling is to make a clean slate (tabula rasa) of it, because it is hard for me to imagine cooperation in a group under these circumstances. I cannot judge whether such a break would be the right political move at the moment. Nevertheless, I suspect that there is quite a bit of bravado in his claims (who is, by the way, the Kurt to whom the letter is directed?). It would also be unpleasant, if – which is probable – Aufhäuser declared himself to be in solidarity with him. But, finally, it's impossible to pay someone and to include him in all decisions, so that he can, ultimately, sabotage the whole thing. But you must make the decision yourselves, since you can better judge the political influence and weight of this group.

Yesterday, I was in Basel to talk to Wirth and a former Zentrum member of parliament, who left Germany temporarily a few weeks ago. After my last conversations, I have the impression that the activity of the Catholic organizations is quite considerable. Nevertheless, further development will depend very strongly on the result of the still pending Concordat negotiations and the view of the Episcopate, about which there are currently certain fears. Others believe that Hitler's presidency and his connection with the Reichswehr denote a relative stabilization compared to the situation on 30 June,[91] but a very relative one indeed, because the overcoming of economic difficulties can scarcely be disregarded. We also discussed the subject of creating a bourgeois center of resistance abroad, with a slogan something like "winning back a state based on law". At the moment, I don't have the impression that the thing will be underway any time soon.

For the rest, it was also confirmed for me that the basis of National Socialism is getting narrower. As before, that is true above all for the peasant and especially the Catholic regions. It was interesting to me, however, that the enthusiasm among the big industrialists, including Thyssen and Krupp, has ebbed a lot. I think it is possible that, as a result of Schacht's new policy, economic difficulties, and probably also conflicts abroad, will rapidly increase. I have the secret hope that Schacht will be dismissed after a time and that a last attempt at an inflationary policy will be made, which could speed up the whole affair a lot.

I now very impatiently await your news, first about the situation with B[öchel], second concerning the form of the next issue, and third your article as well as Klinger's.

Please thank Otto [Wels] for his letter and give him my best.

Best regards to you and your wife.
R

Prague, August 31, 1934

Dear Rudolf,

I am now occasionally spending a day a home to in order to have enough quiet to read and to write the article for the next edition of the *Zeitschrift*. I'm writing this letter, too, from home. Number 11 just came out at the end of last week. You've probably already received a copy.

---

91 The reference is to the infamous "night of the long knives" in June 1934 when Hitler and his allies in the SS and army bloodily purged the leadership of the SA, the NSDAP's paramilitary arm, along with other perceived enemies.

I'm pleased that we are in agreement about the next issue. Meanwhile, I talked with the other comrades regarding the arrangements for the layout that you recently suggested. They agreed with everything. Nevertheless, the foreword should remain unchanged. I declared myself in agreement with that, especially after I'd gotten the impression that anonymity, at a minimum, would only damage Aufhäuser and Böchel. So, matters stand as follows: first, that a double issue will be produced (I'll recommend to Arnold that volume one should be continued until December) and, second, that, at a minimum, you, Klinger, and I will have contributions in the same issue. You did not mention that you want to write an article, but I assume that as a matter of course. Since I don't want you to have to wait for an answer, I can write to you with some suggestions for this article and also with some short comments about the content of my article in the next few days. First, I have to closely read the draft program once again. At the moment, Klinger is still on vacation. I assume that he will be coming into the office in a few days. He can then immediately write to you about his article. I'll make sure that the manuscripts are sent to you on time and thereby make possible the timely publication of future issues.

It is not yet possible to talk to Arthur [Arnold]. Right now, *Die Grenzen der Gewalt* (*The Limits of Violence*) by K[arl] K[autsky], *Revolution* by Julius Deutsch, and *Faschismus als Massenbewegung* (*Fascism as a Mass Movement*) by Historicus, in addition to the book about the concentration camp, are being published. As long as he is busy with these projects, one can't really talk to him, especially since he is very upset because of delays at the printer. In addition, he does not look well, he came to work despite having stomach flu, and is as unwilling to accept advice as before.

You have some articles by Kurt Stechart, who is a very intelligent and above all industrious and well-read twenty-seven-year-old Berlin worker. He visited with me for a few hours recently, which confirmed my positive appraisal of him. Is his article against Miles unsuitable? For the double issue? You should pay more attention to such collaborators, including Ottakar Puls. These people certainly understand as much as Seydewitz and Aufhäuser, and their desire and ability to learn is surely greater.

As is clear from my comments above about the double issue, I have made certain that no consequences be drawn from the conflict with Böchel that would favor the group with which he is involved [The Revolutionary Socialists]. Originally, I had considered it, but, in the end, I agreed that that would be a mistake.

Böchel had answered us with a six-page letter. Therein he accuses us of wielding Gestapo-like methods and does not say a word about the content of his letter to Kurt (I am referring to Dr. Kurt Glaser, a doctor and city councilor in Chemnitz who spent 10 months in a concentration camp and is now in Paris), but instead dishonestly attempts to portray himself as eternally persecuted. At my suggestion, he received a brief reply. We thought it was enough to object to his accusation regarding the Gestapo methods and to note that his letter provides no answer to the question of how he imagines working together. We want to stick with this tactic, which means we want to impute to him the responsibility for an eventual break. For the time being we are calling no meetings of the Executive and [thereby], in a practical sense, are excluding him (and also Aufhäuser, but that is unavoidable). We certainly can proceed with this method for a few weeks and can then make further decisions after the meeting of the three-person commission of [Johan Willem] Albarda, [Louis de] Brouckére, and [Peter] Grimm in Prague, which was called by the SAJ [Sozialistische Arbeiterjugend / Young Socialist Workers Organization] for a reason that remains somewhat mysterious.[92] Are you familiar with the survey circulated by the SAJ in preparation for the meeting? Do you know anything else about the meeting's intentions?

Professor Marck is here now. He was with his relatives in the Tratra [Mountains] and will now participate in the philosophical congress. I've had two conversations with him in which he didn't make a bad impression. He very openly described to me the development of relations among the Parisian emigres, recognized the practical work being carried out in Prague, but underlined the strong desire for a renewal of the leadership while at the same time expressing real concerns, for example, against the councils' system in the A.B.S. program.

---

92 The reference here is to a complex set of circumstances. At a 22 June meeting of the Sopade, Siegmund Crummenerl reported on a May meeting of the LSI Executive Committee in Brussels in which representatives of Neu Beginnen had demanded calling a conference of all socialist groups operating in Germany. This proposal took the Sopade representatives by surprise and they succeeded in getting it withdrawn, but the LSI appointed a commission of three representatives, the Dutch Johan Willem Albarda (1857–1957), the Belgian Louis de Brouckére (1870–1951), and the Swiss Robert Grimm (1881–1958), as well as the LSI Secretary, Fritz Adler to look into organizational issues concerning the German emigration. Meanwhile, over the summer, the Sopade's majority, without the knowledge of the minority, instructed its secretary, Fritz Heine, to put together a report about Neu Beginnen including material on its two sympathizers in the executive, Böchel and Aufhäuser. This report aimed to find grounds that would enable the Executive to break with Neu Beginnen. It was leaked, however, and passed along to Adler who revealed its existence to the entire Sopade Executive when the LSI commission came to Prague on 14 October. The revelation caused a scandal in the Sopade Executive – Hertz, for example, did not know about the report – but had little long-term impact. See Büchholz and Rother (eds.) 1995, pp. 52, 63.

Naturally, he asked about our relations with A[ufhäuser]. I gave him a very precise answer, which then motivated him to offer to mediate between uns. A[ufhäuser] will be visiting me on Monday, so I'll find out whether he stands in solidarity with Böchel or not.

Meanwhile, his position has worsened due to another fact. Among emigres who are more our opponents for personal rather than substantive reasons, there is a plan to establish a local group that is independent from us, will seek connections with groups in other countries, and demand influence on the leadership. About three weeks ago the first meeting of this kind of assembly took place. It was awful and the worst of the speakers was Fritz Bieligk [sic].[93] At the second assembly, which ran more calmly, Vogel spoke. But suddenly Aufhäuser and Böchel appeared. Neither had ever been to an assembly of emigres. Böchel took the floor and spoke cautiously and demagogically. The content: organizational theory and an attack on reformism. The third assembly met yesterday. Fuchs,[94] the first speaker, was factual and unaggressive, but of course also put forward the theory of blame. He wants, above all, to do more to attract thinkers for intellectual preparation. Popp, earlier an independent representative in the Hamburg Citizens' Assembly, spoke next, also critically, but very clearly against creating new special groups or splits. He polemicized above all against Aufhäuser's article calling for a united front in the *Weltbühne*. There can be no united front with Communists. Aufhäuser had sent this article to *N[euer] V[orwärts]*, but because he demanded that Stampfer tell him within twenty-four hours whether he'd publish the article or not, it was rejected. I spoke third and last. I did not limit myself to simply shedding light on the past, but rather I made clear the differences between us and A.B.S. in relation to the united front, old social democracy, dictatorship, the councils' system, and so on. The most important thing about these assemblies, which were introduced by an excellent presentation by Jaksch and will be continued for two to three evenings, is that: 1) instead of resting on personal gossip, the discussions took place on a high level and 2) that we are hardly the accused any longer but are now very much the accusers. Although ten speakers have been signed up, A[ufhäuser] is not among them. I have the impression, that he was

---

93   Fritz Bieligk (1893–1967) was a social democratic journalist who, in the late Weimar Republic, became associated with the left-wing dissidents close to the journal *Klassenkampf*. After his release from the Sachsenhausen concentration camp, he fled to Czechoslovakia and was active in the RSD.

94   Georg Fuchs (1881–?) had been editor of the economics page of the *Leipziger Volkszeitung*. A member of the SPD left wing, in exile he joined Neu Beginnen in 1933 but returned to the Sopade in 1935.

depressed by the unfolding of the discussion and that he is holding himself back because he can't fail to see the outcome. In any case, it proved to be correct for the younger among us to participate in these assemblies (Rinner and Geyer, who in spite or as a consequence of their pseudonyms did not appear, form an inglorious exception). Certainly, it became very clear the that the "Karlin Association of Offices" (Bürogemeinschaft Karlin) is not unified. Yesterday, I defended Wels from a nasty attack by Bieligk [sic], but on the other hand, I also made a number of critical remarks that made clear that I won't accept all the blame for what, in part, was done to us in the past. When it comes to a subsequent vote, the A.B.S. people will scarcely have a majority. They will not succeed in electing an executive committee that consists only of their people. And, since I intend to unify our people more strongly, and because we, doubtless, have the intellectual forces on our side, I feel calm in regard to future arguments. If there was the intention to use this staged movement of emigres here to knock us out of the saddle, it can now be viewed as having already failed.

I agree with your judgement of the general situation. I'd like to advise you to deal with the two speeches by [Hjalmar] Schacht[95] in the next article. Is there anything we can do to sharpen the conflict between Schacht and the foreign states? I think it is a good idea to create a center of bourgeois resistance abroad, but I did not have the impression from Wirth, with whom I also spoke at Marienbad, that he could take something like that in hand or support it. Aren't there other people around who could do it? Couldn't Oskar Meyer[96] prepare something like that?

Best wishes, and from Hannah, too.
　　[Paul]

95　Hjalmar Schacht (1877–1970) was a leading German banker, economist and right-wing politician who served as President of the Reichsbank from 1924–30. A fierce anti-Socialist, he successfully maneuvered to have Hilferding removed as Finance Minister in 1929. After the Nazi seizure of power, he again led the Reichsbank from 1933–39 and served as Minister of Economics from 1934–37.

96　Oscar Meyer (1876–1961) was a Berlin lawyer and liberal politician who represented the German Democratic Party in the Reichstag from 1924–1930 and, with his wife Margarethe, was a close friend of Hilferding.

Prague, September 25, 1934

Dear Hilferding,

I hope successfully to publish the *Zeitschrift* by 1 October. The proofs for the articles by Klinger and myself are being sent to Karlsbad today. I've requested the typesetting be done right away. Aufhäuser told me that his proofs are done. He measures the length of the program at 32 pages. Assuming that this number is correct, the content will look as follows: [Richard] Kern, 7 pages; Program, 32 pages, Klinger, 13 pages; Hertz, 12 pages. Recently, we had mistakenly reckoned on 72 pages. Accordingly, we can accommodate neither the article by Alsen nor the review by [G.D.H.] Cole.

Klinger told me that you have received the carbon copies of three reviews by Stein. We have not yet sent the originals to the printer but are first waiting for your agreement or suggested changes. In my view, we should not publish the reviews by Deutsch and Historicus, if we do not have one of *Grenzen der Gewalt*. Who should undertake that? With so many manuscripts, the next issue can appear on time. Please make your decisions soon. You have articles by Stechert. He is a twenty-eight-year-old worker (the author of a book about Palestine), really smart, and apparently very hard working and eager to learn. Are you of a different opinion about his articles?

I've written to Breitscheid today that we agree to his trip to England. We even desire that he participate in the party congress, which begins on 1. October.

The émigré assemblies have come to a surprising result. When electing an executive board, Vogel received the most votes. Only one member of the opposition was elected. [Otto] Friedländer and consorts received only half as many votes as Vogel.

Best regards,
  [Paul]

October 4, 1934

Dear Rudolf,

Since you are so steadfastly silent, I assume you are doing very well.

The double issue of the *Zeitschrift* should have gone to press yesterday or today. As it was type set the print shop chief noted that he had made an error. The total length of all the articles amounted to 66 pages. Consequently, there was nothing to be done but for me to cut the 88 excess lines largely from my article. You can arrange matters for the next issue, which I hope, if the manuscript can be delivered on time, will be published punctually on the first of the month. Will you be writing an article on the ABS.-Program for the next issue? You have to see the newest issue of *Kampf*. O[tto] B[auer] writes there about and against *Grenzen der Gewalt*. You've not yet told me whether you want to take the three reviews by Stein or not. I think that that in whatever issue these reviews appear, there should also be a review of *Grenzen der Gewalt*. It would make a very bad impression, if the next issue did not discuss this publication.

Comrade Stechert told me recently, that an article by him that he sent to you long ago would possibly contain a polemic against O[tto] B[auer]. He wanted to bring the article up to date, but wondered, of course, why you don't reply to him about whether you want to publish the article or not.

Say something about it.

Best regards,
[Paul]

Prague, October 9, 1934

Dear Rudolf,

Our letters crossed in the mail. The business with the honorarium is done. The honorarium amounts to 25RM. I've given Stein's reviews to Klinger. I remain convinced that it would be a serious error if we don't review *Grenzen der Gewalt* in the next issue. Did you look at the article by O[tto] B[auer] in *Kampf*?

I've just now sent Denike [*sic*] an offset of the ABS-Program, because you had a copy set aside for him in Zürich. Klinger has not said, whether he wants to write a topical article or a commentary.

We agree with your meeting with Bril[l] or Jo.[97] We don't have the edition of the *Zeitschrift* yet. I am giving up quarreling with the printer. Arthur or Klinger should do it.

Best regards,
[Paul]

---

97   Possibly Hermann Brill (1895–1959) who, after joining the USPD in 1918, returned to the SPD in 1922 and served in the Thuringian Landtag. He left the SPD in 1933 and became active in the Deutsche Volksfront and Neu Beginnen. He was arrested in Berlin in 1938

Prague, October 11, 1934

Dear Rudolf,

Yesterday I sent you a copy of my letter to Breitscheid. Additional official conversations with the Commission have not taken place. We now expect only the visit by F[ritz] A[dler] with whom the main theme of the discussion should be financial questions.

Enclosed is a copy of an informational letter that we sent today to our border secretaries. I ask that you view the content of the letter as if it were meant for you personally. If Lange comes to you, try to inquire discretely if his trip concerns financial transactions. We have reason to believe, that the Karlsbader have large sums, the possession of which they are trying to conceal not only from us, but from their own friends.

Best regards,
[Paul]

Prague, November 7, 1934

Dear Rudolf,

I just received your letter of 4 November and I don't know if this letter will reach you before Otto [Wels] and Siegmund [Crummenerl] arrive. Both are leaving tomorrow (Thursday) evening from here and will arrive in Zürich on Friday.

In today's meeting of the Executive we again discussed the delegation to Paris.[98] Böchel had proposed that Aufhäuser be elected as the third representative. Böchel supported Aufhäuser's selection by pointing out that in Paris the Report of the Commission will be discussed, and it would only be fair to provide Aufhäuser and him with the possibility of presenting their standpoint as a special group. When the proposal was rejected, Böchel remarked that he wanted to explicitly ascertain that only two members were traveling to Paris. He made his comment in a very peculiar way. It was blatantly directed either against you or against Breitscheid. In any case, it creates a new obstacle for your delegation,

---

and imprisoned. Liberated from Buchenwald in 1945, he became District President of Thuringia until his dismissal by the Soviets in September 1945. He later moved to Hesse in West Germany where he played a significant role in the SPD. The identity of "Jo" is unclear.

98   The reference is to the upcoming November meeting of the LSI executive committee.

so that this time it is hardly possible. Otto and Siegmund will tell you more. I've long been meaning to write to you in detail. Let me know, please, how long you will be in Paris. I also expect to hear from Breitscheid – I hope you remember his sixtieth birthday on 2 November – about whether he is postponing his trip to London. Then I'll send a report to both of you in Paris.

Best regards,
   [Paul]

Zürich, December 20, 1934

Dear Paul,

I haven't heard anything from you for an eternity and all the promised reports have not appeared. I can hardly imagine that you are coming through here anytime soon. Or am I wrong? Meanwhile, you've had a verbal report from me. The meeting went very well and made a strong impression on me, as the last one, in which you participated, did on you. I was very agreeably moved by the fact that, in spite of all the energy, there was much critical and sober judgement. My main concern continues to be whether the activity can be maintained on such a large scale. That would be desirable, because progress is undeniable, and it appears that the repression has its limits. The development in Germany remains difficult to evaluate. Schacht's "deflationary" policy contradicts not only the agrarian and export interests, but above all the immediate interests of the party in pursuing its struggle against labor, etc. Nevertheless, Schacht's position appears to be quite secure at the moment. The question remains whether it will last because this policy has to make the crisis worse. On the other hand, it seems to be a part of the internal and external stabilization toward which circles in the Reichswehr and in the Foreign Ministry are pushing. After 13 January we'll see whether the push back against the party's interests will continue.

But I'm writing today mainly to ask you to speak to Arnold seriously and at length about the *Zeitschrift*. It is not only that there is no provision for any kind of publicity – I believe, for example, that the November issue of the *Zeitschrift* was advertised neither in [*Neuer*] *Vorwärts* nor in *Freiheit* – but the mailing is also poorly executed. I'm convinced of this, for example, because the November edition, which I received in the middle of the month, never arrived at all at Oprecht's. I've still not received the December edition and, because of my absence from Zürich at the time, I don't know what it contains, because Klinger did not send me the final proofs. That means I cannot make final decisions for the January issue. The worst thing is the irregularity timing of publication. It would not be so bad, on its own, if the issue appeared on the first or the fifteenth, though, actually, publication on the first would really be the right thing. But the production time is impossible. It often takes 14 days or even longer until I receive the galley-proofs for one manuscript and then four weeks pass before publication. So-called current articles mostly take six weeks or longer, under they are in the readers' hands. That has an impact, of course, on the quality of the magazine and makes editing into real torture. I am convinced that when someone really gave the magazine his attention, things could easily be straightened out. That's way I'm asking to you to speak with Arnold about him taking on the matter energetically.

As strange as it is, I have a strong need for suitable collaborators. Of course, there are more articles available from so-called leftists, but I rarely receive good articles despite all efforts. I am writing today to Worker and Friedmann and I'd like to ask you to also speak with them. Worker is, unfortunately, not very clear; Friedmann makes a much more solid impression.

I'd really like to have another article by Jaksch. Perhaps you could talk with Strauss or Franzel about collaborating.

I've decided to publish Karl [Kautsky's] reply, which he wrote to me about at your behest, with some cuts, although I am not happy about publishing polemics that have started in other journals.

In addition, I request that you ask Klinger immediately if he can write an article "Two Years of Hitler" and send it to the printer right away. I would be very grateful to you for that and, in any case, would like to be informed right away. Please tell him it is urgent.

In Paris, Breitscheid was in better spirits than I expected. He is, however, in a very refractory frame of mind and can't decide about going to London. It is also very awkward that the business with [Erich] Alfringhaus has been blabbed about.[99] I am skeptical myself and very mistrustful of the man. Did Klinger tell you about the incident with Toni [Breitscheid]? She was disinvited at the last moment and was furious about it. Completely unnecessarily, one made her into a bitter enemy of Prague, and I very much fear that she will use her time in the United States to stoke anti-Prague sentiment. I was with her for a few hours and vainly attempted to dissuade her. Let us hear from you soon.

---

99   Erich Alfringhaus (1894–1941) was chief of the Social Democratic Press Service under Weimar and an influential adviser to Otto Wels. He fled Germany in 1933 but was arrested in Denmark in 1941 and committed suicide. The "business" referred to here may have been a Sopade effort to raise money with the help of Gottfried Treviranus, a German émigré based in London. See below the letter from Hertz dated 6 February 1935.

Best wishes for the best possible holidays from Rose and me to you and your wife.

Your,
   Rudolf

Prague, December 24, 1934

Dear Rudolf,

You are right that I did not write for a long time and did not send the promised reports. This was due to a whole series of circumstances that I'd rather not lay out in writing. It is possible, that I will be coming to Zürich in the near future. In Saarbrücken, Siegmund [Crummenerl] promised that one of use would be nearby at the time of the referendum. He would like me to undertake the mission. I have not yet been able to decide about it, and it will have to depend, of course, on the decisions that we make in relation to the Saar and the *Deutsche Freiheit*. But I don't think it is out of the question that I'll be in Zürich in mid-January. If that is not the case, then I'll write to you at length.

Today I will only provide a short answer regarding the *Zeitschrift*.

Arthur read your letter and will answer after Christmas. The December edition came out today! I'm sending you a copy along with this letter. I hardly need to tell you about my opinion concerning the irregular publication. I don't just want to blame the slow production process, however, but the editing is at least as responsible. With this current issue the delays did not have to occur. I saw the proofs laying around here 14 days ago. One can't produce a journal with so little interest. Klinger cannot fulfill your request for an article. He is not here. I don't know when he'll return. If he turns up after Christmas, of course I'll tell him about your desire right away. Meanwhile, in any case, send Karl [Kautsky's] reply to the printer. I'm pleased that you made that decision. We've heard several evaluations that make clear that printing [the essay] fulfills an important need.

Toni wrote to me, too, and described her outrage. I could not convince her to change her opinion, especially since I understand that at least the form in which the disinvitation occurred is not unobjectionable. I haven't heard anything from Breitscheid for weeks.

Best regards and best wishes to you and Rose,
   [Paul]

Prague, January 2, 1935

Dear Rudolf,

It was just decided that I will go to the Saar. I must by there by 14 January. I plan to leave here at the beginning of next week. I will, of course, spend two or three days in Arosa, where I have an invitation from relatives. But I'll arrange my trip in such a way that I have a least one day available to talk things over with you. I'll let you know well ahead of time when I will be in Zürich, whether on the 12 or 13 January and whether early or late. Since I just spoke here with Fritz Adler, he doesn't need to know about my presence in Zürich, otherwise, once again, the time won't be sufficient for us.

I am also sending with this letter the most recent manuscript from Karl [Kautsky]: "The Marxist Method". I have just read it and think it is necessary and useful to publish it. I find the last chapter excellent. In contrast, I have the impression that the description in the first part is too broad and risks that frightening off some [people] from reading the whole book.

After having talked to Arthur I ask that you read the manuscript as soon as possible, so that we can discuss it personally. On the way I'll be traveling through Vienna but will only stop there for a few hours. On the other hand, on the way back I'd like to talk with Karl in detail about possible cuts, alterations, and suggestions related to the book.

Best wishes,
 [Paul]
Best wishes for the New Year to you and your wife.

Zürich, January 17, 1935

Dear Paul,

Thanks very much for the news. I am very glad to know that you are in Forbach. I hope that Wilhem Sollm[ann] and [Max] Braun are also out and that the news is correct that the police were, so to speak, expelled.[100] What is with Stampfer,

---

100 A League of Nations supervised referendum on the Saar's return to Germany took place in the territory on 13 January 1935 and, with 90 per cent voting yes, resulted in an overwhelming victory for the Nazis. Anti-Nazi leaders had to rapidly leave the territory, with some, including Hertz, Wilhelm Sollmann, and Max Braun retreating to Forbach, on the French side of the border.

Decker, [...], etc.? It would be nuts to sacrifice even more martyrs, and if there were a bit more human feeling in Prague, they would have officially demanded that S[ollmann] and B[raun] get out in order to be sure. By the way, Braun is the only one who had acquired international esteem and respect, and therefore he is very valuable, which will certainly bother "Prague Otto" [Wels]. The result is horrible. It requires a correction of our perspective and, in regard to Germany itself, it is a dire warning against overestimating the work we've done there. The explanations mean nothing. The terror isn't one, but rather itself requires one. The [nationalist] front did not have state power. First it had to have the masses, because only when it had them could it terrorize effectively. It was, after all, mass [terror] and not state terror. The truth is that the masses joined the Nazis (and not new "Germany"). The workers certainly failed for the most part; they folded miserably. The Catholics are also mostly workers. In Germany it is certainly not so completely unfavorable as in the backward region of the Saar, but, in many areas, it is actually not at all different. Nationally and internationally the consequences will be awful. New blunders by Hitler are the only hope, but that, too, is not certain.

When do you think you'll be coming through here again? I would like to [go visit] Br[eitscheid] this weekend.

Give my very best to S[ollmann] and Braun and express my total admiration. This time even the Communist donkeys can't talk about the failure of the leaders.

Best regards. Send some news soon.
  Your,
  Rudolf

Zürich, January 29, 1935

Dear Paul,

Finally, I have to chance to write to you at length. First, the *Zeitschrift*. I don't like the article by Bienstock at all.[101] On the basis of his "Marxism" and of geopolitics, he wants to prove that the Abyssinian adventure is not an insane undertaking of an adventurer, but rather is the continuation of rational or comprehensible Venetian and later Italian expansionist aims. In any case, it is a kind

---

101   On Bienstock's background see Chapter 4, fn. 43.

of justification of Mussolini or, at a minimum, it places him among the ranks of those continuing foreign policy that is, in itself, rational. I think the effort to show to the bourgeoisie or anyone else that the fascistic Cataline conspirators (Catalinarier)[102] are their best representatives is not only nonsensical, but it contradicts reality. The most energetic opponents of the Abyssinian adventure were and remain circles of the Milanese big bourgeoisie, as their representatives, Balbo[103] and Grandi,[104] spoke against Mussolini in the Fascist Council, and, in league with the General Staff (Badoglio)[105] successfully argued against any expansion of the conflict. I don't want to publish the article at all, and Breitscheid, who read it, is of the same opinion. On the other hand, I would very much like an article by Bienstock on the Far East. That would be interesting and needed, particularly if he briefly characterized the Japanese military dictatorship. See to it that he writes such an article. With the collapse of the London Naval Conference it would be very current. I don't have the articles yet by Wendel (Total War) and Henrickson and will reject them. At the same time, the more recent article of H[endrickson]'s will be the best answer to Heizing, etc. Funny, the people who no longer want to see that, between 1914 and 1924, some things should have been done differently, and [they] don't want to allow it to be pointed out after Stampfer himself went too far for a while in his admission of guilt. But, if they want, they have the possibility to reply in the *Zeitschrift*. The *Zeitschrift* remains, of course, an organ of discussion and the authors are themselves responsible for their articles. Regarding Sering's[106] contribution, I've heard a lot of praise, but also a lot of negative

---

102 Hilferding is referring to the failed conspiracy of the Roman patrician Lucius Sergius Catalina (108–62 B.C.) to overthrow the Roman republic. Catalina attempted to win mass support through policies appealing to the mass of impoverished plebs, such as cancelation of debts.

103 Italo Balbo (1896–1940) was leader of the fascist Blackshirts in the state of Ferrara and a key figure in Mussolini's successful power grab in 1922. He later worked to expand Italian air power, and in 1934 became Governor of Libya.

104 Dino Grandi (1895–1988) was a major fascist leader who served Mussolini as Foreign Minister from 1929–1932, Ambassador to Britain, 1932–39, and thereafter as Justice Minister. As the war effort flagged, he supported Mussolini's removal in 1943.

105 Pietro Badoglio (1871–1956) a leading Italian general, as governor of Libya from 1929–33 he carried out a genocidal campaign against resistance to the Italian occupation and later oversaw the conquest of Abyssinia. As Chief of Staff and Viceroy of Italian East Africa he was a major figure in the fascist regime but turned against Mussolini in 1943.

106 Paul Sering was the pseudonym for Richard Löwenthal (1908–1991). A journalist and academic with broad training in political science, economics, and sociology, was initially a Communist under Weimar but left that party over disagreements with Comintern policy. He joined Neu Beginnen in 1933, fled to Prague in 1935, and later to London. After 1945 he became one of the SPD's most prominent intellectuals.

and critical reactions also from the left. His political remarks seem to me to be open to attack. Hitler as the end point of democracy? Oh, come on, that is too simple. Fascism is not a law of development, and this way of using the "materialist conception of history" leads down the wrong road. The unfortunate thing is that I don't receive any good discussion articles and polemics, just monologues, although I've worked at it. By the way, I have the feeling that the *Zeitschrift* will not be granted a long life, if the [Marx-Engels] archive matter fails, as is likely. (Please don't pass along my remarks to Sering. I'd like to reserve for myself the chance to debate him directly and at length). Has the subsidy for the *Zeitschrift* been reduced? Should one not, if necessary, publish the ads for the products of the émigré press? It would not be uninteresting and might even make the publishing houses more interested in the *Zeitschrift*. Now that it has been aired, I consider the personal stink about Sering to be over and done.

Now on to other things about which I want to express myself to you with total frankness, but also in strict confidence. I wrote to you that I am for Prague, because I believe that the organizational work can best be done there. You reply that the choice of personnel is completely inadequate. That is quite right. That was already a problem during the period of legality. In my experience, workers have very little aptitude for that, and it is a deficiency of their leadership. That is especially noticeable now. It is also the same shortcoming that made overcoming the split so difficult. But how can that be changed? A[ufhäuser], B[öchel], and S[eydewitz] are not suitable; the Miles group is split and confused. Taken together they are still of little significance. A change can only come about when it seems that politics in Germany are possible again, and one can take a political position and fight it out. *One thing* is *decisive* for me. That is the position on democracy and, therefore, on communism. Ever since Bolshevism produced a socialism based on force and oppression, for me there has been only one correct question: freedom or slavery. In any case, socialism can mean both, and the real tragedy is that freedom and socialism are no longer identical, as they were before 1917. I cannot, therefore, compromise on the issue of dictatorship; there can be no equivocation. There can be no "furlough from freedom". Dictatorship is not transitional or educational, but makes the dictators increasingly despotic, and that is the case in Russia as well as in Italy or Germany. For this reason, I reject any cooperation with the Communists, as long as they are for dictatorship and terror. I cannot understand how one can protest together with murderers and terrorists (and today, more than ever, that is what Stalin's worshippers are) against murderers and terrorists. And [I] will not change my mind. I don't care a rap if workers somewhere want to get together or not, because I am not the servant of the workers but rather the representative of an idea. Marx did not ask, what "brother Straubinger" desires or thinks is right; but [what] hinders their understanding. The danger is that the post-war generation of workers, especially in certain countries without a substantial democratic or liberal tradition, have become intellectually reactionary, have no appreciation for freedom and don't fight for it. It is all the more urgent that political and intellectual freedom take center stage, and that can only occur today in opposition to communism. At least Prague offers security against Communism and, therefore, I am for Prague. I am against the groups, against the Trotskyists, the SAP, and the Böchels – all waverers, who now want to set themselves up as left communists. Internationally, the question has been decided. The Belgians have rejected the united front. The émigré groups and the French party remain. We'll soon see how things go there. I believe it [the SFIO] is in a very grave and, in part, ridiculous situation. The French example will in no way encourage other active parties to follow their lead.

Regarding the matter of the archive, there are two points of view that have shaped my thinking from the beginning. The first is that it makes scholarly work possible that I believe is very important, especially now, and, from a practical standpoint, it would make it possible to break Moscow's monopoly. The second is the possibility of continuing the illegal work. Because I am of the opinion that, as things now stand, it [the work] still has to be carried out from Prague – and since I think that the participation of Böchel, the SAP, etc., would be calamity if Prague were completely excluded, then I would favor the sale, and I actually favored it before I had spoken to Fritz and Otto, who were also in favor. I don't have any concerns: the archive today has no actual function. To maintain it for an uncertain future, perhaps for a group of usurpers, would be dangerous and senseless. To whom it is sold is not important, but I can't seek the buyer. Decisive is that there can be no political conditions. If that is the case, then I have no moral concerns; in the end I would use all the money for an impersonal higher purpose, and it is certainly morally justifiable to use it for social democratic, rather than Bolshevik, ends.

There would be a lot more to write about, but an argument in writing is not very much fun. Hopefully, it will not lead to new misunderstandings. I am really quite listless. But perhaps I'll write again, especially if you answer me in the meantime. Despite the great difficulties and the personal resentments, which I understand all too well, I don't want you to get stuck in an irreparable conflict in Prague in which you have interests of all elements on the left and the right. Nothing will come of that other than the loss of your ready influence on *S[ozialistische] A[ktion]* and any of your remaining important influence on the Party Executive. And I don't see the possibility of another organization.

In regard to the congresses in Germany, contact Fritz [Adler] directly. I've forgotten some of the details from the Bureau's meeting. In respect to Danzig, I wanted to tell you that a speaker in Paris said that the Polish view is derived from [the fact] that the opposition (The Catholic Center Party, Social Democracy, and the German Nationals) accuse the Nazis of treason and outdo the latter's nationalism. This is understandable, but, on the other hand, it also makes explicable why Beck[107] would rather do business with the Nazis. Do you have any recent information about the situation in Danzig?

Please tell Crummenerl that he should answer my last letter, which he certainly has received, regarding the bonds that were sold. I also asked him to send me about 200 francs, because I have to make a large payment to Oprecht for the half-year subscription, the reports on the conjuncture, etc.

Does Souvarine [sic] have any prospects?[108] Rose translated part of it, but she doesn't want to undertake the whole thing for no purpose. By the way, I sounded out Oprecht. He will read the book, but I have little hope for a favorable decision, because it is certainly too anti-Communist. These days it is damned hard for the truth to get a hearing.

Best wishes to you and Hannah,
Your,
Rudolf

[P.S.] I had a very interesting visitor from Berlin, a collaborator at the *Gesellschaft*. Crum[menerl] and Oll[enauer] spoke with him here in the summer. He wants to pass along to them that the brother of the woman dentist, who was arrested in the last affair a year ago in Berlin, has gone abroad. One should not abandon him. My visitor views the morale and the outlook in the Berlin factories confidently. But there is still little conscious political insight. One wishes for more discussion of basic principles in *S[ozialistische] A[ktion]*.

---

107 Jozef Beck (1894–1944) was Foreign Minister of Poland in the 1930s. He negotiated a German-Polish Non-Aggression Pact in 1934.
108 Boris Souvarine (1895–1984) was a French journalist, writer, and activist. He joined the SFIO during the First World War and became a major figure in the Communist Party and in the Comintern from 1920–24. A supporter of Trotsky for a time, he was a major critic of Stalin. Hilferding is referring here to the manuscript of his *Stalin: A critical survey of Bolshevism*, which first appeared in French in 1935.

Prague, January 31, 1935

Dear Rudolf,

I returned here yesterday morning. I spoke with Klinger about the article on the Saar. I had the impression that he was already working on it, even though he was not very happy that you were not writing the article yourself. He is not here today, so I assume that he is writing the article at home. He had made highly detailed notes as I described my impressions of the Saar.

From the preview of the February edition of the *Kampf*, I see that this issue will also contain an article on the Saar probably by O[tto] B[auer]. We will have to do everything we can to make sure the February edition of the *Zeitschrift* does not appear so late. Arthur has been bed-ridden for days. He may have a blood clot in the bronchia. I was, of course, shocked when I heard that here, and I went to see him immediately, especially since he was being treated by a regular doctor. I found him with no fever, looking relatively good, and in a very good mood, so I see that my fears were unfounded. Nevertheless, he told me that when he is on his feet again, he will have himself x-rayed and examined by a good doctor. In regard to how the *Zeitschrift* comes out, the propaganda for it, and so on, I can talk to him only after his recovery.

I heard from Arthur that Traute told him three weeks ago that she had received Rose's contribution [to the translation] from Yvonne. I gave Arthur Rose's address. He will communicate with her. But, since I don't know whether Arthur will be coming in over the next few days, it is better if you tell Rose.

In Vienna I found the old fellow [Kautsky] in good shape. In respect to his manuscript, we arranged that Bendel should revise it in line with our wishes. That doesn't make your evaluation superfluous, but rather even more urgent. You should do it all the more quickly, so that we can reach a decision as soon as possible and can make the old man happy. He was very pleased about the reprinting of his reply to O[tto] B[auer] in the *Zeitschrift*. On the other hand, K[arl] and L[uise] complain all the time that they hear nothing from you. At the Kautskys', I met various friends from the old days, who, in the wake of the Saar referendum, judge the situation in Austria rather pessimistically. The [Czechoslovakian] Ambassador, Dr. Fierlinger, is substantially more optimistic, but based largely on observations related to foreign affairs.

You have probably received the exposé on A[ufhäuser] and B[öchel]. I find it very objective and am especially pleased about the recognition of the principle of freedom of expression. Thus far it has not been possible for me to learn about everything that happened in my absence. I'll report about the important stuff in my next letter.

For the moment, I await the evaluation of "Statism" and "The Marxist Method".

Best regards,
  [Paul]

Prague, February 6, 1935

Dear Rudolf,

You probably received this letter only after Siegmund [Cummenerl] had visited you. He has likely told you the most important things. I there are some things I must tell you myself.

I had assumed that you would inform Otto [Wels] by letter about your conversation with Br[eitscheid]. Therefore, I saw no reason to convey any more about it without being asked. By accident, however, Otto told me that you had just mentioned something about it on the phone and that he should get additional information from me. He was surely astounded when I did not say a word. That played out on Tuesday, as Otto told me that Erich A[lfringhaus] has been in Prague since Saturday. I'd already heard about that from Arthur [Arnold], who had met him by chance. Otto told the story, in a very depressed voice, that Erich A. had been informed by Tr[eviranus][109] that, upon the advice of his friends, he should go underground for three months [but] his intentions were torpedoed by Paris (meaning probably by Rudolf [Breitscheid]). One could not even think about money. I merely acknowledged this information, Otto said, because you had promised me to send a written report, and [he] let it be known that I did not intend to concern myself with the matter. What Erich A. wanted and is doing here, I did not know. I haven't seen him, but I think he is still here.[110]

---

109   Gottfried Treviranus (1891–1971) was a member of the DNVP, a member of the Reichstag, and held various ministerial posts in Heinrich Brüning's government. In 1930 he founded the Conservative People's Party. He went into exile in 1934 eventually moving to Britain.
110   According to Hertz's notes from the Executive meetings of 21 December 1934 and 5 February 1935, Wels initially reported that Treviranus had a big office in London, was working with Heinrich Brüning, and hoped to raise 15 million RM, which he planned to share with other émigré groups, including the Sopade. A meeting between Treviranus, Wels, and Hilferding was contemplated for early January. Nothing came of the matter, however. Wels

On the business of A[ufhäuser] and B[öchel] you've surely heard it all from Siegmund. I have the impression that A and B cherish the hope that Fritz A[dler] and Otto B[auer] would intervene along with local friends. The latter is certainly false. I know that Otto B[auer] had rejected such suggestions by Willi M[üller] straightaway.[111] I also don't assume that Fritz longs to be repudiated. In any case, one hears caustic judgements about looking at the papers of strangers. In this respect, one seems to give credence to A[ufhäuser] and B[öchel]'s story.[112]

Today the page proofs for the February issue arrived along with a communication from the printer that the article "Austria 1934" had to be left out due to lack of space. Klinger has the flu and is at home. But since I am unfamiliar with his dispositions and it annoys me that there were thirty empty lines on the last page, I sent everything to his apartment so that he can make the decision himself. Arthur has been sick for three weeks; he has a blood clots in the bronchia but has had no fever since I got back. He has now been x-rayed but I don't know about the result. I am writing that to you to explain why you haven't heard anything about new organizational measures for publishing the *Zeitschrift*.

I doubt very much whether Arthur can do this work at all. He is very unhappy with his entire publishing venture. Things have not gone as he thought they would even with his books. At the moment a balance sheet for [*Neuer*] *V[orwärts]* is being drawn up. It looks grim. If, therefore, we stick to the plan to have the publishing house stand on its own two feet, then surely Arthur will agree to shutting down the *Zeitschrift* as of 1 July. As I told you already, everybody probably agrees about that. If you want to stop it, then you have to talk with Siegmund seriously and urgently about it. I think that would be necessary for another reason as well. If the *Zeitschrift* disappears, then the [*Deutschland*]

---

reported to Hertz that, according to Alfringhaus, "Paris had ruined everything", and there would be no money from Treviranus. See Buchholz and Rother, eds., *Der Parteivorstand im Exil*, 93, 96.

111 Willi Müller (1893–1969), also known as Karl Frank, moved from the KPD through various other political groups until he joined the SPD in 1932. In 1933 he emigrated to Austria and was in the leadership of Neu Beginnen. He eventually moved on to the CSR, France, and eventually the U.S.

112 This remark concerns the "discovery" of Böchel's briefcase, which he supposedly had forgotten and left behind after a meeting of the Executive on 18 December 1934. Many of the documents, which Wel's believed confirmed his conclusions about the Sopade's left wing, were then copied by Fritz Heine and used in the internal conflict between Sopade majority and the left. Böchel, for his part, claimed that he was lured into another room after the regular meeting had ended, thereby giving Wels and others the chance to take his briefcase, which was returned to him on 24 December. Buchholz and Rother (eds.), pp. 92, fn. 6.

Berichte [*Reports from Germany*] will be on firmer ground than was otherwise intended. Gradually, one has come to agree that the effort to finance them through voluntary contributions is scarcely successful. But that won't be an obstacle going forward, because one is now convinced that the *Berichte* are viewed as unique and cannot be replicated. Surely you haven't read the last report. You must do that, especially Part B. What the NSDAP's policy of coordination [*Gleichschaltung*] has dished out is only bearable to me because I believe that no one takes it seriously. But I don't understand your silence about it. In no way does it exonerate you. I can only alter this or some similar phenomenon somewhat if you help me. If you don't, then I'll have to resign myself to the fact that I alone don't have the strength.

My hope that the result of the Saar referendum, the numerous breakdowns over there, the failure of financial plans, and the threatening internal conflicts with all the ugly characteristics that accompany them would create a more thoughtful and less optimistic outlook was based on mistaken assumptions. To be sure, here and there one fact or the other has made an impression. But on the whole, one is convinced of [our] achievements and successes and regards the problems that have to be solved as much more minor and easier than they really are. Siegmund surely told you that it was decided to undertake something similar here – in a larger, more general framework – to what you helped work on in A[ntwerp] on 5 December.[113] I do not agree with this plan at all and fought against it for hours. I demanded that they tell me what new perceptions or goals could be outlined there.[114] Such a thing is unnecessary or harmful just to get a declaration of support. No one was able to answer my question positively. And even when [the plan] was debated, I had the impression that this action was meant to be a blow against A[ufhäuser] and B[öchel]. I fought this battle with great determination, because I want to maintain my own freedom of action. I expect to hear from you about whether Siegmund told you about this affair. If yes, then that's good, and then I hope we will conduct the necessary argument together. If not, then that could be meant to keep you from parti-

---

113   Hilferding had participated in a conference of party border secretaries that took place in Antwerp, where the Sopade maintained a border post. The theme of the conference was the issue of forming a united front with the Communists. Buchholz and Rothfels (eds.) 1995, pp. 80, 88 (footnotes 5 and 50, resp.).

114   Hertz vigorously opposed the calling of a "Reich conference" of party border secretaries operating in Germany, because he did not think the party leadership had laid the programmatic or practical groundwork to make such a dangerous undertaking worthwhile. He also rejected the argument put forward by Hans Vogel to hold the meeting to mobilize the party's supporters against left wing challenges to the Sopade's majority. See ibid., 96.

cipating. I would not accept something like that, as I think about it, if one also demanded the presence of Wilhelm S[ollmann]. I'd like to hear your view of that.

As you can see from the description, there is no lack of things to discuss. I am holding myself back a lot, but there are some issues where that is impossible, as you have seen yourself in the recent argument with Otto [Wels]. I don't know how this has affected him. He is just as reserved as I am. I can only tell you again what I told you in Zürich: either you help me, or the moment will soon come where it makes no more sense to fight or the fight cannot be carried on at all. Talk to Siegmund completely openly – of course, don't mention this letter. You'll be able to tell whether he is for a substantive solution over the long term or not. But don't fall for any promises, the worthlessness of which I know too well.

Hurry up, please, with your evaluation of Karl's manuscript. The sooner we have it, then it will be all the easier to bring about a decision. If it takes so long that it gets caught up in the discussions about saving money, then the decision is unlikely. The old man's evaluation of the "Statism" manuscript pleased Arthur very much. It was written by two authors, by the way, who are more confident than they are able. But here, too, one should not delay the decision.

The *Europäischen Blätter* [*European Gazette*] has reached the end of the line and is seeking a subsidy.

Best wishes from Hanna, too.
[Paul]

[P.S.] Don't leave this letter lying around. Destroy it after you've read it.

Marginal Notes on the ABS-Program[115]

General Preliminary Remarks

There is general agreement that the permanent crisis of capitalism presents socialism with a task for which, in Germany, the overthrow of the National Socialist terror regime is a precondition. Furthermore, there is agreement about the desire for a unified socialist party and an international united front. There

---

115   Signed by the Working Group of Revolutionary Socialists, the ABS-Program appeared under the title "Der Weg zum sozialistischen Deutschland. Eine Plattform für die Einheitsfront", in *Zeitschrift für Sozialismus* (Sept.–Oct. 1934): 375–409. It is unclear whether Hilferding wrote this critique before or after its publication.

are no differences in principle in regard to the first actions that would be taken after the hoped-for revolutionary victory and which are in general agreement with those recommended in the program of the Executive Committee.

However, the authors do not favor a reorganization of the SPD, but rather the formation of groups whose merger would bring about the creation of a new party. Whether they demand that the SPD expressly reject reorganizing itself, or whether they want to recognize the SPD as one group among others, remains unclear. The formation of groups not only should go forward in a planned way among exile groups, but also at home. But it is extraordinarily questionable whether the approximately one million comrades, who in earlier years were loyal to the party, and who, in part, remain loyal today in heroic ways, would greet this call from abroad with much enthusiasm. Perhaps they have totally different concerns and desires under the immediate oppression of the terror. Politically, the p[arty] E[xecutive] acts correctly when it seeks to work together with already established groups and helps them in their effort to join together and collectively fight the dictatorship. This drawing together of organized groups without programmatic hairsplitting serves to mobilize and unify forces to pursue a common aim. But the Executive should not be expected to support the formation of other groups in Germany. That would be disloyal to its mission of being the trustee of party comrades living in Germany.

The authors believe that the new unified party will emerge from the fragmentation of the SPD and the KPD. But they don't provide any appropriate argument to support their belief. One could also imagine that this atomized condition stabilizes and lengthens, rather than shortens, the period of powerlessness.

The authors imagine that the standpoint of the new in-between party would lie somewhere between that of the KPD and that of the SPD. So far, all attempts to create such a party have been sharply rejected by the workers. The English Labor Party, for example, achieved enormous success after it committed itself to democracy and sharply rejected any form of dictatorship, while the International Labor Party drew nearer to the Communists and basically collapsed. In spite of such experiences, the attempt to form such a party could succeed under certain circumstances. But the authors make no effort to provide evidence for such a successful outcome. For them, belief is enough. Distancing the planned in-between party from the SPD is clear, but less clear is its distance from the KPD. Enemies of compromise in practice, they pursue the compromise game when it comes to principles. In doing so, they achieve an ideological vagueness, which cannot be expected to have a strong appeal to the masses.

On Page 5: Crisis of Parliamentarianism

The crisis of parliamentarianism is explained by asserting that the bourgeoisie turned away from parliamentarianism due to Social Democracy's growing electoral success. It is not clear, however, how the stronger parliamentary influence of "reformist" Social Democracy, as it is described in a later chapter, results in the bourgeoisie's fear and moves it to abandon parliamentarianism. Equally unclear is why a crisis of parliamentarianism must necessarily result from the bourgeoisie's turn away from it. On the contrary, wouldn't the bourgeoisie's abandonment of parliamentarianism consequently lead workers to an even stronger commitment to parliamentarianism? Didn't the crisis of parliamentarianism arise as political rights became burdensome to certain social elites, while the majority of the people did not comprehend what these rights meant for them? Wasn't the crisis of parliamentarianism and of democracy not called forth by all those groups and currents who constantly repeated to the masses that democracy had little or no value for them?

"Since the bourgeoisie needs a mass base to implement its violent dictatorship ... fascism is the endpoint of parliament's decline".

Here it is assumed that the class interest of the bourgeoisie supports fascism everywhere. If that were true, then the German bourgeoisie would be about a length ahead of its American, English, French, and Scandinavian, etc., [counterparts]. All these bourgeoisies must be much dumber than the German one. In general, the draft's method, based on a socio-critical analysis that is generalized across the globe and ignores all geographical peculiarities, is portentous.

On page 6: Failure of Reformism, Trade Unions

This chapter is a totally one-sided and purely agitational attack on Social Democracy. Any attempt at what even appears to be a scientific analysis is dropped. There isn't even an attempt to explain how and why the party and unions took the path of reformism and could attract a mass following on that path.

The theme is of decisive importance. Here are some intimations of that.

Theoretical reformism was victorious in Germany. During the war it split. Bernstein, Eisner – USPD; David, Heine – SPD. Almost all the leaders of the republican period had a radical past. They had all the best of radical intentions but were pushed onto the path of reformism by forces that must be observed more closely. As long as these forces of diversion are not scientifically studied and no means are found to counter them, then, unfortunately there is no guarantee that the authors of the draft, when facing the necessity of practical action, would not go down the same road as Ebert, Scheidemann, Legien, Wels, etc.

This urgently needed study cannot be replaced by declamatory nonsense about the "ignorance of class antagonisms", "the belief in a fictional people's community", etc.

The complaint is justified that the revolutionary goal disappeared behind the mountain of daily practical work. But whether a stronger propaganda effort to give prominence to the goal would have hindered the defeat under any circumstances is in no way as certain as the authors would like to have it.

The criticism of the trade unions' perspective in May of last year cannot be sharp enough. Does that mean, however, that all of the achievements of the party and the unions should be disregarded? From Chapters II, III, and IV the reader should get the impression that, at least since 1918, if not earlier, the whole social democratic workers' movement has been led exclusively by cretins and has brought the working class nothing but poverty and shame.

Page 9: KPD

Here the tone changes completely. It becomes subdued. Indeed, it says: "The errors of both proletarian currents balance the scales", but actually the errors of the KPD are excused as reflexive reactions to the failure of reformism. In terms of form, Social Democracy is placed on the same level as the KPD, but in terms of tone it is treated as the latter's inferior. On the desired in-between party see above.

Page 9: Imperialism, Fascism, and War

In this chapter the authors completely drop their usual self-confidence. Throughout it they constantly use terms like apparently, scarcely, not to be excluded, highly opaque, etc. The offer to Soviet Russia had made more sense earlier, when the "reformist leaders" had made it, than now, when the SPD has ceased to be a real force. The claim that, by leaving the League of Nations, Germany has become stronger and is now a much-pursued alliance partner is flabbergasting. First of all, that is wrong, and second of all it is dangerous support for Hitler's propaganda. The position on a future war is unclear. Should the proletarians of the "capitalist democracies" march together against Hitler's Germany or not? What is "socialist militance" in the case of war?

In chapter 6 on page 12 [the authors] put forward rules of conduct in the case of war for the "socialists of countries that are still democratic". They are not beaten or stabbed. Apart from that the central question arises of whether it is the task of a group of German emigres to propose such rules of conduct. If the brother parties involved reject such advice, it would be awkward not only for the authors of this draft program.

Page 13, Chapter IV, 1: The Struggle for Power

"Coalitions with capitalist groups are impossible". It appears, [however,] that not every kind of coalition is criticized. Later on, the necessity of coming together with the peasants and te petty bourgeoisie is discussed. Are coalitions with peasant or petty bourgeois groups then possible?

Page 14

The bourgeoisie never capitulates to the decisions of parliamentary democracy. Consequently, power can never be achieved via a peaceful, democratic path, but only in a "revolutionary struggle for power".

The expression "revolutionary struggle for power" [sic] is unclear. That parliamentary decisions only have meaning if a real force stands behind them is uncontested. That the resistance of the bourgeoisie can only be broken via *civil war* would be a bold claim due to its generality. In this context, what does a "revolutionary struggle for power", mean?

Pages 18–19: Workers' Democracy, Councils' Constitution (Räteverfassung)

In contrast to a "bourgeois democracy", a worker democracy is suggested with a constitutional system of councils. Thus far efforts to create such council systems have failed everywhere. In Germany they were dissolved by the "bourgeois democracy", in Hungary by the white dictatorship, and in Russia by the Bolshevik Party dictatorship. Only their façade continues to exist. The proposal in the draft, too, presents a picture created at the writing desk and incapable of coming to life. It talks about an equal franchise but does not explain how the legal equality of the voters can be achieved in the corporate electoral system. The line between those with the right to vote and those without it is very unclear. Every possible promise is made to those with voting rights, which, however, are made illusory through the [following] condition: excluded from the right to vote are all those "who are guilty of counterrevolutionary behavior". Since there is no objective, comprehensible concept of "counterrevolutionary" behavior, that will lead the respective majority to strip the respective "counterrevolutionary" minority of all rights. The hullaballoo that threatens here can only be increased by the so-called "functional democracy", which the authors recommend on page 26 for the organization of the united revolutionary party. The ability to recall councilors and party leaders at any time will result in long struggles between leaders and cliques until one group sweeps away the "functional democracy" and transforms the councils into a mere façade, behind which they stabilize their own dictatorship.

This road does not lead to freedom, but rather to a new form of enslavement. There is no likelihood that large masses of the people are ready to choose it. The coming revolution will emerge from disgust with a regime that rules by force and suppresses thought and out of longing for the reestablishment of a person's rights. No people has ever made a revolution merely for material goals, but rather only for ideal, transfigured goals, though the forces that drive them [to those goals] may be of a material nature. A future revolution will be fought out under the watchword of freedom, not under the watchword of a new dictatorship.

Page 25: Organization of the Labor Front

The vision of "revolutionary executive committees" is linked at home either consciously or unconsciously with the revolutionary shop stewards of 1918. Those could develop under relatively liberal conditions in which Social Democracy exerted increasing influence on the government. How do the authors imagine the functioning of revolutionary executive committees under current conditions?

Incidentally, the expression armed uprising does not appear in the program of the party Executive Committee, because, at present, it is simply a gift from the gods to the state prosecutor. It sounds radical but is rather premature to speak of armed revolt if all the weapons are in the hands of the enemy.

Conclusion

The draft demonstrates with devastating clarity a total collapse of theoretical-ideological consciousness. The authors spare no effort to sharply condemn those who carried out the material capitulation to Hitler. They are right about that. By they don't notice at all that, by completely abandoning the party's theoretical ideas and all of its most valuable intellectual traditions, they themselves are carrying out a much worse capitulation, namely the ideological one. Material capitulation can leave a way of thinking untouched. Ideological capitulators make the capitulation complete by *intellectually* disarming the opposition to fascism. They want to hinder bringing to bear the only principle with real staying power, the principle of *freedom*, against the principle of dictatorship. They forget that without recognizing this principle every socialism remains a lie. There can be only one answer to their demand that Social Democracy should finally liquidate its own spirit in favor of an in-between party: the clearest and most decisive no.

Zürich, February 14, 1935

Dear Paul,

Thanks very much for your letter. First, regarding Karl, I share your judgement. These are valuable ideas, in part among the best that Karl has written recently. All the more reason that in my opinion the introduction must be substantially cut, because otherwise it runs the risk of frightening people off. Karl himself has already developed these ideas and they are repeated several times in other sections. Incidentally, I find the simple contrasting of Marxist and militaristic thinking not completely satisfactory. To a certain degree, one probably has to resign oneself to providing a psychological explanation, but in so doing one should not completely set aside the psychological-sociological, i.e., Marxist, one. The phenomenon is as psychologically broad in scope as Karl writes. It has to do not only and not even primarily with the shaking up of Marxist thinking, which was, after all, not really at all dominant in the consciousness of the workers. On the contrary, it has to do with the shattering of scientific thought, of its authority as such. The war brought about not so much a reorientation of values, but a devaluation of values. The recognition of scientific knowledge and of the fundamental principles of morality has been superseded by the glorification of violence and the belief in miracles by the military leaders. The spirit of [Erik Jan] Hanussen[116] has replaced the knowledge not only of Marx, but of [Max] Planck[117] and Einstein. And that is not only a negative result of the wartime context, the war experience, the misery of the trenches, etc., and of the post war poverty, the chaos of the inflation, and so on, (the failure of science, of political economy), but also, above all, positively with the shifting of the political focus to the most backward strata – homeowners, artisans, peasants, and the declassed. With Karl, fact is characterized and condemned but not sociologically explained. The result, therefore, is too broad, abstract, and ineffective. So, a thorough cutting of the first 30–40 pages [is necessary], although the arrangement suffers a bit as a result, because the theme of militaristic thinking repeats itself several times as a leitmotiv.

Unfortunately, the role of the "middle class" [Mittelstand] does not get enough attention in the political section. By using electoral statistics, Karl correctly shows how much the working class really resisted fascism. Later in the text, however, he describes the fascist victory as if substantial layers of the proletariat had caused it. He himself correctly says that fascism won because it absorbed the bourgeois parties, but the role of the bourgeois strata is hardly discussed, especially that of the middle classes, the importance of which increased a lot under the post-war democracy, especially since, again in connection with the devaluation of previously accepted values, it emancipated itself from the earlier leadership of the intelligentsia and especially from that of the big bourgeoisie. This is both a prerequisite and a result of unchecked demagoguery, which appears in the form of Hitler as well as Roosevelt.

---

116 Erik Jan Hanussen (1889–1933) was a Moravian Jew who claimed to be a Danish aristocrat and achieved notoriety as an occultist and clairvoyant with close financial and personal ties to a number of leading Nazis, allegedly including Hitler. He was murdered, most probably by SA assassins, a month after the Reichstag fire, which he had "predicted" probably on the basis of inside information.

117 Max Planck (1858–1947) was a leading German scientist whose work provided the foundation of quantum physics.

Some detailed comments: On page 58 and in general: The formulation about economic laws that inevitably take effect is, in my view, too absolute. Economic laws are a scientific abstraction. The economy always develops, however, in a framework of politics that it determines but which also retroactively works upon it. We ourselves want to use state power, in other words politics, to disable the laws of the capitalist economy. Why shouldn't landlords, monopoly capitalists, etc., be able to modify them, contrary to the social ratio, which, again, is an abstraction? – On page 62 there is a repetition of an earlier train of thought. (Page 70 and elsewhere.) The polemic against Lenin as a liar and the moralizing tone definitely weaken the argument. I remember a polemic in connection with Karl's *Ethics* in which he himself conceded substantial limits to the commitment to truth in the struggle against class enemies. But it is also morally difficult to draw a line for [dealing with] the Communists who see Social Democrats as the enemy. I'm on Karl's side, but this kind of polemic has no effect, is regarded as hateful, and does considerable damage to the other excellent polemical arguments.

Page 86: The task of the proletariat is correct; but autarchy is not the goal of "monopoly capital", a catchword, which, unfortunately, Karl borrows uncritically. Once again, the role of the peasants is neglected. Question: whether, aside from the proletariat, other capitalist groups can be mobilized against the continuation of the policy of autarchy? That would mean, however, the consequent rejection of the now usual "anti-capitalist" worker and peasant policy. It's too bad that Karl does not address this topical problem.

Page 98, paragraph 1 is very confusing. Strong agreement with the warning about terrorist illusions, but not in this form. "The next and most urgent task" is the overthrow of the dictatorship. But why warn about things that cannot even be considered today? That can be said differently.

Page 112: I think it is dangerous to demand international agreement on a united front. If one does not want to declare it an impossibility from the start, then *our* conditions must be named: Struggle for democracy, autonomy of organizations, etc.

The formulation on page 118 and elsewhere about party and program can easily be misunderstood. Certainly, the acceptance of the program is the decisive thing, not the class to which one belongs. That, however, can only be viewed from the perspective of the individual, the single person, who joins. In Karl's formulation, it seems as if important groups outside of the working class accept the socialist program. One can raise the old question about the "people's party" anew, but that would require a whole different discussion. So, it looks as if we (in Germany?) have to rely on large, non-proletarian strata and we'll have to do without large, proletarian ones (initially or forever?). And that is claimed without any economic evidence. For our people that is a strange and incomprehensible way of thinking.

Page 163: The *unconditional* excusing of the Social Democrats (the right-wing socialists) goes too far.

Page 165: On cannot talk about a milder regime in Russia after Kirov, Zinoviev, etc. I would have also gladly stressed that the rejection of dictatorship in no way excludes taking certain energetic and ruthless measures, which one once called dictatorial. It is important that our people don't identify democracy with wishy-washiness.

Page 179: Second-to-last paragraph: Reformulate. Otherwise one gets the impression that all we want is to restore legal security.

So, that's enough. I think I've mentioned the most important stuff. I am unconditionally for publication, which, of course, does not mean that I always see everything as Karl does.

February 15, [1935]

Now to your letter. Unfortunately, it only came when Cr[ummenerl] was already gone. Moreover, I had little time alone with him, since [Franz] Neu[mann] from London was here by chance.[118] I hope he also visited you. Neu[mann] told me the following: Voight[119] from the *Manchester Guardian* told him that Otto [Wels] was together with Br[eitscheid] and Tr[eviranus] in Amsterdam and Copenhagen. He didn't ascribe much importance to that and therefore did not publish anything about it! In answer to the question of how he knew about the matter, he said Alf[ringhaus] told him everything when he was drunk in a public bar in Saarbrücken (where Voigt was during the referendum). Apparently [also] in the conversation with Grieß, the former editor of *Germania* and now editor of the Nazified *Landeszeitung*.[120] Neu[mann] told that to Cr[ummenerl], as well, and he will hopefully also tell you. I thought about writing to Otto, but it makes no sense for only Otto, who won't undertake anything against A[lfringhaus], to know. The rest of the Executive must also know, so that A[lfringhaus] is shut out and no longer can travel at the party's expense. The

---

118 Franz Neumann (1900–1956) was a legal specialist who represented the SPD and its allied trade unions under Weimar. He emigrated to London in 1933 and to New York in 1936 where he taught at the New School for Social Research and later at Columbia University.

119 Frederick Voigt (1892–1957) was a liberal British journalist who was the *Manchester Guardian's* German correspondent during the entire Weimar period. In 1934 he became the paper's most important diplomatic correspondent and wrote frequently on Central and Eastern European Affairs.

120 Wilhelm Grieß (1894–1971) was editor of the Catholic Center Party's flagship paper, *Germania*, from 1928–33. After the Nazi seizure of power, he moved to the *Saarbrücker Landeszeitung*, where he remained until 1938 when he left for political reasons.

story is an outrageous scandal. Drinking buddies as political representatives were already disgraceful during the periods of legality but using them under conditions of illegality for any kind of mission is an unconscionable crime. I fear that too little caution is being used when selecting our underground agents. In any case, it is not possible to ignore the Treviranus affair, which is, in any case, now practically wrapped up, as you and Cr[ummenerl] suggest. I don't have anything in the slightest against your using information that I send you, above all when you are dealing with Otto. Accusing Parisian Rudolf [Breitscheid] is stupid slander. It is Alf[ringhaus], who blabs the story all around. Otto places the blame on Rudolf in order to absolve Alf[ringhaus]. In any case, I think it is necessary to elicit what Alf[ringhaus] did in Prague and whether new agreements have been reached between him and Otto.

I read "Part B" on your orders; I did not understand it. The overestimation of Goerdeler[121] is childish; the talk of a "national-socialist economic program" was similar. The political concept, however, is dangerous. What are the personal disputes that are so mightily overestimated? And a lot is incorrect. Darré is still there, as is his core policy, and modifications have no really decisive political significance.[122] Schacht is the best supporter of the system.

The worst is this military prattle by Worker. That [Neuer] V[orwärts] now has become reverent about Schleicher and the generals is really a scandal! Compared to "Part B" and [Neuer] V[orwärts], the last Miles-report is really a political revelation. (Only it degenerates, again, into its opposite of revolutionary illusion, because an illusion does not become reality if one just postpones its realization for X number of years). But the hope placed in the generals is pure idiocy. With all these things we are not dealing with a weakening of the dictatorship as a political institution, which is most important for us, but rather we are dealing with its growing stronger through normalization, through insertion of the party organizations in the state apparatus.

A last example, about which [Neuer] V[orwärts], scandalously, could find not a word, is the municipalities law. Hitler commands the party, and the party commands the state. There is no antagonism between the army and Hitler's

---

121 Carl Goerdeler (1884–1945) was a German monarchist politician. A leader of the DNVP, Mayor of Leipzig from 1930–37, and the government's Price Commissioner under Brüning and Hitler, in the mid-1930s he turned against the government's foreign, economic, and Jewish policies and joined the opposition. He was arrested in connection with his role in the attempt to kill Hitler on July 20, 1944 and executed in February 1945.

122 Richard-Walther Darré (1895–1953) was a leading exponent of the "blood and soil" ideology propounded by the Nazis. In 1933 Hitler named him Reich Peasant Leader and appointed him Reich Food Minister. He was later named head of the Central Office for Race and Resettlement in the SS, in which he held the rank of lieutenant general.

dictatorship, and the bureaucracy obeys the dictator. That intrusions by dilettantes are worked out by negotiation *strengthens* the dictatorship.

That military and bureaucratic organizations have a specific importance in all forms of the state is, of course, a truism, but this changes nothing in terms of the existence of democracy in France and England just as it changes nothing in the dictatorships in Italy and Germany. Miles really has it all too easy when he reveals this nonsense. The most recent issues of [*Neuer*] *V*[*orwärts*] are really annoying. On foreign policy (London!) childish stammering; the military article [is] dumb confusion, and St[ampfer's] proclamation that we remain, as ever, the party of Reich President Ebert is really the peak! By the way, the judgement about [*Neuer*] *V*[*orwärts*] is synonymous with that of Neu[mann] about Hirschfeld[123] to Högner [*sic*].[124]

Crummenerl told me about the "Reich Conference" and added that I should be included. We only spoke fleetingly about it with the proviso that we'd speak further when he returns. Frankly, the business is not clear to me and I'd like to hear your counter argument. On the one hand, maintaining the situation in Prague is impossible over the long term, and on the other hand I also fear, that not much will result from any change. I will talk about it further with Cr[ummenerl]. In any case, everything has to be prepared materially and in terms of personnel, and I am strongly inclined toward your view that it is still too soon. On the other hand, the exclusion of A[ufhäuser] and B[öchel] will not remain without effect. I would demand the inclusion of S[eydewitz]. I have the impression today that the outlook is generally more resigned than it was before the Saar referendum, and it is possibly easier to imagine reckoning on a longer period to realize our vision.

Has the *Zeitschrift* already been published? I had, through Klinger, asked Erich to write about the new municipalities law. I have a very difficult time finding collaborators for such problems. Please ask if he has done it.*[125] If Arthur won't take over the *Zeitschrift*, then things look bleak. You forgot to designate the January edition as the first issue of the second volume and you carried forward the numbering. What should we do now?

---

[123] Hans Hirschfeld (1894–1971) was a Social Democrat who worked during Weimar in the office of the Prussian Interior Ministry. In 1933 he migrated to Switzerland and then to France where he wrote for the *Deutsche Freiheit*.

[124] Wilhelm Hoegner (1887–1980) was a Social Democratic jurist who served in the Bavarian Landtag and in the Reichstag under Weimar. He emigrated to Switzerland where he worked as a writer and was involved with the refugee organization Demokratisches Deutschland. After 1945 he served two terms as Minister President of Bavaria.

[125] *Is there any chance at all that you could write about it right away?

I'll write to you again as soon as I've spoken with Cr[ummenerl]. But write to me again, in the meantime, as quickly as possible.

Arthur [Arnold] wrote to Rose from Amsterdam. He will be in Paris in mid-February and will hand over *Traute's* gift. That is, if he is not precluded from coming by his illness. Can't I get the thing now? I could, after all, probably discuss it with Cr[ummenerl]. Please give my best to Arthur and tell him I hope he gets better soon.

Naturally, I want to help you. We have to come to an agreement about the form as soon as things became a bit clearer. I have not spoken with Fritz [Adler] for some time and want to in the next few days. I will read the manuscript on statism soon, but one can certainly rely on Karl.

Best regards to you and Hanna. Write soon!
Your,
Rudolf

Prague, February 19, 1935

Dear Rudolf,

Siegmund [Crummenerl] has been back since yesterday, but he has not reported about much. He has said nothing about the Voigt/Alf[ringhaus] affair. Neumann was also here yesterday, talked for a long time with Otto [Wels], and "forgot" to mention precisely this issue. He told it to me and asked me to pass it along. But that, of course, gives rise to misgivings, because it is very easy to get the impression that it is gossip. Nevertheless, I'll talk to Siegmund – he, unfortunately, now has the flu and is at home – so that he hears about the thing and can hinder any further assignments for Alfr[inghaus]. It is now my opinion that we have to do this and put a stop to the matter.

Neumann talked to Otto about the case of A[ufhäuser] and B[öchel], etc. He demanded a non-partisan investigation. It is not acceptable for the accuser and the judge to be one and the same person. Otto replied very gruffly and later told Arthur that he will resign if Aufhäuser and Böchel are again brought onto [the Executive]. But others are also demanding the creation of such an arbitration board. For example, that is the view of the local party, which wants to assign the task to the International, because we do not have such a body. It seems to me that everyone is ready to drop Böchel. Aufhäuser is regarded as "capable of improvement". Everything is being done to bring Lange back because he is viewed as an effective and self-sacrificing person.[126] The treatment of the Miles-group has caused the most resistance. Indeed, Willi Müller is not well regarded, but the blow to the group is seen as unjustified.

I view this conflict somewhat differently than I did two weeks ago. We have found a bad echo in our own ranks. But I'm influenced even more strongly by the conviction that this conflict can seriously harm our work here and beyond, and it will lead to such harm when every change for reexamination is stubbornly rejected. I don't think the latter is possible anymore, and I am summoning up all my strength to ensure that an eventual LSI attempt at mediation is not rejected. No threat from Otto can shake my position. A few days ago, I spoke with three friends of Willi Müller for the first time. In the next few days the leading personality of this group will be coming to see me. My overall impression is substantially more favorable that I had earlier assumed. The methods with which this business is operated, its scope, the quality of its personnel, and its products demand respect. It also seems to me that they have dropped the claim to a monopoly and revised some other things. Perhaps [they have done it] only for tactical reasons, because they hope to achieve these aims later on. But that does not repel me. I think one can easily work with these people, who use fairer business practices than A[üfhäuser] and B[öchel]. And if the break with them calls forth a difficult competitive struggle, which would be very damaging if this or the other side wins, than I think it is my task to do everything I can to avoid that. You'll find out more on this subject when S[ollmann] takes his return trip.

S[ollmann]. should tell you whatever is necessary about the "Re[ich] Co[nference]". If the original aim of organizing it one-sidedly is going to be dropped, then I have a different position, as if this would not be the case. Incidentally, it is not at all out of the question that the friends of W[illi] M[üller], who also have strong feelings, undertake something similar, and that this counterblow, which Fritz is supporting, will then unleash a blazing fire.

What you have written about Part B and about *N[euer] V[orwärts]* is completely in line with my view. But both Erich [Rinner] and Curt [sic] [Geyer], as well, are proud of their ingenious notions, and today it seemed to me, when I attempted to gently bring Erich's heresies to his attention, as if he looked down

---

126 Willi Lange (1899–?) was the SPD secretary for Chemnitz-Erzgebirge under Weimar. In 1933 he fled to Czechoslovakia and became an Sopade border secretary for Chemnitz, Zwickau, and Leipzig. He also worked for NV and Graphia Verlag. Accused of disloyalty, he was removed from his secretarial post in January 1935. In 1936 he joined the RSD but was soon expelled. He later worked for the Czechoslovakian and, after moving to Switzerland in 1939, for the British secret services.

upon you and me with a sympathetic smile. I suppose you will get a full taste of the absurdity of his outlook in the essay you requested from him. When we recently discussed this law, he expressed the view, that this is further proof of the expansion of the state power over the power of the party. I fear you won't be happy with his article at all. I think you can see from the essay in the enclosed issue of S[ozialistische] A[ktion]. I would gladly write the essay, if I wasn't always busy with endless, time-consuming, small things.

The *Zeitschrift* has been out for a week. I'm sending you a copy right now. Tomorrow morning, I'll speak with Arthur about Traute's gift. Arthur [Arnold] is here, only his correspondence is sent from Amsterdam.

I hear that Fritz [Adler] is coming at the beginning of next week. It would be good if you would speak to him ahead of time. All forces that want to build something new and better now have to work together.

Best regards from Hanna, too.
Your,
[Paul]

Prague, February 20, 1935

Dear Rudolf,

Arthur [Arnold] received a message from Rose that the handing over of the gift can wait until he comes to Paris. Arthur is now back in the office, so that this way of dealing with the matter is the most expedient. He also thinks that, meanwhile, you have received the *Zeitschrift* and that it isn't necessary to send you a second copy.

Arthur says that the January edition was intentionally not labeled as issue 1 of the second volume. He wants to number them further continuously. By the way, I think it best if you would speak to Arthur personally about the future of the *Zeitschrift* and how it is published. If, as is clear from his comments noted above, he will soon be traveling to the West, then you will be able to speak with him in any case in Zürich.

Erich told me that he has already started working on the article on the municipality law. In addition to his views, you can find more information in Part B of the *Grünen Berichte* [*Green Reports*]. You have to read that without fail! (about 20 pages). Then you'll see that his view is not only the opposite of yours, but it is contradictory to the highest degree. Constructions, nothing but constructions, that have nothing to do with reality.

Best regards,
[Paul]

Prague, February 23, 1935

Dear Rudolf,

Meanwhile, Siegmund [Crummenerl] has reported to Otto [Wels] privately about the Voigt/Alfr[inghaus] affair. Thus, we have not achieved what you wanted, and, at the moment, it does not seem like there will be any possibility of bringing the case to the committee. You must learn from this that, if there are things you think should be made known, then you must write a letter to the Party Executive. This letter would then be circulated and read by all. In order to achieve that, I've had the remarks in your letter to me about Part B and N[euer] V[orwärts] copied and circulated. I'll let you know what I hear back.

The case of A[ufhäuser] and B[öchel] has not made any progress. There was only a conversation between Otto [Wels], Hans [Vogel], Erich [Ollenauer], and [Siegfried] Taub.[127] But, as always, Taub was much more reserved in this most recent discussion than in earlier ones he had had with others, who did not participate [here]. He merely asserted that the Lange case had been cleaned up, and he would mediate with the agreement of our people. Only at the end did he ask how one was thinking about the case going forward and pointed out cautiously that one could not reject the International's mediation if, and as long as, one did not have a control commission available locally. Of course, this instruction annoyed Otto. But, apparently, he has bet that, as before, passivity is the best means of dealing with the dispute.

The Miles man still seems to be around, but thus far he has not yet followed through on his declaration to introduce me to the real leader. Perhaps he did not even come. I'd like to come to that conclusion from the fact that one did not make any further effort to have a discussion with Siegmund after S[ollmann] was first turned down. This attitude toward S[ollmann] is all the more remarkable, because, until now, he also has avoided any conversation with me. He had only officially and very briefly reported even on the conversation with you.

As I understood it from the comments of the Miles man, they intend to answer the Party Executive's memorandum with a very detailed one of their

---

127 Siegfried Taub (1876–1946) was a Jewish Sudeten German Socialist who became General Secretary of the DSAP in 1924 and represented the party in the LSI from 1930–38.

own. I have vigorously expressed my misgivings about this method. If it appeared, it would probably make it more difficult to come to an agreement. I was promised that this memorandum has only been prepared and, initially, should not be circulated. That would only occur if the party Executive sticks to its previous standpoint. Since I've heard that nothing in particular is happening in Brünn that requires Fritz [Adler's] presence, then his trip must be on our account. He'll probably get here on Monday.

This delay surely is in connection with the condition of his mother. Hopefully, you will have a chance in the meantime to speak with Fritz. That's because much depends on how he proceeds here.

February 24, 1935

Meanwhile some things have occurred again. The promised Miles man came to see me yesterday evening. S[ollmann], who was present during the discussion, can describe his impression to you. My impression is favorable. We are dealing with the first mature person who thoroughly understands the problematic of this period. He is, indeed, very taken up with his achievements and those of his friends. He makes demands that overshoot the target and he does not adequately consider the main emphasis of the old [comrades]. But I don't see any decisive obstacle in that, because I have the impression that one understands and respects the arguments. It is remarkable that both people have said not a word about their wish to change the personnel of the party Executive. One might conclude from that at least that they don't wish to press that intention too hard. I don't suppose that they have given it up entirely.

Yesterday we received the news about the death of Emma Adler. Accordingly, one can scarcely imagine that Fritz will be here before the end of this week. Therefore, I have advised the Miles people not to rush anything and to wait until he is here. Still, I'll tell Siegmund tomorrow that the new arrival, with whom he has conferred many times, would like to talk with him. If he says no, I can't change anything. It has nothing to do with factual matters, because it concerns the securing of the work in Germany.

Yesterday your remarks about Part B and N[euer] V[orwärts] made the rounds. The echo was extraordinarily interesting. It can be said, in general, that everyone appeared to be very strongly impressed with the precision and the sharpness of your attack. I must correct myself: it is wrong to say "all" because Erich R[inner] was an exception. He was the first to read your comments and took a lot of notes. Their content and an arrogance that was even more pronounced than usual make very clear that he was not wounded by the withering criticism, but rather felt himself to be quite exalted because one had thanked his work with such a critique. Klinger's reaction was completely different. I had a substantive discussion with him in which he carefully avoided justifying the domestic political tendency in Part B or the parallel comments in *N[euer] V[orwärts]*. His only objection was that you, yourself, bear the responsibility for the foreign policy line, because you did not accede to his request to write about that subject. Also, where you could have taken the lead on the Saar question, you left it to him to write the article. You vilify Worker, in part justifiably, but you published the article even though you were against publishing it. He, too, had already told Worker that the military articles will not be published in coming weeks. My aggressive criticisms, that *N[euer] V[orwärts]* gives one the impression that the editors aim to prevent anything interesting from appearing [in the paper], he answered lamely. Initally, he did not respond at all to my question about why he did not publish his valuable essay from the last part of Part B in *N[euer] V[orwärts]*, but later objected that it was too long. He declared that he wants to write to you.

Stampfer also began a conversation with me, which, however, did not get very far, because I wanted to do dictation and he wanted to go. But he was obviously very affected internally by your critique and horrified when I told him that I felt all aspects were justified. Tomorrow we will talk some more. For the moment, Otto [Wels], Hans [Vogel], Erich O[llenauer], and Siegmund [Crummenerl] haven't said anything to me. They talked among themselves, but I don't know what was said. It is now often the case that they talk among themselves, which in and of itself doesn't indicate a bad intention. I think it shows, rather, a certain insecurity, especially since I think they are all too smart not to assume that they don't clearly understand the limited ability and intentions of Erich R[inner]. Arthur, with whom I spoke today, also says that your comments put the decisive problem on the agenda for discussion and that one won't be able to avoid it. This judgement is based on the impression he got from Stampfer, who read your remarks in his presence.

Sollmann also spoke with Otto about the Reko [Reich Conference]. He, too, was promised that he would be included. Of course, that is great progress. Nevertheless, my misgivings remain. I still think it is of decisive importance only to only to undertake it when one has clearly outlined the material as well as personal aims. But these are still lacking. Despite all my efforts, no one has been able to say to me what the tasks of the Reko will be. I still have the impression, therefore, as if one were led by an unspoken vision to allow one's self to be granted absolution for the past and a mandate for the future. I very much fear that if this intention is realized, it will cause damage. If the Reko confirms the break with the Miles group, then the most severe arguments will be unavoidable. Everything will then retreat behind that viewpoint. One side will do everything to justify this measure, the other will damn it. Any other goal beyond that will disappear. It is a division of the elite, while the task at hand consists of binding the elite with the masses. In this case I also assume that the Miles group will strike a counter blow. What should happen, if a second Reko takes place which lays claim to leadership and to recognition by the LSI? It certainly does not strengthen the Executive's authority that only seven members remain out of nine and that among the seven there are sweeping differences of opinion. I think there is practically no chance that it will be possible to ignore the new situation created by the expulsion of A[ufhäuser] and B[öchel]. Should this matter be discussed at the Reko without giving A[ufhäuser] and B[öchel] a chance to speak? How will one justify that in the face of Otto's declaration that he is sure his friends at home approve of every aspect of his standpoint. I share your opinion that the current situation here cannot be maintained very long. I also believe that we will find much agreement with our long view. But that depends completely on the way it comes together. And on the preparation. Therefore, I will attempt to have these questions discussed. Then there might be a possibility that you could express yourself on these matters in writing.

Luise wrote that Rudolf's epistle, which was naturally very interesting, will be answered by the old man himself, who, by the way, is doing the rewriting in person, because he cannot rest. Someone else, even if it was his own son, can't really do it.

The doctor demands that Arthur [Arnold], whose body is under heavy attack, take a longer vacation. Arthur seems to agree that it is necessary. I am encouraging him in that conclusion. He will just finish the work he has started. That scarcely includes the *Zeitschrift*, however, in which he has little interest. He is waiting longingly for your evaluation of "Statism". It does not have to be as detailed as with Karl's work. For that I suggest this strict standard.

Best regards from Hanna, too.
  Your,
  [Paul]

February 24, 1935

Dear Erich [Rinner],

I just received your article. Since it is now at the printer's, please make sure that it is 1) typeset right away and 2) a proof is sent to me and a second to you.

Correct yours right away and send the corrections to me. The conceptual differences between your comments in the article in the *Grünen Berichte* and my own outlook seem to me to rest upon the following [points]. You start with the fact that the unregulated and arbitrary interventions of party *functionaries* in the economy and administration are restricted, and that that would signify the *separation* of party and state. But limiting such interventions is a condition of a functioning economy and administration, of the necessary normalization and the consolidation of power, not of its tottering. This was precisely the process under Bolshevism and fascism; one does not put the chairman of an electoral committee in command over *our* mayor or give the party cashier power over *our* treasurer. What is decisive is who gives the orders to the bureaucracy and who carries out these orders. There can be no doubt that those who give the orders to the bureaucracy are identical to those who give the orders to the party. The party itself, after all, is not a democratic body, but rather is subordinate to the dictatorship. The bureaucracy lets itself be used; that is the strength of the system, and to want to reveal contradictions there, I think, is politically misleading. The system is so strong, because it has the expert bureaucrats at its disposal, as it does the generals, and thus it counters the danger of dilettantism. Politically, there is no antagonism between the "bureaucracy" and the system. I can't think of anything better for National Socialism, in respect to its essence, which is what we are concerned with here, than the law on municipalities. Popitz[128] has served the National Socialist dictatorship far better than any National Socialist dilettante could ever have, he has strengthened it politically, and that is the key thing. Whether a few Gauleiter more or less become officials is unimportant as long as the officials obey – for the most part effectively and readily. But the same is true for the leading collaborators a la Schacht, Krosigk, Popitz, Goerdeler, and also for the generals. Don't let Worker teach you anything about their social aspirations! That is really intolerable naivete. All these people haven't undermined the dictatorship but strengthened it. If Feder[129] had become Economics

---

128 Johannes Popitz (1884–1945) was a conservative monarchist. Under Weimar he was elected to the National Assembly and then served as a State Secretary in the Finance Ministry, for a time under Hilferding from 1928–1929. He returned to government service as Prussian Finance Minister after 1935 but became disillusioned with Hitler's government after 1938 and collaborated with the German resistance. He was executed in February 1945.

129 Gottfried Feder (1883–1941) was one of the founders of the NSDAP and served as a party ideologist and early economics advisor to Hitler, who he actually had brought into the movement. He rejected modern industrial capitalism and promoted a populist, racist, and peasant-oriented alternative that Hitler first embraced and then rejected. After 1933 Hitler put him on ice.

Minister and head of the Reichsbank and Röhm[130] the Defense Minister, then we would be nearer to the end [of the story]. It is also misleading to speak of a shock to the "totality". The economy (the self-administration they have introduced is not worth mentioning and is completely meaningless) in every system has influence, as does the military organization and the bureaucracy. On this question, however, that is not decisive. It is, rather, who is in command politically. And that is Hitler, and when he wants to replace Fritsch with Reichenau,[131] no rooster will crow about it. Schacht, Popitz, and Krosigk,[132] etc., are not really independent forces, the organization of the bureaucracy itself is endlessly divided up and doesn't really exist, etc. It seems to me there is just enough totality and not too little.

The whole thing might be a fight about words if the danger did not exist of drawing the wrong political conclusions. In regard to the municipalities, one must also add that they become the pure personal booty of the National Socialist mayors, etc.

The "party" has not been maneuvered out of all positions of power, on the contrary, the masters of the party – that they are who matters – are the masters of state power. Because they have state power firmly in their grip, direct party activity, now having become *superfluous*, slides into the background and appears, as you correctly say, more as ruler (and victimizer) over the people than over the state. But that is the consolidation of the dictatorship. You see the matter sometimes from the perspective of the disappointed National Socialist party functionary, of the "old fighter" who has failed. And thus, and God forgive you, you are forced into such lengthy scribbling. Show it to Hertz and Klinger. If you want to take their views into consideration when doing the corrections, I'd be pleased, when no, you sign it (anonymously, of course), not me.

Otherwise, best regards
    Your,
    [Rudolf Hilferding]

---

130   Ernst Röhm (1887–1934) was a former professional solider who headed the NSDAP's massive street-fighting arm, the SA (Sturmabteilung). On 30 June 1934, after many in the SA had called for a "second revolution", Hitler had him and the SA's top leadership murdered to assuage the concerns of Germany's propertied classes and the officer corps.

131   Walther von Reichenau (1884–1942) was an ardent Nazi and one of Hitler's favorite generals.

132   Lutz Graf Schwerin von Krosigk (1887–1977) was a conservative appointed Minister of Finance by Chancellor Franz von Papen in 1932. He remained in this post until 1945. Sentenced to 10 years imprisonment at Nuremberg, he was released in 1951after serving just two years.

Paris, March 2, 1935
Hotel Langham
19 Avenue de Friedland

Dear Paul,

I've been here since Thursday evening and will return to Zürich again on the seventh or the eighth. I spoke with Sollmann in Zürich. [He was] here with [Carl] Spiecker[133] on account of the paper. But nothing happened. Unfortunately, Sp[iecker] has left for three weeks. He claims, that nothing can be done in the meantime, because the most important man won't be back until then. I will try to get something going in this direction perhaps with one of my other local friends.

I spoke at length with Rudolf [Breitscheid]; it is basically the same thing that he told you. I could not speak with Fritz [Adler] at length in Zürich due to the severe illness and then the death of his mother. He did not intend to travel to Prague and only wanted to stay in B[ern]. I assume that, in case he decides to intervene at all, he will consider that only after his return. In any case, I will then talk to him right away. I'll write about everything soon, in the course of which I also hope to be able to report about my local political impressions.

For today, just the following: tell Arthur [Arnold], in my name and in Rose's, that he should send the thing in his possession to me in Zürich. I'd be very pleased if it could be done really soon.

The manuscript for the *Zeitschrift* is done, and I have written about foreign policy. I have to read the proofs, however, and hope to find them in Zürich. Please tell Klinger, he might want to provide a short political commentary and Stein some reviews.

Best wishes from Rose and me to you and Hanna,
 Your,
 Rudolf

---

133 Carl Spiecker (1888–1953) was a leading journalist and politician of the Catholic Center Party. He was a leader of the pro-Republican Reichsbanner para-military formation and held a number of important posts including that of Reich Commissioner for Combatting National Socialism under Brüning. He fled to France in 1933.

Prague, March 2, 1935

Dear Rudolf,

Enclosed is a letter from Karl, which he brought to my attention and wanted me to pass along. It contains a message from him that, instead of having Bendel do it, he decided to rework the manuscript along the lines we suggested, and the work is now done. He is longing for me to come in order to give me the manuscript. I hope that I can make the trip to Vienna in the course of the next week.

At the same time, Luise told me that on 27 February Karl suddenly came down with a fever of 38 degrees, after being tortured by a few days of hoarseness and coughing. "Luckily a few days of bed rest and concomitant care, plus medical treatment by a doctor, brought his temperature down to normal, so that today (28 February) he is on his feet again. But, for a few days one has to be careful. What luck that the flu cases this year have been mild". So, it seems to be nothing serious. I still intend to carry out my plan to travel to Vienna as soon as possible. I am a bit distressed about the old man. Nevertheless, the letter to you testifies once again to his admirable physical and intellectual vigor.

Fritz [Adler] and Otto [Bauer] have been here since yesterday. I have not spoken with them yet. Since Fritz has not called me yet, I also don't know if I will speak to him. He merely talked on the phone with Siegmund [Crummenerl] this morning and proposed a conversation with him over the course of the day. Siegmund is, rightly, very upset, because Fritz, in accordance with a decision of the business committee of the [LSI] Executive, apparently intends to appoint a committee to investigate our financial methods. It is enough for me to communicate this to you. I'll still write to you with my personal view on these matters.

Julius Braunthal has been here since yesterday. He'll be leaving in a few days via Zürich and will look for you there.

My very best regards,
   [Paul]

Zurich, March 16, 1935

Dear Paul,

I can't write to you in as much detail as I'd like, so just a few lines for now.

Yesterday I talked exhaustively to Fritz [Adler]. He only talked to Cr[ummenerl] there and regrets not having spoken to you. Since he had not yet spoken to the other side, he also did not want to speak with you. Now, I'd like to know how you see the whole business. Write to me and then I'll report back immediately.

Nothing major occurred in Paris. Regarding the matter of *Freiheit*, the finances seem to me to be decisive. The politics will follow. Max Braun was very quiet in this business; I don't know, however, what the results of his efforts were.

Now some details. I'd be very pleased if I had the stuff from Arthur here very soon. I need to use some of it now. Further, could I get a bound set of [*Neuer*] *V*[*orwärts*] from 1 May to December or even until 1 April 1935?

Is Cr[ummenerl] coming here soon? I would like that because I have some recommendations to make to him about the matters I've negotiated in Paris.

What is going on with the Re[ich] Co[nference]?

Please write to me in any case about what is going on.

In a rush ...

Your,
R H

[P.S.] Please say hello to Hanna and to Else. I just heard from Fritz that Siegmund is coming next week. I would like it, however, if you would right to me beforehand. Siegmund can bring me the stuff from Arthur.

Prague, March 18, 1933

Dear Rudolf,

Your letter came at the right time. I would have written to you anyway today, because we have had some important discussions and Siegmund [Crummenerl] is leaving for Zürich tomorrow evening. I am sending this letter by airmail and hope you receive it in time.

I had intended to write to F[ritz] A[dler] at length. That he did not speak with me, I understand completely, which I've passed along to him via Julius B[raunthal], who also told him about my conversation with Otto [Wels]. I am very glad, that I spoke with Otto. Julius B. confirmed to me that that O[tto] B[auer] was very impressed by my exposition. I argued with him, that I would do everything to prevent a real split, and I am just as committed to avoiding a break with the LSI. But the other side should not make impossible demands. I see such a demand in the appointment of an investigative committee to review our finances. I reject this investigative committee not only because it could have unforeseeable consequences for the LSI and makes us a special case, but also because it defames us. There are no grounds for that, and I am determined to reject, even as a matter for discussion, any such incitement from A[ufhäuser] and B[öchel] or W[illi] M[üller]. On the other hand, it is acceptable to bring in the LSI to mediate. Because we have no body to which to appeal, one has to be created. Of course, safeguards for an objective process would be needed, to which I would allot not only the task of smoothing over the current dispute, but also of seeking a constructive solution that prevents another dispute over some other reason from erupting in four weeks. That was the weakness of the compromise we reached in October. Otto had the same idea. He is thinking about drawing together the various groups into a broad association that would put the current relationship between the Party Executive and the individual groups, which is the main cause of the differences, on a new basis. Business would be done by a small circle of people appointed for that purpose.

The first discussion of the LSI's letter occurred in the middle of last week. O[tto] W[els] declared his opposition to the investigative committee and against a board of arbitration. I pleaded for rejecting the investigative committee and for accepting the arbitration board. E[rich] O[llenhauer] came to the same result, if also limited to the case of A[ufhäuser] and B[öchel] and not in the case of Lange and Miles. C[urt] G[eyer] pleaded for political agitation: no fear of conflicts, one should act in accordance with the methods of the League of Nations: with every individual and with the greatest possible expenditure of time. O[tto] W[els] himself said that that would have to be puzzled out. Today, however, in the second discussion, O[tto] W[els] accepted C[urt] G[eyer's] recommendation and suggested that Siegmund [Crummenerl] attempt to clarify with F[ritz] A[dler] just what the arbitration board is supposed to decide and how it would be constituted. I pointed out that the first question was answered in the letter from F[ritz] A[dler], and that the delay of our written response over an additional two weeks would make a very poor impression. But I found no support, because apparently preliminary discussions had occurred in which I was not involved and where one had adopted C[urt] G[eyer's] standpoint.

Siegmund is now supposed to find out through a conversation with F[ritz] A[dler] what is the intended scope of the arbitration board's work, how it would be constituted, and what would be its powers. Only after he returns will a final decision be made. My view is that the Lange case does not fall under the purview of such a board. L[ange] is now our paid official and is not the leader of an independent group. Whether one wants to or can include the Miles case completely depends upon whether one wishes to seek guilt or innocence or whether one puts a positive solution for future work into the foreground. Because I support the latter position, I would have nothing against including the Miles case, especially since it hangs together substantively with the case of A[ufhäuser] and B[öchel]. Siegmund has a harsh view of Miles, however, just as he rejects any possibility of coming to an understanding with A[ufhäuser] and B[öchel]. It would be good, therefore, if you could try to make clear to him that the point is not to decide who is right about the various differences. A new organizational solution must be attempted, which can only be achieved if the cause of the differences, the Party Executive on the one side and the independent groups on the other, is removed. Within the context of our reorganization, it has to be possible to build a broad basis of new authority. Otherwise, in a few months will be even more isolated that at present. In any case, the LSI has to be involved. No obstacles can be allowed to arise. Please tell that to F[ritz] A[dler], too.

Siegmund will also tell you that we want you to come here soon. It has to do with the shutting down of the *Zeitschrift*, which is a sharp thorn in the eye. Nevertheless, it was agreed, that one can only make this decision after coming to an agreement with you. It will also provide the opportunity, of course, to discuss political differences, NV, etc. At the moment, one is of the opinion that there is only nonsense in the *Zeitschrift* and wisdom in the *Grünen Berichte*. I urgently ask you not to reject the request to come here, but to come as soon as possible so that you, too, can participate in the decision about the board of arbitration. That means that you will be here at the same time as Siegmund's return. It would be my preference if you could so arrange it to arrive here on Saturday or early Sunday. That way we could talk at length on Sunday.

The Re[ich] Co[nference] has been postponed indefinitely. Ask Siegmund to explain the reasons. He was the only one who did not want to abandon it.

Last week I was in Vienna and brought the revised manuscript back with me. Karl is doing well. He had a cold and had sniffles but is fully able to work. On the other hand, Luise still has painful shingles.

[The letter ends here]

Prague, March 28, 1935

Dear Rudolf,

I just talked to Siegmund [Crummenerl], who told me that F[ritz] A[dler] told him, in your presence, that the English are sending a big delegation to Brussels. Siegmund added that you are interested in the Brussels meeting, but that you did not know if you are available on that day. He asked us to think about whether we wish to consider your becoming a delegate. I had the impression that he was in favor, but his opinion was so vague, that I could only provide my personal impression.

I told Otto [Wels] immediately and explained that, under the circumstances, I am completely in favor of using this opportunity for discussions with the English and that delegating you is absolutely imperative. He did not express an opinion, which does not have to mean that he was opposed, but only reveals that, thus far, the recommendation is not appealing to him. That certainly is associated with a memorandum Stampfer prepared for the meeting in Brussels. Written in accordance with the principle: "Let me have my cake and eat it, too", indeed, it also contains some passages that are contestable, but it exhausts itself in the demand for a "propaganda of truth" against Germany. The discussion of the memorandum is not yet over. It should be continued on Tuesday. I don't have much desire, however, to argue about it again, having stood almost alone just a week ago. Still, this time I had the impression that the rest of them are far more inclined toward my standpoint than that of Stampfer, but they don't think it is right to say so.

I'm prepared to propose you as a delegate in the meeting on Tuesday. But I need to know if that is what you want. It will then also be necessary for you to make the suggestion in a letter to Otto. You know that I have already criticized you several times for your modesty in these political questions, which is all too great. If you, as I assume, are convinced that your participation in the meeting in Brussels is necessary and useful, then you have to express that openly. In the letter you write to Otto, I'd like to achieve that, in respect to the delegation, the vote not be about one person, but rather it should be a decision on the matter at hand, even if only of a general nature.

If you want to write to me about your personal opinion, then please use my private address. Send the letter to Otto directly to the office.

Best regards,
   [Paul]

Prague, March 30, 1935

Dear Rudolf,

I still have not received a reply to my letter of 30 March, but, nevertheless, I have to write to you.

On Friday Siegmund [Crummenerl] called but he expressly asked to be connected with Otto [Wels], so I did not have a chance to speak to him again. I only heard that he would be occupied in Zürich until at least Tuesday and that Otto told him that he might want to stay there [and that] he [Otto] would then come earlier than planned. It seems to me as if he wants to leave here on Monday. To be sure, it was planned to continue the discussion of Stampfer's memorandum for Brussels on Tuesday, but I don't have the impression that one wants to have the meeting. When Otto mentioned his telephone conversation with Siegmund to me, I again raised the issue of your being named to the delegation. But he answered just as recalcitrantly as he had a day ago. There is no doubt that he does not like the idea, and that he and Stampfer will fight against it. In this situation, success here is not possible. Support from the younger members cannot be expected.

If I find out tomorrow from you that you want to be a delegate, then, in spite of everything, I will demand a meeting and make the proposal. To me it is no longer a matter of victory or defeat. It is much more important that, as often as possible, it becomes clear how the others are guided by subjective points of view. I really have no doubt at all that both Otto and Friedrich [Stampfer] are opposed to you because they are not certain of your views in the A[ufhäuser] and B[öchel] affair and, therefore, they are not pleased that you meet with people from the International. If I don't get your letter in time, then I'll have to leave it to you to clarify the issue of your delegation in a verbal conversation with Otto himself. Meanwhile, if a formal decision regarding the delegation issue is made or not doesn't really matter. Because if Otto and Siegmund agree to your being a delegate, then there will be no "resistance". Unfortunately, I can't send you Stampfer's memorandum. I only have one copy and I need it just in case it is discussed. If Otto doesn't say anything to you about the memorandum in your conversation, then you can simply tell him that I had written to you that such a memorandum is available and that it will be put forward in Brussels. Of course, Stampfer had demanded that it be handled confidentially. But I would really like to know if this confidentiality includes your complete exclusion.

Thus far you have not answered my letter of 18 March. When will you come here? If matters are delayed for a while, then I'd like your advice about what I should do with my Swiss securities. I have Swiss railroad and French railroad (Treasury Note A). Both are in Swiss francs. With the collapse of the currency over the past few days I would lose about 5 per cent. But what should I do with the cash following the sale? Should I turn to Hugo Simon[134] about it or what would you advise me to do?

Karl's book is being typeset. Arthur will go on vacation in two weeks. He'll travel from here to Zürich via Vienna.

Best wishes, from Hanna, too.
Your,
[Paul]

Prague, April 10, 1935

Dear Rudolf,

I don't understand at all why you have not answered my letters. In any case, because your selection to the delegation was aborted, I am in a very embarrassing situation. In a conversation with Cr[ummenerl], you say you desire to be a delegate. I take that seriously, fight for it for days, and finally get O[tto] W[els] himself to make the recommendation as a result of his fear of you and me. Stampfer resists the recommendation, because he expects attacks from you in the form of a polemic against the Labor Party, and because O[tto] W[els] and Cr[ummenerl] are not strong enough to influence you. I tell him to his face that that is not only a stupid argument, but it is also untrue, since he refrains from expressing his real reason, which is his social patriotic outlook. He has to concede that and to hear from me that his hate against internationalism so blinds him that he can't recognize what a danger it is for the internal unity of the Sopade if he prevents the expression of any contrary opinion. For O[tto] W[els] this back and forth was, of course, very painful. After all, he knows that I don't allow myself to be stepped all over. Thus, the

---

134   Hugo Simon (1880–1950) was a significant figure in German banking and in left-wing politics. A member of the USPD, during the revolution of 1918 he served as Finance Minister in the Prussian Council of People's Commissars. Co-founder of several successful banking houses, Simon sat on numerous corporate boards including those of the S. Fischer Verlag and of the Ullstein Verlag, and his house was a nexus for Weimar's progressive cultural, scientific, and political elite. He fled to Paris in 1933, founded a new bank, provided aid to the German exile community, and continued his political activities.

argument ended in Stampfer's defeat. In reality, now I am the one who looks ridiculous. With a smirk on his face Stampfer passed along the message to Cru[mmenerl] that you are staying in Zürich, especially since I did not know any more than Cru[mmenerl] why that had occurred. Given the strained relations that exist here, such episodes are unbearable for me. If one assumes that I only speak for myself, then it would soon be better to keep my mouth shut.

I also don't understand your refusal to come here. Stampfer and Geyer have often pointed out that, indeed, you are capable of dishing out abuse, but you aren't prepared to draw the consequences. Geyer made such a remark just a few days ago in connection with your refusal to write about agrarian policy in the Third Reich. I haven't heard anything from Cru[mmenerl] about how you feel about the closing down of the *Zeitschrift*. Should we repeat the comedy of the delegation? To be sure, I am against shutting down the journal, but I am for a form that is appropriate to the current situation. But how should I represent that perspective against all the rest, if I don't even know where you stand on the matter? I think that, in spite of its great shortcomings, shutting down the *Zeitschrift* would be the intellectual death notice of the Sopade. Any leadership would then pass over to the *Kampf*. Meanwhile, here one wants to assign the tasks of the *Zeitschrift* to the *Grünen Berichte*. Do you demand that I should be responsible for and bear that as well? I have no desire to do that.

And now a third matter: In a few weeks, Cru[mmenerl's] recommendations for reorganization will be discussed. We are dealing here with the withdrawal of O[tto] W[els], H[ans] V[ogel], and F[riedrich] S[tampfer] from the office staff, but not from the Party Executive. In this context, the remaining suggestions are irrelevant. Have you ever given some thought to what authority would remain to such a rump? Since the intention of this action is to make it known that those named above are out, one wants to dress it up under the cover of frugality. But as far as I know, one plans severance payments that are more expensive than the salaries that they would otherwise earn as long as there was still money in the treasury. They want to make decisions about this and many other matters among themselves. In other words, only those working in the office get to make the decision since A[ufhäuser] and B[öchel] are gone and all are sworn to secrecy. Do you think I should go along with that? I don't want to come to a premature decision. Since they stopped talking with me about such matters months ago, I also don't know how these intentions have changed. Under no circumstances do I do anything in secret, I don't even think of participating in something that could taint me later, if a confidant starts to talk. And that the reliability of our office personnel is not beyond any doubt is proved by the leaking of the Miles memorandum to Willi Müller, the Schwabe case[135] and others. What should become of the LSI arbitration board? O[tto] W[els] told me curtly before his departure that he would not accept it and would rather sign up for refugee aid. Should I also conceal that?

You will surely complain vociferously when your read this letter and think that it reflects a condition of temporary agitation. But that assumption is wrong. I have told you often that I am prepared to bear everything if my remaining here makes sense. Can you be surprised at my beginning to think differently about it when I repeatedly see that I am alone and cannot change the routine? I want to avoid acting too precipitously, and if you don't come here then I'll come to you before making a final decision. But that every day can produce such a situation you can discern from the following event: a group of good people who want to be Social Democrats, but to work with other methods than we do – not Miles – wants support from us. We are talking about modest means, the amount of which we can determine ourselves. In the discussion about it, Cru[mmenerl] asserted that we should not support any other groups and should now use our money exclusively for our own people. Neither platform nor LSI nor their practice up to the present could change his view.

Best wishes,
[Paul]

Zürich, April 13, 1935

Dear Paul,

Thanks very much for your letter. You have every right to be angry with me because of my long silence. But I knew that I'd have to write you a long novel and, on some issues, matters are not yet clear to me. But I don't regard your letter at all as the momentary expression of your agitation. On the contrary, I understand very well the seriousness of your concerns and can empathize all the more since I share them in part. I will attempt to deal with the various questions successively.

---

135 Reinhold Schwabe (1899–1951), engineer and technical director of the Workers' Radio Association until 1933, went into exile in Czechoslovakia and initially provided assistance to the Sopade in its failed effort to set up a radio transmitter broadcasting into Germany. He later became a Gestapo agent.

I have finally – and that was also a reason for the delay – read the manuscript by Helmut Wickel.[136] The first chapter is interesting. In my opinion, what he calls "statism" needs more analysis and would play a role in the representation of the post-war period, as I remember it. Like most others, the mistake he makes is that he absolutizes the momentary economic and political crises and makes them eternal; he doesn't satisfactorily disentangle economic and political causes; above all he views National Socialism, but also fascism, simplistically as the domination of a supposedly monopolistic capitalism, and he portrays contemporary Germany as the capitalist future. The role of autonomous state power is dealt with all too briefly (despite "statism"), and that leads to incorrect generalizations. It also lacks any analysis of further development and there is no indication of what the task of the proletariat is and how it should derive its ability to meet this challenge from the dynamic of economic development. That is, by the way, what all these views about the "fall of capitalism" have in common, [think of] Sternberg, for example. The description of National Socialist economic policy in the chapters that follow suffers from the same basic mistake of not understanding what this policy is: the power policy of the dictatorship and of war on an anti-capitalist, middle class mass basis, but rather purely as the policy of monopoly capital. Cancel currency controls and tomorrow there would be very little capital remaining in Germany or Italy, these model countries of monopoly capitalism. Instead it would flee to the democratic countries, France and England. If nothing happens, the formula must be saved. The closing chapter on the war economy is historical reminiscence that is not really necessary. Despite this, I would not oppose publishing this work. It provides stuff for discussion. The question is only whether the publishing house should take the risk, since publishing it is not absolutely needed. Finally, the new formulation can be provided in an emergency, and we are in an emergency, in the form of two or three journal articles.

The same can be said about the brochure by Sturmthal, only the risk here would be reduced by the security of sales through the Swiss trade unions. My substantial qualms are also fewer in this case. You will be better able to judge than I am whether it is of less interest for our people since I've been overfed with such books.

Then the *delegation*. That was a particularly unusual bit of bad luck. I could have traveled on the original target date – eight days earlier – and that was also true for any other time. Only not on that particular Sunday. I had taken on a

---

136 Helmut Wickel (1903–1970) was a Social Democratic journalist and deputy editor of the *Chemnitzer Volksstimme*. He went into exile in the CSR and was active in the Revolutionary Socialist group and Neu Beginnen.

firm commitment to represent my friend U., who was counting on that *while away*, on some pretty important business, and to that end I had plans to meet with a third person on that day. I could not reach this person, who was also traveling. Therefore, at most, I would only have been able to travel on Saturday, which we originally had also considered but then backed away from, because Otto had rightly noted that it would not make a good impression. There was nothing political at work here; on the contrary, it was a *purely personal* matter about which I don't want to say anything more because it was not my own affair. Perhaps I could have still changed it if I had known in time about the postponement of the meeting and had been certain of my appointment to the delegation. (But the worst was that my sacrifice proved to be useless. It has been a long time since I was so mad as with this story).

I am really sorry that you had such difficulties. By the way, I don't understand the substance of Stampfer's opposition. Otto [Wels] was really amiable here, at least he appeared so. It seemed like he really wanted me to come, too, and to take the lead on this issue. He told me about your unanimously approved memorandum. It was so well conceived that I could have approved of it, even if I might have interpreted some of it differently. But, thus far, I've still not seen it, and I would *urgently* like you to *send me a copy* as soon as possible. An article about our policy is being typeset. I am waiting impatiently to get it back because I want to add material when doing the corrections. In addition, I want to write another one about the soc[ialist] position.[137] Therefore, I really need the memorandum. From Otto's description – he assured me after his return that I can be pleased to have been spared a useless trip – I can't really get a sense of what happened at the conference. In any case, as expected, the English failed everyone, but recently they appear to want to move a bit further in the direction of "collective security". Along with their government they are always for new negotiations with Hitler. I think that, regardless, it is necessary to take a position on foreign policy. Siegmund [Crummenerl] has suggested to me to write a pamphlet and assures me constantly of his full support. Since the articles in *Kampf* and in the *Zeitschrift* provide a basis for it, I will give it serious consideration. Disconcerting is that I would have to engage in further polemics against the left and against Otto Bauer. For the rest, matters are more than ever in flux. Hitler's most recent sham concession is, on the surface, a retreat. But skillfully done. He accepts what he cannot hinder and strengthens the English – and not only he English – illusions.

---

137   For the two articles see Kern (Hilferding) 1934–1935, pp. 561–68, and idem. 1934–1935, pp. 593–604.

What do you think about the *situation in Germany*? I am convinced, that the 16 March[138] was of tremendous use for the regime. Not only that the idiotic illusions about the Reichswehr have now really become totally senseless. I think, as well, that at present the mass basis is consolidated and that the consolidation is pretty complete. When I indicated that to Otto, he grew very upset [and said]: *That had made no impression upon our people* (as if that what it is all about); of course, you understand everything better. However, since I said that in the article, your view would be of great value to me. But you need to tell me right away, so that I can use it when doing the corrections. Nevertheless, I feel pretty secure in my judgement; for 90 per cent of the Germans, foreign policy has been a wonderful success, which allows them to put up with many economic disappointments – and for some, things are going very well. Danzig was excellent, but one also should not overestimate it and simply transfer it to Germany.

Furthermore, as much as I was annoyed not to be able to come, perhaps some good came out of it. At the moment, it is not very pleasant to put the International in its place arm in arm [with Wels]. He has no points of contact with the others, perhaps the Danes are an exception, and is filled with a mistrust which rises to a level of hate against Bauer, [Fritz] Adler, and others. And against me, too, by the way. He asserts that I said that I alone understand anything about illegal organization (!), I alone have what it takes to lead politically, and similar nonsensical rubbish. Of course, he rejected my demand to reveal who originated this *twaddle*. I told him, if he believes this then he is a Kaffir and I rubbed Alfr[inghaus] under his nose again, whereby I had the distinct impression that he was sticking with him. (Naturally, this is exclusively for you).

I never refused to come to Prague. Still, along with the *Zeitschrift*, it is a burden. It cannot go on as thus far and to demand its continued publication for 300–400 subscribers would be pretty hopeless. Two things would be required. First an administration that was interested in the journal. At the moment there is a total lack of interest and not even [*Neuer*] *V*[*orwärts*] publishes the table of contents any longer. There is no attempt at propaganda. In addition, as I attempted to do in the last issue, the content must be changed. The – with respect – "theoretical" junk makes no sense at all as long as people don't really have anything valuable to say. Instead, politics, and especially the analysis of German reality, as well as the sociological situation in general must occupy more space. There is, indeed, a major shortage of collaborators and

---

138 On 16 March 1935 Hitler reintroduced military conscription and thereby abrogated the size limit placed on the German army by the Treaty of Versailles.

what appears in the section two of the *Gr[üne] Hefte* [sic] should really be in the *Zeitschrift*. Those with an interest in the matter will fight against that and find support. Thus, when it comes to the *Zeitschrift* it doesn't look rosy to me. On the other hand, there is your assertion that then the only German socialist organ would be the well-produced *Kampf* – which has, in Frau B[auer],[139] an editor who does not have to worry about anything else, and who has good assistants immediately around her. That would mean, however, that we would almost give up having any intellectual influence. That could be exercised by neither the *Grünen Hefte* [sic] nor even by [*Neuer*] *V*[*orwärts*], which, after all, generally only does harm to Prague. (What's with the book by Sta[mpfer]?) Thus, I feel like, from the beginning I've been fighting for a cause that is, in reality, already decided against me. Or do you think this judgement is too pessimistic? What else should I do in Prague? I can't really understand Siegmund. Thus, there remains the important reason: you need me. But just tell me for what? (I've read your comments about the *Zeitschrift* over again and see that we agree completely. But is there still *the possibility of fighting and how do you envision the new model*?)

I still have the impression that Otto [Wels], and also Siegmund don't want to know anything at all about an arbitration board. One can think what one wants about the condition of the International today, [but] I think it is tactically awkward. One might need the International again and by rejecting [the arbitration board] only increase the antipathy and give even more support to the gossip. At the same time, it is, indeed, correct that Otto will have to reckon on encountering a great deal of prejudice – more than is justified. But, on the other hand, the material is pretty powerful. But I don't think there is anything that can be done. Also, not much will come of it. If we were dealing with precise, substantive differences of opinion it would be different. But we are dealing with people and with *personal mistrust on the one side and personal ambition on the other*. I don't see any solution, and I also don't believe that Otto Bauer's idea will be so easy to realize. A "Reich Conference" will also not resolve anything. That is because how it is put together and its makeup will, to a large degree, *have to be* arbitrary, since, after all, [sending] a real delegation is impossible. It will be summoned by the "apparatus", and in any case it will be denounced by the opposition. It is the tragic thing with this kind of illegality that it cannot restore authority once it has fallen into doubt. I spoke with Aufhäuser during the trip to Geneva. I have the impression that the solidarity with Böchel is not 100 per cent. In any

---

139   Helene Bauer (1871–1942) was an accomplished Social Democratic journalist, long-time chief editor of *Der Kampf*, and spouse of Otto Bauer.

case, he has no "counter organization", because he has nothing in Germany. It is somewhat different with Miles. But all that is so petty and could, after all, happen to us as well, because in personal matters Otto W[els] is not dominant or generous at all.

What you say about the *reorganization* is also displeasing. I think your position is correct. Only I mean that you should make another attempt to discuss the matter with *Siegmund*. The misfortune is that it is difficult to make a counterproposal. In reality, it is not yet time for politics in the narrow sense, for political action in Germany, and I fear that won't change in the near future. Therefore, the dispute over politics as it is being fought out is so fruitless, since it is only camouflage of the momentary camouflage. Right now, the organizational issue stands in the foreground. One would need then above all a good committee on organization! That would mean Ol[lenhauer], Sigm[und], you, Erich [Rinner] for the *Berichte* and Curt [Geyer] for [*Neuer*] V[*orwärts*]. (Maybe I've forgotten someone, but you know what I mean). One has to let it do its work in peace. Beyond that, one could then create a sort of permanent political commission that would meet quarterly and when possible could include people from inside [Germany]. But that would encounter opposition from the outsiders, and I don't see how that could be overcome. In addition, since this commission would have no authority to make decisions even if one decided to constitute it as liberally as O[tto] B[auer] imagines.

Now, be well, otherwise this letter, which I started two days ago, will keep going. It is, after all, only a discussion, which I would like to continue as soon as you reply. This time, I won't keep you waiting. My very best to you and your family. What is Wilfried up to?

Your,
    Rudolf

Prague, April 17, 1935

Dear Rudolf,

I have to put off answering you at length for a few days but no longer than the end of this week. Today it is enough for me to just answer a few urgent questions.

Stampfer's memorandum is enclosed. I'd like to have it back because no other copy exists, at least one that I could get hold of. Since I don't want you to have to wait, I cannot transcribe the memorandum ahead of time. If O[tto]

W[els] told you that the memorandum was approved unanimously, he was only conditionally accurate. I expressed my opposition [on the grounds] that it contains only one analysis of the situation, it completely forgoes developing its own standpoint, and puts forward, instead, vague compromise formulas that would not change the policies of the LSI or of the parties at all. When my attempt to push through a more concrete position somewhat along the lines of the last French memorandum, economic sanctions, etc., and also in keeping with the idea you expressed at the close of your article – the creation of a superior power – failed, partly due to Stampfer's opposition, and partly due to the apathy of the others, I resigned. I did not say any more about the memorandum and made clear that I regard its content as pretty meaningless. After reading your second article, I am convinced that you would have taken a similar position. You can't imagine how petty Stampfer's points of view have become. He saw, and sees, his memorandum not from the standpoint of winning over others to his perspective, but instead merely from the standpoint of a desire that the Sopade's existence might be remembered devotedly.

When Geyer gave me your new article today, he also remarked that the article was terribly pessimistic. Without knowing the content of the article, I told him that I am also pessimistic and that I assume that there would be no difference of opinion between us when it comes to evaluating the new situation. Reading your article fully confirmed this assumption. The section dealing with domestic politics, in particular, is fully in keeping with the views I have consistently expressed to O[tto] W[els]. Only recently I angered Erich O[llenhauer] and Siegmund, when I expressed the view that broad circles of the working class have been bought by the regime and that our own work would encounter increased difficulty. One doesn't want to see that here, because one would be forced to draw the consequences. Erich R[inner], who then as now is nothing other than a useful specialist, swims completely with the current. And Geyer, who is too smart not to see some of the discomfiting tendencies, has too little character to express this opinion despite the contradictions.

I see no place in part one of your article that needs changing. Merely the concept at the end of the second paragraph, "war becomes hope", seems to me to be expressed too generally. This is because it is exactly in those reports that speak of the enthusiastic effect of the introduction of the military draft that it is simultaneously mentioned that the idea of war also has a widespread depressive impact. Also, I have the impression from the German press that the strong emphasis on peaceful intentions can be traced back to the pretty general rejection of war. Of course, the article by O[tto] W[els] will encounter resistance, especially since he declares that everything reported about the Reichswehr, the bureaucracy, etc., in the "Green Otto" [*Grünen Berichte*] is wrong. But here you can see clearly once more, how impossible it is, that the "Green Otto" becomes our only intellectual mouthpiece. More on that in a couple of days.

Best wishes and from Hanna, too.
   Your,
   [Paul]

[P.S.] Early tomorrow – I have written this letter at home – I'll look in the office to see if the new issue of the *Grünen Berichte* has been sent. Otherwise, you'll get it at the same time.

Prague, April 22, 1935

Dear Rudolf,

I've given your evaluation of the manuscripts by Wickel and Sturmthal to Arthur. He will discuss them with you when he comes to Zürich in two weeks on his vacation trip. I don't think one can count on meaningful sales of Wickel's book. And, since you think that the content could be provided in some articles for the *Zeitschrift*, then I don't know how one can justify the extensive costs a book will incur.

Then as now, Stampfer's book is causing me the most concern.[140] He claims the manuscript will be ready by 15 May. What I've read thus far or what he has told me about it makes me think that it will be not only a terribly one-sided but also a superficial work. St[ampfer] is counting on our publishing it. I don't know whether that is just a wish or if it is based on a firm promise by O[tto] W[els]. On this matter Arthur comports himself very correctly and says little. Since [Arthur] Rosenberg's *Geschichte der Republik* [*History of the Republic*] is now out, then that means, of course, that with the appearance of St[ampfer's] book we have competition in our own publishing house. – But you will soon have the opportunity to talk about that in person with St[ampfer], because I just heard from Arthur – nobody mentioned it to me – that St[ampfer] is planning a trip to the west and north. After he steps down from the Sopade on 1 July, he wants to edit a newsletter, and he intends to create the economic basis for that with personal visits to party newspapers. I have no idea whether the trip is private or official.

---

140   The discussion concerns Stampfer's *Die ersten 14 Jahre der deutschen Republik* (1936).

Siegmund [Crummenerl's] suggestion for a brochure is very good. But you'll have to work it out with Arthur [Arnold] if you want to do it at all. His principle always is to cast multiple works onto the market simultaneously. He claims it reduces the costs and makes marketing easier, especially in smaller publications. Although initially I had big objections to this method, because some new publications are thereby delayed, in the meantime I've become convinced that Arthur's standpoint is correct. A topical brochure must be written so that it can be published immediately. Since at least a few months will have to pass between the current series and the next one – Arthur needs at least three months to recover – then the points of view mentioned above are even more valid.

Concerning the situation in Germany, a few days ago we received information from a new source. A certain Kolar, a party comrade, a German Bohemian, who has been in Berlin since August 1934 for the *Prager Presse*, [*The Prague Press*] reported about his impressions to an inner circle. Geyer represented us there. Nobody told me about it, or I would have gone myself, of course. Geyer reported to us using stenographic notes. I asked him to write them out and, if he does, I'll send them to you. The tendency of Kolar's report was that the Nazis' social demagogy was making a big impression on the workers. On the illegal work of the following three groups he had to say that their significance is revealed in the order listed: The Black Front,[141] Communists, and Social Democrats. The Nazis fear the agitation of the Black Front. It is directed very skillfully at intellectuals, including officers. The work of the Communists has fallen off sharply, but they still have a subdistrict leadership in Berlin. It is deeply unfortunate that one sees nothing from the Social Democratic organization. Its agitation is noticeable here and there, but there is no systematic guidance. On politics in general, K[olar] reported that the introduction of the military draft strongly increased chauvinism, but morale is indifferent again. Unemployment has fallen sharply. The general satisfaction is accumulating with the officials. There is little political interest. The "action-circle" represents a Nazi opposition. Berlin is an oasis for the Jews.

I don't know K[olar], but I will attempt to speak to him. For the moment I have the impression as if he sees things too much through the lenses of a foreign observer who lacks direct personal connections with the people. Nevertheless, his view is interesting, and one must really get the man to have a longer discus-

---

141 The Black Front (Kampfgemeinschaft Revolutionärer Nationalsozialisten) was a Nazi splinter group led by Otto Strasser, who stressed a version of Nazism in which anticapitalism was a central element. Expelled from the NSDAP in 1930, Strasser attempted to build a rival organization but failed. The Black Front was dissolved in 1934.

sion with our circle. That is impossible, however, because as Geyer spoke the first sentence with which O[tto] W[els] disagreed, he made his displeasure very clear, ceased to listen, and cut off any discussion of the report. Your experience with him repeated itself. He does not want to know about anything that might influence his already fixed opinion in any way, and he sees antipathy, hostility, and hate against us in any deviant judgement. Therefore, he is certainly not edified by part one of your new article, but that won't hinder its publication in the next issue of S[ozialistische] A[ktion].

It does not surprise me at all that you had a fierce argument with him. His interpretations of your views go back, perhaps, to the supposition expressed in your letter to me on the *Grünen Berichte*, Worker, etc., from which I circulated an extract, that there is more than he knows. He has never said a word to me about it, just as he has avoided any arguments with me on political questions for months. Your presumption that, then as now, he cultivates the connection with Alfr[inghaus] could be completely right. When I recently told him, very late to be sure, that Stolper[142] – who was here on 15 March – had heard from Trev[iranus] in London all the details about his negotiations with O[tto] W[els], etc., he did not conclude that one should not get mixed up with this man and those like him, but instead he blamed me for not categorically denying these communications from Trev[iranus].

In regard to the *Zeitschrift*, our views are actually fully aligned. I also think that two things are necessary: better administration and propaganda (if Arthur stays, one can definitely interest him and win him over) and the politicization of the content. By that I mean the end of the fruitless theoretical and party-political bull shit. The magazine must be filled with political content that makes possible a real judgement about Germany. That can result from articles, notices, and synopses. Finding the necessary collaborators seems to me to less difficult than you believe. Nevertheless, all these tasks would be easier to achieve if you would make the decision to come to Prague. Then I would not fear the competition from the *Kampf*. Experience shows that Austria's problems are foremost for it, and that interest in Germany is substantially greater everywhere. To be sure, there was unanimity here that the *Zeitschrift* should be shut down. But even Siegmund recognized weeks ago, that that could only be done with your agreement. When it became clear in the Executive that it was a mistake to hope that I agreed with them about the *Zeitschrift*, and when they

---

142 Gustav Stolper (1888–1947) was a leading liberal politician and publicist. Under Weimar he became an editor of the *Berlin Börsen-Courier*, founded the *Deutsche Volkswirt*, and was a member of the executive committee of the DDP. He went into exile in 1933 and moved to the United States.

heard that I was for its continued publication, if with a different content, I did not get the impression at all that there was a majority for a decision. Experience also teaches that one always seeks a compromise, and that nothing is more feared than a majority decision that creates antagonisms. I believe, therefore, that we can achieve success when we both fight together and when care is taken to change the *Zeitschrift*'s content. Naturally, Geyer and Rinner tilt very much toward their *Grünen Berichte*. But I think that this objection can be overcome.

Therefore, I would like it if you would decide as soon as possible whether and when you want to come to Prague to discuss the matter. If you don't want to travel with your own passport, I suggest the following: there is only one control point on the Austrian railroad, which is at the border. If you cross the border with an excursion permit and board in Feldkirch then you won't be checked any more at all. In Vienna you can get a pass with local state citizenship under whatever name you want in half an hour from our friend Dr. F. I see no difficulty for this trip. That this is very necessary will be shown in the description that follows.

I wrote to you recently about the plans for a reorganization of the Sopade, which was intended for 1 July. On Saturday I spoke with Siegmund in detail about it. It is intended that: W[els], V[ogel], St[ampfer], and Siegmund will resign, E[rich] O[llenhauer], E[rich] R[inner] and I, as well as C[urt] G[eyer] for *NV* should remain. However, the resignations should only impact the office of the Sopade, the political body should remain unchanged, no larger and no smaller. Regular business with be done in weekly meetings. Thus, politically, nothing changes. The whole thing is justified as a savings measure. But this argument is merely cover. In reality severance payments are planned which are so high that there will be no savings if one reckons on our means lasting until 31 December 1936. I'm told that you and R[udolf] B[reitschied] are included in this arrangement! Of course, I recognize the obligation of a settlement for those who are stepping down. I take issue only with the amount. But one also wants to pay severance to those who are staying: Party Executive members, border secretaries, office personnel, etc. I can only speculate on why that should happen. It is the desire for security and secrecy. The recommendations by Siegmund go far beyond what I expected. I have the strongest misgivings about them, and I fear that whoever votes in favor will be condemned to permanent silence and, on the other hand, will always have to worry that someone will talk. I will not allow myself to participate in such a situation. I am prepared to do anything that can be justified by decades as a member of the party, by loss of citizenship, and of property. But it cannot rightly be claimed that we have regarded the party treasury as a private treasury.

Tomorrow I'll tell Cru[mmerl] my opinion in a very cautious way. Arthur, who has been really restrained, also says I cannot accept Siegmund's recommendations. But, initially, I will leave the question open of whether I will simply reject them or whether I can be won over with amendments. I need to gain time. In addition, I also have to consider that the reorganization really ought to serve the purpose of political renewal. But there you are right: that meets with the most determined resistance. Here neither O[tto] W[els] nor Siegmund make a concession. They don't want an arbitration board, they don't want any voluntary reconstitution of the Executive, they want to remain among themselves. And, while I believe that, in regard to financial issues, they fear doing anything without my agreement, it seems to me that when it comes to political issues, that is far less the case. In that sphere, the judgement of outsiders has little effect.

You have to let me know soon if you are coming here and when I can plan on it. If you don't come in the foreseeable future – and that would be a shame for the *Zeitschrift* – then I will have to take the position that I can say anything in relation to financial matters without speaking to you and R[udolf] Br[eitscheid] in advance. Even if one officially rejects my taking such a trip, which I don't expect, one can't actually stop me from taking a vacation and traveling with private means.

If your time is short, at least respond to me on the last point.

Best wishes, also from Hanna,
   Your,
   [Paul]

Prague, May 8, 1935

Dear Rudolf,

The April issue of the *Zeitschrift* arrived here today.

Why don't you answer? I can't make any progress on anything if you leave me in the lurch. I have a lot to write you about, but I won't do it until you reply.

Best wishes,
   [Paul]

Prague, May 27, 1935

Dear Rudolf,

Yesterday I heard that you have decided to come here as soon as possible. Hopefully, this news is correct. I am still of the opinion that it is necessary for the two of use to have a thorough discussion of all the unresolved problems. It must be your view as well, as you have said that one would have to write a whole book [about them]. You'll scarcely manage that, but, to that end, I would like to urgently ask that you put your travel plans into action as soon as possible. In no way would you be coming too late, because no decision about the *Zeitschrift* will be made without you.

It would be most preferable if you could arrange your trip so that you arrive here on Saturday. At least write a couple of lines letting me know whether and when I can plan on your being here.

Best regards,
    [Paul]

Zürich, May 27, 1935

Dear Paul,

I have a very guilty conscience and had begun a long letter to you weeks ago, but the idea of having to write a whole essay and a certain indecisiveness kept me from writing. I will limit myself here to the most urgent issues. The reorganization would be necessary. At the moment, the organizational issue stands so much in the foreground and the specific political issues in the background simply because we are still too weak to issue real political slogans, never mind carry out real political actions. The organizational side also suffers all the more when the fragmentation increases. And Wels does not have the wherewithal to pull it all together. I found him last time in a bad state. Even physically he did not seem well. Politically, he confided in me that, on the basis of information [he had received], he was firmly convinced that war was inevitable in the near future, because France (!) and England (!!) wanted it and will not or cannot wait any longer. I avoided any argument, but it is clear that someone influenced by such bar room thinking cannot be the political leader. In the same way, he remains impossible as our representative to the LSI, whatever one might think about it. His mistrust of the "Jews" Blum,

Bauer, and Dan,[143] and his distaste for Fritz [Adler] hinder him and let him see only [a] "conspiracy" against him or Germany or the German party. It makes any effective representation impossible. Finally, at the moment, most concerning are his constantly changing and mostly delusional perspectives on the possibilities and prospects for illegal work, which certainly have damaging effects and, in part, are to blame for an expansion of activity that goes too far on the one hand, and an incautiousness on the other, the impact of which can only be imagined. Therefore, in this context, he is not a unifier, but, on the contrary, a divider, which is, at the moment, hazardous for the organization.

I was somewhat surprised that, before the last meeting in the office for which I had prepared, I had not heard anything about the meeting having been called some time ago to reach a decision on foreign policy. Nevertheless, I would have not agreed to a resolution that was so empty and which so evaded the real issues, just as I would have rejected *the exclusion of Germany from the commission* in which the most disconcerting things could be cooked up. But, after all, Otto [Wels] has no real connection to these problems. However, this is only an aside. But how to change [anything]? Willi [Müller's] visit made a strong impression on me. He wants me to come to Prague, preferably for good, but otherwise for some time, and he offered me loyal cooperation, in which you would also be included. I see no insurmountable obstacles in what he said about his own standpoint and in the way in which his group operates. But how to bring about such cooperation? His view, that my authority is so strong that "those in Prague" would have to yield, I think is much too optimistic. The path of a Reich conference summoned by Prague is not practicable. Who would determine the participants? A real delegation is not possible. Does one want to grant the right to a delegation to each of the various groups (which are quite unequal, and their strength is not ascertainable)? But then the entire apparatus becomes superfluous and agreement can be reached directly by the representatives. As always, that presupposes the will to reach an understanding. Can one count on that with Wels, even when one brings in Sollmann and Dietrich[144] as reinforcements? And how far should an agreement go? Firstly, with what "groups?" Aside from Prague and Miles, do any other serious groups exist? Secondly, materiel. We are talking here less about the basis for a *political* understanding, which

---

143   Fedor Dan (1871–1947) was a long-time Menshevik leader who left Russia for Germany in 1922. He was a co-founder of the LSI and a close collaborator of Otto Bauer.
144   Georg Dietrich (1888–1971) was an SPD district secretary in Groß-Thüringen and a member of the Reichstag from 1924–33. Elected to the Party Executive in April of 1933, he went into exile in Switzerland and eventually moved to the United States.

today is scarcely possible, and more about the basis for *organizational* cooperation. Willi's demands in this respect are quite modest. They would probably increase, just as an *undeniable personal risk* would be included in this cooperation. That Otto [Wels] is not an outstanding personality who can exercise real authority with others and personally bring those involved here together is precisely the problem. But could I do that, or must one not reckon with the fact that new problems will arise that are difficult to overcome? But the central question remains: is it at all possible *to win Prague over to such a coalition, positively, because we have no means of exercising power at our disposal?*

I'd like to know your view about this. I am prepared to come to Prague, personally, when it makes sense. I would simply set off, since my efforts to get information remain fruitless, and I don't think the risk is too great. Wels does not want that; in response to a remark of mine he said it would be a shame about the travel expenses and they could carry out the reorganization on their own. I have the impression that he is generally opposed to me and is very mistrustful. But I have *inhibitions*. Does it make sense to engage in a struggle personally in which you have so little support? Because for Willi, as well, and above all for Aufhäuser, etc., one would simply be a means to an end. In addition, I have concerns of an inner nature. I am, after all, politically not in full agreement with any group and my own conception is incomplete. I see a very serious crisis of socialism, of the workers' movement in general, and today I am not really in agreement with any of the existing labor parties. In this situation, there can be only one reason to allow myself to get involved in a dispute among the factions and parties: if there were any prospect of eliminating the dispute for a time, until new objective facts, objective further development, and, possibly, a new theoretical formulation create a new political foundation. But is cooperation possible, and, for me, does the attempt to bring it about mean not only the likelihood of upsetting both sides, [but also the likelihood] of completely losing the modest effectiveness – somewhat off to the side – that I have today?

I know, that I make demands on your objectivity and friendship. You've made a choice, you are in the middle of it all, you can't escape the whole mess, and you rightfully reproach me for seeking out a much more comfortable position. Thus far, I believed I had chosen correctly. I could scarcely have changed anything in Prague. Above all, I wanted a certain intellectual freedom in order to be able to clarify things for myself. But that takes a while and much longer than I had thought. Now there is a new roll call, a new split, whose size and significance I cannot estimate, and which cannot be stopped through my personal intervention, and my old party comrade makes the decision terribly hard for me, especially since I can scarcely believe in success.

Now something less important. In the details of the reorganization issue, in particular of a material nature, you will have to rely on your own insight and your great conscientiousness. I agree with your principled position. The really difficult thing is that Wels and Stampfer don't want to really step down, otherwise one could certainly bury them in Denmark. But that is something that isn't to be expected from them. I fear, by the way, that Wels doesn't have many years left. What did Stampfer do in Paris? He did not come looking for me. Is there anything new with the *Freiheit*? I was glad not to be there. Wels is filled only with jealousy and mistrust against M[ax] Braun. It is a shame that Decker seems to be lost.

I have great difficulties with the *Zeitschrift*. Until now, the Willi [Müller] circle has rejected collaboration, as Willi told me. The lack of manuscripts is getting ever more serious. It cannot continue like this, although maintaining the *Zeitschrift* is more important to me than ever. What is Arnold doing and is it impossible for him to take the matter in hand? Aside from the administration, it would be necessary to change the title, the signatures of the editors and of the collaborators who can do it, and the current, political, German content. But it has to occur quickly!

Then, I'd also like a *bound* copy of [*Neuer*] *V*[*orwärts*] from 1 May 1934 on. I need it urgently for research purposes and *two*, not a copy of each number, and eight, not five, [copies] of the *Zeitschrift*.

Finally, I need an article for the *Zeitschrift*, and I'd be very grateful if you could supply me with one.

Regarding the investment in securities, good advice is expensive. At the moment I would not change anything. In France there will be a week-long decline (about which I wrote Crumm[enerl] a few lines today). But I suppose that the franc will be maintained and then the Swiss currency will again become more stable. Naturally, there is no absolute certainty, and if Crum[menerl] intends to come here anyway, then he should hurry up his trip. But I would not sell at today's low point. I trust Hugo personally, and I would get his advice on the deposits. If things now calm down, then everything will get simpler, you can leave things as they now are, and occasionally do exchanges when its favorable.

Things in Germany now must be viewed long term. I've never believed in the danger of war and I don't believe in it now, although with these people there is no telling what they might do. But politics cannot be based on the unpredictable. Economically, things are going badly, and the concerns are rising. I don't think that I am greatly exaggerating in [*Neuer*] *V*[*orwärts*]. But that, too, can go on for a long time, until it gets really difficult, and unmanageable consequences follow. For the reorganization that means extreme frugality and reduction of the apparatus.

Best wishes; I started letters to you twice and now it's done. Best regards to Hanna and Else.

Your,
   Rudolf

[P.S.] From Karl K[autsky] I see a nice card with compliments for the last Kern in the *Zeitschrift*.

Prague, May 30, 1935

Dear Rudolf,

Although we've lost a month during which some things could have been taken care of more calmly, that's how it is, and your trip is still not too late. Matters here have actually reached such a point that your trip can now be justified by a completely different reason than before. You can point out with full justification that the last impetus for your trip lay in your intention to give me advice before a step that would be a heavy blow to the Party Executive. Your supposition that there would be conflict here solely on account of your trip is completely unfounded. Otto has never said that he thinks the trip would be superfluous. In all our discussions it was either asserted or assumed that the fate of the *Zeitschrift* would be decided in oral conversation with you. Just yesterday, in a conference of secretaries, Siegmund said the best arguments would decide the fate of the *Zeitschrift*. The assumption is that you will be present for an exchange of views. Therefore, the discussion has been repeatedly postponed.

There can be no doubt that there is still a justifiable motive for your trip. I'll go further: I affirm the appropriateness, and what's more, the necessity of it. Of course, my personal interest plays a role here, but a subordinate one. If I only thought about my personal interest, then I would quit and find new friends by explaining the cause of my action. It is a general interest that you and I have to safeguard. First of all, we have to prevent people here from doing something that will only discredit them and the entire cause. But, additionally, the task is also to prevent the existing substantive antagonisms from getting worse and, therefore, to ensure that this small group of people works together rather than against one another. You will understand that I have to reserve the details of the evidence for the two purposes of the oral discussion. So that you see the seriousness of the situation, I just want to say that the discussion of the reorganization that took place on 21 May was interrupted, because a different negotiation had led to a break with me. Otto [Wels] had already left the meeting and Siegmund [Crummenerl] sought to calm things down by adjourning. Meanwhile, personal conversations that took place between Otto, me, and Siegmund failed to overcome the conflicts. It is the young people who are primarily responsible for this. A moral gulf has opened up here that cannot be bridged by my cooperation, but rather only through the capitulation of the others.

Of course, I know that concrete differences of opinion underlay this dispute. But that is also a point that is ready to be tackled. Perhaps there won't be a 100 per cent solutions right away. But it would be a real advance if one was no longer so far from the correct solution. What you say about Otto's false estimation of the situation and about his leadership abilities is also true of others. It is necessary, for once, to speak openly about the situation. Without you, that won't happen. We have devolved into our own spheres, and each of us represents his own standpoint. There is no desire to achieve agreement. Now you raise the issue of whether it is possible willingly to implement a better solution, because we have no power. I don't share this view. We have neither organizational nor financial means, but we have intellectual power. And that means something. I saw that on 21 May, when I left no doubt that I would rather draw the personal consequences for myself and leave, then cover up something that contradicted my moral and political principles. This language was understood. For the first time in a long time I had the feeling that I was worth something. When we are united, we are stronger than the other side, even when they completely agree among themselves. I hope that I can convince you that this perspective is not too optimistic. But there is something else you must consider. Assuming I draw the consequences, then what will you do? I don't need to tell you that, for me, this idea would be one of the most difficult obstacles to a making a decision. We have to stick together. And I don't really need tell you that I'm inclined to an understanding with you, because I think our agreement about actions and goals is certain.

You fear that we are simply means to an end for W[illi] M[üller] and S[iegfried] A[ufhäuser]. Maybe. I also don't believe that our relationship to these two will be like the one between us. Despite this, I have a different opinion than you. We mean something when, and as long as, we can do something. And, since you are able to provide an answer to this question far more confidently than I am, we don't need to worry. But I don't think that the goal of my efforts is to form a group. I want a coming together; I want the victory of achieving something, of responsibility. If we reach this unity, then we are not diminished but are something greater than before, then our influence would be greater, and we would be less dependent. For this reason, it is also worthwhile to attempt to bring about a constructive solution in which we all work together. By the way, in my conversation with W[illi] M[üller], it struck me that he knew what a serious mistake he had made last year, and, indeed, not only in his personal attitude toward me, but also in his attitude toward substantive problems. It seems to me to a sign of strength if someone openly admits mistakes. I fully understand your wish to have "intellectual freedom". I am ready to stand up for that. But you also don't lose it if others are drawn in so that we can combine forces to solve problems. That must be achieved through the design of the *Zeitschrift*. But that can only be carried out in direct debate. I even believe that we can be successful in breaking up the unity of the six.

But we have to discuss all these things orally. I will prepare everything thoroughly. I will make it known in the office that you will show up mid-week. Please arrange it, so that you get here by Wednesday evening at the latest. If you want to travel during the day, the best connection is at 8:00 in the morning. You'd arrive in Vienna late in the evening, sleep there, and arrive here the next day either at 5:00 in the afternoon, 9:00 in the evening, or 11:30 at night. Send a telegram punctually to my house. Our neighbor has a telephone (72 470) and, if it is absolutely necessary, you could use the number to call us or to work out arrangements. Otto B[auer] always stays in the Hotel Hibernia. It costs the same as the Imperial, where you have stayed, but it is quieter. It lies on the other side of the Masaryk Railway Station (opposite the main entrance to the departure platform).

I received an article from Karl [Kautsky] about Thomas More, which he wants to place in the *Zeitschrift*. The main part does not seem to say much that is new, although for the current generation it would surely be interesting. The concluding section is important. In it, he juxtaposes that More expected the landed aristocracy to fulfill his aims, while today some Socialists place their hopes for salvation in a dictator. Then K[arl] polemicizes against the Russians. I'll hold onto the article here. If you find time to talk to Karl on the trip here, then you are already aware of this.

Arthur will be here next week. Stampfer, who is now in England, will come back via Copenhagen, Stockholm, and Gdingen in Poland. It isn't clear to me what the trip is about.

Now, put aside all your misgivings. I expect you by Wednesday evening, at the latest. Remember that a telegram takes about six hours before it is delivered to my apartment. If we should somehow miss one another, you can most easily reach me if you take streetcar number 7, 11, or 23 to the Siegesplatz in Deyvice (Vitezny namesty). There you can take a car and drive along Sarecka Street to Na Micance. Our house is district number 1044. The street number is 35. However, the sign is not on the house, but the neighbor's house is correctly numbered.

Best wishes, from Hanna, too.

[Paul]

[P.S.] You can come anytime, day or night. I will make sure you get a nice meal. From Hanna.

Zürich, June 1, 1935

Dear Paul,

I just got your letter. Under these circumstances I would leave here early on Tuesday. But now there is a major new difficulty. That is the financial situation. I have access here to the safe and I can't transfer it. Only Siegmund [Crummenerl] can do that. But the situation can develop in such a way that, in the near term, action must be taken, and I have to be here. In any case, it's a very serious business, and I don't think I can leave at the moment. It must be discussed with Siegmund in any case. My opinion is that either he or I must be here and, as unpleasant as it this co-responsibility is for a matter in which there not only isn't 100 per cent certitude, but at most 51 per cent, I can't back out of it.

Please tell Siegmund: I am in constant contact with So[llmann]. He is sticking to his view, that one should wait for at least a few days. The new government is against devaluation.[145] It is likely that on Tuesday it will receive a vote of confidence and full powers. Matters should then calm down. Then one has to think about what needs to be done. To my knowledge, [Maurice] Palmade[146] is against devaluation. I think So[llmann] is right.*[147] [Ludovic-Oscar] Frossard's entry [into the government] is having a disturbing effect.[148] Firstly, it shows the progressive decline of the party and, secondly, he is a determined supporter of devaluation.

---

145 Hilferding is referring to the French coalition government led by the non-partisan politician Fernand Bouisson (1874–1959) which was formed on 1 June and lasted only a week.
146 Maurice Palmade (1886–1955) was a leader of the French Radical Party and a member of Parliament in the interwar period. He served three times as Budget Minister.
147 * One must wait and see.
148 Ludovic-Oscar Frossard (1889–1946) was a founding member of the SFIO and its General Secretary from 1918–1920, when he left to cofound the French Communist Party. He soon returned to the SFIO serving in parliament after 1928 and in several ministerial positions from 1935–40.

I am wondering why Siegmund has not called today and will wait for your call on Monday. The best time would be between 9:30 and 10:30 in the morning or between 3:00 and 4:00 in the afternoon.

Best regards,
 Your,
 Rudolf

Prague, June 4, 1935

Dear Rudolf,

I'm very sad that you have put off your trip again. I am fearful that now nothing at all will come of it. To be sure, in the conversation with Fritz [Adler] I see a certain advantage. But that you first want to let the trips from Erich [Ollenhauer] and Siegmund [Crummenerl] occur and then to come here together with them is a serious disadvantage. If I understood you correctly, from Erich's communication you had the impression that they are holding fast to the plan I am fighting against and that giving way is very unlikely. I have the same impression. The intended continuation of the first meeting will not take place, although I had very intensive, detailed conversations with Otto [Wels], Hans [Vogel], and Siegmund. They believe that by dragging things out the decision can be either totally avoided or, if it is unavoidable, that their position will have been strengthened by agreements made recently with the secretaries, who have a material interest here.

If I find this self-interest and this insidiousness especially hard to take, you should not underestimate my resolve. My trust in the moral and intellectual integrity of the people here is badly shaken. I no longer have hope that they will succeed in favorably impacting the struggle against H[itler], never mind bringing together the divided forces. The latter is no longer the goal. In these circumstances, the question for you and me is whether we can stick to our earlier position. Neither the intellectual nor the organizational renewal will be supported from here. Muddling through will continue. Instead of supporting anything, everything is blocked.

As much as that outrages and pains me, I think even less about capitulation. On the contrary, I would like an open debate with the goal of carrying out a real reorganization that advances everything a step forward. By that I don't at all mean a total solution, like W[illi] M[üller] is thinking about. My aim would be not just to give the appearance of firing W[els], V[ogel], and St[ampfer], as they want, but to really take them down. Because such a decision, carried out in struggle, would naturally lead to bitterness, unless we had a better idea, I'd consider bringing Sollmann into the office. That would create a satisfactory counterweight to the others, and it would also strengthen our position against W[illi] M[üller], S[iegfried] A[ufhäuser], etc. Give these ideas some thought. If you and I don't give in, and, as I am seriously considering, I come out in the executive in favor of an investigative committee, then the resistance could be overcome.

If you happen to see Erich or Siegmund, you can calmly tell them that I've told you everything. If you could add that you are on my side, you'll see the salutary impact of such a declaration. I also agree completely that you tell Fritz.

Don't let me wait too long again. I would like to know how you imagine things going forward. I also can't guarantee you that I will be completely silent in the meantime. It is possible at any moment that these matters come up in a discussion with Otto, the outcome of which cannot be foreseen.

Best wishes,
 [Paul]

Adelboden, Hotel Bellevue
July 18, 1935

Dear Dr. Hertz,

I'm writing to you today behind Rudi's back so that you don't have to wait in vain for a reply. I arrived in Zürich in early July (one day after Rudi) and was appalled at the condition in which I found him. I've never seen him so downcast, hopeless, and disconsolate. He just dragged himself around, couldn't work, slept for hours, ate practically *nothing at all*, was irritable, and unapproachable. In short it was heartrending. Ten days passed like this during which I almost made the decision to leave a hundred times, but I said to myself that I have to hold out and bring him out of this paralysis. Above all, he was depressed about the article for the *Zeitschrift*. He wrote every day and then tore up what he'd written. With difficulty I was able to steer him out of the sticky, hot hotel and this miserable situation, and I think I did the right thing. Over the last three days, he has calmed down markedly, is eating with a good appetite, is no longer so irritable, sleeps well, and yesterday he began to write. Whether it will amount to something this time, I don't know, but I hope so. I wanted him to write to you himself due to the delay, but, well, you know him and know that it is difficult to get him to write letters, especially when he is unsure about what he should say. At the moment, I regard him as ill, and you must do the same and not be angry with him. If he sticks it out here for three weeks, and, above all, when he is done with the article, then I have no doubt that he will be better. Nothing could move forward in Zürich. Luckily, up here the costs are no higher than down below. In the end, the costs of the traveling, which was not all that far, were the only major expenses, but they were simply unavoidable. You know that I am not generally prone to anxiety, but I was not at all prepared and was terribly shocked at the condition in which I found Rudi.

Please keep this letter totally confidential and never say a word to Rudi about it, because he would never forgive this "interference". I'm writing to you to explain the situation, because I know that the long delay of the *Zeitschrift* depresses him, and it must make you very nervous, too.

I'm sorry that you have to bear the heat in Prague. Up here it is so refreshing and cool that you can hardly imagine how we had been sweating down below. Adelboden has the advantage of not being modern and, therefore, you don't encounter fashionable acquaintances, it is not expensive, and it is, in every respect, simple and informal. Anyway, one would not be in the mood to don a tuxedo.

Please give my very best greetings to Hanna and also to Hilde. I was with Arthur M.[149] and his new wife (who is very quiet) in Paris. I found him to be quite nervous and worried. And how miserable Traute must be!

Best wishes from
  Your
  Rose Hilferding

Prague, July 21, 1935

Dear Rudolf,

As you can imagine, the printer asks me every day when the double issue will appear. The colleagues and also the small number of readers are also interested. I console myself as best I can. But I hope that you have already sent off the article or that you will do it immediately.

---

149   The reference is likely to Arthur Müller. See footnote 15 above.

When I get the article, then I will complete the issue right away. I have received some book reviews from Stein. Worker has added 20–30 lines to the conclusion of his article. I have also extended the last part of my article, so that it is now a contribution on the problem of the middle class. If I don't receive any additional manuscripts from you, we can fill space that remains at our disposal – the scale of which I can't estimate until I know the length of your article – with an analysis, which the lawyer Bandmann[150] from Breslau has written at my urging on the responsibility of the courts in Germany. In a strict sense, this description is better suited to the "Grünen Otto" than to the *Zeitschrift*. But surely there are also readers of the *Zeitschrift* who will be interested. Moreover, it would be a first assault on the "responsibility" of the *Grünen Otto*, which does not displease me, especially since, if it doesn't appear in the *Zeitschrift*, I'd have to go on bended knee to the *Grünen Otto* to keep it from being laid aside.

I won't bother you with the decision on this matter. I just wanted to keep you in the picture of what will appear in the issue. I also want to relieve you of the worry, in case you don't have an article that could fill the space. Once again: *everything depends upon the arrival of your article shortly*.

Now to the issue of the next edition. I think it is necessary to do another double issue. It must come out in August at the latest (for July and August), so that we can publish a single issue in September. In this way, not only do we win time to think about the character, form, and title of the magazine, but we would also have the possibility of introducing some changes at the beginning of the new quarter.

Regarding the content of the July/August double issue, it is most important that I tell you about the long conversation I recently had with W[illi] Mü[ller] about the *Zeitschrift* and our intentions. In general, Müller is not pleased about you not being here. But I succeeded in making it clear to him that it is more expedient for him to support us than for him to look for backing from A[ufhäuser] and B[öchel]. He is also prepared to put off the planed founding of his own journal and, at the same time, to reject any obligation to publish the literary output of his group in the *Kampf*. The latter seems to have been a near-term danger.

In order to reach this goal, I had to make some concessions to W[illi] M[üller]. Tomorrow I'll send you proofs of an article "Die Wandlungen des Kapitalismus" ["Transformations of Capitalism"], whose author is named Fehr. The article represents the first of a series, which will be published regularly either

---

150   Eugen Bandmann (1874–1948) was a Social Democratic jurist, a City Councilor in Breslau, and a member of the Silesian Landtag.

monthly or bi-monthly. For the current article, instead of giving the author's name, W[illi] M[üller] wants to include the following introductory remark: the following essay, written by a comrade living in Germany, was placed at our disposal by the foreign policy office of Neu Beginnen! It is an early printing of a part of a larger work, which treats the burning issues of our time and of the current phase of struggle. (The editors)

In principle I've promised him the publication of this article with this preface. Of course, I have made the publication of the article and the wording of the prefatory remarks contingent on your agreement. Naturally, he places great value on the mention of Neu Beginnen. I have no concerns about it.

Above all, W[illi] Mü[ller] desires that the article appear in the May–June issue. Since I took into account that your article would arrive this week – the week that just passed – I feared, due to the need to get your approval, there would be a further delay. In the end, I got his agreement for the article to appear in the July–August issue. Because W[illi] Mü[ller] would like to bring the article to the attention of [Otto] Bauer, [Fedor] Dan, and [Leon] Blum, etc., before the meeting of the [LSI] executive, I promised to send him proofs for this purpose before the end of July. Therefore, I had to have the article typeset, and you have to write to me as soon as possible with your opinion of its content, the preface, and the mode of publication. Much depends on our fulfillment of this agreement with W[illi] M[üller] in regard to other areas of collaboration and cooperation. Of course, such long articles are not easy to include, but the more I think about the *Zeitschrift*, the more I am inclined to the view, that it could better fulfill its tasks as a bimonthly than now. If one further reduces the size of the print and increases the size of the print area, one can include more material and so such long essays would not exceed our limits.

Meanwhile, I've read Sturmthal's book manuscript. Before W[illi] Mü[ller] brought us his manuscript, I wanted to suggest to you that we publish Sturmthal's brochure in two or three parts with separate titles. It contains more valuable ideas than I had originally thought. Publishing it is worthwhile. In the meantime, however, it appears that W[illi] Mü[ller], who was together with Sturmthal in Brussels, is interested in publishing it as a separate brochure. Apparently, it is under consideration as an organizational edition for Switzerland.

You can write to Denicke about a lead article for the July–August issue. Address: Forbach (Moselle) Beratungsstelle, Bahnhofstrasse. Or should I do that?

[The letter ends abruptly with no closing]

Adelboden Park, Hotel Bellevue
July 23, 1935

Dear Paul,

Finally! Yesterday my article went off to "Graphia", along with a second one, by Seeger, called "Amerikanische Eindrücke" ["American Impressions"]. Things have not gone well with me lately. It was the same with the article, which in itself offered no difficulties and is nothing special, but I could not get it going and that made me even more depressed. In Zürich it was also very hot, and I was annoyed by visits to the dentist and treatment for a bad tooth. On 15 July I came with Rose, who sends her best to you and to Hanna, to spend some time here. I'll probably remain here until 29 July or 6 August. I'm starting to feel better, but that I was very low is illustrated by the fact that, despite the beautiful area, I still have not once taken a decent walk, to say nothing of a tour.

You now have plenty of material for the issue. The essay on the "Transformations of Capitalism" is excellent. It is the first really Marxist contribution on post-war development. Surely you got it from [Richard] L[öwenthal] and probably Willi [Müller]. L[öwenthal] has already had an essay [in the *Zeitschrift*], but since I don't have the number here, I can't remember it. In any case, the article must be signed (with the same pseudonym). Without the signature, one could easily ascribe it to me. I agree with most of it and find my good opinion of L[öwenthal] fully confirmed. It bothers me somewhat that he ascribes to Lenin what I myself analyzed, and what Lenin, according to his own notes in his book on imperialism, had based completely on my *Finance Capital*. But one cannot do anything about it.[151]

Now we come to the issue of how you want to do the layout, and that depends again on how, when, and in what length the next issue should appear, above all whether it should appear in a new form. I think this edition should come out as a double issue, and I'm inclined, if really good essays require it, to do double issues, even if one elects not to do double issues generally. Now, I assume that L[öwenthal] will also write the second essay, as he indicated. Then, I think that we should hold onto the current essay for use in the first number of the new format, because it is so good and also because the second installment must follow and not appear in another journal that wouldn't be accessible to new (hopefully!) subscribers. In addition, it will create a guarantee of interest and

---

151 The work was published as planned in two installments. See Paul Sering (Richard Löwenthal), "Wandlungen des Kapitalismus", *Zeitschrift für Sozialismus* (July–August, September–October 1935).

of the indispensability of the magazine. Discuss it, please, with Willy. (I'll send you the proofs directly.) If you share this view, then I would start the current issue with my article. It is called "Das Ende der Völkerbundpolitik". [The End of the Policy of the League of Nations] – you can also change it – and treats the entire foreign policy of recent years, especially the behavior of England and of the soc[ialist] parties. Unfortunately, it is long and amounts to about twelve printed pages. I'd like to get the page proofs, because there might be something to add, but I'll refrain from that if it delays production further. I assume you have provided Graphia with the general instruction to have all the proofs sent to you?

Your letter just arrived, and it clears up a lot. I was right about L[öwenheim] (Fehr). From the beginning, I've placed the greatest weight on his collaboration. In regard to Willy's demand for a preface, I understand his demand. But he undercuts the [essay's] impact and damages the reputation of Fehr. It relegates him to the patronage of a group and gives his essay a sectarian aftertaste. I've already said that not only do I agree with most of it, but frequently what I encountered there I myself have thought. Why proclaim as group property what can be individual property? Talk to Willy about it again in this sense. But if there is no other way, then, of course, with the preface, too. In a different case, if it were a matter of a real group proclamation, I'd have nothing against it, but I think to attach a group insignia to a theoretical analysis (which, by the way, to some extent contradicts "Neu Beginnen" or at least avoids some of its ambiguities) is absurd.

Cooperation with the Willy-People is very important to me and I'm very grateful to you for bringing it about. Hopefully, in doing that you are also doing something of propaganda value for the *Zeitschrift*.

I agree with all your recommendations. In August we'll do a double issue. I will write to Denike [sic]. The only difficulty is that, in this way, the connection of the Fehr article will be severed. But that cannot be changed. On the other hand, one might consider taking out the sentence in order to publish it latter as a brochure. It would be very good if a political commentary about the tightening up in Germany could be written for this issue. Geyer could do it, or is he still too "angry?" Otherwise, Willy or Friedmann could write it. For the next issue I'll call upon [Werner] Thormann,[152] who is, unfortunately, very

---

152 Werner Thormann (1894–?) was a journalist who also served as secretary to Catholic Center Party leader Joseph Wirth. From 1929–33 he was chief editor of the weekly *Deutsche Republik*. He emigrated to France in 1933 and became the Parisian correspondent for press department of the Austrian Embassy.

unreliable. I assume, that for the current issue you will have an abundance of manuscripts. Then you could once again shelve the one from Worker. The table of contents should look like this:

Kern (I'll write under my own name in the new journal)
Historicus
Kautsky
Puls
Worker
Alsen
Hertz, etc.

If you have a better idea, however, I leave it to you.

I recently spoke with my friend from Lugano. He had an extensive conversation with Otto in Ascona and wants to meet with me and Wels. I'll write to Wels about it. What is the situation with the meeting of the Executive planned for mid-August? I think it is important to be there, but it only makes sense if foreign policy is discussed thoroughly and with no holds barred. There is no reason for diplomatic considerations any longer, and I think the time has come for a sharp critique in the Executive. I only fear that the Prague people will simply shunt everything over to their concerns about the delegation to the board of arbitration. But maybe you can talk them out of that. There are, after all, more important things. For the rest, my friend sees the German economic conditions as I do, perhaps even more pessimistically. Politically, however, we differ – it is the old disagreement.

[Franz] Neumann from London wrote to me and reproached me for my reluctance. I should take over the leadership of the opposition! I'll answer him. It would be more important to me to talk again with Willy sometime. Is there a chance that he comes to the West? I hope he agrees that politics must wait until the conditions have reached the point in which politics, and not just organization, can even be pursued. But that is a big subject that is difficult to resolve through letters.

Hopefully, I'll hear from you soon. Will you be staying in Prague the whole time? Best regards to Hanna and also to Else. Again, many thanks for your efforts and best wishes.

Your,
  Rudolf

Prague, July 27, 1935

Dear Rudolf,

I was very happy to receive your letter and only regret that, due to lack the time (editorial deadline for the S[ozialistische] A[ktion]), I am not in a position to answer you at length right away. That will happen with certainty in the middle of next week. Since I assume that the letter will reach you in Adelboden until the end of the week, I'll send it there. In any case, you must make sure, however, that it would be forwarded to you if necessary.

The *Zeitschrift* will be printed on Monday. Unlike you, I find your article to be excellent and hope that a discussion will follow not only in the Executive, but also in the press.[153] That is the best advertising for the *Zeitschrift*. Blurbs have been mailed out. I read the proofs of your article. Everything else for later.

Best wishes, to Rose as well.
  Your,
  [Paul]

Prague, July 30, 1935

Dear Rudolf,

The *Zeitschrift* was mailed today and tomorrow I hope to have the first copies here and will send one immediately to Adelboden, since your regular copy will go to Zürich. To my surprise I discovered yesterday that review copies only go to six local and eleven foreign papers. Consequently, I immediately made a new mailing list and had 100 copies sent to editors, personalities, etc. Of course, that does not replace systematic propaganda, which is necessary if the magazine is to receive any attention at all. But I have to put off this task until Arthur [Arnold] gets back. I wrote to Arthur today and I explained my activity thus far and our plans for the *Zeitschrift*. Since he can gather from that that his pessimism is no longer justified, hopefully he'll energetically collaborate after his return.

We are principally in full agreement about the next issue. Now the main thing is to meet our deadline at the end of August regardless of the circum-

---

153 Kern (Hilferding) 1934–1935, pp. 621–37.

stances. From our mail every day one can see what tremendous damage was done, in intellectual and financial terms, by leaving the subscribers and readers in uncertainty for three months. It even seems as if our own circles have assiduously reported the canceling of the journal as an actual fact.

The author of the article "Wandlungen des Kapitalismus" is now called Paul Sering. The use of his old name is now impossible for conspiratorial reasons. I have spoken in detail with W[illi] Mü[ller] about both the use of the old name and also about the preface. It gives him great satisfaction that the article had pleased you so much. He appears to be very proud of the collaboration with a person whom you view as so qualified. He does not want to acknowledge your objections that the preface would damage Sering's standing, place him under the patronage of a group, and give the essay a sectarian aftertaste. He thinks it is important to him [Sering] not only to share responsibility for the publication, but also to use it advantageously. It should convey that people under a unified leadership are working to create something new. Nevertheless, I could have more strongly influenced him, if I myself didn't recognize the fact that the essays, which represent a unified whole, stem from a number of authors, who, whenever they put forward their names, also have the right to name the group that stands behind the work. Thus, it is in a certain sense a group proclamation. And since you, yourself, agree that in order to ensure further cooperation one must make certain concessions, in the end I accepted the preface.

The essays will be signed each time with the name of the author and the preface will be added the first time (perhaps later as well).

We are talking about five essays altogether. W[illi] Mü[ller] already has two of them. I will receive them, when he is back from a ten-day vacation. The second essay, "Der Faschismus", [Fascism] is also by Sering. The third deals with foreign policy problems (the Soviet Union, the question of war, etc.), the fourth essay is an analysis of the domestic German situation from political points of view, and the fifth essay examines the problem of forming an illegal political organization. That is doubtless a very interesting work. – In any case, I am going to leave this arrangement stand. You are totally right that the first essay already throws much of Miles's thinking overboard. I believe that will also be the case in subsequent essays. Therefore, I would like to contrast your comment, "Am I now a Miles man, because, for the most part, I agree with these ideas?" with: "Soon there will no longer be Miles people. There will only be Neu Beginnen!" You, me, and anyone not wearing blinders belongs to that.

I have even already made progress on the issue of marketing the *Zeitschrift*. W[illi] Mü[ller] is prepared to take 200 copies of the issue with the Sering essay. I've already inquired with Arthur about the price, since it would be the same for the next issue. I have no doubt that sales will rise anyway and can be increased.

We need additional material for the July–August edition. Enclosed is an article by Sollmann and one by Judith Grünfeld. I have written to both that you have the final say about the acceptance of the articles, and that you will write to them directly in case you reject the articles or want revisions. That Sollmann signed his article is progress that puts him in line with us. The content of the article could be laid out in more concentrated form. You will certainly find, as I do, that he sees things somewhat too simplistically. But I think the article is stimulating and should be published. In respect to Judith Grünfeld's article, I'd like to give you a free hand. I have told her that I find the statistical part too broad, and that I am not sure how you would think about her general conclusions, especially about English economic policy. Otherwise, I think the article is interesting. Sollmann's address: Luxembourg, Rue Beaumont 1A. Judith Garland, Paris 13, 7 Square Albin Cachot.

Paul Bernhard, [in] Paris, asked me whether an essay about the two Stalin books by Souvarine and [Henri] Barbusse would be desirable. I told him that his assumption (apparently a misunderstanding in a conversation with Breitscheid) that I now do the journal is an error and that, as before, you decide everything, and that any final judgement about the acceptance of the article depends on agreement with you. Nonetheless, I advised him to send the article as soon as possible, because perhaps it could be considered for the August double issue.

I should also add that I asked Sollmann whether he was prepared to write a commentary on the very readable book, *Das stumme Deutschland redet* [*Silent Germany Speaks*]. I urgently recommend this book (Verlag Die Liga, Zürich) to you. I've ordered a copy already.

I was unable to fulfill your wish to push forward on the matter of the delegation to the Executive. I received your letter after the meeting, when the delegation was decided upon by O[tto] W[els] and S[iegmund] Cr[ummenerl]. By the way, there was no discussion at all about the political problems that are being discussed in Brussels, but only a discussion about organizational matters. There was no interest in anything else. Since you now will be meeting at the right time with O[tto] W[els], I have no misgivings if you speak with him about your being a part of the delegation. He can add you anytime he wants. But I don't think it is right for you to ask or put pressure on him for it. If you think it important that the most important people are familiar with your article, I would be happy to send copies to them.

Have you read the article "Katholische Kirche und Nationalsozialismus" ["The Catholic Church and National Socialism"] by a "German Catholic politician already well known in the pre-war period" (Nr.1268 [in the] N[eue] Z[üricher] Z[eitung])? It seems very interesting to me. Does your friend's desire for a discussion with O[tto] W[els] mean a change in his political views? Your sentence: "politically, we differ" leads me to presume the opposite.

Neumann, [in] London, asked us what was accurate in the rumors about reorganization. A similar question came from Arthur Cr[ispien] in Zürich. Both received the following answer: 1. everything is in order and, 2. nothing at all has changed.

W[illi] Mü[ller] is gone for ten days. I don't know where, but certainly not to the West. You can count on such a trip, however, in the next two months.

I am staying in Prague the whole time, but I'll often be at home to read and write in peace.

Hopefully you were able to catch up with the alpine tours you missed. Our Hilde is now in a holiday camp near Paris.

My very best wishes,
[Paul]

Zürich, August 2, 1935

Dear Paul,

Thanks very much for your letter and your efforts. I'm not happy about the decision on the delegation. On the one hand, I don't think it is appropriate to request something from Otto [Wels] that could appear as a matter of personal preference. On the other hand, I hear that Otto Bauer has worked out theses on foreign policy*[154] and I think it is quite possible that they will be discussed and, under certain circumstances, could result in a decision by the LSI that would not be very welcome. It would be very important for me to present my point of view there, all the more so, since the foreign policy article in the Miles-Correspondence seems flawed to me. Perhaps you could still bring the issue up for discussion. In any case, I'd be grateful if you would send me a copy of the Executive Committee's agenda. I don't have any information, including about the timing of the meeting.

Now to the *Zeitschrift*. I certainly hope that we can publish in August easily. Today I'm sending the essay by Sollmann and one from Bernhard (twelve typed pages – small) to Karlsbad. I assume that you have Willy's second essay at your disposal. Further, I expect an essay by Thormann by 5 August about the Ger-

---

154   *Do you know anything about this? Can you send them to me?

man situation (war of religion, persecution of the Jews, etc.) for which I gave him the catchword: freedom is indivisible. One should also beware of an overestimation of the current crisis. Schifrin will write about the domestic political situation in France. I'll send the article by J[udith] Grünfeld back to her. I'd really appreciate it if you would send me the book *Das stumme Deutschland redet*.

In regard to the mailing of this issue, I would like to know that it is in the hands of all the most important members of the [LSI] Executive. Since I don't know who is coming and who reads German, it would be practical, perhaps, to contact [Adolf] Sturmthal about whether he wants to take on the distribution. In any case, send a copy to Grumbach[155] and Bracke.[156] I've written to Neumann and to Denike [sic]. The latter has not replied.

It is important that the *Zeitschrift* be seriously discussed. Unfortunately, we don't have too many suitable forces for that at our disposal. I'd like it if you could involve little Friedmann (Puls) and get him excited again about writing for the magazine. I think he's well suited, thorough, and conscientious. It would be very nice if we could find someone who properly criticized Worker's dilettantism on military matters. Issues related to the organization of the military are becoming increasingly important, and there is no one available who understands them thoroughly.

I just received a brief personal letter from Arthur [Arnold], but I don't know whether I'll get a chance to speak with him. When do you think that the "new era" will begin? I am enclosing a letter to Willy that I ask you to deliver to him. On Tuesday, 8 August, I will be back in Zürich. The days here did me good and I was able to undertake a couple of minor excursions.

Best wishes to you and your wife, from Rose, too.
Your,
Rudolf

---

155 Salomon Grumbach (1884–1952), member of the SFIO, member of the French delegation to the League of Nations from 1934–39. In 1939 he joined the LSI Executive Committee.
156 Alexandre Bracke (1861–1956), member of SFIO, member of the LSI Executive Committee from 1923–39.

Prague, August 3, 1935

Dear Rudolf,

The printing of the *Zeitschrift* was delayed for a day. Since I assume that you will be back in Zürich today or tomorrow and that you'll find your five copies there, I did not mail the other copies to Adelboden. I find the issue worth reading and rich in content. We got everything in, including a review by Wickel, which I did not like very much but had to accept, because, contrary to our original intentions, I had certain misgivings about taking on the legal piece by Bandmann.

At the end of this edition, I announced the new double issue for the end of August. We have to stick with that, otherwise we'll lose whatever is left of our modest credibility. I am enclosing a circular that we are sending today to the secretaries, etc. From the content you can discern how great the damage was from the delays and rumors of the *Zeitschrift*'s demise.

I hope that, in the meantime, you've written to Denike about the lead article. If you don't get a commitment from him, you will have to plan to write it yourself again. Perhaps that is your intention. About a year ago, you wrote that good article on the logic of 30 June. It seems to me that it would be good if you would describe the distinctions, and also the progress, between this year and last. It is unmistakable that the attitude in the general population today gives evidence of that activist way of thinking that you rightly pointed out was not present last year. That is especially true for the working class. We have interesting reports available to us. They confirm, subsequently, what I wrote in the last issue of S[ozialistische] A[ktion] under the heading, "Es wird gestreikt" ["The Strike is on!"]. In many cases, resistance in Nazi circles against strong criticism of the system and of Hitler personally is already weakening. I have no desire, of course, to preach unjustifiable optimism. The real power apparatus is still functioning. One just needs to compare the verdicts of the judges in Germany with those of the judges in Danzig.

I am enclosing a letter from [Hans] Dill[157] and the two articles it mentions from the *Prager Tagblatt*. I have already responded to Dill that the contradiction does not exist to the extent he fears. I am forwarding his letter to you, because I think it right that you write a popular article on the question "Woher kommt das Geld?" [Where does money come?] as soon as possible. The article on credit policy in Part B of the *Grünen Berichte* is a singular example of how one should

---

157 Hans Dill (1887–1973), SPD district secretary in Franken from 1930–1933, member of the Reichstag in 1933, thereafter in exile in the CSR and the border secretary for northern Bavaria.

not deal with this topic. I don't think that there is a half dozen people either abroad or at home who can understand it or use it. That is specialist work but has nothing to do with politics.

Tell me soon whether you will write this article. I could also use it for the S[*ozialistische*] A[*ktion*]. Make sure you write it language accessible to a broad audience.

Enclosed is also a memorandum, which we sent to the International Congress for Criminal Law and Prison Systems in Berlin. I would like to cover the theme discussed there in an article. As an introduction, one could examine the new criminal law. The memorandum would merely be mentioned in a footnote. What do you think? Do you think it is in keeping with the character of the *Zeitschrift* to publish the Lichtenburg camp regulations in their entirety? Of course, that would only be possible in a double issue.

I don't like Paul Bernhard's article very much. I don't think it is appropriate to treat the problem of illegal organizations in Germany casually with a couple of sentences in a book review about Stalin, especially since we are expecting a major essay on this topic. One needs to train Bernhard to write more succinctly. By the way, if you want to let him write about the "popular front", then the Stalin article will have to be deferred. But couldn't one ask Breitscheid to write about the "popular front, etc.?" The request would have to come from you. His last letter to me was, once again, very laconic and pessimistic. Maybe a nice letter from you would pep him up.

Best regards,
    [Paul]

Prague, August 6, 1935

Dear Rudolf,

Our letters have crossed [in the mail]. I answered you immediately, although after receiving your telegram today I fear that this letter did not reach you before your departure.

I was unable to decide [whether] to speak to anyone about your appointment to the delegation. This is not due to cowardice, but to the feeling that any kind of understanding of political considerations has to start with O[tto] W[els]. Therefore, you should speak to him about the meeting of the [LSI] Executive and let him consider the consequences of your being made a delegate or not. Today we received one copy (from an unknown source) of the theses by

Otto Bauer, Dan, and [Jean] Zyromsky.[158] I'll ask Otto Bauer to send you a copy right away.

You will receive a transcript of the agenda of the meeting of the Executive from us. Let Fritz Alder put you on the mailing list of the *I[nternational] I[nformation]*.[159]

There is not yet enough material for the next issue of the *Zeitschrift*. So far, my calculations are as follows:

Lead article – 300 lines
Wandlungen des Kapitalismus – 1,000 lines
Seger – 300
Sollmann – 400
Alsen – 350
Stein on Engels – 300 but has not yet arrived.

We are still short 300–500 lines, which can be filled through book reviews and a commentary by Sollmann on *Das stumme Deutschland redet*. If necessary, would you like to write a commentary?

The second essay by W[illi] Mü[ller] should appear in the September issue. But it is also impossible to include two big essays by the same author in the same number. By the way, if Schifrin writes the promised article on the French situation, the issue would be full.

Why did you want to send back the article by Judith Grünfeld? Send it to me. Perhaps I can make something out of it. I had urged her to write the article and it pains me that she would have done the work for nothing. But if you think the article is unsuitable for the *Zeitschrift*, then I won't attempt to alter the decision in any way.

Please buy the book *Das stumme Deutschland redet* at our expense. We have no extra copy. But you have to read it.

I will make sure that the last issue of the *Zeitschrift* finds its way into the hands of the most important members of the Executive. Sturmthal receives a dozen copies to distribute. I will send them directly to Grumbach and Bracke.

I've spoken with Puls and assigned him a book review. He has not yet delivered it, however. I'm looking for someone to write about military matters.

Yesterday I received a message that Nathan will come to Europe for a few weeks. He'll land in London, today. He definitely wants to speak with us but cannot come to Prague. He'd like to meet us in Switzerland. I am basically ready to

---

158 Jean Zyromsky (1890–1975), French Socialist, Member of the LSI Executive Committee 1935–36.
159 *International Information* was published in Zürich by the Secretariat of the LSI from 1933–39.

do it and am waiting to hear from him about when and where. Arthur [Arnold] is coming back but is spending a few days in Austria due to a reduction in the travel costs. I have to talk to him before I can say anything to you about when the "new era" will begin. I think on 1 October. But, as I said, I have to talk with Arthur first.

Send me the essays by Thormann and Schifrin as soon as possible, not only so that I can have the issue typeset punctually, but also so that I can undertake the propaganda myself.

Best regards,
 [Paul]

Prague, August 10, 1935

Dear Rudolf,

I already have to write to you again, indeed, because of the *Zeitschrift* and because of Brussels.

I am sending you the article by Stein on Engels. It is a bit long, and I fear that we can't publish it at this length in this issue if we still want to also publish the already announced articles by Thormann and Schifrin. But this question is really only of secondary importance, because the article in and of itself must be published. So, in any case I'd send it to the printer. In my opinion, one can cut the whole introduction to the middle of page two. I also think other cuts are possible. For example, what about the comment on the Labor Party on page 13, which, in that context, does not seem appropriate? Stein was insistent that I not cut anything without his concurrence. I would like to honor the request of the poor guy, who constantly torments himself. Therefore, I recommend that you mark the passages that should be cut and send me the manuscript as soon as possible. Remember, we can't publish all the articles in this issue, and the next issue will comprise only 32 pages, of which 12–14 pages will be taken up by Sering's second article. We have to cut ruthlessly, or we won't be able to manage.

Today a letter from the domestic leadership of Neu Beginnen, which was addressed to the LSI, also arrived here. Its content is pretty much identical to the draft on the Sopade's situation, which recently was sent to you with issue nr. 1 of Neu Beginnen's *Nachrichten der Auslandsbüros* [*Reports of the Foreign Office*]. The letter is signed by Paul Sering, among others. Ollenhauer brought the memorandum to my attention with a casual remark that neither he nor [Siegmund] Cru[mmenerl] or St[ampfer] have any desire for a discussion. I gave the memorandum back to O[llenhauer] with the remark that, even if one does not agree with every idea, one really cannot react negatively to it, as just occurred when, at its recent meeting, the Executive Committee laid down the basic principle for Brussels. Oll[enhauer] replied with the objection that one does not know how much these people have behind them. I sought to make him understand that that is a side issue. The fact that the memorandum doesn't muck about and spread gossip, but on the contrary, raises questions about basic problems and important tactical considerations for discussion, should earn it respect and acknowledgement from any objective person without regard to one's outlook. Under the circumstances, I think that it isn't just a serious error, but it is the surest means of isolating ourselves for the long term, if one simply adopts a negative attitude toward the memorandum and flatly rejects negotiations. I can't say whether my rather forthrightly expressed view made any impression on Oll[enhauer]. He avoided discussion in the way he often does in order to talk about the matter later, privately, with Stampfer and Cru[mmenerl]. However, apparently, a remark I made that one of the signers of the letter, Paul Sering, is the author of an article for the *Zeitschrift* recognized by you as of fundamental importance, caused a certain amount of consternation. In this context I have to advise you most urgently to tell no one anything about Sering's identity. You should never mention either his original name or his earlier pseudonym. We must honor that under any circumstances.

In my absence it was agreed to appoint you to the Brussels' delegation. I was at home for three days. As Else told me, Stampfer appeared to have been strongly opposed. Unbeknownst to me, he also sent a reply to O[tto] B[auer's] memorandum to O[tto] W[els].

But the main thing for me right now is to take advantage of the situation that has arisen as a result of the letter from the Miles group. I've already sent an urgent request to Sollmann to write to O[tto] W[els] in Brussels to accept negotiations about the letter. I think that Sollmann will do it, even if he doesn't like some of the ideas represented by the Miles people. You must speak thoroughly and clearly with Otto and with the other two. Indeed, we don't agree 100 per cent with their ideas and demands but rejecting negotiations in respect to the Miles letter is supportable, not only because it puts us in opposition to objectively thinking people, but also because it will bring on a new struggle within and without. You have to tell them that you can't prevent it and will not prevent it when the organizational issues raised in the letter are discussed in the *Zeitschrift*. You must even tell them that you and I will participate in the discussion and will speak regardless of our allegiance to the Sopade.

Furthermore, in Brussels you must talk with [William] Gillies,[160] Brouckére,[161] and Albarda.[162] A proposal must come from them calling upon the Sopade to enter into direct discussions with the Miles group on the content of their letter. With or without the participation of the LSI, it doesn't matter to me. If such a proposal is made, it cannot be rejected by anybody. The Sopade can't evade it. Please also talk to Fritz [Adler] about it.

Karl [Kautsky's] advice to send your article to Tidens, [*The*] *Daily Forward*, etc., is good. Also, in respect to the fact that the *Reichsanzeiger* has announced that your confiscated property now belongs to the Reich. Something like that had to happen to you. Confirm your receipt of this letter and write to me about what to do with the articles by Thormann, Schifrin, and Stein.

With very best wishes, from Hanna, too, who also sends her best to Rose.
Your,
[Paul]

Zürich, August 13, 1935

Dear Paul,

Rose went to her mother's yesterday, which makes correspondence harder. Stampfer's article is a real affliction. I don't want to hurt him and please don't tell him, but the whole thing is boring and has no fruitful use. Not only are the sources familiar, but they also say nothing. That Engels was against compromise, for class struggle, etc. is well known, and who is interested in the old quarrels with Höchberg[163] and Vollmar,[164] etc. What should people learn from

---

160 William Gillies (1885–1958), Labor Party politician and member of the LSI Executive from 1929–40.
161 Louis de Brouckére (1870–1951), Belgian Social Democrat and member of the LSI Executive from 1929–39. Chair of LSI from 1935–39.
162 Johann Willem Albarda (1877–1957), Dutch Social Democrat and member of LSI Executive committee from 1930–39. LSI Chair in 1939.
163 Karl Höchberg (1853–1884), born in Frankfurt am Main, studied philosophy in Zürich, and committed much of his inherited fortune to the socialist movement as a very young man. Many of the early SPD's most important publications, such as the *Der Sozialdemokrat* and Kautsky's *Neue Zeit* were founded with Höchberg's aid.
164 Georg von Vollmar (1850–1922) was a leading Bavarian Social Democrat. During the era of the Anti-Socialist Laws (1878–1890) he was fiery leader of the party's anti-parliamentary left wing, which often put him at odds with leaders such as August Bebel. After 1890 he joined the revisionist camp, opposed the general strike, and supported the war in 1914.

them today? Taking political positions without examining the whole historical background and problematic is very misleading or, even worse [...] At most the foreign and military policy is of use, but only with further clarifications. On the other hand, the glorification of the German working-class today is grotesque.

I don't know what is to be done. Cuts scarcely do anything and to simply reject it in this case doesn't work either. Moreover, I agreed that he should write an article about Engels. So, convince him to cut it, particularly the passages from the time of the [anti] Socialist Law and the hymns about the German workers. I'll send the manuscript back to you.

The articles by Thormann, Schrifrin, and Schwarz were sent off to Graphia on 7 and 9 August. We have rather too many then too few. We could use some commentaries and reviews. Hopefully the ones from Sollmann will arrive. When is the editorial deadline? I think that the issue should appear in the last days of August, no earlier and no later. How shall we manage the corrections? Should I read them, or you, or as required, meaning in certain, individual cases, by both of us, so that I send my proofs directly to you? Don't you think one could ask Franzen to write a reply to Worker? He [Worker] writes on military-political affairs arrogantly, like a dilettante, half-educated, and confused. A rebuff is necessary. K[arl] K[autsky] apparently is of the same opinion. Still, Franzen is also not ideal. I doubt, if we should do just a single issue in September rather than another double issue in October. That will depend, however, on whether we conclude the publication year with the September number. – Karl's advice about sending my article is good, but I can't do much of anything here, if only for technical reasons. His letter was, by the way, very stimulating. In respect to the Miles memorandum, the critique of the illegal work made a strong impression on me, because it confirmed my own fears. But I don't believe there is much to be done with Otto [Wels] or via the International. I'll write to Brussels about it. I am leaving here on 15 [August] and hope to be back on the 19 [August]. Unfortunately, I'd sent back Judith [Grünfeld's] article to her before your letter arrived. It would make me very happy to see Nathan. What do you think about the situation in Germany? I remain quite skeptical. On the other hand, the Communists (Münzenberg),[165] the Parisian emigres, and Max Braun have obviously gone crazy and appear to want to create a "people's league", or

---

165   Wilhelm Münzenberg (1889–1940), KPD member of the Reichstag from 1924–1933, founder and leader of a very influential press and film company and leading propagandist for the Communist International. In French exile he supported the creation of a "people's front." After 1937 he came into conflict with the KPD leadership and was expelled from the party in 1939. He died mysteriously in southern France in October 1940.

something like that, with the Catholics (namely Saar-Hoffmann [sic]).[166] That would be a wonderful story, which Hitler could not improve upon in order to smother any bourgeois opposition in its infancy. Laughable are the Communists, who, at any cost, want to join with the Catholics to erect a dictatorship of the proletariat; poor Revolutionary Socialists to the united front! Have you read the letter from Max Braun? I was informed a few days earlier, and you are named as someone who could be drawn in! Forgive the brevity and the confusion, but I'm writing in a hurry because I have a lot to do before setting off on my trip. Now I have to go meet O[tto] W[els] in the Metzgerbräu, and at 10:30 the others are coming. "The service of freedom is a hard service", but first there is that of the "Sopade". So, "Freedom!" and best regards and good day!

Your,
   Rudolf

[P.S.] Regards to Hanna and Else.

Zurich, August 14, 1935

Dear Paul,

Please tell Klinger that, because of [the trip to] Brussels, I cannot send him an article for [*Neuer*] V[*orwärts*] this time.

The article by Bienstock is a very pleasant surprise. It is very well done. I have viewed the American problem essentially in the same way and often alluded to it. Only, in regard to his hope for a change in the American attitude, I am more resigned, and, therefore, had not moved it into the foreground. But it's good that this occurs. The most important thing, however, is that the article is an excellent polemic against Bauer's theses, and, therefore, I think it is of the *greatest importance* that it *appears in this issue* even if that means a delay of a few days. So, I'll send it today (Wednesday) directly to Graphia and request that it be inserted with the rest. I view this as most important and can perhaps follow up by writing again to this meeting and that of the Executive.

---

166   Hilferding is most likely referring here to Max Moritz Hofmann (1891–1951), who under Weimar had been a journalist and SPD leader in the Vogtland and a leader of the Reichsbanner. In 1934 he was the business manager for the *Volkstimme* in the Saarland and in 1935 moved to France.

The table of contents would then appear as follows: Thormann, Sollmann, Bienstock, Sering, Nikolajewsky[167] and then Schifrin, Schwarz, and Alsen, whereby the last three could also be held over. Then the next number could possibly be a double issue.

Best regards,
　Rudolf

Zürich, August 20, 1935

Dear Paul,

[I] just returned yesterday evening. To travel to Basel is too expensive for me; it would have been better (half the cost) to go to Luzern, but it is too late. I very much regret not speaking with N[athan].[168] I expect you on Thursday or Friday; it would be nice if you could tell me when you will arrive. It's good that you have received my second letter, and that Bienstock has been salvaged for our side. Should the typesetting be done from here? You could call me tomorrow morning until 10:45 or in the afternoon between 3:00 and 4:00, which wouldn't be expensive and would be something Nathan could do.

Best wishes,
　Your,
　[Rudolf]

167　Boris Nikolajewsky (1888–1966) was a Russian revolutionary and historian. Initially a Bolshevik, by 1907 he had joined the Mensheviks and spent the next ten years as an activist or in Siberian exile. In 1918 he was elected to the Petrograd Soviet and from 1919–1921 served as the Director of the Central Archives for the History of the Revolutionary Movement. Arrested in 1921 and exiled a year later, he moved to Berlin, where he was very active in émigré politics and represented the Moscow-based Marx-Engels Institute. After 1933 he had a similar post in Paris.

168　Otto Nathan (1893–1987) was a German economist who, serving as an official, advised Weimar governments from 1920–1933. A left pacifist, he went into exile in 1933 and moved to the United States where he taught economics at several leading universities, including Princeton, (1933–35), New York University (1935–1942), Vassar (1942–44), and Howard University (1946–52).

Prague, August 30, 1935

Dear Rudolf,

Everything was good in Vienna. Karl and Luise [Kautsky] are doing well. Unfortunately, I did not talk to your Peter and Margaret. But Hanna has arranged to see them, and she'll tell you about it after she gets back.

The address for F.A. Voight is London W C 1, 20 Great James Street.

I found a collaborator on military affairs. Karl had invited our General, but he had to cancel at the last minute. Karl is convinced, however, that Worker's article will spark him to write a reply. He [Karl] had spoken to him recently at length and discerned complete agreement in their views. As soon as the General turns up at Karl's, he will talk to him about the article and tell us what happened.

At Karl's I also met another former officer. I worked out an arrangement with him to write three book reviews for us about Austria. In the discussion with him it became clear that he believes the line [of Kautsky's] *Grenzen der Gewalt* is absolutely right and bases this position on particular supporting arguments. I think that this would be a valuable contribution.

Otherwise, there is nothing new. The *Zeitschrift* will be printed today. All the planned contributions, as well as the commentary and reviews could be included. At the moment, I'm doing the advertising for the issue. Couldn't we get Oskar Mayer, Buchwald,[169] Somary,[170] and other friends of yours to subscribe?

Best regards,
 [Paul]

---

169   Bruno Buchwald (1877–1954) was a journalist specializing in economics. He had worked at various papers including the *Berliner Morgenpost* and *Die Welt am Montag*.

170   Felix Somary (1881–1956) studied law and economics at the University of Vienna and eventually became a leading Austrian-Swiss banker and noted political economist. He had an extraordinarily wide-ranging career advising German, Swiss, and United States governments, teaching, publishing, and co-managing the Blankart & Co. banking house in Zurich, where he lived between 1919 and 1940. His reputation for delivering unvarnished analysis of the German economic predicament under Weimar earned him the nickname "the raven of Zürich.".

Zürich, September 1, 1935

Dear Paul,

The Geneva Conference *can* perhaps have a certain importance but would not be important enough to justify a delegation from Prague. It is, above all, an English and French affair, but tensions could arise, and an arrangement and concord would be all the more urgently needed if there is agitation from the "left". I think it is reasonable if I go, but that would also fully suffice. The line would be similar to that of the last resolution but [...] no united front.

So, talk to the colleagues about it and let me know, by telegraph if necessary, if I must plan on the trip. In this case I should let [Fritz] Adler know right away, so that I can get any printed materials.

The commentary is good. I am only curious about what kinds of positive political concepts should be developed.

Today I was with Staud[inger].[171] He would like to give Wilfried a hand, but he does not seem to be very interested. He would like to offer him a scholarship and urged him to take evening courses, but apparently without much success. He thinks that you should also urge the same course of action to Wilfried.

Have you heard anything from Danzig?

Best wishes to you and to Hanna.
Your,
Rudolf

[P.S.] I have received a somewhat incomprehensible letter from Siegmund [Crummenerl] concerning a telephone call. See what's going on and let me know whether I have something to worry about. It is not clear to me at all why my name was even mentioned in the matter.

---

171 Hans Staudinger (1889–1980) studied sociology and economics under Alfred and Max Weber at the University of Heidelberg. After serving as an officer in the First World War, he occupied important posts in the Reich Economics and the Prussian Trade Ministries and was an SPD member of the Reichstag from 1932–33. Arrested by the Nazis but released in July 1933, he moved to New York and became a Professor of Economics at the New School for Social Research.

Zürich, September 3, 1935

Dear Paul,

In so far as my letter concerned S[eydewitz], A[ufhäuser], [and] B[öchel], it has now become meaningless. I am leaving on Thursday around noon for Geneva and plan to stay at the Cornavin Hotel. I'll be back at the latest by Sunday.

The article by Bienstock and Irlen[172] is interesting and suitable for publication, although I don't agree with the conclusion, which is a panacea. In contrast, Fermin's article on Spain is unsuitable, and I will send it back.

Write to me, please, about the manuscripts you have there or about those you expect and tell me the editorial deadline you have in mind. Ask Sering if he'd like to write an essay about Moszkowska's theory of crisis.[173] On the treatment of Oren and Bauer, I'll let you know after Geneva. Should I send the Bienstock article directly to the printer or wait on that? The wisest thing would be, after the publication of this issue, for the printer to send me the proofs of all the material that remains. Then one could probably still drop the old Rinner article.

[Emil] Lederer,[174] who came looking for me today, gave me ten Swiss francs. He subscribes to the *Zeitschrift*, which should have been sent to him from the beginning of 1935. Address: The New School for Social Research, 66 W. 12th Street, New York.

Sering's commentary is good. However, to attract enough German [Reichsdeutsche] collaborators and to keep the Russians from becoming predominant, we have to see to it that, above all, we get enough articles about German conditions. When will I receive the second essay from the Miles people?

---

172 Irlen was a pseudonym for Boris Sapir (1902–1989), who joined the Menshevik Party in 1919, fought in the Red Army from 1919–1920 and then worked in the Menshevik underground until his arrest in 1921. Imprisoned in the remote Solovetsky Islands, he escaped in 1925 and fled to Germany where he studied law at Heidelberg University. During the 1930s he was employed by the Institute for Social History in Amsterdam.

173 Natalie Moszkowska (1886–1968) joined the Polish Social Democratic Party as an adolescent but moved to Switzerland where she studied economics at the University of Zürich and earned a Ph.D. in 1914 focusing on workers in the Polish coal and steel industries. She joined the Swiss Social Democratic Party and wrote several important works of Marxist political economy, including one on crisis theory, published in 1935.

174 Emil Lederer (1882–1939) studied law and economics at the University of Vienna and sat in many of the same seminars as Hilferding and Bauer. During the Weimar Republic, he held professorships first at Heidelberg and later at Humboldt University. He joined the SPD in 1925, was purged from the university in 1933, and eventually moved to the United States where he co-founded the New School for Social Research in New York.

In respect to Somary (per the address of Blankart & Co., Stadthaus – quoi 7) and Buchwald, whose address you have, it would be best to send this and the last issue of the *Zeitschrift* and well as instructions or directions about how to pay. It would be best to pay into Siegmund's account for a year's subscription.

Best regards,
Rudolf

Prague, September 14, 1935

Dear Rudolf,

I've been back from my trip to Gdingen for some time and today I want to reply at length to your letters of 1 and 3 September.
First, on the Zeitschrift.
We have announced that the next issue should appear at the beginning of October. I'd like to have the galleys ready by 4 October, so that printing and mailing can occur the following week.

Meeting this deadline should not encounter many serious difficulties. I assume that you will long since have finished your article. The article by Sering will also be ready. He told me yesterday that he will finish it up in the next few days and we have arranged it so that he sends it to you directly. Today I heard from Luise that Karl [Kautsky] has written an article that he thinks it is important to publish as soon as possible given the world situation. I told Luise that you intended to write about this subject in the next issue and that the edition is already basically full. Nevertheless, I recommended that Karl send the article directly to you.

Certainly, we once again have too many manuscripts. Here is how things currently stand:

Sollmann:	Sozialistischer Umbruch [Socialist Transformation]– 350 lines
Schwarz:	Zur Demokratie oder zur plebiszitären Diktatur [Democracy or Plebiscitary Dictatorship] – 450 lines
Alsen:	Stalin mit und ohne Maske [Stalin: With or Without a Mask] – 350 lines
Stein:	Engels und die Gegenwart [Engels and Today's World] – (shortened to 300 lines)
Leopold Franz:	Zur marxistischen Staatstheorie [On the Marxist Theory of the State] – 350 lines

In addition, I already have some book reviews by Andreas Hohwald (G. Beyer) and a commentary by Sollmann on *Das stumme Deutschland*. I think, however, it is better to publish the commentary with the reviews. It lacks the sharpness I think necessary for a commentary. One can count on additional book reviews from Stein.

I am not familiar with Irlen's article, which you received from Bienstock. Its author is, unfortunately, a young Russian who I know, but whose name I've forgotten. Send the article, please, directly to the printer with the instruction that proofs be sent to you and to me. Then we can still decide if the article should be placed in the next issue.

By the way, Bienstock intends to write about the congress of the Comintern. As soon as I have the manuscript, I will send it to you for a decision in so far as there are any misgivings on Bienstock's or my part. Otherwise, I'll have it typeset right away so that you can deal with any changes you might want in the proofs.

Since I've provided you with a complete overview of the available manuscripts, and since you have already read all of those on the list above, I don't think it is necessary that the printer send you the proofs again. That is only an unnecessary burden for you.

However, I am sending you manuscripts that have arrived here in the meantime:

1. "Verfall der kapitalistische Ideologie" ["The Decline of Capitalist Ideology"]. It is from Crispien. I don't think it is suitable and recommend sending it back. Address: Frau Claire Lehmuth, Stauffacherstr. 3 mit Innencourvert für A.C. He seems to be prepared for the fact that the article will not be of use for the *Zeitschrift*.
2. "Die Hochschule im Dritten Reich" ["The University in the Third Reich"] by Emil Gross. I discovered nothing new in this article. It is an agitational interpretation that, in my view, also makes it unsuitable for the *Zeitschrift*. I am for rejecting it.
3. "Gibt es eine revolutionäre Bewegung in Deutschland?" ["Is there a Revolutionary Movement in Germany?"] by Helmut Wickel. I cannot really form a judgement about this article. But I have the impression that one could say things much more briefly and concisely, as one might about the book by Schumann, the American professor. I will write to Wickel that I've sent the article to you for evaluation, but that under no circumstances should he count on its publication in the next issue.

I am still waiting to hear from you about the theses of O[tto] B[auer] and Dan. I'll set aside the article by Rinner.

From your suggestion that Sering do a review of Moschkowskas' [sic] book I assume that you've been in contact with him in the meantime. She recently sent us a letter for K[arl] K[autsky], which contained the suggestion that he should review the book. I replied to her that we already intend to review her book but were not considering KK for it. I recommended to her to contact you personally. I've assigned the review to Friedmann, but the Kacha publishing house, like Frau Moschkowska [sic], has not yet sent a review copy. Sering has many other works underway, so I prefer to leave it with Friedmann, especially since you have a very good impression of Friedmann's abilities.

We've put through the subscriptions to the *Zeitschrift* for Lederer, Buchwald, and Somary. You owe ten Swiss francs. Demand for the *Zeitschrift* is getting somewhat stronger. A final overview of the sales of the last two issues is not yet available, however.

We will be talking about the archive on Monday. Wels has very strong misgivings and is inclined to reject the Russian offer. Whether under these conditions it will come to direct negotiations seems very doubtful to me. Professor Posthumus,[175] whom you've perhaps met in Geneva, is coming to Vienna tomorrow. Since he does not wish to travel via Germany, I'll accommodate his desire and will travel to Vienna tomorrow. P[osthumus] thinks it most important that I am present for his conversations with the Kautskys.

Up close the situation in Danzig looks different than we originally thought about it. The capitulation of the Nazis to the Poles has eased the political as well as the economic situation. There are no acute difficulties with no way out. To be sure, in the long term a further fundamental economic decline is inevitable. But, since the Nazi government is most agreeable to the Poles, then it will do everything to keep the Nazi government in place, or at least it won't undertake anything that might accelerate its fall. That is also the opinion of Birnbaum, who would think it unfortunate if the opposition in Danzig came to power.[176] It is fragmented, divided on the issue of the relationship to Poland, and the German nationalists are quite successfully combating the Nazis with the argument of national betrayal. The Poles would make such unbearable demands that it

---

175 Nicolaas Wilhelmus Posthumus (1880–1960) was a Dutch professor of economic history and leading archivist. In 1935 he founded the International Institute for Social History in Amsterdam which became the repository for threatened archival and library collections in Germany, Austria, and Spain. These included the SPD's archive, which contained, among other things, the papers of Marx and Engels.

176 Immanuel Birnbaum (1894–1982) was a Social Democratic journalist and publicist. During Weimar he was a correspondent for several major papers including the *Vossische Zeitung* and the *Frankfurter Zeitung*. After going into exile in 1933, he focused his writing on Polish affairs and, from 1935–38 was the press attaché to the Austrian Embassy in Warsaw.

would soon run aground. Birnbaum is ready to write an article for the *Zeitschrift* in which he discusses the Danzig problem, Poland and Germany, and Poland and Russia.

That Staudinger takes such an interest in Wilfried is nice of him. But after Nathan confirmed to me what Wilfried has written many times – that he rejects further study – Staudinger should give up the attempt to provide him with a stipend. Tell me, please, where Staudinger is right now. I'd happily write to him myself, so that nothing further happens to make Wilfried more rebellious. Vladek,[177] the manager of the Jewish *Forward* in New York, was here recently. He is making a great effort to get Wilfried a job as a book printer. He also said that Wilfried rejects any attempt to get him to return to his studies. He thinks, by the way, that he'll soon succeed in finding a position for Wilfried as a printer.

Best wishes,
  [Paul]

Zürich, September 19, 1935

Dear Paul,

First, send [*Neuer*] *Vorwarts* and the *Zeitschrift* to
1.   Hugo Simon, Paris, Hotel Westminster, Rue de la Pais
2.   Frau Vera Gutmann, Paris 16e, 115 Avenue Henri Martin

Send the marked issues of [*Neuer*] *Vorwärts* with my article: "Die Welt entdeckt den Fascismus" ["The World Discovers Fascism"] and the *Zeitschrift* of 20/21 to A. Buchwald, St. Moritz Dorf – Haus Vinzens, and tell him how to pay for a half or full year subscription.

I.   I have read the big book by Souvarine (founder of the French Communist Party) about "Stalin". It is the first comprehensive, documented, and truthful book about Bolshevism. That is precisely why it is *devastating*. Do you think it might be possible for Graphia to publish the work (500 pages, but it could be shortened)? Since, unfortunately, bourgeois anti-Bolshevism could also exploit it, [the book] *could* be a big success in the

---

177   Baruch Charney Vladek (1886–1938) was a Belorussian Jew who joined the Jewish Bund as an adolescent and was active in the revolutionary underground. Following the Revolution of 1905, he migrated to the U.S., joined the Socialist Party, served in the New York City Council, and managed the *Jewish Daily Forward*. In 1933 he helped found the Jewish Labor Committee to mobilize the Jewish labor movement and allied groups against Nazism.

II. In a broad sense, the Parisian emigration is obviously very active, driven by a very strong sense of optimism. Hugo Simon, with whom I had recently spoken, just write to me and urgently requested me to come to Paris at his expense to participate in discussions. He is primarily in contact with [Leopold] Schwarzschild, who one cannot deny is someone of substance who has to be taken seriously.[178] [Schwarzschild has received a lot of support for his well-known article and it seems that he is striving to apply the "popular front" to Germany. In the background, however, stands [Willi] Münzenberg], who just returned to Paris from Moscow. Hugo's letter also reveals that you have received a letter from Schwarzschild but have not replied. What's in it? I wrote to Hugo that, at the moment, I cannot come. Before I go, I'd like to know your point of view. Since, in any case, I'll be going to Paris in the foreseeable future, it would be senseless once there to not want to hear more. This is all the more the case, because Schwarzschild does not appear to be in overall agreement with Münzenberg. My viewpoint remains that joining up with the Communists is a non-starter for the bourgeois opposition, and the matter can only be about the formation of an independent bourgeois opposition for which the Parisian [opposition] is not suited. Still, one needs to know what is really happening there. So, write to me about what you think, after talking with Wels and Siegmund [Crummenerl] if necessary, about whether you intend to answer Schwarzschild, and about what I should say to the people in Paris if I decide to go.

III. Please tell Crum[menerl] that he should remit my salary. When it comes to money, I have some concerns.

Somary was absent the whole time and is only coming back at the end of the week. I don't wish to bear the responsibility for the investments. To be sure, I don't believe that the French franc is in danger at the moment, even if Holland is carrying out a devaluation. On the other hand, in light of the foreign situation, French stocks could still sink. It would be possible to sell everything and move into dollars. We could hold onto the dollars until matters clear up and they can be reinvested, or they could be invested in

---

178 Leopold Schwarzschild (1891–1950) was the co-founder and later the sole owner of the Tagebuch-Verlag. In 1933 he emigrated to Paris where he founded and edited the *Das Neue Tagebuch*, a weekly.

American securities, about which there would have to be a discussion. In any case, talk to Crum[menerl] about it, so that it can't be said that I ignored the issue.

IV. Karl [Kautsky's] article came yesterday. It is problematic: twenty typed pages and very difficult to cut. In addition, the content is not very concrete or current, and I fear it makes no impression. What should I do? At the same time, Karl wrote as if rejection was virtually impossible. He thinks that something terribly important depends on its publication. In any case, I don't have the heart not to print it. I'll send this article and Irlen's to the printer tomorrow. Didn't you also receive the manuscript from Karl? Naturally that makes it impossible for me to publish an article on the same subject in this issue. I also don't think the exposé by Bauer and Dan has to be published. A polemic can also be conducted in this way. Instead, perhaps I'll write a commentary or a short article on the Abyssinian conflict, just in case it is decided by then. By the end of the week I'll know if I have received anything useful from a local collaborator. If not, who else is there? Klinger? Or Sering? But that is a lot from the same author. When will you get the second article? An article about the Communist International is also necessary. Schifrin offered me one, but I have concerns because of his uncritical outlook. But who else? I've read some stuff, but not enough, to write about it myself, and one has to take a position. And the general question of the united front! Prague won't be able to duck the issue as it has thus far. Now, despite their earlier efforts, the thing is coming to Switzerland initially in the form of unified [electoral] lists. (I've overlooked Bienstock's desire to write about the C[ommunist] Y[outh]. Did it happen? Send me the manuscript right away, please, otherwise send a proof). Regarding other articles, I'll write soon. I agree about Friedmann as a reviewer. Staudinger is probably already back in New York.

Of course, I am also against selling the archive to the Russians and I'm pleased that Wells has the same view. I'm curious about what you have arranged with Posthumus.

Write soon. Best wishes and to Hanna as well.
Rudolf

Prague, September 22, 1935

Dear Rudolf,

I've received your letter of 19 Sept[ember]. I've already taken care of the orders for *N[euer] V[orwärts]* and the *Zeitschrift* for Hugo Simon and Bruno Buchwald. I am also taking care of the order for Vera Gutmann.

I read your comments on the book by Souvarine to Arthur [Arnold]. He is sympathetic to your recommendation. Tell Rose [Hilferding], she should speak to Arthur directly. I was in Vienna from Monday to Wednesday to talk with Posthumus about the archive. K[arl] K[autsky] told me that he has read Souvarine's book and would like to write a review. Naturally, I told him that we already have a review, that will probably appear in the next issue. The book also seemed to have made a great impression on him.

Now to the *Zeitschrift*: Karl gave me a carbon copy of his article, which I read for the first time on my way home. My impression is just about the same as yours. The article says scarcely anything new. I immediately brought it to Karl's attention how difficult it would be to publish the article in the next issue. He then asked me to talk with *[Neuer] Vorwärts* about whether the article could be cut and published there in three installments. He also left it to us to make cuts, because he recognizes that the article had gotten too long and, he hopes, the material will later be available to read in his book. I'll talk to Geyer early tomorrow about whether he will publish the article. If he says yes, then I'll stop the typesetting in Karlsbad. But if it doesn't work out, then we will have to drastically shorten the article. Otherwise there will not be enough room at all.

I am not convinced that, despite everything, you should not write the lead article for this issue. Of course, I understand that your original intention to write a longer polemic against the theses can no longer be pursued. But I assume that there is enough material – the whole development in Geneva, the conflict with Italy, the new relationship between France and England, the threatened fight between Germany, Poland, and Russia/Lithuania – for you to continue to outline your ideas from the article "Das Ende der Völkerbundpolitik". And when you sign your name to this article, then, for the first time, it would get us the exposure we need in the most important papers that is so urgently needed for our sales.

W[illi] Mü[ller], who was in the West for a week, brought me Sering's enclosed manuscript today – unfortunately, he did not meet me at home. I have a carbon copy. But I cannot read it today, so I have to ask you to prepare it for publication yourself and to send it to Karlsbad as soon as possible. I estimate that the article is 24 printed pages long. That seems rather long to me and I ask you to consider cuts. As soon as I talk with W[illi] Mü[ller], I'll tell him that. As necessary as theoretical articles are, it is important for the distribution of the *Zeitschrift* that every issue also contains articles that can be understood by less sophisticated and less theoretically inclined readers.

I hope to get the article about the Comintern from Bienstock tomorrow. I told you how I think I'll handle it in an earlier letter. Yesterday, Aufhäuser asked me if we want an article by him on the united front. He intends to critically discuss the Congress of the Comintern and to link that with observations on the situation in Germany. He also asked if we would be prepared, along with him, to argue that any negotiations with the Communists must include all social democratic groups. So, not just the Sopade should participate, but also Miles, the Revolutionary Socialists, etc. When I told him that we already have arranged for an article by Bienstock, he decided not to write an article himself, especially since I also reminded him of your skepticism about an alliance with the Communists. He was not annoyed, however, especially because I repeated the promise of freedom of discussion.

I would welcome it if you favored the writing of the article about the [NSDAP's] Nuremberg Party Congress, which I think is urgently needed. I don't think Klinger is capable of it. He is completely disoriented and swings uncontrollably back and forth between the illusions of O[tto] W[els] and F[riedrich] St[ampfer], his own illusions about the gradual transition to a system of bureaucratic domination, and the occasional recognition of the real relations of power. I much prefer Sering, although I admit to having substantive and personal misgivings about using him too often. Let me know if you receive the article. Then we'll consider things further.

If you don't write an article, you definitely have to send a commentary. After considerable cutting, I'll publish the book review by Sollman on *das stumme Deutschland*. I've also sent the two enclosed reviews by Friedmann. I don't like them. I especially dislike the one on Moszkowska. I've read other reviews elsewhere on this book which were shorter and more illuminating, because they only focused on the main issue: "do crises have technical or social causes?" It is impossible to publish these extensive reviews. Each is two pages. I had asked Friedmann only for a review Moszkowska and told him it could be one page. His opinion opposing short reviews as a matter of principle is ridiculous, because a short review can also have valuable content. Since we have at most two or three pages for book reviews in each issue, with double issues we have five to six pages. Thus, we have to squeeze all the reviews we have into this space. I can do that with the reviews by Stein, Beyer, [and] Sollmann, which I can evaluate myself. In Friedmann's case, you have to do it. I will tell him that in writing tomorrow. If we can't fit the reviews into the next edition, that is also not a misfortune. If we cannot train collaborators to write succinctly, we will never create anything useful.

I think your trip to Paris is appropriate. If it lasts for 8–10 days, then you'll meet Breitscheid, as well, who is in the Geneva area at the moment. He is staying on the French side but can be reached using Wertheimer's Geneva address. You are right that I got a letter from Schwarzschild at the beginning of August. He sent me his article from the NTB [*Das Neue Tagebuch*] and asked me what I think. I thought I'd told you about this letter, which was just a few lines. I did not reply, because, like you, I have great misgivings about allowing myself to get involved in something the context and significance of which I cannot judge from here. Since I also have the impression that Schw[arzschild] has become a serious man whom I don't wish to offend, I will write to him tomorrow. Still, I think I'll avoid taking a substantive position and tell him that I'll only be able to develop a substantive viewpoint after I've learned more from you about it.

I ask that you also talk about the problem in detail with Breitscheid. I believe that, like me, he would have little objection to a personal discussion with Schw[arzschild]. I think contact is necessary in any case. We don't have any opinion here. A few days ago, we decided to refrain from answering in writing for as long as possible. Neither O[tto] W[els] nor S[iegmund] Cr[ummenerl] have an opinion on the issue. As important as relations to the bourgeois groups seem to them, their doubts are equally significant about whether Schw[arzschild] and consorts, especially in connection with Münzenberg, are the appropriate personalities for it. Therefore, your task is to get a sense of things on the spot and to provide us with the information necessary to make a judgement. O[tto] W[els] said recently that we would never get free of the Communists and their offers of a united front. If what I heard recently is confirmed – that the Scandinavians and the Dutch have taken the same position at a special meeting in Brussels, and that, in Holland, there was also vocal support for an agreement with the Communists within the party – then that would certainly influence not only the opinion of the LSI, but also that of O[tto] W[els]. I personally think that we can hardly continue to completely reject negotiations with the Communists. On the other hand, however, I also see a great deal of resistance among our own people to cooperation in Germany. But that does not prevent you from speaking personally with the people in Paris.

Regarding the matter of the archive, you can discern our sharply negative attitude in our letter to the LSI, etc. If O[tto] W[els] was guided by different motives than I was, we were still united in our arguments. Only Siegmund took a different position. He is tortured by the worry that we are running out of money much faster than he thought we would. From the materially completely unlimited Russian offer (Nikolajewsky was told 10 million French francs) it seems to me that the inner motive is to make us materially independent from Moscow. For the moment nothing will happen, including further negotiations with Posthumus. He believes the Dutch will offer 50,000 Gulden. After one has heard sums in the millions, the effect of that offer is disappointing. Just so you know, I want to tell you that I also spoke with Posthumus about you. He does not think a position is possible, but, in the framework of an agreement, he would be prepared to support your receiving ongoing compensation that would equal your current salary. The pursuit of scholarly work would be your only obligation. But I have not said anything about this to Arthur [Arnold]. For the time being, anyway, it is theoretical.

I'll tell Siegmund about your view of the investments tomorrow. You'll hear from him directly.

W[illi] Mü[ller] was just here. He has been hit very hard. His group has recently suffered severe losses of people very close to him personally. In addition, the domestic conflicts are beginning to create a bit stir abroad. When [Kurt] Menz[179] or someone else turns up near you, see what he says. I'll be able to ascertain whether the story is correct through a confrontation with W[illi] M[üller. Until then, I'll keep my cards very close to the vest and I suggest the same to you.

W[illi] Mü[ller] has misgivings about cuts to Sering's article. On the other hand, he agrees that Part v, "die faschistische Revolution" ["the Fascist Revolution"], should be deferred to the next article. If that happens, then the length of the second article would not go beyond that of the first.

I spoke to Margret and Peter in Vienna, who both send their warmest regards […] Peter impressed me as a mature person. He claimed to be very much engaged in political economy, so I recommended that he send the initial results of his work to you. If you had direct contact with Peter, it would benefit him a lot. Reply to me soon so that the *Zeitschrift* doesn't get delayed.

Best regards, from Hanna too.
   Your,
   [Paul]

---

179   Kurt Menz was another pseudonym for Walter Löwenheim, also known as Miles.

Zürich, September 30, 1935

Dear Paul,

First, Richard Neumann urgently requests that you tell his wife (the address is enclosed). The poor devil himself has to leave tomorrow for Brussels, without a red cent, because he cannot get his permit to stay here extended. He brought me a short, essentially informational, article about the Comintern Congress, which, unfortunately, I cannot accept, but perhaps I can use parts of it for one of my own. However, I can't give him money for that ...

[I received] an angry letter from Karl [Kautsky] in Vienna. I thought you had straightened everything out with him. I'm very sorry to have annoyed him – after all, it would have worked out with the cuts. I'll write to him directly. The hard thing is that my original intention to take a position on war has been messed up. That will have to wait until the next issue. I thought about possibly writing a commentary on Abyssinia. But the thing is too risky. By the time it gets into the hands of the readers, all the important decisions would have been made long ago. In addition, changes would have occurred to such an extent that a more thorough treatment is essential.

Yesterday I sent the "Nuremberg" article and a very good little commentary, which must be published under any circumstances, to Graphia. Sering's article – he should make more of an effort to write for working-class readers – is interesting, but I am curious about the real political conclusions. It would be nice to receive his next article; one could still correspond with him about it. I was unable to cut anything from the manuscript, and it also seems to be impossible to divide, because the conclusion definitely belongs in the context and would be too meagre left standing alone. But what about a device to which Willi [Müller] would have no apparent legal claim? What is Sering's address?

Bienstock's article is acceptable. I don't agree with everything. For example, I don't think the "world revolution" is a motive of Russian foreign policy, as it undoubtably was for Trotsky. On that there will occasionally be some things to be said. In any case that article can be published as it is. I will write to Puls directly about his reviews, not in regard to their length – in principle I agree with his opinion – but rather their content. I am sending all the other articles back to you; they are unusable. Worker constructs a [view of] history and of the future according to fantasies garnered from a pair of anthologies. There was no talk of hatred of Russians in Germany's ruling strata. Bismarck had always conducted politics *with* Russia and for that reason old [Wilhelm] Liebknecht had named him the Russian bootblack. For this policy, B[ismarck] always had the support of the conservatives and when Caprivi dropped the Russian Insurance Treaty, he came under withering attack by the right. It is correct that the agrarians opposed any easing of grain imports, but that was not a decisive determinant of foreign policy before the war and today it is less so than ever. The whole construction – [General] von Seeckt as an exponent of industrial capital – is childish. Who is Müritz? The review is not only long, but its execution is too speculative. Nevertheless, it appears that he knows something and perhaps is useful. I'm also sending Crispien back. I'm sorry to always have to reject him – that is really our only relationship. So, do it for me this time. The other is not interesting.

I spoke with Siegmund [Crummenerl] about Stalin and he is interested. For me it is a political problem more than anything. Precisely now, as we experience difficult times with the Communists, it is of particular importance to make the book accessible to German readers, despite all of the bourgeoisie's triumphant cries. It could also be shortened a bit. I only fear that the other foreign publishers can scarcely be considered, because they are mainly friendly to the Bolsheviks. I have asked Rose, who went to Paris yesterday, to contact Souvarine via Nikolajewski to discuss translation rights. I'd like to know whether you think this is at all possible. Ask Arnold about it.

Crum[menerl] told me in detail about the conversation with Miles, and I spoke with Miles and his companion at length yesterday. Both made a good impression on me. I can imagine how hard you must have been hit by what he said. Bearing in mind that the description was one-sided, it seems certain that Wi[lli] [Müller] has reported to us incorrectly about many things. Most important is the false description of M[iles] as one of the liquidators, and most disconcerting are the divisive methods Willi used. You know that I have consistently had more extensive reservations about him than you or Fritz [Adler] and Otto [Wels]. I am very curious about what Fritz will say about their report. The argument with them shows me that, in any case, there are no deeper differences present. But the split has put the two of us in a somewhat uncomfortable position and I can imagine Wels's triumph rather well. Naturally, I am very excited about your view of the conversations with Willi and I'd like to hear about it soon, because I will probably see the two of them again after their return from Brussels. In any case, it woud be important to maintain contact with them and perhaps to bring them gradually into a relationship with the Sopade, for which Siegmund has some sympathy. It seems to me, however, that neither Miles faction is strongly for a split.

I don't have any new information about Paris and therefore I also don't know when I'll be going there. Aufhäuser's idea about the participation of all the groups in negotiations with the Communists is foolish and in the current situation won't even be considered by the Sopade.

The archive matter is damned hard. On the one hand, I'm very pleased with Wels's view. But I also understand Crum[menerl's] concerns and fear the pressure that will be exercised by our people in Germany and elsewhere for the sale. I am not so absolutely sure. If one imagines that everything could be photocopied and carefully checked, then scholarly misuse can be avoided. Wels's political misgivings are very strong and are, in part, very well grounded, but perhaps not decisively, when you are faced with the intent of stopping the work. I would love to talk with Karl K[autsky] and Fritz [Adler] about the issue. In any case, I'm glad that the first, initial decision is to reject [the sale]. Please, for the moment, don't speak with anyone about my doubts.

Of course, it would be really nice if something worked out for me with Posthumus, but you, yourself, are skeptical in this regard. In any case, thanks very much.

I'll leave the page proofs to you. It is clear that Bienstock's article must be included. Right, I forgot to sign the "Nuremberg" article. I added the first page myself and believe the article is now acceptable. But I need a pseudonym for the article. Please provide something. By the way, the issue is very topical and really interesting after all.

Write soon and best wishes. I'm not sure about whether I can see Hilde since I'll be spending the evening with Crumm[enerl].

Best regards and to Hanno, too.
    Your
    Rudolf

[P.S.] After setting the pages, send me the proofs of the overset, because otherwise the content of the articles is no longer current. In the future, perhaps we want to do it in such a way that, unless we decide differently, the proofs and manuscripts are sent to you and to me and, in any case, also an offprint.

Prague, October 3, 1935

Dear Rudolf,

I have to put off responding at length to your letter until next week. Today, just a few lines about the journal.

I don't think that Karl [Kautsky] is upset. I've recently received a card from Luise from which one cannot discern that. Nevertheless, I've written to him today and I hope that, if he has become upset, he realized that publishing in *N[euer] V[orwärts]* is not worse for him than publishing in the *Zeitschrift*.

It is very regrettable that you have not written your article. But at least remain true to your original intention and write it for the next issue. Today I energetically exhorted the printer to immediately send me all the proofs. But one can already see that we won't be able to accommodate all the articles. As soon as I have an overview, I'll write to you about what I will accept for this number and see to it that the offsets from the overset are sent to you.

I have to stay home for the next few days, because I finally have to end the saga of my tooth, which meanwhile has been getting more complicated. I will then sketch my thoughts on the Miles-complex. You are right, that M[iles] and his companion make a good impression. Nevertheless, their description contains lies and contradictions, which, in spite of all my efforts, I've not been able to explain. If the two of them should return to you before you've received my notes, then I ask you to remain doubly reserved. Especially since, for you and I, there is only one task: to prevent any sharpening of differences between the groups.

Schiff has recently already written a letter to Stampfer, in which he expresses support for the connection with Münzenberg, etc. Today, a personal letter arrived for O[tto] W[els] in which Schiff urgently pleads for Wels to go to Paris to personally participate in the negotiations. He believes that the Communists have genuinely changed. I don't know whether O[tto] W[els] will do [anything] or what that might be. A few days ago, I received a letter from Kirschmann. He's heard that I would shortly be meeting with you. He wants to talk to me because what he has on his chest cannot be expressed on paper. Since I see in the letter from Schiff to O[tto] W[els] that Kirschmann was present for the discussions on 26 September in Paris, there can be no doubt that his desire for a conversation is in connection with the issue of the united front. Münzenberg is also always working on Sollmann to come to Paris at his expense. If you go to Paris, you must first talk with Salomon Schwarz about what happened in the meetings that occurred at the end of September between Münzenberg and our people.

Very best wishes,
    [Paul]

Zürich, October 5, 1935

Dear Paul,

Among the manuscripts I sent back to you that is one about the trade union movement that I'd like you to take a look at. Still, I don't think it is something we should take. I ask that you send it back to the author, perhaps with the explanation that topics concerning the details of illegal organization are not suitable for discussion, as soon as they go beyond general principles. In this case there can be no difference of opinion about that. I'm enclosing the author's letter.

Hopefully, the *Zeitschrift* is done. Are you thinking, again, about a double issue? For when?

The last S[*ozialistiche*] A[*ktion*] is good, only I don't think that Schacht was victorious. Firstly, one should not forget that these debates only concern *relative* antagonisms and, secondly, Schacht conceded on every point. We are dealing with inflation when it comes to what Schacht does, and when it comes to what his opponents demand. That is not the difference. [It is] rather, that Schacht wants to reduce the scale and tempo and has failed. Voila tout [That is all]. The ruminations of Klinger and Erich [Rinner] about the party and the state are becoming increasingly childish and the differentiation between the economic state, the military state, and the actual state more confused. What's that about?

Best regards,
 Rudolf

[P.S.] Hopefully, your letter is already on its way, because I'm curious about your judgement of the Menz business.

Prague, October 7, 1935

Dear Rudolf,

Your letter of 5 October just arrived. Meanwhile, you have probably received my letter of 3 October in which, aside from some awkward grammatical errors – I did not proofread the letter – there are also some troubling mistakes. It should not read "lies and contradictions" but rather "gaps and contradictions".

Just yesterday I received the proofs of the articles by Bienstock and Sering. Although I sent them on immediately, creating the page breaks can only begin tomorrow at the earliest. The magazine won't appear before Friday or Saturday. I made the following arrangements: first, "Nürnberg" ["Nuremberg"] by Richard Stichling; 2. "Sozialistische Machtpolitik" ["Socialist Power Politics"] (Sollmann); 3. "Faschismus" ["Fascism"] (Sering); 4. "Komintern" ["Comintern"] (Bienstock); 5. "Plebiscitäre Diktatur" ["Plebiscitary Dictatorship"] (Schwarz); 6. "Stalin" (Alsen); 7". Engels" (Stein); 8. book reviews. The only one left out is the one by Franz on the theory of the state. I will write to him about it. Since he'd already received his honorarium in advance, there are no complications.

I will have a discussion with Sering today and let him know your desires. His address is: Post Office Box 408, Prague II, Main Post Office. (Don't use any name). The article "Der Parteitag der Totalität" ["The Party Congress of Totality"] in S[ozialistishe] A[ktion] is by him. He can also write for a popular audience. I will expressly require him to do the same for the *Zeitschrift*. In the same way, I'll insist that you receive the next article very soon. This time, I'm publishing the article without cuts. It is 1024 lines, so about 22 lines too long. I won't publish the phrase about legal claims.[180] Neither Sering nor Willi [Müller] asked for it.

I've told Worker about your view. He was annoyed and again very arrogant. It is precisely because we are dealing with such a talented but also overly self-confident person that I am for strictly evaluating his contributions. Otherwise, the guy will never amount to much. "Müritz" is H. Wickel. You know him from his book about *I-G Deutschland* and from his work on statism, which he is doing together with Bergner. Both are now Willi supporters. I suggest that you instruct and advise Müritz. I think he would be grateful. I have a better impression of Bergner, too, whom I have gotten to know, than I had from his articles. I'll send back the useless manuscripts, including Crispien's, with some kind remarks.

Do you have any preference to whom I should assign the review of Wolfgang Hallgarten's *Vorkriegsimperialismus*. [*Imperialism before 1914*]. From the *Gesellschaft* I gathered that he had published some good contributions there.

I don't yet have a firm opinion about the next issue. Both the deadline as well as the length will have to rest on two considerations: 1. on whether the ongoing world situation – Abyssinia, Italy, England-France – demands elucidation soon. And second, on whether the next article by Sering will be as long as the first two. From the publisher's perspective it is hard to get a clear picture about what is more advantageous, a double or a single issue. Willi [Müller] has already paid for 300 copies of the earlier issue, but he can only take 100 cop-

---

180   See Hilferding's comment to Hertz on possible legal claims in his letter of 30 September 1935.

ies of the next one. In my view that is fine, because I think that prospects of selling individual copies at full price will improve. In general, there has been no meaningful increase in sales. If we next decide to do a single-issue, then I would foresee a deadline of mid-November with early December for a double issue. This time I will refrain from any announcement about the next number.

I hope that today or tomorrow I'll finally get to dictate the presentation about Miles. Until then I'll spare you my remarks on my impressions. In the last few days I've had many visits from over there [Germany], so my time has been short. In addition, the saga of my tooth, which I began on Saturday and which will continue until tomorrow or the next day, is taking more out of me than I'd anticipated.

I'm very pleased with your judgement of S[ozialistische] A[ktion]. With the next issue, I hope to make it even better, because this time the collaboration with Sering occurred without the right preparation, and I hope that with the next issue even Stein's old bottles will be filled with some new wine. There is no talking to Klinger and Erich [Rinner]. They both think of themselves as terribly important and imagine that their scribblings make an impression on the whole world. Therefore, they take any criticism from me as a personal affront. The question, then, is whether one shouldn't for once publish an essay in the *Zeitschrift* that criticizes, even if indirectly, this mistaken train of thought. By the way, it is worth noting that our agent in Copenhagen, who has especially good connections to Reichswehr circles and, thus far, has always maintained illusions about the Reichswehr, Stahlhelm,[181] and the German Nationals, has issued a markedly pessimistic report. The context of the report is as follows:

> Within the Stahlhelm and among the monarchists there is, to a minor degree, outrage, and to a large degree, dejection. In Kiel, the Chairman of the Stahlhelm – an old admiral – wanted to resign after the change of flags.[182] He recommended self-dissolution. One criticizes the generals for betraying the common cause for the pottage of rearmament. The Flag Law is regarded as the result of secret negotiations in Kiel. One sees the Nuremberg Party Congress as a victory of the left. The use of armed

---

181   The Stahlhelm Bund der Frontsoldaten (The Steel Helmet League of Front Soldiers) was a powerful right-wing paramilitary formation that operated as part of the illegal "Black Reichswehr" following Germany's defeat in 1918 and as the armed branch of the monarchist German National People's Party.

182   In addition to passing laws stripping Germany's Jews of full citizenship, the Nuremberg Party Congress of September 1935 also replaced the imperial black, white, and red national flag, which had in 1933 superseded the black, red, and gold flag of the Weimar Republic, with the Nazis' swastika flag.

force against Hitler and the party is insane as long as Hitler has the masses behind him. Today the generals reject a military dictatorship more decisively than two years ago. The Reichswehr has always taken only a passive position in the struggle with the left wing, indeed, with the emphatic agreement of the civilian opposition. This failed completely. Fritsch is now condemned just like Blomberg.

The dejection among the former German Nationals is particularly great. The Jewish Laws are not regarded as a tragedy, but the Reich Citizenship Law all the more. It is certain that not only the Marxists, but also the bourgeois opposition will lose its right to vote.

The consistently optimistic outlook of many of the people from over there [Germany] is remarkable. I've now had a number of lengthy conversations with the man who is in close contact with Hans Hirschf[eld] and who has visited him many times. We are dealing here with an intellectual who apparently lived in proletarian conditions. He certainly possesses very good knowledge of the old and new movement, is courageous but not reckless, optimistic but not uncritical. He is more inclined to the party Executive's way of thinking than to that of Miles, although he makes substantial human and material demands on his collaborators. To be sure, this man thinks that the optimism of those working illegally does not match completely with their conviction but is simply a condition of their work. Whoever does not have this optimism or cannot convince himself of it, is unable to carry out the difficult work over there. But he was insightful enough to advise us not to make this optimism into a single guiding principle of our action and thought. I introduced this man to Siegmund [Crummenerl]. He also had a very favorable impression of him. Among other things, we also continued the conversation that you had with Siegmund on the issue of the future. Our friend said it is urgent that one not only place general political and human considerations against the dictatorship more in the foreground than economic concerns, but instead he also wishes that the goals of the struggle for democracy and freedom could be made more concrete than hitherto.

Meanwhile, Kirschmann sent us an exact protocol about affairs in Paris. In two meetings at the end of September, Koenen and Münzenberg explained that the KPD has put into place a policy favoring the broadest possible anti-fascist coalition with the goal of establishing a democratic republic with broad political freedoms, especially religious freedom. The idea of a National Assembly should stand at the center of all anti-fascist political activity. Max Braun proposed to the meeting recommendations and guidelines for a supra-party league [called] "das kommende Deutschland" [the Germany of the future]. Schiff expressed that he was personally in favor of cooperation. The Kaminsky group, which sees its goal as the socialist revolution and demands an examination of the past before working with Prague, was only a small minority. No discussion at all about these things has occurred in our circle. Apparently, O[tto] W[els] and F[riedrich] St[ampfer] are discussing everything in private letters. For the time being, their behavior seems to indicate a negative attitude. I think that is still urgently necessary that you form a personal impression on the spot.

On the matter of the archive, I am in no way guided by concern that the Russians could misuse the material in the sphere of scholarship. My concerns are purely political. The Russians are recognized as the intellectual heirs of Marx and Engels. This greatly strengthens their position in the working class. If we continue to reject political cooperation with them, but take money from them and, indeed, so much money that no one can speak any longer of a "purchase", in which one payment stands in correct proportion to a reciprocal payment, then our moral standing will suffer enormously. The replies to our message to the parties of the International concerning the Russian offer basically all agree with our view. O[tto] B[auer] still leaves the question of whether one can sell the archive to the Russians open and only agrees about the need for the LSI's consent. The most important parties, the French, the English, the Belgians, the Scandinavians, and Fritz A[dler] have not yet answered. Karl K[autsky] agrees with our position. His decisive argument was that these materials must be preserved in a country in which there is freedom to conduct research. – I think that your fear that concerns about lack of money to continue the work would push back all other considerations is fully justified. I see that not only in Siegmund's outlook, but also in that of Arthur [Arnold]. Initially, he agreed completely with me and O[tto] W[els] but has started to vacillate. The people from over there will, of course, initially see the continuation of the work as decisive, especially since they cannot see in full measure the full impact of the baiting that will set in afterward. In addition, there are all the misgivings that result from the émigrés' desperate situation and the conflicts among the political parties. Without a real re-organization of the leadership, after the new money flows there will be an atmosphere that makes me anxious and worried.

As I see in a letter from Luise, the business with Karl's article is still unresolved. He is a little mad at me for publishing his article in *N[euer] V[orwärts]* in two installments and for making numerous necessary cuts. I spoke with Arthur about Richard Neumann. There is no clear answer from him. I don't know anything about his publishing intentions. At the moment, he is busy with Sturmthal's manuscript, but it is not clear if he will publish it before Christmas together with Karl's manuscript, which is not yet type set.

Arthur finds the Stalin book appealing. As we spoke recently, F[riedrich] St[ampfer] offered to translate it. When he made the attempt, he stumbled on the first line. Even a dictionary couldn't help him get on his feet. My conclusion: not 61 but 122 [years old]! That is why you need to just take a look at his correspondence. Also, read the mailbox-notice in the last issue of the *Weltbühne*. Dirty but uncomfortable.

For the Nuremberg article, to whom do we pay the honorarium and how much?

Best,
 [Paul]

Zürich, October 25, 1935

Dear Paul,

I am very troubled that the letter I sent you from Paris on 17 October has not arrived. In it I provided a report about the discussions with Münzenberg to be passed along to the comrades. Please tell Wels that I mailed off the report *immediately*. Today I am enclosing another and hope that I did not forget anything in spite of the time interval. My perspective emerges from the report. The Congress of the Comm[unist] Internation[al] marks the complete intellectual capitulation of the Comm[unists].[183] The situation must be exploited to the advantage of Social Democracy. One should not rebuild the prestige of the Communists by remaining silent about the capitulation and rehabilitating them by means of the united front. An energetic tactic on our side, within an international framework, could probably achieve not only the Communists' unconditional espousal of democracy, but also the liquidation of the small Communist Parties in the western countries and thereby make negotiations with the Communist International feasible for the first time. Unfortunately,

---

183 The Seventh World Congress of the Communist International met from 25 July to 30 August in Moscow. Its most important decision was to endorse the formation of a "popular front" of Communist and non-Communist forces against the growing threat of fascism. This approach reversed the position of the Sixth World Congress of 1928 which had announced the coming of a "third period" of intensified class warfare and capitalism's impending collapse. It also asserted that Social Democrats were "social fascists" whose organizations needed to be destroyed, a strategy that proved catastrophic as fascism grew stronger across Europe.

that is not understood on the left or on the right. On the left one proceeds to support Moscow's foreign and domestic policies; on the right one wants to prevent any discussion at all. As for us, in any case for the moment, I would not go beyond the declaration of a truce.

The second part of the letter concerned the Stalin translation. I will write to Rose today and ask that she rewrite the substantive content of the letter and send it to you. I am asking you, however, to consider yourself as our trustee, so to speak, in this matter. I know that only a fraction can be paid of what used to be expected for the translation. But we are dealing here with a difficult and large-scale work. Rose has received the rights to the translation from Souvarine and his publisher, Plon. Naturally, in this matter I am guided solely by political considerations, but I'm more convinced than ever of the necessity of the translation, and I have, by the way, heard the same opinion from others, such as Denike [sic]. I think considerable sales in Germany are possible. Therefore, the publishing house has to be camouflaged. A joint edition with another publisher (Opprecht?) could also be considered.

If I undertake them, Souvarine would agree to some cuts and is prepared to add an up-to-date conclusion on the most recent developments. In order not to lose any time, Rose has already started with the translations and requests that matters proceed as quickly as possible. She'll write to you about the rest herself.

I spoke with Bernhard and comrade Kroner (?) about the Miles shit, to use Marxist language. From her description I am not very convinced that Menz only wants his organization to continue in order to have an effective point of departure in democratic countries. That he has a secret program, etc., sounds not only rather implausible but quite fantastic. Moreover, my impression is strengthened that the effectiveness [of the organization] is very limited. In any case, I'd like to know, finally, what you think about it.

Denike [sic] is at the end of his resources. Crum[menerl] seems to have offered him certain prospects, but not followed through. In any case, Den[ike] is now in Paris looking for some way to make a living, but the prospects are not great. Do you know whether there is anything that can be done?

Meanwhile, you've received the memorandum by Nikolajewski. What he says about the scholarly side of the matter is, by and large, in keeping with my view. The politics are more difficult, and it is doubtful whether Nikolajewski's suggested way out will suffice. But the problem remains: what should happen when the resources have run out and the issue is raised about the continuation of illegal work? Without money we are thrown back into the situation of the Italians and the Mensheviks. It is also questionable, whether *then* a more advantageous arrangement would be possible. Breitscheid is passionately against the sale, but I believe mainly because [he thinks] the Party Executive, which stole the Sender letters,[184] should not come into possession of such large sums. But that is not a point of view. With others, such as Fritz [Adler], Otto B[auer], and Denike, I encountered more minor concerns. All this is confidential, but write to me about it, please, and not as you have recently with only short blurbs.

Regarding the *Zeitschrift*, I'll have read the manuscripts by the beginning of next week. I've commissioned articles from Thormann, Schifrin, Wendel, and Breitscheid. Whether and when I'll receive something is doubtful. – The last [*Neuer*] *Vörwarts* is beneath all criticism. In this situation there is nothing about foreign policy, nothing serious about Germany!

Best regards .... reply quickly, to Rose as well.
Your,
Rudolf

Discussions in Paris

I had two discussions with [Willi] Mü[nzenberg], the first on 15 October and the second on 21 October. The latter was pretty short and, when compared with the first, was mainly supplemental.

Mü[nzenberg], who also had learned about the content of the discussions between Schiff and Wels last Monday, initially asserted that the Communist International intended to have official negotiations with the Sopade in Prague. Ulbricht[185] and Dahlem[186] were proposed as representatives. They would talk

---

184   According to Breitscheid's biographer, Peter Pistorius, in January 1935 Toni Sender, a prominent left-wing Social Democrat, left her correspondence with Siegfried Aufhäuser and Karl Böchel with a comrade for safekeeping while she traveled in the United States. This comrade, whose identity is unclear, supported Otto Wels against the left in the Sopade and he or she photographed the letters and sent them to Wels, who then used them against his opponents in the factional infighting. See Pistorius (1970), pp. 353–54; Hild-Berg (1994), p. 170.

185   Walter Ulbricht (1893–1973) joined the SPD in 1912, the USPD in 1917, and the KPD in 1920. After working as a KPD organizer, he moved to Moscow in 1923 to serve in the Comintern's Executive Committee. Returning to Germany in 1925, he was elected to the Reichstag from 1928–33 and joined the KPD's Politburo in 1929. In exile after 1933, he represented the KPD in Paris and in Prague before returning to Moscow in 1938. After 1945 he became the most important leader of the German Democratic Republic until forced from power in 1971.

186   Franz Dahlem (1892–1981) was a member of the KPD's Politburo and Secretary of the Central Committee. From 1928–33 he was also a member of the Reichstag. After 1933 he served the KPD in in Czechoslovakia, France, Spain, and the Soviet Union. Arrested in France in 1942, he was sent to the Mauthausen concentration camp. He later became a leading figure in the German Democratic Republic.

about a joint declaration against the danger of war and German rearmament., about the necessity of the struggle for the achievement of democracy, and about the possible organization of an association for mutual aid, perhaps along the lines of Red Aid, a project about which Hertz had already been informed. He himself thinks it most important to make a statement declaring a truce. That would be consistent with the establishment of an actual relationship. Then, [even] if attacks on Social Democracy still occur occasionally in the illegal press, they would certainly soon cease entirely. I am familiar with the draft he worked on with Schiff, which could be enhanced. It would be useful preliminary work if I worked on a revised draft together with him.

In his opinion, the second [most important thing] would be a joint declaration on the struggle for democratic rights. He showed me an article in the *Rote Fahne* [*Red Flag*] (reprinted in *Gegenangriff* [*Counterattack*]) about the possibility of a mutually agreed upon action program. It would demand democratic rights, beginning with freedom of assembly and freedom of association, and include free local elections. Mü[nzenberg] added that it must also demand the creation of a parliament, preceded by the calling of a National Assembly to write a constitution. The agreements on the truce and the fight for democracy seem more important to him than declarations against war.

It is natural that, after 16 years of bitter struggle, the Communist proposals met with the greatest mistrust. But in his opinion, Otto Bauer, in the last issue of the *Kampf*, had correctly put forward the causes that had determined a change in Moscow's attitude in the interests of its foreign policy. The reasons were so forceful that one should not doubt Moscow's interest in the reestablishment and maintenance of democracy. Therefore, the desire to reestablish the unity of the workers' movement is not a simple maneuver. The fight against fascism also requires allies beyond the working class.

I told him that, basically, I am not in any way authorized to engage in negotiations, but instead I simply wish to inform myself personally. Therefore, I don't want to work with him on recommendations for negotiations – that is a matter for official negotiators. My personal standpoint is as follows: that the change in the Communist standpoint is a result of the pressure Moscow feels in its foreign policy. In that respect, Bauer is right. The mistrust exists, however, not only in our ranks and in the working class in general, but far beyond in strata which could be of great importance in the fight against Hitler. And one has to be attentive to that when considering German conditions, which in their current state exclude applying the popular front model developed in France. In regard to the question of a "united front", matters are very clear especially for the countries, particularly for Germany, where operations are underground. The fundamental condition for the German movement must be its total autonomy.

It would be impossible that the German underground movement would receive its slogans, etc., from Moscow in accordance with the needs of Moscow's foreign policy. In any case, I could imagine, instead, an "organic unity", of course with full autonomy from Moscow, as a "united front". Furthermore, agreements about real actions, which thus far in Germany have not seemed possible, are impossible under current conditions. I don't have any major concerns about a declaration of a truce. In regard to a declaration on the struggle for democracy, I have strong inhibitions about a joint statement. One has to reckon with the mistrust that is awakened by the Communists' change of heart. Our position would not be strengthened and that would damage the cause. As a first step I think it would be more practical if the KPD issued a declaration for the fight for democracy. We could then issue an agreed upon, parallel one. That, next to the declaration of a truce – which, however, should not preclude a principled, substantive discussion, would be enough with which to start.

Mü[nzenberg] was not very pleased by these limitations, but I had the impression that one should not step beyond this line, and that the comrades, who seemed extraordinarily pliable, would be satisfied with that, at least initially. Such a process, however, would be a considerable relief for us also in our relations to various [other] groups, which is why I would not reject the planned conversations in Prague from the outset.

The other part of the discussions revolved around the committees and the Popular Front game in Paris. I asserted as strongly as possible that these things are just damaging. It would be important if a bourgeois opposition formed and maintained a center abroad. But that must be accomplished completely independently by bourgeois representatives, not outsiders, who would really be viewed as such in Germany. It would only create more support for Hitler if a bourgeois opposition is created "under the overt protection of Moscow". Mü[zenberg] appeared to understand that very clearly as did Schwarzschild and Bernhard, to whom I said the same thing. In any case, I think that our participation is useless and would compromise us. Denike, who is broke and came to Paris looking for a means of making a living, told me that he was initially in favor of our participation in order not to abandon the field to Mü[nzenberg]. It would be important to have a hand in the game in order to influence international public opinion and to influence intellectuals. These things are scarcely important for Germany, but they are significant for foreign countries. I was skeptical about this view, because we lack the necessary means and people. Breitscheid is for deciding on a case to case basis, in so far as it concerns certain international matters such as the prevention of the Olympics and the agreement for a truce.

From the Mü[nzenberg] discussion it is also interesting [to note] that he thinks our cadre – for the moment – are stronger than theirs, but the mood among the workers is now more inclined toward the Communists.

To summarize I'd like to say: no rejection of negotiations from the outset; possible declaration of a truce stipulating the struggle for democracy, but no joint declaration beyond that, no "united front", and no application of the "popular front" tactic to Germany.

There was a major difference of opinion in Paris regarding the international situation. While one side expects the Abyssinian conflict to soon be set aside, many competent observers are skeptical and don't believe that England is happy to compromise and come to an agreement. Meanwhile, French popular sentiment is unanimously opposed to war and I have the impression that the left would damage itself severely with the demand for military sanctions. Perhaps to some extent it has already done so.

The domestic situation is confused. The Popular Front doesn't yet have a unified program and it has no real leader. It could bring down Laval,[187] but it fears taking power, especially if it cannot immediately dissolve [parliament]. Nevertheless, the elections themselves will strengthen the left unless something unexpected happens between now and then. The country is really radical in the sense of the Radical Socialist mystique! Under these conditions the possibility remains that Laval's government could continue, or perhaps a transitional government under Herriot. Matters will be clearer following the Radical Socialist Party Congress.

Fritz Adler was in Paris. I had an appointment with him, but he had to cancel at the last minute. As Breitscheid told me, the conversation with Brouckeres and [Marcel] Cachin[188] was only of an informational nature. The Communists intend to invite Adler and Brouckeres to Moscow for a discussion with Dimitrov.[189]

---

187 Pierre Laval (1883–1945) began a long political career as a socialist lawyer prior to the First World War. Elected to parliament in 1914, he left the SFIO after his defeat in 1919 and moved steadily rightward. During the 1920s he was reelected to parliament and then to the Senate and served in a variety of ministerial posts first as an independent and then as a conservative. He served as Prime Minister three times. His last term was under the pro-fascist Vichy regime headed by Philippe Petain.

188 Marcel Cachin (1869–1958), cofounder of the French Communist Party, was a member of parliament from 1914–35 and a Senator from 1935–40. Chief editor of the Communist flagship paper L'Humanité.

189 Georgi Dimitrov (1889–1949) was a Bulgarian trade unionist and Social Democrat who held a seat in parliament from 1913–1923. He joined the Bulgarian Communist Party, made a career in the Communist International, and became its General Secretary in 1935. Arrested in Germany following the Reichstag fire of February 1933, his acquittal at the subsequent trial made him a figure of international renown.

Prague, October 30, 1935

Dear Rudolf,

I received your registered letter of 26 October. You've probably received my short letter and the registered packet of manuscripts. I have not yet received your letter of 17 October from Paris. Did you address it to my apartment or the office? This is the second letter that did not reach me. The first was a letter from Hilde in London at the beginning of October.

I have circulated the outline of the Paris discussions. I can't say anything yet about the impression it has made on the others. We have not yet had a meeting, and there are ever fewer personal conversations on such matters. For the most part, I agree with your views. You can see that in the most recent issue of S[ozialistische] A[ktion], which had already been prepared beforehand. The first article about the united front rests on the approaches contained in the "First Commentary" by Fritz Adler, distributed in Brussels. Like you, I also view the liquidation of the Communist Parties in the western countries as the most important prerequisite if the Russians really are serious with the whole campaign. The second article, written by Sering, draws the consequences for Germany. His main assertion is: what is the point of unity of action if there are no actions? Not action, but organization, is the main task right now.

In this context, first a frank word about Mü[nzenberg's] remark that our cadre are stronger their theirs, but the mood among the workers inclines toward the Communists. I hear the last point from many directions, but only in the last few months has it been more pronounced. It seems to me, therefore, to be an effect of the improving economic conditions in Russia and also an effect of the congress of the Comintern. It is said virtually unanimously that the fear of listening to Radio Moscow has evaporated. The effect of this propaganda is increasing a lot. But, in regard to Mü[nzenberg's] first assertion, it seems to me that hidden behind it is the intention of saying something pleasing to Prague. Of course, it is extraordinarily difficult for me to ascertain objective clues about the strength of the Communist movement in Germany. But when I consider the enormous number of trials, at which hundreds of accused appear who are accused of being associated with the Communist Party; when I read the official announcements, in which Communist leaflets in Germany are confiscated and printers are closed for producing them, then those are facts to which one must pay attention. Even if one does not think much of them, and if one does not want to draw conclusions about how the two sides compare in strength, it is still true that the Communists are engaged in unmatched levels of daily activity. From information I receive from people involved with "Red Aid", who have frequently sought me out recently, and which I view as accurate, I see what enormous resources are flowing to Germany. According to this information, the Communists spend as much for support in Germany alone as we do both at home and abroad.

After all that I personally have the impression that the Communists are substantially stronger than us. You know that I am always extraordinarily suspicious of the assertions of our people. I find that my skepticism has not gone far enough. Since the conflict with A[ufhäuser] and B[öchel], we have lost virtually all of our connections in western Saxony and central Germany as well as Thüringen. We are completely cut off from Berlin. Subsequently, the statements by the Miles people about spies proved to be 100 per cent correct. (This remains very confidential!) Since the arrests, the connections with Hamburg, etc. have been very few. I fear that I have to say the same is true for the Rhineland and for a part of southern Germany. To be sure, the three people, Sh., F., and R., report on the heavy blows but don't want to draw the consequences.

I recently had a conversation with Camille H[uysmans], who is certainly an unsuspicious and sympathetic witness.[190] He knew quite a bit about the Communists' work and had witnessed some of it. He has not heard anything about our work for over a year. Since the arrest of one of our men who had occasionally sought him out, he was so completely cut off that he remained in the dark about the actual fact of this man's arrest. I have to write to you so openly about these facts, because they are equally important for evaluating another complex situation, which I'll discuss later.

I agree with your conclusion: no absolute rejection of negotiations, a truce, a declaration for democracy, but separate and each one independent of the other. On the other hand, I am more inclined to Breitscheid's view in regard to action in Paris. It is also my view that these matters are of no importance for Germany. But it is tremendously important for foreign countries that we attempt to break through the intellectual encirclement in which we find ourselves, if it is possible without unbearable concessions. Therefore, I would also prefer making decisions on a case by case basis, especially if one can bring the initiators to the point where they limit themselves to practical actions, such as the struggle to block the Olympics.

I'd hoped that W[illi] Mü[ller] would speak to you in Brussels. Then you probably would have had a different impression than via the discussions with

---

190 Camille Huysmans (1871–1968), Secretary of the Belgian Workers' Party and, from 1905–1922, Secretary of the Second International. From 1931–40 he served in the LSI Executive Committee and was its last chairman in 1940. After exile in Britain, he became Prime Minister of Belgium in 1946.

Bernhard, etc. You might remember that I've always stressed that the numerical effectiveness of the Miles group should not be overestimated. Over the past year, a change seemed to occur. Since I've been maintaining a connection to W[illi] Mü[ller], I knew that his conceptions about organizational methods had changed. What I've learned here about practical connections confirms this impression. There is no question that the connections W[illi] Mü[ller] had to Berlin and the Rhineland were far more numerous and were better than those of the Sopade. I've often received reports from him that come to us via some other route and only arrive here weeks later. At the moment that is no longer the case. The arrests, which don't have any connection with the organizational conflict, the causes of which go back quite far, have been very destructive. But as you have seen from my description above, the numerical significance has been overestimated everywhere. This point cannot be used for an assessment.

Menz is here again. I won't get to talk to him, however, until tomorrow. But, meanwhile, I've talked with Paulsen,[191] who is now staying here for a while, and that has enabled me to round off my judgement. Especially after the testimony by Paulsen, who, together with Menz signed the disclaimer of 28 June, it is certain that Menz had really maintained the theoretical conceptions for which W[illi] Mü[ller] reproached him [such as] the formation of narrow circles, and of organization only for the sake of appearances for the democratic countries. To that extent, W[illi] Mü[ller] would be fully justified. By the way, that was also my opinion when I made the attempt to bring both of them into a discussion about their differences in my presence. W[illi] Mü[ller] was ready, but Menz refused without providing any reasons and finally left soon afterward for reasons that were not really very convincing. With that it was not yet said whether it was necessary and expedient to hold this debate about theory or fundamental principles internally, even if the price was a split. After the initial conversations with Menz, I had already told W[illi] Mü[ller] very clearly that on this point I inclined more toward the view of Menz and Magold that one should not go through with the discussion. W[illi] Mü[ller] objected that this was out of his hands. Menz's plans had become public and led to great indignation and counteractions. To be sure, Paulsen claims that the basic difference of opinion was still without practical effect, and that the elimination of the differences would have been possible via other approaches, since it had already been decided to transfer a part of the domestic headquarters. Both statements may be right. Since, according to Paulsen's statements everything was initially for W[illi] Mü[ller], except for the leadership – only later did the power rela-

---

191   Paulsen was a Neu Beginnen activist.

tions change – I'd like to assume that W[illi] Mü[ller] has been pushed to his action from below. In spite of everything, he was unable to lead the counterthrust as long as the practical realization of the new theoretical intentions had not begun.

I judged that part of the events that I witnessed myself very differently. Once things over there [in Germany] had been decided in W[illi] Mü[ller's] favor, there was and is no reason to continue the dispute abroad and to make use of the Sopade's help. The struggle among the groups does not interest the Sopade from the standpoint of ending it in the interest of the whole movement, but rather only to draw advantages from it. If Menz declares today that his line was always one of cooperation with the Sopade, while W[illi] Mü[ller] wanted to more strongly safeguard the special existence of the group, my own experience stands in the way as do the basic outlooks of both people. Menz stresses that he completely supports New Beginnen's old program. W[illi] Mü[ller] has made basic changes, which make clear in practice his substantial movement in the direction of our conceptions and methods of work. To be sure, I don't know W[illi] Mü[ller's] final intentions and motives. But, nevertheless, I assume that he has learned from earlier mistakes and in the meantime has realized that, if one is weak, an agreement is better than endless struggle.

Regarding the expediency of W[illi] Mü[ller's] approach, one can certainly have doubts. Paulsen, too, thinks he is too flexible and conspirative. But he thinks he is absolutely honest, smart, agile, and courageous. He ascribes attributes to him which are especially important at just this moment. Therefore, I see no reason to change my behavior toward him. Nevertheless, I won't give up trying to bring him and Menz together. This is because, as I was a year and a day ago, I am today still of the opinion that the Miles group is called to take on important tasks due to its good methods of work and the quality of its people.

Nikolajewski's plan to create an international research center is not bad. It is certainly suited to reducing scholarly misgivings, but the political ones remain. I still regard it as impossible for us to do business with the Russians if one thinks that any political contact with them to be dangerous, especially for political development in Germany. In addition, I still fear that this business won't stay secret, and it would be a terrible weapon in the hands of the regime against the underground. Above all, I fear the moral damages. Both at home and abroad, this money will widen the gap between the leadership and its supporters. That is unavoidable when a leadership doesn't stand high above such attacks. Unfortunately, we see every day that the opposite is the case. You can already discern from these remarks that my earlier outlook has not changed. I won't try to hide that I not only understand Breitscheid's concerns, but in large part share them. It is certainly an insidious question: What should happen when the money runs out? But we will always face this question. And as little as I underestimate how important it can be that one can work again for two or three years without being bothered by material concerns, it seems to me that the most decisive thing is what kind of work and by whom? My fear that, with its current methods, the Sopade is not in a position to create a long-term foundation has not been reduced but rather has increased. Therefore, the bottom line for our support for the financial deal concerning the P[arty] A[rchive] would have to be tied to the reorganization of our political [structure] and personnel. That F[ritz] A[dler] and O[tto] B[auer] have fewer concerns I've also heard from the latter in person. Still, he conceded that my objections are weighty and require attention. Nikolajewski's offer to come to Prague for personal conversations was accepted. We expect him any day.

I'll write to you about Denicke and the *Zeitschrift*. Of course, on the matter of the translation I regard myself as the trustee for you and Rose. By the way, the others have fewer misgivings than I do. It seems to me that, based just your description of the book's content, it is practically out of the question that Graphia can undertake the thing.

Best wishes, from Hanna, too.
  Your,
  [Paul]

Prague, November 5, 1935

Dear Rudolf,

I hope that, in the meantime, you've received my letter of 31 October. I am just getting to the dictation of the follow up letter because I had to transcribe some important documents, which I've enclosed with today's letter.

The first is a letter from Reinbold. It is superfluous for me to give you my opinion of its content. I don't intend to answer this letter. One cannot combat anti-Semitism with arguments. It is the same with Nazi thinking. From comments made by Stampfer and Cummenerl – others haven't expressed their views to me – I take it that this letter is also very unpleasant for you. Stampfer wanted to make it the object of a confrontation, but he seems to have given up the idea, as has Cru[mmenerl], who originally announced that he would tell R[einbold] what he thought in writing. I don't intend to demand that a position be taken on this letter. Even harder to take, however, is the fact that I simultaneously got a letter from Sollmann, in which – with the exception of the anti-Semitic vulgarities – he is thinking along similar lines as Reinbold. I think it would not be unjust to view Sollmann as the originator of this whole line of thinking. My reply to him will leave nothing to be desired in terms of clarity. Please take a look the *Basler National-Zeitung*, number 501 on 1 November. This article, too, is surely by S[ollmann]. By the way, I doubt even less today than at the time that S[ollmann] is also the author of the article on Marxism in the *N[euer] Z[üricher] Z[eitung]*. I know W[ilhelm] S[ollmann] better than you.

The second document is an excerpt from a very long report sent to us by the man from the north, who has maintained a connection with the military for two years and who was the main bearer of the illusions about the Reichswehr. In transmitting the content of the report, I don't know if I've succeeded in conveying the catastrophic impression which the hopelessness of the Reichswehr had made on the reporter – and also on me as I read the report. In short, the report is a singular confirmation that total peace reigns between the regime and the Reichswehr.

Arthur [Arnold] has received a letter from Rose. I know neither the content nor Arthur's opinion. At the moment, I cannot do anything regarding this matter.

The information from you about Denicke's situation has saddened me greatly. I don't know anything about promises that Cru[mmenerl] might have made. I've never heard that he had spoken with him. By the way, in Zürich we won the first round of our lawsuit with a splendid finding in our favor. The *Volksstimme* wants to appeal. But at the suggestion of our lawyer, their acceptance will be subject to a deposit of 3000 Swiss francs. However, the outlook for the second round remains favorable. It would not be out of the question that something could be done for the Saar people with the resources procured in this way. We have a promise along these lines. Cru[mmenerl] wants to hold to [the promise] as well.

Regarding the *Zeitschrift* I also have to have a thorough answer soon. I assume that you concur that we should do a double issue this time, which appears at the beginning of December. But we must stick to this deadline if we want to start the new year at least somewhat on time. Now that I see that double issues are much harder to sell than single issues, I also have the goal of publishing as many single issues as possible.

I'm also enclosing here an article by Carwy and one by Worker. I've already responded to Carwy that reprinting his article, which has already appeared in the *Russischen Bote* [*Russian Messenger*] cannot be considered. If you agree, then you need neither to answer him nor to send back the manuscript. I have not yet expressed myself on Worker's article. If it contains some correct ideas,

I still think it is much too broad and also says a lot that does not belong in the *Zeitschrift*. You will have to answer the letter form W[orker]. One should not yet abandon as hopeless the attempt to teach him and to bring him around. What about the other articles by Puls, Friedrich, etc.? Puls was recently here and said he was astounded that you had not yet written to him about the reviews (Moszkowska, Niekisch).

You received [Konrad] Heiden's Hitler book from Oprecht. We will have to review it in the next issue. Who should do the review? It must be a review that attempts to compare our view with that of Heiden's notion of the "victory of the declassed". In my view it would be best if you undertook the review yourself. If you don't intend to do that, write to me, please, about whether I should draw on Sering. I'll review the book by Seger myself. Who should review the book by Hallgarten? By the way, we have a series of reviews beyond our available space.

I have the same opinion about *NV*. But I've cured myself of the habit of talking to anyone about it, because no one seems to share my opinion. In contrast, Stampfer recently expressed his clear dissatisfaction with the *SA*.

Nikolajewski says he is coming tomorrow. If he does not stop to see you on the way, I'll urge him to do so on the way back. I got a long letter from Breitscheid with a report about the discussion with Münzenberg. Basic tendency: The same as yours.

Best wishes,
 [Paul]

Prague, November 9, 1935

Dear Rudolf,

Hopefully, you'll soon answer my letters of 31 October and 5 November.

In the meantime, the following has occurred: a few days ago Walter (Ulbricht) appeared at my apartment to talk with me. Since I wasn't home, he said he'd call me the next day. I informed the Executive at its meeting that Ulbricht wanted to talk to me, and said I'd only speak to him if it was in accordance with the wishes of the committee. O[tto] W[els] immediately rejected having any such desire. Stampfer said I could talk with anyone with whom I had an interest in speaking. I insisted that I would refuse to talk with Ulbricht if the Executive did not make very clear that it regarded this discussion was expedient and that, later on, no partisan political consequences would be drawn from such a meeting. Since W[els] bluntly rejected any statement along these lines,

I drew the consequences and told Ulbricht on the phone that I would not have a conversation with him.

You'll be surprised that I made my action so dependent upon the attitude of the Party Executive, but I did that for well-considered reasons. I want to avoid any appearance of having a political discussion with the Communists behind the Executive's back, indeed, not only because that could give rise to awkward discussions, but also because it damages the cause. If the Communists want to reach a substantive agreement with the Sopade, as Münzenberg told you and Breitscheid, then there is only one road: open discussion with the Sopade. But the Communists are not there yet. In its last issue, on page one, in capital letters, *Gegenangriff* [*Counterattack*] published an open letter to me in which an attempt was made in the old manner to take partisan political advantage of the substantive differences of opinion within the Sopade. In the last issue of the *Weltbühne*, Walter Ulbricht wrote an article that, to be sure, did not offer any particular grounds for attack, but also was not very expedient if one wants to have sincere and confidential negotiations. These two articles in the press strengthened my view that private negotiations between Ulbricht and me could only do damage.

I'm providing all these details about the facts, because I fear that incorrect conclusions about the Sopade's attitude and also my personal attitude will be drawn from them. If you get the chance to speak to Münzenberg or someone else, then you know in any case what happened between me and Ulbricht.

As I already wrote to you, I've been circulating your outline of the discussion in Paris. Although, in the meantime, we've had several meetings of the Executive, the issue of the "united front" did not come up for discussion. From some brief comments by O[tto] W[els], I gather that he is not inclined to have any sort of discussions with the Communists, a view with which Stampfer seemingly does not agree. Thus far I have remained very reticent, because the steps that Münzenberg had proposed to you and Breitscheid had not been taken. Today a letter arrived from Emil Kirschmann reporting that on 21 November a second discussion on the popular front will take place, and that he urgently recommended that we participate. As long as this private letter is all we have, naturally no position will be taken on this second conference. I also don't regret that, because on this point – the people's front – I am in full agreement with you and Breitscheid, who wrote to me in the meantime about his conversation with Münzenberg.

Best wishes,
  [Paul]

Zürich, November 16, 1935

Dear Paul,

I've received your letters. Forgive me for not replying sooner and today I can't write fully as I originally intended. I've had a ton of stuff to take care of. First, I'd like to ask you to send me the honorarium for the article about the Nuremberg Party Congress in the *Zeitschrift*, plus the article "Deutsches Recht und Deutsche Richter" ["German Law and German Judges"] in number 123 of [*Neuer*] *Vorwärts* on 20 October, so that I can give it to the author. I've sent the articles by Sering and Karl K[autsky] to the printer; I have a very good (lead) article by [Karl] Henriksen about German power relations, which I'll soon be sending in, and I expect another one from Breitscheid about German-French relations (possibilities of negotiation, etc.) and possibly from Schifrin on foreign policy and Polish military strength. Sering's article is too long and difficult, but I could not cut it because I don't know where its thrust actually lies. He undercuts himself with all-too-detailed detours that are not always necessary. I'll try my luck again when doing the corrections but talk to him about whether he could undertake cuts himself when reading the proofs. I find (but please don't tell him all this) that Henriksen basically says things much more clearly, more simply, and more correctly. But I'll make a judgement when I see the whole thing in context and have read it in print. I don't want him to know about these preliminary comments. In general, I'd like to ask you to not to pass along my summary judgements, which are meant for *you*. I now have the pleasure of arguing with the touchy Worker after you transmitted the "terrible nonsense" to him and that costs me a whole essay.

In regard to Karl, after a lot of difficulty I've cut out 5–6 pages of about 27 (?): on Stalin and on the united front, but the latter is again very vague, out of place, and non-psychological (this, too, is not to be passed along!). But, after all, Karl has the right to give his opinion.

I'm writing today mainly about the translation and the archive. You will have received Rose's letter. Nikol[ajewski] told me the translation would be done. I am not surprised at all about O[tto] Bauer's resistance, but I think it is all the more necessary. Even if one thinks that a certain change in our relationship to the Communists is indicated, advocacy of our basic principles is especially important and, above all, one must tell the truth.

I'm very curious about the further development of the archive business. In general, I agree with the procedure; caution is needed regarding the details. Those who all-too-conveniently are against Moscow should not get too much influence when forming the various committees. How much do people think I should be involved? Nik[olajewski] places great weight on that, but what does Prague think? Is it being considered whether I, perhaps with Crum[menerl] and Wels, should go to Paris soon, and what about you? Please write to me about this point right away.

Reinbold's expectoration is scandalous, but it is hard when there is no reply from Prague. In any case, I'll talk to Crum[menerl] about it. I'd be very happy if you came here soon yourself since there is so much to talk about. If the business with the archive turns into something and I, like Nikolajewski, would need to be there and involved from a scholarly standpoint, then I'd probably have to go to Paris for a while. By the way, that might become necessary, if the story there continues. I have no new information about the most recent discussions there. What do you know?

Enough for today. I'll write again soon. What is the final deadline for the journal? I have commissioned the articles that have not yet arrived for 22 November. I'd very much like to look at Hallgarten myself. I could let the author of the article on the Nuremberg Party Congress review the Heiden book.

Best regards and to Hanna and Else, too.
Your,
Rudolf

Prague, November 18, 1935

Dear Rudolf,

Today I received your letter of 16 [November]. However, I don't have time for a long reply. It is already late in the evening and I'm leaving tomorrow for Vienna. Yesterday I received an express letter from Luise [Kautsky]. I should come immediately. Karl is unhappy with the information from Nikol[ajewski] about the archive. In addition, they have now received an offer from Posthumus about which they must make a decision right away. Luise writes that Karl was very sick, had a high fever and is still really weak. If I conclude that there are no immediate concerns about his health, then I'll happily use the opportunity to get a breath of fresh air one more time.

I am still very dissatisfied regarding the archive issue. If the new plan mitigates the original concerns, enough still remain. Above all a double, political party concern. The more money that flows, the less utility will result from it. The war among the groups becomes eternal and the sterility of the apparatus wins. But above all the intellectual barriers to Moscow are broken. If the party Executive is paid by Moscow, where else should concerns about the Russian ruble arise? In the face of F[ritz] A[dler's] attitude, there is nothing left for me to do at the moment than to keep my misgivings about the new plan to myself. But I want you to know that they won't go away.

Concerning your participation, it seems that O[tto] W[els] thinks it is necessary both for the negotiations and for scholarly guidance later on. He doesn't place any value on me, on the contrary, he makes no secret of his desire to cut me out completely. If it comes to negotiations in Paris, one will surely call upon you to come. I don't at all value being involved in these negotiations with the Russians. I don't envy the responsibility that F[ritz] A[dler] bears if he brings about this agreement with the Russians. Perhaps then he will have simultaneously established a scholarly institute for the International and [dug] the German movement's grave, as its intellectual life dies out under the heavy weight of the party Executive's refilled money bags.

If you think that judgement is too hard and unjustified, then please remember that no one here found the letter from Reinbold scandalous. Expressions of indignation from Stampfer and Cru[mmenerl] only came from the concern that this letter could be put on their account. In reality, they never considered distancing themselves from its content. Under these circumstances, what is the point of your talking to Cru[mmenerl]? If these people don't feel the need to distance themselves from such an outlook, then this way of thinking cannot be all that foreign to them.

I really do need to speak with you. Every day I experience so much here that I don't accept that I can well imagine that one day my patience will come to an end. Today, for example, we dealt with a letter from the Communists that requested negotiations about a united front. O[tto] W[els] stuck with his opinion not to reply in the sole company of Max Klinger!!! Stampfer was for a written reply, which one could orally elucidate without getting involved in a long discussion. Cru[mmenerl] supported my view, that, to be sure, there could be no talk of a united front, but one must initiate friendly rather than hostile relations. Originally, we discussed appointing three negotiators. Through a trick, however, O[tto] W[els] was able to get just Stampfer and Vogel appointed, while declaring from the beginning that he opposed my appointment. This is how the hope for a full treasury reveals itself.

I showed the letter from Rose about the translation to Arthur [Arnold]. He told me that he'd replied, but I suspect that his answer was very diplomatic. The starting point at the meeting was the view that Graphia could not publish the book. Then Cru[mmenerl] recommended that, in the best case, 400–

500 Swiss francs could be spent for a translation that could then be sent to our own people in the form of typed copies. Arthur did not pass this suggestion along because he thinks it is too shabby. (That is just for you and Rose, however.)

I will talk to Sering. Hopefully, the article by Schifrin about Poland won't arrive. Birnbaum promised me to write about all the problems in the east. But we won't be able to consider that article until the January issue, at the earliest. I have a good article about Austria. It treats various books (Pertinax, etc.) and analyzes well the damage caused by the division [of the movement] into the Schutzbund (fighting) and party (non-fighting). I'll have the article type set. You can then raise objections. I'd like you to let me know as soon as you can, because of the other contributions (Körner, etc.) I'll send you Hallgarten. Please have the review of Heiden done there. We definitely have to have it, however, for this issue. The final deadline for the next issue should be 1 December.

After January we have to do single issues. I have no doubt at all that each double issue sets back our sales a lot. With double issues you can only get subscriptions, but they hardly sell as individual copies in the book shop. More on that later.

Best wishes. Hanna returns your greetings.
   Your,
   [Paul]

Prague, December 20, 1935

Dear Rudolf,

I wrote to you five weeks ago. You did not reply. Therefore, I don't understand why, as Breitscheid wrote to me, you "wonder [why] you don't hear anything from me". I am all the more astounded by this statement since, after all, everything important that has happened in recent weeks occurred where you were on the spot. Consequently, I'd assumed that you would keep me appraised about the course of the events in which you were involved and about which I have scarcely had an accurate, or at least no exhaustive, overview. Siegmund [Crummenerl] has been back for a few days and today he'll give a report. But in no way does that replace the direct knowledge of your evaluation. From the content of my last letter you can imagine how important your judgement is for me and my decisions.

I am sending you the new issue of the *Zeitschrift* today. You'll see that, with Sering's agreement, I have cut five pages from his article. The footnote in the Henrichsen article was included at Sering's request. He was initially astounded, to put it mildly, that the article appears at the same time as his series. I calmed him down and successfully made clear to him the difference in the form of representation, which undoubtedly speaks in Henrichsen's favor. I assumed your agreement with the footnote in Henrichsen's article, because it did not influence the article's impact. On the contrary, it points to Henrichsen's and Sering's agreement, which seems to me to be very useful in respect to Sering's petty and superficial critics. I thought that Henrichsen's article was really excellent. It is, without doubt, very effective and I am especially pleased that you did not strike his critical sentences about the past. I hope that you have a similarly favorable view of Sering's commentary, through which the article by Henrichsen is effectively supplemented according to the current page. I think his review of the book by Heoden is outstanding, so I am very satisfied with the content of this issue. You have to send me Henrichsen's address so that I can send him his money for the article.

With respect to the next edition, there are two issues. First: *from now on we have to do single issues*. We have not only lost individual subscribers because of the double issues, but primarily bookshops have cancelled their subscriptions because the double issues cannot be sold. I have Arthur [Arnold's] basic agreement that the typescript be changed in such a way that we can fit more on the page. But the enlargement of the space will be modest and won't amount to, at most, more than 15 per cent. So, instead of 1,500 we'll have about 1,700 lines.

Second: the following articles are available: F. Alsen, "Jakobinerlegende" ["Jacobin Legends"], 284 lines; Hans Seitner, "Faschistisches Österreich" ["Fascist Austria]", 341 lines; A. Schifrin, "Wohin treibt Polen?" ["Whither Poland?"], 434 lines.

Sering's new article, which should have programmatic content, will take up 500 lines. With that, along with the book reviews, our available space is exhausted. If Breitscheid writes the article that was agreed upon, then it has to appear in this issue. Have you considered that an article on Hitler's first three years would also be fitting for a New Year's issue? Don't you want to write that article yourself? If you signed that article, which I would welcome for other reasons, as you know, then this number would be just right for a propaganda action, which I've long had in mind. Perhaps you'll let me know what you think.

I find it troubling that I cannot answers questions from Worker, Friedländer, and Puls about the fate of their contributions. Under these circumstances, there will be nothing left but for me to make the decisions about articles sent here on my own.

Rose has not held it against me for not answering her letter of 9 November about Souvarine. But there was nothing else for me to write, since Arthur had already written.

My very best wishes and to Rose, too.
Your,
[Paul]

Paris, December 25, 1935

Dear Paul,

It makes no sense when you are sulky with me. It would have been much more prudent if, in the meantime, you'd urged me to reply. You probably would have gotten it much sooner. Sometimes, when it comes to writing, I am terribly inhibited.

Now, first, to the journal. Please see to it that Schifrin receives an offprint as soon as possible. Further, on my behalf, ask Bienstock if he would like to write an article on China and the repercussions for Russia, England, and America. I hope to soon get the article by Breitscheid and possibly another one by Henrichsen (perhaps about Hitler's first three years). Please send the honorarium for Henrichsen to Dr. Werner Thormann, Nogent sur Marne (Seine), 15 rue Bayine de Perreuse. Why can't I get the honorarium for the Nuremberg Party Congress article? I think it is right that you now do single issues. When is the editorial deadline?

Sering's articles are becoming a burden. The article by Henrichsen shows how clearly and effectively everything essential can be said without the clumsiness of Sering's style. I still don't know exactly where he wants to go. One can share Crummenerl's sentiments when he says that [Sering's article] "will exert little influence on the opinions of our people. Very little is said in a lot of words". Hopefully, we are approaching the conclusion, the shorter the better. The Henrichsen notation is not important.

Why Siegmund's report would be like a blow to the head for you is beyond me. You were familiar with the content and the aim of the negotiations. I assume that the negotiations will continue in January and lead to a positive result, even if it is very doubtful that we'll get the desired amount. I've never subscribed to the illusion that in the long run the sale would not be forthcoming. Like Otto B[auer] and Fritz [Adler], whose initiative led to the current negotiations, I have regarded the possibility of establishing a scholarly institute to be desirable. Naturally, my political misgivings are major, but for now I see no possibility of basic changes in Prague and it is still preferable to me that the organizational work be done there, rather than by the various groups. I am also pleased that you are being somewhat cautious in respect to the Miles people. Already the gossip is that Miles disposes over half of the S[ozialistische] A[ktion]. Of course, I know that's nonsense, but it could occasionally have unpleasant consequences. I respect Sering, even if I don't know how he will develop politically. In this respect he is, to me, too constructive and too doctrinaire and perhaps overestimates the economic to the detriment of the political. I can only repeat that, to me, freedom is the main issue and that, after the Bolshevik and other experiences, a change in the organization of the economy doesn't guarantee freedom, not by a long shot. As much as I am for attracting individual, able people, at the moment at least, I think little of the groups. The whole thing doesn't have much significance.

Except for the negotiations, there was nothing important here to report about to you. I spoke once with Münzenberg, who was very annoyed about the collapse of the negotiations in Prague and, in particular, about the clumsy actions of his people, to whom he ascribes the main guilt for the unfavorable result. That is also my opinion. And, furthermore, I have the impression, that in Moscow one is getting cold feet about the new tactic. I still don't think much of the united front. In France it unnecessarily led to a far-reaching capitulation to Communism, and in fascist countries there cannot be any united front but only a unified party. For completely different reasons the latter is true also for all of Western Europe, where it can only mean the liquidation of the Communist Parties. I have rejected a call to sign the protest against the execution of [Rudolf] Claus[192] with Breitscheid and Schiff. I won't protest with murderers against murder. In fact, totally infamous acts of terror against politically independent people and Mensheviks have recently come back onto the agenda in Russia which are in no way different from those in Germany. On the other hand, I would consider it right if the Prague leadership itself protested against the most recent judicial killings.

Arnold recently asked what should happen with Wickel's book. I remember that we discussed this at length. In any case, Graphia shouldn't undertake anything that would unnecessarily lose money. In the future perhaps these kinds of

---

192   Rudolf Claus was a Communist functionary of the Red Aid organization. Based in Berlin, in July 1935 he was arrested, charged with high treason, and sentenced to death. Breitscheid and Schiff joined with Münzenberg in an effort to circulate a petition protesting against his execution, which was carried out on 20 December. See Winkler (2007), p. 41.

brochures can be published by the new research institute. The essential ideas of the brochure can be expressed in the *Zeitschrift*. W[ickel], to whom I'd communicated that, then sent me the first article. Unfortunately, in this form it was scarcely ready for printing, but I myself have to write to him about it, which I'll do in the next few days. I spoke at length with Friedmann in Zürich. I'll write to Friedländer and Worker soon. Worker is a real calamity. His material is a mixture of correct and incorrect, and whole essays are required in response. In addition, the man is touchy and conceited and, by telling him what I think, you've made him really obstinate.

Rose is working, if at a slower pace, on the Stalin translation. I fear that a decision will only be made when the archive matter is further along. But I still think it is very important that something come of the thing. I believe that, with skillful camouflage in Germany, it not only won't be banned but will meet with strong sales.

A different chapter than that of the united front is the participation in such events as those of the International Association of Jurists or the Conference of Parliaments. On that I essentially share Breitscheid's view. We will lag behind, if we don't attend or rely on chance. I assume that you have been informed about these things by Breitscheid and will close now. Write soon and don't be annoyed if my reply is delayed. It really isn't intentional but results from a certain depressed mood, during which I don't like to say anything. I don't know if you wanted more or different questions answered, but I will happily catch up, if you raise them again.

Hopefully, you and Hanna have been able to relax a bit during the holidays. Our very best wishes and heartfelt New Year's greetings to both of you from both of us.

Your,
    Rudolf

[P.S.] Best regards to Else.

Prague, December 30, 1935

Dear Rudolf,

I have to put off an extensive reply to your [letter] of 25 December until next week, when I have the editing of the new number of *SA* behind me. Today I want to write to you about the *Zeitschrift*. Schifrin has already received an offprint of his article. I've spoken to Bienstock about the desired article on China. He came to me to offer an article on England, Italy, and France. But both articles depend upon whether we receive the articles by Breitscheid and Henrichsen. I think you should make effort to get these two articles. I would like to make the editorial deadline 10 January, so that the January issue comes out in January. So far, I've not received the article from Sering. If I don't get it in the first few days of January, I intend to defer it until the February issue, so that the January edition would appear as follows:

Henrichsen: "Drei Jahre Hitler" [Three Years of Hitler]
Breitscheid:
Schifrin: "Wohin treibt Polen?" [Whither Poland?]
Alsen: "Die Jakobinerlegende" [The Jacobin Legend]
Hans Seitner: "Faschistischer Österreich" [Fascist Austria]
and possibly some book reviews.

In order to maintain this program, I would like your reply as soon as possible about whether and when the two articles are expected from Breitscheid and Henrichsen. I am really supportive of an article by Henrichsen. If you don't get it on time for the January issue, then you will have to talk to Breitscheid about writing his article in such a way that I can place it first.

I've sent the honorarium to Henrichsen to the address you sent me.

The honorarium for the article by Richard Stichling will go to his Nuremberg address.

Best regards,
  [Paul]

Prague, January 3, 1936

Dear Rudolf,

I'm waiting for your decision on the next number of the *Zeitschrift*. Meanwhile, I have gently prepared Sering for the deferral of his article to the February issue if the articles from Henrichsen and Breitscheid arrive on time. Please see to it that the articles by B[reitscheid] and H[enrichsen] arrive at the printer as soon as possible and please note the enclosed letter to Graphia. We only gain a tenth more space through the new layout, but when you consider that, at that time, the typescript was only selected because one wanted to produce a smaller edition of the *Zeitschrift*, then this layout is not only necessary but expedient. In the future I ask that, with all future arrangements you note that our goal has to be to publish the issue at the beginning of each month. The editorial deadline, therefore, must always be between the twentieth and the twenty-fifth of the month before.

I want to tell you today that I intend to write an article for the February issue with the title "Selbstvertrauen, Solidarität, und Einheit" [Self-Confidence, Solidarity, and Unity]. It will be a discussion which, more than my article in the *Sozialdemokrat*, which I've enclosed, provides proof that self-confidence and solidarity, which for six decades were the foundation of the German workers' movement, have been lost, and that only their restoration will make political progress in Germany possible. You need to tell me your view when you get the article.

The reason for my letter today lies in the enclosed transcription of the letter by Dr. Demuth. Following my recommendation, the Executive has decided to ask you and Breitscheid to travel to Geneva and act there in accordance with the Dr. Demuth's suggestions.[193] To be sure, I have certain doubts about whether we will be able to achieve anything in Geneva. But, in any case, it cannot do any harm and since it is appropriate to place ourselves in the foreground again, then I'd like to ask you not to refuse our request. Please contact Breitscheid, who I'm also notifying, immediately. If you come to the conclusion that one of the two of you would be enough to accomplish the task, they you can make the decision about who should go.

I'll reply to your earlier letter as promised during the coming week. Meanwhile, the substantive differences here have become much sharper.

The enclosed outline is by Sollmann. In addition, for your personal information, I want to tell you that I've rejected a request from the *Weltbühne* to collaborate on an issue focused on Hitler's first three years. I've done the same with the A[rbeiter] I[illustrierte] Z[eitung].

Best regards,
 [Paul]

---

[193] Fritz Demuth (1876–1965) was a left-liberal economist and politician with the German Democratic Party during the Weimar Republic. He migrated to Switzerland in 1933 and founded the Emergency Committee of German Scholars Abroad. It is unclear why Hilferding and Breitscheid were asked to visit him.

Paris, January 3, 1936

Dear Paul,

I'll receive Henrichsen's article "Drei Jahre Hitler" [Three Years of Hitler] on Monday and the one from Breitscheid on Tuesday and I'll send both of them to Graphia right away with a note that you [should] receive the galleys. Thus, they'll be in Karlsbad on time on 9 [January]. If Bienstock has already written the article about England, he should definitely send it to me. In any case, however, please ask him to write the article about the Far East. He is a specialist in that area.

I am sending you two letters for Worker and Wickel. I'm turning the manuscripts over to you as office business. Perhaps you might read Worker's article and talk to him about it. I think the thing is too confusing to be published, but I'd like to have your opinion. And finally, the article by Friedrich. I must have overlooked it but, luckily, I came across it in a file. I don't really know what to do with it. In itself it is mediocre. If necessary, one could publish it, but I don't think that anyone would be very interested in it. That one has gone down the wrong track, psychologically, and that some so-called Marxists have done so much too one-sidedly and directly, is, of course, correct, but the point is to show this through the use of concrete events and not limit oneself to abstract proclamations of methodological principles. Now, I've always handled the poor guy badly and I'd really like him to have the floor just once. But this consideration is too subjective to be final and, therefore, I'd like to ask you to read the article yourself and to decide whether to return it to Friedrich. Wendel just telephoned to tell me that he will write an article about the new book by [Erich] Ludendorff about total war and a brief review of Leon Blum's remembrances of Dreyfus. Both contributions can only be considered for the February issue. Please ask Friedmann if he would like to revise the review about Moszkowska in the manner we discussed. I'd like to publish that review, but not [the one] about the Italian.

Now something else. For understandable reasons, Souvarine is becoming really impatient. His publisher, Plon, has an offer from the Frankfurt Societäts-druckerei and would like to accept it. Souvarine is not sure if he can prevent the acceptance, which would be highly uncomfortable for him if he cannot present a counteroffer. Naturally, I know that as long as the local business is not resolved, it is hard to make a decision. Nevertheless, it would very desirable if one could at least get a decision in principle. If I were in Zürich, then I would see if there might be a publisher there to which you possibly could sell a certain number of copies. But I'll probably be staying here for reasons that you will discern from the letter to Wels. But I'd like to urgently ask you to take up the issue, to speak with Arnold, and in any case get me an answer that I can use with Souvarine. [*Neuer*] *Vorwärts* did not publish my article, which I mailed from here on 21 December. It was registered and must have arrived. If it was not used, then I'd like to have the manuscript back for revisions. Please send the honorarium for the Nuremberg article here.

Best wishes to you and Hanna. From Rose, too.
Your,
Rudolf

[P.S.] Write soon.

Prague, January 9, 1936

Dear Rudolf,

I received your letter of 3 January plus the enclosures. I've forwarded the letter to O[tto] W[els]. I assume that he has replied to you. Since there still has been no news about the archive, the inclination to travel to the west solely on account of the LSI meeting seems minimal.

At the moment, there is nothing that can be done here on the Souvarine matter. To be sure, I've have spoken with Arthur [Arnold] about it, but any kind of opinion from him was not forthcoming. I suppose that is also not the case with the others as long as the whole finance problem is not cleared up. Consequently, I think it is neither in your interest nor in mine to do anything in this matter.

I spoke with Bienstock today. He'll deliver the article on England by early Saturday. Nevertheless, I was unable to promise him that the article will appear in this issue. That probably won't happen for reasons of space if the lengthy piece by Schifrin is included. I'd also like you to read Bienstock's article beforehand. I'll deal with the remaining issues with Worker, Wickel, Friedrich, Friedmann, etc. in accordance with your desires. I am in favor of accepting neither Worker's article nor Friedrich's. I'll write to you about it after I've spoken to them. What's up with the manuscript by Körner? He wrote a letter to me a few days ago in which he also discussed the article by Sollmann. In regard to his own article, he said it would only usable as an indirect reply to W[orker's], because it was intended as a lesson for W[orker]. It does not seem really suitable as an independent article. "The main goal of my brief note is to express my opinion to you about my own product and to free you of any hesitation that you might have to discard my article. If it instructed the young man, W[orker], as you indicated to me, then it would have fulfilled its aim".

This high-minded and modest approach is fully in keeping with Körner's character.[194]

In case you are also of the opinion that the article cannot be published, even if revised, then you must write a few lines to him. He certainly does not attach any importance to it. But, in my last conversation with him he made such a wonderful impression that I think it is very important to recognize the great effort he made in his elaboration through a brief note.

Best regards,
 [Paul]

[P.S.] The address is: Theodor Körner, Wien I, Mahlergasse 5.

Prague, January 14, 1936

Dear Rudolf,

I'm finally responding to your letter of 25 December. You are entirely correct that it makes no sense to sulk. But you have to understand the situation in which I find myself here, and how it affects me when I am out of contact with you. I have this feeling creeping up on me more and more that all my intellectual efforts here are in vain.

You don't understand [why] Siegmund [Crummenerl's] report was like a blow to the head for me. I was, after all, already familiar with its content and purpose. That's right. But you also know that I have not given up my original, negative standpoint and, in the face of the fact that I am completely isolated in my misgivings, I've merely dispensed with allowing my concerns to be discerned. I also refrain from doing that because I spoke to F[riedrich] A[dler] in great detail about how my concerns still could be taken into account.

---

194 Theodor Körner (1873–1957) had had a successful career as a military officer and as leading official in the Austrian military bureaucracy before joining the SDAP in 1924 and serving as a Viennse delegate to the Bundesrat and as an advisor to the Republican Schutzbund. Despite multiple arrests after 1934, he did not emigrate. After serving as Mayor of Vienna from 1945–51, he became Austria's first popularly elected President from 1951–57.

At this point I have to clarify an essential substantive difference that now exists between us. You see no possibility of changing things in Prague in any substantive way and, therefore, you still prefer the organizational work to be done there rather than by various groups. Unfortunately, as a result of my intimate knowledge of things, I have to contradict you on that. Organizationally, nothing is done here other than keeping the old apparatus busy with publishing newspapers and making reports. I won't say anything about the reporting. because, aside from costing money, it at least does no damage. The newspaper publishing lacks one decisive thing: it is disconnected with the selection of people, their training, and the conscious formation of new organizations. The Miles group, despite its divisions, has been able to achieve some things in that regard. I don't want to make any claims for the other groups. But I am not claiming at all that the work of the groups is exemplary or better than that of the party Executive. Something totally different is decisive for me. As long as the current fragmentation in the social democratic sphere continues, all the work is fruitless. Conflict among the groups consumes so much of their energy that there is nothing left for the other important tasks. These matters are still viewed totally differently in the Party Executive. One behaves as if one is alone in the world, as if all the [other] groups are insignificant and, consequently, there is no reason to attempt to work together.

Just look at the results of our work. Instead of bringing the forces together, which we designated as our task in the manifesto of January 1934, we have achieved fragmentation. In spite of the dominance of the money bag, a small group has started to gather around A[ufhäuser}, B[öchel], and S[eydewitz]. Instead of winning the emigrants to the Sopade, broad alienation and atomization has set in. Earlier, during our travels to Zürich, Amsterdam, etc. we had conferences with emigres. That has ceased. In Prague, where we once had leadership, we now have a wild struggle with suspicions, expulsions, etc.

At the border there is constant skirmishing between our people and the people around A[ufhäuser], B[öchel], and S[eydewitz], which also draws in the local [Czech] party and requires constant visits by E[rich] O[llenhauer] and H[ans] V[ogel]. In the bourgeois press reports on foreign rallies against Hitler we are less influential than we were earlier. And, finally, the most important thing: we have fewer connections over there [in Germany] and our work is less effective than earlier. Repeated efforts to create a domestic headquarters have failed and their fate sealed by two large trials before the People's Court and the Prussian Supreme Court. But everything abroad has also become more difficult. Among other things, the large number of arrests can be traced back to the fact that our people only slowly learn to protect themselves against the refined methods of the Gestapo.

I am not seeking to blame anyone personally for these realities. Under the prevailing conditions, many of these difficulties simply cannot be mastered. But you have to understand that it is important to draw conclusions from this. We have too little authority and too few forces to be able do the work alone and better. We also have too little money to be able to bear this costly fragmentation and the fraternal struggle. Since this realization will arrive here when it is too late, I was and remain of the opinion that the sale of a good, one that belongs to the whole party and not to any single current, is an appropriate occasion to redress the current shortcomings of the leadership. I blame you for having not yet recognized this situation and for doing nothing to support me. Without your help the new plan to raise money will not be realized. In this respect, you not only had far more reason, but also greater right, then F[ritz] A[dler] to get active. Instead, I heard straight from the mouth of Siegmund [Crummenerl] that one had watered down F[ritz] A[dler's] modest recommendation to divert ten per cent for special purposes. To combat this recommendation, Siegmund and Curt G[eyer], who, in taking his turn now really functions as his [Crummenerl's] wing man, dismissed it with the assertion that nevertheless not a penny could be used without the agreement of the party Executive. That is the real attitude.

Under these circumstances, my hope that new money will give rise to a new spirit and that new work will be undertaken with new aims, has reached its nadir. I must have really deceived myself to overcome my fear, that with new money an even greater intolerance would take hold.

I think as little of the united front with the KP [Communist Party] as you and O[tto] W[els]. But it is a fact that under fascism one-time Social Democrats and one-time Communists, who trust one another, are working together. It is nothing other than stupidity or stubbornness if one does not want to see that. Of course, there are old Social Democrats who only orient themselves on the past, because they count on the return of the past. I don't think a pact with the Communists is possible. Nevertheless, I have a different position on the whole issue than the party Executive. In regard to our people in Germany, I wish neither to force them to work with the Communists nor to forbid it. On the other hand, I think it necessary to outline the prerequisites under which cooperation is safe, so as not to let our people run willy-nilly into the arms of the Communists. And abroad a certain cooperation is necessary in respect to all the tasks that one cannot deal with alone. In this regard we agree. In contrast, here I find either active resistance or apathy when it comes to participation in all events in which the Communists are also involved.

If Münzenberg describes the behavior of his people as "clumsy", then he is only somewhat correct. They were so "clumsy" that they prevailed upon our representatives for a non-aggression pact, which is not foreseen in the memorandum, and caused Vogel to say that he was happy about the cooperation between our comrades in Germany, while the memorandum states the opposite. For me, the Communist representatives are not ideal. But they certainly don't bear the guilt for the failure of the negotiations. The failure resulted from our decision in the meeting of the Executive Committee, and it was affirmed in the selection of the negotiators. Before the selection of Stampfer and Vogel, Wels declared that anyone is fine with him as a representative, but under no circumstances would he accept me.

I have to frankly point out another difference of opinion between us, especially since it hurts me deeply and I fear that here that might be no compromise. You rejected the call to sign the protest against the execution of Klaus. If I'd been asked, I would have signed. I condemn terrorist acts in Russia against independents and Mensheviks just like you, but I cannot endorse your conclusions. When Communists protest with me against the death penalty for the crime of stating one's opinion, then, in the end, this protest works against them when they themselves carry out such actions. But I have to go another step further: you don't want to protest together with murderers against murder, although in this case that would only happen indirectly. But you have no misgivings to do business with murderers if it rests on a non-business basis. I've thought about this matter for a long time. Your position had me wracking my brains, but I still don't understand it. You can discern how much this tortures me from the fact that I am still struggling with myself about whether I can reconcile my convictions with being paid from an unappealing source.

Enclosed is the copy of a letter from Sering. I have no idea who stands behind this slander. O[tto] W[els] attacked me first, backed by Siegmund and Heine. But it was a defeat, which was underlined by the gruffness of Sering's reply. My personal relationship to Sering rests on my recognition of his ability. I don't have a close relationship to him. Over five months we've not grown closer. I know that your advice to be cautious in respect to the Miles people is well meant. But I base my political relations neither only on expediency nor on the accountant's pen. To say that Miles disposes over half of the *SA* leaves me completely cold. *I* dispose over the paper and there is not a line that I do not approve. In this regard nothing has changed, and it will not change. But, meanwhile, the measure of discomfort that some have about the content of the *SA* has given rise to wholly different slanders. There has not been an Executive Committee meeting for over a year in which *policy* or the meaning and unity of our work was discussed. Every conceivable kind of rubbish could be talked about. Now one is outraged about the article I wrote in the last issue of *SA*, "Einheit and Solidarität" ["Unity and Solidarity"]. For weeks Stampfer has had it in mind to introduce censorship to the paper. This bill was made without a host. I recognize intellectual authority. But no censor. My own feeling of responsibility and my sense of duty are my decisive guides. But I'll write to you about it, when the matter is over.

You can discern how wrong Crummenerl's low opinion of Sering is from the fact that we have marketed not only the 120 copies with Sering's article that the Miles people sold, but also, on average, an additional fifty copies. In that [number] I have not included the general increase – it is not very much – that has resulted from my own propaganda. And, I can tell you that just yesterday Emil Franzel[195] said that the *Zeitschrift* is now considerably better than the *Kampf*. Should one not combine the two? This conversation took place after Franzel had given a lecture on the fascist party, which had borrowed some material from Sering's train of thought. But I am also working on Sering to be more succinct and to finally come to his political conclusions.

Have you received my memorandum about the "International Congress on Criminal Law/International Assembly of Cities"? I am in contact with Wibaut, so that first there can be a meeting of the Social Democratic members of the Assembly in order to work out a unified position. Then I'd travel to the west.

Meanwhile, it appears that the prospects for the archive had not improved. I heard from Luise [Kautsky], in any case, that Nikolajewsky has written very pessimistically. By the way, what should be understood by Karl's announcement of a visit? Do you want to go to Vienna? I had no idea about your trip.

You were surely amazed, today, when you called. That is a nice illustration of the local methods of work and of the existing "relations of trust". The telegram arrived yesterday. Of course, one could not know that it was meant for me. But also no one asked. One assumed that it was somehow connected with a matter about which I should not be informed. Therefore, the phone call was reported with such secrecy that I only heard about if after it was over.

Reply soon. Best wishes, also from Hanna to Rose.
Your,
[Paul]

195　Emil Franzel (1901–1976) was a Sudeten German Social Democratic politician, historian and journalist.

Prague, January 15, 1936

Dear Rudolf,

The new issue of the *ZfS* is now being printed. I've included Henrichsen, Breitscheid, Schifrin, Seitner, and book reviews. I've had to shorten Schifrin and Seitner somewhat, but that made it possible to add more reviews, which I think are interesting. Among those is a review of Olden by Sering.

I did not include the review by Wendel. I have to say very openly that I don't like Wendel disguising himself in such a way that even the initiated cannot recognize him. Everyone abroad knows that he collaborates at *Tagebuch* and under which pseudonym. Here he submits a new pseudonym every couple of weeks so that nobody knows that he is associated with us.

Articles by Alsen and Bienstock are also still available for the new issue of the *ZfS*. Regarding the Bienstock article, in addition to your telegram, I'll expect to receive additional instructions about your intentions. I hope to receive the next article by Sering in a few days. You'll get it, before it is typeset. We still lack a political article to use as a lead. I'm grateful to you for the reviews, but I also can procure some here. I reject the Friedrich article. In my view, friendship alone is not a satisfactory reason to publish this article.

The letter from Sering was received here with silence. I ask that you tell me frankly, whether you see the matter as closed or whether you think that we should make inquiries with Mitnietsky, who is at *Pester Lloyd*,[196] or Lederer. I don't think it is necessary. But I don't want to be criticized for neglecting to clarify something.

Best regards,
   [Paul]

---

196   *Pester Lloyd* was an independent German language daily newspaper based in Budapest and covering Hungary, Central, and Eastern Europe. Founded in 1854, the paper is still published online today.

Prague, January 23, 1936

Dear Rudolf,

Enclosed is a copy of a letter from Kurt Heinig.[197] I am bringing it to your attention not with the intention of avoiding any kind of co-responsibility. But, since I don't think I'm wrong to assume that you duly considered whether to accept Henrichsen's article, then I don't think it would be justified to keep Heinig's criticisms from you.

I don't expect you to reply to these criticisms directly with Heinig. On the other hand, I think it would be expedient if you would answer them for us, especially since I have to know whether you still stand by the sentence you wrote in your inaugural article:

> Revolutionary, not only in the struggle against enemy, but also in the ruthless criticism of our own movement, it puts forward its goals: to debate, in a free discussion, the great problems of socialism and its realization, to learn from laying bare the mistakes of the past, and to prepare to shape the future by analyzing the present.

For the same purpose I'm sending you a copy of a letter from comrade Hansen-Kopenhagen, which contains views similar to those in the letter from Heinig.

I probably don't particularly need to emphasize, that it would be easy for me to produce the opinions of many comrades, also from newspapers and magazines, that have the opposite judgement.

Best regards,
  [Paul]

Zürich, January 24, 1936

To the Party Executive Committee!

[Below] are a few observations to be added to the official report on the meeting of the Bureau of the International.

---

197   Kurt Heinig (1886–1956) was a financial expert and SPD member of the Reichstag from 1927–33. After fleeing to Denmark, he collaborated on the production of the *Deutschland-Berichte* for the Sopade.

The political debate about the Abyssinian war initially gave Modigliani[198] reason to report that growing amounts of reliable information indicate that the organization of antifascist forces is making progress. The core of the reporting organizations is in education; mainly intellectuals, but also workers. Clear rebellion in capitalist circles. Contrary to the expectations of the Communists, thus far the opposition is coming from the right, rather than the left. Mussolini's intention to break diplomatic relations failed in the face of resistance from Balbo, Grandi, etc. At the beginning there was great fear of the appearance of the English fleet; later things calmed down as a result of Laval's policy. There is strong anti-English opinion in the lower strata. The improvement of workers' morale has resulted from the reduction of unemployment by the [military] draft and employment in the arms industries. For that reason, there is frequently support for Mussolini in these circles. Personally, he favors only a petroleum embargo for an immediate and certain impact. Anything else would strengthen nationalist sentiment.

Regarding Gillies'[199] long exposition on the complicity not only of Hoare but of the whole English government in respect to the Laval-Hoare Plan,[200] contrary to official claims the English government knew about the plan. Blum thought that Laval's part was more significant. By the way, there was unanimity on the demand to intensify sanctions. In the plenary meeting Mertens[201] and Jouhaux[202] demanded adding something about the need to deal with the raw materials problem as the fundamental cause of the war. I vehemently opposed this position, because that would have recognized Germany's new colonial demands as justified, and I was well supported by Gillies and Citrine.[203] Jouhaux energetically insisted, however, on his demand. Finally, after the dangerous formulations were removed, the passage was put forward in a form that seemed harmless and, therefore, I let it pass.

---

198 Guiseppe Modigliani (1872–1947) was an Italian Socialist, cofounder of the United Socialist Party in 1922 and its leader from 1928–30. He was a member of the LSI Executive Committee from 1923–38.

199 William Gillies (1885–1958) represented the British Labor Party in the LSI executive committee from 1929–1940.

200 The Laval-Hoare plan was put forward by the Conservative British Foreign Secretary, Samuel Hoare (1880–1959), and the right-wing French Foreign Minister, Pierre Laval, to end the Italo-Abyssinian War essential by handing Abyssinia over to Italy. The outcry against the proposal led their resignations.

201 Cornielle Mertens (1880–1951) was a leading Belgian trade unionist and member of the Belgian Labor Party's executive committee.

202 Leon Jouhaux (1879–1954) was a top French trade unionist during the Popular Front era and after 1945. He was awarded a Nobel Peace Prize in 1951.

203 Walter Citrine (1887–1983), was a British Labor Party leader and president of the International Federation of Trade Unions from 1928–1945.

The second point of unanimity was that the action against events in Germany must be maintained and strengthened. Concerning the Assembly of Cities, the behavior of Wibauts was described as incomprehensible and sharply [criticized] by Albarda and Soukoup. It was decided that the business commission should get in touch with Wibaut, Vink, etc. and make it clear to them that participation is impossible. Support for refugees was discussed briefly. I made the point that, thus far, advocacy on this matter by the ISB has been unsatisfactory. Fritz [Adler] explained that that would be changed. Under Broucheres' chairmanship, it will form its own committee and representation will be established after a new commission is named.

I'd like to request, therefore, that you contact Fritz directly and, in that connection, examine the question of how we should relate to the organizations that are engaged with refugee matter, such as the Comité Franco-Allemande in Paris. This [committee] no longer merely wants to represent Jewish [refugees], but refugees in general. I don't know about the details of these matters, but perhaps it would be very good to request a report about them – especially on new developments – from comrade Friedländer.[204]

Abramovitch's reports about the intensification of the terror in Russia were also interesting, while practically nothing was said about the promised democratization.[205] Comrade Broido, who has just returned from 5 years of banishment in Turkestan – after she had already sat in prison for years – has now been sent to the border of Outer Mongolia. The appeals of the English Women's Association have all been in vain. Gillies explained that there is nothing else to be done other than to answer the campaign to liberate Thälmann with one to free Broido.[206] It was decided to give Bulgaria a small amount of support – I'm not in error, Wladek = money. The completely insignificant socialist movement in the U.S.A. – probably 15,000 members – supposedly faces a split.

These are these essential points.

Best regards,
R.H.

---

204 Otto Friedländer (1897–1954) was the secretary of the Socialist Student International until 1932. In 1933 he moved to Czechoslovakia and worked with the German League for Human Rights.
205 Raphael Abramovitch (1880–1963) was a veteran member of the Jewish Bund and of Russian Social Democracy. A Menshevik Internationalist during the First World War, he served in the Central Executive Committee of the Soviets in 1917–18 and later in the Moscow Soviet. Exiled in 1920, he became a leading Menshevik intellectual and served on the Executive Committee of the LSI from 1923–40.
206 Eva Broido (1876–1941) was long-time Menshevik activist. The western campaign to gain her release failed, and she was shot in Orlov Prison in September 1941.

Prague, February 11, 1936

Dear Rudolf,

We are again encountering delays with the *Zeitschrift*. We cannot count on Sering. He had a minor run-in with the police during which his manuscripts were taken away. Thus far I only have the article by Alsen. When will I receive the articles promised by Wendel and Henrichsen? We can't count on the article from Bienstock on the Far East. Although I conveyed your criticisms of his article on Italy very gently, it appears that, at the moment, he has lost his desire for further collaboration. He wrote me a very moody letter. He admits that what he intended was a serious error against Marxism and now believes he is scarcely in a position to achieve our journal's high Marxist standard. I will soon have reconciled with him, but for the moment there is nothing to be done. You must write to me immediately about how you envision the next issue of the *Zeitschrift*, because I don't want it to unceremoniously disappear.

I hear rumors from various quarters that the *Zeitschrift* will soon disappear. Besides Heinig, other forces are also at work to annihilate the only social democratic place where, in spite of the party secretary type, one can still speak openly. I'm not surprised about it, because the social democratic movement of the old stamp actually needs no discussion of problems. Of course, I can understand that the *Zeitschrift* should also take a hit as expenditures are reduced in general. But I fear that a blow also is planned against the *Zeitschrift* if we come into lots of money. There is no balance sheet yet for the second half of 1935. But I have no doubt that the *Zeitschrift*'s balance has become more positive. We have certainly doubled our (small) sales. At the same time, no advertising has been carried out that cost money. Arthur [Arnold] always strongly opposed that, and I did not insist as long as I did not know whether the *Zeitschrift* would be granted a long life.

The personal gossip against Sering has finally ended after Scheidemann, as you can read in the enclosed copy, belied the claim.

Besides the letter from Heinig and [one] from Handen, a letter from Schumacher has also arrived. In part, it contains the same criticisms of the *Zeitschrift* and of S[ozialistische] A[ktion] as in the other letters. I replied with a letter, a copy of which is enclosed, and I hope that one will see throughout that I do not intend to respond to such idiotic agitation quietly and patiently.

By the way, in another letter from Schumacher demands that the party Executive intervene against Breitscheid because he has not loyally and obediently joined the ranks of the anti-Communist front. We have happily returned to the intolerance that, twenty years ago, was the starting point of the split. I think it is regrettable that these and similar utterances are answered as rarely as the discipline-mocking cessation of the distribution of *SA*. It is developing just as it did earlier with tolerance for attacks from the right and, at the same time, the gruffest attitude toward the left. You can include in the same chapter that all those who stand in any type of association with the Popular Front in Paris are described as "bought by Bolshevik money". One can easily imagine how the other side will reply when the archive matter is brought to a conclusion in the way that has been foreseen. Can one still speak of "leadership" if such things are not checked from the start?

On the decisive issue: freedom or slavery there are no differences of opinion between us. I agree that, in this regard, we should not make any concessions. But, on certain fundamental points, I draw different practical conclusions than you did in you last letter.

1. You reject any collaboration with the Communists. That was not always your standpoint. In the discussion with Münzenberg, about which you reported in detail, you took a fundamentally more forgiving position. You supported the autonomy of the German movement, the calling of a truce, and separate declarations of both parties for democracy. Above all, you demanded that negotiations not be rejected from the start. You described the Popular Front as a frivolous game, but here you also said collaboration could be considered on a case to case basis. I still think this earlier position is correct. It is also fully compatible with unconditional support for freedom and democracy. It does not mean that you become a "servant of the workers" and stop being a "servant of an idea". It only means that we don't lead the fight for our ideas in isolation. On the contrary, we'd be closely connected with those forces that we need for the implementation of our ideas.

2. You are for Prague, because Prague at least offers the certainty of being against the Communists. I greatly fear that you are only momentarily correct. When the situation looked different two years ago, Prague was no bulwark against the Communists. At that time Stampfer was prepared for every concession. I don't know if such a situation is out of the question in the future, but apart from that, it isn't enough for me to know that Prague is against this or that. I would much rather know what Prague is for. Unfortunately, no clear answer has been given except, if one thinks about it, Prague avoids anything that looks like cooperation with other groups, even when they don't have anything at all to do with the Communists. You say the issue of the Popular Front has been decided internationally. At the moment, I also have that impression. Nevertheless, I want to contradict your reference to Belgium. It seems to me to be more than a symptom

when Vandervelde said, "... in France I would be for the Popular Front, in Belgium I'm against it". Doesn't that apply to Germany to a much greater extent? Can you imagine any progress at all, as long as the workers in Germany are split? And I recognize more every day that we share a part of the blame for the countless victims sacrificed to no avail. Today it is even more the case that fragmentation and side-by-side existence are greater sources of danger than cooperation. I'll give you an example of the current, fateful situation. In the elections to the Trust Councils (Vertrauenräte) the Communists put out the slogan that one must put Socialists on the lists and vote yes. We put forward the opposite slogan as sharply as possible. On this matter I fully asserted my standpoint, but O[tto] W[els] took a more conciliatory position, which reflected a more reformist approach. Thus, in no way can I be suspected of wanting to make substantive concessions to bring about cooperation with the Communists. But the harsh, confrontational slogans were a terrible disaster – neither the one nor the other could be followed, because, after all, at home there is no possibility that Socialists and Communists can come to an understanding with such different slogans. Wouldn't it be more reasonable for us, who live in safety abroad, to engage in this tactical dispute and not to leave to those people at home who have to pay with jail and prison time.

3. You are for Prague, because you are against the groups. I don't understand that either, because you cannot support this standpoint with reference to achievements. Of course, Prague can do more today than all the other groups put together. You know the reason for that as well as I do. It is only financial superiority and nothing more. Our organizational and intellectual achievements are, unfortunately, not of the type about which you can boast. What I regret most about your standpoint, however, is that it makes the split into a principle. As long as Prague had the tendency – and that was still the case in 1933 and 1934 – to absorb the groups and to become an organizational and intellectual center, one had to argue for Prague. But now that one lives a life apart and keeps others at a distance, whether good or bad, whether similar or different politically, the unconditional support for Prague means eternal struggle among the groups and the impossibility of concentrating our forces.

I could list more objections to your point of view, but I'd like to avoid our writing past one another. Still, I'd say that my influence is much less than you would. I don't imagine that I can actually improve the situation through my presence. It only puts a good face on things to the outside world. What you recommend is the theory of the lesser evil, which, after the shipwreck, I can no longer recognize as the right tactic.

We don't need to argue about the archive. You have no moral misgivings, because the money will be used for an impersonal, higher purpose, and for social democratic goals. But then, may I not I treat money differently which is provided without conditions also for an impersonal, higher purpose and for social democratic goals, when it doesn't pass through my own hands? The fact is that, for example, the local [Czech] party has rejected money from "Red Aid", which also would have been given unconditionally. And, furthermore, the fact is that the local party greatly fears would it be used by the reactionary parties for massive agitation against it.

You reported that you are very pleased with the appeal, especially its last section, and that you fully agree with it. In reply I want to say that I was not against anything that was in it. I opposed what was missing. Stampfer had left no doubt that, with this appeal, he wanted to completely negate that of January1934. In other words, he no longer believes that the path to freedom is Hitler's violent overthrow. He hopes for some kind of miracle. I combated this belief in miracles and, because others also thought that a 100 per cent swing was a bit too much, as a concession to me, they added the reference to the platform of January 1934. But the whole thing is, after all, a total waste of time. I found scarcely a paper in which our declaration was noted. Even here in Prague only the *Sozialdemokrat* did. Stampfer's book will be published. A decision on it was made without considering financial developments. I did not oppose the book's publication, because I don't view it as my task to block a truthful description of the causes of our catastrophe. Moreover, during the discussion, I had the rare satisfaction of hearing Kurt Geyer judge Stampfer's book and its impact as even more ill-fated than I. Indeed, and not because it is superficial and wrong about many things, but because its fundamental outlook confirms that Social Democratic policy between 1914 and 1933 was guided by inadequacy, weakness, and faintheartedness.

As far as I can tell, there are no prospects for Souvarine. But talk personally with Siegmund [Crummenerl] or O[tto] W[els]. If the news from Nikolajewski proves to be true, both will soon be traveling to the west.

W[illi] Mü[ller] has been back for a few days. I have only spoken with him once. He is satisfied with the financial results of his trip. And he made so many friends over there that he thinks he can count on financial support for his work in later years without another trip. He also energetically promoted the *Zeitschrift*, so that we can now begin propaganda for it over there.

My very best wishes. Hanna also says hello.

Your,

[Paul]

Zürich, March 5, 1936

Dear Paul!

I am very worried because of the lack of manuscripts. I only have the prospect of one article from Wendel and that's not a sure thing. I would prefer to not turn to Thormann, Schifrin, or Alsen again in order to avoid making the journal too monotonous. It is a miserable situation, and I just hope you have something. Maybe you can talk to Friedmann. Hopefully, Bienstock will write. In any case, the *Zeitschrift* must be maintained until a decision is reached concerning the business in Paris. Then it will be easier to get collaborators. Thanks a lot for the Jaksch [article]; I hope to get to it today or tomorrow. And what is with your article?

First of all, I spoke with Siegmund [Crummenerl] only about Danzig and the Frankfurt trial. He'll report on that himself. After his return, we'll want to discuss all the financial and political problems thoroughly. – The address for the *Zeitschrift für Sozialforschung*, to which you should send a sample copy in exchange for one of theirs, is Geneva, 91 Rue de Lausanne. Wendel requests three more copies of the last issue and Thormann wants a sample copy of the December issue.

Now to your letter. It is difficult to answer by letter, because, actually, a radical new reconsideration of all our views would be necessary. So, first of all, I do not fear that we have differences. I have not changed my view of the Communists; I can understand declaring a truce. But it almost looks as if another change of course is underway in Moscow. Dimitroff appears to be on ice. In principle, what is decisive for me is as follows: the great contradiction today is not socialism and capitalism, as Dan, among others, writes. On the contrary, it is freedom or slavery. That sounds ideological, but it isn't. The tragedy for socialism and what is counterrevolutionary in Bolshevism is just that the connection between freedom and socialism, which we all took for granted earlier, has been torn asunder. In Russia itself any idea of the dictatorship as transitional stage has been dropped. The supporters of the united front have already capitulated intellectually. In France they are casting about for a conception of the proletarian dictatorship that would be acceptable to the Communists in the program for a new unified party, which, moreover, is utopian. The maintenance of intellectual independence is all the more difficult for us, since we have Communists in our own ranks. The party's Second Secretary, Zyromski, writes articles in *Populaire* in which he speaks supportively not only of Lenin, but also of Stalin. A few ambiguous reservations change nothing. For the workers, any differentiation between dictatorship and democracy disappears. Quite a number of functionaries in various countries would have gone over to the Communists if they hadn't feared for their later removal. Their main concern isn't political freedom, but rather "party democracy" in which their own power is secured. But the most crucial and dangerous thing is that the events in Italy, Germany, and, above all, Russia itself have shown very clearly that the workers' own longing for freedom is not as strong as we once imagined. The freedom of science, the development of individuality, the self-determination of one's personality, in short, all the things that led me to socialism, because I thought that the securing of material [existence] via the social control of the economy would mean the consummation of freedom, is hardly a vital factor which, under all conditions, actually drives the historical behavior of today's labor movement. Instead, in its agitation, Communism sees all ideals of freedom as a bourgeois swindle. Russia as an ideal? "The proletarian state"? Bauer and Dan use such terms. No, Russia is a disgrace, an abasement of humanity, and it would remain so even if wages and productivity per acre were much higher. The consciousness of freedom must be obtained by or reawakened in the working class. For that reason, I oppose a united front that is international in scope. As little as the English and Scandinavian parties are in accord with my ideals, their standpoint on democracy is crucial and should not be obscured by any compromise with Bolshevism. There is only one policy: the complete liquidation of the Communist International. Associating with the Communists is especially dangerous in Germany, not because of its impact on the enemy, but because of workers' lack of a sense of freedom. If any hope is still justified, then it is that, at last, a real feeling for freedom grows out of the fight against Hitler in Germany, too. And we should undermine that, as well, by opening our ranks to the preachers of dictatorship?

And one more thing. I know of nothing more detestable than the Communist leaders. In order to save their paid positions, these guys have adhered to or denied any way of thinking prescribed or forbidden to them by Lenin or now the wretched Stalin beginning with Zinoviev and Radek right on down to Cachin and Köhnen.[207] And we should work together with them? And recommend them to the workers as leaders in the new world? These people should be given control over the new society? No, I am sticking to what I said at Halle: between us and them there is an unbridgeable moral chasm. You say, Prague is not firmly against the Communists. But it is now and, therefore, for the moment I'll have to make do. My standpoint does not prevent participation in events like

---

207   Probably Bernard Koenen (1889–1964), who joined the KPD in 1920 and rose into the leadership after 1923. Escaped to the Saarland in 1933 and migrated to the USSR. After 1945 he was part of the leadership of the GDR.

that of the anti-fascist lawyers under certain circumstances, but that is a purely practical matter. You ask, what does Prague actually stand for? However, I have never expected an answer to this question from Prague: we have to provide it. The objective problem here is that concrete political problems are still not posed. You took from my letter to Geyer that I am optimistic. Unjustifiably. I do think the system's ability to resist has been severely shaken. But the mass action that would be required simply cannot be carried out and that is the horrible thing. That is not the fault of Prague or any other group, and it will not be eliminated through the addition of more groups that all have no influence. Of course, I think the unification of the bulk of the working class is necessary, but when and how that will occur will only emerge when concrete actions once again move into the realm of possibility.

I remain critical of Prague's attitude toward the groups, but even today I don't think it is very important. I did not understand your remark about the election of the shop stewards. What actually prevented agreement if the Communist determination of the Trojan horse tactic really isn't a genuine Moscow jackass.

Since you have made such a great sacrifice to go to Prague, I don't want you to give up the cause. I can empathize with everything. But, outside of Prague, I see no possibility of action. At the moment, there is not much more to do than you are already undertaking with SA. But the moment can come, when you will have to fight to get a policy started and to determine its content, and then you will need the apparatus the current nature of which I consider much the same as you do. If you fail, then you can always draw the consequences.

Ugh, I've had enough of writing by typewriter. I'll never learn it and it hinders me from thinking. The letter is meant for you. I am actually in the midst of an intense process of internal upheaval that is not at all over and at this stage I don't want any of my statements to be [regarded as] settled. There is ever more tension internationally. Hopefully, it won't come to war. It would be the end for a long time. English armaments are a ray of hope. I spoke with Unterleitner. He overcame the thing better than I thought he would. Write to me again, soon. What is Willi Müller up to? I'd be happy to see Sering again. Best wishes to you and Hannah. Say hello to Else.

Your,
   Rudolf

[P.S.] Write very soon!

Prague, March 6, 1936

Dear Rudolf,

The matter with Sering is cleaned up. It cost him two days. He promised me, however, that the article will definitely be in my hands by Monday. I have to then immediately have it set. In the middle of next week, however, Sering is traveling to London, where he is settling down, and he will visit you in Zürich. You'll have the chance, then, to talk to him at length about his article and to work out any changes, which can then be taken care of in the galleys.

What about the rest of the *Zeitschrift*'s content? Especially with your article about Jaksch's book?

Siegmund [Crummenerl] reported as follows about his conversation with you: "Hilferding thinks the political discussions in P[aris] are wrong. There is a "moral chasm" between us and the other partners that cannot be bridged. He fully shares our view".

Best regards,
 [Paul]

Zürich, March 12, 1936

Dear Paul,

Yesterday I forgot to ask you if you received my letter of eight days ago. I read Wickel's article and favor publication. It is interesting, furthers the discussion begun by Sering, and, after all, I had, in principle, promised him. It is also very nice to have manus[cripts]. I don't have his address at hand, so I'd like to ask you to come to an agreement with him about the printing. Cuts in certain places are possible, the Czech example could be somewhat tightened up, but it doesn't amount to all that much. Luckily, the thing is easily divided into sections and is very readable. There is much with which I don't agree, but that can be cleared up in the discussion later on. So, please, get in touch with W[ickel] and send me the galleys. I assume that he has a copy, otherwise I'd send the manus[cript] back to you if you request it.

Crum[menerl] isn't here yet and I'm a bit impatient, because I have to make decisions about financial investments. The political situation is moving toward a climax. I've been right about everything; what was still easy in 1933 is now bound up with a major war. The workers' parties bear much of the blame for this situation; there is nothing more pitiful than the behavior of the Labor Party and the recent behavior of the French party. It has to dance to the tune of the Communists, and they are for a war that would be to Russia's advantage – now with the West, as it has been since 1918 and even more so after Rapallo: a war of German nationalism against the West. Blackguards! But the Socialists are dilettantes, ignoramuses, and demagogues. We look terrific. I'm afraid that where you are nothing is prepared, although if things get serious – I'm not sure about it, but I also would not exclude the possibility – it could become impossible to stay in Prague.

It is telling that instead of the Executive, only the [LSI's] office staff is meeting; obviously, Fritz [Adler] fears being helpless. But the thing would only make a certain amount of sense if, in terms of foreign policy, the SA seriously engaged the pro-Hitler *Daily Herald*. In reality, the Second International is dead and continuing the fraud is becoming increasingly deceitful. On the one side stands the crazy left which is fleeing from the romance of revolution to the romance of war. On the other side stand the pacifists, who do Hitler's business. On the day after Hitler's action [in the Rhineland], in addition to the babble of Faure[208] and Rosenfeld (!), *Populäire* published a dumb, erroneous article by Dan and a discussion piece by Pivert, his secretary (!), under the title: "We won't march!" Criminals!

Best regards and write soon!
Your,
Rudolf

Prague, March 13, 1936

Dear Rudolf,

You will be overrun these days with visitors from Prague, but I hope you will retain the required degree of skepticism. Sering, too, will tell you some things that you won't hear from the others. Of course, that would be no substitute for a personal discussion between us, which I still think is necessary and want to make happen in the near future. Meanwhile, with this letter I'll make the attempt to carry on the process of clarification between us.

---

208 Paul Faure (1878–1960) was a long-time leader of the SFIO, editor of *Populaire*, member of parliament, and a leading proponent of French pacifism and appeasement in the interwar period.

There is scarcely any contradiction between us on fundamental principles. I also believe that the basic antagonism is not socialism and communism, but freedom and slavery. And yet, in the face of your blunt postulate, I cannot suppress some doubts. Since you cited Halle in your letter, I read through your speech again. There I came upon the following passage:

> If we are for the dictatorship of the proletariat, then I'd like to say that it is precisely German conditions that move us to tell the working class that it cannot manage with democratic means because the nature of historical development in Germany makes a period of proletarian dictatorship inevitable. If we don't fight with all means, then the bourgeoisie would use all means to quickly overthrow us. Therefore, we need a period of the dictatorship of the proletariat. That is because it is not possible to gain a foothold in a country that was as reactionary as Germany, where the belief in the power of violence is so firmly anchored in the minds of the bourgeoisie. The proletariat must hold onto power for as long as it takes to consolidate [its position] economically and politically so that no one can later wrest it away.

I am not a literalist and I would not think of binding you to every word from that time. But I assume that today, even more than in 1920, you would maintain the view that formal democracy is not enough to secure power once it is conquered. And, therefore, I'm compelled to ask whether the idea of freedom that we thought was necessary is also subject to change. I believe that freedom under socialism has to look different than under liberalism. It will probably have to be substantially limited for the benefit of society. Do I not understand you much more correctly when I assume that, above all, you oppose arbitrariness, the lack of rights, and inequality?

You write: "the consciousness of freedom must be obtained by or reawakened in the working class". Agreed, but we are already on our way to that goal. For that reason, I have a different opinion about associating with Communists in Germany. First of all, you have to drop the idea that in Germany you can still orient yourself according to the party divisions. That applies at most for some people in the apparatus on both sides, but not to the broader strata. Unless my impression is wrong – and I've had more personal contact with people from over there in the last six months than the whole Party Executive and its apparatus put together – there are just as many Communists, who want to free themselves from the dictatorship of Moscow and from the split, as there are Social Democrats, who see the serious damage caused by powerlessness and democracy's lack of a will to power. I have no fear at all that we are handing over our people to the preachers of dictatorship if we don't hinder them from working together with all the socialist forces they trust. It is a completely false schema to think we have to give the command for cooperation from here. Wherever there is serious underground work that goes beyond the framework of friendly cohesion, unity is practically restored. Not, however, on the basis of dictatorship, but rather on that of militant democracy. Interventions carried out from here against the united front haven't been effective or they have shaken the cohesion between us and our comrades (that is the case in Berlin) or caused disintegration that made the Gestapo's job easier. If we had the possibility of a conference where we could speak freely with our people, that is, with those not tendentiously selected, then this view would be one hundred percent confirmed.

I view the international side of the united front movement just as skeptically as you do. You only need to observe the events in Czechoslovakia to know that dependence on Moscow causes corruption everywhere and represents nothing other than a repeat of the events we experienced in 1920. The liquidation of the Comintern, therefore, is in fact the only possibility for unity to come. But I strongly urge you to look at your allies on this issue. I don't think much of those who insult the Communists today in same unbridled fashion as they did to us back then. I doubt whether convictions today are more genuine than at that time.

Recent days have shown how strongly your conception of the truce declaration stands in contradiction to the local conception and practice. In a letter, the Communists have requested a discussion of the new situation. They received no answer. When Stampfer raised the question very cautiously at a conference of secretaries of whether one should at least send a brief reply saying that we had already reached a decision, O[tto] W[els] bit his head off like a schoolboy. Of course, I took the position that it is impossible for us to have relations with every reactionary, but conversations with Communists are treasonous. O[tto] W[els] understood that and remained silent, trusting that I could not cause a fight about every kind of rubbish. Now, our people are supposed to carry the enclosed message into Germany. Even if there is nothing to object to in the text, one must still consider that the "Front of Decent Germans" is associated in Germany with the Black Front.[209] What does that have to do with Social Democracy? Stampfer is now fighting for the "German Free Thinkers" Front. You see from this example how weak one feels here. On 23 November Vogel and Stampfer supposedly recommended a non-aggression pact with the Com-

---

209 On the Black Front see footnote 141 above.

munists. In reality that was only in a report in *NV*. A few days ago, in a long letter, Kreyssig explained the necessity for the party Executive to seize the initiative and recommend a non-aggression pact to the Communists. That is necessary in order to win back friends, who participated in the Lutetia Conference, but now have doubts. That did not change anything in respect to the local stubbornness, however.

"Russia is a disgrace": isn't that a terrible exaggeration? I hate the Russian terror, the whole single party rule of the C[ommunist] P[arty] and everything associated with bossism and the lack of principle as much as you do. Nevertheless, everything in me resists thinking that your label is correct. Even K[arl] K[autsky], in his recent article about war and socialism in *NV*, resists equating National Socialism and Bolshevism and points out having to evaluate the dictatorships according to their origins. In general, there are many voices in the recent literature that judge Bolshevism differently. Think about Henrichsen, Gurian, and Ernst Karl Winter in *Europa*, Nr. 6. – In the *Zeitschrift*, too, we will have to deal with the Webbs' book on Russia. Did you already assign that task?

I also find your assertion: "I know of nothing more detestable than the Communist leaders. In order to save their paid positions, these guys have adhered to or denied any way of thinking prescribed to them by Lenin or now the wretched Stalin beginning with Zinoviev and Radek right on down to Cachin and Köhnen" to be one-sided. Do you only find such people with the Communists? Of course not, weakness of character can be found in every camp. We have met many in our own. I don't hold any higher standards than you do, but I apply them to everyone and not only to the Communists. Certainly, I agree with you completely when you want to say that Bolshevism as a system breeds this lack of character. But isn't the lack of character and conviction just as condemnable where is isn't caused by the system?

I've enclosed the translation of an article from the *Manchester Guardian*. I think this description – I don't know the author – is essentially correct. There is no question at all that the illegal movement over the last year has shrunk both in scope and influence. For example, E[rich] O[llenauer] frankly admitted that to me in a private conversation, although a few days before I had said it during a conference of secretaries and was then labeled from all sides as a hopeless pessimist. In an oral discussion I would be able to shower you with more examples. One single fact will suffice here: The circulation of the *SA* on 1 January 1935 was 28, 500. On 1 March 1936 it was 8, 500. Parsing these numbers results in a picture that is even grimmer. We are cut off from entire parts of the country, even from those that were formally our best districts. (R[ein]bold). But I'd rather leave that for a personal conversation. Here it is enough for me to say that what I have always told you has now already set in: a leadership without authority or expertise must suffer shipwreck. You might think my judgement is too harsh. Perhaps, with lots of money, this or that could be improved or changed. But that would alter nothing in my general outlook. Money is very important, but it is not enough by itself. The Communists spend millions and make no progress. Valuable human ability can be procured less than ever by money.

And with that I've arrived at what is for me the most crucial point. What separates me from the local friends is much less [our] political differences of opinion than the principles of our work. There can be no progress without attracting valuable forces without regard to their tactical position on party matters. As long as the groups continue to struggle and are not drawn into common work, there will be no authority, no leadership, no success. Equally damaging is the policy of isolation pursued against those anti-fascist forces that are not on the right, but rather on the left. A leadership that unhesitatingly works together with monarchists, three-quarter anti-Semites, neo-fascists, etc., but rejects working with genuine anti-fascists, because one or the other Communist is among them, can't move forward at all. I am enclosing copies of letters related to our relationship to the local "Union for Law and Freedom". I didn't think the difference of opinion was large enough to oppose the majority, but I left no doubt that our position is stupid and rigid and sharply contradicts our interests. This applies primarily to Siegmund [Crummenerl].

Some other things have played out here about which you've been informed one-sidedly and incorrectly, but I think the matters are too irrelevant to bother you with them. I am reluctant to assure you in particular that I have done and will do nothing that I cannot stand up for. I only wish that each of the others could also say that.

Only one more thing: let me know whether anything has been discussed with you about the discontinuation of the *Zeitschrift*. My vision and my opinion about that remain unchanged. If no new money comes through, my resistance will not be insurmountable, especially since I'm absolutely sure that others will pick up the banner if we drop it. I only demand one thing: the opportunity to discuss this decision with you and Breitscheid. If necessary, I'll make the trip privately.

My very best wishes and from Hanna, too.
　Your,
　[Paul]

Prague, April 2, 1936

Dear Rudolf,

I assume that this letter will reach you in Paris, and that, meanwhile, the proofs of the articles by Wickel and Alsen probably have arrived in Zürich.

Regarding the next issue of the *Zeitschrift*, I have to have a timely reply from you. It hurt us that we published a week late this time. When we don't come out on time, the bookstores lose interest in selling the *ZfS*. Thus far, I have manuscripts from Wickel, 860 lines; Alsen, 250 lines; and book reviews of 200 lines. That is in no way enough, and we have to seek out new manuscripts.

I assume that you will write the lead article and for that you'll need 7–8 pages or 350–400 lines. I don't think it is expedient to publish the article by Wickel. The issue would be dull. Do you have other articles in view? What about the article by Sering? Is he writing one and is it being considered for this issue? I have two other articles available, one on the problem of the military, which I'd like to publish when you've read it, and an article [called] "Vor einem revolutionären Kurs in Polen" ["Before a revolutionary course in Poland"], which, in respect to the current escalation of the social situation, is very interesting. It is authored by a young Jewish worker who appears to be very talented. He lived in Germany until 1933. I gave the article to Birnbaum, who was just here, to look it over and he told me today that he'll talk to the author in the next few days about some changes. I will try to get the manuscript back quickly enough to consider its publication in the April issue if necessary. But, in any case, we still could use a short topical article.

I've enclosed the draft of a review of the Jaksch book, which Stein undertook at my request, in order for you to decide if he should do it. If you tell me right away, then this contribution could also be considered for the April issue.

I also spoke with Birnbaum about collaboration. He let me know his thinking on the matter in a letter, a copy of which is enclosed. Write to me about how to answer him. I am inclined to encourage him to write the article. His ideas interest me even if I have certain qualms about their correctness.

Enclosed is a circular and a letter from which you will see that we are attempting to attract subscribers in the U.S.A.

Answer me as soon as possible. Everything else orally.

Best wishes,
  [Paul]

[P.S.] Greetings from Else L.

Prague, April 24, 1936

Dear Rudolf,

I got back from Danzig yesterday and want to write to you about the outcome [of my trip].

The general political situation in Danzig has not essentially changed over the last six months. The party is maintaining itself relatively well. The condition of its press and of its organization has improved somewhat. Recently, in spite of the terror in the countryside, some progress was made. However, nothing has changed in respect to the Nazis' decisive position of power. The effects of the devaluation have almost been overcome. They hardly play a role in the consciousness of the masses. The opposition to the Nazis stems primarily from the sense of unfreedom. Economic considerations are moving decisively into the background. Since 7 March the public's attitude is dominated by the whispered slogan "now it's Danzig's turn". It is so strong that the German Nationalists, who were weak in and of themselves, now speak of being "just cut off". They are considered a group of civil servants, who exercise no influence on the bourgeoisie. It is, of course, different with the Center [Party], whose ideological foundation has held up, like that of the socialists.

The May meeting of the Council of the League of Nations will simply receive the quarterly report of the High Commissioner, but it won't make any decisions on the Danzig question, and the proposal for dissolution [of the city assembly], in particular, won't be raised. The Senate's promise that it is prepared to negotiate directly with the opposition should have been extraordinarily well received in Geneva. Poland's position is unchanged. Lester,[210] whose time in office is coming to an end, intends to act in accord with Valeras' wish,[211] which the Irish Foreign Ministry made to him. Eden[212] favors his remaining, as do the Poles. Our friends have the impression that Lester has little hope that, with Geneva's help, matters in Danzig can be settled. One expects nothing to come of the dir-

---

210 Sean Lester (1888–1959) was appointed Ireland's representative to the League of Nations in 1929. He joined the League's Secretariat in 1933 and served as its High Commissioner in the Free City of Danzig from 1934–1937. Lester protested strongly against the German government's persecution of Jews and, as tensions grew between Poland and Germany over Danzig, he warned of looming disaster. He was boycotted by representatives of the Nazi government and by the Nazi Party in Danzig.
211 Éamon de Valera (1882–1972) was at that time Prime Minister of the Irish Republic and President of the Council of the League of Nations.
212 Anthony Eden (1897–1977) was a Conservative British politician who served as Foreign Secretary in the government of Stanley Baldwin from 1935–1938.

ect negotiations with the Senate, especially since, in a 22 February speech to officers of the security police [Schutzpolizei], Greiser[213] expressly said the only thing to be done was to prevent all incidents until the May meeting and even issued precise instructions for the dispersal of assemblies.

Under these circumstances, our friends also see only [the option] of self-help through the dissolution of the Volkstag [Assembly]. Their motion for dissolution has no chance of success. So only the referendum remains. They have already used it as a threat in their propaganda. In the face of the progress that the opposition has made in the countryside, they think the prospects for the referendum are somewhat better than six months ago. They concede, however, that overcoming the difficulties of the devaluation and Hitler's fait accompli have had a negative impact on the outlook. Our friends agree unanimously that any action aiming toward a referendum requires thorough and long preparation. The possibilities of written and oral propaganda through the press and the organization will have to be fully utilized for months before the referendum can actually be carried out. In the face of expected strong counter pressure from the Nazis, this increased activity will demand great material and personal sacrifices. Support for the victims is one of the most important prerequisites for holding on. Only long-term solidarity can overcome the fear of the terror.

Long-term and close contacts exist between the opposition parties. Nevertheless, our friends don't think it is useful, at this point, to establish contacts with the Center [Party] or the German Nationals. The influence of the German Nationals right now is so minimal that it isn't worth risking the discovery of our plans. In regard to the Center, one thinks it expedient to make a direct offer when the funder is a personality close to the party.

This cautious judgement doesn't change anything in respect to the willingness of our friends to accept any unobjectionable help. I've taken on the task of informing you of the results of our discussions, but the friends in Danzig would also be happy to come to come to Switzerland before the Council meeting in Geneva to inform you and the financial sponsors, respectively.

But, before that, a great danger must be overcome. In May 1936 the *Volkstimme* [in Danzig] was saddled with an unexpected tax debt of 42,000 guilders. 12,000 guilders have been paid and a further 20,000 are available (including the 5,000 from the LSI). Ten thousand more must be raised. Aside from the tax debt, there is the threat of a penalty that is two to three times higher than the total tax itself. It would break the firm. One intends, therefore, to pay the 42,000 guilders and hope that the finance department will then release the machines. Mean-

---

213   Arthur Greiser (1897–1946) was the leader of the NSDAP in Danzig and President of the Danzig Senate. In 1939 he became the Gauleiter of the Wartheland, the area of northwestern Poland annexed by Germany.

while, the plant will be sold before the tax penalty is levied. To do this, a total of 10,000 guilders is required. The sum is not needed as a grant, but rather could be provided as a loan against the machines as collateral. The Danzig friends request your help in raising the money. Since Siegmund [Crummenerl] will be there when you get this letter, we ask you to do everything to fulfill the Danzigers' request. We have to do everything to maintain the *Volkstimme*, whose circulation and influence is greater today than ever before. Because the Danzigers have raised 75,000 guilders by their own efforts over the last 21/2 years (from October 1935 to April 1936) – that is the sale price for the enterprise, which was acquired in bankruptcy – the task of paying interest on or paying back a loan of 10,000 guilders is not impossible for them. The paper and printer shops are active.

Best regards,
  [Paul]

                                                            Prague, April 24, 1936

Confidential

Dear Rudolf,

This letter is for you alone.

The Danzig friends told me that in February and March Alfringhaus turned up there. He wanted to be put in touch with the Center [Party] and with the German Nationals. He refused to say whom he was representing but mentioned that the Sopade was aware of his trip and his plans. No one cooperated with him and he made a bad impression. The first time, A[lfringhaus] traveled back to Copenhagen, though he claimed to be on a trip to Prague. In March, however, he did continue on to Prague, and he told the Danzigers that he would look for you in Zürich.

I knew neither that the Danzigers and O[tto] W[els] had engaged in a correspondence about this question, nor that A[lfringhaus] was in Danzig and Prague, respectively. I never made any secret out of my view that A[lfringhaus] was a shadowy type with shadowy relationships and declared that he neither had an assignment from the Sopade nor any kind of relationship to it. I declared this again, today, in the Executive where no objections were raised. Wels had merely remarked, briefly, that he answered questions from the Danzigers and that A[lfringhas] was in Prague.

The Danzig friends suppose that there is a connection between the action you started and the action by A[lfringhaus]. That is proven by the fact that a sum of 200,000 Danish kronen is being discussed. Why Danish kronen, when one lives in Switzerland and normally calculates in francs?

I'd very much like to know if you know anything about A[lfringhaus].

Paul Bernhard [in] Paris writes to me that he intends to write a fundamental work for the new issue of the *ZfS*, which will appear right after the French elections, on the Popular Front experiment, the domestic impact of the Popular Front's views on foreign policy questions, and the essence of French democracy in general. He differs on almost every point with Schifrin, whose essay in issue 22/23 was rather unfortunate. I'll write to Paul Bernhard that you will send him a note immediately.

So, what's with the next issue? Will you now finally write the promised article? When can I count on it? We are once again publishing a week late. What other articles do you have?

Luise and Karl [Kautsky] send their very best regards. Karl has written two articles in *NV* in response to Tejessay, Howald, etc. He remains in excellent shape – only his legs don't quite work right anymore. The birds in Türkenschanzpark long to be fed by him again. Otherwise, he is working hard, as he has been for his entire life. Luise is in good shape again.

With best wishes,
[Paul]

Zürich, May 3, 1936

Dear Paul,

Tomorrow I'm sending two articles to the printer: Abramovitch on the united front and another one on Keynes's new book, theoretical but very lively. I assume that you have also sent Karl's article to the printer; one cannot, after all, really do anything else. It is totally abstract and, when it comes to the International, illusionary. But what can one do? You've surely had more than enough of that. And the future? In the wake of the collapse of the [archive] negotiations I think it looks very grim for the *Zeitschrift*. And you?

Paul Bernhard writes to me that you'd like to let him know directly, because you are easier for him to reach. In God's name he ought to write, but I want to see it beforehand. I already had written to him, but I don't know if my letter reached him.

Best regards, I'll write again later in the week. Let me know what you think about the prospects in Danzig. If the business goes wrong, which is what I almost want to fear, then it would make no sense to start it. I'll probably discuss your concern tomorrow, [...] .

Best wishes,
R

[P.S.] Menne's commentary was good.

Prague, May 4, 1936

Dear Rudolf,

You have in the meantime received my letter of 29 April. I urgently need an answer about the *ZfS* and, indeed, on the following questions:
1. Are you writing the lead article?
2. Are you in favor of printing the article from K[arl] K[autsky]? I've kept a copy of the article here and already received some corrections from Karl. Therefore, the article will have to by typeset here.
3. What do you think of the commentary by Menne? Should I publish another from him in the next issue?

Since I assume that you are in agreement about the article from Alsen, which you suggested, and that Alsen will send in the article this week, then the issue would contain an article by you, the article by K[arl] K[autsky], Alsen, and the conclusion by Wickel. Let me know as soon as possible. The printer is overburdened, and I have to cut the pages on the tenth if we want to publish by the fifteenth. If necessary, I'll call you in the next few days in the morning.

I'm sending the enclosed copy of a letter from Danzig. Siegmund [Crummenerl] reported briefly about your discussion of Danzig and said that you expect another statement from me in respect to our friends starting negotiations with the Center and the German Nationals and in respect to the prospects of a referendum. But upon rereading my description of 24 April, I see that I've really written everything necessary to judge the situation. The immediate initiation of a referendum is impossible. It would with infallible certainty end in failure and negatively influence the prospects for the opposition. Its effects would be the same: a negative vote would be the same as a positive victory for the Nazis.

If your agent wants to have a direct discussion and assumes the costs of the trip to Switzerland, then it could take place either, as we think is correct, with a

Social Democrat and a representative of the Center, or, more problematic but not a deal breaker, also with a representative of the German Nationals.

I can only underline once more that, beforehand, the *Volkstimme* must be protected at all costs from the danger of financial strangulation by the tax office. Even if our financial condition is disastrous, in my opinion, if it gets serious and no one else will assist, there will be no other choice but to provide the help ourselves. Therefore, see whether you can reduce this burden. Our Danzigers are good people, who will fulfill all the contractual conditions to secure the money.

Best regards,
 [Paul]

Prague, May 7, 1936

Dear Rudolf,

Our letters crossed. I've already replied to your questions on Danzig.

The two expected articles had not yet arrived in Karlsbad yesterday. Hopefully they have been delivered in the meantime. I sent in Karl's article yesterday to be typeset. But I don't feel good about it. Aside from the content, I don't like it that the article is signed by "the author of the Limits of Violence" rather than K[arl] K[autsky]. I think we'll lose respect with the next issue. I should get Bernhard's article tomorrow. I'll then send a copy of the article to you immediately.

You ask about the future of the *Zeitschrift*. It is very difficult to answer that question. After all, it is a part of our future in general. There is a growing tendency here not to talk about uncomfortable things. I've only heard a few personal remarks from Siegmund [Crummenerl] about his last trip and he has not made any official report. And, while earlier it was widely envisioned that we would immediately go on austerity if the negotiations over the archive collapse, there is no trace of that now. Today's meeting of the party Executive did not say a single word about it. Since O[tto] W[els] and E[rich] O[llenhauer] will be traveling westward again in the next few days, nothing can be expected before Pentecost.

I don't need to go into details about my feelings regarding this behavior. But I've given up any hope that the tendency to just let everything go could be changed by an attitude that is substantive and urgent. As I've long been telling you, it applies to everything. Moreover, a contributing factor is that the "cost-savings" undertaken last year scarcely saved any money. I don't know much about the details of last year's financial decisions, but I just found out today that the settlement for a low-level employee consists of his receiving a year's salary at a higher level than that of a member of the Party Executive.

No one has spoken to me about the future of the *ZfS*. I see no reason to bring it up for discussion. Arthur [Arnold] told me, just today, that Stampfer told him that we can no longer afford the *ZfS*. If he makes such a remark to me, then I will borrow your judgement about Jaksch – in terms of meaning, not word-for-word – in respect to his book. He assesses his *Korrespondenz* correctly. The fact that no one prints or pays for it has led him to conclude that it is useless.

Regarding the *ZfS*, I remain steadfast in my opinion of past years: if you and I take the position that the *ZfS* should not be canceled, no other decision will be taken. Today, through comments in the press and by individual personalities, it is easy for me to show that the achievements of the *ZfS* are recognized. It could be demanded that we reduce expenses, but we don't need to concede more than that. From your sorrowful tone in raising the question I surmise that you have little desire for this fight. I remain convinced that the cancelation of the *Zfs* is a sign of the party's intellectual suicide. Perhaps I cannot hinder the Party Executive form this action. But I think it is crucial to distance myself from it on this matter. Therefore, I'll make every effort to retain the *ZfS* and I'm convinced I'll succeed. Maybe that's tied up with relationships that are the increasingly tense anyway. But that does not frighten me. I've said it to you often enough that I can only justify my remaining here if it has some use for the movement as a whole. Therefore, I don't have the slightest inclination to allow myself to be dragged into the general political and moral collapse that I believe is unavoidable without our resistance.

In today's meeting, the attitude toward the International Conference of Refugee Commissioners was remarkable. Nothing could have been more important [to me] than my being assigned to handle preparations and possibly representation. Instead, it was decided to ask the LSI and the IGB [Internationale Gewerkschaftbund] to take the matter in hand. Of course, the disinclination to work with the émigré organizations in Paris plays a role in determining this attitude. This is another case in which the right approach to representing the interests of German refugees is neglected for no good reason. This is because the LSI and the IGB lack the apparatus and knowledge to effectively contribute to the Commission's preparatory work in Geneva and it is in the preparatory work where the decisive steps are taken. All experience shows that this insight is absolutely right. In addition, the antipathy toward my traveling to the west plays a role.

I have firmly decided, however, to take the trip to the west. I think it is urgent to keep Breitscheid and others from getting themselves too mixed up with the Communists. Barring unforeseen circumstances, I'll make the trip in June. Will you be in Zürich at the beginning of June or do you have plans to travel? Let me know as soon as possible.

Best wishes,
  [Paul]

Prague, May 8, 1936

Dear Rudolf,

Alsen's article is enclosed. I assume that it conforms to your expectations. In any case, I don't see any difference between what you wrote to him and the tendencies in the article. The stylistic changes that I made to the text are not visible in the carbon copy. They are unimportant for you. I will negotiate today with Alsen about two small changes. For example, I think the last sentence is superfluous.

I am enclosing a copy of Stein's review. I think the review is lousy. I don't want to return it to him, however, after having accepted his help. I am also counting on still getting articles that will critically challenge Jaksch's way of thinking. Can I count on your writing about Franzel? If not, then I'd like to call upon Sering to deal with both Jaksch and Franzel and to write a fundamental article on both books in which the basic position on Otto Strasser's Black Front is clearly developed. This task is very urgent, because close relations exist between us (O[tto] [Strasser] and O[tto] W[els]), which are widely known and have led to the most disconcerting political assumptions.

As far as I can tell – I still did not get the galleys from Karlsbad – the next issue of the *ZfS* will appear as follows: 1. Alsen, 2. K[arl] K[autsky], 3. Abramovitch, 4. Wickel.

Best wishes,
  [Paul]

Prague, May 18, 1936

Dear Rudolf,

Number 32 of the *ZfS* was mailed today. You can discern the content from the enclosed blurbs. Happily, the *ZfS* is now finding a favorable echo. Even in the local party it is beginning to slowly win through.

I hope that you spoke at length with O[tto] B[auer] in Brussels. I was very satisfied by my last conversation with him. He also expressed a favorable opinion of the *ZfS* overall. He even told me that he wants to support its sales abroad, even if that would mean a certain competition with the *Kampf*. We talked about many other things, but I'd like to reserve passing along further information for an oral conversation between the two of us.

This conversation between us is becoming increasingly urgent. The local spy story is tragic.[214] It is the hardest blow that we could suffer. When lessons are drawn from this case, one can then overcome the breakdown, otherwise it looks bleak. Thus far, unfortunately, my efforts to use this case to push for a reexamination of our methods of work have met with no success worth mentioning. If you read the last circular from the party Executive critically, you'll see how big the breakdown is.

The main goal of this letter, however, is to ask you to tell me what you think of the upcoming issue (number 33) of the *ZfS*. The three articles by Sering, Abramovitsch, and Bruggers take up 1230 lines. I am still missing 400 lines. I could fill them with two commentaries (one on foreign policy and one on domestic policy) as well as book reviews. In case you don't have an especially important article, I'd recommend proceeding in this way. That would have the great advantage that, instead of publishing in mid-June, we could publish number 33 in the first week of June. I'd like to do that with the intention of moving the regular publication date forward to the first of the month. Tell me what you think of that, so I can act accordingly.

And now yet another idea. The problem of Volkssozialismus [Popular Socialism] is in no way exhausted by Stein's review of Jaksch. We also have to take a position on the book by Franzel and on the *Aufbau des Sozialismus* [*Construction of Socialism*] by Otto Strasser. In addition, a review of the book by

---

214 Hertz is referring to the case of Peter Ochmann, a German émigré arrested by the Czech authorities on 26 April for suspected military espionage. It turned out that Ochmann, who was employed by an institution helping German refugees, was actually a spy working for the Nazis since the fall of 1935. He successfully passed refugees' personal information on to the Gestapo. See Buchholz and Rother, eds., *Der Parteivorstand im Exil*, p. 151.

Otto Bauer, *Zwischen den Weltkriegen* [*Between the World Wars*] seems urgently needed. How much confusion was caused, for example, by Branzel's book, is illustrated by a review that Bienstock just sent me. Essentially, he took Franzel's position, so I gave it back to him. I believe we should deliver a fundamental analysis of the three books named above, perhaps also including Bauer's book. I would prefer it if you would deliver such an essay. I desire it also in your interest. A fundamental analysis that provides clarification and lifts the problems out of the fog would provide you with a position of intellectual leadership, which I regard as extraordinarily necessary and useful for the interests of the movement as a whole.

If this work from you will not be forthcoming, which I would find most regrettable in every respect, then I'd like to ask Sering to undertake it. To me, the fact that you have submitted his article to be printed without changes does not mean that you agree with every word. I don't either. I think that Sering's analysis lacks a discussion of transitional solutions which will very probably [be necessary]. But I assume that you consider Sering's work as an essential contribution to the discussion of the issues and as an achievement of which he and we can be proud. I would trust him, then, with taking on this new task.

For the [continued] existence of the *ZfS* it is very important to intervene in current affairs. I still don't know what one intends to do with the journal. Outside of our narrow circle, I've heard recently only regret about the plans to halt the *Zeitschrift*'s publication. Taub, for example, expressed such regrets just yesterday. Therefore, at all costs I'd like to ensure that the cancellation of the *ZfS* can only rest upon financial causes and not upon the argument that it is insignificant and will not be missed. I won't repeat what I wrote to you recently: that I can't stand idly by as the intellectual banner slips from our hands. I want to take up the flag again. At least help me with that, so it isn't made all too difficult.

Best regards,
 [Paul]

Langham Hotel
19, Avenue Friedland, Paris
May 28, 1936

Dear Paul,

Due to the Pentecost holidays, I've stayed longer than I intended, although I'm not happy about being here. I'll be traveling back to Zürich next Wednesday. I spoke at length with O[tto] B[auer]. We agree on the analysis, but not so much in our evaluation of tactical means. I completely agree with your intention to finish the *Zeitschrift* with the available articles and also with giving the assignment of the critique of Jaksch, who I spoke with briefly in Brussels, Franzel, and Bauer to Sering. Tomorrow I'm sending a really good critical article on the League of Nations by Zoltan Ronay to Graphia and want to see whether I can get one from Thormann for the issue after the next one.

I spoke with Crum[menerl] about his austerity plan. Cutting cannot be avoided following the failure of the archive saga and the doubts about any resumption [of negotiations]. Crum[menerl] wants to cancel the *Zeitschrift*. The subsidies cannot be justified by 260 subscribers. I heard the same from Oll[enhauer]. Of course, I talked about the loss of intellectual leadership, etc., without making an impression.

Yesterday Ulbricht appeared at my place. The savages of yore are hardly recognizable. You've already been informed that he spoke with Stampfer at length. He'd like a joint declaration against the danger of war. One would have to most strongly oppose the increasingly dominant view in Germany that war is the only way out and call for propaganda against nationalist agitation. In terms of this position as such, I don't see any conflict with our own views. The tactical issue remains, however, and all the more so because Ulbricht doesn't want to push on organizational matters, cooperation in Germany, etc. In this regard I stand by my earlier opinion. Declaration of a non-aggression pact and perhaps also a clarification of our foreign policy position, which would allow the Communists to follow along parallel lines. Above all, U[lbricht] would like a discussion with Otto W[els] among others, in strict confidence. W[els] could talk to him or with someone else of his choosing.

Please officially inform the party Executive about this conversation. People here are pretty optimistic; I am extremely worried. I am very depressed, actually. I'd be very happy to talk with you, but whether you would like to see a lot of me under the current circumstances is, unfortunately, another matter. I had called Breitscheid, but he is in London. I'll still probably get to see him. Will you be coming here to the congress on asylum?

Best regards, and to Hanna and Else, too.
Your,
Rudolf

Prague, June 5, 1936

Dear Rudolf,

I've received your letter of 28 May. I've passed along your communication about the conversation with Ulbricht. I don't assume that O[tto] W[els] has any desire to speak to him and that one will undertake anything else in regard to the non-aggression pact.

Austerity plans were discussed in yesterday's meeting of the Party Executive and it was decided to stop publishing the *ZfS* after the June issue. I did not expect anything else. Of course, I laid out my position there and spoke openly of the efforts to establish an intellectual journal outside of the Sopade. An argument followed (in which Stampfer, in particular, accused me of wanting to use it to organize a struggle against the party Executive). I replied to this criticism by declaring that it was never my intention to open a conflict against a body to which I belong. O[tto] W[els] then immediately brought the debate to an end with the assertion that matter was resolved.

The relaxation that was thereby achieved was illustrated today when we discussed the delegation to the Conference on the Right of Asylum and O[tto] W[els] recommended me. According to the previous division of labor, this delegation should have been a given, but I had not counted on the matter going so smoothly.

I'll take the trip as soon as I can, because I have a lot to do in the west. That also relieves me of the task of presenting my views and intentions regarding the *ZfS* and all other problems to you in writing. If I don't hear anything else, then I assume that you will be in Zürich from 13–15 June, which is probably the time that I can be there.

Today we only have to deal with the June issue of the *ZfS*, which will be printed in the next few days. The content is: Sering, Abramovitch, Bruggers, Fritz Brügel: "Bücher gegen die Barbarei" ["Books against Barbarism"], a review of foreign policy by Menne, and a review of politics in which I will consider the book *Ich kann nicht schweigen* [*I cannot be Silent*].

Best regards,
 [Paul]

[P.S.] Warmest regards from Else, too. I would love to also come to Zürich this time.

Hotel Post
St. Anton Am Arlberg, Tirol
July 21, 1936

Dear Paul,

Dr. Br[ett] was here on Saturday for a few hours.[215] In his opinion, as matters now stand, it doesn't make sense to make substantial means available at present, because the press is banned, and assemblies are not possible. I argued that, in Poland's unstable conditions, matters are not yet decided, and it would depend upon using far less money to make it possible for the parties to survive and possibly organize smaller, closed meetings where they could distribute flyers. He agreed with that and told me that he was in contact with Bro.[216] for that reason. He should write to him about what, under the current circumstances, is absolutely required.

I myself believe that, right now, politics is most important. Everything has to be tried, in London and in Paris, to mobilize what is possible. I discussed with Br[ett] that T[reviranus] should speak with [Winston] Churchill and [Neville] Chamberlain in London. He had already had that idea. Unfortunately, his exposé is not yet ready, because he is still waiting for the promised copy of the Danzig court's judgement on the last elections. I think it would also be very useful if O[tto] W[els] wrote directly to T[reviranus] and, if possible, also sent him the appropriate material.

Paris is important. Rosenfeld published a good article in *Populaire*. You might write to him again and, in any case, Fritz [Adler] must be constantly pushed. The matter goes beyond Danzig and, depending on circumstances, could be of decisive European importance.

What should happen to the sum that my American friend placed at our disposal? My Zürich friend, who requests, by the way, not to be named under any circumstances, rightly says that it would make no sense for the money to sit there without earning interest. In any case, my the American had not previ-

---

215 Dr. Brett was most likely one of the people from whom the Social Democrats hoped to raise funds to resolve the financial crisis at the *Volksstimme* in Danzig. See Hertz to Hilferding, April 24, 1936.
216 The identity of "Bro." is unclear.

ously instructed us. Perhaps write to him directly in a cautious way at the Hotel Karersee. You could directly dispose over half of the sum for Paris.

What is the situation with the *Zeitschrift*? How many issues do you think could still be published? Tell Klinger, please, he should tell me why my last article did not appear. In any case, he should send back the manuscript to me (I mean the article about Danzig).

Otherwise, nothing else is new with us. Unfortunately, the weather is very variable. I'll be back in Zürich next Monday or, at the latest, Wednesday.

Best wishes to Hanna, too, from Rose and me.
Your,
Rudolf

Prague, July 24, 1936

Dear Rudolf,

I got your letter of 21 [July].

We hear very little from our friends in Danzig. They are incredibly busy. We really have to put a capable person in Gdingen or Dirschau, who can maintain connections with our Danzig friends and simultaneously keep people abroad informed. In the next few days, after O[tto] W[els] gets back – he has been traveling for some time – I'll speak with him about it again. Given the lack of people who support us, it is not easy to find a suitable personality. This and similar cases show how fateful it is that thinking people who find themselves in the emigration don't want to have anything to do with Prague.

I am busy because of the judgement of the Danzig court. It was announced on 14 November. There is a notice about it in [*Neuer*] *Vörwarts* Number 128. I've enclosed it. Perhaps this offprint is enough for T[reviranus]. I'll pass along the suggestion that Otto W[els] write to him. I'll write to Rosenfeld. I'm pleased that you judged his article so favorably. You, yourself, should maintain a good connection with him. He is interested in our affairs and of good will. I again told Fritz [Adler] on the phone today how concerned we are about Danzig. But he does not see many possibilities for active intervention. Fritz declared that he is ready to publish an article "Danzig und Europa" ["Danzig and Europe"]. I'd think it would be good if you'd write to him. Then we could at least count on him finding an echo.

Klinger has published the part of your article concerning Danzig in the newest issue of *NV*. He told me to tell you that he cannot use the remaining part, because at the time of its arrival the agreement between Berlin and Vienna had changed the whole situation.

We are having bad luck this time with the *ZfS*. So far, I have neither the article by Sering nor the one by Henrichsen. I've sent reminders to both. I should receive Sering's in the next few days. but Henrichsen does not reply. I've spoken to W[illi] Mü[ller] about shortening and deepening his article on O[tto] B[auer]. He agreed that a simple abstract with a reference to his article in *Kampf* is not possible. The article by Bergner cannot be considered. It was already published in New Beginning's foreign news. I still hope that the issue can appear at the beginning of August. If that doesn't happen, I'm thinking about a double issue. I don't have any confirmation from Luise [Kautsky] about whether she had received the money, but I assume so. In any case, I don't want to take responsibility for publishing more than two issues or one double issue as long as the prospects for financial support don't improve. The first [person] with whom I'll talk about continued financing is Vladek. We expect him here in mid-August. If necessary, I'll turn to your friend Gustav in America. Still, I'd like it if you or I first talked with Otto Nathan about it. I'm also thinking of asking Vagts if he is interested and wants to help.[217]

By the way, the business with the archive is underway again. The offer was made through the embassy at 7.5 [million]. Nikol[ajewsky] suggests a counter-offer of 8 [million]. Modigl[iani] wants to demand 8.5 [million]. Fritz has the last word. Around here the inclination is toward an accommodation, in other words one is more for Nikolajewsky than Modigliani.

Wilfried arrived in London on Monday. Both kids are traveling together via Zürich. When I know the time and that you won't have to come through Zürich at 8 o'clock in the morning, I've be very pleased if you would take the opportunity to meet them at the station for a chat.

Best wishes,
 [Paul]

---

217 Alfred Vagts (1892–1986) was a poet and historian. A highly decorated officer during the First World War, under Weimar Vagts joined the SPD, taught at the University of Hamburg, helped build up the pro-Republican Reichsbanner para-military force, and promoted cooperation between liberals and socialists to defend the Republic. Married to the daughter of American historian Charles Beard, Vagts left Germany for the United States in 1932.

Prague, July 31, 1936

Dear Rudolf

Enclosed are two copies of a letter from Birnbaum. I've taken out some passages marked confidential. I want you to know, however, what this is about.

The first missing passage contained news that a discussion was planned with the Inspector of the Army, Orlicz-Dreszer, "who, as chair of the Polish Navy League was accessible and had emerged as one of the strongest voices among leading military figures against allowing the National Socialists in Danzig, of course purely for reasons of national power politics. As you might know from the newspapers, this man, upon whom the strongest hopes had been placed, was in a fatal accident three days before the planned visit. Previously, there was no access to the higher military circles that are also critical of [Poland's] friendly policy [toward Germany], because no one else had simultaneously emerged in such an organization. These two actions occurred in strict secrecy; even in Germany only a few key people had known about them".

The second missing passage concerned the news that Berlin "has explicitly pointed out several times – unfortunately that must also remain confidential! – that the opposition in Danzig would be dangerous for the regime in the Reich. This domestic anxiety was probably paraded around so explicitly in order to be able to deny any intention of foreign aggression as convincingly as possible".

I think it would be right for you to pass along a copy of the letter from Birnbaum to Dr. Brett. It would be expedient if he would again put his connection in London to use. What do you think about the possibilities in that regard? We have none here. However, I'm sending a copy of B[irnbaum's] letter to Breitscheid and Schiff, too, so that they can utilize their London connections.

O[tto] W[els] will be back on Monday. I am still of the opinion that the current situation is unbearable, because we don't hear anything at all directly from Danzig. Br[?] cannot possibly maintain their connection with us along with all his other tasks. I know a Polish citizen, who I think is smart and skilled [enough] to take on the job of keeping us appraised daily of what is going on. That is J. Landau, the author of the article "Poland vor der Krise" ["Poland before the Crisis"]. Birnbaum also thinks highly of him. If we sent him to Danzig, there would be no major expenses. Can you ask Brett if he is prepared to cover the costs if the Sopade does not want to do it? I estimate it would cost 200–300 Gulden per month.

The archive matter is underway again. Supposedly the buyers are prepared to pay 7.5 [million]. We have declared our agreement.

Powerful attacks are coming from Holland against our view of the unified organization of emigrants. The driver is its secretary, Schumacher. Bird brain! Reply soon.

Best wishes,
 [Paul]

Zürich, August 4, 1936

Dear Paul,

Bringing in Br[eitscheid] seems to me to be unnecessary. In any case, he doesn't need to be told where the money comes from. That is because it would be irresponsible to possibly expose St.[218] to a new discussion and, given Br[eitscheid's] current state of mind, that could easily happen. Couldn't Friedländer, the former city councilor, be entrusted with the distribution? In any case, it must be ensured that the money is distributed without regard to party membership, because St. expressly desired its charitable rather than political use. I completely agree with the donation to Deniki [sic]. I am thinking about a one-time transfer of 1,500 French francs that could done directly from here. Or are you thinking of more, about 2,000? I don't know the address, but Niko[lajewsky] knows it.

In regard to Müller's review, the point of view is not difficult for me. I still haven't read Otto [Bauer's] book. I am somewhat anxious about it, but I'll do it now. Müller's critique is a Communist perspective, since, going beyond Otto, he is expressly for dictatorship. That is decisive for me and I reject it. I also remain an opponent of the Popular Front and don't regard that as "integral socialism" or radicalism, but rather as dangerous and damaging opportunism. But what do we do with the article? Since you have taken over matters related to the *Zeitschrift*, you have to bear the responsibility and I leave the decision entirely to you. To nominate O[tto] B[auer] as the theoretician of the International is childish. Today he has as little influence on the International as any of us.

For the rest, I'm despondent about Spain. It's bad and will have far reaching consequences. The victory of reaction is a decisive victory for Muss[olini] and

---

218 It is unclear to whom "St." refers. Possibly Friedrich Stampfer. It appears that Hilferding and Hertz were directing charitable relief to Denicke (George Decker), who had been experiencing particularly hard times. See Hilferding to Hertz, October 25, 1935.

Hitler over France and England. I am convinced more than ever that the French Popular Front government is ruining France. My pessimism is deep.

What is happening with the archive negotiations and will there be a branch for scientific work, if also to a reduced extent? Please talk to Crum[menerl] about my salary and the other matter about which we have spoken.

Best wishes to you and Hannah.
 Your,
 Rudolf

[P.S.] I haven't heard from Thormann.

Prague, August 8, 1936

Dear Rudolf,

I'm sending you the enclosed article by Menne. I don't like it much. And if I didn't have such a shortage of contributions for the *ZfS*, I would have given it back. I am asking you to look at it right away and to send me your opinion. Menne has agreed to some changes. If it's the case that only individual parts of the article are promising, one could consider making a commentary out of it. Please send the manuscript back.

Sering's article should be in my hands by Monday. Urgent work for the institute, where S[ering] receives a stipend, had prevented him from submitting it on time. I also have not heard anything from Thormann. I will publish W[illi] M[üller's] article about O[tto] B[auer]. Some changes have been made. Above all the passage about O[tto] B[auer] as the theoretician of the International is now formulated in a way that is unobjectionable. I don't think that the rest of your complaints are as serious as you do. Without a certain degree of tolerance – when the authors sign their work and assume responsibility for it – we would not have survived previously.

Due to the late date, I would have been happy to do a double issue. But I lack material. Thus far, I only have the articles by Sering, W[illi] M[üller], Menne, and Ronai Zolnay. Do you still have some articles? Otherwise there will be no other choice but to produce a single issue.

I, too, am most worried that things will go badly in Spain. Once, again, we are experiencing how the world's fascist forces are fully deployed, while the democratic forces are fractured and stand aside passively and hesitantly. One should not deceive oneself: the wave of reaction that will sweep over the world if the Spanish fighters are defeated will be just as destructive as that of 1933. It seems to me that your judgement of the French Popular Front government is too one sided. Czech told me that B said to him that Leon Blum now enjoys great authority in England. Also important is his report that no one here is thinking of a special agreement between Prague and Berlin, but rather only about a European solution in which all existing treaties are maintained.

According to reports from F[ritz] A[dler] and B[oris] N[ikolajewsky], the buyers are prepared to close with 7.5 [million]. Supposedly, the signing of the contract and the payment of the first installment should take place on 5–6 of August, respectively. But we still don't have any news. At the moment, B[oris] N[ikolajewski] can't be reached by phone. He appears to be outside of Paris. We have not yet discussed whether, with the signing of the contract, internal agreements will remain in place and money will be diverted for scholarly work. But I believe that that will be the case if F[ritz] A[dler] and the Commission insist upon it.

Siegmund [Crummenerl] will talk to you about your salary. In any case he will be coming to Zurich in the near future.

Another trip is also in the offing for me, because the party Executive has decided that I should participate in the negotiations in Geneva dealing with refugee issues.

I'll follow your suggestion to ask little Friedländer and not Breitscheid. Wait just a little while, and I'll make a precise recommendation about what should be done. I agree completely with your recommendation about Denicke. I'll provide his address. It is not expedient to include a third person.

Wilfried and Hilde are here. Around 25 August they will start the trip back and seek you out.

Congratulations on your birthday. Hopefully, things will look better at 60.

Best wishes,

[Paul]

Copy

Zürich, August 28, 1936

(Hilf[erding] to Stampfer)

Thanks very much for your letter. It confirms, once again, that our political views, as always, since we've known one another, are at odds and cannot be reconciled.

First of all, you are fooling yourself completely in ascribing my motives. On the possibilities of influencing public opinion in general or the opinions of foreign parties through articles in *NV*, I am just as skeptical as you are – our single point of agreement. It is very simple: I want to tell *the truth*.

In my life I have always viewed the search for knowledge and discussion of what is known as the function and duty of the intellectual, especially in politics. [They are] a *raison d'etre*, and I've always striven to fulfill them even at the risk of being "disciplined" by the right-wing socialists [and] later, occasionally, by the USPD. Now, at a time when consideration of certain actions or situations of a living party no longer applies, when, therefore, discipline during the action is no longer an issue, the restrictions also disappear that must be imposed upon anyone active in an organizational context, so that he does not express misgivings during the action. I have never knowingly gone beyond that even when I was politically active.

I also cannot alter the situation when the truth is bitter and shatters illusions. The foreign policy successes of the German and Italian dictatorships are crucial facts. When illusions evaporate about help from the Reichswehr or from abroad, then that can only be beneficial. In any case, it hastens the recognition that overthrowing the dictatorship requires your own work and not a hoped-for miracle. Whether your own work will be successful [and] how long it will take is another matter, but it will at least be furthered by not denying reality.

What I say about the L[abor] P[arty] and the French Socialists is very considered. I won't let anyone take away my right to say it. It would be the worst dereliction of duty to refrain from criticism at a time when the life and death of freedom [and], perhaps, of the workers' movement is at stake. I derive the right to do that from the right of every discerning person to make use of his critical understanding. Whether one's perception is correct – and that's what we are talking about here – can only be determined by discussion and, in the end, history.

But our difference is, after all, also of a factual nature. Your judgement of foreign policy reminds me vividly of the domestic policy after Hitler's seizure of power. I am thinking of that speech in the Party Council, on the Lindenstraße, in March 1933, where you explained your happy mood. You returned to the time of your youth at the *Volksfreund* in Brünn as the confiscated copies were distributed in spite of the police, etc., and how, at the time, the party would rise again more gloriously than ever. It was after the Reichstag fire, after the beatings in the concentration camps, which you did not want to be true. You delude[d] not only yourself about the situation, but also the others, and, during the short time that we still had available, you prevented us from using it to create illegal cadre. When you, yourself, were then in exile, your concern was to hinder publishing about illegal German weapons, and I have not forgotten your somewhat strange agitation about me and Breitscheid, who you accused of supporting propaganda for a preventative war. You evaluate foreign policy today in exactly the same way. You write that Hitler has nothing. To me, that is simply grotesque, and I feel unable to discuss it. First of all, Hitler disposes over the strongest military power in the world even in the face of Russian strength, which is extraordinarily exaggerated in Russian propaganda. Since 7 March France has been "imprisoned in its own borders". Consolidated by military agreements, the strong German and Italian bloc, with its vassals in Austria, Hungary, and Bulgaria, militarily dominates Europe. Why you deny the cooperation with Italy, which has brought Italy Abyssinia, and allows it to safely defy England, is incomprehensible. That there will be an agreement about Austria has long been clear to me. It is there, and the cooperation continues, becomes closer, and more successful. But, of course, these low-life foreigners [Katzelmacher] have no loyalty. Hitler wants all of Austria for himself, because he comes from Braunau, and antagonisms exist among all great powers. That has never hindered their [forming a] coalition – Russia and England, for example, before 1914 – if there was a common goal to pursue. As I said, Germany and Italy dominate Europe militarily, above all in the west. Today England can scarcely send one division to the continent. By the time it is able to assert its strength militarily, the war could already be decided. Poland has Germany, Italy, and Russia to choose from. It is out of the question for it to choose Russia, as long as that can be avoided. France is too weak to be a lone ally. In an emergency, Poland will face a German and (perhaps) a Russian ultimatum. We cannot know what it will do. But it makes no sense to talk about details. Your mistake is that you see "Hitler", the person, and not his function. German state power has its own laws, which it obeys, and which not "Hitler", but a collective of leading men carry out, who are at the disposal of the whole apparatus of the Foreign Ministry and of the military. This policy is simple, not so hard to understand, and does not require overmuch intelligence on the part of its exponents, because they have the primitive logic of violence as their guiding principle. When you say it will bring about a catastrophe, I wonder what you mean by catastrophe. For Mussolini and Hitler war is not a catastrophe when they win it. And today there is already much that indicates they will win it, even if they have fewer allies than is probable –Titulescu[219] in Romania hovers in

---

219 Nicolae Titulescu (1882–1941) was a Romanian diplomat who served for long periods as that country's representative to the League of Nations and was twice its President. He

mid-air and Yugoslavia is hemmed in between Germany and Italy. Do you think, then, the growing fear of war in England and France is simply fantastical? The comparison with Wilhelm II is childish. Hitler and Mussolini's current foreign policy is not only far more solid, but it encounters no strong and determined governments like England and France had before the World War. Instead they have become almost incapable of action.

Thus, you can see that we judge matters in fundamentally different ways. But at least I can claim for myself that, in the course of the *Kampf* articles in 1934, I predicted that if Germany's rearmament was not prevented, it would mean the total transformation of power relations, which you ignore. That was easy then, and it is the crime of the LP and of the French Socialists to have spoiled that. Now it is all too late. France has become a second rank power, and its behavior on a vital issue like that of Spain shows how helpless it is in Western Europe, to say nothing about the East. England has lost its crucial position, and it will scarcely be able to restore it even after rearmament. The dumb, ignorant Hitler is now using the same methods in foreign policy that he used successfully in his domestic policy. Since England and France don't grasp that, they will pay just as dearly as we did. Unfortunately, we will be sacrificed for a second time. If Hitler should reach Vladivostok, which he does not intend and will not do, then, indeed, I will certainly no longer write, but I'll expect a letter from you in which you argue that we should not overestimate Hitler. What does he have, if he has the icy wastes of Siberia? In reality, Hitler has *nothing*!

With best regards,
   Respectfully yours,
   R. Hilferding

P.S. The letter was written on 24 August, but I had no opportunity to have it copied. Since then Titulescu has fallen. The more dangerous thing is that the chances for the seizure of power by Romanian fascists allied with Berlin are much improved. Events in Spain have had devastating effects and strengthened reaction everywhere, including in the West. The Flemings in Belgium, for example, are mostly pro-German, and in Holland, too, the pro-German orientation is growing. Greece under Metaxus has become an uncertain factor. The only good news is the Polish turn, presuming that it lasts. But it should not be overlooked that, after the occupation of the Rhineland, the Poles cannot take a firm

---

attempted to promote peaceful relations, stable borders, and collective security. As Hilferding intimated would happen in his letter, was removed by King Carol II in 1936 and sent into exile.

position against Germany, but at best can tone down Beck's policy toward Hitler. The Moscow trial has had a catastrophic impact and compromised the Popular Front policy. In that regard, I'll stress again that today everything in foreign policy is more unstable and unpredictable than before 1914. But, increasingly, on the dictators' side order is replacing the previous chaos and their efforts are more and more concentrated on a decision in the West, where what they need economically is to be had: rich areas, which alone can restore their shattered economies.

That is some of what I have to say to you. I don't think you'll misunderstand me. You know that I hold you personally in high regard, not only your abilities as a publicist, but also your dedication to the cause. Personally, things are and remain fine. But politically our old antagonism remains.

Again, best regards.
Respectfully yours,
R.H.

Zürich, August 14, 1936

Dear Paul,

In my view, the article by Menne is totally unusable. That a man from the coast of Flanders (page 3) is writing makes him untenable as a commentator on foreign policy. Also, we don't need to discredit our own foreign policy, which (after unification) was the only reasonably good thing we had going. But, above all, I think Menne's basic position that it is not the West, but rather the East that is threatened, is an outlook shared by some of Hitler's top people. The offensive plans of the French general staff serve beautifully as justification for fortifying the Rhineland. I don't think even Goebbels has gone that far.

I thought you'd publish the W[illi] Mü[ller] article. Meanwhile, I've read Otto [Bauer's] book and find all my fears confirmed. It is romantic communism bound up with incomprehensible optimism. The victory of socialism is no longer expected [to be carried out] by the working class in the developed countries, but rather by the Soviet army in a new world war, and it is expected that the English and French bourgeoisie makes itself into the dupe of Stalin, etc. It's possible, but there is nothing here for me. W[illi] Mü[ller] has only to object that O[tto] B[äuer] does not devote enough attention to Leninist organization, the legacy of which W[illi] Mü[ller] feels himself heir. You understand that I am in even less agreement with the critic than with the author.

For the rest, you see how difficult it has become for the *Zeitschrift* to get manuscripts. Unfortunately, that is no accident and cannot be traced back to my lack of ability as an editor. It is, rather, a sign of the inferior intellectual capacity and reduced participation. That might make the continuation of the *Zeitschrift* more problematic than the financial difficulties. I have no manuscripts. Today, however, comrade Dr. Fritz Bauer, Copenhagen, S Ridder Stig Vej 3, wrote to me that he had sent an extensive manuscript, which, upon my recommendation he has divided into four independent parts, to [*Neuer*] *Vorwärts*, but had not received a reply. Perhaps you could go and take a look at it to see if there is anything usable there.

Br[eitscheid] was here on his way back from London. In Paris he spoke with the most important people. I don't have the impression, however, that the matter is hopeful. In London nothing will be done that could disturb the planned conference. According to Br[eitscheid's] information, it seems that the planned call for a conference about Danzig collapsed not because of Poland, but England. It would be different if Poland's position changed. That seems rather improbable given the long-term strengthening of the German position. Naturally, this unfavorable outlook also terrifies my friend from Melide [Switzerland]. I myself, [...] have repeatedly talked to him on the phone and I wanted to meet with him. But, again, nothing has come of it, and I cannot write to him in detail because he is in Austria and I have reason to suppose that he is closely watched. I will try again to convince him of the necessity to do something in the meantime. If and when I'll succeed, I don't know. Apart from that, I'll make an attempt here, the outcome of which is uncertain.

I am annoyed that neither Fritz [Adler] nor [Hans] V[ogel] find it worthwhile to discuss the archive matter with me. Please write to me about it right away as soon as you have news. In contrast to you, I would be very pleased with the realization [of an agreement], but I hope that at least something is set aside for scholarly activity – it would be more necessary than ever. It would be very nice if you would discuss my personal business with Siegmund [Crummenerl] in advance. After all, you know how awkward I am in such matters. If possible, tell me about it before his arrival [here]. When is that to be expected?

For the rest, things look terrible. In any case, the Spanish business is a disaster. Spain is becoming a defenseless and, therefore, more desirable object of Italian and German striving for power and expansion. The behavior of the western powers is the strongest encouragement. France has broken international law to the disadvantage of the Spanish government – perhaps because it is already too weak for another policy and would have no English support for anything other than to give Hitler and Mussolini a free hand. England, too, following the Abyssinian catastrophe, appears to see backing away as its salvation.[220] Perhaps that is also no longer possible. But that is the precisely the terrible thing, that the Western powers today are already inferior. I believe that, with Blum is now persona grata in England, Macdonald, Baldwin, Eden, and Attlee couldn't wish for a more amenable and spineless partner. It is not for nothing that Siegburg is also dissatisfied with Blum and Ducloz. Regarding French domestic politics, too, there is nothing to revise in my judgement, as damned happy as I'd be to be wrong. I cannot see how France can get out of the crisis without inflation and that is political death for the left.

The manuscript will be sent commercial rate.

Best regards to you and Hannah!
Rudolf

[P.S.] Thanks for the wishes and greetings to Else. And one more thing: after sending my best regards, tell Arthur [Arnold] that I'd be very grateful if he would send [*Neuer*] *Vorwärts* to me [already] bound. I have the last volume, which ends on 31 March 1935, but I no longer have all the loose copies since then and need them for reference. It would be very important for me to have them in bound form since 1 April 1935.

Zürich, September 10, 1936

Dear Paul,

I'm in a pretty tight spot financially. I had counted on Cr[ummenerl] coming, but that seems to be taking forever. I'm also getting anxious because the Paris negotiations have stalled. Please tell Crum[menerl] either to pay me my salary for the fourth quarter now or to give me an advance. My expense money has also run out. If my salary will remain at 300 francs – I also cannot live on that – then he should pay me 900 francs plus 100 for expected expenses. It would be enough if he wrote me a letter agreeing to that, because I can withdraw money directly and it would be cheapest, but I won't do it without his approval. I would just like to ask that this be taken care of right away. Have you spoken about the balance or should one wait for the results in Paris?

---

220 "Auch England scheint nach der Abyssinian Katastrophe im Zurückweichen sein Heil (Hitler!) zu sehen.".

Have you spoken with Arthur [Arnold] about the bound copies of [*Neuer*] *V*[*orwarts*] and will I receive them?

I've paid P[aul] Bernhard 400 Swiss francs. He should give fifty Swiss francs to Mehring.[221] I urgently was asked to do this, because he was in miserable shape and I was very happy that there was an opportunity to do something for someone who was not a party comrade. I spoke at length with Bernhard and Sering. I was satisfied to be able to ascertain that they were pretty much in agreement with my view of Otto Bauer's book. The disgraceful Moscow trial is the clearest refutation of Bauer's apologia for the Bolsheviks. At the same time, it makes any association with the Communists undiscussable and shows *what* despotism is: Stalin-fascism is deadly for freedom.

When are you coming through here? And what is going on with the *Zeitschrift*? Sering left me the manuscript about people's socialism which is a brochure after all. I will get to it in the next few days.

I'm enclosing a letter to Stampfer that I'm asking you to give him because I don't have his private address. Please read it through. In case you would like a carbon copy, I can send it to you.

Best regards,
 Your,
 R.H.

Prague, October 18, 1936

Dear Rudolf,

On Friday I sent you an article from the *D.A.Z.* [*Deutsche Allgemeine Zeitung*] about the devaluation and I'm enclosing its continuation here. If you haven't used the clipping, send it back to me since I can use it for the sa.

I have not learned anything about the conversations between you, S[iegmund] Cr[ummenerl] and E[rich] O[llenhauer]. Siegmund Crummenerl only reported that he had come to an agreement with you about material matters and that you are working on a book about "democracy". You apparently impressed him very much. But I cannot discern whether he has come to any conclusions or what they are.

---

221 Walter Mehring (1896–1981) was a well-known German satirist. Despised by the Nazis, he fled into exile in May 1933.

When I got back from my trip, I found the Party Executive's circular on Neu Beginnen. I've enclosed a copy of a letter to Fritz Adler, from which you will learn all the details. Meanwhile, 14 days have passed. They have proved to me that my view was totally right. If I had not made perfectly clear that I would fight hard against any renewed conflict among the groups, we would scarcely have been able to avoid it. Currently I think that O[tto] W[els] has recognized that he had not carried out a master stroke. Apart from C[urt] G[eyer] and E[rich] R[inner], it seems that none of his other friends stand fully behind him. Certainly, no one will say that to him openly. But a series of signs leads me to believe that one wishes to avoid a renewed conflict among the groups.

The unfavorable echo caused by O[tto] W[els's] action, may underlay this opinion. While earlier on such occasions the grief-stricken people inside and outside the apparatus hurried to express their enthusiasm, this time they were all silent. Not a single letter of approval has arrived. On the other hand, we've received many letters of protest. I've enclosed two examples. I also want to say that these protests were not encouraged from here. They originated independently.

W[illi] Mü[ller] originally intended to answer publicly, indeed, through an article in the *Nachrichten*. He realized that that would be a mistake and satisfied himself with a letter to O[tto] W[els]. I assume that you have received this letter, so you can convince yourself that he is substantive and has actually offered to come to an understanding. If O[tto] W[els] were well advised, he would seize the opportunity. It would be useful for the whole movement. You could be active in this effort. If you were to decide to write a private letter to O[tto] W[els] on the subject, it would surely get him thinking. He seems to me currently to be in a situation in which he recognizes that the time has passed when he can act solely on his own.

In the Sudeten German party, the chaos cannot be exaggerated. Taub was recently on top and Jaksch was on his heels, but then Jaksch decided to defend himself and Taub capitulated. With the plan to put Franzl out of business, it seems to be over. I am the one who suffers. The arrangement for the special printing never existed. Now I am advertising the journal. The demand is there. The letter from Osterroth is just one of many in which the echo can be heard.

Strasser appears to understand that. In the last issue of *German Revolution*, he attacked me by saying that the *ZfS* is financed by the Third International. I sent him a correction and, in doing so took O[tto] W[els's] concerns into consideration. Nevertheless, I believe that the end has come for the *ZfS*. To be sure, I'm still not done mulling things over, but I'm now inclined to think that it is not worth the effort of a big fight with the party Executive.

From Hansen's letter,[222] which I've enclosed, you can see that, long before the decision [was made], one had already promised the northern idiot to halt publication. I've not answered Hansen's letter. But O[tto] W[els] left no doubt that Hansen is the second anti-Semite in the apparatus, and that his antisemitism is just as well known in northern Germany as Reinbold's is in western Germany.

If you, S[iegmund] Cr[ummenerl], and E[rich] O[llenhauer] have said anything interesting about your future intentions in respect to reorganization, let me know. In the meantime, things are calm, and the work continues as if the treasury were still full or as if in a few months one would be back in his old place.

Best regards,
 [Paul]

Zürich, October 21, 1936

Dear Paul,

First, some personal stuff. Have you already spoken with [Ambassador] Fier[linger].[223] about the passport? It becomes invalid at the end of December and it would be great if you could get one that was valid for a longer time. It is just as important for me to get a Czech passport for Rose. Her registration in Paris as a German refugee and the surrender of her German passport is very disagreeable. Her freedom of movement as a result of the visa requirements (the Swiss!) has been put into question, and the document, similar to the Nansen Passport, is like an arrest warrant. I'd be very grateful, if you look into both of these matters *very soon* and let me know what happened as soon as possible. In addition, could you also determine whether repatriation would be an option for Rose, or whether there is some way to make it possible, because she was born in what is now Czechoslovakian Nove Mesto nad Vahom.

Of the 700 shillings, I've sold 500 at 70 [French francs], after they'd fallen as low as 62, and held onto 200. An invoice for the money came from Bernhard in Paris. If you are interested, I'll send it to you when I can.

---

222   Richard Hansen (1887–1976) was a top SPD official, a leader of the Reichsbanner, and delegate to the Landtag in Schleswig-Holstein. After 1933 he became an SPD border secretary in Copenhagen.
223   On Zdanek Fierlinger see fn. 17 above.

Politically, I don't have much to tell you. It's too bad that the circular hadn't arrived when you were here. I am only familiar with paragraph VI, which was cited, and today I cannot remember very well what was in it. It did not have a very positive impact on me. But that is also not important. For me the decisive divide is between the supporters of democracy and those who support dictatorship. I feel separated from Otto Bauer, my best friend, and I'll never come near W[illi] Mü[ller]. He is and remains a Communist. Not only his identification with O[tto] Bauer proves that, but also the article in his *Nachrichten*, where it says "the question of democracy or dictatorship" can no longer exist. Today, for me, it is *the* question, and I regard working together with Communists, as well as the "Revolutionary Socialists", etc., as a mistake. I don't think anything of "international class war" – what idiocy, to convince the English and French bourgeoisie that it is in their class interest for England and France to be defeated by Hitler and Mussolini, and themselves to be annihilated in the process. These left socialists are even more idiotic than the Communists. I don't believe in revolutions in which one workers' party after another is crushed, and I believe that a united front with Communists doesn't weaken fascism but, on the contrary, strengthens it. The goal cannot be a united front or a united party that demands dictatorship, but rather the liquidation of the Communist Parties in Central and Western Europe. I also think the "Moscow disgrace" was a real disgrace,[224] and that shooting hostages is murder. In short, I can't associate myself with people for whom freedom and humanity are not absolute values.

I have not written to O[tto] W[els] because I don't want to unnecessarily get involved in this argument, but, in principle, I stand with Wels. On the other hand, I'd like to ask that you not say anything to W[illi] Mü[ller] about my views. I have the greatest mistrust in him, and it is not necessary to mobilize him against me now. I would like to determine the timing of an eventual argument myself.

I think it is right that you no longer want the *Zeitschrift* to appear. It certainly isn't worth the fight. I have not spoken with Crum[menerl] in detail about the reorganization, because he obviously wants to make his plans dependent on the negotiations with the Scandinavians. He talked to me about writing up my thoughts on democracy, etc., [but] I left it open. He [also] talked to me about

---

[224] The reference here is to the first of the show trials organized by Stalin in Moscow between 1936 and 1938 to destroy his perceived enemies, mainly the core of the "old Bolshevik" leadership that had made the revolution of 1917. In the so-called "Trial of the Sixteen", the key figures accused of "terrorism" and conspiring with Trotsky to wipe out the Soviet government were Grigory Zinoviev and Lev Kamenev. After "confessing", all were executed.

1,000 francs and transferred 500 (Swiss and, unfortunately, devalued) with 500 to come later, possibly in December. Did you talk to Rose about 2,000 RM?? She says so. I accepted Cr[ummenerl's] offer without discussion. Anyway, it was not pleasant.

At the beginning of last week, I was in Melide for four days, but I was unable to achieve anything in the Danzig matter. Breitscheid is on a trip to America. I wanted to write to you beforehand but did not get to it. Otherwise, it gets worse and worse.

Best regards. Don't get all too annoyed with me, but I just stand by democracy, like my old K[arl] K[autsky], and I cannot see anything but ruin in any pact with Bolshevism.
Your,
R.H.

Prague, October 26, 1936

Dear Rudolf,

Today I was at Fie[rlinger's], who was extraordinarily friendly, and we talked for 45 minutes. Regarding your concerns, I achieved the following result: At some point in November the Consul in Zürich will receive instructions from the Foreign Ministry to extend [the validity] of your passport at any time without making a request in advance. The business with Rose is much more difficult. In his personal opinion – he is unfamiliar with the official regulations – naturalization could only be considered if you get a divorce. But, even then, it is very difficult, as we know from a number of cases we've experienced. I asked, therefore, if Rose could get a passport, just as you have. Since I had to conclude from his remarks that the answer would be no, I asked whether Rose could be a co-registrant in your passport. He agreed to that. So, the Consul will also receive an instruction along those lines. In my view it is not ideal, but it is a fortunate solution. The officials in France don't need to know anything about the entry in your passport. It will always be possible [for her] to travel without a visa, as long as you don't need the passport for yourself alone.

I'll return later to the general remarks in your letter. I am neither wholly in agreement with your basic remarks nor with your current conclusions. I don't have time today to explain anything in more detail. I have to say, however, that, at present, it really hurts me not to be able to follow you. Of course, just as it is with K[arl] K[autsky], I know that it is your most deeply held conviction that has caused this difference of opinion. By the way, K[arl] K[autsky] was sick on 16 October, his eighty second birthday. He was hoarse and had a fever, etc., but he appears now to have put that behind him and he's working hard on the memoirs.

The article by F[riedrich] A[dler] on the Moscow Trial impressed me deeply. His evidence was completely convincing. I also agree with his political conclusions in respect to the Soviet Union. Do you have a different opinion?

Next to its disagreeableness, the polemic with Otto Strasser has also done some good. His open unmasking has motivated the party Executive to reply, which will be published in the next issue of *NV*. It is authored by C[urt] G[eyer] and approved by all. With that, the evil rumors about the close relations between Str[asser] and Social Democratic elements will be completely eliminated. Politically, however, the reply to Strasser is clear. That is a success of Sering's article.

Of course, I won't say anything about the content of your letter to W[illi] Mü[ller].

Indeed, I have spoken with Rose about 2000 RM but also with you. I don't think the arrangement with Siegmund [Crummenerl] is factually correct. But I know, that you are a poor advocate in your own affairs. Therefore, I'll give it my attention.

Paul Bernhard requests that the matter of the money be dealt with. I agree with his recommendations. He'll find you and talk with you directly about everything.

Best regards and to Rose as well.
[Paul]

Zürich, February 28, 1937

Dear Else [Lehmann],[225]

Please tell Paul that he should finally get in touch. Then tell Crumm[enerl] that I spoke briefly with Som[ary][226] – next time it will be at greater length. He has the same view as I do and thinks that, essentially, no changes are advisable. Ho[egner] is traveling. I'll speak to him next week.

---

225   See fn. 72 above.
226   Felix Somary. See fn. 170 above.

I'd also like to know whether a decision was made about the deputation of the Executive [Committee]? I would be grateful if Oll[enhauer] or someone else could send me a view words about their understanding of the situation in Germany, about the fate of V[orwärts] in Czechoslovakia, and also about the results of the last trip.

Best regards to all!
R.H.

Prague, March 30, 1937

Dear Rudolf,

I was in Vienna for a few days, where I met with the Stolpers.[227]

Karl and Luise [Kautsky] are well. Karl is much livelier than he was in December, although he did not leave the apartment for the whole winter. The legs are weak, the mind is strong. His book, *Sozialismus und Krieg* [*Socialism and War*] is being typeset at Orbis. Karl is now working on his memoirs.

I spoke with Peter [Hilferding]. He is satisfied with his business. It pays the bills. Karl [Hilferding] is also in Vienna but I did not talk to him. Peter only told me that he is negotiating with a South American university. Margarethe had the flu and I could not talk to her. I was glad to see Peter, [he is] knowledgeable and thoughtful. It's too bad he is in Vienna.

Enclosed is a description of the economic situation in Germany, which originated in Germany and was sent to Fritz Adler. I am also enclosing some other materials, which should be destroyed after reading. Tomorrow we are having a meeting about the reorganization. That will stimulate me to send you the promised letter.

My very best regards,
[Paul]

---

227   Gustav Stolper (1888–1947) was an Austro-German economist, journalist, and politician. He founded *Der Österreichische Volkswirt* (1913) and, with Toni Stolper (1890–1988), *Der Deutsche Volkswirt* (1926). Gustav represented the German State Party in the Reichstag after 1930. The Stolpers emigrated to the United States in 1933.

Prague, April 2, 1937

Dear Rudolf,

There is not much to say about the Party Executive's meeting on our financial situation. Crummenerl merely gave a treasurer's report for 1936. Expenditures amounted to 1.3 million Kc [Czechoslovakian crowns]. The publishing house required a subsidy of 202,000 Kc, *NV* needed 136,000 Kc, the *ZfS* 25,000 Kc, and the book business 41,000 Kc. He merely added that the available money should last until the end of September. Wels told us about the conversation with Höglund,[228] about which you surely know. He evaluates the Scandinavian action positively and thinks that a contribution is forthcoming that will allow expenditures at the previous level until the end of 1938. He also sees a silver lining for the business with the archive. It seems to me that Cr[ummenerl] is more pessimistic. It was interesting to me that no plans exist for cuts. When the terribly expensive costs of Stahl's car were criticized, one actually defended them.[229]

But that was the only point that caused a discussion. There wasn't a word about politics and nothing about the organization, in short nothing that could disturb the grave-like silence of our office. It has been like this for months. There are no more conferences with secretaries at all and there are only Executive Committee meetings to discuss questions of support or delegations. Everything rests upon not discussing issues that would require taking some kind of active step.

In the process, decline progresses inexorably. The book publishing house is dead. Only 107 copies of Stampfer's *14 Jahre* [*14 Years*] have been sold. Maybe over the course of the year that number will double or triple. Sales of other books are also practically zero. On average, the sale of *NV* came to about 4,500 copies per issue in 1936. Now, that number refers to the print run; sales are actually at about 3,000. The ban on colportage in the CSR and in Poland has reduced sales to about 1,000 copies per issue. Besides that, sales are decreasing in other countries.

---

228 Zeth Höglund (1884–1956) was a long-time leader of the left-wing of Swedish Social Democracy and a co-founder of the Swedish Communist Party. After a falling out with the Comintern, he returned to the Social Democrats in 1926 and was a member of the LSI Executive Committee from 1932–40.

229 Emil Stahl (1879–1956) was a Weimar labor leader in the transport sector. Regularly reelected to the SPD executive after 1924, he also served in the Prussian Landtag from 1928–1933. From 1933–38 he was the Sopade's border secretary in Reichenberg. Later, he represented the Sopade in Sweden.

The shortfall at NV was 136,000 Kc in 1936 and will be 100,000 more this year and thus will reach 60 per cent. In that regard, even the *ZfS* would be in a better position if it hadn't been dealt a death blow for political reasons. According to Cr[ummenerl's] data, the total costs for the first half of 1936 were 40,000 Kc, income was 18,000 Kc, thus the subsidy was 22,000 Kc. Even if you take these numbers as a basis, forty per cent [of the costs] could be covered by income. Actually, the proportion is much more positive. Above all, however, it could have been improved even more if one hadn't intended to axe a publication that caused discomfort. I still don't have the invoices for the last two issues. It is clear that there are only 30 copies of number 36 available and money will probably be paid for about 700 copies. The result is similar for the preceding issue.

I haven't changed my view that the *Zeitschrift* is necessary. I also believe that one could get the necessary subsidies. I estimate them today at no more than forty dollars per month. I still don't know what Breitscheid told you about Willi Müller's supposed plans for a journal. Consequently, I also can't take a position on it. That Breitscheid would oppose such a magazine would not bother me in the least. If in recent months I've made no particular efforts to drive these plans for a journal forward, the reason is primarily organizational. Without a compelling reason and without a guarantee of success I don't want to intensify the current strains in the body of our organization. Finally, I think it is a prerequisite of the plan's success that domestic collaborators be won over to the journal. The work has begun, but it is going forward slowly.

Organizationally, I think the Sopade's situation is increasingly unfavorable. The number of connections is constantly declining. The quality of reports is getting worse. The reports are made almost exclusively from this side of the border and most of the secretaries base them on information in the press. The *SA* is maintaining its previous print run. But I would really be fooling myself if I assumed that the distribution matched the print run. I don't think you can imagine them small enough. Previously, however, in some strata there was a need for an illegal paper. It is now greatly reduced. The Strasburg radio transmitter has gotten markedly better. The Communist short-wave transmitter on frequency 29, 8 is widely heard and has earned the Communists a great deal of sympathy. Now the question on the tip of everyone's tongue is: why the great sacrifice if we can safely educate via the radio? Nevertheless, it is out of the question that anything here can be done to solve this problem.

There are two considerations that are decisive for the total sterility: the first is that there was, is, and supposedly will be enough money available; and the second is that one is convinced that one will only get this money if a Scandinavian policy is pursued that is oriented according to the requirements of the German situation. Hence, total inactivity in the Spanish question; hence, disinterest in French developments; hence, rejection of the ever more urgent calls in Germany for loyal cooperation with the Communists and of a joint solution to radio programming, etc. In January, there was a delegation from Berlin here. It consisted of friends, whose political, moral, and intellectual qualifications were unquestionable. It was the first time that a part of the illegal movement, which had arisen under its own steam, and not been pumped up from the outside, came into contact with us. While we have seen our effort to create a headquarters in Berlin fail six to eight times at great cost in blood and treasure, such a headquarters was standing here before us. Our friends demanded that we on the outside work together with the Communists as loyally as those at home are doing. The cooperation at home is occurring under the guidance of Social Democratic principles. Our influence and our slogans would have all the more impact the more resolutely we take over the leadership on the issue of unity. Stampfer and H[ans] V[ogel] were very impressed by these discussions and suggested that we should emphasize the idea of unity more strongly. O[tto] W[els] rejected everything. The two folded and nothing changed. The external result is that the Communists mechanistically repeat in publications and radio programs that we want to play the same old dirty game. In our discussion, St[ampfer] correctly recognized that such a criticism will fatally wound us. The internal result is that the friends let it be known to me that they would not undertake a second effort to reach an understanding with the Party Executive and would definitively distance themselves from it. Because of that, the ongoing development is intensified: the Sopade's connections with valuable, political, and intellectually independent people is coming to an end. Relations continue on the basis of old friendship, conservative rigidity, and material considerations. I assume that you now think politically differently than I do about the united front and the popular front. But all I can tell you is that those are the only living currents there are in the German working class. If you deny them, then you separate yourself from them. Spain and France have created feelings that have called forth a fresh new vigor in contrast to the slogan: raise wages! It has merely deepened the perception that not the slightest intellectual and political connection exists between the émigré leadership and the underground movement.

You surely know that Sollmann is in America. He has developed nationalist emphases there in interviews and speeches and so strongly elevated Otto Strasser as a future force that he has become the target of attacks. He himself talks about a "slander campaign" against him emanating from Europe. But to make that claim he can only introduce one piece of evidence: the article from Sering in the *ZfS* was translated into English and distributed. I don't know if it is right. But even if it is, that does not justify one word in a slander campaign. I told

S[ollmann] my opinion in a lengthy letter. I reproached him there for stressing his connection with Otto Strasser, for his silence about his membership in the party Executive, and for his remark that, for him, divisions between the parties don't exist. He had done the opposite of that which he agreed to do with the party Executive. He went to England and the USA as an exponent of the Executive. We paid for his trip, his English lessons, etc. I can appreciate that he did not want to speak for Executive. But, then, the only consequence is that he cannot accept any assignment or payment from it. There can be no doubt that he did not go to America intending to raise money for the underground movement. He wants to build a basis for his existence, which is something I cannot hold against him. My letter, which was firm and in no way personally hurtful – that was Beyer's judgement, for example – hit S[ollmann] terribly hard. I only have one explanation for that; he sees that he'd been recognized, and he is, at the same time, somewhat horrified that he can no longer move in the half light, which was necessary, because he doesn't want to hurt anyone and wants to stand in good stead with everyone.

The fate of Georg Beyer is terrible: the daughter's appendix operation, the difficult financial situation of the factory, disagreeable personal battles with his traveling companions, and, above all, the worst thing – Beyer cannot use his limbs. He has been in under doctors' care for months with no improvement in his condition. He has been advised to take a cure in Pistyan. But he cannot travel alone, thus the costs are double. Nathan has contributed fifty dollars for him. From Paris, Toni Stolper sent me 150 dollars, which the Stolpers made available from their own means. Really laudable.

So, it has become a long litany. If the letter speaks to you, then maybe you'll want to reply.

Best regards,
[Paul]

Prague, August 8, 1937

Dear Rudolf,

I hope this letter reached you in time. If you want to let your sixtieth birthday pass by without much fuss, I still want to assure you that I'll always be grateful for everything I've learn from you after having worked together for twenty years, and that I hope you will retain your intellectual and physical vigor for a long time to come.

Nevertheless, I cannot express this recognition and my wishes without at the same time saying what I've often told you in person. I regret that, these days, we don't agree on many issues and that you have stood aside in respect to what is currently the most important problem we have to solve.

You have consistently pointed out that, in the current period, in which the organizational and agitational tasks stand in the background, there are two tasks that above all others must be solved. It is important to put the tactical problems of the party and of socialism up for discussion and to draw the intellectual consequences from the stormy political and economic transformations of the current epoch. That would only be possible, however, through the concentration and cooperation of the few intellectual forces still at the movement's disposal.

You can't hold it against me if I ask you today what you have contributed to the solution of this task. If I tell you what I think with complete frankness, then that occurs in the expectation – in which I've never been disappointed – that you are convinced of my good intentions. For sure, you helped found the *Zeitschrift*. But you did not resist at all when threadbare reasons were used to end the only attempt to solve the intellectual tasks and to bring people together. I recognize the shortcomings of the *Zeitschrift* as well as you do, but I am more convinced today than ever before that its content was not negative and that only it put before the public the most valuable beginnings toward renewal. The *Zeitschrift* is dead, the publishing house is closed down, and the intellectual face of Social Democracy is only provided by the *Deutschland Berichte* [*Reports from Germany*]. Two years ago, in a justified fit of anger, you polemicized against the shallowness that was expressed there at the time. Now, it appears to have escaped you completely that in the May *Bericht* the idea was put forward that intellectual resistance to National Socialism can only be promoted to a small degree through theoretical schooling. Hence, polemics are carried out there against the danger of "narrow minded half education and pigheaded attachment to principles", and against the "cancer of theoretical armor". It fits perfectly into this picture that, a few days ago, in a polemic about our basic attitude toward National Socialism, Stampfer said to me that everything we said in 1933 and 1934 about the prerequisites for overthrowing National Socialism was humbug. I assume that you, too, no longer stand by everything we wrote at that time about Social Democracy's revolutionary tasks. But I don't believe that you would make Rinner and Stampfer's opinion your own.

And what about the concentration of forces. My answer: inside of the Sopade it is hopeless. That is true for Germany and for abroad. The Sopade has no such forces within Germany and abroad it is losing those it still has. There was once a time when you thought about it as I did, but that is long in the past. Two years ago, you wrote to me from Adelboden, when you had read Sering's manuscript, [that] "it is important that we cooperate with Willi's people and I am grateful to you that you have brought it about". Much more recently you said to me (to be sure in an unjustified fit of anger) that you'd rather associate with Otto Wels than with Willi Müller. At that moment, in the letter just mentioned, I did not think that you had posed the rhetorical question [to me]: "am I now a Miles man, because I largely agree with these ideas?" I recently read Karl K[autsky's] critique of the brochure *Neu Beginnen* [*New Beginning*] in the *ZfS*. His criticism applied mainly to the theoretical and critical part. He agreed almost completely with the positive part. "The program Miles put forward for discussion is reasonable and can be accepted".

When I decided to work together with the New Beginning people, it was not Karl's theoretical insight that I was thinking about, rather it was the practical necessity to prevent people valuable to the movement from diverging completely and my just bearing witness to the group wars that constituted the existence of Social Democracy. I know I can probably only say of my activity over the last two years that I have prevented some bad things. I have not achieved much that is positive or valuable, but I believe the reason for that was because I had to follow the correct path alone; not because I was on the wrong path. Without support from you or Breitscheid, perhaps I can't make further progress. That's because, after four years of failure, I no longer harbor the hope that this can be achieved within the Sopade.

I hope that, despite everything, this letter has not spoiled the good spirits of your sixtieth birthday. I would not have written it if our last conversation just before my departure did not keep running through my head. But I'll tell you just as bluntly as in this entire letter, that, in spite of all the bitter experiences of the last four years, I would never think of making you responsible for my situation. The path I have taken was prescribed by my convictions and my sense of duty. The same motives will determine whatever I do in the future – which today is not yet discernable.

You don't need to reply to this letter. We'll have a chance to talk at length again.

Your,
    [Paul]

[P.S.] Dear Rudolf, I also want to wish you all the best on your birthday. I can also do that unconditionally and let Paul argue with you. Spend the day happily with Rose, to whom I also send warm regards. [Hannah]

Zürich, August 19, 1937

Dear Paul,

I was very pleased with your letter. I always prefer openness, especially between people who are close. But first one thing: I have consistently assumed, and I am still of this opinion, that in conversations with you, as someone who knows me, I can not only be open, but I can also sometimes exaggerate a bit. At the moment when something is problematic, one has the need to express it absolutely just to trigger the contradiction that one wants inwardly. It is also possible that I've sometimes chosen wording that easily could lead to misunderstanding. Now, someone recounted to me that you told someone else that I have become a capitalist liberal. Really? Even if you had had that suspicion, it would have been, first of all, more proper for you to discuss it with me, and, second, it was unnecessary to say that to a third person who is not in a position to make a judgement. Such a thing gets around very fast and is very welcome to many people, who, having a guilty conscience after capitulating to Stalin, would feel better after my treason. Now, I know you much too well in order not to know how easily you launch into abuse and, conversely, again too well, in order not to appreciate your personal feelings for me. But, objectively, it is disagreeable. Precisely because there are few people today to whom you can speak openly and with whom you can discuss the ideas that are running through your head, it's bad to also force these few to become restrained and cautious. Still, I recently was right to have the feeling that you have allowed yourself to be guided by restraint and caution with me. I viewed that as a result of your close relationship to W[illi] Müller, and I judged it as a certain doubt about my loyalty, but, in the end, I did not find it incomprehensible, I only felt bad that you had made that choice. But, on the other hand, I had also counted on your also not doing anything – not even in anger – that would pointlessly hurt me. You see, I am writing to you with total openness and that shows you that I still trust you and only recommend a bit more caution.

You reproach me for doing too little and, more recently, nothing at all to concentrate our intellectual forces. From your perspective, that is, perhaps, to a certain degree an understandable criticism. But I don't think much of "concentration" when it comes to intellectual forces. First of all, they have to be there, and they form themselves initially. Then they make themselves heard. In the *Zeitschrift* they scarcely made an appearance and, indeed, the journal could not carry on. The best evidence was the scandalous last issue.

I think that, instead of organizing what does not yet exist, it is more fitting to think things over for yourself, even at the risk of being accused of liberalism and of treason. In regard to concentration, however, I am in favor of the concentration of those who, today, hold onto what is most important: ethics and character, morality without a double standard, and the uncompromising advocacy of freedom. Today, more than ever, that means relentlessly distancing yourself from all forms of Bolshevism and Communism, the unmasking of Communist functionaries as paid scoundrels, combatting the so-called left socialist opportunists, in short, the uncompromising advocacy of freedom. Morally, the unmasking of Stalin as a criminal is imperative, as is showing the ever-greater similarity of Bolshevism and Fascism. Immediately after the split in Halle, I was already talking about the chasm that separates us from the Bolsheviks, and I've continued to do so, just like Karl, whose writings against Trotsky and Lenin were truly prophetic. Even today that is the salient point. That is what I value in Wels. Neu Beginnen started by rejecting the Communists. (The brochure wasn't by W[illi] M[ülller] and he rejected it). W[illi] M[üller] is now being led around by O[tto] Bauer, even after the gruesome series of murders, after the deepest decay. O[tto] B[auer] goes furthest today defending Stalin's crimes and denying any morality. He has sacrificed the idea to his mania for power and W[illi] M[üller] is running after him. (By the way, is it true that O[tto] B[auer] and W[illi] M[üller] intend to create a kind of Austro-German united party to displace and replace the SPD? That would be damned familiar to W[illi] M[üller], who has betrayed every party to which he has belonged.)

But that's enough. I feel it makes no sense to go on about it. I fear that you are closing your eyes to certain problems that seem most important to me. Recently, I read the works of W[ilhelm] Schlamm.[230] It's a shame that one has to leave it to an outsider to say what has to be said by Social Democracy. I don't know anything about the man, I don't like his style, but sometimes he says exactly what I think. (One thing, on page 141, the Appeal of the Italian Communist Party, [he] uses documents to show the degeneration of the Communists that goes beyond anything imaginable. And the united and popular front people want to unleash this pack of Communist functionaries on the

---

230   Wilhelm Siegmund Schlamm (1904–78) was an Austrian writer and journalist. After joining the KPÖ as a youth, he became an editor of the Viennese *Rote Fahne*. Expelled in 1929 as a right-wing deviationist, in 1933 he became editor of the *Weltbühne* after it moved from Berlin to Vienna. Horrified by the Moscow trials, he broke completely with Soviet Communism in 1937 in his book *Diktatur der Lüge: eine Abrechnung* [*Dictatorship of Lies: a Reckoning*], published in Zürich. He later emigrated to the United States where he became an intellectual of the far right and a protégé of Joseph McCarthy.

confused workers!) I'd like it if you would read the work attentively and without prejudice. But I fear that you won't do it. Hopefully, we'll talk again soon personally.

Many thanks to you and Hannah and best regards,
 Your,
 Rudolf

Prague, October 7, 1937

Dear Rudolf,

Through a fortunate accident I found out that you are now in Paris. But perhaps I myself am guilty for not knowing how you are doing and what your plans are because I neglected to answer your letter.

As you can see from the enclosed sketch of the Relewo trial in Zürich, I'll be in Zürich during the second half of November. I assume that Dr. Meyer had put you down as witness with your permission and that you will also be back in Zürich at that time.

Tony Stolper writes that you and Gustav Stolper are taking a European trip on 20 October, and that in due course you'll be in Vienna in November. So, you should be in Zürich at the beginning of November.

Best regards,
 [Paul]

Paris, January 12, 1938
Langham Hotel
19 Avenue de Friedland

Dear Paul,

It was dumb that I did not reply to you right away, but I thought that you knew. I was notified that I would receive an "Interim-Passport", in other words one for former German citizens. Since I could neither remain in Switzerland with such a passport nor could I get here in time (because of the visa), I came here on the 23 [December] using my still valid passport. I then wrote to Denesh in detail and sent the letter via a diplomatic courier. It was sent on 27 December. Meanwhile, I received a letter dated 27 December in which, on Krofta's order,[231] I was again informed about the approval of my interim passport. Oddly, I haven't heard a thing from Denesh. I can scarcely explain that; I would have understood a rejection, but not this silence. I was told that my letter to [President] B[enes], which was sealed, was given to Krofta, who wanted to pass it along. I can't imagine that that didn't happen. Meanwhile, I've tried to get a *titre de voyage* [travel pass] here. I hope I can get it. Everything takes so terribly long that I doubt I'll get it in time to come to Brussels.

That is disagreeable enough, but it is not my main concern, [which is] how and when will I get to Zürich. Dr. M is still sick, misses me a lot, and it I think it terrible to leave him in the lurch.

By the way, I am not very inclined to stay here. The situation among the local emigres is really confused. The "Popular Front" has broken down and is only outwardly (and dishonestly) continued although the break with the Communists is practically done. Champions of the united front are now Robert Breuer and Rud[olf] Leonard. Münz[enberg] came to see me. Only my authority (!) could unite the various socialist groups. Breitscheid had a falling out with [Max] Braun and claims to want to withdraw completely [from politics]. I also spoke with M[ax] Braun, who is now the "leader" here. I think it might be possible to accomplish something here because the political issue – popular or united front – no longer plays a role. But to do that the people have to be more suitable than they are at present, and so the grotesque situation of there being two Social Democratic weeklies will probably last a while.

But now to you. After our last conversation, I thought it was out of the question that such misunderstandings could arise that now afflict you. When have I ever let it be known that you don't seem trustworthy? And on the basis of "information?" I judge neither politics nor people on the basis of information. And if I did not think you were trustworthy, I'd have spoken to you less. In reality, I only argued with you about why *those in Prague* don't regard you as trustworthy, and my efforts aimed to create a basis upon which you and the others would be able first to talk things out and then work together. Thus, I don't believe myself either earlier or later to be the victim of any false information, all the less so since I never had any doubt in the truth of your statements to me. But you are obviously mistrustful of me, about which I really have a right to complain. How could you suppose I would take seriously the claim that you are an agent of the KPD Central Committee? That is just so foolish.

---

231   Kamil Krofta (1876–1945) was a Czechoslovakian historian and diplomat. He served as Foreign Minister in the cabinet of President Edvard Benes from 1936–1938.

I had written to O[tto] W[els] – as I also told Crum[menerl] – that I think a discussion is necessary, possible, and promising. What you tell me about your view of the supposed situation in Prague strengthens this conviction because in many respects Geyer and Crum[menerl] have said the same thing and are just as frustrated with the postponement of decisions as you are.

By the way, I don't have anything against your aim of concentration, if you don't pursue a united front or a popular front, which you are not. I have stronger doubts then you about carrying it out in the face of the people involved and the conditions of emigration. But I don't want to hinder you in the pursuit of your goals. I have to close, however. I wanted to write immediately, because otherwise it would be questionable when I'd answer. But my mind is so full of this passport business, which might possibly force me to stay here. When I've gotten over it, then I'll write a longer and more orderly letter to you. Meanwhile, write a few lines to me here.

Best regards to you and Hannah and also from my wife.
Your,
Rudolf

[P.S.] What do you hear about how the Kautskys are doing?

Paris, January 24, 1938
Langham Hotel
19 Avenue de Friedland

Dear Paul,

Thanks so much for your telegram, which was forwarded to me in Brussels. Unfortunately, the expected decision and any other news from you did not come. There is a lot riding for me on a favorable outcome, above all I would like to know if Benes has received the letter that I wrote to him personally and sent on 27 December. I am afraid that Krofta, who had taken it with him personally, may still have it, since otherwise I cannot explain why B[enes] has not responded. Have you been able to discern anything about it?

There is not much else that is new to report. Nothing especially important happened in Brussels. The conditions in Spain are judged with more confidence as a result of the strengthening of the government's military power. I fear, however, that the Italians and Germans will soon strengthen their intervention again. Yesterday, my fears were confirmed by an especially well-informed man, who nevertheless also indicated that the reports he'd received about the Italians now sending regular troops require verification. Not much has changed in the local situation. You probably know that Bernhard has definitively withdrawn from the *P[ariser] T[ageblatt]*. In any case, the Communists' money will not last very long, and it is thought that the paper will soon fold. I spoke to Max Braun, but I didn't know how, given the personal relations, an understanding could be reached with him in case Schiff's idea to create a monthly paper or Münzenberg's [idea] for a daily cannot be realized. At the moment I have strong doubts about pulling it off. Denike [*sic*] claims that the *Deutsche Freiheit* is at least viable.

If I find out anything more important, I'd write to you and answer fully any questions you might want to ask. Meanwhile, I hope for information from you as soon as possible.

Best regards to you and Hannah from me and my wife.
Your,
Rudolf

Prague, February 3, 1938

Dear Rudolf,

I still cannot tell you anything about the final decision regarding your passport. Thus far, my inquiries have brought the following results:

Krofta passed along your first application to the Passport Department, which issued a legal opinion. The matter then landed in the hands of the bureaucracy and the interim passport was issued as a solution. I have not been able to ascertain whether your letter ever found its way into Benes's hands. The Ambassador Rejholec, who replaced Fierlinger, has now promised me that he'll speak with Krofta and communicate to him all the reasons I provided on your behalf. At the same time, he'd ascertain the whereabouts of your letter to Benes. I should receive the information on Monday. Given this brief delay, today I won't describe any of the other possibilities that might result in the fulfillment of your wish. But, after having received this information, I'm not very optimistic. Your cause has landed in bureaucratic channels and you know what that means.

Otherwise, not much is new. Supposedly, our concern is being discussed today in the Council of Ministers. If it is correct that such a discussion will take place, then at is already an unfavorable sign. Internal problems are not discussed in the party Executive, neither the issue of whether and how the SA should appear, nor the other questions related to work within Germany. That is getting to be unbearable. Yesterday, there was an assembly of emigres at which Aufhäuser spoke about "social democratic concentration". Vogel participated in the discussion and spoke so negatively that he strongly disappointed Aufhäuser, who, as you know, currently has a very familiar relationship with O[tto] W[els] and F[riedrich] St[ampfer], etc. The atmosphere is dominated by purely personal resentments. I'm afraid that all attempts to change that are in vain, as I've feared for a long time.

You'll hear from me at the beginning of next week.

My very best greetings,
[Paul]

Prague, February 10, 1938

Dear Rudolf,

Unfortunately, I can't tell you anything new concerning the matter of your passport. There is no doubt that my connection, who was previously Fierlinger's secretary, wants to be helpful, but he is now reliant on his current boss. This person, the envoy Rejholec, also means well, but he has not yet taken care of the matter. I call every day and always get the same story.

Yesterday I sent a memorandum to you that was discussed over the last two days in the party Executive. Yesterday, O[tto] W[els], St[ampfer], E[rich] O[llenhauer], H[ans] V[ogel], and E[rich] R[inner] spoke. While the first four made an effort to discuss my ideas substantively, E[rich] R[inner] wanted to give me a moral talking to, indeed on your authority and that of Breitscheid. Of course, my rebuttal was short and sweet. But perhaps you are interested in what Arthur [Arnold] thinks. He has written it down [as follows:].

> I was ashamed of *Rinner*. Until this evening, I was never exactly sure of why so much. I was familiar with his ideas and I encountered them often with O[tto] W[els], Ollenhauer, and above all Stampfer. When *Stampfer* talked about them, I had to agree completely, because in spite of my efforts, I could not contradict him. But that *Rinner* would preach to you about morality – and in this form – is incomprehensible to me, despite my knowledge about what happened. The whole meeting was *at an unusually high level*. Whether or not you were able to convince O[tto] W[els] and Siegmund [Crummenerl], their statements revealed their deepest

inner conviction. Hans Vogel and Ollenhauer followed up, expanded, and delimited. But Rinner? [Preaching] morality to you? The manner of the substantive and impressive teacher, who one can forget, along with all the school fees, and who, lacking tact and advice, didn't learn to be tactful? Is this, perhaps, politics? "A debt of thanks is the most oppressive of all debts". (That approximates what I read a few days ago in the *Basler N[ational-Zeitung]*) Perhaps you did not notice at the time, but he attended a lecture in which one was able to hear about tact. That is *your* fault.

Dear Dr. Hertz don't let yourself be discouraged in any way by moral preaching. O[tto] W[els], Siegmund, Hans Vogel, Friedrich Stampfer, and Ollenhauer hung their heads ever lower. I cannot tell if Heine, who always applauded and expressed agreement with Rinner, spoke from the soul or whether they were as ashamed of the Sopade as I was. But the Sopade did actually hang its head lower and lower during Rinner's appeal.

So that you don't misunderstand me, Rudolf, I don't want to overdo the criticism of Rinner. After our last conversation and your last letter, I no longer falsely suspect you. I am only writing this to you in order to acquaint you with the atmosphere.

O[tto] W[els] had to go home during today's meeting. Arnold called and said he has the flu and a temperature of 40 degrees Celsius. The arguments hit him hard. He can scarcely hide his dislike of having such discussions at all. E[rich] O[llenhauer] just assured me that he had made an effort to get Wels to talk to me personally. But he failed. It is clear, however, that if O[tto] W[els] is now sick there will be even less leadership than before, and the hope to do something reasonable steadily dwindles. It is my firm conviction in that regard that only a trifle is required in order to bring about the concentration. Of the two people required for that to happen, Crum[menerl] is too stubborn and E[rich] O[llenhauer] maddeningly weak. I avoided any sharpness and, of course, laid down no ultimatum. I declared myself ready to find our way out of our political crisis upon another basis. But the hope for Swedish money and the sale of the archive lingers on and paralyzes any rational thinking.

I, too, have been in better health. I am very tired, sleep worse than usual, and am rarely able to work in the evenings. I need a few weeks to relax, but how can I do that now?

Best regards,
    [Paul]

Prague, March 6, 1938

Dear Rudolf,

E[rich] O[llenhauer] told me that you are back in Zürich. Unfortunately, I still cannot tell you anything about your passport. I'm constantly trying but get no information. I cannot press any harder. The attitude toward me has not become unfriendly, but one has other concerns and is not happy to be continually pressured. I'll try again in the next few days, but if it doesn't work, I'm going to drop it.

Hopefully, you've heard that our move to the west is basically decided. Whether to Brussels or Paris has not been determined and neither has the point in time. I reckon that it won't be long. The events in Austria are unfolding very quickly and it is necessary to move fast. The move will take place in stages. Mine will hopefully be in March.

I recently sent you my memorandum. It was discussed at length in a number of meetings of the party Executive. The debates provisionally concluded with the acceptance of the enclosed resolution. It is a complete "about face" as H[ans] V[ogel] rightly said. While it was argued during the initial debates that concentration via an agreement among the groups would not lead to unity, but rather to the perpetuation of the group system, it was later realized that only by this means can the liquidation of the groups be achieved. Another positive element of the discussion was that both sides expressed all of the many resentments that had piled up over the years. (Including a personal episode with E[rich] R[inner]). My friends and I also used the opportunity to say with complete openness what we have done in recent years. Under the impression of this information, efforts to belittle and underestimate our achievements had to be given up. It is now known that a very large part of the connections established with the Sopade were actually connections provided by N[eu] B[eginnen] or had adopted its standpoint. From the perspective of those who dominated the old party Executive that is a very bitter lesson and realization. If you think about the future of the whole movement, then that is reason for great hope. That's because it has to do with qualitatively highly developed connections.

The resolution was put forward by the majority. Originally, a sentence was to be included expressing disapproval of my behavior. During the debate it was also asserted that "sanctions" were necessary. In line with my view, which I've explained to you many times, I left no doubt that I was unwilling to accept any moral or moral-political condemnation. What I did, I did out of substantive, not personal, considerations. It was for the goal for which now everyone is striving, and that never would have been achieved had I not undertaken this dangerous tightrope walk in which my political life was threatened hourly. I won't allow myself to be proscribed for that. It appears to have worked, because article 16 disappeared.

The form and timing of the publication of the resolution still needs to be determined. Although the resolution represents unanimity of purpose, there are still big differences of opinion, however, about the path forward. The "about face" has many causes: 1) the transfer of headquarters to the west and the recognition that the position maintained thus far would have no roots there. 2) The fact that much more of the work will be shifted to foreign countries than was previously the case and will have to be adapted accordingly. 3) The finances are declining, and refinancing can only occur via concessions to the idea of unity and the creation of a broader basis.

The reason that the resolution has not yet be published is as follows: I demand that a body be convened consisting of representatives from all currents so that discussions about concentration can go forward in a democratic form. I think that this resolution will only be taken seriously if the announcement about the decision, in principle, to move toward concentration is made along with a call for the formation of such a committee. The majority, in contrast, at most wants to have loose, private discussions about concentration that would take place over a period of months. One hopes that the resolution alone would elevate [the group's] authority with the LSI, the French party, and the émigré community. I have the impression that it is believed some kind of agreement with Max Braun is possible, that an agreement can be reached at least with one part of the émigré community and thereby be able to avoid a really democratic fresh start for the movement. I think that would be unfortunate. I don't believe in a long-term, personal agreement with M[ax] B[raun]. That would be an agreement with a clique and not one with the part of the movement with which we are concerned. If we go west, then the task of maintaining connection with domestic German forces will be much harder than previously. The danger of becoming detached from it will increase. Whoever wants to avoid this danger will have to come to terms with those forces whose roots are in Germany.

That is as far as I wrote on Sunday. Meanwhile, the situation has changed. It was originally assumed that H[ans] V[ogel] and S[iegmund] C[rummenerl] alone would hold the discussions with the LSI about the move and finances. I took the position, however, that that could lead to the same attitudes as in December, when Siegmund Crummenerl and E[rich] O[llenhauer] were commissioned. In addition, I wanted to represent my position alone. Since I stuck to my guns, in the end no one contradicted me once I had replied affirmatively to Hans Vogel's question about whether I would go as a representative of the

Party Executive rather than NB. Still, they could not bring themselves to grant me full equality. Only you and Hans Vogel have been delegated to the LSI, even though the invitation has expressly allowed the right of expanded representation. The intention behind my exclusion at the meeting remains unclear to me. One wants to simply exclude me from the initial contact. I would not bother about it any further if I hadn't had to draw the conclusion that the desire for an agreement is very narrowly delimited. Furthermore, a danger is bound up with the party Executive's behavior. I am coming to Paris on Monday. No one will be able to keep me from speaking with friends from the LSI. What should I reply when I'm asked why I'm not coming into the negotiation room, but instead remain standing at the door? Today I alerted Erich Ollenhauer to the situation. My question made him very worried, and he promised to speak with Hans Vogel and Siegmund Crummenerl. But both disappeared before the discussion could take place.

I did not mean to bother you with our disputes. But I believe it is my duty to keep you informed. It could be that you are also asked when I'll appear. I'll phone you in any case at Rose's on Monday and hope to talk with you then.

I will reserve providing any more information about our local discussions for our conversation. For the present, I'll just give the following summary appraisal: the discussion straightened out many personal misunderstandings and cleared up an atmosphere that had become unbearable for both sides. In any case, I'd like to say that, as far as I am concerned, the possibility exists to begin cooperation on a new basis. Furthermore, complete clarity has been established about my relationship to NB [and] the relations and functions of the border secretaries to NB. The party Executive wants to make a clean break with the past, since it has recognized that the work we've done is valuable, and that any other behavior would only lead to its separation from the politically and numerically most significant parts of the German workers' movement. It's basis in Germany would then be narrower than that of any other group.

But future cooperation is not yet certain. The agreement on a resolution regarding the issue of concentration is not enough by itself. Drawing the groups together must also be connected with an attempt at a democratic renewal of the movement. It has become clear that it would be a mistake to remove the party Executive and to replace it with a new one. But the current situation can't work. You have told me yourself that a party Executive without me is impossible. The majority thinks differently about that. Its goal is to exclude me, and all the pretty words don't change a thing. You know that I am not attached to my paid position and I've relinquished it. But I did it not to let myself be excluded, but rather in order to eliminate the obstacles that stand in the way of creating a new, viable representational body. My recommendation is that the party Executive should begin the concentration [process] by calling for the formation of a small advisory group. Its composition should include the following: party Executive, Social Democracy in the west, the Mühlhausen group, the Neu Beginnen Group, and representatives of autonomous districts, like Württemberg. This approach would prevent émigré interests from dominating the group. It represents the form of representation that is possible today for forces operating in Germany. Without this body, the resolution of the party Executive remains a theoretical commitment. If the party Executive insists on this standpoint, a concentration of forces under its leadership could scarcely occur.

It you want to contribute to the establishment of an effective nucleus of a new movement from the fragmented remains of the current one, you have to clearly tell Hans Vogel and Siegmund Crummenerl that 1) a rump party Executive without me is not a body with enough authority and 2) that a theoretical commitment to the concentration of forces is not enough; the creation of an advisory body is required.

Today I learned only by accident that Hans Vogel and Siegmund Crummenerl have already departed, while yesterday they had said Vogel wanted to leave tomorrow or Friday and Crummenerl on Sunday or Monday. Their intention is clear: I now know what I should think about their assurances of total loyalty.

Best regards,
 [Paul]

[P.S.] Today the Foreign Ministry informed me that all your requests have been passed along to the Presidential Chancellery. My confidant is no longer in a position to do anything directly. I am having difficulties with my own case.

Bibliography

Archival Sources

International Institute for Social History

Paul Hertz Papers
Rudolf Hilferding Papers (TH 1–22)
Karl Kautsky Papers (KDXII 577–670)

Published Sources

Adler, Friedrich (ed.) 1954, *Victor Adler: Briefwechsel mit August Bebel und Karl Kautsky*, Vienna: Verlag der Wiener Volksbuchhandlung.
Adler, Friedrich 1933, "Zur Diskusison über Sowjetrussland. Ein Briefwechsel mit Karl Kautsky", *Der Kampf* XXVI: 58–69.
Adolph, Hans J.L. 1971, *Otto Wels und die Politik der deutschen Sozialdemokratie 1894–1939. Eine politische Biographie*, Walter de Gruyter & Co.: Berlin.
Appelius, Stefan 1999, *Die SPD und Der Lange Weg zur Macht*, Essen: Klartext Verlag.
Bauer, Otto 1909–1910, "Das Finanzkapital", *Der Kampf* 3: 397.
Bauer, Otto 1931, *Kapitalismus und Sozialismus nach dem Weltkrieg: Rationalisierung, Fehlrationalisierung*, Berlin: Büchergilde Gutenberg.
Behring, Rainer 2007, "Oprion für den Westen. Rudolf Hilferding, Curt Geyer und der antitotalitäre Konsens", in Mike Schmeitzer (ed.), *Totalitarismuskritik von links: Deutsche Diskurse im 20. Jahrhundert*, Göttingen: Vandenhoeck & Ruprecht.
Behring, Rainer 2019, "Vom marxistischen Theoretiker zum politischen Denker: Rudolf Hilferdings Konzept des 'organisierten Kapitalismus' und die angelsächsischen Demokratien", in Detlef Lehnert (ed.), *Soziale Demokratie und Kapitalismus: Die Weimarer Republik im Vergleich*, Berlin: Metropol Verlag.
Benz, Wolfgang, and Graml, Hermann (eds.) 1988, *Biographisches Lexikon zur Weimarer Republik*, Munich: Verlag C.H. Beck.
Bernstein, Eduard, "Rezension Marx-Studien", in Bernstein, Eduard (ed.) 1969, *Dokumente des Sozialismus, Band IV*, reprint, New York: Burt Franklin.
Blum, Mark E. and Smaldone, William (eds.) 2016/2017, *Austro-Marxism: The Ideology of Unity, Vols. I & II*, Leiden & Boston: Brill.
Blumenberg, Werner 1960, *Karl Kautsky's Literarisches Werk: eine bibliographical Übersicht*, Amsterdam: Mouton & Co.
Bottomore, Tom, and Goode, Patrick (eds.) 1978, *Austro-Marxism*, Oxford: Oxford University Press.

Braunthal, Julius 1978, *Geschichte der Internationale, Band 1*, Berlin/Bonn: Verlag J.H.W. Dietz.

Braunthal, Julius 1965, *Victor und Friedrich Adler: Zwei Generationen Arbeiterbewegung*, Vienna: Verlag der Wiener Buchhandlung.

Buchholz, Marlis, and Rother, Bernd (eds.) 1995, *Der Parteivorstand der SPD im Exil. Protokolle der Sopade 1933–1940*, Bonn: J.H.W. Dietz Nachfolger.

Calkins, Kenneth R. 1979, *Hugo Haase. Democrat and Revolutionary*, Durham: Carolina Academic Press.

Cohnstaedt, Wilhelm 1904, *Die Agrarfrage in der deutschen Sozialdemokratie von Karl Marx bis zum Breslauer Parteitag*, Munchen: Ernst Reinhart Verlagsbuchhandlung.

Cole, G.D.H. 1956, *A History of Socialist Thought, Volume III, Part I: The Second International, 1889–1914*, London: Macmillan & Co. 1956.

Cole, G.D.H. 1956, *A History of Socialist Thought, Volume III. Part II. The Second International: 1889–1914*, London: Macmillan & Co.

Deutscher, Isaac 2015, *The Prophet. The Life of Leon Trotsky*, London & New York: Verso.

Dowe, Dieter, and Klotzbach, Kurt, (eds.) 2004, "Prager Manifest der Sopade 1934: Kampf und Ziel des revolutionäre Sozialismus. Die Politik der Sozialdemokratischen Partei Deutschlands", in *Programmatische Dokumente der deutschen Sozialdemokratie*, Bonn: J.H.W. Dietz Nachf.

Edinger, Lewis J. 1956, *German Exile Politics: The Social Democratic Executive Committee in the Nazi Era*, Berkeley & Los Angeles: University of California Press.

Emil, Karl (Hilferding) 1907/08, "Der deutsche Imperialismus und die innere Politik", *Neue Zeit* 26, 1: 148–163.

Emil, Karl (Hilferding) 1906/07, "Der Internationale Kongress in Stuttgart", *Neue Zeit*, 25, 2: 660–67.

Emil, Karl (Hilferding) 1916/17, "Handelspolitische Fragen", *Neue Zeit* 35, 1: 5–11, 40–47, 91–99, 118–26, 141–46, 205–16, 241–46.

Geary, Dick 1987, *Karl Kautsky*, New York: St. Martin's Press.

Gottschalch Wilfriled 1962, *Strukturveränderungen der Gesellschaft und politisches Handeln in der Lehre von Rudolf Hilferding*, Berlin: Dunker und Humblot.

Gilcher-Holtey, Ingrid 1986, *Das Mandat des Intellektuellen: Karl Kautsky und die Sozialdemokratie*, Berlin: Siedler Verlag.

Graml, Hermann (ed.) 1994, *Widerstand im Dritten Reich. Probleme, Ereignisse, Gestalten*, Frankfürt am Main: Fischer Taschenbuch Verlag.

Grasmann, Peter 1976, *Sozialdemokraten gegen Hitler, 1933–1945*, Munich: G. Olzog.

Grau, R., Hortzschansky, W., et. Al. (eds.) 1970, *Geschichte der deutschen Arbeiterbewegung: Biographisches Lexikon*, Berlin: Dietz Verlag.

Grebing, Helga and Wickert, Christl (eds.) 1994, *Das „andere Deutschland" im Widerstand gegen den Nationalsozialismus. Beiträge zur politischen Überwindung der nationalsozialistischen Diktatur im Exil und im Dritten Reich*, Essen: Klartext Verlag.

Greitens, Jan 2012, *Finanzkapital und Finanzsysteme: "Das Finanzkapital" von Rudolf Hilferding*, Marburg: Metropolitan Verlag.

Greitens, Jan 2013, "Marxian and non-Marxian Foundations of Rudolf Hilferding's Finance Capital", *The History of Economic Thought* 55: 1: 18–35.

Gronow, Jukka 2017, *On the Formation of Marxism: Karl Kautsky's Theory of Capitalism, the Marxism of the Second International and Karl Marx's Critique of Political Economy*, Chicago: Haymarket.

Hass, Gerhard, Obermann, Karl, et. Al. (eds) 1970, *Biographisches Lexikon zur deutschen Geschichte: Von den Anfängen bis 1945*, Berlin, VEB Deutscher Verlag der Wissenschaften.

Hebel-Kunze, Bärbel 1977 *SPD und Faschismus. Zur politischen und organisatorischen Entwicklung der SPD*, Frankurt am Main: Röderberg-Verlag.

Hild-Berg, Annette (1994), *Toni Sender (1888–1964): Ein Leben im Namen der Freiheit und der sozialen Gerechtigkeit*, Köln: Bund-Verlag.

Hilferding, Rudolf 1954, "Das historische Problem", edited and introduced by Benedikt Kautsky, *Zeitschrift für Politik* (new series) 1: 293–324.

Hilferding, Rudolf 1908–09, "Der Revisionismus und die Internationale", *Neue Zeit* 27, 2: 161–174.

Hilferding, Rudolf 1915a, "Europäer nicht Mitteleuropäer!" *Der Kampf* 8: 357–65.

Hilferding, Rudolf 1981, *Finance Capital. A Study in the Latest Phase of Capitalist Development*. Edited with an introduction by Tom Bottomore. From Translations by Morris Watnick and Sam Gordon, London: Routledge & Kegan Paul.

Hilferding 1930, "In die Gefahrenzone", *Die Gesellschaft* 7, 2: 290–97.

Hilferding, Rudolf 1916, "Phantasie oder Gelehrsamkeit", *Der Kampf* 9: 54–63.

Hilferding, Rudolf 1982, "Revolutionäre Macht oder Machtillusionen", in Cora Stephan (ed.), *Zwishen den Stühlen, oder über die Unvereinbarkeit von Theorie und Praxis: Schriften Rudolf Hilferdings*, Bonn: J.H.W. Dietz Nachf.

Hilferding, Rudolf 1903/04a, "Die ersten Elemente der Wirtschaftslehre", *Neue Zeit* 22, 2: 700.

Hilferding, Rudolf 1915b, "Die Sozialdemokratie am Scheidewege", *Neue Zeit* 33, 2: 489–99.

Hilferding, Rudolf 1914/15, "Sozialistische Betrachtungen zum Weltkrieg. Besprechung von Max Adler, Prinzip oder Romantik?" *Neue Zeit* 33, 2: 840–44

Hilferding, Rudolf 1903/04b, "Staatswissenschaftliche Abhandlungen", *Neue Zeit* 22, 2: 497–500.

Hilferding, Rudolf 1904/05a, "Untersuchung über die Gründsätze der für das menschliche Glück dienlichen Verteilung des Reichtums", *Neue Zeit* 23, 2 (1904/05): 329.

Hilferding, Rudolf 1903, "Werner Sombart, 'Der moderne Kapitalismus,'" *Zeitschrift für Volkswirtschaft, Sozialpolitik und Verwaltung*, 12: 446–553

Hilferding, Rudolf 1903/1904, "Zur Frage des Generalstreiks", *Neue Zeit* 22, 1: 134–142.

Hilferding Rudolf 1904/05b, "Zur Problemstellung der theoretischen Ökonomie bei Karl Marx", *Neue Zeit*, 23, 1: 101–112.

Hilferding, Rudolf 1919, *Zur Sozialisierungsfrage. Referat auf dem 10. Deutschen Gewerkschaftkongress vom 30. Juni bus 5. Juli 1919 zu Nürnberg*, Berlin.

Hilferding, Rudolf, and Adler, Max (eds.) 1904, *Marx-Studien: Blätter zur Theorie und Politik des wissenschaftlichen Sozialismus, erster Band*, Vienna: Wiener Volksbuchhandlung.

Jones, William 1999, *The Lost Debate: German Socialist Intellectuals and Totalitarianism*, Urbana & Chicago: University of Illinois Press.

Kampfmeyer, Paul (ed.) 1947, *Das Heidelberger Programm*, Offenbach am Main: Bollwerk Verlag Karl Drott.

Kautsky, John H. 1994, *Karl Kautsky: Marxism, Revolution, & Democracy*, New Brunswick & London: Transaction Publishers.

Kautsky, Karl 1927, "De Man als Lehrer", *Die Gesellschaft* 4, 1: 62–77.

Kautsky, Karl 1918, *Demokratie oder Diktatur*, Berlin: Cassirer.

Kautsky, Karl 1916/17, "Der Eispalast", *Die Neue Zeit* 35, 1: 609–613.

Kautsky, Karl 1927, *Die Materialistische Geschichtsauffassung*, 2 Bde., Berlin: J.H.W. Dietz.

Kautsky, Karl 1925, "Eduard Bernstein zu seinem fünfundsiebzigsten Geburtstag", *Die Gesellschaft* II: 1–22.

Kautsky, Karl 1918, *Franz Mehring und die deutsche Sozialdemokratie. Ein Beitrag zur Parteigeschichte*, Dessau: Self-published.

Karl Kautsky, 1910–1911, "Finanzkapital und Krisen", *Neue Zeit* 29, 1: 883

Kautsky, Karl 1935, "Gedanken über die Einheitsfront", *Zeitschrift für Sozialismus* 26, 7: 825–38.

Kautsku, Karl 1933, "Heinrich Braun. Ein Beitrag zur Geschichte der deutschen Sozialdemokratie", *Die Gesellschaft* 10, 2: 155–72.

Kautsky, Karl 1932, *Krieg and Demokratie. Eine historische Untersuchung und Darstellung ihrer Wechselwirkungen in der Neuzeit*, Berlin: J.H.W. Dietz.

Kautsky, Karl 1918, *Kriegsmarxismus. Eine theoretische Grundlegung der Politik des 4. August*, Vienna, Wiener Volksbuchhandlung.

Kautsky, Karl 1918. *Sozialdemokratische Bemerkungen zur Übergangswirtschaft*, Leipzig, Leipziger Buchdruckerei.

Kautsky, Karl 1937, *Sozialisten und Kriege. Ein Beitrag zur Ideengeschichte des Sozialismus von den Hussiten bis zum Völkerbund*, Prague: Orbis-Verlag.

Kautsky, Karl 1971, *The Dictatorship of the Proletariat*, Ann Arbor: The University of Michigan Press.

Kautsky, Karl 1919, *Was ist Sozialisierung? Referat gehalten auf dem 2. Reihskongress der Arbeiter-, Soldaten-, und Bauernräte am 14. April 1919*, Berlin: Linden Drückerei u. Verlags-Gesellschaft

Kautsky, Karl Jr. (ed.) 1971, *August Bebels Briefwechsel mit Karl Kautsky*, Assen: Van Gorcum & Co.

Kern, Richard (Hilferding) 1934–1935, "Das Londoner Abkommen", *Zeitschrift für Sozialismus* 2: 561–68.

Kern, Richard (Hilferding) 1934–1935, "Das Ende der Völkerbundpolitik", *Zeitschrift für Sozialismus*, 2: 621–37.

Kern, Richard (Hilferding) 1934, "Die Internationale vor der Entscheidung", *Der Kampf* 27, 2: 41–47.

Kern, Richard (Hilferding) 1934, "Karl Kautsky", *Zeitschrift für Sozialismus* 1, 12/13: 369–75.

Kern, Richard (Hilferding) 1934–1935, "Macht ohne Diplomatie – Diplomatie ohne Macht", *Zeitschrift für Sozialismus* 2: 593–604.

Kern, Richard (Hilferding) 1933–1934, "Die Zeit und die Aufgabe", *Sozialistische Revolution* 1, 1: 1–3

Klozt, Johannes 1983, *Das "kommende Deutschland": Vorstellungen und Konzeptionen des sozialdemokratischen Parteivorstandes im Exil 1933–1945 zu Staat und Wirtschaft*, Cologne: Pahl-Rugenstein Verlag.

Kurata, Minoru 1978, "Rudolf Hilferding, Wiener Zeit: Eine Biographie (2)", *Economic Review* 29, 2: 25–35.

Langkau-Alex, Ursula 1988, "Paul Hertz (1888–1961): Realpolitiker im Dienste der sozialdemokratischen Utopie", in Peter Lösche, Michael Scholing and Franz Walter (eds.), *Vor dem Vergessen bewahren. Lebenswege Weimarer Sozialdemokraten*, Berlin: Colloquium Verlag.

Langkau-Alex, Ursula 1977, *Volksfront für Deutschland. Band 1: Vorgeschichte und Gründung des 'Ausschusses zur Vorbereitung einer deutschen Volksfront,' 1933–1936*, Frankfurt am Main: Syndicat.

Lederer, Emil 1915, "Zur Soziologie des Weltkriegs", *Archiv für Sozialwissenschaft und Sozialpolitik* 39: 347–84.

Lewis, Ben (ed.) 2020, *Karl Kautsky on Democracy and Republicanism*, Leiden & Boston: Brill.

List, Eveline 2006, *Mutterliebe und Geburtenkontrolle – Zwischen Psychoanalyse und Sozialismus. Die Geschichte der Margarethe Hilferding-Hönigsberg*, Vienna: Mandelbaum Verlag.

Liebich, André 1997, *From the Other Shore: Russian Social Democracy After 1921*, Cambridge & London: Harvard University Press.

List, Eveline 2006, *Mutterliebe und Geburtenkontrolle – Zwischen Psychoanalyse und Sozialismus. Die Geschichte der Margarethe Hilferding-Hönigsberg*, Budapest: Mandelbaum Verlag.

Lösche, Peter, Schöling, Michae, and Walter, Franz (eds.) 1988, *Vor dem Vergessen bewahren: Lebenswege Weimarer Sozialdemokraten*, Berlin: Colloquium Verlag.

Mammach, Klaus 1974, *Die Deutsche antifaschistische Widerstandsbewegung 1933–1939*, Berlin, Dietz Verlag.

Mammach, Klaus 1984, *Widerstand 1933–1939. Geschichte der deutschen antifaschistischen Widerstandsbewegung im Inland und in der Emigration*, Berlin: Pahl Rugenstein.

Matthias, Erich (ed) 1968, *Mit dem Gesicht nach Deutschland. Eine Dokumentation über die sozialdemokratische Emigration. Aus dem Nachlaß von Friedrich Stampfer ergänzt dürch andere Überlieferungen*, Düssseldorf: Droste Verlag.

Marx, Karl 1967, *Capital. A Critique of Political Economy. Volume II*, Moscow, Progress Publishers.

Marx, Karl, and Engles, Friedrich 1985, *The Communist Manifesto*, New York: International Publishers.

Mehring, Franz 1918, *Karl Marx. Geschichte seines Lebens*, Leipzig: Verlag der Leipziger Buchdruckerei.

Meyer, Thomas, Klär, Karl-Heinz, et. Al. (eds.) 1986, *Lexikon des Sozialismus*, Cologne: Bund-Verlag.

Morgan, David W. 1975, *The Socialist Left and the German Revolution. A History oft he German Independent Social Democratic Party, 1917–1923*, Ithaca & London: Cornell University Press.

Morina Christine 2016, *Die Erfindung des Marxismus: Wie eine Idee die Welt eroberte*, Munich: Siedler.

Nenning, Günther 1973, "Biographie Carl Grünbergs", *Indexband zum Archiv dür die Geschichte des Sozialismus und der Arbeiterbewegung*, Graz: Limmat Verlag.

Nettl, J.P. 1969, *Rosa Luxemburg*, New York, Shocken Books.

Patch, William 1998, *Heinrich Brüning and the Dissolution of the Weimar Republic*, Cambridge: Cambridge University Press.

Osterroth, Franz 1960, *Biographisches Lexikon des Sozialismus. Band I: Verstorbene Persönlichkeiten*, Hannover: Verlag J.H.W. Dietz Nachfolger.

Palmier, Jean-Michel 2006, *Weimar in Exile. The Antifascist Emigration in Europe and America*. Translated by David Fernbach, London: Verso.

Pierson, Stanley 1993, *Marxist Intellectuals and the Working-Class Mentality in Germany, 1887–1912*, Cambridge, MA: Harvard University Press.

Pistorius, Peter 1970, *Rudolf Breitscheid 1874–1944. Ein biographischer Beitrag zur deutschen Parteiengeschichte*. Nuremberg: Druckschnelldienst Nürnberg.

Prager, Eugen 1970, *Geschichte der USPD*, Berlin: reprint of 1921 edition, Glashütten im Taunus, Auvermann.

Regneri, Günter 2013, *Luise Kautsky: Seele des internationalen Marxismus – Freundin von Rosa Luxemburg*, Berlin: Hentrich & Hentrich Verlag.

Renner, Karl 1946, *An der Wende Zweier Zeiten*, Vienna: Danubia-Verlag.

Renner Karl 1917, *Marxismus, Krieg und Internationale: Kritische Studien über offene*

Probleme des Wissenschaftlichen und des praktischen Sozialismus in und nach dem Krieg, Stuttgart: J.H.W. Dietz.

Riazanov, David 1927, *Karl Marx and Friedrich Engels: An Introduction to their Lives and Work*, New York: International Publishers.

Röder, Werner, and Strauss, Herbert A. (1980–1983), *Biographisches Handbuch der deutschsprachigen Emigration*, New York, London, & Paris: K.G. Saur.

Rosner, Peter 1988, "A Note on the Theories of the Business Cycle by Hilferding and Hayek", *History of Political Economy* 20, 2: 309–19.

Salvadori, Massimo 1979, *Karl Kautsky and the Socialist Revolution, 1880–1938*. Translated by Jon Rothschild. London: NLB.

Scharlau, Winfried B. and Zeman, Zbynek A. 1964, *Freibeuter der Revolution: Parvus-Helphand. Eine politische Biographie*, Koln: Verlag Wissenschaft und Politik.

Service, Robert 2009, *Trotsky: A Biography*, Cambridge, Harvard University Press.

Smaldone, William 1998, *Rudolf Hilferding: The Tragedy of a German Social Democrat*, Dekalb, Northern Illinois University Press.

Smaldone, William 2008, *Confronting Hitler: German Social Democrats in Defense of the Weimar Republic, 1929–1933*, Lanham: Lexington Books.

Stein, Alexander 1946, *Rudolf Hilferding und die deutsche Arbeiterbewegung, Gedenkblätter*, Hamburg: Hamburger Buckdruckerei und Verlagsanstalt Auerdruk.

Steenson, Gary P. 1978, *Karl Kautsky, 1854–1938. Marxism in the Classical Years*, Pittsburgh: University of Pittsburgh Press.

Stephan, Cora (ed.) 1982, *Zwischen den Stühlen oder über die Unvereinbarkeit von Theorie und Praxis*, Bonn: J.H.W. Dietz Nachfolg.

Trotsky, Leon 1906–1907a, "Die Arbeiterdeputiertenrat und die Revolution", *Neue Zeit*, 25, 2: 76–86.

Trotsky, Leon 1906–07b, "Die Duma und die Revolution", *Neue Zeit*, 25, 2: 377–85.

Trotsky, Leon 1907–1908a, "Das Proletariat und die russische Revolution" *Neue Zeit* 26, 2: 782–91.

Trotsky, Leon 1907–08b, "Frank Wedekind", *Neue Zeit* 26, 2: 63–70.

Trotsky, Leon 1984, *My Life: An Attempt at an Autobiography*, Singapore: Penguin Books.

Van Roon, Ger. 1994, *Widerstand im Dritten Reich. Ein Überblick, sechste überarbeitete Auflage*, Munich: Verlag C.H. Beck.

Vliegen, Willem Hubert 1903–04, "Der Generalstreik als politisches Kampfmittel", *Neue Zeit* 22, 1: 193–99.

Volkoganov, Dmitri 1996, *Trotsky: The Eternal Revolutionary*, New York: The Free Press.

Wagner, F. Peter 1996, *Rudolf Hilferding: Theory and Politics of Revolutionary Socialism*, Atlantic Highlands: Humanities Press International.

Winkler, Heinrich August (2007), *The Long Road West, Volume 2*, Oxford: Oxford University Press.

Index

Abramovitch, Raphael   149, 434
"ABS program"   268n, 274, 290, 307–312
   see also Böchel, Karl and Aufhäuser, Siegfried
Abyssinian conflict   298–299, 386, 391, 405, 433, 469
Adler, Emma   97n, 322
Adler, Fritz   see Adler, Friedrich
Adler, Friedrich ("Fritz")   99n, 101, 108, 279, 288n, 416
   Assassination of Austrian Prime Minister   99n, 104, 105n, 117n
   Danzig and   461, 462
   Socialism and dictatorship   26
Adler, Max   39, 75, 150
   Relationship with Hilferding   5, 7, 38
Adler, Victor
   Editor of *Arbeiter-Zeitung*   43
   Leadership of SDAP   6, 42, 46, 51, 53, 67, 70–71, 76, 91
   Support for strike   56–59
   World War I and   110
AfA-Bund   240n, 257
Albarda, Johan Willem   288n, 374n
Alfringhaus, Erich   295n, 304, 315, 451–452
Anti-semitism   398, 410–411, 476
Arbeiter-Zeitung   43
   Aschaffenburg, Gustav   38n
   Association for Social Policy   55n, 142–143
Aufhäuser, Siegfried
   Revolutionary Socialist   224, 240, 268n, 274, 285, 289, 293, 318, 388, 392, 493
Augagneur, Victor   85n
Austerlitz, Friedrich   63, 65, 75–76
Austria
   Comparison to Germany   72
Austrian Social Democratic Workers' Party (SDAP)   see Social Democratic Workers' Party of Austria
"Away from Rome" movement   46n
Axelrod, Pavel   187
AZ   see *Arbeiter-Zeitung*

Badoglio, Pietro   299n
Balbo, Italo   299n

Bandmann, Eugen   359
Bauer, Helene   340n
Bauer, Otto   276–277
   Communist sympathies   477
   Imprisonment   117n
   Political involvement   5, 189
   Russian Revolution and   141, 403, 474, 477, 488
Bavaria   21, 112
Bavarian People's Party   21
Bebel, August
   Position on strikes   37, 56, 57
   Role in SPD   3, 4, 54n, 62, 135
Beck, Jozef   302n, 470–471
Bendel   see Kautsky, Benedikt
Bernhard, Georg   269–270, 370, 474
Bernhard, Paul   366, 367, 452
Bernstein, Edward   3, 4, 89n, 119, 132, 136–137, 235, 309
   Revisionism   7, 8, 13, 14, 29, 48, 85
Bieligk, Fritz   289n
Bienstock, Gregor   161, 162, 376, 380, 419, 435
Birnbaum, Immanuel   383–384, 464
Black Front, The   344n, 445, 446
Bloch, Josef   73, 84n, 85
Blum, Leon   133n, 171, 260, 264, 348–349, 433, 467, 473
   Leadership of the Popular Front   172n
Böchel, Karl
   "ABS Program"   see "ABS Program"
   Revolutionary Socialist   223, 224, 268n, 301, 305
   SPD activity   25n, 245, 285, 287–289, 293, 318, 340–341
Bogdanov, Alexander   134n, 138, 204
Böhm-Bawerk, Eugen
   Criticism of Marx   5–6, 29, 31–32
Bolsheviks   see Russian Revolution
Bömelburg, Theodor   60n
Bouisson, Fernand   355n
Bracke, Alexandre   368
Braun, Adolf   97n, 112, 128n, 145–146
Braun, Heinrich   31n, 57
Braun, Max   252, 375–376, 398–399, 490, 496

Braunthal, Alfred   147
Braunthal, Julius   150n
Brazil   145
Breitscheid, Rudolf   105n, 140, 229, 230n, 269, 490
Brill, Hermann   292n
Bringmann, August   60n
Broido, Eva   434
Brouckére, Louis de   288n, 374n
Brügel, Fritz   268n
Brüning, Heinrich   22, 23, 155–156, 158, 159, 221
Buchwald, Bruno   378n
Bülow, Bernhard Wilhelm Otto von   59, 62, 234n
Bylandt-Rheidt, Count Artur M. Graf   71n

Cachin, Marcel   405n
Calwer, Richard   80, 82
Cartels   13, 16, 41–42, 46, 55, 130
Cassirer, Paul   141
Catholic Center Party   22, 136, 155–156, 158, 302, 449
  Coalition with SPD   21, 113n, 140n, 221
Center Party   see Catholic Center Party
Chamberlain, Austen   171n
Chamberlain, Neville   461
Churchill, Winston   27, 171n, 461
Citrine, Walter   433
Claus, Rudolf   420n
Clemenceau, Georges   84n
Comintern   see Communist International
Communist International   18, 181
Communist Party of France   260
Communist Party of Germany (KPD)   131n, 166n, 224, 241, 271n, 404, 428
  Anti-fascism   398
  Distinction from SPD   18, 308, 310
  Electoral share   22, 23, 138, 141, 152
  Relationship with Russia   18
Crispien, Arthur   128n, 382, 392, 396
Crummenerl, Siegmund
  Arbitration board   330–331
  Sopade activity   232n, 236–239, 317, 328, 332, 353, 419, 428, 442, 447, 498
Cunow, Heinrich   87n, 100, 116n
Czech, Ludwig   265n

Dahlem, Franz   402–403
Dan, Fedor   349n
Dannenberg, Robert   123
Danzig
  Sovereignty of   302, 383–384, 449–454, 462, 464
Darré, Richard-Walther   316
Daszynski, Ignaz   196
David, Eduard   39, 91, 113
Déat, Marcel   262n
Decker, Georg ["Denicke"]   254, 256, 465n
Delcassé, Théophile   60n, 62n
De Man, Hendrik   143n, 144
Demuth, Fritz   423
Denicke   see Decker, Georg
Der Kampf   11, 13, 87
Der Sozialdemokrat   3
Deutsch, Hans   42n
Diefenbach, Hans   96n
Die Freiheit   235n, 252
  Hilferding's editorship of   17, 100n, 217, 220
Die Gesellschaft
  Hilferding's role in   6, 19, 26, 130, 139, 162–163, 239, 245
Diehl, Karl   44, 53
Die Neue Zeit (The New Age)   4, 12, 38
Dietrich, Georg   25, 223, 349
Die Zeitschrift für Sozialismus (ZfS)   25–26, 222, 268, 300, 331, 335, 345–346, 352, 435, 455, 458, 460, 475, 482, 485
Die Zukunft   10
Dill, Hans   369n
Dimitrov, Georgi   405n
Dissman, Robert   131
Dollfuss, Engelbert   263n, 265n
Doumergue, Gaston   260, 261
DVP   see German People's Party

Ebert, Friedrich   137n
Eckstein, Gustav   61, 68, 87, 97, 120
Eden, Anthony   171, 449n
Eisner, Kurt   53–54, 56, 62, 67
Emil, Karl   see Hilferding, Rudolf, "Karl Emil" pseudonym
Erfurt Program of 1891   4
Erzberger, Matthias   113n

Fascism   261, 400n
  Connection to Stalinism   viii, 474, 477, 488
  French Fascism   171
  Socialist resistance   225, 227, 240, 242, 312, 403, 428
  Rise to power   3, 27, 28, 164–165, 221, 313
  Theoretical understanding of   256, 271, 300, 309, 325, 337
Faure, Paul   443
Feder, Gottfried   325–326
Fey, Emil   265n
Fierlinger, Zdenek   237
Finance Capital   7
Flag Law   397
Fourniere, Eugene   84n
France
  1934 Crisis   259–264
Franzel, Emil   430n
Friedeberg, Raphael   54
Friedländer, Otto   273n, 291, 434n
Fritsch, Werner Freiherr von   283n, 326, 398
Frossard, Ludovic-Oscar   355n
Fuchs, Georg   289n

German Communist Party (KPD)   *see* Communist Party of Germany
German National People's Party (DNVP)   233n, 302, 397–398
German People's Party (DVP)   21
German Social Democratic Party (SPD)   *see* Social Democratic Party of Germany
Gesellschaft   *see Die Gesellschaft*
Geyer, Curt   170, 240n, 342
  "Max Klinger" pseudonym   255–257, 258, 388, 395, 397
Gillies, William   374n, 433–434
Goerdeler, Carl   316
Goldendach, David Borisovich   *see* Riazanov, David
Goldscheid, Rudolf   38n
Göppinger Affair   211
Göring, Hermann   234
Gradnauer, Goerg   62n, 74
Grandi, Dino   299n
Great Coalition   21, 140n
Great Depression   21, 22, 155, 233 n6
Greiser, Arthur   450

Grieß, Wilhelm   315n
Grimm, Robert   288n
Grumbach, Salomon   368n
Grünberg, Carl   5
Grünfeld, Judith   366, 371

Haase, Hugo   14, 17, 89n, 235
Halle Congress of 1920   18
Hanecki, Yakov   115n
Hansen, Richard   476
Hanussen, Erik Jan   313n
Heidelberg Program   19, 20
Heine, Fritz   248
Heine, Wolfgang   39
Heinig, Kurt   432, 435
Helphand, Alexander   *see* Parvus, Alexander Lvovich
Henderson, Arthur   238
Herriot, Edouard   138, 261n, 405
Hertz, Paul   25, 26, 155, 228–229
  Biography   217–221, 229
  Collaboration with Communists   428–429, 436–437, 444–447
  Criticism of the Sopade   224–225, 482
  Democracy   444
  Relationship with Hilferding   220, 484–489
  Work for SPD   217, 220–221
Hertz, Wilfried   249n, 384
Hervé, Gustave   85n
Herz, Friedrich Otto   129n
Hilferding, Anna   4
Hilferding, Emil (Rudolf's father)   4
Hilferding, Karl Emil (Rudolf's son)   11, 57n
Hilferding, Maria   4
Hilferding, Rose   134n, 357–358
Hilferding, Rudolf
  Cartelization   13, 16, 46, 130
  Democracy and   7, 15–16, 26, 34, 52–53, 70
  Depression   22, 27, 165, 173, 222–223, 357–358
  Early life   4–7
  Fatherhood   12, 12n
  Finance Capital   7, 12–13
  Flight from Nazis   28, 229–230
  Imperialism   20, 243, 271–272
  "Karl Emil" pseudonym   86n, 94n, 100, 105, 120, 121

INDEX 509

Marriage to Margarethe Hönigsberg 10, 11–12
Marriage to Rose Lanyi 20
Opposition to Bolsheviks 10, 15–16, 21, 49, 63–67, 111, 117, 121–122, 141, 148–149, 156, 164, 377n, 439–441
Opposition to Communist Party 16, 18, 152, 226, 300, 420, 477, 478, 488
Opposition to World War I 14, 16, 60
Post-war reconstruction 18
Relationship with Kautsky 3–10, 14, 19, 168
Socialist theory viii, 9–10, 226–227, 270–272
Hilquit, Morris 238n
Hindenburg, Paul von 22, 23, 24, 159, 282n, 283
Hirschfeld, Hans 142, 317, 398
Hitler, Adolf
  Resistance to 356, 398
  Rise to power 23, 24, 158, 159, 221, 283
  Totalitarian control (or "dictatorship") 316–317
Hoare, Samuel 171, 433n
Höchberg, Karl 3, 374n
Hoegner, Wilhelm 317n
Hofmann, Max Moritz 376n
Höglund, Zeth 481
Holst, Roland see van der Schalk, Henriëtte Roland Holst
Hönigsberg, Margarethe 10, 11–12, 12n, 20, 68
Horkheimer, Max 267
Hugenberg, Alfred 155, 233n, 234
Huysmans, Camille 407n

Imperialism 16, 20, 196, 224, 243, 271
Independent Social Democratic Party (USPD)
  Anit-World War I stance 14, 112n
  Membership 18
International Socialist Bureau (ISB) 110n
ISB see International Socialist Bureau

Jaksch, Wenzel 273n
Jews 4, 7, 11, 181, 218
  see also anti-semitism
Jouhaux, Leon 433

Kautsky, Benedikt (Bendel) 21, 101–102, 118, 146–147, 149
Kautsky, Karl
  Biography 3–4, 6–7
  Democracy and 7
  Imperialism 16
  Mentorship of Hilferding 8, 10
  Opposition to World War I 14, 16
  Post-war reconstruction 18
  Socialist theory 9–10
  View of Bolsheviks 15–16, 21, 146, 147
Kautsky, Luise 19, 28, 68
  Letters from Margret Hilferding 68
  Letters from Rudolf Hilferding 47, 87–88, 90–92, 106–107, 139–140
Kelles-Kraus, Kazimierz 49
Kerensky, Alexander 15, 113–114, 181
Kiel Party Congress of 1927 21, 397
Kirschmann, Emil 258, 413
Klatschko, Samuel 69, 212n
Klein, Franz 76, 108n
Klinger, Max see Geyer, Curt
Klopfer, Ernst 258
Koenen, Bernard 440
Koerber, Ernest von 108n
Körner, Theodor 425–426
KPD see Communist Party of Germany
Kraus, Karl 282–283
Krofta, Kamil 490, 491, 492
Krosigk, Lutz Graf Schwerin von 325, 326n
Kunfi, Zsigmond 149n

Labor and Socialist International (LSI) 224, 330, 455, 496–497
Lange, Willi 293, 318–319
Lanyi, Rose 20
Lassalle, Ferdinand 160
Laval, Pierre 405, 433
League of Nations 310, 449
Ledebour, Georg 124n
Lederer, Emil 89, 380n
Legien, Carl 81, 91
Lehmann, Else 267
Leichter, Otto 131n
Leipart, Theodor 166–167
Leipziger Volkszeitung (LVZ) 49, 53–54, 56n
Lenin, Vladimir Ilyich 16n, 113, 182, 187, 188, 212, 361
Lensch, Paul 87, 95

Lester, Sean 449
Leuschner, Wilhelm 240
Leuthner, Karl 45n, 206
Levi, Paul 131n
Liebknecht, Karl 3, 96n
Liebknecht, Sophie "Sonja" 96n
Liebknecht, Wilhelm 31
Litvinov, Maxim 234
Löbe, Paul 166–167, 223, 266n
Löwenheim, Walter
   "Miles" pseudonym 166n, 251n, 390n
   "Kurt Menz" pseudonym 390
   Leader of the "Miles group" 251, 273, 276, 300, 323–324, 365, 373, 392, 407, 420, 427, 429
Löwenthal, Richard
   "Paul Sering" pseudonym 299n, 300, 365, 373, 420, 429–430, 435, 442, 458
LSI *see* Labor and Socialist International
Luxemburg, Rosa 10, 13, 14, 64–65, 96n, 131n, 187n, 200n, 270
LVZ *see* Leipziger Volkszeitung

MacDonald, Ramsey 84n, 138
Mach, Ernst
   Influence on Hilferding 5
Marquet, Adrien 262
Martov, Julius 53, 182, 188n
Marx, Karl
   Historical materialism 29, 177
   Nachlaß 4, 51, 69
   Value theory 5–6, 7
Mauerenbrecher, Max 83n
May Day Rally of 1893 5
Mehring, Franz 32n, 59, 60, 81, 123, 199
   Anti-revisionism 56n
   Biography of Marx 123
   Controversial reputation 37n
   Edition of Marx's works 148
   Leadership role in SPD 62, 72, 83, 84, 187
Mehring, Walter 474n
Mensheviks 182–183, 186–187, 199
Menz, Kurt *see* Löwenheim, Walter
Mertens, Cornielle 433
Meyer, Oscar 290n
Miles *see* Löwenheim, Walter
Miles group *see* Löwenheim, Walter
Modigliani, Giuseppe 433, 463
Morina, Christina 6

Most, Johan 128n
Moszkowska, Natalie 380n, 383, 388
Müller, Arthur (Arnold) 236, 358n
Müller-Franken, Hermann 133, 140, 152, 156
   Leadership of SPD 21, 22, 92, 128n, 211
Müller, Willi (Karl Frank) 361, 391, 465, 482, 486, 487
   Communist sympathies 477
   Party activity 305n, 319, 349, 351, 359, 392
Münzenberg, Wilhelm ("Willi") 375n, 385, 394, 402–405, 406, 413, 420, 428–429
Mussolini 263, 298–299, 433, 469, 472

Nachlaß 4
Naphtali, Fritz 249n
Nathan, Otto 377n
National Socialist German Workers Party (NSDAP) *see* Nazi Party
Nazi Party (NSDAP)
   Invasion of France 229
   Rise to power 22, 23–24, 152, 223, 255–256, 286n, 297n
   SPD accommodation 231
   SPD resistance 24, 223–225, 228
Nemec, Anton 196
Nestriepke, Siegfried 100n
Neu Beginnen (NB/New Beginning) 26, 224, 288n, 486, 488
Neu Beginnen (pamphlet) 166n, 251
Neumann, Franz 315n, 318, 363
Neumann, Richard 391, 399
New Age, the *see Die Neue Zeit*
Nikolajewsky, Boris 377n, 409, 410, 415, 430, 463
NSDAP *see* Nazi Party
Nuremberg Party Congress 388, 397, 397n
NZ *see Die Neue Zeit*

Ochmann, Peter 457n
Olivier, Sydney 85n
Ollenhauer, Erich 223, 240n, 356, 372–373, 493–494
Oppenheimer, Franz 36
Oprecht, Emil 236–237, 249, 265, 302

Pahl, Walter 249
Palmade, Maurice 355n
Papen, Franz von 23, 24, 161, 164

INDEX

Parvus, Alexander Lvovich   37n, 115, 183
Pernerstorfer, Engelbert   53
Pester Lloyd   431
Pissin, Raimund   196
Planck, Max   313n
Plehve, Vyacheslav   201n
Plekhanov, Georgi   42n, 64, 182, 204
Poland   43, 64, 66–67, 469
Polish Socialist Party   43, 47, 49, 64, 66, 200n
Pölzer, Johann   131n
Popitz, Johannes   325
Popular Front   172n, 436–437
  Anti-fascism   400n
  Formation   27, 400n
  Hilferding's critique of   27, 171–172, 405, 465–466, 490
Posthumus, Nicolaas Wilhelmus   383n, 386, 387, 390
PPS   *see* Polish Socialist Party
Pravda   186–188, 205, 209, 213
Prussia   12, 66, 70, 72, 73, 78
Puls, Ottakar   287

Radek, Karl   115n, 211, 440, 446
Randa, Antonin Ritter von   70
Reich conference   306, 317, 323–324, 340, 349
Reichenau, Walther von   326n
Reinbold, Georg   274n, 410–411, 476
Reko   *see* Reich conference
Renaudel, Pierre   262n
Renner, Karl
  Political involvement   75–76, 189
  Political views   14–15, 91–92, 101, 120, 198
Reparations   131n, 159
Revisionism   7, 8, 13, 14, 29, 31, 48, 54n, 56n, 85
Revolutionary Socialists   224, 225–226, 249n
Riazanov, David   20–21, 123n, 132, 145–148
Ricardo, David   44
Rinner, Erich   223, 240, 324–326, 395, 397, 493–494
Rodbertus, Johann Karl   51
Röhm, Ernst   326n
Roosevelt, Franklin Delano   242, 267, 313
Rosenberg, Schaja   40
Rosenberg, Alfred   234n
Rosenfeld, Kurt   155, 249n, 271

RSDLP   *see* Russian Social Democratic Labor Party
Russian Revolution
  Effect on SPD   18
  Hilferding's perception of   10, 15–16, 21, 49, 63–67, 111, 117, 121–122, 141, 148–149, 156, 164, 377n, 439–441
Russian Social Democratic Labor Party   182–3, 186–187, 205n

SA   *see* Sturmabteilung
SAP   *see* Socialist Workers Party of Germany
Sapir, Boris ("Irlen")   380n, 382
Saar referendum   235n, 258n, 296, 297n, 303, 306, 315, 317, 450, 453
Saxony   70, 72, 73
Schacht, Hjalmar   286, 290n, 294, 316, 325, 395
Schäfer, Valentin   269
Schalk, Henriëtte   *see* van der Schalk, Henriëtte Roland Holst
Scheidemann, Philip   113n, 126, 238, 247, 435
Schertz, Hugo   53
Schifrin, Alexander   240n
Schippel, Max   63, 80, 85
Schlamm, Wilhelm Siegmund   488
Schleicher, Kurt von   23, 161, 280n
Schönlank, Bruno   56
Schüller, Richard   51
Schwabe, Reinhold   336n
Schwarzschild, Leopold   385, 389
SDAP   *see* Social Democratic Workers' Party of Austria
Sedova, Natalya   183
Seitz, Karl   108n
Sering, Paul   *see* Löwenthal, Richard
Severing, Carl   269
Seydewitz, Max   249, 268n, 274
Simon, Hugo   334n, 385
Social Democratic Party of Germany (SPD)   3, 4, 14, 18, 19, 21, 22, 23, 24
  Nazi accommodation   231
  Nazi resistance   24, 223–225, 228
  World War I stance   14, 89n, 235
Social Democratic Party Executive in exile (Sopade)   25, 26, 223–225, 228–229, 279, 409, 410, 413
  Diminishing influence   481–485

Reorganisation   224–225, 308, 331, 335, 341, 346–357, 410
Social Democratic Workers' Party of Austria (SDAP)   5, 45n, 301
　Kautsky's activity in   3
　Party influence   58, 72, 46n, 189, 265n
　Relations with SPD   10, 213, 266
　Role in workers' strikes   9
　Support for WWI   99n
Socialist schools
　Party schools   6, 10, 12, 80–81, 190
　Trade union schools   11, 43, 79, 80–81, 82, 217
Socialist Workers Party of Germany   268n, 270n, 301
Sollmann, WIlhelm   25, 223, 245, 323, 357, 366, 373, 410–411, 483
Somary, Felix   378n
Sombart, Werner   31, 44–45, 111
Sopade   *see* Social Democratic Party Executive in exile
Souvarine, Boris   302n, 384–385, 401
SPD   *see* Social Democratic Party of Germany
Spiecker, Carl   327n
Spilka   205
Stadthagen, Arthur   57, 62
Stahl, Emil   481n
Stahlhelm Bund der Frontsoldaten   397
Stalin, Joseph   viii, 181, 226, 300, 474, 488
Stampfer, Friedrich   240n, 343, 374, 416, 467–471
　Dictatorship   273
　Letters to Hilferding   254–255, 280
　Sopade activity   25, 272, 274–275, 299, 332–335, 342, 351, 413, 429–430, 436, 438, 445–446
Staudinger, Hans   379n, 384
Stein, Alexander   125n
Stennes, Walter   152n
Sternberg, Fritz   270n, 337
Stolper, Gustav   345n, 480
Stolypin, Pyotr   209
Strasser, Otto   344n, 456, 479
Ströbel, Heinrich   56, 71
Stürgkh, Karl von   99n, 104, 108n, 117n
Sturmabteilung   326n, 344n, 450n
Sturmthal, Adolf   280, 360

Tarnow, Fritz   267
Taub, Siegfried   279n, 321, 475
Thälmann, Ernst   271, 434
Thomas, Albert   114n
Thormann, Werner   362n
Titulescu, Nicolae   469–470
Trade unions   9, 45, 77–78, 80–81, 217–218
　Nazi suppression   25, 27, 165, 167n, 221
　Schools   11, 79, 80–81, 82, 217
　Strikes   24, 42, 46
Treviranus, Gottfried   295n, 304n, 316
Troelstra, Pieter Jelles   110n
Trotsky, Leon   113–114, 121
　Biography   181–183
　Bolsheviks   199
　Pravda   185–187
　Relationship with Hilferding   113–114, 121, 184–186, 188–189
　Relationship with Lenin   182
Tscherevanin, V.   202–204
Tsereteli, Irakli   113n
Tucholsky, Kurt   247n

Ulbricht, Walter   402n, 412–413, 459
Unions   *see* Trade unions
United front   260, 261, 272, 289, 306n, 307, 420, 428, 440, 445, 477
University of Vienna   4, 6, 11, 129n
Untermeyer, Samuel   238
USPD   *see* Independent Social Democratic Party

Vagts, Alfred   463
Valera, Éamon de   449
Van der Schalk, Henriëtte Roland Holst   31, 50–51
Vandervelde, Emile   133, 240, 436–437
Verein für Sozialpolitik   *see* Association for Social Policy
Vladek, Baruch Charney   384, 463
Vliegen, Willem Hubert   38n, 39
Vogel, Hans   25, 231n, 291, 445–446, 493, 496–498
Voigt, Frederick   315n
Volksstimme   258n, 450–451, 454
Vollmar, Georg von   374n
Vorwärts   9, 12, 13, 14

Vossiche Zeitung   21
Voting rights   9, 34, 35, 52–53, 58, 60, 65, 70, 72–73, 75, 78, 311

Wallfisch, Hermann   201n
Warski, Adolf   212
Wedekind, Frank   196
Wels, Otto   25, 128n
   Leadership of SPD   153, 223, 225, 245, 271, 272, 274, 280n, 282, 304, 318, 332, 338, 340, 348–351, 353, 356, 367, 383, 429
   Relationship with Hilferding   339
Wendel, Hermann   247, 431
Westmeyer, Friedrich   122n
Wickel, Helmut   337, 343, 382, 420–421
   "Müritz" pseudonym   392, 396
Wilson, Woodrow   110n

Winarsky, Leopold   75
Wirth, Karl Joseph   264n
Witte, Count Sergei Yulyevich   66
Wolf, Julius   157
Workers' strikes   9, 33–36, 39, 42, 60–61, 73
World War I   14, 95, 114, 121, 126
Woytinsky, Vladimir   139
Wurm, Emanuel   10, 55n, 218

Zeitschrift für Sozialismus   see *Die Zeitschrift für Sozialismus* (*ZfS*)
Zetkin, Clara   47n, 187, 209
Zetterbaum, Max   38n, 49, 64
ZfS   see *Die Zeitschrift für Sozialismus* (*ZfS*)
Zinoviev, Grigori   18, 315, 440, 446, 477n
Zyromsky, Jean   371n

Printed in the United States
by Baker & Taylor Publisher Services

Printed in the United States
by Baker & Taylor Publisher Services